Scientology

Scientology

EDITED BY
JAMES R. LEWIS

OXFORD
UNIVERSITY PRESS

2009

OXFORD

UNIVERSITY PRESS

Oxford University Press, Inc., publishes works that further
Oxford University's objective of excellence
in research, scholarship, and education.

Oxford   New York
Auckland   Cape Town   Dar es Salaam   Hong Kong   Karachi
Kuala Lumpur   Madrid   Melbourne   Mexico City   Nairobi
New Delhi   Shanghai   Taipei   Toronto

With offices in
Argentina   Austria   Brazil   Chile   Czech Republic   France   Greece
Guatemala   Hungary   Italy   Japan   Poland   Portugal   Singapore
South Korea   Switzerland   Thailand   Turkey   Ukraine   Vietnam

Published by Oxford University Press, Inc.
198 Madison Avenue, New York, New York 10016

www.oup.com

Oxford is a registered trademark of Oxford University Press.

Library of Congress Cataloging-in-Publication Data
Scientology / edited by James R. Lewis.
   p. cm.
Includes bibliographical references and index.
ISBN 978-0-19-533149-3
1. Scientology.   I. Lewis, James R.
BP605.S2S29 2009
299'.936—dc22   2008026684

9 8 7 6 5 4 3 2 1
Printed in the United States of America
on acid-free paper

Acknowledgments

In the process of compiling this book, I have incurred debts of gratitude to numerous people, not all of whom I can acknowledge here
without generating a chapter-length document.

First and foremost, I owe a debt of gratitude to Evelyn Oliver, my
wife and partner of two decades, who participated in my informal
field research with the Church of Scientology and who supported me
during this project in ways too numerous to mention.

Thanks are especially due to the contributors. I anticipate that
this will become an important collection—one to which all future
scholars writing on Scientology will refer—thanks to the high-quality
chapters these individuals have contributed.

I would also like to acknowledge the many Scientologists I have
known over the past two dozen years. In no particular order, these
include: David Aden, Sue Taylor, Gail Armstrong, Nancy O'Meara, Rick
Moxon, Andrew Miln, Leisa Goodman, Janet Weiland, Sarah Burrough,
Sheila McDonald, Glenn Barton, Jennifer Robinson, Kay and Lee
Holzinger, Cindy and Steve Conway, Frank Molinaro, Sue Strzewski,
Tony Klarich, Dave Klarich, Dan Costello, Nick Broadhurst, Yoko
Takeda, Atushi Tojo Koji Minami, Chika Sakimoto, Heber Jentzsch and
numerous other L.A. Scientologists whose names I have forgotten,
and, finally, certain ex-Scientologists who prefer to remain nameless.

Thanks to Cynthia Read, my acquisitions editor, who took interest
in the initial proposal and supported it through the approval process at
Oxford University Press. Also, thanks to the manuscript's anonymous
reviewers whose feedback led to improvements in the final product.

I am grateful for the indirect support I received from the Philosophy Department at the University of Wisconsin Milwaukee. Particular
thanks are due the office staff, Georgette Jaworski and Diane Grubisha.

Régis Dericquebourg's "How Should We Regard the Religious Ceremonies of the Church of Scientology?" was first published in *Acta Comparanda* (Antwerp-Belgium), Faculty for Comparative Study of Religions, 2006. Also, Carole M. Cusack and Justine Digance's "Pastoral Care and September 11: Scientology's Nontraditional Religious Contribution" originally appeared as a section in their "Religious, Spiritual, Secular: Some American Responses to September 11," which was published in the *Australian Religious Studies Review* 16:2 (Spring 2003).

Finally, thanks to Signature Books for permission to reprint "Birth of a Religion," the first chapter of J. Gordon Melton's *Church of Scientology* (2000), and to Paragon Books/Rose of Sharon Press for permission to reprint Frank Flinn's "Scientology as Technological Buddhism," which originally appeared in Joseph H. Fichter, ed., *Alternatives to American Mainline Churches* (1983).

Contents

Contributors, xi

Introduction, 3
James R. Lewis

Part I. Introductory Essays

1. Birth of a Religion, 17
   J. Gordon Melton

2. The Cultural Context of Scientology, 35
   William Sims Bainbridge

3. Researching Scientology: Perceptions,
   Premises, Promises, and Problematics, 53
   Douglas E. Cowan

Part II. Theoretical and Quantitative Approaches

4. Making Sense of Scientology:
   Prophetic, Contractual Religion, 83
   David G. Bromley

5. Scientology and Self-Narrativity:
   Theology and Soteriology as Resource
   and Strategy, 103
   Dorthe Refslund Christensen

6. The Growth of Scientology and the
   Stark Model of Religious "Success," 117
   James R. Lewis

Part III. Community and Practices

7. Community in Scientology and among Scientologists, 143
   Peter B. Andersen and Rie Wellendorf

8. How Should We Regard the Religious Ceremonies
   of the Church of Scientology?, 165
   Régis Dericquebourg

9. The Development and Reality of Auditing, 183
   Gail M. Harley and John Kieffer

Part IV. Sources and Comparative Approaches

10. Scientology as Technological Buddhism, 209
    Frank K. Flinn

11. Scientology, a "New Age" Religion?, 225
    Andreas Grünschloß

12. Scientology: "Modern Religion" or
    "Religion of Modernity"?, 245
    Gerald Willms

Part V. Controversy

13. The Nature of the New Religious Movements–Anticult
    "Culture War" in Microcosm: The Church of
    Scientology versus the Cult Awareness Network, 269
    Anson Shupe

14. Scientology in Court: A Look at Some Major Cases
    from Various Nations, 283
    James T. Richardson

15. The Church of Scientology in France:
    Legal and Activist Counterattacks in the "War on *Sectes*," 295
    Susan J. Palmer

Part VI. International Missions

16. Scientology Missions International (SMI):
    An Immutable Model of Technological Missionary Activity, 325
    Bernadette Rigal-Cellard

17. The Church of Scientology in Sweden, 335
    Henrik Bogdan

18. Scientology Down Under, 345
    Adam Possamai and Alphia Possamai-Inesedy

Part VII. Dimensions of Scientology

19. "His name was Xenu. He used renegades . . .":
    Aspects of Scientology's Founding Myth, 365
    Mikael Rothstein

20. Celebrity, the Popular Media, and Scientology:
    Making Familiar the Unfamiliar, 389
    Carole M. Cusack

21. Sources for the Study of Scientology:
    Presentations and Reflections, 411
    Dorthe Refslund Christensen

Part VIII. Appendix

22. Pastoral Care and September 11:
    Scientology's Nontraditional Religious Contribution, 435
    Carole M. Cusack and Justine Digance

Index, 439

Contributors

Peter B. Andersen is Associate Professor of History of Religions, University of Copenhagen. His main interest is the modernization of religion. He has participated in surveys on religion in the educational system and among Scientologists.

William Sims Bainbridge is the author of 11 books, 4 textbook-software packages, and about 180 shorter publications in information science, social science of technology, and the sociology of religion. At the National Science Foundation since 1992, he represented the social and behavioral sciences on five advanced technology initiatives. Currently, he is program director for Social Informatics, after having directed the Sociology, Human Computer Interaction, Science and Engineering Informatics, and Artificial Intelligence programs.

Henrik Bogdan is Professor of Religion at the Göteborg University, Sweden. His main areas of research are Western esotericism and new religious movements, and he is secretary of FINYAR (The Swedish Association for Research and Information on New Religious Movements). Bogdan is the author of *Western Esotericism and Rituals of Initiation* (2007).

David G. Bromley is Professor of Sociology at Virginia Commonwealth University. Among his recent books on religious movements are *Cults, Religion, and Violence* (2002) and *Toward Reflexive Ethnography: Participating, Observing, Narrating* (2001). He is former president of the Association for the Association of Religion; founding editor of the annual series *Religion and the Social Order*, sponsored by the Association for the Sociology of Religion; and former editor of the *Journal for the Scientific Study of Religion*.

DORTHE REFSLUND CHRISTENSEN has taught at Aarhus University, Southern Denmark University, and the University of Copenhagan. In 2004 she held a postdoctoral scholarship from the Danish Research council for the project Religion in Popular Culture and Everyday Life.

DOUGLAS E. COWAN is Assistant Professor of Religious Studies and Social Development Studies at Renison College, the University of Waterloo. In addition to numerous books and articles, he has written specifically about issues related to the Church of Scientology and the Internet, and the question of whether Scientology qualifies as a legitimate religion.

CAROLE M. CUSACK is Senior Lecturer and Chair of the Department of Studies in Religion at the University of Sydney. She trained as a medievalist, and her doctorate was published as *Conversion among the Germanic Peoples* (1998). She has since specialized in contemporary religion, publishing on pilgrimage and tourism, the pagan revival, new religious movements, and the interface between religion and politics.

RÉGIS DERICQUEBOURG is Professor of Psychology at Charles De Gaulle University in Lille, France, and a member of the group Society, Religions and Laicite (CNRS). He is concerned with the conflict between society and minority religious groups in pluralist societies. He is the author of *Healing Religions* (1988), *Minority Religious Groups: Aspects and Problems* (1992), *The Antonianists* (1993), *Christian Science* (1999), and *To Believe and to Heal* (2001).

JUSTINE DIGANCE is Senior Lecturer in Tourism Management at Griffith University, Queensland, Australia. Her research interests are secular pilgrimage, theme parks, and tourism management. Her doctorate (University of Sydney) was based upon research into modern secular pilgrimage.

FRANK K. FLINN is Adjunct Professor of Religious Studies at Washington University in St. Louis. He also serves as an expert in forensic religion, testifying on the legal definition of religion and religious practices here and abroad. He is the author of numerous articles on issues relating to Catholicism, the new religions, Waco, the militia in the United States, Heavensgate, church and state, and religious violence.

ANDREAS GRÜNSCHLOß is Professor of Religious Studies at the University of Göttingen. His publications include *Religionswissenschaft als Welt-Theologie: Wilfred Cantwell Smiths interreligiöse Hermeneutik* (1994), *Der eigene und der fremde Glaube: Studien zur interreligiösen Fremdwahrnehmung in Islam, Hinduismus, Buddhismus und Christentum* (1999), as well as contributions to academic journals, encyclopedias, and anthologies.

GAIL M. HARLEY teaches Religious Studies at the University of South Florida. She is the author of *Emma Curtis Hopkins: Forgotten Founder of New Thought* (2002) and *Hindu and Sikh Faiths in America* (2002).

JOHN KIEFFER is a graduate student at the University of South Florida with an interest in new religious movements. A former member of the Church of

Scientology, from 1985–1990 he received auditor training and auditing. His career includes twenty years of service in the U.S. military.

JAMES R. LEWIS is a Lecturer in Philosophy at the University of Wisconsin. His extensive publications in the field of new religious movements include *The Oxford Handbook of New Religious Movements* (2004) and *Legitimating New Religions* (2003). He is also general editor of the Brill Handbooks on Contemporary Religion series and coeditor of Ashgate's Controversial New Religions series.

J. GORDON MELTON is Director of the Institute for the Study of American Religions and a Specialist in Religion in the Religious Studies Department at the University of California, Santa Barbara. He is a leading scholar of new religious movements and the author of such standard reference works as the *Encyclopedia of American Religions*.

SUSAN PALMER is Adjunct Professor at Concordia University and a tenured professor at Dawson College, both in Montreal, Quebec. She has written over sixty articles and authored or edited eight books on new religious movements, including *Aliens Adored: Rael's UFO Religion* (2004).

ADAM POSSAMAI is Senior Lecturer in Sociology at the University of Western Sydney and past president of the Australian Association for the Study of Religions. He was the Programme Coordinator for the Research Committee for the Sociology of Religion at the XVI World Congress of Sociology. He is the author of *Religion and Popular Culture: A Hyper-Real Testament* (2005), *In Search of New Age* (2005), and a book of short stories, *Perles Noires* (2005). His latest book, *Sociology of Religion for Generations X and Y*, will be published in 2009.

ALPHIA POSSAMAI-INESEDY has recently completed a Ph.D. in Sociology at the University of Western Sydney. She is one of the editors of *The Chameleon and the Quilt: A Cross Disciplinary Exploration in the Social Sciences* published in 2005. In 2006, she co-organized a workshop sponsored by the Academy of Social Sciences in Australia on "Risking Motherhood in the 21st Century: The Politics of Maternity Care in a 'Risk Society.' " This workshop led to the publication of a special issue of the *Health Sociology Review*, which she coedited.

JAMES T. RICHARDSON is Professor of Sociology and Judicial Studies at the University of Nevada, Reno, where he directs the Grant Sawyer Center for Justice Studies as well as the Judicial Studies degree programs for trial judges. He is the author or coauthor of nearly 200 articles and chapters, as well as 7 books, including his latest, *Regulating Religion: Case Studies from around the Globe* (2003).

BERNADETTE RIGAL-CELLARD is Professor of North American Studies at the University Michel de Montaigne-Bordeaux 3 (France). While researching how American and Canadian religions interact with their surrounding culture, she also studies the transformations undergone by religious groups in their transatlantic passage from Europe and Africa to the Americas and vice versa. In the field of religious studies, she has organized several international conferences and published many articles and books.

MIKAEL ROTHSTEIN is Professor in the Department of History of Religions at the University of Copenhagen. He specializes in the study of new religions, and is the author or editor of several books on the subject. His is a member of the board of the Research Network on New Religions (RENNER), Denmark, and editor-in-chief of *CHAOS*, a Danish-Norwegian journal on the history of religions.

ANSON SHUPE is Professor of Sociology and Anthropology at the joint campus of Indiana University and Purdue University in Fort Wayne. He is the author of numerous professional articles and over two dozen books, including *Six Perspectives on New Religions, Born Again Politics and the Moral Majority,* and *Wealth and Power in American Zion.*

RIE WELLENDORF received her M.A. in the Sociology of Religion and Minority Studies from the University of Copenhagen in 2001. She subsequently worked as Coordinator of the Eures Initial Training from 2002 to 2004. At present she is Research Assistant at the Center for Youth Research, Danish School of Education, University of Aarhus.

GERALD WILLMS is a social scientist who has taught political sciences and sociology of religion the University of Göttingen. His thesis, *Scientology: Kulturbeobachtungen jenseits der Devianz,* was published in 2005.

Scientology

Introduction

James R. Lewis

In midsummer 2007 as I was finishing up the manuscript for this book, Tom Cruise was in the news again. It seems many Germans objected to a Scientologist playing Col. Claus von Stauffenberg, a national hero, in the upcoming film *Valkyrie*. As a consequence, the German government refused to allow the production company to shoot parts of the movie in certain historic buildings. (Cruise, by the way, bears a striking resemblance to Stauffenberg.) All too predictably, a number of cable news programs used this incident as yet another opportunity to heap scorn on the Church of Scientology.

During the lead-in to a cable news program I watch on a semi-regular basis, it was announced that they would be including a segment on the Cruise-Germany incident that would feature a research professor from a respected university. The researcher was billed as a "Scientology expert." This piqued my curiosity. In the early stages of the present book project, I had invited most of the relevant mainstream academicians to contribute chapters. I was thus quite surprised that I did not recognize the name of the guest expert.

When I finally saw the interview, I was even more surprised to hear this "expert" mouthing popular simplistic stereotypes about "cults," rather than presenting reputable, scholarly information. He emphasized standard negative information about Scientology, such as the Guardian Office's covert infiltration program (neglecting to mention that the Church eventually shut down the Guardian's Office and disciplined the individuals responsible for illegal activities). He even went so far as to depreciate Tom Cruise's intelligence, as if Mr. Cruise's membership in the Church of Scientology was prima facie evidence that he was not very bright. I found this latter item especially distasteful. Whatever one's personal evaluation of a particular religious group, no responsible academician would give voice to unsupported insults about a member of such a group in a public forum.

So after the program concluded, I looked up the guest online and discovered he was a computer scientist rather than a sociologist or a religious studies scholar. I also discovered he had never written anything on Scientology that had appeared in a scholarly publication (though I did find out that he had previously spoken about Scientology on prior episodes). Obviously, the mere fact that he is affiliated with a good university in no way qualifies him to speak as an authority on nontraditional religions any more than—in the absence of an appropriate background—my affiliation with a university qualifies me to speak authoritatively about computer science.

When it comes to controversial new religions, however, the normal standards for what constitute legitimate expertise are frequently tossed to the winds. In the case of this program's treatment of Scientology, the guest speaker had a university affiliation (implying authoritative objectivity) and a negative attitude toward the Church, and that was apparently all that counted.

Though other nontraditional religious groups that have been involved in dramatic incidents have attracted more public attention for short periods of time, the Church of Scientology is arguably the most *persistently* controversial of all contemporary new religious movements (NRMs). As a consequence of its involvement in numerous legal conflicts, Scientology has acquired a reputation as a litigious organization, ready to sue anyone who dares criticize the Church. Partly as a consequence of this fierce reputation, academicians have tended to avoid publishing studies about Scientology outside the esoteric realm of scholarly journals. Thus, at present, there exist only two scholarly, English-language monographs about the Church, Roy Wallis's out-of-print, and now outdated, *The Road to Total Freedom* (1977) and Harriet Whitehead's similarly outdated *Renunciation and Reformulation* (1987). The present collection thus fills an important gap in the NRM literature.

Despite the obvious need for such a collection, certain critics will object to any treatment of this religious group that does not adopt a critical, debunking stance. I have, in fact, been cautioned that any "neutral" study should be avoided because such a study might lend some legitimacy to this (by implication illegitimate) organization. This kind of objection is, however, patently absurd. Even the harshest critic should be able to acknowledge that the task of constructing an accurate *understanding* of the Church must precede any meaningful *criticism*. The point is so obvious that it merits no further comment. Thus, throughout this introduction, I will attempt (to the extent that this is actually possible) a descriptive rather than an evaluative overview of Scientology and the various controversies in which it has been involved.

At the same time, it should immediately be noted that this is not an apologetic collection. Within the bounds of normal academic conventions, contributors have been free to include critical observations and to discuss matters deemed off-limits by the Church of Scientology (e.g., the Xenu narrative). This volume will thus likely end up pleasing no one engaged in the Scientology/anti-Scientology conflict, which is perhaps as it should be.

Overview of Scientology

The Church of Scientology grew out of Dianetics, a popular therapy movement founded by L. Ron Hubbard (1911–1986) in the mid-twentieth century. Hubbard was a talented writer and adventurer with a consuming interest in the human mind. In 1950, he published *Dianetics: The Modern Science of Mental Health*. This book described techniques designed to rid the mind of irrational fears and psychosomatic illnesses. *Dianetics* quickly became a best seller, and groups were soon formed so that individuals could assist each other in the application of Hubbard's "auditing" techniques. He lectured extensively, and wrote more books. In 1951 he announced the birth of Scientology. It was described as a subject separate from Dianetics, as it dealt not only with the mind of an individual, but also with one's nature as a spiritual being.

In 1954, the first Church of Scientology was established in Los Angeles, California. In 1959 Hubbard moved to Saint Hill Manor, in Sussex, England, and the worldwide headquarters of Scientology was relocated there. In 1966, Hubbard resigned his position as executive director of the Church and formed the "Sea Organization," a group of dedicated members of the Church who lived aboard large, oceangoing ships. In 1975 these activities outgrew the ships, and were moved onto land in Clearwater, Florida. From this time on until his death in 1986, Hubbard continuously wrote and published materials on the subjects of Dianetics and Scientology, as well as a number of works of science fiction.

The Church of Scientology believes that "Man is basically good, that he is seeking to survive, (and) that his survival depends on himself and his attainment of brotherhood with the universe" (from the Creed of the Church of Scientology). This is achieved in Scientology by two methods, referred to as "auditing" and "training." Dianetics and Scientology auditing (counseling of one individual by another) consists of an "auditor" guiding someone through various mental processes in order to first free the individual of the effects of the "reactive mind," and then to fully realize the spiritual nature of the person. The reactive mind is said to be that part of the mind that operates on a stimulus-response basis, and is composed of residual memories of painful and unpleasant mental incidents (termed "engrams") that exert unwilling and unknowing control over the individual. When the individual is freed from these undesired effects, he or she is said to have achieved the state of "Clear," which is the goal of Dianetics counseling. An individual then goes on to higher levels of counseling dealing with his or her nature as an immortal spiritual being (referred to in Scientology as a "thetan"). Scientologists believe that a thetan has lived many lifetimes before this one and will again live more lifetimes after the death of their current body (the doctrine of reincarnation).

Scientology training consists of many levels of courses about (1) improving the daily life of individuals by giving them various tools (e.g., concerning communication) and (2) learning the techniques of auditing so that one can counsel others. Scientologists refer to a Supreme Being, but do not worship any deity as such, instead spending their time on the application of Scientology principles to daily activities. One unusual aspect of the Church is that members are not discouraged from being active participants in other religions.

The Church of Scientology International consists of over 1,000 separate churches, missions, and groups, spread over seventy-four countries. Its membership includes people from a wide variety of ages and backgrounds. There are also over 500 community action and social reform groups affiliated with Scientology that concern themselves with human rights, education, drug rehabilitation, and other issues.

Hubbard's publications number in the hundreds (all of his lectures were recorded and later transcribed into publications). They cover a wide variety of subjects from communication and the problems of work to past lives. *Dianetics: The Modern Science of Mental Health* has continued over the years to be a best seller. There are numerous Church magazines published on a regular basis, the principal ones being *Source, Advance, The Auditor,* and *Freedom.* These serve to inform the membership of current events, the activities of celebrity and other Scientologists, and the availability of classes and Scientology materials.

Controversy

In terms of its willingness to undertake legal action, the Church of Scientology was in the latter half of the twentieth century what the Jehovah's Witnesses had been earlier in the century. Like the Witnesses, Scientology early set up a strong legal wing. One of the first new religions to be embroiled in controversy, Scientology eventually prevailed in the majority of its legal suits in North America and played a leading role in demolishing the Cult Awareness Network (CAN), the most important anticult organization in the United States. Although the Witnesses had attracted controversy as a consequence of their very public proselytizing, Scientology's initial point of friction with the larger society was its challenge to the medical and psychotherapeutic establishment.

During the early stages of the Dianetics movement, Hubbard naively contacted medical and psychiatric associations, explaining the significance of his discoveries for mental and physical health, and asking that the AMA and the APA investigate his new technique. Instead of taking this offer seriously, these associations responded by attacking him. The subsequent popular success of Dianetics did nothing to improve the image of Hubbard in the minds of the medical-psychiatric establishment, and was likely instrumental in prompting an FDA raid against the Church.

On January 4, 1963, the Founding Church of Scientology in Washington, D.C., was raided by United States marshals and deputized longshoremen with drawn guns, acting in behalf of the Food and Drug Administration (FDA). Five thousand volumes of Church scriptures, 20,000 booklets, and 100 E-Meters (electrical machines that record galvanic skin response that are sometimes used in Scientology counseling) were seized. In 1971, after years of litigation, the U.S. District Court for the District of Columbia issued the *Founding Church of Scientology* v. *United States* decision. The Food and Drug Administration was ordered to return the books and E-Meters that had been taken in the 1963 raid. In its decision, the court recognized Scientology's constitutional right to protection from the government's excessive entanglement with religion. Though the raid was declared illegal, the documents remained in government possession and were open to public scrutiny. According to these documents, the Church was keeping files on people it considered unfriendly, and there had been various attempts by Scientology to infiltrate anticult organizations.

After the raid, the Church's Guardian's Office sent a number of top officials incognito to selected government agencies that were collecting data on Scientology. However, several members were indicted and convicted for theft of government documents. The convicted members were released from their offices. The Church then closed the Guardian's Office, which had been responsible for initiating illegal activities.

In 1991, *Time* magazine published a front-page story attacking the Church of Scientology, which subsequently responded with a massive public relations campaign and with a lengthy series of full-page ads in *USA Today*. Early in 1992 the Church filed a major lawsuit against *Time*, after discovering that the maker of Prozac—a psychiatric drug Scientology had been active in opposing—had been the ultimate prompter of *Time*'s assault on the Church. This suit was eventually rejected by the court as baseless.

The Church of Scientology was also involved in extended conflicts with the Australian, French, and German governments, and problems with the IRS through the 1980s and 1990s. Hubbard was charged with criminal tax evasion, and the IRS often moved against the Church in ways that questioned its tax-exempt status. These problems terminated in a landmark decision in 1993, when the IRS ceased all litigation and recognized Scientology as a legitimate religious organization. Following this decision, the Church redirected its legal resources against CAN, and managed to sue the group out of existence by 1996. Scientology in North America then entered a period of relative calm, but the Church has recently been in the news again because of the activities of Scientologist Tom Cruise, a high-profile episode of the TV show *South Park* that led to the resignation of Isaac Hayes (another celebrity Scientologist) from *South Park*, and an exposé article that appeared in *Rolling Stone* in early 2006.

Scientology, Science, and the Utopian Impulse

One of the interesting aspects of the Church is how certain elements of the popular culture of the 1950s were preserved within the Scientology subculture. For instance, even female members typically refer to other adult women as "girls"—a linguistic convention the larger society has abandoned. Also, until relatively recently, the majority of full-time Church staff members smoked cigarettes, as did the majority of adults in the '50s.

A more subtle, but far more significant, mid-century theme preserved in the time capsule of the Church's subculture is reflected in its name. Prior to the blossoming of cold war nuclear concerns and the emergence of the ecology movement's critique of runaway technology, the general populace accorded science and science's child, technology, a level of respect and prestige enjoyed by few other social institutions. Science was viewed quasi-religiously, as an objective arbiter of "Truth." Thus any religion claiming to be *scientific* drew on the prestige and perceived legitimacy of natural science. Religions such as Christian Science, Science of Mind, and Scientology claim just that.

There are, however, a number of differences between popular notions of science and science proper. Average citizens' views of science are significantly influenced by their experience of technology. Hence, in most people's minds, an important goal of science appears to be the solution of practical problems. This aspect of our cultural view of science shaped the various religious sects that incorporated "science" into their names. In sharp contrast to traditional religions, which emphasize salvation in the afterlife, the emphasis in these religions is on the improvement of this life. Groups in the Metaphysical (Christian Science–New Thought) tradition, for example, usually claim to have discovered spiritual "laws" that, if properly understood and applied, would transform and improve the lives of ordinary individuals, much as technology has transformed society.

The notion of spiritual laws is taken directly from the laws of classical physics. The eighteenth- and nineteenth-century mind was enamored of Newton's formulation of mathematical order in the natural world. A significant aspect of his system of physics was expressed in the laws of gravity. Following Newton's lead, later scientists similarly expressed their discoveries in terms of the same legislative metaphor—for example, the "law" of evolution.

One of the first and, at the time, most influential of the nineteenth century new movements to adopt a rhetoric of establishing religion on a scientific basis was spiritualism. Spiritualism was and is a religious movement emphasizing survival after death, a belief Spiritualists claim is based upon scientific proof through communication with the surviving personalities of deceased human beings by means of mediumship. In the Spiritualist view, communicating with the dead allowed one to conduct empirical (in the broadest sense) research into the spiritual realm. Like the later New Thought movement, Spiritualists also expressed their discoveries in the spiritual realm in terms of a series of laws.

This legislative rhetoric was carried over into Metaphysical religions, particularly New Thought. Rather than presenting themselves as empirically investigating the spiritual realm via communications from the dead, groups in the Metaphysical tradition view themselves as investigating the mind or spirit in a practical, experimental way. The aim of this "research" was a kind of "science of mind" (the title of Ernest Holmes's 1926 classic book, as well as the name of the denomination he founded).

The Church of Scientology is in this same lineage, though Scientology takes the further step of explicitly referring to their religio-therapeutic practices as religious *technology*—in Scientology lingo, the "tech." In much the same way as the 1950s viewed technology as ushering in a new, utopian world, Scientology sees their psycho-spiritual technology as supplying the missing ingredient in existing technologies—namely, the therapeutic engineering of the human psyche.

Where most utopian thinkers converge is in the notion that humanity is basically *good:* Just remove the corrupting influence of the modern, dysfunctional social order, and a healthy society will emerge. This macrocosmic utopianism is reflected in the microcosmic ideal of Dianetics therapy: Just clear individuals of the corrupting influence of their engrams, and healthy psyches will emerge. This is not to say that Scientology focuses entirely on individuals. In fact, much of the Church's energies go into reforming and otherwise impacting the larger society, a focus that stands in marked contrast to most other nontraditional religions.

Scientology's social outreach is a significant and highly interesting aspect of the Church's activities, yet one that observers—particularly hostile observers—almost always ignore. If mentioned at all, critics dismiss Scientology's social outreach as being nothing more than a token effort at improving its public image. If this is the case, however, it is surprising how little the Church has done to attract attention to its public service activities.

Rather than an elaborate public relations exercise, it is evident, particularly if one is familiar with Hubbard's thinking, that Scientology's social outreach flows rather naturally out of the ideas and ideals bequeathed to the Church by its founder. For example, Narconon, Scientology's drug rehabilitation program, is a natural extension of Hubbard's purification program. Hubbard devised a regime of physiological purification focused on impurities such as drugs, which tend to interfere not only with one's health, but also with one's thinking and perception of the world. The residues of the drugs one has ingested and other impurities that have been taken into the body must be purged before an individual can become a healthy, fully functioning human being. The parallel between this physiological treatment process and the auditing of psychological engrams should be transparent.

Another activity the Church supports is the World Literacy Crusade, which focuses on bringing Scientology "study technology" to the inner cities. Scientology celebrities such as Isaac Hayes and Ann Archer have been especially active in this crusade. Among the other principles of this "study tech" is the notion that when readers skip over a word they do not understand, they tend not to grasp anything else they read past that particular word. Consequently, one of the core processes of Hubbard's study technology is going back over a text until one finds the problem word, learning its meaning from a dictionary, and then proceeding to read forward from that point. Like the drug residues cleared by the purification program, the word skipped while reading comes to play a role similar to an engram—a warping factor that must be "cleared" before one can enjoy optimum learning. Solving problems by removing blockages even carries over into what we might call Hubbard's "sociology": When an organization is not working properly, Scientologists attempt to identify a "suppressive person"—a negative, dysfunctional individual who acts as a sort of "social engram" fouling things up.

Other Church outreach programs include educating young people about the dangers of drugs, Criminon (the application of Hubbard's technology to the reform of criminals), human rights advocacy, exposing abuses by governmental agencies (in the United States and abroad), exposing abuses by the psychiatric establishment (the Church of Scientology is the chief critic of drugs like Prozac), as well as more traditional kinds of community service. Via these activities, Scientologists contribute to the task of "clearing the planet"— applying the "tech" to the whole spectrum of human ills in a utopian effort to restore humanity to its natural state of happiness. In Hubbard's words, "A civilization without insanity, without criminals and without war, where the able can prosper and honest beings can have rights, and where man is free to rise to greater heights, are the aims of Scientology" (http://www.scientology religion.org/).

Survey of Contents

I began exploring the possibility of compiling an anthology on Scientology in early 2006. The initial responses I received were discouraging; some of my close colleagues thought that few "objective" (a problematic term) researchers were currently studying the Church. I was thus pleasantly surprised to discover numerous people—including some of the top scholars in the field—who were either already researching Scientology or who were interested in writing something on this intriguing organization. Subsequently, I decided to expand this project into a larger-than-usual anthology that would seek to incorporate a wide range of different approaches. One consequence of this way of proceeding is that chapters in the present collection run the gamut from descriptive overviews of different aspects of the Church to chapters utilizing Scientology as a case study for certain theoretical formulations.

As a backdrop to the other chapters, J. Gordon Melton's "Birth of a Religion" provides a concise overview of L. Ron Hubbard and the Church of Scientology's history up to the time of Hubbard's death in 1987. The chapter consists of three components: (1) a summary of Hubbard's life, (2) a basic introduction to Scientology's beliefs, practices, and organization, and (3) an overview of the main features of the conflicts in which the Church has been involved.

Williams Sims Bainbridge's "The Cultural Context of Scientology" charts Scientology's cultural origins and affinities based on extensive data from participant observation, historical documents, questionnaire survey research, and other sources of quantitative information. The chapter outlines part of the complex cultural influences on Scientology in terms of four formative phenomena: (1) science fiction, (2) science adventurism, (3) systems of honor, and (4) the cyberculture. Of particular interest is the story of Joseph ("Snake") Thompson, an important influence on Hubbard, and the best friend of Bainbridge's great uncle.

In "Researching Scientology: Perceptions, Premises, Promises, and Problematics," Douglas E. Cowan explores the research problem of the Church of Scientology, and does so from three interrelated angles: (1) some of the premises on which such research ought to be conducted, (2) some of the promises that are implicit in it for the field of NRM studies, and (3) some of the problems encountered because of the paucity of data, and either the unwillingness of Scientology to cooperate in research or interference from the Church as research proceeds.

Scientology is a response to structural changes in Western societies, and particularly the United States, in the latter half of the twentieth century. In "Making Sense of Scientology: Prophetic, Contractual Religion," David G. Bromley discusses the Church of Scientology as an example of a quasi-religious organization that blended religion and therapy in a way that created a heightened sense of individual empowerment for practitioners. This chapter analyzes how its myth, ritual, organization, and leadership are constructed to sacralize individual essence.

In "Scientology and Self-Narrativity: Theology and Soteriology as Resource and Strategy," Dorthe Refslund Christensen reflects on the extent to which a rigid soteriological organization leads to a uniformity in the representations made by the individuals engaged in a system. Scientologists might share certain representations that make it possible for them to feel part of a group, but it might just be that these representations are fewer than one might expect. In fact, this chapter will argue that there are only three basic ideas shared by all Scientologists.

On the basis of census and other data collected in a variety of different Anglophone countries, a clear pattern emerges showing that Scientology is experiencing healthy growth—though it is also clear that the Church is not the "world's fastest growing religion," as is sometimes claimed. In "The Growth of Scientology and the Stark Model of Religious 'Success,'" the present writer applies Rodney Stark's model of religious "success" to the Church of Scientology. This discussion is preceded by an extended analysis of the shortcomings of Stark's model.

Peter B. Andersen and Rie Wellendorf's "Community in Scientology and Among Scientologists" examines belief, commitment, and community among Scientologists on the basis of a survey among core Scientologists in Denmark. The authors use a number of indicators of belief and social attitudes that are suitable for an analysis of individualism and utilitarian attitudes among Scientologists in Denmark—values that are lauded in Hubbard's writings.

Regis Dericquebourg's "How Should We Regard the Religious Ceremonies of the Church of Scientology?" examines the role of the ceremonies of the Church of Scientology. Scientology aims at personal, spiritual self-development and does not a priori need a religious service. Hubbard may, in fact, have invented these ceremonies to imitate the major confessions and denominations of the Western world and give his movement the appearance of being a religion. On the other hand, perhaps the founder invented them because a religious community needs to mark important moments in the lives of its members.

In "The Development and Reality of Auditing," Gail M. Harley and John Kieffer examine auditing, the Church of Scientology's core practice. Hubbard postulated that the systematic application of auditing would lead the practitioner and believer to higher levels of thought revealed in the advancement of not only their cognitive abilities but major lifestyle changes that offered salvation from misery. This chapter undertakes a close analysis of the auditing process, demonstrating that there is more complexity to this practice than meets the eye.

Frank Flinn's "Scientology as Technological Buddhism" examines Scientology's affinities with, and roots in, Buddhism and Hinduism, and its employment of technological language. This is followed by a historical section on the transition from Dianetics to Scientology proper, and concludes with specific comparisons and contrasts between Scientology terminology and standard Western theological concepts—research versus revelation, standardness versus infallibility/inerrancy, engrams versus sin, et cetera.

Andreas Grünschloß's "Scientology: A 'New Age' Religion?" examines Scientology in terms of its parallels with the so-called New Age movement. These parallels are not accidental, but arise out of the influence of common predecessor movements. Theosophy, for example, is the source of certain interpretations of Asian religions like Buddhism that influenced both Hubbard and the New Age.

Grünschloß also picks up on the same theme as Willms covers in his chapter, namely that both the New Age and Hubbard have been influenced by modern Western culture, an influence reflected in, for instance, such themes as the emphasis on using "spiritual" practices to help one achieve practical, this-worldly goals. In "Scientology: 'Modern Religion' or 'Religion of Modernity'?" Gerald Willms analyzes some of the deep-rooted cultural influences on L. Ron Hubbard that shaped the Church of Scientology. Willms is systematically critical of Hubbard's claim that Scientology is a religion, a point that is still hotly debated in Europe. The reader should not allow Willms's critique to overshadow the insightful contributions of his chapter, such as the observation that the Church has sanctified and ritualized modernity in such expressions as science and technology, as well as basic Western (particularly, American) values like individualism and capitalism.

For anyone interested in the conflict in which many contemporary new religions have been engaged, Scientology is especially important for its role in destroying the Cult Awareness Network (until it declared bankruptcy, the latter organization was the primary "anticult" group in North America). In "The Nature of the New Religious Movements–Anticult 'Culture War' in Microcosm: The Church of Scientology versus the Cult Awareness Network," Anson Shupe provides a historical overview of this conflict, particularly focusing on the events that led to the demise of the Cult Awareness Network.

In "Scientology in Court: A Look at Some Major Cases from Various Nations," James T. Richardson analyses the experience of Scientology in court in terms of two issues: (1) cases in which Scientology has attempted to define and defend itself as a genuine religion and (2) cases concerning registration in societies that demand registration of religious groups before they can achieve tax exempt status and other privileges. These types of cases, and others where relevant, are discussed by country, with certain countries being selected that are particularly significant in terms of legal precedents and the impact of their decisions.

Continental Europe, especially since the murder-suicides conducted by the Order of the Solar Temple in Switzerland in 1994, plus the small-scale group suicide of some surviving members in France in 1995, has been a hotbed of anticult (anti-"sect") activism. In "The Church of Scientology in France: A History of Legal and Activist Responses to the Forces of Anticultism and the Government-Sponsored 'War on *Sectes*,'" Susan J. Palmer presents an historical overview of Scientology's (and other alternative religions') various conflicts with the French government.

In "SMI: Scientology Missions International, An Immutable Model of Technological Missionary Activity," Bernadette Rigal-Cellard examines the way religions undergo transformations when they migrate from the country in which they were born to other cultures, using the Church of Scientology as a case study. The chapter asks, how do its missionaries react to their new environment, particularly in terms of how they try to adapt—or resist adaptation—to their new country? In the course of her analysis, Rigal-Cellard presents the foundation of SMI, its European missions, its franchise system, and the expected duties of mission holders.

As reflected in the title, Henrik Bogdan's chapter focuses on "Scientology in Sweden." International new religious movements such as the Church of Scientology are usually discussed in the light of the context in which they have originated, and often little attention is given to the variations and idiosyncrasies that tend to develop within the movements when they are established in other parts of the world. This chapter sets out to discuss the development of the Church of Scientology in Sweden from its inception in 1969 and how it has adapted to the Swedish religious climate.

Adam Possamai and Alphia Possamai-Inesedy's "Scientology Down Under" uses the Church of Scientology as a case study of Australia's approach to new religious movements. It analyses Australian legal and government opinions on Scientology such as the Anderson report and the Hansard inquiry on religious freedom in Australia. It is argued through this case study that although Australia is a success story of religious settlement and is home to many new religious movements, the official way groups like Scientology are portrayed often lapse into popular stereotypes.

Mikael Rothstein's "'His name was Xenu. He used renegades . . .': Aspects of Scientology's Founding Myth" is the first extended academic treatment of the Xenu narrative. Though the Xenu story is at the heart of Scientology's vision of the universe, it is part of the Church's secret, inner teachings, reserved for members initiated into the Operating Thetan levels. In addition to analyzing the cultural influences informing Hubbard's religious vision, Rothstein provides a compelling argument for why scholars should legitimately be able to discuss Xenu. He also discusses the central role this narrative has played in efforts to debunk Scientology.

One of the most prominent aspects of the Church of Scientology to average citizens is its ability to attract high-profile celebrities, particularly Hollywood celebrities. In "Celebrity, the Popular Media, and Scientology: Making Familiar the Unfamiliar," Carole M. Cusack examines this phenomenon in terms of contemporary scholarship about the role celebrities play in contemporary popular culture. She argues, among other things, that despite the critical slant taken in many media stories about Scientology celebrities, this coverage also serves to make the Church seem more familiar and thus helps to normalize the image of Scientology in the public consciousness.

In "Sources for the Study of Scientology: Presentations and Reflections," Dorthe Refslund Christensen provides researchers with an introduction to, and overview of, several different categories of Scientology material. Her chapter prioritizes books by their importance and provides thorough presentations of *The Technical Bulletins of Dianetics and Scientology*, the basic books of Dianetics and Scientology, and a few additional books. She also presents an overview analysis of the video recordings of two major annual events. Finally, she briefly covers Scientology periodicals, magazines, booklets, and pamphlets.

Carole M. Cusack and Justine Digance's "Pastoral Care and September 11: Scientology's Non-Traditional Religious Contribution" is excerpted from their longer article, "Religious, Spiritual, Secular: Some American Responses to September 11." It is reproduced here as an appendix because it provides a concise overview of the Church of Scientology's participation in the post-9/11 response at ground zero in New York City.

PART I

Introductory Essays

I

Birth of a Religion

J. Gordon Melton

As the twenty-first century opened, the Church of Scientology[1] has emerged as one major focus of the ongoing controversy on new religions and their role in the rise of religious pluralism in the West. The teachings of founder L. Ron Hubbard enjoyed some immediate success with the public following their initial appearance in 1950, but one could have hardly predicted Scientology's meteoric rise or its history of public conflict from its modest beginning. The controversy over Scientology has extended at times to almost every aspect of the church and its founder, and although those issues have been largely resolved in North America, the very status of Scientology as a religion continues to be seriously questioned in some quarters and has been the subject of multiple court cases. True, it has been recognized as a religion in many countries of the world, including the United States; but opposition continues in some quarters. In the modest space allowed, this chapter cannot cover every point at issue but does attempt to provide (1) an overview of the life of L. Ron Hubbard anchored by the generally agreed upon facts; (2) an introduction to the church's beliefs, practices, and organization; and (3) a summary of the major points of the controversy.

The Founder

Lafayette Ronald Hubbard (1911–1986) began life in the rural Midwest, born in Tilden, Nebraska, to U.S. naval officer Harry Ross Hubbard and Ledora May Waterbury.[2] Six months after his birth, the family moved from Nebraska to Oklahoma, then settled for a time in Montana, eventually establishing itself on a ranch near Helena.

The land was still frontier country, and the youthful Hubbard learned to be at home on a horse. Befriended by the local Blackfoot Indians, he was made a blood brother at the age of six.[3] After some five years, the family was on the move again, and in October 1923 headed for Washington, D.C. Memorable on the trip East to the twelve-year-old Hubbard was a meeting with U.S Navy commander Joseph "Snake" Thompson. Over the next couple of months, Thompson, a student of Sigmund Freud, introduced Hubbard to the inner workings of the mind being explored by depth psychology, and the youth felt encouraged to begin his own independent explorations.[4]

In March 1925 Hubbard returned to the family homestead in Montana and was still residing there when, in the summer of 1927, he made his first excursion to foreign lands, a summer trip that included brief stops in Hawaii, Japan, China (including Hong Kong), the Philippines, and finally Guam, where he taught school with the native Chamorros for several weeks. Returning for a last year at Helena High School, he got a start on his writing career with articles submitted to the school newspaper (including stories of his summer travels). He also became an editor for the newspaper. In 1928 he returned to the Orient for a longer visit. For fourteen months he journeyed around China (including at least one inland trip), Japan, the Philippines, and Indonesia, and for a period served as helmsman and supercargo aboard a twin-masted coastal schooner. In September 1929 he returned to finish his high school education at Swavely Prep School in Manassas, Virginia (February 1930), and Woodward School for Boys in Washington, D.C. (June 1930).

After graduating from Woodward, in the fall of 1930 he enrolled at George Washington University (GWU). He led a varied student life that included singing and scriptwriting for the local radio station, writing dramas, and taking a course in subatomic physics. As flying captured the imagination of the nation, Hubbard became an accomplished pilot and president of the GWU Flying Club. In fact, his flying enthusiasm occasioned his first sale of a piece of writing, a nonfiction article, "Tailwind Willies," to *Sportsman Pilot* (Jan. 1932). He soon followed it with his first published fiction stories, "Tah" (*The University Hatchet*, Feb. 1932) and "Grounded" (*The University Hatchet*, Apr. 1932). As the school year closed, he won the GWU Literary Award for his one-act play "The God Smiles."

Although writing had clearly manifested as Hubbard's primary talent, his early travels as a teen also prepared him for what was to be a significant subtheme—exploring. He was still in his early twenties when in 1932 he organized and led more than fifty students on a two-and-a-half-month tour of the Caribbean aboard a 200-foot, four-masted schooner. Amid the fun of the trip, a scientific team that joined the cruise gathered a selection of tropical plants and animals later deposited at the University of Michigan. Soon after the trip, Hubbard left again for the West Indies to work on a mineralogical survey in the new American territory of Puerto Rico.

Hubbard left the university after only two years, and in 1933 married. It was time to settle down and make a living, and the popular pulp magazines provided employment. His first story, "The Green God," appeared in *Thrilling Adventures* in February 1934. He wrote rapidly (a talent his fellow authors would always envy) and turned out story after story that frequently appeared under a variety of imaginative pen manes (Winchester Remington Colt, Bernard Hubbel, René Lafayette, Scott Morgan, Kurt von Rachen, and John Seabrook). It was a common practice for pulps to rely upon a few valued writers while appearing to draw from a much larger stable of writers than they actually possessed.

Through the mid-1930s, Hubbard produced many different kinds of stories for the pulps, from westerns to supernatural fantasy. He also turned out his first novel, *Buckskin Brigades*, in 1937. That same year Columbia Pictures purchased the film rights to a second novel, *Murder at Pirate Castle,* and Hubbard moved to Hollywood for a few months to work on the screenplay. His book was seen on the big screen as the serial *Secret of Treasure Island*. He remained in California to work on two additional serials produced by Columbia, *The Mysterious Pilot* and *The Adventures of Wild Bill Hickok,* and on *The Spider Returns,* an early superhero adventure done by Warner Brothers.

Shortly after his return to New York from the West Coast, he came into touch with the publishers of *Astounding Science Fiction*. Though continuing to write in other genres, he would find his greatest fame in science fiction (and the related fields of fantasy and horror) and would become one of the noteworthy voices in that primal generation that created the field as it is known today. Over the next few years he would become friends with *Astounding*'s editor, John W. Campbell, Jr., for whom he produced an initial story, "The Dangerous Dimension," for the July 1938 issue. He also became a regular contributor to Campbell's fantasy magazine, *Unknown,* for which Hubbard produced one of his greatest pieces of fiction, *Fear,* originally published in the June 1940 issue. He quickly established himself in the community of writers of popular fiction, a fact signaled in 1935 by his election as president of the New York chapter of the American Fiction Guild. Increasingly, during his spare time, he was sought out by aspiring writers looking for words of advice, encouragement, and assistance.

The Disruption of War

Though writing consumed his time, Hubbard never lost his adventurous spirit, and, with war already a reality in Europe, he found new uses for his interests. In 1940 he was elected a member of the Explorers Club and in June sailed under its banner as head of the Alaskan Radio Experimental Expedition. His group charted the coastline north of Seattle to the Alaskan panhandle for the U.S. Navy Hydrographic Office, experimented with radio directional finding, and included some anthropological observations of the Native American peoples of the region. As the expedition was drawing to a close, in December the U.S. Bureau of Marine Inspection and Navigation awarded him a "Master of Steam and Motor Vessels" license. Three months later he received his "Master of Sail Vessels" license for any ocean.[5]

Hubbard was commissioned as a lieutenant (junior grade) in the U.S. Naval Reserve in late June. He was called to active duty following the attack on Pearl

Harbor and ordered to the Philippines. With the subsequent Japanese takeover of the Philippines, he began his wartime service with naval intelligence
in Australia. His later posts during the war included command of convoy es-
cort YP 422 in Boston; command of the sub chaser PC 815 in the North Pacific;
and navigation officer aboard the USS *Algol*. It appears that PC 815 did engage
and sink a Japanese submarine off the Oregon coast, a fact only recently sub-
stantiated because of the American government's reluctance to admit that the
Japanese were in fact operating off America's Pacific Coast during the war.
He spent the last months of the war at Oak Knoll Naval Hospital in Oakland,
California.[6] While recovering, he had time to give consideration to the larger
questions of the nature of the human mind and to help some of his fellow
patients who had not survived the war in the best of mental health. It appears
that the months in Oak Knoll provided an occasion during which the earlier
ruminations on the human problem were intensified and a period of more
systematic consideration of the human condition was launched.[7]

Following his release from active duty in February 1946, Hubbard to all
outward appearances returned to his prewar life. His first marriage having
ended, he married again and picked up his writing career. He churned out a
number of short stories, among the most enduring being the "Ole Doc Methu-
selah" series, a collection of seven short stories that originally appeared in *Astounding Science Fiction* under Hubbard's pen name René Lafayette and more
recently gathered and published as a single volume. The stories centered upon
a 700-year-old Soldier of Light who traveled throughout the galaxy performing
astonishing medical feats and, contrary to standard professional ethics, involving himself in interesting areas of interplanetary politics.

Immediately after the war, in December 1945, but while still a commis-
sioned officer and on active duty, Hubbard became involved in one of the most
intriguing episodes in his long life, participation in the activities of the Ordo
Templi Orientis. The OTO is a ritual magic group, then headed by the aging
Aleister Crowley (1875–1947), the famous and somewhat notorious occultist.
It practiced what it saw as real "magick" (as opposed to stage magic); the se-
cret ritual of the group involved the use of sex to raise magical energies. After
World War II, the Agape Lodge of the OTO was opened in Pasadena, California,
and one John W. (Jack) Parsons (1914–52), an explosives expert and key man at
the California Institute of Technology, emerged as a leader of the small group.
Soon after his discharge from Oak Knoll, Hubbard showed up at the Pasadena
OTO headquarters.

According to accounts published by the OTO, Parsons developed an immediate liking for Hubbard and invited him to participate in the OTO work,
though Hubbard refused to become a member. Even though Hubbard was not
properly initiated, he assisted Parsons on several magical operations in what
he would later claim was in fulfillment of his military intelligence function.[8]
For whatever reason, early in 1946 Parsons and Hubbard had a parting of the
ways. Parsons claimed that Hubbard had persuaded him to sell the property
of the Agape Lodge, after which Hubbard, along with Parson's sister-in-law
Betty, allegedly absconded with the money. Hubbard reappeared on a newly

purchased yacht off the Florida coast. Parsons pursued him, and on July 5, 1946 a confrontation occurred. Hubbard had sailed at 5:00 P.M. At 8:00 P.M., Parsons performed a full magical invocation to "Bartzabel." Coincidentally, a sudden squall struck the yacht, ripped the sails, and forced Hubbard to port, where Parsons was able to recover at least a small percentage of the money.[9]

Hubbard's account (and that of the present-day Church of Scientology) denies any attachment to the OTO. Rather, Hubbard claimed that in his capacity as a U.S. intelligence officer, he was sent to scrutinize Parsons and the lodge. The building that served as the lodge's headquarters also housed a number of nuclear physicists living there while working at Cal Tech (and these physicists were among sixty-four later dismissed from government service as security risks). Hubbard asserted that due to his efforts, the headquarters was torn down, a girl was rescued from the group, and the group was ultimately destroyed.

Both stories stand and, in fact, may be genuine perceptions of the events because Hubbard obviously would not make any undercover "investigative" operation known to Parsons. These events also appear to be the source of charges that Hubbard based Scientology's teachings in part on Crowley's. It should be noted that whatever happened during Hubbard's association with Parsons, the teachings of the Church of Scientology are at wide variance with those of Crowley and that the practices of the church show no direct OTO influence.[10]

Quite apart from the OTO, however, in light of the later emergence of the Dianetics movement and the Church of Scientology, it is obvious that Hubbard was spending the greater part of his energies during these postwar years on his personal research aimed at finding a technology of the human mind. He was synthesizing all he had read and learned into what would be a novel approach to the problem.[11] He first compiled his thoughts in 1948 into a short book, *The Original Thesis*,[12] which he circulated privately. It contained his basic conclusions concerning the nature of human aberrations and his early ideas about handling them through the counseling technique called auditing. Knowledge of his new ideas within his friendship network led to his initial published articles on Dianetics, "Terra Incognita: The Mind," in *The Explorers Club Journal* (Winter/Spring 1948/1950) and the far more influential one in *Astounding Science Fiction*.[13]

Favorable response to *The Original Thesis* led to his expanding it into a more substantial volume, *Dianetics: The Modern Science of Mental Health*,[14] whose publication on May 9, 1950 is considered by Scientologists a seminal event of the century. The appearance of Dianetics has, they believe, ushered in a new era of hope for humankind. The next month it hit the *New York Times* best-seller list and there remained for the rest of the year. Concurrently, Hubbard founded the Hubbard Dianetic Research Foundation in Elizabeth, New Jersey, where he held classes to train people as auditors. He also toured the country lecturing on the principles presented in the book.

Overnight Hubbard had become the leader of a popular movement that was growing faster than anyone had expected. Above and beyond responding to people who wanted to know more or wished to be audited, he faced an immediate need to provide guidelines for auditors (from the Latin *audire*, "to listen"). People were purchasing his book and auditing each other with the instructions they found in its pages. Hubbard launched a series of training lectures and had the notes from his "Professional Course" (Nov. 1950) transcribed and published.

During 1951 he intensified efforts to offer direction to the growing movement. He increased the number of public lectures, but concentrated teaching time on the training of auditors. He also found time to write two important new texts—*Science of Survival*[15] and *Self-Analysis*.[16] Possibly the most important addition to Dianetics during the year, however, came with the incorporation of the electropsychometer, or E-meter. Developed by Volney Matheson, following Hubbard's designs, the small device measures emotional reactions to a tiny electrical current. To Scientologists, the changes in the E-meter measure changes in the mind and tell what the pre-Clear's mind is doing when the pre-Clear is induced to think of something, though its indications must be interpreted by a trained auditor. The E-meter gave Scientology a means of quantifying the counseling experience (a possibility about which most psychotherapists are extremely skeptical).[17]

Not everyone inspired by their reading of *Dianetics* came into association with the foundation. A number of organizations, each with its own variation on Hubbard's ideas and practices, arose. At the same time Hubbard's own investigations brought him up against the phenomenon of past lives. Through the first half of 1951, the subject of reincarnation became a matter of intense debate on the board, and in July some members of the board sought to pass a resolution banning the entire subject.[18] Most notable among those supporting the resolution were John Campbell, who had supported Hubbard since the publication of the Dianetics article in his magazine, and Dr. Joseph Winter, a physician who had written a book on Dianetics and who had hoped to see Dianetics eventually accepted by his physician colleagues.[19] With the changing personnel, his organization went through various corporate changes, and in 1952 Hubbard founded the Hubbard Association of Scientologists (later adding the word International) as a more permanent corporate structure. He also launched the *Journal of Scientology* to keep followers abreast of the growing movement and issued a regular series of technical publications to further the auditors' training and keep them abreast of the latest developments.

The appearance of the term *Scientology* indicated the emergence of a distinct new emphasis in the movement Hubbard had founded. Dianetics concentrated on the mind, believed to be the mechanism that receives, records, and stores images of experiences. In several years since the publication of Dianetics, amid the time-consuming task of training auditors, Hubbard shifted his attention away from the mind itself to the entity observing the images that the mind was storing. That entity—he called it a thetan, from the Greek letter theta, for thought or life—closely resembled what other religions had called the soul or spirit. Hubbard was clearly venturing into theological realms, inspired somewhat by Eastern religious perspectives, especially manifest in his acceptance of past lives.

The development of a more comprehensive understanding of the human being that included consideration of humanity's place in the cosmos suggested the emergence of Scientology into the field of religion. By 1954 students of Dianetics and Scientology were already acknowledging that Scientology functioned for them as their religion. Thus it came as no surprise when, in February 1954, some of Hubbard's followers, operating independently of him but clearly with his blessing, organized the first local Church of Scientology.[20]

While the movement was expanding rapidly in the United States, Dianetics was also finding an audience overseas. In late 1952, when Hubbard first traveled to England, he found a group of people already using his book. And as he was opening the training center in London, he discovered that there were similar responses to his teachings throughout the English-speaking world, from Ireland to Australia to South Africa. There were eager students even in far-off Israel, and the second local Church of Scientology was opened neither in Chicago nor New York, but in Auckland, New Zealand.

In March 1955, Hubbard moved east where the Founding Church of Scientology in Washington, D.C., was opened, and he assumed duties as its executive director. From that post, he began the process of developing the church's administration procedures. He also formed a distribution center to oversee the publication and dissemination of Dianetics/Scientology literature (the seed of what is now Bridge Publications).

The international spread of Scientology during the last half of the 1950s was capped by the opening of churches in Johannesburg, South Africa (1957), and Paris, France (1959), the first in a non-English-speaking country. World headquarters was moved to England where Saint Hill, a rural estate, had been purchased at East Grinstead, Sussex. Hubbard would live there for the next seven years. However, before he really settled in, he finished off the decade with a round-the-world tour, highlighted by stops in Greece and India, and a series of lectures in Melbourne and London. The new decade began on an optimistic note, but storm clouds had gathered and a deluge was about to burst upon the young church.

Encountering the Powers That Be

When Hubbard first circulated his ideas on the mind, its operation, and the implications for medicine, he offered his findings to both the American Psychiatric Association and the American Medical Association. He found them uninterested.[21] They declined to take Dianetics seriously. Hubbard's approach to the mind did not connect with the state of psychiatry at the time, and the American Medical Association looked askance at nonprofessionals they considered were attempting to enter their ranks with magic bullets. They had a long history of examining similar claims only to label them worthless. As a matter of fact, once Hubbard published *Dianetics,* he found no less a person than Dr. Morris Fishbein, well-known for his exposés of quack medicine, dismissing his book.

With the opening of the Founding Church of Scientology in Washington, D.C., the stage was set for further confrontation. Washington was the headquarters of the Food and Drug Administration (FDA), the federal agency charged with preserving the quality of food and drugs. Although Dianetics as presented in 1950 did not particularly interest them, the introduction of the E-meter, with accompanying claims of marked improvement resulting from auditing, did attract their attention. Here was something to which possibly unwarranted medical claims were being attached. They began an investigation.

The FDA attention had not arisen in a vacuum, however. As additional congregations of the church were founded each received its tax-exempt status almost as a matter of routine. However, in 1958 the Internal Revenue Service began to call that status into question. The Church of Scientology did not look like a traditional church, and the language it used to describe its activities was unfamiliar. The initial withdrawal of tax-exempt status (with a resultant demand for back taxes) started a string of appeals, investigations, and litigation that would last for a quarter of a century, the longest set of related litigations in the agency's history.

The questioning of the church's status as a religion (the only long-term grounds for withdrawal of tax exemption) would have dramatic effects. It would lead to the circulation of numerous memos to other government agencies and no doubt lay behind actions that at first glance appeared to be completely unrelated to tax issues. Thus it was that on January 4, 1963, deputized agents of the FDA moved into the Founding Church of Scientology and seized all of the E-meters and thousands of pieces of church literature. It would take eight years for the issue to be resolved in the courts, which would eventually declare the E-meter a legitimate religious artifact and order the return of the Scientology literature.

The circulation of material relative to the IRS action was also used to support the actions of the British and Australian governments. As early as October 1962, psychiatrist E. Cunningham Dax, the chair of the Mental Health Authority in the State of Victoria, recommended the curbing of Scientology, in part by banning its advertisements. He found allies in Labor Minister J. W. Galbally and Kevin Anderson, Q.C. The latter prepared a lengthy report that led the government of Victoria, Australia, in 1965 to pass the Psychological Practices Act that prohibited the practice of Scientology, the use of its name, and the dissemination of its teachings. Western Australia and South Australia soon followed suit. At the beginning of 1969, Scientology churches in Melbourne, Sydney, Perth, and Adelaide reorganized as the Church of the New Faith to pursue their cause. The first step in reversing the legislation occurred in 1969 when the High Court of Western Australia ruled the ban illegal. The law was formally repealed in Western Australia and South Australia in 1973, but it would take almost two decades to reverse all of the negative legislation.[22] The law in Victoria was repealed in 1982, and the following year the High Court of Australia in a unanimous decision ruled that the Church of Scientology (still operating as the Church of the New Faith) was undoubtedly a religion and deserving of tax exemption. The final ruling addressed a number of challenges alleged against the church's religious status and dismissed them. Over the next several years, the tax-exempt status of the church was granted in the various states of Australia.[23]

In 1968 the United Kingdom moved against the church, which had expanded its facilities at East Grinstead to include an advanced training center. The health minister barred the entry of noncitizens coming into England specifically to study or work at Saint Hill. A subsequent inquiry into the situation by Sir John Foster recommended a lifting of the ban in 1971; however, it was not acted upon until 1980.[24]

The public controversy over Scientology through the 1960s led to extensive newspaper coverage and finally to a set of books that highlighted the charges being made against the church—George Malko's *Scientology, the Now Religion* (1970), Paulette Cooper's *The Scandal of Scientology* (1971), and Robert Kaufmann's *Inside Scientology* (1972).[25] A more sympathetic treatment appeared in Omar Garrison's *The Hidden History of Scientology* (1974).[26] Church leaders were especially offended by Cooper's work, and favorably settled a major libel case against her.[27]

In 1966, in order to cordon off the attacks on Scientology to some degree and prevent them from interfering with the central activities of counseling and training, the church established the Guardian's Office. It was assigned the mission of protecting the church against outside attacks and ensuring that the organization moved ahead according to the policies laid down in the writings of its founder. The Guardian's Office was designed to handle the obstacles (primarily legal and public relations) to the church's growth. In isolating the rest of the church from any disturbances, theoretically, the day-to-day work of teaching and auditing could continue smoothly. As the number of issues placed on its agenda grew, especially with the addition of the "anticult" agitation in the 1970s, the Guardian's Office developed an activist stance. It eventually would oversee an extensive program of intelligence gathering, infiltration of organizations seen as enemies, and the spread of information that it hoped would disrupt actions being taken against the church (black propaganda). Unfortunately, the small group running the Guardian's Office, quite apart from the awareness of the rest of the church's leadership and membership, began to see itself above the laws of both the church and the state. In the end, this group and its operatives committed a number of morally questionable and even illegal acts.[28] It is significant that the majority of accusations against the church refer to actions taken by the Guardian's Office in the 1970s.

The same year that the Guardian's Office was founded, Hubbard resigned all official administrative positions with the church, most notably his post as executive director and his membership on the board of directors. He was given the title "founder" and withdrew to continue his development of Scientology and to write. He, of course, retained a number of significant ties to the church. His Scientology writings had attained the status of scripture; and as he completed new materials for the church, they were regularly incorporated into its curriculum. He owned the copyrights to all his writings, and received royalties on their sales. More important, he remained and remains the source of the spiritual practices and doctrines of the religion, and retained the loyalty of the leadership, who regularly looked to him for continued guidance and direction.[29]

The 1960s and Beyond

Hubbard's turning over the reins of the church to others actually coincided with a significant redirection of his concerns. Through the mid-1960s, he had authored a set of books laying out the overall perspective of the church, had spoken and written extensively on the process of Dianetic and Scientology training, had outlined the church's internal structure, and had created the organizational flowchart now utilized in all church centers. All of this foundational work reached a culminating point in 1965 with the publication of *The Bridge to Freedom*, the "Classification and Gradation Chart" that outlines the steps to be followed by church members as they pursue their study of Scientology. The chart succinctly summarizes the results of all of the development and experimentation that had been conducted since the founding of the Hubbard Dianetics Research Foundation fifteen years previously. Although further additions and adjustments would be made over the years, the program for reaching the state of Clear and beginning the process of becoming an Operating Thetan was essentially and clearly delineated.

With the basics completed, Hubbard could turn the movement over to the leaders he had trained and redirect the greater part of his energies to a more complete elucidation of the advanced levels of training. To accomplish this task, in 1967 a new church unit was established, the Sea Organization, or Sea Org. The Sea Org was located aboard three ships, the *Diana*, the *Athena*, and the *Apollo*, with the last serving as the flag ship. Membership was drawn from among the most dedicated of church members. Unlike Hubbard, the average Sea Org member had no experience as a sailor, and the running of the ships had to be learned from scratch.

Soon after the Sea Org was founded, actually less than a month, Hubbard announced that he had discovered an important breakthrough, the means of erasing those mental factors that stand in the way of peace and toleration of humankind. The material he was releasing to the advanced members would constitute the substance of OT III, a new level on the upper end of the Bridge to Freedom.[30] The release of the materials necessarily involved the training of people who not only had mastered the new levels but who were prepared to teach it. As the teaching spread beyond the ships, those who formerly resided on the ship were reassigned to staff the several Advanced Organizations in which the OT teachings would be disseminated to the church.

The Sea Org has attained somewhat of a mythical character among Scientologists. Many are the stories of the hundreds of people who spent time aboard the ships, and those who remain in the church value their opportunity to have been among the chosen few. At the same time, some who left the ships reported bad experiences that eventually provided the church's detractors with scandalous material. In fact, life aboard the Sea Org was a strenuous test of commitment and loyalty to Hubbard and Scientology. Notwithstanding the negative reports, the Sea Org has grown from just those few aboard the ships in the beginning years to more than 6,000 members today.

Life aboard the ships came to an end in 1975. On the one hand, the work for which the Sea Org was created had been completed and the emphasis had once again shifted from the discovery and outlining of the advanced grades to the actual delivery of them to the church membership. Church staff from around the world had been brought on board to learn of the developments, but the ships' facilities were proving inadequate to handle the flow. On the other hand, various governments around the world were reacting to the negative information about the church generated through several international government agencies. These reports, later shown to have been fabricated, created incidents in some ports where the ships were berthed. Both factors led to the shifting of the Sea Organization to the new Flag Land Base established in Florida.

Quietly, through 1975, the church acquired various properties in downtown Clearwater, Florida, a sleepy resort community whose downtown was going through a period of economic decline. Primary purchases included the Fort Harrison Hotel and the former Bank of Clearwater building. The move of the personnel from the ship into their new facilities on land was marred by intense local reaction to the purchase of the property that had occurred through a third party. Suddenly, city fathers became aware that the town was to become the new headquarters of the church. The Scientologists' attempts to settle in their new home were not helped by the attacks of a local radio station comparing the church to a mafia group and other people simply opposed to the church.[31] In retaliation, a few members of the Guardian's Office attempted some "dirty tricks" against several of the antagonists. When their schemes were uncovered, a decade-long war was set off between the church and its local critics.

The actions of the Guardian's Office in Clearwater, as reprehensible as they were, were overshadowed by the massive disclosure of its activities following the July 8, 1977, raid on the churches in Washington, D.C., and Los Angeles. These raids came a week after a former operative with the Guardian's Office who had been involved in an extensive infiltration operation into various government offices in Washington surrendered to the FBI and told his story. As the full account of what had occurred was uncovered, it read like a Cold War spy novel. It appears that several years after the Guardian's Office was established, a plan was put in place to gather material from the files of various government agencies including the Internal Revenue Service and the Federal Bureau of Investigation. The object was twofold. In part, it supported the church's attempt to clear government files of what it considered false material about Hubbard and Scientology. Through the 1970s the church filed a variety of Freedom of Information requests in order to locate material that was informing government attitudes toward the church and that was being circulated overseas and causing problems in other countries. Frustrated at times by agencies unwilling to surrender copies of their files, these Guardian's Office staff felt justified in locating and copying them. However, they also had a second, less justified, purpose. It appears that agents began to gather files on various potential enemies of the church and planned to use the information to embarrass, smear, or otherwise render them harmless.

As a result of the raids, the seized files, some 48,000 documents, were made public, and eleven officials and agents of the Guardian's Office were indicted. Included were Jane Kember, the international head of the office, and Hubbard's wife Mary Sue (his third). In the end, the actual crimes for which they were convicted were relatively minor, though the sentences, handed down in December 1979, ranged between four and five years in prison with additional fines of $10,000. (They may have been given relatively heavy sentences because of the embarrassment of their having infiltrated major government security agencies.) Far beyond the legal penalties, however, the actions of the Guardian's Office opened the church to broad censure from both religious and secular leaders who questioned the morality of the church's allowing the gathering and use of confidential files. It must be said in the church's defense, however, that following the convictions, the church stripped the eleven of all offices in the church, and those later found to have had some role in aiding or covering their actions were either dismissed from their position and/or expelled from the church. The incident became a moment of great soul searching for the remaining Scientology leadership and resulted in a major international reorganization. Among the first acts, the leadership of the Sea Org disbanded the Guardian's Office.

The Church of Scientology International

The disclosures of the activities of the Guardian's Office created a severe crisis. Public access to the seized files provided a basis for a series of civil lawsuits (though most of these would ultimately be rebuffed). At the same time, the bad publicity also created problems for the public image of the church. Thus, even as the trial proceeded, internal changes were initiated. Among the leaders in the efforts to reform the church, with Hubbard's sanction, was David Miscavige, a relatively young leader who had emerged in the Sea Org. Housecleaning began with those convicted in the court case, but soon led to the demotion of other officials in the Guardian's Office and eventually to the discontinuance of the office itself. Through 1980 and into 1981, a number of personnel shifts occurred, followed by a significant revamping of the church's structure at the highest levels.[32] That revamping included consideration of the future of the copyrights of Hubbard's books and the church's trademarks.

Reorganization resulted in the birth of two key corporate entities. First, in 1981 the individual churches and organizations of Scientology were realigned with a new mother church structure, the Church of Scientology International, that now oversees the expansion of Scientology around the world, guides local churches in the application of the teachings (i.e., the technology), and has assumed many of the duties formerly assigned to the Guardian's Office, such as public relations and legal affairs. The second new corporation, the Religious Technology Center, appeared in 1982. It has ultimate ecclesiastical authority in the church. Through the church's first generation, Hubbard personally owned all of the trademarks and service marks utilized by Scientologists, but these were turned over to the new center, which has since controlled the licensing of these items to other church (and nonchurch) entities.

In spite of the controversy that followed the church through the years, it continued to grow and spread. At the beginning of the 1960s, it had just begun to break out of the English-speaking world. However, from the initial non-English-speaking church in Paris (1959), new churches were founded successively in Denmark (1968), Sweden (1969), and Germany (1970). Through the 1970s, Scientology spread through Europe, with churches being opened in Austria (1971), Holland (1972), Italy (1978), and Switzerland (1978). Groups and missions that would become churches would be found in most of the remaining European nations. Scientology centers could be found in fifty-two countries in 1980. That number had expanded to seventy-four by 1992 and included all of the countries of the former Soviet bloc.

Step by step, beginning with his withdrawal from administrative duties, and especially after the removal of the Sea Org to the Flag Land Base in 1975, Hubbard relinquished control of the church to the new generation of leaders. By 1975 most of his research incorporated into the higher OT levels of the church program had been completed, though they would be released to the advanced membership in stages through the remainder of the decade. During the last years of his life, only a small number of close associates had contact with him. He settled first in Florida, but eventually took up residence in rural California in a home outside San Luis Obispo.

During these last years, his consideration of two major social problems led to the development of the church's drug rehabilitation program, the Purification Rundown, and his writing of a concise moral code in response to the perceived decline in public morality, *The Way to Happiness,* which church members have circulated widely. Hubbard also revisited his earlier writing career and celebrated fifty years as a professional writer by authoring a massive science fiction novel, *Battlefield Earth,* which enjoyed good reviews from the genre press. Accompanying the book was an album of music he composed. He followed *Battlefield Earth* with a ten-volume science fiction novel, *Mission Earth,* each volume of which also made the *New York Times* bestseller list.

Hubbard died on January 24, 1986, and has remained as newsworthy in the years since his death as he was during his life.[33] After a suitable pause to acknowledge its founder's life and accomplishments, the church continued its forward march. As a memorial to the founder, each Church of Scientology now maintains an office room, complete with a collection of Hubbard's books, a desk with writing instruments, and a picture of Hubbard, as if one day he might walk into the building and need a place to continue his work.

NOTES

1. Scientology and Dianetics are trademarks of the Religious Technology Center, and the works of L. Ron Hubbard quoted in this work are copyrighted by the L. Ron Hubbard Library.

2. The Church of Scientology has yet to produce a biography of Hubbard, though it has put out a series of biographical booklets that highlight important areas of his life through his own writings and added commentary, and a photographic biography: *L. Ron Hubbard, Images of a Lifetime: A Photographic Biography* (Los Angeles: Bridge Publications, 1996). A comprehensive biography is due out soon. The best of the several biographies attempted by critics, *The Bare-Faced Messiah,* by Russell Miller (New York: Henry Holt, 1988), is seriously lacking as Miller did not have access to many of the documents relating to the rise and progress of the church.

3. On the seventieth anniversary of Hubbard's becoming a blood brother, a ceremony commemorating that event was held among the members of the contemporary Blackfoot tribe. Cf. Letter from C. Emerson Fisher, Aug. 27, 1985, copy in the American Religions Collection, Davidson Library, University of California–Santa Barbara, Santa Barbara, California.

4. Indicative of the continuing relationship between Thompson and Freud is an interesting postcard found in the Freud papers at the Library of Congress in which Thompson is thanked for sending his mentor a "charming photograph of the 3 beauties at the Pacific Ocean." Postcard from Sigmund Freud to Thompson, July 27, 1923, in Library of Congress; copy in the American Religions Collection of the University of California, Santa Barbara.

5. In 1970 an officer of the Explorers Club wrote of Hubbard, "His extensive experience in aerial mapping by camera under almost every type of condition was one of the many qualifying factors for membership. To his credit is the first complete mineralogical survey of Puerto Rico in 1932 and 1933; survey flights throughout the United States to assist in the adjustment of field and facility data; and a Caribbean expedition resulting in valued data for the Hydrographic Office and the University of Michigan. In 1940 he went to Alaska to rewrite *U.S. Coast Pilot, Alaska, Part 1,* and to investigate a new method of radio-positioning entailing a new aerial and a new mathematical computation and instrument." Letter from Marie E. Roy, Feb. 4, 1970, copy in the American Religions Collection, Davidson Library, University of California, Santa Barbara.

6. Hubbard left the service in February 1946 with twenty-one citations, letters of commendation, and medals on his record. It should be noted that the details of Hubbard's naval career have been called into question by the critics of the Church of Scientology. Critics rely on an alleged copy of Hubbard's notice of separation deposited at the Veteran's Administration and accessible through the Freedom of Information Act. This copy, inter alia, mentions four medals and awards rather than twenty-one. The church has replied by filing in a number of court cases both the original notice of separation dept in the church's archives and expert evidence by military specialists explaining why discrepancies may occur for a number of reasons between an original notice of separation and the copy kept by the Veteran's Administration, insisting that the original should prevail.

7. Along with the assistance he offered to some of his fellow patients at Oak Knoll, Hubbard saw two prior events as forming the trajectory that led to Dianetics. While in college, he became curious about the nature of poetry and wondered why poetry affected us differently from prose writing. Of interest were not so much his results as the method he adopted to answer his question. He used a Koenig photometer (which shows the vocal patterns when held against the diaphragm) and produced graphs of the two kinds of vibration patterns. He then posed the question of how the mind might respond to different patterns. Second, in 1938 he authored an essay,

"Excalibur," which concluded with what became a basic Dianetics/Scientology insight that all life is directed toward survival.

8. Space does not allow a detailed discussion of Hubbard's involvement with the Agape Lodge. I have included a more detailed discussion in the most recent editions of my *Encyclopedia of American Religion* (Detroit Gale Research, 1996), 162, and in my paper published as "Thelemic Magic in America: The Emergence of an Alternative Religion," in Joseph H. Fichter, ed., *Alternatives to American Mainline Churches* (Barrytown NY: Unification Theological Seminary, 1983), 67–87.

9. The story of Parsons and Hubbard has been recounted in several books over the last thirty years, but most definitively in the following: Jack Carter, *Sex and Rockets*, Los Angeles: Feral House, 1999; George Pendle, *Strange Angel: The Otherworldly Life of Rocket Scientist John Whiteside Parsons*, San Diego: Harcourt, 2005.

10. In an off-the-cuff remark during the Philadelphia Lectures in 1952 (PDC Lecture 18), Hubbard referred to "my friend Aleister Crowley." This reference would have to be one of literary allusion, as Crowley and Hubbard never met. He obviously had read some of Crowley's writings and makes reference to one of the more famous passages in Crowley's vast writings and his idea that the essence of the magical act was the intention with which it was accomplished. Crowley went on to illustrate magic with a mundane example, an author's intention in writing a book.

11. Critics of the church have gone into great detail to point out possible sources for the various aspects of the teachings of Dianetics and Scientology, and there are certainly numerous points of convergence between Hubbard's teachings and individual ideas and practices available elsewhere. At present, it is not known which aspects of Dianetics Hubbard actually encountered in previously existing sources and subsequently incorporated them into his system and which parts occurred to him independently. The essence of Hubbard's originality, however, lies not so much in the sources of the individual elements as in the synthesizing of them into a finished system.

12. *The Original Thesis* is currently available under the title *The Dynamics of Life* (Los Angeles: Bridge Publications, 1983).

13. The article, "Dianetics: The Evolution of a Science," appeared in the May 1950 issue of *Astounding Science Fiction*, and editor Campbell was for several years a major supporter of Hubbard's new approach to mental health.

14. L. Ron Hubbard, *Dianetics: The Modern Science of Mental Health. A Handbook of Dianetics Therapy* (New York: Hermitage House, 1950).

15. Los Angeles: Bridge Publications, 1989.

16. Los Angeles: Bridge Publications, 1982.

17. The E-meter has frequently been compared to a lie detector, but such a comparison is misleading. Their only common denominator is a Wheatstone bridge, but the two instruments are designed for completely different purposes.

18. See the discussion of the board's inner turmoil in chapter 9 of Hubbard's early work, *Science of Survival* (Los Angeles: Bridge Publications, 1989), 74 (first edition, Wichita, KS: The Hubbard Dianetic Foundation, 1951).

19. Winter had written the preface to the original edition of *Dianetics* and then penned an early favorable account of Hubbard's work, *A Doctor's Report on Dianetics, Theory and Therapy* (New York: Julian Press, 1951).

20. In 1954, through the *Professional Auditor's Bulletin*, Hubbard issued a most enlightening statement on the foundation of the Church of Scientology, the existence of which he had to explain against the criticisms of some of the students of Dianetics. See "Why Doctor of Divinity," *Professional Auditor's Bulletin 32* (Aug. 7, 1954).

21. Hubbard later opined about his offer of Dianetics, "The AMA simply wrote me, 'Why?' and the APA replied, 'If it amounts to anything I am sure we will hear of it in a couple of years.'" Quoted in *Ron the Philosopher: The Rediscovery of the Human Soul* (Los Angeles: L. Ron Hubbard Library, 1996), 14–15.

22. A similar report was prepared in New Zealand though with less hostile conclusions and no recommendations for legislative action.

23. For a discussion of the Scientology situation in Australia, see *Discrimination and Religious Conviction* (Sydney: New South Wales Anti-Discrimination Board, 1984).

24. In 1978 in France, four Scientologists (three, including Hubbard, in absentia) were tried and convicted for fraud. The conviction was reversed on appeal in one of the French decisions in which Scientology was pronounced "religious." French anti-cult movements, however, continued their attacks against the church. The substance of their criticism was later incorporated into the French parliamentary report *Les Sectes en France* (Paris: Les Documents d'information de l'Assemblé Nationale, 1996). For a scholarly criticism of this report, see Massimo Introvigne and J. G. Melton, eds., *Pour en finir avec les sectes: le débat sur le rapport de la commission parlementaire* (3rd ed., Paris: Dervy, 1996). This book includes a detailed critical discussion of the report's comments about Scientology by British sociologist Bryan Wilson ("La Scientologie et le rapport," 277–287).

25. George Malko, *Scientology, the Now Religion* (New York: Delacorte Press, 1970); Paulette Cooper, *The Scandal of Scientology* (New York: Tower, 1971); Robert Kaufmann, *Inside Scientology* (London: Olympia Press, 1972).

26. Omar Garrison, *The Hidden History of Scientology* (London: Arlington Books, 1974).

27. Copies of the original documents, including Cooper's signed statement renouncing her "libels," are in the American Religions Collection at the University of California Santa Barbara. This was discussed by Cooper herself during the Clearwater, Florida, hearings in the 1990s. See also http://www.cs.cmu.edu/~dst/Krasel/cooper/index.html.

28. In the court case that followed the 1979 raid, all of this material was made public for the first time. It was a secret operation obviously done without a general awareness, even through the Guardian's Office representatives around the world. Nobody except the few conspirators knew it until it was revealed in court.

29. His withdrawal from immediate administrative concerns, an act quite common among founders of religious groups, has been viewed by critics as merely a convenient way to shield himself from what they hoped would be definitive actions to be taken by the government and/or courts against the church. Such actions, of course, did not occur.

30. The materials and teachings for the Operating Thetan levels of Scientology are considered confidential. They are discussed only in the most general of terms in the literature and by the leadership of the church when talking to nonmembers. At the same time, they have become the subject of a massive controversy. Over the past twenty years, several members who had access to the higher level materials have left the church and stolen the materials. These former members have tried in various ways to harm the church by circulating copies of these materials. At the same time, fake documents purporting to be OT level material have also been produced and circulated. In response, the church has taken a variety of legal steps to prevent the publication of these, claiming copyright ownership.

31. This conclusion is drawn from the 1980 court case against the Guardian's Office leadership. Only a few people were ever indicted and less than fifty ever

implicated in the illegal actions. Those implicated were later fired by the church. In spite of the fact that the church of Scientology has a certain responsibility for what occurred, just as the whole Catholic Church has some responsibility for what occurred in the Diocese of Boston relative to child abuse, to date no evidence has been presented that more than a small group of people were aware of the crimes under discussion prior to their disclosure in court documents, and the leadership of the church apart from the Guardian's Office acted as if they did not know. Given the hatred against the church, if others had been implicated, they surely would have been called out.

32. Several people, formerly in the church and negatively affected by the reorganization, left the church at this time and joined the ranks of its critics. Chief among these was Jon Atack, author of *A Piece of Blue Sky* and at the center of an anti-Scientology network in the United Kingdom. As might be expected, those most affected for good or ill by the changes in 1980–1981 view what occurred in a very different light.

33. Several years earlier his estranged son had filed a lawsuit claiming that his reclusive father was already dead and that the church leadership was concealing the fact. Rather than appear in court, Hubbard submitted a letter to prove that he was still very much alive.

2

The Cultural Context
of Scientology

William Sims Bainbridge

I must be clear. I am not myself a Scientologist. As an atheistic
Futurist and Transhumanist, I do not share the beliefs of Scientology
or of any other religion, but I do agree with Scientology about the
possibility of achieving transcendence through technology. Where
Scientology seeks to promulgate a spiritual technology, I believe that
physical technologies based in computer science and cognitive science would be required. A more sociological way of expressing this
is to say that I am a member of the same post-Christian cyberculture
as L. Ron Hubbard, but not a member of the Scientology subculture
within it. My personal position is relevant for this scholarly essay for
two reasons. First, members of the archaic Judeo-Christian-Islamic
culture—including some mercenary secular journalists—are so
hostile toward Scientology that a special effort must be made to see
this novel religion's real virtues. Second, it is essential for someone
familiar with the wider culture to which Scientology belongs to place
it in its proper cultural context.

The Science Fiction Subculture

I first learned about Scientology's precursor, Dianetics, through a
1950 issue of *Astounding Science Fiction* that belonged to my maternal
grandfather, and a 1951 issue of *Marvel Science Stories* that I myself
bought at a newsstand (at age ten). Mr. Hubbard published articles
titled "Dianetics: The Evolution of a Science" in *Astounding*, and
"Homo Superior, Here we Come!" in *Marvel*. Already by 1951,
Mr. Hubbard's work was controversial, and the issue of *Marvel* also

included critical appraisals by leading science fiction writers Lester del Rey and Theodore Sturgeon.

It is well known that L. Ron Hubbard was a science fiction writer, but the significance of this fact is seldom realized. Science fiction is a redoubt of deviant science. A *redoubt* is a cultural enclave in which cultural elements can survive, despite being rejected by the wider culture. In part, "redoubt" is a pun, referring to doubting again, or doubting one's very doubts, or undoubting undoubtable falsehoods. But it is also a serious technical concept describing an essential component of any great cultural system. A great culture must be diverse, but some cultural elements contradict others. Partly, we solve this through the division of labor, for example, allowing poets to describe human beings in a different manner from psychologists or political scientists. But some contradictions are so striking or concern such important areas of life that we must exile one or more of the cultural alternatives to a redoubt. Over time, conditions change, and a previously exiled cultural element may sometimes reemerge from the redoubt to take a respected place in conventional culture.

Art, as Coleridge remarked, requires the willing suspension of disbelief. We would agree that maxim applies to science fiction, except that Coleridge missed an important point. There are serious ambiguities about the meaning of the concept *belief.* This is especially true in the area of religion, in which the Judeo-Christian-Islamic tradition placed heavy emphasis on exclusive loyalty to one set of statements, symbols, and formal organizations. That tradition assumes that the truth is known, unique, and expressable. Although all religious traditions have some room for doubt and mysticism, the Judeo-Christian-Islamic has been exclusive to the point of tyranny.

In my recent book *God from the Machine,* I used artificial intelligence computer simulations to model belief not in terms of a dichotomous YES–NO, but as varying probabilities of acting upon myriad combinations of particular ideas. Except for members of highly particularistic religions that demand total belief, people hedge their cognitive bets. Rather than believing in one dogma, they have varying degrees of positive or negative feelings toward a range of doctrines, depending somewhat upon the concrete situation in which they find themselves at the moment.

Scientology, like the Judeo-Christian-Islamic tradition, seems to stress loyalty to a particular set of beliefs, to "100 percent standard tech." However, other maxims in Scientology communicate a kind of relativism, notably, "Your reality is your reality." Indeed, Scientology defines reality in terms of social agreement, a perspective entirely in tune with the sociological concept of social construction (Berger and Luckman, 1966). Incidentally, Earl Babbie's (1977) classic textbook, *Society by Agreement,* seems to have been influenced to some degree by Werner Erhard's EST movement, which in turn drew heavily upon Scientology. Mr. Hubbard's conception of reality as agreement is well illustrated by his *Hymn of Asia,* which has been set to music in the form of a rather attractive oratorio.

Given the present incomplete state of scholarship on the origins of L. Ron Hubbard's thought, it is difficult to know the extent to which Scientology was directly influenced by Buddhism. An alternate possibility is that Mr. Hubbard discerned certain affinities after developing Scientology. One passage of *Hymn of Asia* ("Am I Metteyya?") is a nice example of a Scientology process, apparently training the audience to perceive Mr. Hubbard as very real, while he stands on a stage lecturing them, part of a general program to help Scientologists gain beingness, a grip on a reality that is both solid and positive.

Metteyya is the way the Pali language renders the Sanskrit name Maitreya, the future Buddha who will bring the world ultimate enlightenment. One way to conceptualize many Asian religions, and a way Scientology conceptualizes itself, is as technological religion (Braddeson, 1969). That is, they seek to employ spiritual techniques to accomplish definite goals, notably advancement in personal wisdom, power, and invulnerability.

Science fiction is filled with supermen—including the comic book character explicitly named Superman and created by science fiction fans. Some, like Superman himself, are born superior. Mr. Hubbard's *Marvel* essay, "Homo Superior, Here We Come!" reflects the fact that stories about human evolution to a higher plane were common. For example, *Odd John* by Olaf Stapledon (1935) and *Slan* by A. E. Van Vogt (1946) imagine that ordinary humans will defensively seek to destroy superior beings, and this is one explanation for current hostility against Scientology. In the mid-twentieth-century science fiction subculture, the slogan "fans are slans" reflected a debate about whether the members of the subculture were themselves harbingers of a future posthuman species (Bainbridge, 1986).

Many science fiction stories concerned possible means for becoming superior through physical or spiritual technologies. In *The Alien*, by Raymond F. Jones (1951), the only chance to defeat an extraterrestrial who has taken political control over the Earth is to transplant an alien organ into the brain of a human scientist, to give him the mental power needed for the climactic duel of the novel. In *The World of Null-A* by Van Vogt, mental training techniques derived from the actual General Semantics movement of Alfred Korzybski (1921, 1941) were employed to strengthen the mind of the protagonist. Mr. Hubbard's first Dianetics book cited Korzybski's General Semantics as a precursor of Dianetics, and Van Vogt (1961) himself joined the Dianetics movement.

Mr. Hubbard really had two careers as a science fiction writer. First, from about 1938 until the establishment of Dianetics in the early 1950s, he was one of a stable of authors associated with *Astounding Science Fiction*, edited by John W. Campbell, Jr., the flagship of the so-called golden age of science fiction (Rogers, 1964). His second career consisted of a series of epic novels, beginning in 1982 with *Battlefield Earth*, which was made into a movie in 2000 starring John Travolta, a Scientologist. Among the other authors in the *Astounding* circle who were close to Mr. Hubbard especially worth mentioning are the "dean" of science fiction writers, Robert A. Heinlein, and A. E. Van Vogt.

Astounding, later renamed *Analog*, carried a monthly poll asking readers to rank each story on a 1,000-point scale, with low numbers being good, as in the game of golf (Bainbridge, 1980). Figure 2.1 graphs the thirty writers who published at least ten rated stories or novel episodes. The mean publication years of these items ranged from 1944 to 1966, and for L. Ron Hubbard the mean date for twenty-three items was the very beginning of this range, 1944. The horizontal dimension of the graph is the *Astounding/Analog* ranking, with the most popular writers at the left and least popular at the right. Robert A. Heinlein's ranking is 145 on the 1-to-1,000 scale, the average is 392, and L. Ron Hubbard's ranking is 441, better than the 500 average of all stories but below the mean for these thirty popular writers. The vertical dimension is preference scores on a 0-to-6 scale (from "do not like" to "like very much") from a questionnaire I administered to 595 science fiction fans at the 1978 Iguanacon World Science Fiction Convention. Heinlein's average score was 5.05, the mean for these writers was 4.16, and Mr. Hubbard's score was only 2.15

Heinlein was the highest rated author in the magazine's poll, with a mean publication date of 1947, and Isaac Asimov was near the middle of the pack with a ranking of 351 and mean date of 1950. But by 1978, Asimov had edged out Heinlein for the top spot, having a mean score of 5.08. The classic "space opera" writer E. E. "Doc" Smith was in second place in the magazine polls, but had dropped well below average (rating 3.48) by 1978. Two authors, A. Bertram Chandler and Algis Budrys, were rated somewhat negatively by *Analog* readers in the 1950s, but by 1978 had earned ratings near the middle of the pack. Coincidentally, a brief autobiography written by Budrys in 1997 notes, "From the late 1980s to date, his work is often under the auspices of L. Ron Hubbard's

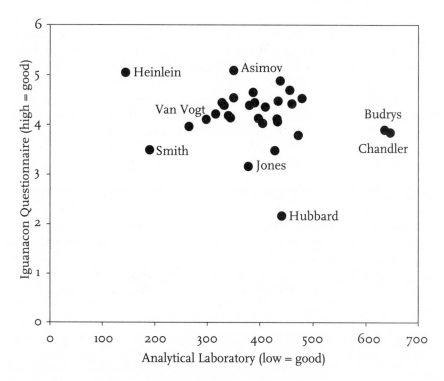

FIGURE 2.1. Popularities of Golden-Age Science Fiction Writers

Writers of the Future program."[1] I once had a private lunch with Budrys and Heber Jentzsch, president of the Church of Scientology International.

Thus the graph allows us to see how the subculture of science fiction "fandom" has changed its views of some of the older writers. Mr. Hubbard, notably, dropped from the middle of the pack to the bottom, possibly because fans had become hostile to Scientology as it developed during the intervening years. In my study of the social movement that produced space technology (Bainbridge, 1976), I described fandom as a somewhat retreatist redoubt, capable of preserving and even creating new ideas, but incapable of organizing to bring them to reality. Thus, fans may paradoxically resent Scientology's attempt to bring their dreams to reality.

Science Adventurism

Critics of Scientology sometimes disparage L. Ron Hubbard's love of adventure, implying that it was an unrealistic residue of his experience writing action-adventure fiction. I would suggest something quite different: The image of adventurer-scientists undertaking dangerous expeditions is quite realistic, and illuminates much about Scientology, although this image has gone somewhat out of style. Few people will today recall that Alexander von Humbolt heroically combined scientific research with bold exploration of uncharted territories two centuries ago, but perhaps they know that Charles Darwin had to go literally to the ends of the Earth to do the research reported in *Origin of Species*. L. Ron Hubbard may or may not have risked his life, but scientists and scholars in my own family did so, in one case connecting to Mr. Hubbard's personal story.

According to several Scientology publications, Mr. Hubbard first learned about psychoanalysis, and thus took the first major step toward creating his own science of the mind from a flamboyant Navy doctor and scientist named Snake Thompson. Opponents of Scientology imagine that Snake Thompson was a figment of Mr. Hubbard's imagination (Miller, 1987), but as I explained in a statement posted by others on Internet, he was entirely real:

> Snake Thompson was the best friend of my great uncle, Con (Consuelo Seoane). Together, around 1911, they spent nearly two years as American spies inside the Japanese Empire, charting possible invasion routes and counting all the Japanese fortifications and naval guns. It was an official but top secret joint Army-Navy spy expedition, with Con representing the Army, and Snake, the Navy. They pretended to be South African naturalists studying Japanese reptiles and amphibians, and Con was constantly worried that Snake had a camera hidden in his creel, which would get them shot if the Japanese checked too closely. Thompson habitually wore a green scarf fastened with a gold pin in the shape of a snake.[2]

After fighting in the Spanish-American War and helping to suppress the Philippine Insurrection, Con received specialized training in mapping and

military engineering, and he published a book on international law (C. S. Seoane, 1904, 1960; R. L. Seoane, 1968). Immediately after the Japanese victory
over Russia, he was assigned back to the Philippines as a staff officer command-
ing a team that prepared detailed military charts of the islands. There was much
concern among Army leadership about Japanese expansionism, and many expected that eventually war would break out between the Japanese Empire and
the United States. Con learned that General Wood wished he had an agent who
could scout possible invasion routes into Japan without being caught. Con took
it upon himself to find the right man for this impossible job. Playing cards with
his fellow officers, he sized each of them up. Quickly he realized Joseph "Snake"
Thompson was his man. Of average height, with blond hair and blue eyes, he
had a rapier-like wit. Snake got his nickname because he had an all-consuming
interest in reptiles, amphibia, and hard-shelled beetles. On one Navy ship, he
amused himself by placing a frantic snake in the officers' bathtub.

Like my great uncle, Thompson was an adventurer, having been attached
to the U.S. forces in China during the Boxer Rebellion. Snake's father had been
a missionary in Japan, and he himself had served two years at the naval hospital in Yokohama, so he was fluent in Japanese. Snake had an exceedingly alert
mind, which made Seoane think of Sherlock Holmes, but he was also quick in
action. Con asked Snake what he would do if a card player pulled a pistol on
him. "I would have it out of his grasp before he realized what was happening,"
Thompson replied confidently. Top-level approval was needed for the plan to
send Snake as a spy into Japanese territory. Wood and Seoane prepared a paper
for signature by future president William Howard Taft, who was then secretary
of war and traveling in the Orient, then slipped it into a pile of papers for Taft's
signature. Perhaps without fully realizing what he was doing, Taft signed it.

Both Con and Snake understood how dangerous the mission would be,
but the doctor had the advantage of a good cover story for his travels. He would
pretend to be a South African naturalist named Victor Kuhne, tramping the
shores of the Pacific in search of scientific specimens. Thompson's favorite
book was Darwin's *Origin of Species,* and he was fascinated by the question of
why species have different geographic ranges. Thus he was well prepared to
tell a convincing story that would explain his movements while concealing his
real purpose.

Thompson traveled with Taft's party as far as Vladivostok, where he disappeared. After a few months, he reappeared in the Philippines, explaining to Con
that he had been able to penetrate the Japanese Empire but discovered he was
not well trained to collect militarily useful data. "Will you go with me?" he asked
Con, knowing that Seoane had just the knowledge of maps and military engineering that he himself lacked. Instantly, Con agreed. He would also pretend to
be a South African naturalist, John G. Nurse. Together, they would chart all of
Japan's shore defenses, in the captured territories as well as the home islands.

In June 1909, they did a dry run. Pretending to collect butterflies, they
scouted Hong Kong's outer fortifications. They did not dare write down the
information about guns and forts they gained, so Con developed a system of
making little scratches on the side of his shoe, which would later remind him

of the information and help him memorize it. After a few days training themselves for espionage, Snake and Con went to Shanghai, and from there to Kobe, Japan, where they would further develop their methods. They had business cards printed in English and Japanese, bearing their false names and explaining they were South African scientists, which they would give to every hotel as their identity papers.

The British had recently won a war in South Africa against the Dutch settlers they called Boers, and Snake pretended to be the son of a Boer mother and English father, a ruse he had successfully used in an earlier escapade. There was no way the two men could conceal themselves in Japanese society, so they followed the opposite strategy, being extremely obvious in a way that would prevent the Japanese from suspecting their real mission. Whenever they entered a major city, Snake would very loudly present himself at the British consular office, earning visible British scorn and thereby fooling the Japanese.

After a few days adjusting in Kobe, they headed for the Ryukyu Islands and Okinawa, with five gallons of medical alcohol in their luggage for preserving snakes they would collect. Indeed, their ghastly specimens deterred the police from finding any incriminating evidence against them. Every day was a battle of wits against suspicious police spies, and the two Americans were constantly on alert. Espionage then took them to Japan's home islands, beginning with the southern island, Kyushu, followed by the Tsushima islands and then Yokohama in the heart of the Empire. From there they examined dozens of potential invasion points, memorizing as much as they could and using a code to insert a few crucial facts into an apparently harmless naturalist's diary. For example, when they viewed the Sendai Temple they wrote that there were 135 steps in the approach, referring actually to the total number of artillery field pieces they had seen in the area. Another time, references to fifty-four green polypedates and seventy-eight tadpoles meant 5 four-inch guns and 7 eight-inch guns.

Their perilous expedition took them to Korea and deep into Manchuria, where they observed the Japanese military occupation, some distance into China, then finally back to the Philippines in the spring of 1911, nearly two years since they had begun their mission. During the expedition, Thompson had in fact assembled 11,787 specimens of reptiles, amphibians, and insects, which he gave to the museum of the California Academy of Sciences, half under his own name and half in his guise as Victor Kuhne.[3] In 1913, he published a scientific article about the *hibikari* snake, concealing the fact he had collected the specimens during his espionage tour with Con. A 1923 article proves his knowledge of psychoanalysis, and Silas Warner (1993) reports that Thompson was a practicing psychoanalyst for many years. Warner implies that Thompson was the primary influence leading to Mr. Hubbard's development of Dianetics, and suggests that Scientology's epistemology (Hubbard, 1956) was influenced by Thompson's dictum, "If it's not true for you, it's not true."

I have told this true story at some length, both because Thompson was so influential in Mr. Hubbard's intellectual development, and because it illustrates a little-appreciated fact. A very few adventuresome souls really do have the fantastic experiences described in science fiction or action-adventure stories.

I count among them my great grandfather William Folwell Bainbridge (1882a, 1882b), who carried out a social-scientific world tour of Protestant missions in 1879–1880, my grandfather William Seaman Bainbridge (1919), who studied surgical practices on both sides of the western front in World War I, his cousin Louis Livingston Seaman (1905, 1906), who studied military medical practices in the Russo-Japanese War, plus my cousin Christopher McIntosh (1987, 1992) and myself, both of whom have carried out extensive field observation of esoteric religious groups. Our uncle John Seaman Bainbridge (1972) devoted ten years to the intellectual and physical adventure of developing law schools throughout sub-Saharan Africa.

In particular, I spent six months in 1970 doing covert participant observation inside Scientology for my senior honors thesis, even trying Con's method of using shoe scratches to record data, and two years intermittently from 1971 to 1975 inside a nominally Satanic offshoot of it called the Process (Bainbridge, 1978). Subsequently, I felt it was my duty to provide court affidavits for the Church of Scientology—at no cost, of course—affirming that many members really did consider it to be their religion. Scientology was wise enough to notice that the fact I had done covert research without their permission or guidance added credibility to my affirmations, and our relationship has been on cordial but unbiasing terms ever since.

One way to look at membership in the Church of Scientology is as a great adventure. Very few people infiltrate it as I had done, given that espionage runs in my family. However, a large number undoubtedly gain from their spiritual processing sessions many of the benefits of adventure: anticipation, excitement, a sense of stretching one's capabilities, intense emotions, a series of unusual perspectives on life, and a treasure trove of vivid memories to look back upon. Adventure builds competence and a sense of efficacy. Mr. Hubbard's personal interest in the sea, in wild adventures in exotic lands, and in combining science with spiritual questing may in some significant measure have been inspired by Snake Thompson. Contrary to rumor, Thompson was entirely real and he lived the kind of life that bland folk imagine only fictional characters experience. Scientology cannot fully be understood, unless we realize that it is an adventure comparable to science fiction, but real.

A Ludic System of Honor

A science-oriented adventure is very much like a game, but all of life can be conceptualized in ludic terms, especially in highly competitive societies such as ancient Greece and modern America (Huizinga, 1949; Gouldner, 1965). Mr. Hubbard has said, "Life can best be understood by likening it to a game" (Hubbard, 1956: 45) and "The highest activity is playing a game" (Hubbard, 1956: 103). Competitive games are a quest for status—winner preferred over loser—within a system of rules.

Today, Scientology says it seeks to increase a person's ability rather than status: "The goal of auditing is to restore beingness and ability. This is accomplished by (1) helping the individual rid himself of any spiritual disabilities and (2) increasing individual abilities. Obviously, both are necessary for an individual to achieve his full spiritual potential."[4] Beingness is the ability to say confidently, "I am." Ability is the ability to say confidently, "I am able." Yet spiritual abilities cannot be measured outside the framework of assumptions of the particular spiritual movement, so spiritual ability is a status, relative to a socially constructed framework of meanings.

In secular society, status is marked by money and power. In the ivory towers of universities, professors imagine they have status despite the lack of money and power, but their honor tends to evaporate when they leave the tower. Similarly, every religious sect confers a subjective sense of honor upon members, because they are the salt of the Earth, the chosen of God, or in some other way supernaturally better than their status in secular society justifies.

In an often quoted passage, Erving Goffman (1963: 7) asserted, "In America at present, however, separate systems of honor seem to be on the decline." Forty-five years ago may have been a low point, because in earlier decades many flourishing fraternal societies like the Masons had given American men a sense of position in a status hierarchy. Scientology is to a significant extent patterned on them, their Rosicrucian or Golden Dawn variants, or on the conventional university system that may have the same historical origins. These groups assign members to a long series of statuses, often using the term *degree* to describe each level. In 1950, Mr. Hubbard announced his intention to develop the spiritual technology to attain an advanced state he called *Clear*. Sixteen years later, when he finally announced success, his movement offered a whole series of degrees of spiritual advancement, and they continued to grow for at least another decade. Degrees below clear were called *Release*, and degrees above clear were called *Operating Thetan*, or *OT.*

When Dianetics was first publicized, the press developed the habit of calling it "the poor man's psychoanalysis." This ironic slander suggests that Dianetics is an inferior variant of psychoanalysis, without quite affirming that psychoanalysis itself was any good (Bakan, 1958; cf. Cuddihy, 1974). It was useful for its practitioners because for a while it enabled intellectuals who immigrated to the United States to gain somewhat high status serving high-status clients (Hollingshead and Redlich, 1958). Against the formidable opposition they faced, Dianetics and Scientology needed to develop a strategy to assert the reality of the clear status that only they could attain. As Rodney Stark and I described it in 1980, this strategy consisted of four stages:

1. Prohibition of independent creation and evaluation of clears.
2. Development of a hierarchy of statuses below clear.
3. Isolation of the preclear at the crucial stage in upward progress.
4. Development of a hierarchy of statuses above clear.

A game or separate system of honor requires a boundary, within which the rules apply. The triumphant act of seizing a chess piece has no meaning outside the rules of chess. Just as only the Roman Catholic Church can decide who is a Catholic saint, only Scientology can decide who is clear.

The many release statuses below clear commit a person to the system. A person who fails to achieve clear is at risk of losing the release grades, as well, which certainly happens if the person leaves Scientology. The release grades are also a training ground in the norms and values, and a series of tests of the individual's willingness to play the game.

If self-esteem and the respect of other people are the real goals of playing a status game, then the individual must somehow be convinced to stop whining, complaining, and being dependent. All of the steps up to clear require the preclear to depend upon other people, but at the last moment, the clear must learn to depend upon himself.

After going clear, a Scientologist may still wish to gain added abilities and status, so a ladder of further degrees is provided. Lingering doubts may be handled by hopes that the additional benefits will finally provide complete satisfaction. However, humans did not evolve to be perfectly happy, but to continue to struggle for advantage, as in games. Additional degrees above clear allowed Scientologists to continue attaining successes and the increasing subjective status associated with them.

Cyberspace Culture

In "Dianetics: The Evolution of a Science," Mr. Hubbard contemplated modeling the human brain on "the optimum computing machine" such that "it should be *always* right, its *answers* never wrong" (Hubbard 1950a: 46). The status of *clear* was named by analogy with pressing the clear button on a calculator, clearing it of bad data. Mr. Hubbard was certainly not the only person to advocate applying computer engineering to the problems of the human mind, but was among the first to try to do it (cf. Maltz 1960). Recently, a number of cultural and technical developments have created a massive *cyberculture* with profound religious implications, poorly organized, poorly understood, but profoundly important.

Science fiction has played a role, providing both inspiration and terminology. Notably, the word *robot* came from the classic drama *R.U.R.* by Karel Capek (1923); *cyberspace* came from William Gibson's (1984) novel *Neuromancer,* and *avatar* came from Neal Stephenson's (1992) novel *Snow Crash*. I cannot guess who was the first science fiction writer to imagine transferring a human personality from a biological brain to a computer, but *The Shockwave Rider* by John Brunner (1975) is an influential example. Crucially, respected leaders in computer science and engineering have argued that this wild idea is actually feasible, desirable, and possibly inevitable (Moravec, 1988; Kurzweil, 1999). Much of my own research in recent years has been devoted to developing methods to accomplish what I call personality capture (Bainbridge, 2003, 2004, 2006a, 2006c), the first step on the way toward emulating human personalities inside computers, information systems, and robots.

Without in any way endorsing Scientology's specific procedures, I can report that some of them are potentially relevant to personality capture. From the very beginning, Scientology has emphasized preserving data from auditing sessions. The auditor running an E-meter session on a preclear is supposed to keep a written record that becomes part of the preclear's case file, which may guide a different auditor in future. Unlike psychoanalysis, Scientology has not traditionally built a transference relationship between a client and a particular practitioner, but attempted to employ precise procedures that could interchangeably be applied by different trained practitioners. The E-meter has its own very special design features and operational procedures, but fundamentally it measures galvanic skin response, something also done by today's researchers in *affective computing*, which means incorporating the user's emotions in human-computer interaction (Picard, 1997). Thus, records of auditing sessions, which include E-meter readings associated with things the preclear said, could be data for personality capture because they reflect what stimuli produce emotional arousal in the individual.

Around 1984, I was able to interface an E-meter with a computer and write software that would display the E-meter reactions on a screen in the form of a moving bar graph that could be saved along with typed text describing what the person was saying. I did not follow up on this line of personality capture research, but did demonstrate it at the time in a colloquium at Harvard University that the public relations officer of Scientology of Boston attended. I have no reason to believe that Scientology was in any way influenced by my experiments, and certainly the idea would have occurred to its technical people quite independently. But I was interested to see when I toured all the Los Angeles facilities of the church in 2000 that computer output from E-meters was used in auditor training sessions.

Another connection to personality capture was also revealed on that 2000 trip. The Church of Scientology was already working to transfer approximately 3,000 recorded lectures by Mr. Hubbard to media designed to last thousands of years. I was shown the technical methods that had been developed to that point, and told about Scientology's own software to remove noise from the historical recordings, many of which dated from the early 1950s. Among the unfair negative publicity of 2007 have been CNN news broadcasts that mocked a facility the church has established in New Mexico, believed to be a vault to preserve Scientology's archives.[5] From the cyberculture viewpoint, it is quite reasonable for Scientology to preserve its technology, its historical archives, and its members' auditing records against the possibility of world war, catastrophic natural disaster, or even another Dark Age.

Recent research has documented the huge gulf that exists between cyberculture and traditional religion. Notably, videogames are practically never based upon traditional religious myths, but many of them promulgate pagan, exotic, or innovative supernatural ideas, as well as occasionally disparaging traditional faith (W. S. Bainbridge and W. A. Bainbridge 2007; cf. W. A. Bainbridge and W. S. Bainbridge 2007).

A striking example of how novel cyber-religion can become a prominent part of many peoples' lived experience is the massively multiplayer online game, *World of Warcraft* (Lummis and Kern, 2006; Ducheneaut et al., 2007), which has eight million subscribers. The player creates one or more characters, each of a distinctive race and class, and over a period of months undertakes quests inside a vast pseudo-medieval world. As part of a large research project, I am currently running many characters, several of which are priests, either in the Holy Light cult of Humans, the Elune lunar cult of Night Elves, or the Voodoo cult of the Trolls. The priests cannot only cast spells that actually work, but resurrect dead characters, and study at least the rudiments of exotic doctrines. *World of Warcraft* is a separate system of honor, including not only seventy levels of general experience in questing and five degrees of proficiency in alchemy, but also ranks within guilds and possession of distinctive spiritual abilities, not unlike those described by Scientology.

Researchers are only just beginning to chart the outlines of the emerging cyberculture, and one very rough way to connect it provisionally to Scientology is to look at Scientology's geographic distribution. In the past, I have used geographic data to document the negative correlations between new religious movements (including Scientology) and conventional church membership (Stark and Bainbridge, 1985; Bainbridge, 1989). Figure 2.2 maps the density of Scientology clears across regions of the United States based on data given me by the church in 1985, and figure 2.3 maps the personal Web sites of individual Scientologists in 1998.

The Pacific region (which includes Alaska and Hawaii) has the highest rates for Scientology, but many studies show it has exceptionally low rates for membership in conventional churches. The Mountain region is also somewhat low on church membership, whereas the other seven regions tend to be at about the same level as each other, and the rate of Scientologists is somewhat high in the Mountain region. Both maps show New England below the

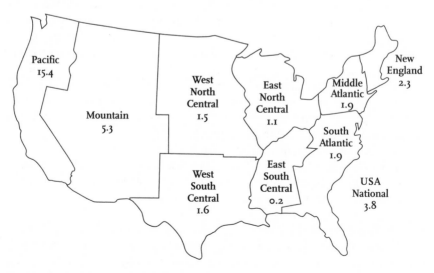

FIGURE 2.2. Scientology Clears per 100,000 in 1985

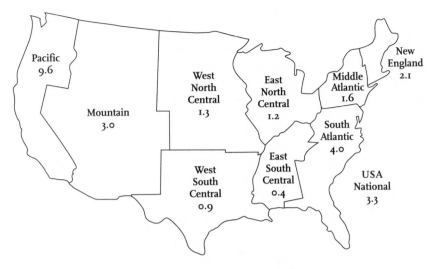

FIGURE 2.3. Scientologist Web sites per 100,000 in 1998

national average but above five or six other regions in density of Scientologists. In these measures and others like them, the South Atlantic region would be at about the same low level as the East South Central region if we removed Florida and the area near Washington, D.C. As it happens, the Founding Church of Scientology is in the District of Columbia, and a major center is in Clearwater, Florida.

The Pacific region, of course, includes "Silicon Valley," high-tech industries like Microsoft in the Seattle area, and computer companies up and down the coast. For example, the home of the company that produced *World of Warcraft* is in Irvine, California, just south of Los Angeles, whereas the Scientology headquarters in Hollywood is just a hair north of the city. The slightly high rates of new religions in New England, despite the fact that the church member rate there is not low, may be the effect of the university communities in New Haven, Providence, and Boston, and Boston's high-tech Route 128 is a slightly older version of Silicon Valley. These connections are only suggestive, of course, but to me they imply a positive correlation between technologically innovative regions and interest in Scientology, in addition to the well-known negative correlation with traditional religion.

Conclusion

This chapter has outlined some of the complex sociocultural history of Scientology in terms of four formative phenomena: (1) science fiction, (2) science adventurism, (3) ludic systems of honor, and (4) the emerging cyberculture. Scientology is not an isolated phenomenon, but can best be understood in terms of these cultural origins and affinities. People who are not attuned to these influences may misunderstand what they are getting into when they encounter Scientology, occasionally leading to unpleasant results.

Scientology has affinities with a wide range of other techniques for training the human mind, including Asian religions and Western psychological treatments, but it is entirely at odds with the dominant Judeo-Christian-Islamic religious tradition. Christians, especially, should be careful when they criticize the factual correctness of Scientology's claims, given the flimsy nature of their own claims about the divinity and resurrection of Jesus. Outsiders of all kinds tend to underestimate the extent to which Scientology could harmonize with major sociocultural trends likely to be important in postindustrial societies. It is impossible to predict whether Scientology will grow to become a major religious tradition, become merely one of many small scientistic faiths, or be overshadowed by technological accomplishments based on the cognitive and computer sciences. We can only hope that all will come clear in time.

NOTES

1. http://www.alamo-sf.org/lonestarcon2/budrys.html
2. http://www.solitarytrees.net/cowen/misc/auto2.htm or http://www.cs.cmu.edu/~dst/Library/Shelf/miller/bfm01.htm
3. http://www.calacademy.org/research/herpetology/history.php
4. http://www.scientology.org/en_US/religion/auditing/pg002.html
5. http://www.youtube.com/watch?v=ooaMq3CEJ2Q or http://www.youtube.com/watch?v=fB87IJT78M8

REFERENCES

Babbie, Earl R. 1977. *Society by Agreement: An Introduction to Sociology.* Belmont, California: Wadsworth.

Bainbridge, John Seaman. 1972. *The Study and Teaching of Law in Africa.* South Hackensack, New Jersey: F. B. Rothman.

Bainbridge, William Folwell. 1882a. *Along the Lines at the Front.* Philadelphia: American Baptist Publication Society.

Bainbridge, William Folwell. 1882b. *Around the World Tour of Christian Missions.* New York: C. R. Blackall.

Bainbridge, William Seaman. 1919. *Report on Medical and Surgical Developments of the War.* Washington, D.C.: United States Naval Medical Bulletin (special issue bound as a book).

Bainbridge, William Sims. 1976. *The Spaceflight Revolution.* New York: Wiley-Interscience.

Bainbridge, William Sims. 1978. *Satan's Power: A Deviant Psychotherapy Cult.* Berkeley: University of California Press.

Bainbridge, William Sims. 1980. "The Analytical Laboratory, 1938–1976," *Analog* 100(1): 121–134.

Bainbridge, William Sims. 1986. *Dimensions of Science Fiction.* Cambridge, Massachusetts: Harvard University Press.

Bainbridge, William Sims. 1987. "Science and Religion: The Case of Scientology."
Pp. 59–79 in *The Future of New Religious Movements*, edited by David G. Bromley and Phillip E. Hammond. Macon, Georgia: Mercer University Press.

Bainbridge, William Sims. 1989. "The Religious Ecology of Deviance," *American Sociological Review* 54: 288–295.

Bainbridge, William Sims. 1994. "General Semantics." P. 1361 in *The Encyclopedia of Language and Linguistics*, edited by R. E. Asher and J. M. Y. Simpson. Oxford: Pergamon.

Bainbridge, William Sims. 2001. "Scientology." In *Concise Encyclopedia of Language and Religions*, edited by J. F. A Sawyer and J. M. Y. Simpson. New York: Elsevier.

Bainbridge, William Sims. 2003. "Massive Questionnaires for Personality Capture," *Social Science Computer Review* 21(3): 267–280.

Bainbridge, William Sims. 2004. "The Future of the Internet: Cultural and Individual Conceptions." Pp. 307–324 in *Society Online: The Internet in Context*, edited by Philip N. Howard and Steve Jones. Thousand Oaks, California: Sage.

Bainbridge, William Sims. 2005. "Scientology." Pp. 1499–1500 in *The Encyclopedia of Religion and Nature*, edited by Bron Taylor. London: Thoemmes Continuum.

Bainbridge, William Sims. 2006a. "Cyberimmortality: Science, Religion, and the Battle to Save Our Souls," *The Futurist* 40(2): 25–29.

Bainbridge, William Sims. 2006b. *God from the Machine*. Walnut Grove, California: AltaMira.

Bainbridge, William Sims. 2006c. "Information Technology for Convergence." Pp. 347–368 in *Managing Nano-Bio-Info-Cogno Innovations: Converging Technologies in Society*, edited by William Sims Bainbridge and Mihail C. Roco. Berlin: Springer.

Bainbridge, William Sims, and Rodney Stark. 1980. "Scientology: To Be Perfectly Clear," *Sociological Analysis* 41: 128–136.

Bainbridge, William Sims, and Wilma Alice Bainbridge. 2007. "Electronic Game Research Methodologies: Studying Religious Implications," *Review of Religious Research* 49: 35–53.

Bainbridge, Wilma Alice, and William Sims Bainbridge. 2007. "Creative Uses of Software Errors: Glitches and Cheats," *Social Science Computer Review* 25: 61–77.

Bakan, David. 1958. *Sigmund Freud and the Jewish Mystical Tradition*. Princeton, New Jersey: Van Nostrand.

Berger, Peter L., and Thomas Luckmann. 1966. *The Social Construction of Reality: A Treatise in the Sociology of Knowledge*. Garden City, New York: Doubleday.

Braddeson, Walter. 1969. *Scientology for the Millions*. Los Angeles: Sherbourne.

Brunner, John. 1975. *The Shockwave Rider*. New York: Harper and Row.

Capek, Karel. 1923. *R.U.R.* Garden City, New York: Doubleday, Page.

Cuddihy, John Murray. 1974. *The Ordeal of Civility: Freud, Marx, Lévi-Strauss, and the Jewish Struggle with Modernity*. New York: Basic Books.

Del Ray, Lester. 1951. "Superman—C.O.D.," *Marvel Science Stories* 3 (May): 116–119.

Ducheneaut, Nicolas, Nicholas Yee, Eric Nickell, and Robert J. Moore. 2007. "The Life and Death of Online Gaming Communities: A Look at Guilds in World of Warcraft." Pp. 839–848 in *Proceedings of CHI 2007*, April 28—May 3, San Jose, California. New York: Association for Computing Machinery.

Gibson, William. 1984. *Neuromancer*. New York: Ace.

Goffman, Erving. 1963. *Stigma*. Englewood Cliffs, New Jersey: Prentice Hall.

Gouldner, Alvin. 1965. *Enter Plato*. New York: Basic Books.

Hollingshead, August, and Fredrick C. Redlich. 1958. *Social Class and Mental Illness.* New York: Wiley.

Hubbard, L. Ron. 1950a. "Dianetics: The Evolution of a Science," *Astounding Science Fiction* 45(3): 43–87.

Hubbard, L. Ron. 1950b. *Dianetics: The Modern Science of Mental Health.* New York: Paperback Library.

Hubbard, L. Ron. 1951. "Homo Superior, Here We Come," *Marvel Science Stories* 3 (May): 111–114.

Hubbard, L. Ron. 1956. *The Fundamentals of Thought.* Edinburgh: Publications Organization World Wide.

Hubbard, L. Ron. 1982. *Battlefield Earth: A Saga of the Year 3000.* New York: St. Martin's Press.

Hubbard, L. Ron. 2000. *Hymn of Asia.* Los Angeles: Golden Era Productions.

Huizinga, Johan. 1949. *Homo Ludens: A Study of the Play-Element in Culture.* London: Routledge and Kegan Paul.

Jones, Raymond F. 1951. *The Alien.* New York: World Editions.

Korzybski, Alfred. 1921. *Manhood of Humanity.* New York: E. P. Dutton.

Korzybski, Alfred. 1941. *Science and Sanity: An Introduction to non-Aristotelian Systems and General Semantics.* Lancaster, Pennsylvania: International non-Aristotelian Library Publishing Company.

Kurzweil, Ray. 1999. *The Age of Spiritual Machines: When Computers Exceed Human Intelligence.* New York: Viking.

Lummis, Michael, and Ed Kern. 2006. *World of Warcraft: Master Guide.* New York: BradyGames.

Maltz, Maxwell 1960. *Psycho-Cybernetics.* Englewood Cliffs, New Jersey: Prentice-Hall.

McIntosh, Christopher. 1987. *The Rosicrucians: The History, Mythology, and Rituals of an Occult Order.* Wellingborough, England: Crucible.

McIntosh, Christopher. 1992. *The Rose Cross and the Age of Reason.* New York: E. J. Brill.

Miller, Russell. 1987. *Bare-Faced Messiah: The True Story of L. Ron Hubbard.* London: M. Joseph.

Moravec, Hans P. 1988. *Mind Children: The Future of Robot and Human Intelligence.* Cambridge, Massachusetts: Harvard University Press.

Picard, Rosalind W. 1997. *Affective Computing.* Cambridge, Massachusetts: MIT Press.

Rogers, Alva. 1964. *A Requiem for Astounding.* Chicago: Advent.

Seaman, Louis Livingston. 1905. *From Tokio through Manchuria with the Japanese.* New York: Appleton.

Seaman, Louis Livingston. 1906. *The Real Triumph of Japan: The Conquest of the Silent Foe.* New York: Appleton.

Seoane, Consuelo Andrew. 1904. *Syllabus of Davis' International Law.* Kansas City, Missouri: Hudson-Kimberly.

Seoane, Consuelo Andrew. 1960. *Beyond the Ranges.* New York: Robert Spellar.

Seoane, Rhoda Low. 1968. *Uttermost East and the Longest War.* New York: Vantage.

Stapledon, Olaf. 1935. *Odd John.* London: Methuen.

Stark, Rodney, and William Sims Bainbridge. 1985. *The Future of Religion.* Berkeley: University of California Press.

Stephenson, Neal. 1992. *Snow Crash.* New York: Bantam.

Sturgeon, Theodore. 1951. "How to Avoid a Hole in the Head," *Marvel Science Stories* 3 (May): 114–116.

Thompson, Joseph C. 1914. "The Variation Exhibited by Mainland and Island Speci-
  mens of the Hibakari Snake, Natrix Vibakari [Boie]," *Proceedings of the United
  States National Museum* 46: 157–160.
Thompson, Joseph C. 1923. "Psychoanalytic Literature," *United States Naval Medical
  Bulletin* 19(3).
Van Vogt, A. E. 1946. *Slan.* Sauk City, Wisconsin: Arkham House.
Van Vogt, A. E. 1948. *The World of Null-A.* New York: Simon and Schuster.
Van Vogt, A. E. 1961. "Predisposition and the Power of Hidden Words," *Journal of the
  Dianetic Sciences* 1(1): 1–18.
Warner, Silas L. 1993. "The Psychoanalytic Roots of Scientology," lecture presented at
  the winter meeting of the American Academy of Psychoanalysis New York City.
  Online at http://www.aapsa.org/forum/forum43_1.html#4312.

3

Researching Scientology: Perceptions, Premises, Promises, and Problematics

Douglas E. Cowan

When at last we have our way, man's inhumanity to man will have ended. We have the answers. Authority belongs to those who can do the job. And Scientology will inherit tomorrow as surely as the sun will rise.

—Church of Scientology, "Scientology's Future"

Introduction

This chapter began, as I suspect many do, in a bar.

A number of years ago, at the annual meeting of the American Academy of Religion, three colleagues and I were sitting over drinks with a representative of the Church of Scientology, and at one point she asked, "Why don't academics write more about Scientology?" With neither hesitation nor consultation, we all answered virtually in the same breath, "Because you threaten to sue us if we say things you don't like!" Although that may have overstated the case a wee bit, the point was clear: Among academics there is the *perception*, at least, that research into the Church of Scientology does not come without costs, and that for many scholars those costs appear simply prohibitive. Media stories about the difficulties encountered by journalists who write about the Church, clear if relatively isolated incidences of attempted interference in the academic process, and watercooler conversations about different experiences colleagues have had all contribute to this perception. And this is extremely unfortunate, because the Church of Scientology is an important new religious movement for a number of reasons, and one that is deserving of the kind of careful social scientific investigation that has been conducted in other groups.

Four interrelated elements comprise what I am calling the research problem of the Church of Scientology: (1) the perceptions of the Church, both positive and negative, that inevitably inform any research agenda; (2) the premises on which such research ought to be conducted; (3) the promises that are implicit in it for the field of NRM studies (and, not insignificantly, I would suggest, for the Church itself); and (4) the problems encountered because of a paucity of data, and either the unwillingness of Church members and officials to cooperate in social scientific research or interference from the Church as research proceeds. Obviously, then, this is not a report on research that has been completed, per se. It is, rather, one set of preliminary statements about research that I believe ought to be conducted, and is guided for the most part by the kind of questions in which I am interested. Although some of these could certainly be turned into testable hypotheses, most of them are designed simply to raise the issues for further discussion. Within each section, however, I hope to make a few concrete suggestions for elements of a useful research agenda.

In many ways, this chapter is about perceptions. A fundamental principle of a sociology of knowledge is that social action of any type is not based on *reality as it is,* but on *reality as it is perceived to be.* And perceptions are often much more powerful and much more compelling than the reality they allege to represent.[1]

Perceptions: The Church of Scientology

In a wide variety of publications and advertisements, the Church of Scientology claims to be "the fastest growing religious movement on Earth" (Church of Scientology International [hereafter CSI] 2004c: 3; 2006),[2] and the "only major religious movement to emerge in the twentieth century" (CSI 2004c: 3; Jentzsch 2002: 141). From the opening pages of *Dianetics* (Hubbard [1950] 1990) to the nearly 100 sermons contained in *The Background, Ministry, Ceremonies and Sermons of the Scientology Religion* (CSI 2002), Scientological literature is filled with similar claims—both falsifiable and nonfalsifiable. Although scholars might challenge the empirical accuracy of many of these statements, and I will have more to say about the nature of those challenges below, few of us would contest Scientology's importance as a new religious movement—as much for the growth that it *has* achieved in the past half-century as for the numerous controversies it has generated.

Both falsifiable and nonfalsifiable claims are valuable to social scientists, providing rich resources for research into the Church of Scientology itself and other new religious movements to which insights gained from the study of Scientology might be applied. It is important, of course, both to differentiate these types of claims and to recognize that something of a gray area exists between them. Falsifiable claims such as membership statistics, growth rates, and historical statements help establish a picture of the religious group as it is (or as it perceives and presents itself) organizationally, whereas nonfalsifiable, often hyperbolic claims based on the religious experiences reported by adherents—or on Church claims to the character of Scientology and the benefits of Scientological practice—contribute to an understanding of the worldview through which group members perceive the world around them, and on which they base their actions in the world. Given my own interest in the ability of religious believers to maintain belief in the face of disconfirming evidence—a lower-order management of cognitive dissonance, as it were—it is this kind of claim that I regard as most significant.

Among the many nonfalsifiable claims contained in *The Background, Ministry, Sermons and Ceremonies of the Scientology Religion,* for example, are the following: "Scientology is the most vital movement on Earth today" (CSI 2002: 166); "Scientology eventually delivers all it says it can. And that is what is new about it and why it grows. No other religion ever given man, delivered" (CSI 2002: 173); "We are the only group on Earth that does have a workable solution" (CSI 2002: 483); "You can learn to straighten out *any* relationship simply by studying *The Scientology Handbook*" (CSI 2002: 419); "We have the only workable new civilization and technology since Rome fell" (CSI 2002: 436); "To the degree Scientology progresses in an area, the environment becomes calmer and calmer" (CSI 2002: 476); and "Anything religious teachers said or Buddha promised, even the visions of Christianity, are all attained in Scientology as *result*" (CSI 2002: 503; emphasis in original). During his address to the 2003 International Association of Scientologists gala aboard the MV *Freewinds*, David Miscavige, the chair of the board of the Religious Technology Center, told the assembled glitterati about the "new civilization that only we can bring, the likes of which has never been before" (Miscavige 2003). That these claims may appear hyperbolic and hubristic to outsiders has not been lost on Scientologists. Indeed, on the copyright page of *The Background* and in a note "To the Reader" in *Dianetics*, we find the disclaimer that "this book is presented as part of [L. Ron Hubbard's] personal research into life, and the application of same by others, and should be construed only as a written report of such research and not as a statement of claims made by the Church or the Founder."

Although some might argue that some of these claims are, in fact, empirically falsifiable, it is important to recognize them as theological constructions, statements of faith no different from those made by any number of other religious leaders and organizations throughout history. Indeed, it is in the nature of religion to make hyperbolic claims based upon the belief in an exclusive or superior access to the divine mind or will. For more than a thousand years, *extra ecclesiam nulla salus* was the Roman Catholic Church's claim to universal significance and particularist efficacy. "No one come to the Father but through me" (John 14:6), when interpreted through the particularist lens of John 3:16, has become the *extra ecclesiam* claim of evangelical and fundamentalist Protestantism. Similar examples could be multiplied across religious traditions, both large and small.

On the other hand, although it appears to epitomize the falsifiable, the Church of Scientology's claim to (at this point) nearly ten million members worldwide is a prime example of the zone of ambiguity that lies between the strict poles of falsifiability and nonfalsifiability. On the surface, it seems preposterous, but, if accurate, would go along way to validating some of Scientology's more hyperbolic claims. It would place Scientology, for example, alongside the Church of Jesus Christ of Latter-day Saints as an emerging world religion. How, though, is the concept of membership constructed in Scientology, and how is it deployed as a mechanism of legitimation? Beyond those who are active Scientologists, for example, if membership is construed as comprising every person who has ever signed up for an introductory course in auditing, attended a film presentation or lecture at an org (and left some record of their attendance), purchased Scientological materials, or taken the Oxford Capacity Analysis™ test online, then perhaps ten million is not unreasonable. It is well established in the social scientific literature that religious movements of all types—both established and new—regularly inflate membership and attendance figures, sometimes by an order of magnitude or more. That said, if few of these alleged ten million pursue their Scientological involvement no further than an initial contact, it poses the question of how devout Scientologists, in the Church hierarchy, but especially in the rank-and-file, resolve the contradiction on an ongoing basis. As a low-level experience of cognitive dissonance, how does one maintain faith in an organization when some of the most basic claims are contradicted by evidence and ordinary experience? We can theorize these relationships, of course, but the empirical data required to test these theories remain elusive.

Although the Church of Scientology has been the subject of scholarly attention for decades now,[3] I do not believe that such attention has been as sustained, as systematic, or as comprehensive as its prominence as a new religious movement warrants. The last major sociological studies, for example, are Roy Wallis's *The Road to Total Freedom* (1976), which though valuable is now nearly a generation old, and Harriet Whitehead's *Renunciation and Reformulation* (1987), which is similarly dated and appeared years before such high-profile controversies as the 1995 death of Lisa McPherson.

A number of other significant new religious movements, on the other hand, have been closely studied by social scientists, and important, often groundbreaking results obtained. One need only mention here Eileen Barker's research on the Unification Church (1984), Burke Rochford's study of ISKCON (1985), Phillip Lucas's research on the Holy Order of MANS (1995), and the work of William Sims Bainbridge (2002) or James Chancellor (2000) on The Family International. Although they may not have been universally thrilled with the end products, each of these groups opened themselves up to scholarly observation in ways that the Church of Scientology, unfortunately, has not.

Researching Scientology: Premises

I would like to suggest that research into any religious movement, but especially one that makes the kind of exclusive religious claims made by the Church of Scientology, must, among other things, be guided by a creative tension between at least one of Durkheim's rules of sociological method, a healthy hermeneutic of suspicion toward both emic and etic voices, and a keen awareness that ours is not necessarily the task of authentication.

Professor Durkheim Visits the Org

"*When one undertakes to explain a social phenomenon,*" Durkheim wrote in *The Rules of Sociological Method* ([1895] 1982: 123), "*the efficient cause which produces it and the function it fulfills must be investigated separately*" (emphasis in the original). That is, the vagaries of origin do not necessarily determine the nature or value of something as a social fact apart from those origins. Although *The Rules* may not be regarded as Durkheim's most sophisticated theoretical work (cf. Lukes 1982: 23), the importance of this particular *régle* in terms of many religious movements is clear. Explaining (or explaining away, whether sociologically or psychologically) the origins of a religious tradition—even if such origins are found to be entirely fabricated or drawn from distinctly questionable sources—does nothing to diminish the cultural force those facts carry for participants today. In fact, I would suggest that this is one of the most fundamental mistakes made by many in the Christian countercult and secular anticult movements—trying to invalidate a target religious tradition by exposing the alleged flaws in its social origin or foundational mythistory. How much ink, for example, has been spilled "exposing" the problematic origins of the LDS Church or pointing out Charles Taze Russell's exaggerated claims to proficiency in Greek and Hebrew—all with an eye to discrediting Mormonism or Jehovah's Witnesses as viable religious traditions?

The situation is little different with Scientology.

"The Church of Scientology is a commercial enterprise that masquerades as a religion," writes Anton Hein (2001), a rather notorious Dutch countercultist. And he is hardly alone in his evaluation. Both Stephen Kent (1999a, 1999c) and Benjamin Beit-Hallahmi (2003) have published lengthy articles in the *Marburg Journal of Religion* arguing that Scientology is a multinational business that purports to be a religion only for the purpose of securing the social benefits that accrue to "official" religious organizations—most notably, tax relief, but in some countries state recognition and access to educational systems. Although Kent chooses to take his research in a very different direction than I am proposing here, he at least recognizes the implications of Professor Durkheim visiting the Org, and concedes that "the historical reasons behind Scientology's religious claims, as well as the organization's selectivity in making the claims, do not diminish the probability that many Scientologists view their commitment as a religious one" (1999c: 2). I would suggest that the evidence indicates the certainty that such a commitment on the part of Scientologists is religious—for many, profoundly so.

In terms of Durkheim's rule, though, I would like to put Kent's comment even more bluntly, recognizing that the research principle that emerges obtains regardless of the religious tradition to which it is applied. To illustrate, let me suggest two hypothetical questions, both of which are predicated on the question, "OK, so how much more do we know?"

On the one hand, let us assume that Kent and Beit-Hallahmi are correct, that whatever its claims, Scientology is *not* a religion, or at least was not in the beginning. Further, for the sake of argument let us assume that Hubbard was a complete, conscious, and utter fraud who, whether through megalomaniacal hubris or simply an interest in avoiding his fair share of the tax burden, created the "Scientology religion" as a thoroughgoing hoax. How much more do we know? How have we substantially increased our understanding of those adherents—especially the rank-and-file—who call themselves "Scientologists" and base their religiously motivated behavior on that identification?

On the other hand, and again for the sake of argument, let us assume the polar opposite, that Scientology *is* a religion. Let us assume—say, by dint of a combination of the Stark and Bainbridge psychopathological and entrepreneurial models of new religious formation (1979)—that from the very beginning Hubbard was entirely sincere about what he was doing, that he believed everything he wrote and taught completely and without reservation. Once again, how much more do we know? How much further does that go to explaining the growth and activities of the Church of Scientology both before and after Hubbard's death?

Indeed, how does either of these versions of the "efficient cause" of Scientology explain its function and importance in the lives of hundreds of thousands of adherents who now believe that it *is* a religion and conduct their lives accordingly? How does either explain the Sea Org—dedicated religionists who base their behavior in the world on their belief in the religion of Scientology and their billion-year contract with it? How do they explain that young woman at the bar in Boston, who has raised her children as religious Scientologists? Or one of the staff members at the org in Kansas City who has been a Church member since the late 1970s and has homeschooled his daughter as a religious Scientologist?

It's simple. They don't.

And they don't because, in many respects, they are simply asking the wrong question, one that is based on a fundamentally flawed premise: If the efficient cause can be demonstrated false (or true), then the social organization that has proceeded from that cause is defective (or not) almost by definition.[4]

From my perspective, I would much rather learn how those who are happy, healthy Scientologists account for themselves as religious actors, how those who are no longer affiliated with the organization account for their departure, and what internal and external factors contributed to the difference. As a research problem, obviously, although this particular aspect could be approached only through in-depth ethnographies and participant observation, it also raises the thorny issue of competing voices, especially emic advocacy versus etic antagonism.

Emic and Etic Voices in Contention

In a number of cases of either perceived or actual interference by the Church of Scientology in academic research and discussions, the claim is often made that Scientologists only want what they regard as the truth about their religion to be on the agenda. Please note, though, the double entendre: at the least, they *merely* want their perspectives included; at the most, they *only* want their perspectives represented.

At a basic level, of course, they want mistakes corrected, misstatements modified, and the "real" story of Scientology foregrounded. And I think that's perfectly reasonable, if not always realistic. That is, if believers are not willing to stand up in defense of what they believe, one has to wonder just how strong their commitment is or how compelling the belief system to which they are committed. What this position ignores, however, is the social reality that emic voices are invested voices, and for that reason may not always be the most reliable or the most accurate. This principle, as well, holds whether we are dealing with Scientologists, fundamentalist Christians, Ibo diviners, or members of the local Ordo Templi Orientis.[5]

On the one hand, if we are discussing the dynamics of one's personal religious faith and spiritual journey, then I would suggest that the *a priori* research position should be that the emic voice is paramount. As a social scientist, I certainly don't have the right to tell someone, "Your faith isn't real; it isn't authentic"—which is often one of the hardest concepts for my students, both undergraduate and graduate, to grasp, and, I suspect, the logical extension of positions held by scholars such as Kent and Beit-Hallahmi. On the other hand, etic voices—whether they are obviously disgruntled or merely disinterested—are not any more or less reliable necessarily.

This is, of course, the "member-versus-ex-member" debate that has been raging in the field of new religions studies for a few decades now. Recognizing that, stated thus, "emic" and "etic" are both imperfect categories, my contention here is two-fold: first, there must be an healthy hermeneutic of suspicion displayed toward each side in the debate; but, second, and this is the more important point, as many of these different and disparate voices as possible must be included in a comprehensive research program. Anything less, it seems, especially in the case of an emotionally charged topic such as Scientology, simply perpetuates the problem of vested interest influencing the process and product of research.

But Are They Really Religious?

Finally, another of the concepts that many students—and a few academics—find difficult to grasp is that our primary task is not that of authentication. Especially when we consider new religious movements, many students seem stuck on questions like, "Are online Druids *really* Druids? Are American converts who chant the sutras in English *really* Buddhists? Are Scientologists *really* people of faith, and is theirs *really* a religion?" Except under rather specific circumstances, this is not a call we get to make.[6] More important to the sociology of new religious movements is *why* religious adherents believe what they believe, *how* that belief informs their social action, and how they *maintain* their belief in the face of challenge or disconfirmation.

Because this particular point informs so much of what follows in this chapter, I want to be very clear about this next statement, so that there is no misunderstanding. As a subject of intellectual inquiry, in terms of the kinds of research questions I am interested in, I do not care what Scientologists believe, any more than I care what Christians or Druids or Buddhists believe. That is, I am not invested in proving or disproving the content of their belief insofar as they believe it. A religious group could suddenly proclaim that the moon is made of foam rubber and is inhabited by, as Neil Simon (1977) would put it, "one-eyed Episcopalian kangaroos," and I could not care less. What I do care about, what I am intensely interested in, and what I take very seriously, is *that they believe* it. I'm interested in how those beliefs have *evolved and developed*, what *social practices* have grown up around them and what *social function* they serve in terms of the religious group, and how religious groups *maintain belief* in the face of challenge, opprobrium, and the occasional conclusive disconfirmation of their particular religious claims.

All this leads me to some of the promises that I think are implicit in more detailed and comprehensive research into the Church of Scientology.

Researching Scientology: Promises

There a number of areas in which more comprehensive research into the Church of Scientology could yield significant benefits. These range from data on basic institutional issues to more intentionally theorizing the variety of new religions, from the process of mythmaking and hagiology to the inclusion of concepts such as conspiracism as an integral component of religious culture.

Basic Institutional Issues

First, obviously, there are a number of basic institutional issues about which we have very little information, or such data as we have are long out of date. These would comprise the foundational data on which more sophisticated analyses would inevitably depend. Using the Stark and Bainbridge audience-client-cult movement model, for example, how often do inquirers move into the auditing process? How many of those who take the Oxford Capacity Analysis™ test on-line make personal contact with a local org? How many of those actually take courses? How far do those who begin auditing tend to go on the Bridge, and what are the various rates of attrition and further commitment? How have these rates changed over time, if they have, and how has the institution responded to those changes organizationally? What factors facilitate the transition from an auditing client to a full-fledged member of the Church of Scientology, especially in a high investment branch like the Sea Org? How often do in-group ties form, and what role do they play in commitment, continuation, and attrition or disaffiliation? How do rank-and-file Scientologists feel about such organizations as the office of Inspectors General or the Rehabilitation Project Force?

Generationally, in what ways do Scientologists who have been raised in the Church differ from converts (cf. Lattin 2001)?

The Church of Scientology is well known for promoting its success on the basis of its various building programs throughout the world. Certainly, many of its properties are large, often aesthetically stunning, and built (or renovated and remodeled) to very high standards. Put simply, then, where does the money come from? What is the cash flow of the Church of Scientology and its various interrelated organizations? Who controls it? Although the financial aspects of new religions have been the subject of some study (see, for example, Bromley 1985; Richardson 1988), clearly more work is needed, especially in terms of such an ostentatiously high profile group like the Church of Scientology.

Of Scientology's numerous outreach programs—literacy campaigns, drug treatment programs, and criminal rehabilitation projects—how many Scientologists actually participate in program delivery, and how do the empirical data on the success of these programs square with Scientology's own claims? If there are significant differences, and the data we have indicate there are, what accounts for them? Finally, there is the question that my students always seem to raise whenever Scientology enters the classroom conversation: Why are so many cultural celebrities attracted to it?

In terms of my own particular research perspective—and, as I have said, I am interested in how religious groups construct and maintain meaningful identity in the face of social challenge, cultural opprobrium, and the inevitable cognitive dissonance that accompanies them—a more comprehensive research program could yield valuable data in a number of areas: (1) the nature of religion; (2) the process of religious evolution; and (3) the dynamics of religious boundary maintenance.

Scientology as a Closed Source Religion

In *Cyberhenge: Modern Pagans on the Internet* (Cowan 2005), I introduced a modest theoretical approach to understanding further certain aspects of religious organization, development, and behavior. Based on the open source model of computer programming, I make a distinction between what I am calling "open source" and "closed source" religious traditions. Although these are endpoints on a heuristic continuum and not meant to represent any kind of ontological duality, put simply, open source traditions are those in which the "source codes," the fundamental building blocks of the religion, are open to adaptation and modification by religious participants; closed source traditions, on the other hand, restrict deviation from the source codes either partially or entirely.

In this theoretical model, the Church of Scientology is the quintessential closed source tradition. In closed source terms, for example, and despite the fact that it has been modified over the course of the Church's development, the foundational practice of Scientology—auditing—is believed to be 100 percent effective only so long as it proceeds in strict accordance with the instructions laid down by Hubbard himself, principally in *Dianetics*, but also in the voluminous reports, updates, and memoranda he issued throughout his career. In

"Any Reasons for Difficulties and Their Correction," for example, part of *What Is Scientology?* (CSI 1998: 215), we read that "when Scientology appears to go wrong, there is invariably a specific error that has been made in the application of technology which, when remedied, enables it to then work and achieve the expected result. The fact is: *Scientology works 100 percent of the time when it is properly applied to a person who sincerely desires to improve his life*" (emphasis in the original).

Invoking the nonfalsifiability common to religious beliefs and practices worldwide, lack of success in the auditing process or stunted progress in one's spiritual development are often attributed either to a lack of seriousness on the part of the practitioner, or to deviance from the protocols established by Hubbard and guarded by the Church through an aggressive program of copyright enclosure and infraction surveillance.[7] To ensure uniformity and avoid what the Religious Technology Center regards as "the nemesis of alteration and reinterpretation" (2003b), during auditing sessions participants pause frequently to "word clear," that is, to look up the precise meaning of a word in its Scientological context. This precludes the kind of multiple interpretations that are anathema to the closed source tradition. Similarly, during Church worship services, sermons are read verbatim from a master text (CSI 2002), and neither innovation nor deviation is permitted.[8]

Institutionally, on the other hand, Scientology as a closed source religion—one in which the source codes for the religion provided by Hubbard are, at least ostensibly, unavailable for challenge or modification in any way—is best demonstrated through the Religious Technology Center, the organization charged with safeguarding Scientological orthodoxy. "Scientologists across the globe," reads part of the RTC's online mission statement (2003a), "view the maintenance and incorruptibility of their religious technology—in precise accordance with the founder's source writings—to be essential to their very salvation." Although this is no doubt due in part to the host of Scientological imitators that have appeared since the 1950s (see Stark and Bainbridge 1979; Wallis 1976) and the problem of unauthorized reproduction of Church esoterica that has only been exacerbated by the Internet (Cowan 2004; Peckham 1998), it would be hard to imagine a clearer statement of a closed source religious tradition.

More comprehensive research into the Church of Scientology could yield important socio-historical data on how this situation arose, how closed source traditions form and endure through generational transmission, and how they respond to cultural change, institutional evolution, and an almost inevitable degree of cognitive dissonance.

Mythistory in the Making

It could also tell us a tremendous amount about how some traditions construct, maintain, and reinforce their religious mythistory.[9] Here, I am not thinking of such things as Scientology's esoteric cosmogony, but rather the larger patterns of their emerging *Heilsgeschichte* into which a particular religious identity becomes embedded, and on which it later draws for maintenance and reinforcement. Let me suggest just three examples of this developing mythistory: (1) the emergent hagiology of L. Ron Hubbard; (2) the cognitive dissonance occasioned by the clear disconfirmation of religious and mythistorical claims; and (3) the manner in which a conspiracist understanding of culture has both become embedded in and now serves the evolution of Scientological mythistory.

Hagiologizing L. Ron Hubbard

When I visited the Hollywood Celebrity Center in 2002, our first stop was the American Saint Hill Organization on L. Ron Hubbard Way, a couple of blocks off Santa Monica Boulevard. At one point as we were being shown around, our guide pointed to one of the Hubbard busts that are prominent in the orgs, and cautioned us, "Now, we don't worship Mr. Hubbard as a god." My immediate thought was, "Not yet, you don't, but give it a hundred years or so. After all, look what happened to Jesus."

Anyone who has spent any time visiting various Scientology orgs, reading Scientological literature, listening to tapes, or watching DVDs will recognize the ubiquitous presence of L. Ron Hubbard. Auditing practices are designed to follow Hubbard's instructions without deviation. The chapel arrangement for Sunday worship services calls for the same large bust of Hubbard to be placed at stage right, between the lectern and the Scientology cross. Over half of the ninety-six official Scientology sermons reference Hubbard directly, and every one concludes by referring congregants either to Hubbard's own works or to Scientology books based on those works. In the manner of setting a place for Elijah at the Passover Seder, every Scientology org, large or small, maintains an office for Hubbard in perpetuity. The Author Services Center is a virtual shrine to Hubbard's writings in all their manifold versions, editions, and translations, something that is exceeded only by the Hubbard Life Exhibition in Hollywood, a museum celebrating the life of Scientology's founder. As a sociologist I would suggest that its value lies less in the insight that it provides into that life than the ways in which the Church constructs that life and continues the process of hagiography.

Indeed, try to imagine for a moment a Church of Scientology without L. Ron Hubbard. It's unthinkable. It makes no more sense than trying to imagine Christianity without Jesus. In Scientology, Hubbard is the founder of the practice, the author of the scriptures, the touchstone of belief, and the guarantor of salvation. What I suggest a more comprehensive research program would reveal is the manner in which, in Weberian terms, for example, Hubbard's charisma is being routinized, institutionalized, and sacralized. Hubbard's is an emerging hagiography like very few that I can think of in a new religious movement, and one that has the considerable financial resources of the various Scientology organizations thrown completely behind it. In terms of emic advocacy and etic antagonism, we have once again the process of competing propagandas. As a religious movement that is so integrally linked to its founder, how does the Church create and maintain its vision of

Hubbard in the face of ongoing countermovement challenges to his honesty and legitimacy (see, for example, Atack 1990, Corydon 1995, Miller 1987)?

On the other hand, the institutional Church of Scientology claims that "there are millions of people around the world who consider they have no greater friend" than L. Ron Hubbard (CSI 2004a). In this regard, there is significant ethnographic work to be done to see how (or even whether) this approbation is reflected in the lived practice and faith experience of rank-and-file Scientologists. Certainly the material culture of Scientology—from perpetual offices and busts in the chapels to the myriad of adulatory literature produced by Author Services and the unfolding hagiography that is the Hubbard Life Exhibition—foregrounds Hubbard at every turn, but that still leaves open the question of how he is regarded by the Scientological laity, by those Scientologists who function outside the domains of institutional power.

And, there is yet another issue. Since his death in 1986, books, pamphlets, magazines, courses, and other components of Scientology's expanding religious and therapeutic entrepreneuria—including the massive *Scientology Handbook* (CSI 2001)—have been issued with the caveat that they are "based on the works of L. Ron Hubbard." However, as theorists ranging from Noam Chomsky and Michel Foucault to Jacques Ellul and Pierre Bourdieu have so trenchantly demonstrated, any claims that access to "correct" or "accurate" information can cure a variety of personal and social ills ignore the crucial reality that all educational philosophies, all heuristic frameworks according to which information is chosen, and all technologies by which those philosophies are enacted are ineluctably embedded in a web of contested power relations. Given this, the question for the Church of Scientology becomes, "After 1986, who did the choosing?" Who is selecting which of Hubbard's works are included in various products? What are the criteria on which such selections are based—and who established those? And, more to the point, because absolute fidelity to the Founder's work is paramount—indeed, according to the Religious Technology Center (2003a), "essential to their very salvation"—how can rank-and-file Scientologists be assured that they are getting the original material? The copyright page of *The Scientology Handbook,* for example, says that it was "compiled by the LRH Book Compilation Staff of the Church of Scientology International." But who are they? Who appointed them to those positions, and who oversees their work? It is not insignificant, I think, that a recent Google search for the phrases "LRH Book Compilation" and "LRH Book Compilation Staff" returned not one, single substantive result.[10] More comprehensive research into the Church could potentially tell scholars—and Scientologists—quite a bit about the emerging hagiography of L. Ron Hubbard on the one hand, and an increasingly closed source religion on the other.

On Finding the Bones of Jesus

As Peter Berger points out in *The Sacred Canopy* (1967: 29), "All socially constructed worlds are inherently precarious." That is, they are constantly open to the threat of challenge and disconfirmation. And, indeed, as I indicated earlier, this is one of the principal means by which both the evangelical Christian countercult and the secular anticult seek to discredit target traditions, to disenchant religious adherents, and to encourage either conversion to evangelical Protestantism or at least disaffiliation from the group in question. Creatively misreading Durkheim for a moment, their argument runs that if the "efficient cause" can be demonstrated flawed, then the social product must be similarly defective. A reasonable premise, perhaps—there just doesn't seem to be a lot of empirical evidence for it so far.

Consider the Mormons. If an authentic "Salamander letter" were to be uncovered, if an undisputed document in Joseph Smith's own handwriting declared the whole thing an elaborate hoax, does that mean that the Church of Jesus Christ of Latter-day Saints as we know it today would simply collapse? Unlikely. Or, consider Wicca. If despite an elaborate mythistory that includes religious survivals dating to the Neolithic period and stages of unprecedented persecution, as scholars such as Ronald Hutton contend, the origins of Wicca and modern Witchcraft extend no further back than Gerald Gardner, and do not represent anything like a Pagan revitalization movement, does that mean that these aspects of modern Paganism—which also claim to be among the fastest growing religious traditions in the world—will disappear? Similarly unlikely. Or, finally, to take perhaps the most trenchant example, if in the dusty hills outside Jerusalem an ossuary were to be found, and its contents indisputably verified as the bones of Jesus of Nazareth (perhaps by means of a scroll tube included in the ossuary containing the Gospel of Joseph of Arimathea), does that mean that one-third of the world's population would simply fold up its religious tents and go searching for the nearest dharma center?[11]

I rather suspect not.

In the last case, at least, I would like to suggest that, metaphorically speaking, the bones of Jesus have been found, and have been available for viewing roughly since the middle of the nineteenth century. As soon as thinkers like Lamarck and Darwin appeared on the scene and suggested a view of creation other than that delineated in the Bible; as soon as the German Higher Critics pointed out that Moses did not, in fact, write the Pentateuch; as soon as Schweitzer began the search for the historical Jesus and Bultmann divorced him from the Christ of faith; and as soon as liberal theologians began to consider the social and theological value of religious pluralism, the bones of Jesus were placed on public display. That is, the theological grounding on which the notion of *extra ecclesiam nulla salus* was based for more than a thousand years was suddenly called into question, and much of the Christian church was forced to reconsider its positions, to deal with the cognitive dissonance these discoveries and theories and challenges presented.

As Karl Mannheim wrote in his classic essay, "The Problem of a Sociology of Knowledge" ([1925] 1952: 147), "after one class has discovered some sociological or historical fact . . . all other groups, no matter what *their* interests are, can equally take such a fact into account—nay, *must* somehow incorporate such fact into their system of world interpretation." Some streams of Christianity chose to reinvent themselves, to rethink theology and to reexamine the Church's position in the world. Others chose to retrench, to dig in and hold the high ground of salvation through Christ alone. Obviously, though, they did not disappear.

For my part, however it plays out, it is precisely this process of *incorpora-tion*, of interpretation, explanation, and integration that interests me intellectually. For example, how do religious groups deal with claims that are open to immediate and conclusive disconfirmation? How do they handle on a day-to-day basis the cognitive dissonance generated by disparate data and competing interpretations of their religious legitimacy and identity? Though there are numerous others we could choose in terms of the Church of Scientology, consider this one small, yet rather revealing, example.

In Heber Jentzsch's contribution to *New Religious Movements and Religious Liberty in America,* he claims that both L. Ron Hubbard and the Church of Scientology were on the notorious Nixon White House "enemies list," and that congressional hearings following the Watergate scandal "revealed previously secret and illegal IRS programs against individuals and organizations, including the Church of Scientology. Of the 213 names on the Nixon list, 211 were left bankrupt, collapsed, disbanded, or dead. Indeed, of the individuals and organizations on that infamous 'enemies list,' only two survived intact: Hubbard and the Church of Scientology" (2002: 154). This claim is repeated in numerous places throughout the Scientological literature (see, for example, CSI 1998: 509–10; 2004b).

In terms of claims that are open to immediate and conclusive disconfirmation, and how religious groups incorporate them into their worldviews, three things are important to note about this particular statement.

First, it is worth considering some of the people who were on the Nixon list and where they are now. Of the original twenty collected in 1969 by Charles Colson, number nineteen was actor, race car driver, and salad dressing entrepreneur Paul Newman. Number seventeen was Daniel Schorr, currently a senior news analyst for NPR and a 2002 inductee into the American Academy of Arts and Sciences. Political figures on the expanded list included the following: Edward Kennedy, George McGovern, Walter Mondale, Edmund Muskie, Shirley Chisholm, and Bella Abzug. The Southern Christian Leadership Convention was on the list, as were performers such as Bill Cosby, Jane Fonda, Gregory Peck, and Barbra Streisand. Although we might question Streisand for inflicting *Yentl* on the movie-going public, few would consider her life unsuccessful. Ramsey Clark, former Attorney General; Robert McNamara, former Secretary of Defense; Sargent Shriver, former U.S. ambassador to France—all were on the list. And there were academics: Noam Chomsky, John Kenneth Galbraith, and Arthur Schlesinger notable among them, and hardly "bankrupt, collapsed, disbanded, or dead."[12]

Second, though, and equally important, neither L. Ron Hubbard nor the Church of Scientology appears on the Nixon "enemies list." It is important to note here that, whether knowingly or unknowingly, Jentzsch and the authors of similar claims in Scientological literature are referring to two separate and distinct lists. At the time, the IRS did maintain a running list of organizations it believed were likely to try to evade taxation, and the Church of Scientology was

RESEARCHING SCIENTOLOGY 67

on that list. The Nixon "enemies list," however, which was produced originally by senior White House staff, detailed political enemies specifically opposed to the president and his administrative policies.

Third, and most important in terms of a sociology of knowledge approach to the Church of Scientology, neither of these other facts appears to matter.

Conspiracism as Religious Culture

One of the theoretical and methodological dicta that I urge my students to take to heart when considering any religious tradition is Berger and Luckmann's observation that we are dealing with "whatever passes for 'knowledge'" in that tradition, "regardless of the ultimate validity or invalidity (by whatever criteria) of such 'knowledge'" (1966: 15). Scientology's place as the sole survivor of Nixon's "enemies list" is part of what passes for knowledge in their particular religious culture. Further, I believe that it is a good example of how conspiracism has come to play an important role in the emerging salvation history of the Church, and represents another aspect of Scientology's development that is well worth further exploration—not to disprove it, but to understand how it is integrated into and deployed in the service of an evolving religious worldview.

What Is Scientology? contains the chapter "Those Who Oppose Scientology" (CSI 1998: 503–15), which details what the Church regards as a coordinated program of harassment by an assorted cast of villains, including the American Medical Association, the American Psychiatric Association, the Food and Drug Administration, the Internal Revenue Service, the secular anticult movement (which the Church regards as "a variety of antireligious front groups" deployed by the psychiatric community worldwide "to assault Scientology and other churches" [CSI 1998: 513]), ex-members of the Church, the media, and, occasionally, scholars. Much of this history, not surprisingly, is reprised in Jentzsch's contribution to *New Religious Movements and Religious Liberty in America,* and which it tellingly subtitled, "Separating Truth from Fiction."

References to this legacy of harassment, persecution, and inevitable triumph are also found in Scientology sermons. In "Scientology's Future," for example, parishioners are told, "Do not blink when you ask your doctor, your psychiatrist, your savant in the humanities, and he says we are vile. Who has ever admired their own executioner? Do not blink when you read how terrible we are in the papers" (CSI 2002: 448–49). Rather, congregants are exhorted "to laugh at frantic efforts to block our way" (CSI 2002: 449).[13] In "Why Feel Guilty?" they are reminded that "ridicule, wild rumors, bad press, lies and even attacks by governments have failed to suppress the technology" (CSI 2002: 485), and in "The Value of Scientology": "Not all the screaming apes of press or the cold sadists who run the 'learned societies' are likely to be able to stop man's first chance for immortality and the sun" (CSI 2002: 503).

Numerous other examples could be offered, but at this point it is worth remembering that these are drawn from *sermons.* That is, they are the texts for *performative acts* meant to inform adherents of the content of their religious belief, and exhort them to action based on those beliefs.

Almost from its very inception, Scientology's claims to systematic persecution and harassment have become part of its religious culture and mythistory—something that, when considered in the context of an increasingly closed source religious tradition, goes a long way toward explaining the overt suspicion with which the Church regards any attempts at investigation, and their own ongoing attempts to influence or to prevent the publication of anything even remotely critical of the Church or its founder. Although, obviously, there is considerable work to be done in this area, I would like to suggest that this conspiracism is one of the ways in which the Church of Scientology has explained and integrated precisely the kinds of cognitive dissonance referred to by Mannheim.

Researching Scientology: Problematics

At least as important as these perceptions, premises, and promises, however, are the problems that have come to be associated with research into the Church of Scientology and its various organizations. These problems cluster around three principal dynamics: (1) lack of access to relevant Scientological data and materials; (2) lack of understanding on the part of the Church about the social function of scholarship; and (3) lack of trust on the part of academics that research into the Church will not put them or their institutions in jeopardy.

Lack of Access: The Problem of Data Collection and the Resulting Chorus of Voices

Unfortunately, there are no scholarly studies of the Church of Scientology that even approach those accomplished by Bainbridge (2002), Barker (1984), Chancellor (2000), Lucas (1995), and Rochford (1985). At the very least, such a study would require reasonably unimpeded access to Church archives and records (including membership and finances), recruits and recruiting practices, and leadership in the various orgs (especially Author Services, the Guardian Office, the Office of Special Affairs, the Church of Spiritual Technology, the Sea Organization, the Religious Technology Center, and the Rehabilitation Project Force). Further, in some fashion, it would require access to the auditing process itself. Many of these, I suspect, the Church would be unlikely to permit except under the most restricted circumstances, especially because it conceptualizes auditing sessions as part of the confessional practice of the Scientology religion.

In terms of the more controversial aspects of the Church of Scientology, especially the history of the Guardian Office and the Rehabilitation Project Force, we encounter what might be called the "Area 51 paradox," named for the secret U.S. military base in the Nevada desert that everyone knows exists, but which does not show up on any official map and whose existence is denied by the government. If, as Church officials consistently maintain, all the controversy that surrounds Scientology is the result of adversarial propaganda disseminated by some of the groups and organizations named above, and that in its fifty-year history the Church has done nothing for which it needs to atone or repent, one would think that they would be delighted to open archives, orgs, and depositories to scholarly research, if for no other reason than to address the criticisms leveled at them by detractors. To date, at least, this has not been the case.

Continuing from one of the points I made earlier, a comprehensive research program would require the participation not only of happy, healthy emic voices, but also disgruntled, even vitriolic etic ones. That is, one thing that the Church of Scientology would have to recognize is that no picture of a religious organization is complete without some consideration of those who were less than satisfied with the religious product, and how the organization responded to that dissatisfaction. This brings us to the second issue: co-optation and the Church's lack of understanding about the social function of scholarship.

Lack of Understanding: The Problem of Co-optation and the Social Function of Scholarship

How do we communicate to new religious movements that the social function and responsibility of scholarship is considerably broader than simple due diligence to their beliefs and organization? Especially when there is a fine line between reporting and interpreting phenomena in ways that are intellectually credible and academically valuable, and maintaining access to those among whom we carry out our research? Although I am delighted to speak in defense of religious movements when I believe they have been inaccurately portrayed or wrongfully accused—and I have done so on behalf of a number of groups, including the Church of Scientology—that willingness does not include serving as a court stenographer or facilitating particular movement agendas. That is, among other things, scholarly responsibility requires that I satisfy myself that "X" group *has* been inaccurately portrayed in these situations, and simply taking the word of the group in question is often not enough. Occasionally, academics are asked to validate groups in ways that to me, at least, fall clearly outside the boundaries of responsible scholarship.

Consider these few personal examples. I have no doubt that they could be multiplied many times over across the profession. A number of scholars, for example, report being contacted by members of the Church and asked if they would participate in a variety of protests organized by (and not infrequently on behalf of) Scientology. In 2003, I was asked if I would be willing to participate in a commemorative video on Hubbard's life that was being produced to celebrate the fiftieth anniversary of the founding of the Church of Scientology. That is, would I be willing to be interviewed about Hubbard's achievements, his accomplishments, and the contributions he has made to the betterment of the world? I replied that I would be happy to talk about what Scientologists believe Hubbard has done, about the regard in which Scientologists hold him, but that was as far as I would be comfortable going. A subtle, but not insignificant, difference. I was not contacted on this again. Later that year, I was asked to contact the head of the Google corporation to protest the fact that that their search engine protocols do not adequately discriminate between anti-Scientology Web sites and official Church sites, and to register my complaint that this situation was unacceptable. This, too, I refused to do. Finally, in 2004, as the initial draft of this chapter was being written, one of the senior staff at the local org asked if I would facilitate space on my university campus for a traveling version of the Hubbard Life Exhibition. He said that this would be the best way that the university could help expose our students to the "truth" of Scientology. That Scientologists appear to so completely misunderstand the social function of scholarship could be a co-constructed problem: their inability or unwillingness to do so, and our failure to communicate that responsibility adequately or clearly enough when interacting with new religious adherents.

What, then, is the social function of scholarship? I tell my graduate students that it is the asking and answering of significant questions. An easy thing to say, perhaps, but often a very hard thing to do. Not least because sometimes the significance of a question is measured precisely by the amount of resistance it generates when one tries to formulate an answer. Which brings me to the third issue in the problematics of researching the Church of Scientology: lack of trust on the part of academics that such research will not put them or their institutions at risk.

Lack of Trust: The Problem of Perception and the Perception of Intimidation

Put bluntly, the Church of Scientology has something of an image problem. From Tom Cruise going "off message" while trying to promote *The War of the Worlds* and dressing down Matt Lauer on the evils of psychiatry to Scientology officials in confrontation with a British journalist over an interview for a recent BBC *Panorama* program (an incident that revealed, admittedly, the worst of both sides), the Church of Scientology has been fighting an uphill battle for public sympathy for nearly half a century. That battle extends to its interactions with sociologists and historians of religion, some of whom are among the most sympathetic to new religions in the entire academy. My best friend, on the other hand, is not an academic. He doesn't own a television, barely has access to the Internet, knows next to nothing about new religious movements, and would rather be in the woods with his dog than just about anywhere else. When I told him about the conference presentation on which this chapter is based, however, his initial and immediate response was, "Be careful, man, they walk softly, but they carry a big lawyer." And, in point of fact, I got variations of this from virtually everyone I consulted about the initial draft—scholars (both NRM specialists and not), laypeople, even a practicing Scientologist in the Church's Volunteer Ministry program.

From my perspective, there are some concrete reasons for this perception. Setting aside such high-profile issues as litigation over copyright infringement on the Internet and the 2004 settlement in the Lisa McPherson wrongful death suit (the details of which remain undisclosed), let me offer three quick examples that bring the issue closer to home.

First, new religions scholar Ben Zablocki has accused the Church of Scientology of attempting to stop one of the sessions at the 1997 meeting of the Association for the Sociology of Religion, a session in which one of the panelists was a former Cult Awareness Network deprogrammer. According to a post Zablocki made to the Nurel-l electronic discussion list (1998):

> The executive officer of the ASR complained to me of receiving a rather frightening [very early morning] visit from a courier carrying a request from Scientology to reconsider whether the session (that was scheduled for 8 AM that same day) should be allowed to take place. The executive officer agreed with me that such unprecedented interference with freedom of academic expression was totally unacceptable.[14]

Second, John Morehead (1998), then a staff member and the former Executive Director of Evangelical Ministries to New Religions, reported on Nurel-l a similar situation in regard to a seminar he was scheduled to present at his own local church. Intended to contrast Scientological beliefs with those of conservative Christianity, Morehead wrote:

> Prior to the seminar, the CoS caught wind of the event, and the Office of Special Affairs pressured my church not to allow the seminar. At least two Scientologists appeared in the seminar, yet were polite during my presentation. Afterwards, my pastor and the church were again pressured for allowing a seminar which allegedly promoted religious intolerance. I was personally contacted by the OSA and "warned" of copyright violation and alleged misrepresentation of Scientology. . . . Just last week, the day after my post in Nurel, a sister organization informed me that they had received a call from the Arlington, TX branch of the CoS looking for information on me![15]

Third, there is "Contested Spaces," my contribution to a collection of essays called *Religion Online*, that Lorne Dawson and I edited (2004). In this essay, I used the Church of Scientology as an example of the ways in which the Internet has become a contested information space, an arena for competing propagandas, and why, in my opinion, such a space inevitably favors the dedicated countermovement. I dealt with well-known issues such as the unauthorized reposting of Scientological esoterica, Scientology's various battles over Internet remailers, and the large number of anti-Scientology sites on the Web. Overall, both Dawson and I thought it a fairly sympathetic piece, one that argued for a religious organization's fundamental right to the privacy of its own esoteric teachings, and one that was certainly far more critical of the anticult and countercult movements than of Scientology.

In conversation with Heber Jentzsch one evening—he had called to encourage me to contact the head of Google and complain about their search protocols—I mentioned that I had just written this paper. Jentzsch asked that I send him a copy, and, perhaps naïvely, I did. He called back a couple of days later, telling me that he had some "serious trouble" with a lot of what I had written, and wanted to send me "more correct and up-to-date information." I agreed, though I cautioned him that he needed to act quickly because the book manuscript was due at the publisher in a few days. The next day, Dawson telephoned to say that he had received a similar call from Jentzsch, this one framed more in the manner of a "senior editor" being expected to control the actions of a junior colleague. Indeed, I received no more communication from the Church. A few weeks later, though, Dawson received some material from the Church, notably a heavily copyedited version of my chapter, complete with suggested emendations, deletions, and additions. The Church, for example, wanted all references to the work of Stephen Kent deleted from the paper, and a section on their earlier Internet battles on alt.religion.scientology rewritten in a manner that clearly favored Scientology's position. As Dawson put it, there was no overt threat, but the legalistic language of the three-page cover letter was sufficiently aggressive to put us on our guard.

Fourth (though by no means finally), when I was preparing the conference presentation on which this chapter is based, and Jentzsch learned of it through the published conference agenda, he requested that I provide him with further information—presumably he wanted an advance copy. He noted that I had not communicated with him what I intended to present, and, therefore, had had no opportunity to discuss what might be needed in terms of documentation (presumably to support the claims I intended to make). He pointed out that that the title of my presentation—which, with the exception of "Perceptions," is the same as this chapter—seemed controversial and that any controversy resides solely with those who would oppose Scientology. He also requested further information about my presentation from conference organizers, something that quite distressed the local arrangements assistant who contacted me about Jentzsch's request.

Without wanting to read *too* much into this, it is worth asking whether Jentzsch (and by extension the Church of Scientology writ large) expects to be routinely "kept in the loop" on such matters as conference presentations, academic articles, and so forth. The wording of his communications to me in this instance could certainly be read as though he expects the Church to be notified of presentations or forthcoming publications, and to be actively involved in their preparation. I still hold out hope that he does not expect that scholars will seek the Church's approval—or of any new religion, for that matter—before presenting or publishing, but who knows?

These particular episodes foreground for me a couple of important issues. First, although in principle I have no trouble letting subject groups see copies of scholarly material prior to publication, such inspection is at the scholar's discretion and we should avoid giving the impression that these groups are somehow vetting the material or that they will be allowed final approval on either content or presentation. Second, and this is more regrettable because it goes to the very heart of this paper, Dawson and I had mused about researching and writing more substantially about the Church of Scientology—something I have tried to suggest in this chapter is desperately needed. We both arrived at the conclusion, however, that, problems of access to data and ethnographic field sites notwithstanding, neither of us was willing to endure what we suspected would be the inevitable interference from the Church in the final scholarly product. That is, we were right back to that conversation in the bar, now so many years ago.

And, to that earnest member of the Church of Scientology, I say this:

Many scholars have either experienced or become familiar with the varying levels of interference of which the Church of Scientology is capable. And, however accurate or inaccurate their individual perceptions, there is a fear among some academics that producing research critical of the Church will result in some measure of legal opposition. In the face of this, rather than invest significant amounts of time and energy in a project that may be stalled by litigation or some other form of obstruction, scholars simply choose to research something else. What the Church of Scientology does not seem to grasp in all this is how any attempt at interference or intimidation only exacerbates the problem, and can, indeed, result in the creation of decidedly antipathetic scholars such as Stephen Kent and Benjamin Beit-Hallahmi. This has been put perhaps most trenchantly by J. Gordon Melton. As he noted in a *New York Times* interview, "Scientology has probably received the most persistent criticism of any church in America in recent years. But [Melton] said the Scientologists bear some of the responsibility. 'They don't get mad, they get even,' Mr. Melton said. 'They turn critics into enemies and enemies into dedicated warriors for a lifetime'" (Frantz 1997).

If there is a thesis statement for this chapter, it is this: Comprehensive socio-historical research into the Church of Scientology is desperately needed in our field and would be invaluable to new religions scholarship. But such research cannot (and likely will not) usefully proceed until the Church commits itself to refrain from interference or intimidation of any kind, regardless of the scholarly product. *Respond* to the product, certainly, disagree with it, debate it, excoriate it, if that's what Scientologists want to do—that kind of exchange lies at the heart of the scholarly dialectic. But do *not* interfere with its production.

NOTES

1. Parts of this chapter have appeared in both *Cyberhenge: Modern Pagans on the Internet* (Cowan 2005) and *Cults and New Religions: A Brief History* (Cowan and Bromley 2008). A preliminary version was presented at the 2004 international meeting of CESNUR (Center for Study on New Religions), held at Baylor University in Waco, Texas, and, in places, I have retained aspects of that idiom. A little more than a decade after the tragic BATF/FBI siege of the Branch Davidian residence just ten miles east of the town, the importance of distinguishing perception from reality—or at least recognizing that such a distinction is necessary—could hardly be clearer.

2. Of course, this claim is hardly limited to the Church of Scientology, and is also made by a number of other groups. On the basis of recent statistical data, many modern Pagans claim that theirs is the fastest growing religion in Canada, the United States, and Australia (cf. Cowan 2005: 193–96), whereas Carolyn Wah writes that "Jehovah's Witnesses are one of the world's fastest growing religious groups" (2001: 61).

Even the tiny United Nuwaubian Nation of Moors, which is clearly not a contender, maintains that it is "one of the fastest growing organizations on the planet" (United Nuwaubian Nation of Moors n.d.).

3. See, for example, Bainbridge 1980, 1987; Beckford 1980; Bednarowski 1995; Beit-Hallahmi 2003; Berglie 1996; Black 1996; Bromley and Bracey 1998; Bryant 1994; Chidester n.d.; Christensen 1999: Cowan 2004; Cowan and Bromley 2006, 2008; Dericquebourg 1988, 1995, 1998; Flinn 1983; Frigerio 1996; Heino 1995; Kelley [1980] 1996; Kent 1996, 1999a, 1999b, 1999c; Melton 2000, 2001; Pentikainen and Pentikainen 1996; Ross 1988; Sabbatucci 1983; Safa 1996; Sawada 1996; Sivertsev 1995; Urban 2006; Wallis 1973, 1976; Whitehead 1974, 1987.

4. Once again, it is important to point out that this dynamic is hardly limited to the Church of Scientology. One of the basic criticisms of the Christian Church since the advent of German higher criticism in the late nineteenth century has been that powerful members of the early Church crafted the religion to suit their own emerging needs, and that what developed as "the Christian Church" bears little resemblance to anything envisioned by its putative founder. That is, the efficient cause of Christianity must be researched and interpreted separately from Christian social, cultural, and ecclesiastical organizations it evolved to embody. On this, see, for example, Bauer 1971; Ehrman 1993, 2003, 2005; Lüdemann 1995.

5. Consider, for example, the translator's preface to Lévi-Strauss's *Structural Anthropology,* in which she refers to "the author's oft-repeated point that, although informants' accounts of institutions [to which we might legitimately add beliefs, practices, and rituals] must be taken into consideration, they are rationalizations and reinterpretations, not to be confused with the actual social organization" (Jacobson 1963: xiii).

6. Such circumstances include, but are not limited to, media interviews, testimony on behalf of (or in contest with) religious organizations involved in litigation, and/or information regarding religious organizations seeking official state recognition.

7. Among other things, the Religious Technology Center Web site (http://www.rtc.org) includes a link to report infractions electronically, as well as a detailed listing of "matters of RTC concern." These include the following: "Any suppressive act against Scientology or Scientologists"; "Any misrepresentation of Dianetics or Scientology"; "Any person who is hypercritical of Scientology or the Church" (http://www.rtc.org/matters/ethics.htm); "Willful perversion or corruption of the tech" (http://www.rtc.org/matters/tech.htm); "Any calculated efforts to disrupt Church services or the flow of public up the Bridge through the Churches"; and "Any actions or omissions undertaken to knowingly suppress, reduce or impede Scientology or Scientologists" (http://www.rtc.org/matters/admin.htm).

8. I confirmed this during a conversation with Church of Scientology International vice president Janet Weiland following a worship service at the Hollywood Celebrity Center, September 2002.

9. I borrow this term from a colleague at the University of Missouri–Kansas City, Gary L. Ebersole, who coined it to avoid imposing a modern bifurcation of myth and history back onto ancient Japan. It seems no less useful for late modern religious traditions like the Church of Scientology.

10. In June 2004, when this paper was first drafted, a Google search for these phrases returned not a single result. In May 2007, as I revise it for inclusion in this volume, the only three results are to the Web version of my 2004 CESNUR presentation, and two bibliographic entries for *The Scientology Handbook.*

11. This is an example I have used for years in the classroom to explore the principle of religious resiliency in the face of disconfirmation. It has only been reinforced by recent public discussions about the significance of the Talpiot tomb.

12. The standard documentary source for this list is found at Knappman 1973: 96–97.

13. Similar comments are integral to the sermons "Dangerous Environment" (CSI 2002: 475–77), and "The True Story of Scientology" (CSI 2002: 478–81).

14. Used with permission of Benjamin Zablocki (2004). On other problems the Nurel-l list had as a result of Scientology—from both detractors and supporters—trouble that ultimately led to a ban on discussion of the topic, see Cowan 2000.

15. Used by permission of John Morehead (2004). Morehead's seminar was designed to contrast "Scientology beliefs with orthodox Christianity." His original Nurel-l post, though, questioned the response of a Scientologist on the list to allegations that the Church of Scientology had used the offer of a sympathetic portrayal of the Bill Clinton character in the film *Primary Colors*—a part played by prominent Scientologist John Travolta—in return for White House pressure on foreign governments that were investigating or otherwise interfering with Scientologist within their jurisdictions (cf. Kent 2002). Interestingly, that very same week, in response to its five-part series on the Church of Scientology, the *Boston Herald* claimed that the Church had "hired a private investigator to delve into the Herald reporter's private life," a fact, the article continued, that had been confirmed by Church of Scientology International president, Heber Jentzsch. " 'This investigation will have to look at what's driving this coverage,' " Jentzsch is quoted as saying (MacLaughlin and Gully 1998)—a position that suggests at least that any investigation into the Church that is likely to produce critical results is somehow motivated by malice on the part of the researchers. A decade earlier, journalist Russell Miller faced similar difficulties during the preparation of *Bare-Faced Messiah*. In the "Author's Note," he writes, "I would like to be able to thank the officials of the Church of Scientology for their help in compiling this bibliography, but I am unable to do so because the price of their co-operation was effective control of the manuscript and it was a price I was unwilling to pay. Thereafter the Church did its best to dissuade people who knew Hubbard from speaking with me and constantly threatened litigation."

REFERENCES

Atack, Jon. (1990). *A Piece of Blue Sky: Scientology, Dianetics and L. Ron Hubbard Exposed*. New York: Lyle Stuart Books.

Bainbridge, William Sims. (1980). "Scientology: To Be Perfectly Clear." *Sociological Analysis* 41: 128–36.

_____. (1987). "Science and Religion: The Case of Scientology." In *The Future of New Religious Movements*, ed. David G. Bromley and Phillip E. Hammond, 55–79. Macon, GA: Mercer University Press.

_____. (2002). *The Endtime Family: Children of God*. Albany, NY: State University of New York Press.

Barker, Eileen. (1984). *The Making of a Moonie: Choice or Brainwashing?* London: Basil Blackwell.

Bauer, Walter. (1971). *Orthodoxy and Heresy in Earliest Christianity*, 2nd ed. Trans. Philadelphia Seminar on Christian Origins; ed. Walter A. Kraft and Gerhard Krodel. Mifflintown, PA: Sigler Press.

Beckford, James A. (1980). "Scientology, Social Science and the Definition of Religion." Los Angeles: Freedom Publishing.

Bednarowski, Mary Farrell. (1995). "The Church of Scientology: Lightning Rod for Cultural Boundary Conflicts." In *America's Alternative Religions*, ed. Timothy Miller, 385–92. Albany, NY: State University of New York Press.

Beit-Hallahmi, Benjamin. (2003). "Scientology: Religion or Racket?" *Marburg Journal of Religion* 8 (1); retrieved from http://www.uni-marburg.de/ religionswissen schaft/journal/mjr/beit.html, May 30, 2004.

Berger, Peter L. (1967). *The Sacred Canopy: Elements of a Sociological Theory of Religion.* New York: Doubleday Anchor.

Berger, Peter, and Thomas Luckmann. (1966). *The Social Construction of Reality: A Treatise in the Sociology of Knowledge.* Harmondsworth, U.K.: Penguin Books.

Berglie, Per-Arne. (1996). "Scientology: A Comparison with Religions of the East and West." Los Angeles: Freedom Publishing.

Black, Alan W. (1996). "Is Scientology a Religion?" Los Angeles: Freedom Publishing.

Bromley, David G. (1985). "Financing the Millennium: The Economic Structure of the Unificationist Movement." *Journal for the Scientific Study of Religion* 24: 253–74.

Bromley, David G., and Mitchell L. Bracey, Jr. (1998). "The Church of Scientology: A Quasi-Religion." In *Sects, Cults, and Spiritual Communities*, ed. W. W. Zellner and Marc Petrowsky, 142–56. Westport, CT: Praeger Publishers.

Bryant, M. Darrol. (1994). "Scientology: A New Religion." Los Angeles: Freedom Publishing.

Chancellor, James D. (2000). *Life in the Family: An Oral History of the Children of God.* Syracuse, NY: Syracuse University Press.

Chidester, David. (n.d.) "Scientology: A Religion in South Africa." Los Angeles: Freedom Publishing.

Christensen, Dorthe Refslund. (1999). "Rethinking Scientology: Cognition and Representation in Religion, Therapy and Soteriology." Ph.D. dissertation, University of Aarhus, Denmark.

Church of Scientology International. (1998). *What Is Scientology?* Los Angeles: Bridge Publications.

———. (2001). *The Scientology Handbook.* Los Angeles: Bridge Publications.

———. (2002). *The Background, Ministry, Ceremonies and Sermons of the Scientology Religion.* Los Angeles: Bridge Publications.

———. (2004a). "L. Ron Hubbard: Founder of Scientology"; retrieved from http:// www.lronhubbard.org.au, May 10, 2007.

———. (2004b). "On Government"; retrieved from http://freedom.lronhubbard.org/ page010.htm, May 15, 2007.

———. (2004c). "Scientology Effective Solutions: Providing the Tools for Successful Living." Brussels, Belgium: Church of Scientology International.

———. (2006). "L. Ron Hubbard: The Founder of Scientology"; retrieved online from http://www.aboutlronhubbard.org, May 3, 2007.

Corydon, Bent. (1995). *L. Ron Hubbard: Messiah or Madman?* Fort Lee, NJ: Barricade Books.

Cowan, Douglas E. (2000). "Religion, Rhetoric, and Scholarship: Managing Vested Interest in E-Space." In *Religion on the Internet: Research Prospects and Promises*, ed. Jeffrey K. Hadden and Douglas E. Cowan, 101–24. Amsterdam and London: JAI/Elsevier Science.

————. (2004). "Contested Spaces: Movement, Countermovement, and E-Space Propaganda." In *Religion Online: Finding Faith on the Internet,* ed. Lorne L. Dawson and Douglas E. Cowan, 255–71. New York: Routledge.

————. (2005). *Cyberhenge: Modern Pagans on the Internet.* New York and London: Routledge.

Cowan, Douglas E., and David G. Bromley. (2006). "The Church of Scientology." In *New and Alternative Religions in the United States,* ed. Eugene V. Gallagher and W. Michael Ashcraft, vol. 5, 169–96. Westport, CT: Praeger Publishers.

————. (2008). *Cults and New Religions: A Brief History.* London: Basil Blackwell.

Dawson, Lorne L., and Douglas E. Cowan, eds. (2004). *Religion Online: Finding Faith on the Internet.* New York and London: Routledge.

Dericquebourg, Régis. (1988). *Religions de Guérison: Antoinisme, Science Chrétienne, Scientologie.* Paris: Cerf

————. (1995). "Scientology." Los Angeles: Freedom Publishing.

————. (1998). "De la thérapie à la spiritualité et inversement: l'exemple de la scientologie et du rebirth." *Recherches Sociologiques* 29 (2): 37–51.

Durkheim, Emile. ([1895] 1982). *The Rules of Sociological Method,* ed. Steven Lukes, trans. W. D. Hals. New York: The Free Press.

Ehrman, Bart D. (1993). *The Orthodox Corruption of Scripture: The Effect of Early Christological Controversies on the Text of the New Testament.* New York and Oxford: Oxford University Press.

————. (2003). *Lost Christianities: The Battles for Scriptures and the Faiths We Never Knew.* New York and Oxford: Oxford University Press.

————. (2005). *Misquoting Jesus: The Story Behind Who Changed the Bible and Why.* New York: HarperSanFrancisco.

Flinn, Frank K. (1983). "Scientology as Technological Buddhism." In *Alternatives to American Mainline Churches,* ed. Joseph H. Fichter, 89–110. New York: Rose of Sharon Press.

Frantz, Douglas. (1997). "Boston Man in Costly Fight with Scientology." *New York Times* (December 21): 24.

Frigerio, Alejandro. (1996). "Scientology and Contemporary Definitions of Religion in the Social Sciences." Los Angeles: Freedom Publishing.

Hein, Anton. (2001). "The Church of Scientology"; retrieved from http://www.apolo geticsindex.com/204.html, May 30, 2004.

Heino, Harri. (1995). "Scientology: Its True Nature." Los Angeles: Freedom Publishing.

Hubbard, L. Ron. ([1950] 1990). *Dianetics: The Modern Science of Mental Health.* Los Angeles: Bridge Publications.

Jacobson, Claire. (1963). "Translator's Preface." In *Structural Anthropology,* by Claude Lévi-Strauss; trans. Claire Jacobson and Brooke Grundfest Schoepf. New York: Basic Books.

Jentzsch, Heber C. (2002). "Scientology: Separating Truth from Fiction." In *New Religious Movements and Religious Liberty in America,* ed. Derek H. Davis and Barry Hankins, 141–62. Waco, TX: Baylor University Press.

Kelley, Dean M. ([1980] 1996). "Is Scientology a Religion?" Updated ed. Los Angeles: Freedom Publishing.

Kent, Stephen A. (1996). "Scientology's Relationship with Eastern Religions." *Journal of Contemporary Religion* 11 (1): 21–36.

————. (1999a). "The Creation of 'Religious' Scientology." *Religious Studies and Theology* 18 (2): 97–126.

———. (1999b). "The Globalization of Scientology: Influence, Control and Opposition in Transnational Markets." *Religion* 29: 147–69.

———. (1999c). "Scientology—Is This a Religion?" *Marburg Journal of Religion* 4 (2); retrieved from http://www.uni-marburg.de/fb11/religionswissenschaft/ journal/ mjr/kent.html, May 30, 2004.

———. (2002). "Hollywood's Celebrity-Lobbyists and the Clinton Administration's American Foreign Policy toward German Scientology." *Journal of Religion and Popular Culture* 1; retrieved from http://www.usask.ca/relst/jrpc/article-scientol ogy.html, May 28, 2007.

Knappman, E. W. (1973). *Watergate and the White House: June 1972–July 1973*, vol. 1. New York: Facts on File.

Lattin, Don. (2001). "Leaving the Fold: Third-Generation Scientologist Grows Disillusioned with Faith." *San Francisco Chronicle* (February 12): A1.

Lucas, Phillip Charles. (1995). *The Odyssey of a New Religion: The Holy Order of MANS from New Age to Orthodoxy.* Bloomington, IN: Indiana University Press.

Lüdemann, Gerd. (1995). *Heretics: The Other Side of Early Christianity,* trans. John Bowden. Louisville, KY: Westminster John Knox Press.

Lukes, Steven. (1982). "Introduction." In *The Rules of Sociological Method,* by Emile Durkheim, trans. W. D. Hals. New York: The Free Press.

MacLaughlin, Jim, and Andrew Gully. (1998). "Church of Scientology Probes *Herald* Reporter—Investigation Follows Pattern of Harassment." *Boston Herald* (March 19): News, 4.

Mannheim, Karl. ([1925] 1953). "The Problem of a Sociology of Knowledge." In *Essays on the Sociology of Knowledge,* ed. Paul Kecskemeti, 134–90. London: Routledge & Kegan Paul.

Melton, J. Gordon. (2000). *The Church of Scientology.* Torino, Italy: Signature Books.

———. (2001). "A Contemporary Ordered Religious Community: The Sea Organization." Paper presented at the international meeting of CESNUR (Center for Study on New Religions), London, England.

Miller, Russell. (1987). *Bare-Faced Messiah: The True Story of L. Ron Hubbard.* Toronto: Key Porter Books.

Miscavige, David. (2003). "Address to International Association of Scientologists"; DVD presentation viewed by author at Kansas City Church of Scientology, June 2003.

Morehead, John. (1998). Email communication to Nurel-l electronic discussion list (March 11).

———. (2004). Personal communication with author (June 4).

Peckham, Michael H. (1998). "New Dimensions of Social Movement/Countermovement Interaction: The Case of Scientology and Its Internet Critics. *Canadian Journal of Sociology/Cahiers Canadiens de Sociologie* 23 (4): 317–47.

Pentikainen, Juha, and Marja Pentikainen. (1996). "The Church of Scientology." Los Angeles: Freedom Publishing.

Religious Technology Center. (2003a). "Guaranteeing the Future of Dianetics & Scientology"; retrieved from http://www.rtc.org/guarant/page06.htm, September 14, 2003.

———. (2003b). "The Guarantor of Scientology's Future"; retrieved from http://www. rtc.org/guarant/page01.htm, September 14, 2003.

Richardson, James T., ed. (1988). *Money and Power in the New Religions.* Lewiston, NY: Edwin Mellen Press.

Rochford, E. Burke. (1985). *Hare Krishna in America.* New Brunswick, NJ: Rutgers University Press.

Ross, Michael W. (1988). "Effects of Membership in Scientology on Personality: An Exploratory Study." *Journal for the Scientific Study of Religion* 27: 630–36.

Sabbatucci, Dario. (1983). "Scientology: Its Historical-Morphological Frame." Los Angeles: Freedom Publishing.

Safa, Hajji Muhammad al-Qaaim. (1996). "Scientology and Islam: An Analogous Study." Los Angeles: Freedom Publishing.

Sawada, Fumio. (1996). "The Relationship between Scientology and Other Religions." Los Angeles: Freedom Publishing.

Simon, Neil. (1977). *The Goodbye Girl*, dir. Hebert Ross. Metro-Goldwyn-Mayer.

Sivertsev, Michael A. (1995). "Scientology: A Way of Spiritual Self-Identification." Los Angeles: Freedom Publishing.

Stark, Rodney, and William Sims Bainbridge. (1979). "Cult Formation: Three Compatible Models." *Sociological Analysis* 40: 283–95.

United Nuwaubian Nation of Moors. (n.d.). "The United Nuwaubian Nation of Moors"; retrieved online from http://www.geocities.com/Area51/Corridor/4978/unnm.html, May 3, 2007.

Urban, Hugh B. (2006). "Fair Game: Secrecy, Security, and the Church of Scientology in Cold War America." *Journal of the American Academy of Religion* 74 (2): 356–89.

Wah, Carolyn R. (2001). "An Introduction to Research and Analysis of Jehovah's Witnesses: A View from the Watchtower. *Review of Religious Research* 43 (2): 161–74.

Wallis, Roy. (1973). "A Comparative Analysis of Problems and Processes of Change in Two Manipulationist Movements: Christian Science and Scientology." In *Contemporary Metamorphosis of Religion: Acts of the Twelfth International Conference for the Sociology of Religion*, 407–22. Lille, France: Edition du Secrétariat CISR.

———. (1976). *The Road to Total Freedom: A Sociological Analysis of Scientology*. New York: Columbia University Press.

Whitehead, Harriet. (1974). "Reasonably Fantastic: Some Perspectives on Scientology, Science Fiction, and Occultism." In *Religious Movements in Contemporary America*, ed. Irving I. Zaretsky and Mark P. Leone, 547–87. Princeton, NJ: Princeton University Press.

———. (1987). *Renunciation and Reformulation: A Study of Conversion in an American Sect*. Ithaca, NY: Cornell University Press.

Zablocki, Benjamin. (1998). Email communication to the Nurel-l electronic discussion list (March 6).

———. (2004). Personal correspondence with author (June 2).

PART II

Theoretical and Quantitative Approaches

4

Making Sense of Scientology: Prophetic, Contractual Religion

David G. Bromley

Many scholars analyzing the cohort of new religious movements (NRMs) that appeared or gained popularity during the 1960s and 1970s have linked their growth to a major sociocultural dislocation in the United States and western Europe. As Robbins (1988: 60) puts the matter, there is "some acute and distinctively modern dislocation which is said to be producing some mode of alienation, anomie or deprivation" that in turn leads to individuals "responding by search-ing for new structures of meaning and community." Some of these analyses have emphasized the cultural and others the social struc-tural dimensions of this dislocation. Bellah (1976) and Tipton (1982) argue that the moral crisis during this era involved a repudiation of the two dominant elements of American culture through which in-dividuals constructed moral meaning, utilitarian individualism, and biblical religion. Bellah argues that the American civil religious myth has been eroded, leading to a crisis of moral meaning and a variety of attempts to create new mythic systems. Tipton argues that youth-ful protesters have rejected utilitarian culture and its central values (power, money, technology) in favor of expressive culture values (self-actualization, interpersonal love, and intimacy). By joining NRMs, young adults resolved the historic tension between utilitarian and expressive culture. Hunter (1981) describes an erosion of traditional social order that has divided the contemporary world into public and private spheres. The public sphere (governmental, legal, corporate institutions) is highly rationalized, impersonal, and bureaucratically organized, which undermines any sense of personal uniqueness and increases the individual's sense of vulnerability and expendability. By contrast, the private sphere (intimate, friendship, familial, spiritual relationships) has been progressively deinstitutionalized. The result is that the most central emotional relationships in people's lives have become unstructured, leaving individuals confronted with an overwhelming array of choices. NRMs therefore constitute a protest against modernity.

Whichever approach is adopted, the implication is that sociocultural dislocation provided a recruitment base for a set of prophetic NRMs that shared in common a contesting of the established social order and calling for a radical restructuring of that order. NRM scholars have also noted that there have been diverse responses to the sociocultural dislocation. Wallis (1984) distinguishes between world-affirming and world-rejecting movements, and Bromley (1997) distinguishes between adaptive and transformative NRMs (see also Tipton 1982). This means that understanding specific NRMs involves understanding both the qualities they share with the NRM cohort as a set and the distinctive qualities of the particular type of NRM that they represent.

Drawing on the assumption that prophetic NRMs are most likely during periods of dislocation and that movements may develop alternative or opposed responses to this dislocation, I will use the Church of Scientology to examine how one of these alternative responses is socially constructed. I shall argue that prophetic groups develop through a process of constructing a prophetic figure whose persona symbolizes the proposed alternative to prevailing logic, a mythic narrative that offers a new and contestive version of cosmic history, a novel ritual system that allows adherents to connect with the transcendent power source and validate the myth, and a new organizational and relational system that models the envisioned social order. The prophetic form occurs in specific sociohistorical contexts. In this instance, I shall argue, the dislocation associated with the contemporary NRM cohort may be described as tension between contractual and covenantal forms of social relations. This means that NRMs responding to the dislocation will exhibit both prophetic characteristics and some novel combination of contractual/covenantal characteristics that address the nature of the sociocultural dislocation.

In the case of Scientology, the movement shares prophetic logic with other contemporary and NRMs and is distinguished by the way that it has intermixed predominantly contractual logic characteristics in a novel fashion. That is, Scientology is best understood sociologically as a prophetic, contractual religion.[1] The issues to be addressed here are *how the logic of the prophetic method is developed* and *how contractual and covenantal characteristics have been juxtaposed*. Specifically, I shall argue that as a prophetic, contractual religion, Scientology has engaged in a project of (1) creating a prophetic persona for its founder/leader that legitimates his authority in a manner that resonates with contractual individualism; (2) constructing a mythic narrative that depicts massive discontinuity between the original, godlike qualities of individuals, described in terms of rational/analytic qualities, and their currently degraded state; (3) instituting a ritual system that combines religion and therapy to effect spiritual healing and transformation by restoring the individual's rational, analytic abilities; and (4) establishing a network of movement organizations that merges religious and economic organization and offers a contractually based model of individual-institutional relationships. The chapter begins with a brief rehearsal of the prophetic method and contractualism/covenantalism and then turns to the matters of prophetic persona, myth, ritual, and organization in Scientology.

The Prophetic Mode and Contractual Logic

There are two primary methods of authorizing religious social relations, priestly and prophetic (Bromley 1997), with the latter being of primary interest here. In contrast to the priestly method, which is most effective in settled times and locations when the continuity of tradition buttresses the existing structure of social relations, the prophetic method is most likely to be invoked during periods of dislocation when the existing structure of social relations is losing legitimacy and/or effectiveness. Through a mythic narrative, the prophetic method depicts a fundamental discontinuity between the natural order of things and the present, degraded state of affairs in the world that accounts for both personal and collective troubles. This narrative interweaves traditional and novel cultural themes in such a way as to create a new vision that "makes sense" to those experiencing dislocation. It is the energy generated by discontinuity, rather than continuity, that mobilizes and directs prophetically oriented groups. Rather than proposing progressive change within the existing structure of social relations, as the priestly method does, the prophetic method seeks to delegitimate the existing structure and calls for an immediate, radical restructuring of the social order and new forms of religious authorization. The discovery of a new truth that is the basis or prophetic mythology is revolutionary in its implications and constitutes the authority base for the prophetic founder/ leader. Personal transformation rituals create a destructuring/restructuring experience that transforms individual identity. Individuals gain new identities and membership in the vanguard of a new social order. Ritual experiences provide adherents with confirmatory experiences, and movement organizations model the shape of the dawning social order.

One of the primary abilities of prophetic leaders is to interpret the dislocations that individuals are experiencing in a culturally appropriate fashion. This means recasting elements of the cultural worldview and the social structure so that they offer an innovative alternative to the existing state of affairs but at the same time "make sense" in terms of working with the existing culture understandings and social practices. Two of the major sociocultural forms that prophetic leaders of NRMs have reworked are contractualism and covenantalism, both of which have been foundational to the development of Western societies over the last several hundred years. The covenantal tradition has biblical roots and expression in both the Jewish and Christian faiths. For the first Americans covenantalism was the reflexive form through which they organized themselves. From a Puritan perspective, God stood as witness to and authorized human affairs; America constituted a land and people, a community of the elect; and the community was compelled by conscience to fulfill the plan divinely ordained for them. In the covenantal tradition, community rather than the individual is the elemental unit of human organization because individuals are the product of the communities of which they are part. Individuals are therefore expected to give priority to the collective good and to pursue individual aspirations and actions in that context. The contractual tradition has equally deep roots but finds its most recent and influential expression in the work of contractarian philosophers. Put simply, the social contract consists of an agreement by participants to give up some rights to a sovereign in order to promote social order. Common to strands of contractual thought are the postulation of *autonomous, voluntaristic, self-directed individuals* as the basic constituent unit of human groups; *interests* (individual needs mediated by cognitive ordering) as the natural form of human intentionality; and *institutions* as derivative units legitimated by and responsive to individual interests. In the contractual tradition it is thus assumed that collective good is the product of individual actions in furtherance of personal interest.

The dynamics of contractualism and covenantalism create very different types of relationships (Bromley and Busching 1988: 18). The objective of interaction in contractual social relations, in which pledges are to specific activity (e.g., purchase, employment), is mutual agreement on terms of exchange (e.g., price, wage). In covenantal social relations, in which pledges are to one another's well-being (personal happiness, spiritual enlightenment), the objective is mutual commitment to one another (e.g., mutual caring, nurturance, love). The process through which individuals express their intentions in contractual social relations is negotiation (e.g., bargaining, bidding), whereas the corresponding process in covenantal social relations is bonding (uniting, fostering community, worship).

Historically, contractual logic has been a key element in the growth of corporate, bureaucratic forms of organization. One outgrowth of this process is that contemporary Western societies have divided between a contractually oriented public sphere (the state and economy) and a covenantally oriented private sphere (religion, family, community, ethnicity). This trend accelerated following World War II with the rapid expansion of the bureaucratically organized governmental and corporate sectors. The tension between the two traditions intensified as the public sphere has gained strength and solidity while deinstitutionalization has weakened the private sphere. Commenting on the impact of this trend on the family, for example, Glendon (1981: 1) concludes that "Changes in the legal regulation of family relationships increasingly reflect the perishability and fluidity, if not the transience, of these relationships, while legal changes in the workplace recognize and reinforce the durability and centrality, if not the permanence, of the work relationship." With the increasing regimentation of the public sphere, individuals have increasingly sought meaningful, authentic, personal relationships in the private sphere. It is therefore not surprising that in searching for alternative ways of living during the turbulent period of the 1960s and 1970s, prophetic leaders frequently formulated mythic narratives and organizational relationships grounded in some new combination of contractualism and covenantalism.

The Creation of Prophetic Authority

The creation of prophetic authority in a contractually oriented group involves reshaping the prophetic founder/leader's life history from biography to hagiography, with the emphasis on individual empowerment. The result is a persona that transcends the biographical person and that exemplifies the ultimate, spiritually self-actualized person.[2]

Lafayette Ronald Hubbard

Hubbard was born in Tilden, Nebraska, on March 13, 1911, to Harry Ross Hubbard and Ledora Mary Hubbard. Because his father was a naval officer, Hubbard's family moved often during his childhood. Hubbard was an adventurous youth who traveled the globe as a navigator, sailor, pilot, surveyor, and explorer. He also cultivated a range of intellectual interests, reading and writing both fiction and nonfiction while a student at George Washington University for two years. During the 1930s Hubbard supported himself by writing fiction and became a moderately successful science fiction writer. During World War II, Hubbard served as a lieutenant in the Navy and toward the end of the war was hospitalized. Hubbard reports that it was during this period that he began contemplating the nature of the human mind, immersing himself in Freudian psychoanalytic theory and Eastern philosophy that he had encountered in reading and travels earlier in his life. The basic principles of Dianetics and Scientology represent his personal synthesis of philosophy, physics, and psychology.

Hubbard's ideas received their first public exposure in 1950 when the popular magazine *Astounding Science Fiction* featured an article on Dianetics. In that same year Hubbard's book *Dianetics: The Modern Science of Mental Health* was published; *Dianetics* almost immediately became a best-seller and Hubbard a popular lecturer. Dianetics attracted a large following of practitioners because it offered a do-it-yourself alternative to individuals interested in improving their own mental health. In contrast to psychotherapy, Dianetics was much more accessible, promised more immediate progress, and placed the practitioner rather than a therapist in control of the therapy process. Within a year of the publication of *Dianetics*, Hubbard was developing Scientology.

He established the Church of Scientology in Los Angeles in 1954, and the following year moved to Washington, D.C., where he established the Founding Church of Scientology. In 1959 Hubbard moved again, this time to England, where he remained until the mid-1960s. Since founding his church, Hubbard provided it with both administrative and spiritual leadership, but in 1966 he resigned his organizational positions and devoted himself to further research and writing. At this juncture he formed what came to be an elite unit within Scientology, the Sea Organization (Sea Org), a church unit staffed by advanced, committed members. Sea Org derived its name from its initial design as a flotilla of oceangoing vessels that cruised international waters for several years. Sea Org moved to a land base in Clearwater, Florida, in 1975. During this decade

Hubbard continued to relinquish formal control over church organizations, and by 1980 he had withdrawn completely from public view. He retained the title of "founder" and remained the driving force behind the movement but lived a reclusive life until his death in 1986. Hubbard was succeeded in an administrative capacity by David Miscavige, then a twenty-six-year-old, second-generation Scientologist, a member of the church's elite Sea Organization, and chairman of the board of the Religious Technology Center.

The LRH Persona

Prophetic NRMs construct hagiographies (sacred biographies) of founder/ leaders that establish their prophetic authority. Prophetic authority involves claims to moral superiority on some dimension such that those acknowledging the authority are obligated to align their behavior with the prophetic leader. The essence of this process is to create a prophetic persona, in this case referred to as LRH, whose extraordinary qualities transcend those of the actual person. In the case of Scientology, LRH claimed to have discovered both the source of human misery, an insight that had escaped all previous cultural understanding, and a technology for realizing the godlike potential that all individuals actually possess. During and after LRH's life, the church has actively sought to document those extraordinary qualities. For example, according to church-sponsored publications, LRH was a very precocious child and an extremely learned young man, perhaps even a child prodigy. His life-long quest for spiritual knowledge began when he became blood brother to the Blackfoot Indians, through his relationship with an Indian shaman. By the age of twelve, LRH began studying under Commander Joseph C. Thompson, the first U.S. military officer to study under Freud in Vienna. As a young man LRH became a world traveler, exploring countries from Guam, Java, and, India to the Philippines, Japan, and China. From his investigation of these ancient cultures he is said to have gained further insight into the mysteries of the universe and concluded that existing explanations offered for the obvious condition of human misery were all inadequate. In 1930, LRH began his education at George Washington University, where he studied mathematics, engineering, and nuclear physics. LRH withdrew from the university, disillusioned with the potential for a secular education to answer the broader questions that he was posing.

The thrust of the church hagiography is that LRH was a particularly gifted individual who from an early age "possessed exactly the orientation and the personal characteristics necessary to one day discover and communicate a special knowledge to others" (Christensen 1999: 161). LRH foresaw his own potential to live an extraordinary life, possessed exceptional personal talents, recognized that he was on a path to making a major impact on history, and was received by other notable individuals because they, too, perceived his unique gifts. He recognized the inadequacies of existing cultural explanations for the problems of humankind, and in the process of his research he discovered knowledge that transcended the existing stock of cultural wisdom available in any culture

(Christensen 1999: 151–72). This depiction of LRH is contained in the church-produced biography and photo history of his life (1996), the L. Ron Hubbard Life Exhibition in Los Angeles, and the RON Series (a series of magazines reviewing different periods of Hubbard's life). In addition to the hagiographic content of these official biographies, the structure is also accommodated to hagiography. As LRH produced new writings, the "data contained in the written material was gradually edited according to Hubbard's new findings and ideas" (Christensen 1999: 49–50). The result is that LRH's life and work are depicted seamlessly, as if they were a continuous set of predetermined events and discoveries that unfolded through his lifelong research. His death has been treated in the same fashion. The church announced that Hubbard had "dropped his body" and moved to another planet to pursue higher levels of research that were not possible while he was encumbered by his body. The sacred status of LRH's discoveries in Scientology is indisputable. The church maintains a calendar that begins in 1950, the year that *Dianetics* was first published. His writings have been placed on disks and secured in a vault hewn from a mountainside so that they will be available to intergalactic travelers should Earth's population perish.

Although the basic outline of L. Ron Hubbard's life is not contested, the LRH persona has been a subject of particularly intense debate. Church critics have charged that many of the claims that Hubbard made about his own life and accomplishments are empirically false (Atack 1990; Corydon and DeWolf 1987; Miller 1987), and some social scientists have challenged certain of Hubbard's claims (Bainbridge 1987; Wallis 1976; Whitehead 1987). The empirical status of Hubbard's, Scientology's, and critics' truth claims is not, of course, what is at issue here as these essentially constitute rejection of charisma claims (politically) or narrative deconstruction (sociologically). The hagiography created by Hubbard and the church is the basis for the prophetic authority attributed to Hubbard within the movement. Together they produced a prophetic persona, LRH, that transcended Hubbard's biographical history. At its core, this process involves constructing an extraordinary persona that transcends normal human qualities and acts through the actual individual. In this case, the socially constructed persona, LRH, acts through Lafayette Ronald Hubbard. The successful process of constructing LRH as a prophetic leader has involved establishing the reality of LRH over Lafayette Ronald Hubbard.

There are some covenantal elements to this LRH persona. He is described by church members as a "friend" and is affectionately referred to as "Ron." His discovery of Scientology, the product of a lifelong search, is depicted as motivated by a personal commitment to humanity's well-being and is sometimes described as a "gift." The predominant orientation, however, is contractual as his discoveries were a "technology" that was itself the product of "research." Although Scientology may be a gift in the abstract, on an individual level Hubbard quickly established an economic exchange relationship with practitioners. Further, in many respects Hubbard is presented as the epitome of the autonomous, voluntaristic, self-directed individual, one who is able to stand outside of the social order and uses his creative abilities to realize the truly extraordinary selfhood of which everyone is to some degree capable. LRH's persona exemplified the process of discovering the true self that practicing Scientologists can emulate by following his technology. His presence continues through the "Standard Technology," which constitutes his personal embodiment in the counseling process (Christensen 1999: 155).

Scientology Mythology

Consistent with their prophetic stances, NRMs typically reimagine the mythic narrative describing the origin and ultimate destiny of humankind and the universe. By juxtaposing the original purpose of creation with the subsequent separation from that original purpose, prophetic mythology creates a sense of discontinuity that mobilizes movements and their adherents. The myth then offers resolution of this discontinuity by detailing the requisite path to salvation or restoration to the originally intended state. The prophetic qualities of Scientology increased dramatically with the transition from Dianetics, and the narrative took on an increasingly contractual character.

Themes in Scientology Mythology

In the early Dianetics, the focus of counseling was practitioners' minds and the negative experiences that had occurred within their current life lifetimes. According to Hubbard, the mind contains three components—analytic, reactive, and somatic—with the first two being of primary importance. The analytic mind is a conscious, completely rational mechanism that processes information with all the efficiency and infallibility of a computer. However, it is also very delicate, and its functioning can be disrupted by traumatic experiences. The reactive mind, by contrast, operates on a stimulus-response basis and protects the analytic mind from traumatic experiences. In times of great stress, injury, or threat, the analytic mind shuts down and the reactive mind takes over. The reactive mind is an extremely precise recording device that stores every detail of sensory experience—emotion, touch, sight, sound, smell—that occurs while the analytic mind is inoperative, even if the individual is unconscious at the time. The reactive mind consists of "engrams," the individual memory records of traumatic events, and at that time was understood to be the source of individual suffering and limitation. Clearing out the reactive mind, Hubbard claimed, significantly heightened practitioner ability and well-being.

With Hubbard's acceptance of practitioner reports of memories of experiences from previous lives and his introduction of Scientology (whatever his motivation for doing so), the mythology became more prophetic. Hubbard had now discovered the ultimate source of human misery and the means of its remediation. The emphasis of the mythology shifted from the individual's current life experience to the "whole track," accumulated experiences across countless lifetimes. The potential now existed for a narrative that incorporated an original, natural condition, a separation from that condition, and the potential for restoration to the original state.

According to Scientology doctrine, each human being is actually a thetan or spirit, an immortal, godlike expression of the life force (*theta*).

> A thetan is the person himself, not his body or his name or the physical universe, his mind or anything else. It is that which is aware of being aware; the identity which IS the individual. One does not *have* a thetan, something one keeps somewhere apart from oneself; he *is* a thetan. (Church of Scientology 1992: 8)

In his writings, Hubbard traces the existence of this life force back trillions of years. In the beginning theta was separate from the physical universe. Theta had no energy or mass, time or location; it was simply energy. Thetans therefore existed before and are the original source of the material universe. At one time thetans were godlike, celestial entities, possessed their own distinctive individuality, and created and controlled their own "Home Universes." It was a collision of these many universes that created an interchange among them, resulting in the physical universe that humans currently inhabit.

It was thetans who created the material world, which is composed of four elements—matter, energy, space, and time (MEST). Because MEST is the creation of thetans, it possesses only the reality they attribute to it. This means that the material universe actually is an illusion that becomes reality only through the action of thetans. However, once thetans had created the MEST universe, they began experimenting with taking on a corporeal human form. In the process, thetans gradually lost knowledge of their higher origins and became trapped in the bodies of humans (referred to as beings) and in the material universe. When the mortal being that a thetan inhabited died, the thetan simply entered another body around the time of its birth. Scientologists refer to this succession of lifetimes as a thetan's "time track." Having lost an understanding of their true identities, thetans came to accept the illusion that they are simply human.

In addition to the universal problem of loss of understanding of one's true spiritual essence across one's time track, there have been "universal incidents," events that have further undermined thetans' ability to recognize and actualize their true essence. There have been a number of such incidents through cosmic history; in many such cases thetans have been captured and implanted with false information that has left them more easily controlled. Briefly, one such event is what is known as "Incident 2," which occurred seventy-five million years ago. In this incident the leader (Xenu) of a group of seventy-six planets (the Galactic Confederation) responded to massive overpopulation by transporting large numbers of people to Earth (Teegeeack) and detonating hydrogen bombs in volcanoes to kill the people. Although the bodies were destroyed, the thetans survived. These thetans were implanted with false information that continues to afflict thetans who, millennia later, are living in different lifetimes and bodies (see Atack 1990). Vast numbers of traumatized thetans without bodies cluster on or around thetans inhabiting bodies. Each of these "body thetans" retains traumatic experiences that negatively impact the individual to whom the body thetan is attached. Much of the attention in advanced Scientology counseling is therefore on auditing body thetans sufficiently that they release from the host individual.

In Scientology individual salvation is achieved progressively; Hubbard identified an increasing number of levels of freedom from MEST that together are designated as the "Bridge to Total Freedom." Everyone begins Scientology practice as a "preclear," and there are two benchmark achievements along the Bridge. The first is reaching a state of Clear. Scientology defines a Clear as "a person who no longer has his own reactive mind and therefore suffers none of the ill effects that the reactive mind can cause" (Church of Scientology 1992: 811). Once the reactive mind has been emptied and therefore no longer exists, individuals are capable of a new level of spiritual awareness. The highest level of spiritual development is that of Operating Thetan. To achieve this level is to cease being "in effect," unable to control one's own mind, and to become "at cause," in control of one's mind as well of the MEST world. Thetans thus are spiritually perfect beings who transcend all limitations, assuming total control and responsibility in all their actions. As Scientologists put it, the person is "(and discovers himself to be) a BEING (spiritual agent) of infinite creative potential who acts in, but is not part of, the physical universe" (Thomas 1970: 8). Scientologists believe that as Operating Thetans they will have restored themselves to their original, natural condition ("native state"). In their native state individuals can think and act rationally and be "at cause" in dealing with events and relationships in their everyday lives.

The quest to restore oneself and others to a native state is pivotal in Scientology. Indeed, committed members identify their goal as "clearing the planet," and there are even expectations of clearing other planets. Hubbard was very explicit about Scientology's role in cosmic history:

> We're not playing some minor game in Scientology. It isn't cute or something to do for lack of something better. The whole agonized future of this planet, every man, woman and child on it, and your own destiny for the next endless trillions of years depend on what you do here and now with and in Scientology. (Christensen 1999: 173)

This sense of urgency is reflected in church claims that it is the fastest growing religion on the planet and the expectation among many committed Scientologists that they will indeed clear the planet in the immediate future.

Prophetic and Contractual Themes in Scientology Mythology

Scientology offers a prophetic challenge to traditional religion, and particularly Christian theology. Contrary to Christian doctrine, individuals as theta beings are themselves Creators. The fall of humankind involved not a separation from God but from the essential self, not sinfulness but misinformation. Much of the degraded state of the world and its accompanying human misery is attributable to this historic separation of thetans from their native state. What Hubbard has discovered, then, is the ultimate source of human misery, an insight that has eluded all previous religious knowledge systems and renders them basically irrelevant. Scientology offers the only sure path to salvation both for individuals and for humanity collectively. Further, salvation can be achieved immediately in this world, and Scientologists can control the process by employing Hubbard's technology. This discovery has created a sense of urgency within the movement that mobilizes core members to make a total, personal commitment to the cause.

Scientology's mythic narrative constructs root reality and the individual nature in contractually compatible terms that resonate with a social world organized technologically, scientifically, and bureaucratically. Practitioners learn that the material reality they inhabit is not the work of a transcendent deity but simply the product of an agreement among thetans themselves. In this sense, the sovereign in the social contract is the individual theta being. The self is conceptualized in scientific, technological terms, as the basic adaptive mechanism of the individual is the analytic mind, a mechanistic device that resembles a computer. The structure of the mind resembles any ordinary bureaucratic organization; it contains a set of memory records, referred to as files, that are constantly being gathered, processed, and stored by the mind. The individual is at risk when the analytic mind is unable to function normally and there is a loss of cognitive control that results from unrecognized and uncontrolled emotional responses. The solution to these problems is to root out unruly emotions and to reassert and heighten cognitive control. In this sense, the essence of the thetan shares much in common with a variety of New Age groups that postulate a true self, whose qualities transcend those the current individual is capable of manifesting. The Operating Thetan very much resembles the autonomous, voluntaristic, self-directed individual writ large, who is the building block of the contractual social order. The project of individual empowerment is not simply self-serving, however, as fully empowered individuals will be motivated to create mutually meaningful and rewarding social relationships and further the collective good.

Scientology Ritual

One of the challenges facing prophetic NRMs is demonstrating the existence of the alternative reality that is depicted in their mythic systems. Ritual observances are constructed so as to provide practitioners with direct, personal experience of this reality, and are particularly likely to be found where status or identity transformations are being created. The ritual process follows a destructuring-restructuring sequence as practitioners shed their prior status/identity and assume the new one. During this process there are breakthrough moments when practitioners experience the new reality. In Scientology the emphasis is primarily on the destructuring process as the practitioners' true identities are assumed to be intact and simply need to be released.

The Patterning of Scientology Ritual

When individuals first begin practicing Scientology, they participate in training routines (TRs) that develop skills they will use throughout their Scientology careers. TRs for beginning-level practitioners have twin objectives—enhancing individual awareness and self-control while simultaneously building responsiveness and sensitivity toward others. For example, practitioners learn the capacity for "just being there" by simply maintaining nonverbal presence and attentiveness with a partner for an extended period of time ("confronting"). In another exercise, participants try to maintain focus in a situation despite concerted efforts by their partner to disrupt concentration ("bull-baiting"). More advanced TRs create the capacity for meaningful communication with others, as well as building auditing skills.

As already noted, auditing and training processes are organized in a complex series of levels. At each level practitioners encounter and gain release from a certain set of problems; they then expect to experience enhanced abilities. The grading of the rituals is designed to address the most immediate sources of trauma first and then move on to more fundamental issues over the whole track. Initially, in Dianetics auditing, the emphasis was on clearing traumatic incidents through the preclear's present life, although even then Hubbard was concerned with prenatal experiences. Currently, Dianetics focuses on clearing away traumatic incidents from the preclear's present and past lives. Once practitioners have reached the state of Clear, they begin to move through the eight of the fifteen OT (Operating Thetan) levels that have been released to date. The emphasis in much of this auditing is on body thetans and necessarily involves experiences in previous lives. For example, at the OT III level (Wall of Fire), the Clear learns about the Xenu incident and focuses on auditing body thetans related to that cosmic incident.

The key piece of diagnostic technology employed in auditing is the Electropsychometer (E-Meter). This instrument is a skin galvanometer that sends a small electrical charge through the body and then registers the electrical flow on its display. Negative memory records are thought to possess an actual mass and so offer resistance to the electrical charge. The E-Meter is used during auditing sessions to identify resistance created by negative memory records. The auditor assists the practitioner in eliminating negative memory records by first locating points of resistance, converting the form that they take into energy, and then discharging that energy. When a stored emotional charge (negative memory record) is identified and is discussed sufficiently (audited), it will no longer produce an emotional response (the charge it contains will be released), and the E-Meter needle will "float" (it has been cleared). Once the negative memory record is cleared, the past event is refiled in the standard memory bank of the analytical mind.

The auditing process itself consists of the auditor posing a list of questions to the preclear or Clear. The individuals search their memory banks for a related memory record and report that experience to the auditor, who observes responses on the E-Meter, makes notes on the substance of those responses, and acknowledges the responses. The auditor goes to great lengths not to influence the nature of the practitioner's responses. In a typical lower level auditing session the auditor begins by asking preclears if they are comfortable, well fed, and well rested. If so, the auditor inquires whether the preclear has experienced an upset, which is described as an ARC (affinity, reality, communication) break. Affinity involves liking or loving another person, reality is an agreement with another person about what is, and communication is an exchange of ideas with another person. Together these three dimensions comprise understanding, and reduced levels of any dimension reduce individual understanding. Any such event reported by the preclear in response to the ARC break query is then briefly discussed. If the preclear does not experience relief, the ARC break is further assessed using the E-Meter to identify the exact nature of the upset. If resolution is achieved and the needle floats, the auditor then proceeds to checking for present time problems (something that worries the preclear). This problem is then discussed in the same fashion. Finally, the auditor asks whether the preclear has committed any moral transgression that has almost been discovered (a missed withhold). That incident is then discussed with the objective of resolving it. In each of these three cases (ARC breaks, present time problems, and withholds), if the problem does not resolve, the auditor inquires as to whether there was an earlier incident, which is then probed until the needle floats. Beyond the Clear level and at the upper OT levels, practitioners are trained to communicate with and set free the troublesome clusters of body thetans that have attached themselves to practitioners. By awakening these thetans from their amnesia and liberating them, the practitioner frees these thetans to find other bodies in which they can reside or to enjoy their freedom as entities detached from any body. Progressive clearing of negative memory records and of body thetans allows the individual to relate to experiences directly rather than through the distorting filter of those memory records.

Prophetic and Contractual Patterns in Scientology Ritual

In contemporary society it has become commonplace for individuals to turn to therapeutic services when they experience feelings of self-doubt, loss of self-esteem, diffuse anxiety, loneliness, alienation, lack of personal competence, dissatisfaction with social relationships, and inability to realize personal aspirations. The goal of conventional therapies is to restore autonomy, voluntarism, and self-directedness but within the context of a contractual social order. As Bellah et al. (1985: 47) observe:

> the therapist takes the functional organization of industrial society
> for granted, as the unproblematical context of life. The goal of living
> is to achieve some combination of "lifestyle" that is economically pos-
> sible and psychically tolerable, that "works." The therapist . . . takes
> the ends as they are given; the focus is upon the effectiveness of the
> means.

Nickolas Rose (1990: 228–29) concurs, commenting that "the rationale of psychotherapies is to restore the individuals the capacity to function as autonomous beings in the contractual society of the self."

Scientology ritual takes a prophetic turn by merging secular therapy from the public sphere and religion from the private sphere. Therapy becomes religion and religion becomes therapy. In contrast to secular therapy, which seeks to fold a functioning individual back into the conventional social order, Scientology seeks to empower practitioners to experience themselves as standing outside of and independent of that order. Indeed, they are ultimately the Creators of whatever order exists. This therapeutic transformation becomes possible because the practitioner is not mortal but rather is an immortal theta being. The progressive process of restoring what one truly is focuses on destructuring, much like a Christian deliverance or exorcism ritual. Traumatic memory records from one's present lifetime and whole track, as well as those from traumatized body thetans, must be eliminated. During this painstaking process, individuals experience breakthrough moments when they recall experiences from previous lives or "exteriorize" (experience the thetan independent of the body). Movement up the Bridge to Total Freedom does provide empowering experiences that restructure practitioners' lives, at least within the movement. Practitioners are entrusted with more advanced doctrines, can conduct more advanced auditing, and are eligible for higher status positions within church affiliated organizations.

The counseling process in Scientology is technologically and bureaucratically organized, taking those regulatory elements of the conventional social order and reversing their effects so that they become mechanisms of liberation. The counselor is referred to an auditor, a role that in conventional society is created to reveal record-keeping errors and violations for which individuals are held accountable. In Scientology the auditor searches out misinformation that has victimized the practitioner and assists the practitioner in releasing any related trauma and in refiling the experience in the analytic mind's files. The device that is used in locating the misinformation, the E-Meter, closely resembles a lie detector, an instrument frequently used by bureaucratic functionaries to discover concealed prevarications and initiate sanctioning. In Scientology the E-Meter is used to locate misinformation that is harmful to the individual. The auditor assists the individual in identifying harmful misinformation and refiling the reconstructed memory record in the proper file. In this way, technology and bureaucracy become mechanisms of empowerment rather than repression.

Scientology Organization

In corporate capitalist societies, of which the United States is the preeminent example, religious organizations have initiated a variety of innovative connections between religious and economic activity. For example, megachurches, one of the fastest growing group of churches in the United States, have consciously adopted the shopping mall as the model for their churches in order to place parishioners in a comfortable, familiar atmosphere. A number of NRMs have adopted more radical innovations. The Unificationist Movement created integrated corporate and religious organizations by developig an elaborate network of corporate organizations that funneled profits to not-for-profit outreach organizations that further the movement's religious agenda (Bromley 1985). Amway, a quasi-religious corporation, has linked business and family in part through a gospel of prosperity ideology and evangelistic style organization (Bromley 1998). A variety of New Age groups treat practitioners as clients and charge fees for enroll them in workshops, courses, or trainings, essentially establishing producer-consumer, buyer-seller relationships with practitioners. For example, Transcendental Meditation marketed its meditative techniques to practitioners and also sought markets in a variety of public institutions before being enjoined by the courts. Scientology has extended this logic through its own unique blending of religion and capitalism.

Scientology Organizations

Three major categories of Scientology organizations are those dedicated to practice and training, technology application, and social reform. Because Scientology has been granted tax-exempt status as a religious organization, most of its affiliate organizations are established on a not-for-profit basis. The practice and training organizations are all part of the church structure. The technology application and social reform organizations are formally separate from the church but are staffed by Scientologists and report to Sea Organization administrators. The various Advanced Organizations are staffed entirely by Sea Organization members.

Scientology practice and training is carried out on several different levels. At the local level there are hundreds of Scientology missions and organizations (orgs) around the world where introductory level training is offered by trained Scientologists. The vast majority of Scientology practitioners participate in the church at this level. Above the mission/org level are a number of other organizations that offer advanced training or perform specialized functions. For example, Saint Hill Organizations resemble religious colleges and seminaries as they train auditors and ministers who provide religious leaders for the church. Higher levels of Scientology technology are offered to senior practitioners in Advanced Organizations, such as the Flag Ship Service and the Flag Service Organization. All of these organizations are united under the umbrella of the Church of Scientology International.

The network of technology application organizations creates model programs that apply Hubbard's technologies to a variety of societal problems. For example, Narconon International offers drug education and rehabilitation services. Narconon administers a drug treatment program based on Hubbard's theory that drugs and toxins stored in the body inhibit spiritual growth. The program consists of auditing combined with a regimen of exercise, saunas, vitamins, and diet management. Criminon seeks to rehabilitate criminals by teaching the teaching them how to study, to communicate more effectively, to avoid what Scientology terms antisocial personalities, and to adopt more appropriate personal values. Applied Scholastics employs Hubbard's educational technology to teach students how to learn and to study effectively. Each of these technology application organizations claims success rates that exceed their conventional counterparts. The Way to Happiness Foundation distributes Scientology's moral code to the public. The technology application organizations also address business-related problems. The World Institute of Scientology Enterprises (WISE) is a not-for-profit organization that licenses the use of Hubbard's business technology. Licensed business training organizations, of which Sterling Management is the best known, offer training in specific skills such as hiring, logical decision making, plan implementation, and organizational streamlining.

The most prominent social betterment organizations opposing what Scientology judges as abusive practices by public and private agencies are the Citizens Commission on Human Rights (CCHR) and the National Commission on Law Enforcement and Social Justice. Based on Hubbard's unequivocal hostility toward psychiatrists, CCHR has been an unremitting opponent of psychiatry. *What Is Scientology?* (1992), for example, asserts that psychiatry is a "conglomeration of half-baked theories" espoused by a "priesthood" that has its mission not healing but control. The National Commission on Law Enforcement and Social Justice combats what it defines as abusive practices by national and international agencies, such as the Internal Revenue Service, Central Intelligence Agency, and Department of Justice, and Interpol.

Scientology as Corporate Religion

Scientology has adopted a prophetic turn in its reorganization of the public-private sphere relationship. Rather than maintaining the separation of the public and private spheres, Scientology has merged and unified the economic and religious. For Scientology, the business is a church and the church is a business. Although the various church affiliated entities are formally constituted as not-for-profit organizations, their corporate, capitalist characteristics are nonetheless paramount. For example, the church protects its logos, technology, and Hubbard's various signatures through copyrights, trademarks, and service marks. Each of the missions and orgs is a corporate entity set up as a licensed franchise. These units retain the right to market church services to individual practitioners so long as they meet the qualitative and quantitative standards established and rigorously monitored by upper level administrative units (Religious Technology Center and Commodore's Messenger Organization). Missions and orgs offer practitioners beginning level auditing services for a "fixed donation," and they then return a (sometimes very substantial) percentage of the gross revenues and payment for other services to International Management. Other organizations, such as the technology application groups, operate on a similar basis. Within all of the major Scientology organizations, the emphasis is on individual and organizational unit productivity. Each organization systematically gathers "stats" on individual and collective performance so that a valuable final product (VFP) is produced. Operating budgets within organizations are based on performance indicators and are reviewed weekly; internal funding for these units is adjusted weekly based on these performance indicators. Positive stats ("up stats") are an indication that an individual or organization is in one of the more favorable Scientological conditions, and failure to perform adequately or show continuous improvement is defined as a spiritual problem that may invoke the Scientology ethics system. An entrepreneurial incentive system also pervades these organizations. Both individuals and organizations receive direct payment for bringing new practitioners into church-affiliated organizations or for prompting them to register for more advanced services.

Although the various missions/orgs, technology application groups, and social reform organizations are legally separate, independent entities, they are controlled by the church. The primary management unit within the church is Sea Org, which consists of five to seven thousand committed Scientologists. Although Sea Org in some respects resembles a traditional monastic order and hence could easily have assumed a covenantal form, it is in fact an elaborately organized bureaucracy based on contractual principles. Upon joining Sea Org, members agree to "employment" that commits them to a "billion-year contract" for very nominal compensation in pursuit of organizational goals. Sea Org members constitute the religious management of Scientology as they deliver the advanced auditing and provide spiritual advice (that is, manage) the various technology application and social reform groups. Sea Org is subject to the same performance requirements and assessments as the groups that it oversees. In essence, the Sea Org merges clerical and bureaucratic roles, producing a spiritual bureaucracy the goal of which, from an insider standpoint at least, is individual and planetary transformation.

Conclusions

In this chapter I have argued that Scientology may be productively understood from a sociological perspective as prophetic, contractual religion. Scientology has created a hagiographic portrayal of L. Ron Hubbard's life that yields the LRH persona, which authorizes Scientology's salvationist project. The myth rewrites cosmic history to create godlike qualities for practitioners that model the requisite characteristics of individuals in a contractual social order. Two dynamics of the prophetic method are particularly evident in the ritual practices and organizational structure. First, elements of the conventional order are combined in a novel fashion. In this case, therapy (from the public sphere) and religion (from the private sphere) are conjoined. This permits Scientology to offer extraordinary individual empowerment in a contractually compatible form. Similarly, business and religion are unified, creating a corporate religion where the spirit of capitalism and spiritual salvation are harmonized, where spiritual salvation can be earned and purchased. Second, repressive elements of the conventional order are transformed into mechanisms of liberation as technology, therapy, and corporate bureaucracy become means of promoting both individual and collective salvation. Both the role of therapeutic client and religious consumer are sufficiently plausible extensions of individualism, capitalism, and therapy to provide practitioners a cultural bridge to what otherwise might be a radical and alien tradition. The irony is that the innovations that Scientology has made by merging therapy, business, and religion has at once been the source of practitioners' attraction to the movement and the source of the intense opposition that it has evoked.

NOTES

1. In treating Scientology as prophetic contractual religion I am analyzing the way that the organization presents itself to the overwhelming proportion of individual practitioners who are involved as lower level consumers of Scientology services. The organization and dynamics of the Sea Organization and its members and upper levels of Scientology practice require a separate analysis.

2. There is considerable controversy surrounding Hubbard's biography, and numerous competing accounts have been produced. Critics have amassed considerable evidence that challenges the hagiographic depiction of Hubbard. Here a basic outline of Hubbard's life is used as the baseline for interpreting the Hubbard hagiography. The degree of persona construction would obviously increase were critics' accounts used as a baseline.

REFERENCES

Atack, Jon. 1990. *A Piece of Blue Sky: Scientology and L. Ron Hubbard Exposed*. New York: Carol Publishing.

Bainbridge, William. 1987. "Science and Religion: The Case of Scientology." Pp. 59–79 in David G. Bromley and Phillip Hammond, eds., *The Future of New Religious Movements*. Macon, GA: Mercer University Press.

Bellah, Robert. 1976. "New Religious Consciousness and the Crisis of Modernity." Pp. 333–52 in Charles Glock and Robert Bellah, eds., *The New Religious Consciousness*. Berkeley, CA: University of California Press.

Bellah, Robert, et al. 1985. *Habits of the Heart: Individualism and Commitment in American Life*. Berkeley: University of California Press.

Bromley, David G. 1985. "The Economic Structure of the Unificationist Movement." *Journal for the Scientific Study of Religion* 24: 253–74.

Bromley, David G. 1997. "A Sociological Narrative of Crisis Episodes, Collective Action, Culture Workers, and Countermovements." *Sociology of Religion* 58: 105–40.

Bromley, David G. 1998. "Transformative Movements and Quasi-Religious Corporations: The Case of Amway." Pp. 349–63 in Nicolas J. Demerath, Peter Dobkin Hall, Terry Schmitt, and Rhys H. Williams, eds., *Sacred Companies: Organizational Aspects of Religion and Religious Aspects of Organizations*. New York: Oxford University Press.

Bromley, David G., and Bruce Busching. 1988. "Understanding the Structure of Contractual and Covenantal Social Relations: Implications for the Sociology of Religion." *Sociological Analysis* 49: 15–32.

Christensen, Dorthe. 1999. "Rethinking Scientology: Cognition and Representation in Religion, Therapy and Soteriology." Ph.D. Dissertation. University of Aarhus.

Church of Scientology. 1992. *What Is Scientology?* Los Angeles: Bridge Publications.

Church of Scientology. 1996. *L. Ron Hubbard: Images of a Lifetime.* Los Angeles: Bridge Publications.

Corydon, Bent, and Ronald DeWolf (L. Ron Hubbard, Jr.). 1987. *L. Ron Hubbard: Messiah or Madman.* Secaucus, NJ: Lyle Stuart.

Hubbard, L. Ron. 1950. *Dianetics: The Modern Science of Mental Health.* Los Angeles: Church of Scientology of Los Angeles.

Hunter, James. 1981. "The New Religions: Demodernization and the Protest against Modernity." Pp. 1–19 in Bryan Wilson, ed., *The Social Impact of the New Religious Movements.* New York: The Rose of Sharon Press.

Miller, Russell. 1987. *Bare-Faced Messiah: The True Story of L. Ron Hubbard.* New York: Henry Holt.

Robbins, Thomas. 1988. *Cults, Converts and Charisma.* London: Sage.

Rose, Nickolas. 1990. *Governing the Soul: The Shaping of the Private Self.* London: Routledge.

Thomas, Robert. 1970. *Scientology and Dianetics.* Los Angeles: Church of Scientology.

Tipton, Stephen. 1982. *Getting Saved From the Sixties.* Berkeley: University of California Press.

Wallis, Roy. 1976. *The Road to Total Freedom: A Sociological Analysis of Scientology.* London: Heinmann.

Wallis, Roy. 1984. *The Elementary Forms of the New Religious Life.* London: Routledge & Kegan Paul.

Whitehead, Harriet. 1987. *Renunciation and Reformulation: A Study of Conversion in an American Sect.* Ithaca, NY: Cornell University Press.

5

Scientology and Self-Narrativity: Theology and Soteriology as Resource and Strategy

Dorthe Refslund Christensen

Many religious groups, whether we choose to refer to them as New Age or new religions or new religiosity, seem to be organized around ideas and practices that aim at organizing the self of the individual practitioner.[1] Here, religious individuals blend with many secularly oriented individuals following individual practices for self-development. Scientology is no exception. Although it may be said—and many *have* pointed to this fact—that the social and soterio-logical organization of Scientology is rigid and—apparently—without space for individual interpretation and decision making, it might be more correct to say that Scientology, as a religion and religious orga-nization, offers a mythological and ritual framework that leaves a big open space within which individuals can develop their own narratives of their lives and selves, and that this open space seems very suited to meet the challenges of postmodern, Western culture. In this chapter I will argue that a rigid soteriological organization does not necessar-ily lead to uniformity in the representations made by the individuals engaged in that particular system.

In order to establish the cultural setting for today's religious practitioner I draw on sociologist Anthony Giddens (1990, 1991, 1992) and his idea of self-reflectiveness as one of the most funda-mental issues of our times, the concepts *religion as a chain of memo-ries* and *memories in bits* offered by sociologist of religion Danièle Hervieu-Léger (1998, 2001) to account for the function of incorpo-rating religious bits and pieces into the postmodern production of identity and self-narrativity, and cultural analyst John Storey (2003a) to explain the interrelatedness of identity and culture. Furthermore,

I point to theories from cognitive anthropologist Pascal Boyer (1993, 1994a, 1994b) and cognitive psychologist Justin Barrett (1999) in order to suggest why rigidity does not necessarily lead to uniformity in the representations made by individual practitioners of a religion.

Self-Narrativity and Reflectiveness: A Postmodern Perspective

It is, of course, outside the scope of this chapter to analyze in depth any of the theoretical positions that I use to establish the cultural diagnosis typical of Western postmodern culture. I will only stress a very few central points:

In his analyses of the social and cultural backgrounds of New Age ideas and practices and their appeal to modern individuals, sociologist of religion Paul Heelas has suggested that postmodern spiritual ideas can be considered radicalized versions of themes and values present in postmodern culture (for instance, Heelas 1996). Which values and themes are these? Many a writer, including sociologist Anthony Giddens, has focused on the *self-reflexiveness* of our times. In Giddens's analyses of *The Consequences of Modernity* (1990) this concept is the point of departure. He does not, of course, imply that individuals have not always, to some extent, reflected on who they are. But people in present-day Western culture are reflecting on every aspect of life to the extent that the individual is seen as a "work in progress." The separation of time and space and the disembeddedness of individual life in a close cultural setting have produced a state of affairs in which individual identity is established according to the different roles and positions in which individuals are engaged. These different roles do not correspond to one another, and the individual is therefore urged to be flexible in the creation of—not *a self*—but multiple *selves*, if the individual is to be successful in life. This prompts reflection, not only on the different aspects of life but on reflection itself. Sociologist Zygmunt Bauman has said that "it is easy to adopt an individual identity but very very difficult to hold on to it" (1994: 57).

Cultural analyst John Storey (e.g., 2003a) also points to the necessity of viewing identity as processual, reflexive, and fragmented, and—following from this—he suggests that rather than speaking of a singular *identity*, we speak of *identities*. Identities are something that each of us is continuously producing *culturally* rather than something we act out on the basis of something *natural*.[2] According to Storey our identity work is relational and goes on in the context of an exchange with institutions, ideologies, and people (significant others). Telling stories of oneself in Storey's theory is not a question of remembering how things actually happened in order to find the *truth* about oneself but rather negotiating fruitful bits of stories that seem useful here and now. That is, our personal stories change over time. Memories are storytelling with a purpose in order to produce *roots* that can explain and put into perspective our self-representation and also by locating *routes* that can help us transform ourselves according to ambitions, goals, and desires.

Scholar of religion Russell McCutcheon (2000) has suggested a reconceptualization of *myth*. Instead of defining myth by a certain kind of substance, he suggests thinking of myth as a tool by which any agenda can be set as authoritative and unique, as something you cannot imagine differently. Thereby, mythological storytelling becomes a social strategy, a storytelling tool, a social kind of argumentation through which individuals represent and legitimate themselves and their social and cultural reality (McCutcheon 2000: 199f). This process McCutcheon refers to as *mythologization*.

Religious practice might be explained by referring to the resources religious myths and ritual practices offer to the process of creating the self.[3] Scientological ideas and practices, one might argue, seem perfectly fit to meet the challenge of the reflective individual: Both the immortal kernel of the individual is represented (as the *thetan*—see below), and a mythological time track is provided containing every bit of information and stories about the individual's large-scale history. Thereby the system leaves plenty of space for the individual to experiment with whom he or she has been and wants to be in the future. Roots and routes become mythologizing strategies in personalized transformation stories.

Another important characteristic of our times is pluralism and the blurring of cultural genres. Increasingly, all kinds of cultural knowledge and information are available for individuals. Clear-cut distinctions between elite culture and popular culture, and between culture and market, are not drawn in the sense that any kind of cultural representation can be utilized in individual self-representations.[4] The same goes for religion and other cultural categories. Furthermore, religious narratives and ritualized behavior are blended with other (secular) cultural repertoires in order to provide the individual with aesthetic forms, mythological and psychological contexts, and fragmented pieces of meaning.[5] One very close relative of religious mythologies these days is therapy, and the secular cousins of ritual are found in all kinds of ritualized behavior and practical forms using elements from ritual or borrowing the transformative, altering potential of the ritual room. These are found, for instance, in performance theater, in high-risk sport activities, and in dieting and fitness subcultures.

In Scientology, therapy and religion are two interacting cultural repertoires, whereas management rhetoric and religious discourse are joined to form yet another mixed couple. The aesthetics of Scientology derive from American popular culture, such as TV shows, and the interior decorating of Scientological facilities seems inspired as much by IKEA as by the aesthetics of the romanticized nineteenth-century English countryside. The resources seem limitless, and the frames for individual representations are suggestive and highly flexible.

Norwegian psychiatrist Finn Skårderud (1999) has pointed to *restlessness* as a fundamental premise for postmodern lives and individuals. In his analysis of individual strategies in contemporary Western culture, inspired by the ideas of, amongst others, philosopher Jean-François Lyotard and sociologists Christoffer Lasch and Thomas Ziehe (besides the inspiration from modern popular fiction), he points to two dominant and interrelated strategies by which the individual finds his or her places in life: *self-narrativity* and *staging of the self*. To Skårderud, no matter whether the object is the teenager suffering from anorexia, the modern primitive having his or her body pierced and tattooed, or the homemaker seeing her psychotherapist or crystal healer on a regular basis—these people are coming to terms with the existential conditions of our times by, more or less pragmatically, choosing a strategy: a way of *telling* themselves, of finding narratives to make sense of who they are or who they want or need to be, *and* a set of practices through which they can find room for obtaining resources or practical tools for handling their lives. The concepts of self-narrativity and staging of the self seem to me very useful tools in the interpretation of many contemporary religious activities. Scientology is no exception. As argued below, the soteriological and ritual strategies of Scientology leave space for individuals to tell and stage themselves in a mytho-evolutional perspective that might take away some of the pressure and pain generated by a superfragmented, individualistic, success-oriented culture of everyday modern life because it offers room for action—not only in this life but in relation to one's mythological past. Karmic past experience is a very instrumental idea in the modern making of identity.[6]

The *fragmented* character of contemporary Western culture is also stressed by sociologist of religion Danièle Hervieu-Léger when she speaks of the short term memory of Western culture (*memories in bits*) and the call for fragmented, mythological constructs of the past that anybody needs as a sort of existential context but which is not present without the process of constructing it (1998). Continuity has been replaced by a thoroughly event-centered orientation in modern Western culture. This goes for the media as well as for our conceptualization of history. The individual, coping with this situation, constructs him- or herself *in bits,* in fragments: "a modern ideal of continuity is (possibly) reshaping itself by intertwining shattered 'small memories' which are formed from bits and pieces, and which are sometimes invented memories" (1998: 39). According to Hervieu-Léger—and in line with Heelas—modern Western culture implies a constant demand of personal and cultural growth and change and this calls for strong resources. Religion, according to Hervieu-Léger, offers chains of memories and, in Scientology, these chains of memories are the mythological resources brought to the mind of the individual in the ritual sphere.

Scientology and Scientologists

When studying the material written by or ascribed to founder L. Ron Hubbard,[7] it is possible to establish an understanding of how the different elements of Scientological theology are interrelated in a number of ways. My Ph.D. dissertation, *Rethinking Scientology: Cognition and Representation in Therapy, Religion and Soteriology,* was an attempt to develop a theoretical framework for analyzing the written material with a focus on how the therapeutic and religious elements interplay in the Scientological soteriological system and in the written representations of founder L. Ron Hubbard from 1950 to 1986.[8]

However, interpreting texts does not give us any understanding of how actual individuals in Scientology organize the knowledge they gain from studying the Hubbard material or how different sets of knowledge interplay. The study and interpretations of texts is limited in its explanatory scope because it, of course, can reflect how different mythological elements interplay only at a *systemic* level. Therefore such studies must be supplemented by analyzing actual individuals and their representations of their religious ideas and practices.

Since 1991 I have done fieldwork among Scientologists in Denmark and in the United States. My fieldwork varies from interviews and informal conversations with Scientologists to hanging out with Scientologists and participating in all kinds of religious festivals and ceremonies, social gatherings, and other informal activities. A large number of Scientologists have, during the years, generously shared their self-narratives and ideas and emotions with me. Hanging out with people is a great way of making oneself aware of what is actually going on in people's everyday representations of the world: getting to know people in the sense that the conversations with them do not constitute formalized communication such as interviews but simply implicitly reflect how they think of themselves and the world at small and at large. Going to the movies, hanging out at parties, chatting over a cup of coffee. Everyday practices.

This kind of communication has made several things obvious to me: First, Scientologists are, of course, Scientologists, but they are, more important, people in the community, in society, in the world: citizens, lovers, parents, friends, employees, and so on. Second, their representations do not follow a simple pattern of deduction from, for example, the writings of Hubbard (the systemic or theological level of Scientology) to their own lives. Not all the teachings of Hubbard are actual factors in the individual lives of these people. Third, the ideas produced by these individuals seem to be produced to meet the overall cultural challenges of Western, modern culture. And, fourth, even though these people represent things differently, it is possible to point to certain key representations that are—implicitly or explicitly—present in their ideas with regard to their being Scientologists. This last point leads me to suggest that Scientologists share three basic ideas to which I shall return below.

On Knowledge and Representations

Scientology is an individualistic religion with a hierarchical organization of the soteriological system, called *the Bridge*.[9] The Bridge is pictured as a comprehensive series of soteriological steps, and each step consists of a certain type of *auditing* (the primary ritual activity) or training, addressing a certain kind of physical, mental, or spiritual trauma from the individual's mythological past. At each step the individual receives a formal certificate and is supposed to feel—or, socially speaking, to *perform*—a changed awareness of his or her own development as a human being and as a spiritual being.

It might be said, therefore, that, on the one side, the Scientological soteriological system is rigid and hierarchical because individual Scientologists are not supposed to intuitively feel their way through the different steps or intuitively choose which step might be suitable for them and their specific life situation. Furthermore, the texts and other materials studied at each step by the initiate (referred to in Scientology as the *pre-Clear*) are strictly prescribed in a firm order as are the questions asked by the *auditor,* that is, the person trained to carry out the rituals within the framework of Scientology's *standard technology* (the canonized, ritual practice).

But, at the same time, although material is continuously published in which the Scientologist can read about experiences of others at the different ritual steps of the Bridge[10] and *despite* the fact that the comprehensive oral tradition in Scientology on ritual experience is known by Scientologists,[11] the normativity of these written and oral traditions do not seem to be closed. Individuals can easily find room for their own understanding of themselves and their lives, and find relevant contexts in Scientological reality. The Scientological material, in this sense, seems to be a resource of terminology, mythological frameworks, and stylized forms—a vessel of resources from which Scientologists draw needed bits and pieces in the specific ritual situation, as in daily life situations serving ad hoc needs.

But if the system invites individuality and fragmentality, one might ask, what is it then that Scientologists have in common? How do Scientologists represent their religious and other ideas, and what do these individual representations have in common? I will return to these questions below. First, I will introduce two sets of cognitive theoretical ideas on human representations.

Religion in Mind

The American anthropologist Harriet Whitehead has suggested that a differentiation among Scientologists must be made according to their position on the Bridge[12] in the sense that moving up the steps of the Bridge must be seen as a learning process within a larger framework of conversion. At each step the Scientologist "learns" the teachings of Hubbard that are available at that particular step. This implies, according to Whitehead, that Scientologists, at each step, have a knowledge of the religious ideas at that particular step *and* of the steps below this step in the hierarchy. According to Whitehead, this further implies that at each step the Scientologist's internalization of a particular set of ideas brings about a reformulation of the way this person sees him- or herself and the world—a process in which individuals therefore gradually internalize the Scientological system are led to *reformulate* more and more of the knowledge of the world they had prior to their Scientological activities and commitment. As they move up the Bridge, their worldview will gradually change.

My interviews and conversations with Scientologists from all over the world tell me differently. Although Scientologists eagerly socially engage in performing a changed awareness according to the social demands within Scientological society, and although they have, of course, studied the material prescribed for each soteriological step, it is by no means certain that it is accurate to talk about a change of worldview as the person gradually moves up the Bridge. In fact, talking to Scientologists through the years has convinced me that for most individuals no actual change seem to take place that can be connected directly to their moving up the Bridge. The changes lie somewhere else—in fact, outside the ritual, soteriological system itself. By deciding to be a Scientologist, one might say, in the conscious process of conversion, individuals decide, by joining Scientology, that "from now on" this system is important to them and is to influence the way they represent things. This decision mainly seems to imply that the language by which they make their representations is heavily influenced by the Scientological vocabulary and, thereby, of course, their representations bear witness to their religious orientation. But how this change is actually taking place in each individual's representations is much more complicated than Whitehead suggests. Why is this?

Within recent years, cognitive anthropologists such as Pascal Boyer (1993, 1994a, 1994b) have argued that no human being—religious or not—has a coherent worldview. We experience the world, make sense of it, and categorize it according to our cognitive system in a rather fragmented and ad hoc way. New knowledge or information of the world *might* affect the way we represent the world explicitly, but it might just as well *not* affect it whatsoever. There is no automatic transfer between cultural inputs and mental representations. New information or new ideas are categorized by means of complicated cognitive processes in the mind-brain and thereby play the role of a reservoir of knowledge that *can* be used in a person's representations of the world in certain situations in which this kind of knowledge or these ideas are usable or seem intuitively plausible. In other words, when new information actually affects our representations of the world it is always in ad hoc cognitive processing. It is incorrect to talk about an existent worldview that is affected every time new knowledge or information is acquired. Therefore, we cannot, as Whitehead does, theoretically explain differences in the ways individual Scientologists represent the world in ad hoc situations by referring to their actual position on the Bridge. Nor, and more fundamentally, can we take for granted that being initiated into a certain step on the Bridge actually affects the ways a given Scientologist represents his or her world.

My fieldwork affirms this. If Whitehead's hypothesis were to be supported by empirical evidence, this would imply that talking to, say, twenty Scientologists at the level Clear on the Bridge would represent certain aspects of their lives in equal terms and with the same set of implications. Furthermore, their representations would rather narrowly reflect the knowledge they were supposed to have internalized through studying the Hubbard material at the relevant levels. The point is, of course, that they do *not*. Although Scientologists at the level of "Clear" are supposed to have—and in some respects do have—a certain knowledge that people further down the Bridge have not yet acquired, this knowledge is not necessarily a part of actual representations these Scientologists make in, for instance, a conversation. But this again, depends on the kinds of questions posed by the interviewer. How can this be?

Cognitive psychologist Justine Barrett (1999) has pointed to two different kinds of representations that seem to be in play when religious practitioners make statements that utilize or refer to the religious ideas and practices in which they are involved. The first kind reflects what Barrett refers to as *theological correctness*. This means that the individual reproduces some kind of idea or explains it theologically according to the theological teachings of the religious system. This often has the character of a short resumé of a certain aspect of the teachings that has recently preoccupied the individual, often in response to a certain kind of question asked by the interviewer. This kind of representation is frequently in play when the speaker is actually *aware* of representing the religion in some way and feels prompted to answer the question in a way that is *theological correct*. Relating this to the Scientological situation, one might say that, as Scientologists move up the Bridge, they will be capable of making new theologically correct representations of their religion because they acquire a more detailed knowledge of its mythology, and so on. They might say, for instance, "Ron says . . ." or "Ron has written . . ." this and that, making theological representations where they entertain their memories in order to reproduce sentences from the Scientological written and oral traditions.

The second kind of representation, referred to as *subjective representations*, is brought about when the speaker is not necessarily aware that he or she is representing religious ideas. This means the person is in some kind of communicational situation in which the person relaxes, or the situation has no direct connection to the religious system and its theological teachings or practices. These kinds of representations are the most interesting and the most revealing because the person makes spontaneous statements about this and that, and it is thereby possible to analyze which ideas of, in this case, the religious system, the person is *actually* using to represent his or her life—that is, which ideas this particular individual has not only achieved *as knowledge* but is in fact using in communication with and about the world. This is why the more informal aspects of fieldwork have proven so valuable in regard to my Scientological studies. According to Barrett, these kinds of subjective representations are—and I find this particularly intriguing—very often *not* in accordance with the person's theological representations. Actually, they often contradict what the person knows about the system. The explanation for this, which I cannot elaborate on in this chapter, is that human cognitive mechanisms cannot intuitively cope with all of the ideas and causal mechanisms dealt with in religious theologies. They can be *remembered*, but, when the person is not aware, that is, when representations are spontaneously made, the representations are produced according to basic intuitive cognitive principles and processes. And the basic causal connections within our cognitive system are not only different from any religious idea, but they are also more fundamental. Religious systems in this manner cannot compete with the intuitive ontological knowledge human beings have about the world from very early in their lives.

This theoretical knowledge challenges our way of studying, for instance, *conversion*, setting aside the sociological mechanisms involved. What kinds of processes are actually involved in conversion when it comes to the religious ideas and practices entertained in a particular religious system? And what are the interrelations of a religious system and its individual practitioners?[13]

Three Basic Representations

What exactly is it, then, that Scientologists do, in fact, share? Which representations are basic? I have tried to analyze and systematize the representations on all kinds of issues from Scientologists I have talked to across a ten-year period in order to figure out which basic premises or fundamental ideas these individuals share. How can Scientology as a soteriological system be a rigid, hierarchic, and thoroughly organized system with apparently *no space* for individual strategies and, at the same time, be an open system with *plenty of space* for individual strategies?

I will argue that there are (only) three basic ideas shared by all Scientologists no matter at what level at the Bridge. These ideas are always, implicitly or explicitly, in some way present in their representations and *must be* in order to make sense of the ritual participation standing in the center of Scientological religious practice.

First, every Scientologist has a notion of him- or herself as a spiritual being, in Scientology referred to as a *thetan*. The thetan is immortal and, in his[14] native state, capable of being "at cause" in all kinds of decisions and actions with no physical, mental, spiritual or practical boundaries or limitations to realizations of his will. No matter how Scientologists formulate this idea—some can represent it in a very sophisticated and theologically correct way according to their stage on the Bridge, whereas others only have a certainty, however vague, that they are indeed spiritual beings who have, for some reason, come out of the ideal state—the notion of the thetan is always present, and without this notion the fundamental premise for the second common notion is totally lacking.

This second notion is the *time track*. The time track is, basically, a set of ideas about reincarnation and karma. The thetan, that is, the individual as a spiritual being, has coexisted with physical bodies throughout the history of this and other planets.[15] Every single experience, be it physical, mental, or spiritual, that the individual has had throughout his or her total history, makes up the time track—and millions of millions of units of experience are affecting the life of the individual in this actual incarnation. Experiences are restimulative—that is, they are activated in situations that the individual, in his or her present state, is not capable of controlling. This is damaging, not only to personal well-being and down-to-earth happiness in the present incarnation, but, in a larger perspective, to spiritual and personal development and ultimate salvation.

The notion of the time track is fundamental to the ritual practice of auditing because auditing sessions, according to Scientology, help the individual address his or her large-scale past in order to become aware of his or her history and reorganize it as ordinary experience free of self-triggering mechanisms. In the perspective of this chapter, I see auditing not as a process for *actual* transformation as Scientologists see it, but as providing room for the *production* of individual mythological bits and pieces that make sense of the individual's present life and condition in a perspective in which roots and routes can be produced—a ritual space in which the individual can experiment with different kinds of representations about her- or himself. He or she tells stories—inventing pieces of past, *memories in bits*, roots, to decide whom to be (routes)—to make a personal reservoir of ideas about oneself and one's past. This reservoir for self-narrativity can be drawn from when necessary.

The third idea shared by all Scientologists is that founder L. Ron Hubbard was a very special human being who educated himself in all kinds of wisdom (Eastern religion and Western science and philosophy), thereby making available for his fellow men a safe path to mental and spiritual freedom.[16] According to Scientology, Hubbard did not *invent* the truths taught by Scientology—he *discovered* them. He streamlined the salvational path so that today everyone can walk the Bridge and cross the gap from misery, pain, and lack of awareness and presence to the other side, increasing spiritual awareness of one's true self. This notion of Hubbard is the reason for the gratitude Scientologists feel for Scientology's founder and originator—or, to put it Scientologically, *the Source*.[17] One might say that Scientology is selling roots and routes for the individual's personal transformation and self-narrative strategies by making each individual's life perspective infinite, and to do this, the most important *brand* is L. Ron Hubbard. Therefore he is the central object in the branding and marketing promotions of the church. If people are not demanding LRH products, Scientology is not the answer to people's needs because this is what the church is selling. It is therefore important to keep this brand vital.

These three sets of ideas are the basic premises all Scientologists share—premises that are needed in order to be able to take part in life as a Scientologist, whatever step on the Bridge has been achieved.

What does this imply? It does not imply that Scientologists themselves point to these three notions as central, even though most Scientologists might point to them if asked in a certain way. Neither does it imply that these notions are always explicitly a part of Scientologists' representations, though of course the interviewer calls for theologically correct representations. But they are always implicitly present. Being a practicing Scientologist involves entertaining these notions in some way or the other. The idea of being a spiritual being, a thetan, is necessary in order to be able to join the ritual sphere of representing the mythological past that is basic "knowledge" to Scientologists about themselves, their past, and their present conditions of existence because it is causally fundamental to the karmic ideas of the time track. The idea of Hubbard as a special person with very special skills is fundamental to the specific philosophy taught in Scientology because this, in many ways, does not differ fundamentally from many other religious ideas of the individual and his or her relations to the cosmos exposed by many religions and New Age groups and networks.

Concluding Remarks

In this chapter I have suggested that a rigid soteriological organization does not necessarily lead to uniformity in ideas and representations of the individuals engaged in that particular system. Most of the ideas exposed in New Age today are centered around "the organization of the self" in some way or another, and

Scientology is no exception. Whether individuals find themselves engaged in everyday problems such as feeling sad, being poor, having bad relationships, or, in a larger perspective, wanting answers to the deeper questions of life, Scientological mythology seems to be a pool of resources. In the auditing rituals the mythological fragments can be experimented with by the individual, thereby exploring not only "Who am I? Where do I come from?" but also "Who could I possibly be, and how far can I realize my potentials?" Even though Scientological soteriology is rigid and hierarchical, the suggestive and highly flexible mythological resources entertained in these rituals seem highly potent in the individual's creating of a self.

NOTES

1. Paul Heelas has, among others, pointed to this self-orientation of modern spirituality, as has Wouter Hanegraff (see, e.g., Heelas 1996, 2005; Heelas and Woodhead 2003; Hanegraff 1999).

2. See also the work of Judith Butler, for instance, Butler 1993.

3. Compare to, for example, Hanegraff 1999; Hammer 1997; Gilhus and Mikaelsson 1998, Refslund Christensen 2005.

4. See, for instance, Pine and Gilmore 1999.

5. See Thomas Luckman 1992.

6. Historian of religion Ingvild Sælid Gilhus has put it this way: "It is with reincarnation [and karma] as with the potato: you can use it for almost anything" (Gilhus 1996, my translation).

7. See my other chapter (21) in this volume.

8. Refslund Christensen, in press.

9. See, for example, WiS 1992 for descriptions of the Bridge and of auditing.

10. The first book accounting for auditing experiences was *Have You Lived before This Life?* (Hubbard 1960).

11. Although it is not *comme il faut* to share with others what is going on in the auditing sessions, individuals find a way to share some of these experiences, and all kinds of gatherings are arranged through the week in Scientology facilities to spread the oral tradition of exchanging success stories.

12. See Whitehead 1987. Whitehead's theoretical framework is primarily the works of cognitive psychologist Jean Piaget. This implies viewing cognitive development as domain general, that is, similar and simultaneous to all cognitive domains. See Refslund Christensen in press for a discussion of the consequences of this approach. See Hirschfeld and Gelman 1994 for a discussion of domain generality versus domain specificity.

13. The information available in cognitive theory might encourage us as scholars to, once and for all, ban the idea of brainwashing as a characteristic typical of new religions. Brains are simply not designed to be washed!

14. The thetan is always referred to as *he* even though both women and men are thetans, that is, spiritual beings that have taken refuge in a physical body.

15. L. Ron Hubbard, *Scientology: A History of Man* (1952b/1989) lays out the mythological evolution of man.

16. A comprehensive hagiographic tradition in Scientology continuously promotes Hubbard's claimed character and skills; see, for example, the Ron mags, that is, magazines each providing the reader with thorough information on a particular aspect

of Hubbard's life. See also WiS 1992 for the basic hagiography on L. Ron Hubbard and Refslund Christensen 2005 for an analysis of these hagiographical activities.

17. I have argued elsewhere that the crucial reason for Scientology as an organization to maintain the construction of Hubbard in all his different aspects—both mythological and when it comes to authority—is that he is the only legitimation of why to choose Scientology over other spiritual paths available (Refslund Christensen in press).

BIBLIOGRAPHY

For an extensive bibliography on Scientology material see my other chapter (21) in this volume.

Scientology Material

Hubbard, L. Ron. 1950. *Dianetics: The Modern Science of Mental Health*. Repr., Copenhagen: New Era Publications International Aps., 1989.

———. 1952a. *Scientology 8–8008*. Repr., Copenhagen: New Era Publications International Aps., 1989.

———. 1952b. *Scientology: A History of Man*. Repr., Copenhagen: New Era Publications International Aps., 1989.

———. 1956. *Scientology: The Fundamentals of Thought*. Repr., Copenhagen: New Era Publications International Aps., 1989.

———. 1960. *Have You Lived before This Life?* Repr., Copenhagen: New Era Publications International Aps., 1989.

———. *The Technical Bulletins of Dianetics and Scientology* (TB). Copenhagen: New Era Publications International, 1991. (New edition of the Technical Bulletins.)

———. *Dianetics and Scientology Technical Dictionary* (TD). Copenhagen: New Era Publications International, 1983.

———. *What Is Scientology?* (WiS 1992). Copenhagen: New Era Publications International, 1992. (Compiled by LRH Book Compilations Staff of the Church of Scientology International.)

The Ron Mags (a large number exist besides the titles mentioned here)

L. Ron Hubbard: A Profile. Los Angeles: L. Ron Hubbard Library, 1995.

Ron. Letters and Journals: Early Years of Adventure. Los Angeles: L. Ron Hubbard Library, 1997.

Ron. Letters and Journals: Literary Correspondence. Los Angeles: L. Ron Hubbard Library, 1997.

Ron. Letters and Journals: The Dianetic Letters. Los Angeles: L. Ron Hubbard Library, 1997.

Ron. The Adventurer/Explorer: Daring Deeds and Unknown Realms. Los Angeles: L. Ron Hubbard Library, 1996.

Ron. The Auditor: From Research to Application. Los Angeles: L. Ron Hubbard Library, 1991.

Ron. The Humanitarian: Rehabilitation of a Drugged Society. Los Angeles: L. Ron Hubbard Library, 1996.

Ron. The Humanitarian: Freedom Fighter, Articles and Essays. Los Angeles: L. Ron Hubbard Library, 1997.

Ron. The Philosopher: Rediscovery of the Human Soul. Los Angeles: L. Ron Hubbard Library, 1996.

Ron. The Writer: The Shaping of Popular Fiction. Los Angeles: L. Ron Hubbard Library, 1997.

Literature

Barrett, Justine. 1999. "Theological Correctness: Cognitive Constraints and the Study of Religion," in *Method and Theory in the Study of Religion*, vol. 11–4, pp. 325–339. Leiden: Brill.

Bauman, Zygmunt. 1992. *Intimations of Modernity.* London: Routledge.

Boyer, Pascal. 1993. "Cognitive Aspects of Religious Symbolism," in Boyer, Pascal (ed.), *Cognitive Aspects of Religious Symbolism.* Cambridge: Cambridge University Press.

———. 1994a. *The Naturalness of Religious Ideas: A Cognitive Theory of Religion.* Berkeley: University of California Press.

———. 1994b. "Cognitive Constraints on Cultural Representations: Natural Ontologies and Religious Ideas," in Hirschfeld, Lawrence A., and Susan A. Gelman (eds.), *Mapping the Mind: Domain Specificity in Cognition and Culture.* New York: Cambridge University Press.

Butler, Judith. 1993. *Bodies that Matter: On the Discursive Limits of "Sex."* New York: Routledge.

Christensen, Dorthe Refslund. 1994. *Fra Terapi til Religion. En religionshistorisk analyse af centrale begreber i henholdsvis Dianetics og Scientology med særligt henblik på forskellene i diskurs og mål.* Department for the Study of Religion, Aarhus University.

———. 1997a. *Scientology: Fra Terapi til Religion.* Copenhagen: Gyldendal.

———. 1997b. *Scientology: En ny religion.* Copenhagen: Forlaget Munksgaard.

———. 1997c. "Legenden om L. Ron Hubbard—et eksempel på en moderne hagiografi. Om konstruktionen af et mytologisk livsforløb og brugen af det i Scientology" in *CHAOS, dansk-norsk tidsskrift for religionshistorie*, no 28, 1997.

———. 1999. "Rethinking Scientology: Cognition and Representation in Religion, Therapy, and Soteriology." Ph.D. dissertation, Faculty of Theology, University of Aarhus, Denmark.

———. 2002. "Church of Scientology," in Melton, J. Gordon, and Martin Baumann (eds.), *Religions of the World: A Comprehensive Encyclopedia of Beliefs and Practices*, pp. 331–332. Santa Barbara, California: ABC Clio.

———. 2005. "Inventing L. Ron Hubbard: On the Construction and Maintenance of the Hagiographic Mythology on Scientology's Founder," in Lewis, Jim, and Jesper Aagaard Pedersen (eds.), *Controversial New Religions*, pp. 227–259. Oxford: Oxford University Press.

Giddens, Anthony. 1990. *The Consequences of Modernity.* Cambridge: Polity Press.

———. 1991. *Modernity and Self-Identity.* Cambridge: Polity Press.

———. 1992. *Transformation of Intimacy.* Cambridge: Polity Press.

Gilhus, Ingvild Sælid. 1996. "Sjelevandring—et nytt nøkkelsymbol," in Mikaelsson 1996, pp. 47–61.

Gilhus, Ingvild Sælid (ed.). 1997. *Miraklenes Tid*, KULTs Skriftserie nr. 95. Oslo: Norsk Forskningsråd.

Gilhus, Ingvild S., and Lisbeth Mikaelsson. 1998. *Kulturens refortrylling. Nyreligiøsitet i moderne samfunn.* Oslo: Universitetsforlaget.

———. 2001. *Nytt Blikk på Religion: Studiet av religion i dag.* Oslo: Pax Forlag A/S.

Hammer, Olav. 1997. *På Spanning efter helheten: New Age—en ny folktro?* Stockholm: Wahlström & Widstrand.

Hanegraff, Wouter J. 1999. "New Age Spiritualities as Secular Religion: A Historian's Perspective. *Social Compass* 46 (2), 145–160.

Heelas, Paul. 1996. *The New Age Movement: The Celebration of the Self and the Sacralization of Modernity.* Oxford: Blackwell Publishers.

———. 1998. *Religion, Modernity and Postmodernity.* Oxford: Blackwell Publishers.

———. 2005. *The Spiritual Revolution: Why Religion Is Giving Way to Spirituality.* Oxford: Blackwell.

Heelas, Paul, and Linda Woodhead. 2003. *Religion in Modern Times: An Interpretive Anthology.* Oxford: Blackwell.

Hervieu-Léger, Danièle. 1998. "Secularization, Tradition and New Forms of Religiosity: Some Theoretical Proposals," in Barker, Eileen, and Margit Warburg (eds.), *New Religions and New Religiosity.* Århus: Aarhus University Press.

———. 2001. *Religion as a Chain of Memory.* Cambridge: Polity Press.

Hirschfeld, Lawrence A., and Susan A. Gelman. 1994. "Towards a Topography of Mind: An Introduction to Domain Specificity," in Hirschfeld, Lawrence A., and Susan A. Gelman (eds.), *Mapping the Mind: Domain Specificity in Cognition and Culture.* New York: Cambridge University Press.

Lasch, Christopher. 1991. *The Culture of Narcissism: American Life in an Age of Diminishing Expectations.* New York: W. W. Norton.

Luckmann, Thomas. 1992. "Shrinking Transcendence, Expanding Religion?," *Sociological Analysis* 50 (2), 127–138.

Lyon, David. 2000. *Jesus in Disneyland: Religion in Postmodern Times.* Cambridge: Polity Press.

Lyotard, Jean-François. 1992. *The Postmodern Explained to Children: Correspondence 1982–85.* London: Turnaround.

———. 1999. *The Postmodern Condition: A Report on Knowledge,* Manchester: Manchester University Press.

McCutcheon, Russell T. 2000. " Myth," in Willi Braun and Russell T. McCutcheon (eds.), *Guide to the Study of Religion,* pp. 190–208. London: Cassell.

Mikaelsson, Lisbeth. *Myte i møte med det moderne,* KULTs Skriftserie nr. 63, Oslo: Norsk Forskningsråd.

Pine, B. Joseph, and James H. Gilmore. 1999. *The Experience Economy: Work Is Theatre and Every Business a Stage.* Boston, Massachusetts: Harvard Business School Press.

Skårderud, Finn. 1999. *Uro. En rejse i det moderne selv.* København: Samlerens Bogklub.

Storey, John. 1998a. *What Is Cultural Studies? A Reader.* London: Prentice Hall.

———. 1998b. *Cultural Theory and Popular Culture: A Reader.* London: Prentice Hall.

———. 1999. *Cultural Consumption in Everyday Life.* London: Arnold.

———. 2001. *Cultural Theory and Popular Culture: An Introduction.* Harlow: Prentice Hall.

———. 2003a. *Inventing Popular Culture: From Folklore to Globalization.* Malden, Massachusetts: Blackwell Publishing

———. 2003b. *Cultural Studies and the Study of Popular Culture.* Edinburgh: Edinburgh University Press.

Wallis, Roy. 1976. *The Road to Total Freedom: A Sociological Analysis.* London: Heinemann Educational Books Ltd.

Whitehead, Harriet. 1987. *Renunciation and Reformulation: A Study of Conversion in an American Sect.* Ithaca: Cornell University Press.

6

The Growth of Scientology and the Stark Model of Religious "Success"

James R. Lewis

While it is impossible to predict the fate of Scientology as a particular religious organization, we must suspect that some religion very much like Scientology will be a major force in the future of our civilization.

—William Sims Bainbridge (1987: 75)

As a specialist in the field of new religious movements, I regularly encounter claims that such-and-such a religion is the world's fastest growing. Paganism (in the sense of contemporary Neo-Paganism) is a case in point; a number of different Pagan spokespeople have asserted that Paganism is the fastest growing religion in the world. Upon examination of the data, it turns out that Paganism actually did enjoy *spectacular* growth in the late 1990s and in the first few years of the twenty-first century. I have examined this "Pagan explosion" in a number of publications (e.g., Lewis 2002, 2007), but more recent data I have seen (e.g., Jung 2006) indicate a slowing—if not an actual leveling off—of this movement's rate of expansion since about 2003.

A front-page story about the Mormons in *Time* magazine in 1997 highlighted the claim that the Church of Jesus Christ of Latter-day Saints (LDS) was the world's fastest-growing religion (Van Biema 1997). This claim was based on the work of Rodney Stark, an influential sociologist of religion who predicted the LDS would become a "major world faith" by the year 2080 (1987: 11). It is difficult not to be impressed by the statistics marshaled in support of this analysis. However, Stark depends heavily on the Church's own statistics, and LDS statistics appear to have been misleading, as we shall see.

Yet another religion claiming to be the fastest growing—or, more modestly, *among* the fastest growing—is Baha'i. Baha'i, a nineteenth-century spin off of Iranian Islam, is a medium-sized religion of seven million adherents. According to figures compiled by the authors of the *World Christian Encyclopedia*, Baha'i is growing at an annual rate of 2.28 percent—faster than any of the larger world religions and second only to Zoroastrianism among medium-sized world religions.

However, as an examination of table 6.1 will quickly show, a fractional percentage advantage over other religious traditions does not mean very much if

TABLE 6.1 Status of Religions in World Population, 2000–2050

Followers	2000 total	%	rate	2025	2050
Christians	1,999,564,000	33.0	1.36	2,616,610,000	3,051,564,000
Roman Catholics	1,051,328,000	17.5	1.29	1,361,965,000	1,564,609,000
Independents	385,745,000	6.4	2.49	501,641,000	752,092,000
Protestants	342,002,000	5.7	1.44	460,633,000	574,419,000
Muslims	1,188,143,000	19.6	2.13	1,104,816,000	2,229,281,000
Hindus	811,336,000	13.4	1.69	1,049,231,000	1,175,290,000
Nonreligious	768,159,000	12.7	0.83	875,121,000	887,995,000
Chinese folk-religionists	384,807,000	6.4	1.02	440,843,000	454,333,000
Buddhists	359,902,000	6.0	1.09	410,345,000	424,607,000
Ethnoreligionists	228,367,000	3.8	1.33	277,247,000	303,599,000
Atheists	150,090,000	2.5	0.30	159,544,000	169,150,000
Neoreligionists	182,356,000	1.7	1.03	114,120,000	110,045,000
Sikhs	23,250,000	0.4	1.87	31,378,000	37,059,000
Jews	14,434,000	0.2	0.91	16,053,000	16,694,000
Spiritists	12,334,000	0.2	1.96	16,212,000	10,709,000
Baha'is	7,106,000	0.1	2.28	12,862,000	10,001,008
Confucianists	6,299,000	0.1	0.73	6,018,000	6,953,080
Jains	4,210,000	0.1	0.87	6,116,000	6,733,000
Shintoists	2,762,000	0.1	-1.09	2,123,000	1,655,080
Taoists	2,655,000	0.0	1.00	3,066,000	1,172,000
Zoroastrians	2,544,000	0.0	2.65	4,440,000	6,965,000
Other religionists	1,067,000	0.0	1.03	1,500,000	1,938,000
Total population	6,055,049,000	100.0	1.41	7,823,703,000	8,909,095,000

Table reproduced courtesy of ABC-Clio. From J. Gordon Melton and Martin Baumann, eds. 2002. *Religions of the World: A Comprehensive Encyclopedia of Beliefs and Practices,* Vol. 1, p. xxx. Santa Barbara: ABC-Clio. The data for this table was taken from the *World Christian Encyclopedia* (2001).

your initial membership is less than 1 percent of your competitors'. This point becomes clearer if we consider a hypothetical religion—which we will refer to as "Badmashism"—that begins with, let us say, five charter members. If over the next year the Badmashis recruit ten new members (to make a total of fifteen), then they can claim an annual growth rate of 200 percent. However, a spectacular *rate* of growth is difficult to maintain. Thus the Badmashis must bring in 30 new members, 90 new members, 270 new members, 810 new members, and 2,430 new members in the succeeding five years in order to be able to continue to claim a 200 percent annual growth rate. Also, though a 200 percent growth rate looks impressive, the actual number of new adherents to join a tiny religious group is minuscule in comparison with the major world faiths.

An alternate way of measuring growth is in terms of actual numbers of new adherents. In practice, the brute numbers approach is usually discussed in terms of net growth—meaning new members by birth and by conversion minus older members lost from death and apostasy. In order even to be admitted to this kind of numbers contest, a tradition must already be a major world religion with hundreds of millions of members. This means the only serious contenders for the distinction of being the world's fastest growing religion in these terms are Christianity, Islam, Buddhism, Hinduism, and maybe one or two others. However, the only two major religious traditions that seem seriously interested in claiming this title are Christianity and Islam.

Though Christianity is the world's largest religion, Islam, the second largest, has the edge in terms of its rate of expansion (e.g., in table 6.1, 1.36 percent versus 2.13 percent). This situation led many observers in the late twentieth century to predict that Islam would overtake Christianity sometime during the twenty-first century, though some have called this prediction into question.[1]

At this juncture in the discussion, we can change tack and ask, why have people concerned themselves with this question? Or, to restate this more bluntly, so what? Islam might be catching up with Christianity or Christianity might be maintaining its lead. But, in real world terms, neither scenario will ultimately make much of a difference. Having a slight numbers edge certainly does not mean that one religion has vanquished or will vanquish the other. However— and this is the heart of the issue—people debate the point *as if* being the fastest growing really did mean that one religion was winning out over all the others.

This attitude is partially captured in LDS sociologist Rick Phillips's remarks about Mormonism, as cited by Reid L. Neilson in his introduction to *The Rise of Mormonism*:

> Phillips argues that his church "uses membership growth as a principal benchmark of its success. Church publications and the speeches of LDS leaders often cite the expansion of Mormonism as evidence of the validity and legitimacy of church doctrines and programs." Noting that nearly every LDS periodical chronicles growth, he also argues that "Mormon apologists . . . use the work of sociologists [especially Rodney Stark] to substantiate Mormonism's bandwagon appeal" and claims that the LDS Church has "seized on Stark's predictions,

and has disseminated them widely." Phillips continues, "While I
was doing research in Salt Lake City several years ago, rank-and-file
Mormons sometimes mentioned Stark's work to me in passing. They
had heard of the eminent, non-Mormon sociologist who concurs
with their own assessment of the church's destiny." (Stark 2005: 10;
brackets in original)

The reference to "bandwagon appeal" brings to mind a late-twentieth-
century television ad by the long-distance telecommunications carrier MCI. This
particular commercial stated absolutely nothing about MCI's rates or services.
Instead, the message was about the expanding numbers of new consumers who
were dropping their old carriers and signing up with MCI. I recall that there was
something like a giant odometer on the wall in the background, with the numbers spinning rapidly as it quickly added up new customers. The implied message was, "Everyone else is switching to MCI, so shouldn't you switch too?"
    Similarly, the message of calling attention to the growth statistics of one's
religion seems to be, "Everyone is switching to my religion, so shouldn't you
switch too?" As implied by Phillips's remarks, such statistics can also be cited
to encourage the faithful. Additionally, the mere fact of impressive growth appears to *validate the truth* of one's religion. The unstated argument here seems
to be: The true (or best) religion will win out over false (or less adequate) religions. The fastest growing religion is the one that will win. Therefore the fastest growing religion is the true religion.
    Scientology is no exception to this general pattern (though I should quickly
add that, unlike the traditional Abrahamic faiths, the Church's vision of the
future is pluralistic). Thus, for example, a few years ago the Church of Scientology put out a DVD under the title, *This Is Scientology: An Overview of the World's
Fastest Growing Religion*. Though Scientologists can present some impressive
statistics, various census data, as well as certain non-Scientology survey data I
have examined, reflect a healthy—but not a spectacular—rate of growth.
    Scientology's self-perception of being the "fastest growing" is likely based
on an uncritical reading of its own statistics. During his tenure as organizational head, L. Ron Hubbard established the tradition of each branch sending
in reports on Thursdays. He then spent Fridays reading them. This is the origin
of the "Thursday Report" that is the bane of many staff members. The ideal
Thursday Report embodies a measurable increase over the preceding week's
report, which is referred to as being "Up Stat." A decrease is referred to as
"Down Stat." All Scientology staffers are motivated to be Up Stat, resulting (not
necessarily consciously) in exaggerated statistics.
    The governments of Canada, New Zealand, and Australia all included
a religion affiliation item in their more recent national censuses. The Canadian census reported that in the ten-year period between 1991 and 2001, self-
identified Scientologists grew by 26.5 percent, from 1,215 to 1,525 adherents. In
New Zealand during the same period, Church membership expanded from 207
to 282—an almost 37 percent increase. And in Australia, the number of self-
identified members rose almost 37 percent from 1,488 to 2,032 in the *five-year*

period between 1996 and 2001 (Australia did not collect data on alternative religions prior to 1996).

The United States census does not collect religion membership data, but in 1990 and 2001 the Graduate Center of the City University of New York conducted national surveys of religious self-identification via randomly dialed phone numbers. During this eleven-year period, Scientology grew from 45,000 to 55,000 adherents, which represents a bit more than a 22 percent rate of expansion. Though it would be possible to question generalizations based on only one of these four data sets, taken together they add up to a compelling case for the conclusion that the Church of Scientology is growing. At the same time, it is clearly *not* the "world's fastest growing." Nevertheless, Scientology's growth statistics are impressive. Reflecting on the movement's expansion naturally leads to questions about Scientology's prospects for future growth.

Rodney Stark (the same Stark mentioned above in connection with the LDS) has invested significant energy into developing and elaborating a model of how emergent religions "succeed." He further claims that based on the proper application of his model, we can assess a religious movement's prospects for expansion. Given the ambitious scope of this claim, the task of determining how Scientology "measures up" could be illuminating. In the present chapter, I will discuss the Church's future prospects in terms of Stark's model. First, however, a fairly lengthy discussion needs to take place about problems with Stark's specific formulation.

The Stark Model

To begin with, Benton Johnson—one of the participants in a published discussion of an early version of Stark's model (Bromley and Hammond 1987)—observes that terms like *success* and *failure* have "strong evaluative connotations that make them poor candidates for technical terms in a scientific model" (1987: 252). Johnson suggests alternate terms like *domination* or *impact*. The former designation, *domination*, derives from Stark's definition of religious success as the *"degree to which a religious movement is able to dominate one or more societies"* (emphasis in original). Stark clarifies his use of the word *domination* by noting, "By dominate, I mean to influence behavior, culture, and public policy in a society" (1987: 12). The evaluative connotations of *domination*, however, are only slightly less objectionable than the connotations of the original terms. Furthermore, despite their connotations, *success* and *failure* have become established as standard terms in relevant academic analyses (e.g., refer to Lucas 1992: 37–51 and to Palmer 2004: 77–79). I will thus adhere to this terminological convention, despite my misgivings and the misgivings of others.

Another consideration voiced by (among others) Bryan Wilson is that the ultimate goal of most religions is supramundane: "Since religion is a matter of faith, its goals might be expressed in transcendental or metaphysical terms" (1987: 30). Consequently, it is not difficult to find religious movements that sociologists would likely judge failures but that participants would judge successes—successes in terms of these movements' internal, spiritual standards. Stark's response to this kind of reasoning is, "I suspect that few movements ever begin with such modest aims; they adopt them only after they have lost hope of doing any better" in terms of growth (1987: 12). In support of this provocative assertion, he cites his and Roberts's article in which they note that after a decade or two of growth, many groups "turned inward and ceased to seek converts" (Stark and Roberts 1985: 351 [1982]). They explain this inward turn as a response to "the small absolute numbers of recruits gained during the first generation" (1985: 347)—in other words, movements turn inward in response to the perception that they have failed as mass movements.

Despite his dismissal of internal, spiritual measures of success, I believe Stark's argument has merit as long as we distinguish between groups that start out aspiring to become popular movements, and groups that come into being with more limited—and, especially, local—membership goals. There exist numerous independent churches and other kinds of small spiritual groups that never envision themselves becoming international or even national movements. (It may be that some churches in this category eventually find themselves growing beyond local bounds, but that is another issue.) So we should confine our analysis to groups that start out with the aim of becoming world-transforming movements before we can meaningfully evaluate Stark's ideas on this point.

Stark's interest in religious success grew out of his study of the LDS. On the basis of available statistical data, in combination with his theoretical model, he projected that the Mormons would become the next great world religion before the end of the twenty-first century. This study was the background for a conference that became the basis for the 1987 Bromley and Hammond collection mentioned earlier. Almost ten years later, Stark authored an article in which he revised his original model (2003 [1996]). At the end of this piece, he outlined his new model in the form of ten propositions, which I will refer to as *growth factors* (not Stark's term). For ease of reference, I will reproduce this outline here. Stark asserts:

> Other things being equal, religious movements will succeed to the degree that:
>
> 1. They retain cultural continuity with the conventional faiths of the societies within which they seek converts.
> 2. Their doctrines are non-empirical.
> 3. They maintain a medium level of tension with their surrounding environment—are strict but not too strict.
> 4. They have legitimate leaders with adequate authority to be effective.
>   a. Adequate authority requires clear doctrinal justifications for an effective and legitimate leadership.
>   b. Authority is regarded as more legitimate and gains in effectiveness to the degree that members perceive themselves as participants in the system of authority.
> 5. They can generate a highly motivated, volunteer, religious labor force, including many willing to proselytize.

6. They maintain a level of fertility sufficient to at least offset member mortality.

7. They compete against weak, local conventional religious organizations within a relatively unregulated religious economy.

8. They sustain strong internal attachments, able to maintain and form ties to outsiders.

9. They continue to maintain sufficient tension with their environment—remain sufficiently strict.

10. They socialize the young sufficiently well as to minimize both defection and the appeal of reduced strictness. (Stark 2003 [1996]: 268–269).

Stark's original formulation consisted of only eight statements. Item 2 in the above outline is the only completely new proposition. Some of the issues embodied in items 5 and 6 above were covered in the original model by the proposition that a movement needs to "attract and maintain a *normal age and sex structure.*" Similarly, some of the other issues covered in items 4 and 5 were stated as the need to achieve *"effective mobilization:* strong governance and a high level of individual commitment" in his first version (Stark 1987: 13).

After publishing his revised model, Stark then proceeded to apply it to a series of case studies—the Jehovah's Witnesses (Stark and Iannaccone 1997), the early Christian Church (Stark 1996), Christian Science (Stark 1998), and American religious history more generally (Finke and Stark 2005). Though the model has been "very well received and widely cited" (Stark 2003: 259), few scholars have independently applied the model in a detailed way.[2] It is, however, not uncommon for researchers to refer to one or two of these growth factors. One item of particular note is that Stark and his long-time collaborator William Sims Bainbridge seem to have popularized the notion of "medium tension" (derived from the earlier work of Benton Johnson 1963) among sociologists and other scholars of alternative religions (refer to Bainbridge and Stark 1980).

This is an impressive body of work. In particular, it is difficult not to be impressed by the variety of statistics Stark marshals in support of his analyses of specific movements. Unfortunately, Stark assembled the data for his case studies of the LDS, the Witnesses, and Christian Science (the former two churches were portrayed as examples of religious success, and the latter as a case of failure) before 2001. In that year, an important survey of American religion was conducted and a variety of census data in other English-speaking countries were gathered that undermined Stark's case studies. These new data sets indicate that Mormon growth has slowed, the Jehovah's Witnesses are declining, and Christian Scientists, though declining, are not likely to go out of existence anytime soon.

Stats versus Stark

Australia, New Zealand, Canada, and the United Kingdom all collected data on religious affiliation in their respective 2001 censuses. The U.K. census did not contain an item about religious preference prior to 2001, so the British data throws no light on the expansion or decline of particular religious bodies. Canada, on the other hand, has collected information on religion every ten years. And Australia and New Zealand have collected religious affiliation data every five years. The scope of Australia's census data improved in 1996 when smaller, nontraditional groups began to be included in the census reports. Also, prior to 2001, New Zealand collected data on only five nontraditional movements (in 1991 and 1996).

The U.S. census does not measure religious affiliation. However, in 1990, the Graduate Center of the City University of New York conducted a National Survey of Religious Identification (NSRI) via randomly dialed phone numbers (113,723 people were surveyed). Eleven years later, in 2001, the same center carried out the American Religious Identification Survey (ARIS) in the same manner (over 50,000 people responded), though callers probed for more information than they had in the earlier NSRI. Categories were developed post facto. The contrast between the 1990 data and the 2001 data allows one to make judgments about the growth or decline of select religious bodies in a manner comparable to the census data from Canada, Australia, and New Zealand.

To obtain an overall sense of the relevant statistics, I have arranged the data on Stark's three case study groups into four tables (tables 6.2–6.5) that display NSRI-ARIS data for the United States and census data for Canada, New Zealand, and Australia. Additionally, I have included data on the Unitarian Universalist Church because this denomination is arguably the most secularized religious group of significant size—in terms of Stark's model, the Unitarians should be declining even more sharply than mainline Christian denominations.

In the course of his case studies, Stark also mentions a number of other groups that he either depreciates as declining or dismisses as insignificant. For

TABLE 6.2 NSRI and ARIS (Adults 18+)

	1990	2001	Change
Unitarian	502,000[a]	629,000	+25%
Christian Science	214,000	194,000	–9%
LDS	2,487,000	2,787,000	+12%
Jehovah's Witnesses	1,381,000	1,331,000	–4%
Spiritualism[b]		116,000	+?
Pagan[c]	8,000	307,000	+3738%

[a] Numbers have been rounded off to the nearest 1,000. Unlike a census, which attempts to reach the entire population, these figures represent statistical extrapolations.

[b] Spiritualism did not emerge as significant in the 1990 NSRI survey, so no relevant data is available.

[c] Designated "Wicca" in 1990, the 307,000 figure represents a collapsing of Wicca (134,000), Druid (33,000), and Pagan (140,000) in 2001.

TABLE 6.3 Canadian Census 1991–2001

	1991	2001	Change
Unitarian	16,535	17,480	+6%
Christian Science[a]			
LDS	100,770	104,750	+4%
Jehovah's Witnesses	168,375	154,745	–8%
Spiritualism	3735	3,295	–12%
Paganism[b]	5530	21,080	+281%

[a] I have thus far been unable to locate statistics for Christian Science in Canada.

[b] The Canadian Census table contains a footnote stating that the Pagan category "includes persons who report 'Wicca.'"

TABLE 6.4 New Zealand Census 1991–2001

	1991	2001	Change
Unitarian	255	327	+28%
Christian Science	318	258	–19%
LDS	48,009	39,915	–17%
Jehovah's Witnesses	19,182	17,826	–7%
Spiritualism	3,333	5,853	+76%
Paganism[a]	318	5,862	+1743%

[a] In the 2001 Census, the Pagan category was broken down into Animism, Pantheism, Wiccan, Druidism, and Nature and Earth-based Religions.

TABLE 6.5 Australian Census 1996–2001

	1996	2001	Change
Unitarian	719	868	+21%
Christian Science	1,494	1,666	+11%
LDS	45,112	49,915	+11%
Jehovah's Witnesses	83,414	81,069	–3%
Spiritualism	8,140	9,279	+14%
Paganism[a]*	8,490	22,309	+163%

Note: Prior to 1996, the Australian Census did not include categories for such "exotic" religions as Christian Science, the Unitarians, and so forth, which is why this table uses a five-year rather than a ten-year span.

[a] The Paganism category represents a collapsing of four categories from the 1996 and 2001 censuses: Wicca/Witchcraft, Druidism, Paganism, and Nature Religions.

example, in his article on Christian Science, he characterizes Spiritualism as a "dead end" (1998: 213). Additionally, the last paragraph of Stark and Innaccone's study of the Jehovah's Witnesses disparages (at least implicitly) contemporary neo-paganism as unworthy of study where the authors assert that they hope they have convinced scholars that their time would be far better spent studying a sizable group like the Witnesses instead of "documenting the rites of a coven of 13 Dutch Witches" (1997: 155). I may not be fairly interpreting Stark's views, but these remarks prompted me to include data on Spiritualism and on modern Paganism.

The advantage of bringing together data from a variety of different sources is that it overcomes objections that might arise from using only one source. If all or most sources agree, then we can be far more confident that trends indicated by our statistics correspond with the state of affairs in the "real" world. Thus, for example, all four data sets indicate that the Unitarian Universalist Church is growing. What is particularly interesting about this denomination is that it lacks so many of the components Stark deems essential for church growth. In his first article setting forth the religious success model, he asserted that "failure minimally to fulfill any single condition [referring to the model's various propositions] will doom a movement" (1987: 13). Because the Unitarian denomination is one of the most secularized, "unstrict," nonproselytizing groups one could imagine, it should, therefore, be "doomed" according to the Stark model. However, just the opposite seems to be the case.

What about Stark's three case studies? He seems to have been correct about the Christian Science Church, though this denomination is declining less precipitously than many mainline churches, and appears to be gaining ground in Australia. In a published response to Stark's article on Christian Science, Richard Singelenberg pointed out that a scandal that broke out at the end of the 1980s and early 1990s might subsequently have been responsible for a drop in membership. Described as "the most traumatic period in the movement's history," this conflict was apparently so intense that the church might have been "on the brink of a major schism" (1999: 127). In other words, the decline in Christian Science membership during the 1990s might have had little or nothing to with the factors discussed by Stark. In fact, the rise in membership indicated by the Australian data during the five-year period 1996–2001 might even reflect a movement recovering from this trauma.

Similarly, the Mormon data initially seem to support the religious success model, though not in the powerful way one would anticipate from Stark's prediction that the Church of Jesus Christ of Latter-day Saints will become a "major world faith" by the year 2080 (1987: 11). In Canada, the LDS grew by a slim 4 percent between 1991 and 2001, and in the United States by about 12 percent between 1990 and 2001. However, LDS growth in the United States was relatively insignificant, considering that the total U.S. population grew by almost 19 percent during the same eleven-year period. This means Mormonism actually *lost ground* in terms of its percentage of the total population. In New Zealand, the LDS *declined* by almost 17 percent. The only bright spot in this picture seems to be Australia, where Mormons increased by 11 percent between 1996 and 2001 (though Christian Science, the denomination Stark labels a "failure," also grew by 11 percent during the same period). Mormonism is probably doing better in other countries beyond the four we have been considering, but likely not so well as to become the next world religion to take its place alongside Christianity, Islam, Buddhism, and the like.

The worst news for Stark's set of case studies is the decline of the Jehovah's Witnesses in the United States, Canada, Australia, and New Zealand. Though I am confident the Witnesses are continuing to grow in other countries, particularly developing countries, this fact does not negate the challenge to the Stark model posed by these statistics.

To turn now to the religion Stark disparaged as a "dead end," we can see that Spiritualism is growing at quite a nice rate in Australia and New Zealand (keep in mind that the Australian Spiritualism figures are for a five-year rather than for a ten-year period). The only nation where this religion appears to be losing ground is Canada. As for the United States, it is hard to decide exactly how to interpret the NSRI-ARIS data for Spiritualism. There were obviously Spiritualists in the United States in 1990 (e.g., according to the 1992 *Yearbook of American and Canadian Churches,* the National Spiritualist Association of Churches—the oldest Spiritualist body in North America—reported 3,406 members for 1990). Perhaps Spiritualists were collapsed into another category, such as nondenominational, in the NSRI. Whatever happened, we can probably infer that Spiritualism experienced remarkable growth between 1990 and 2001. We should further note that this growth took place *before* TV programs like *Crossing Over, Medium,* and *Ghost Whisperer* became popular. If a similar poll was to be conducted today (mid 2007), I am confident one would find Spiritualism has grown considerably since the ARIS survey.

Finally we come to contemporary Neo-Paganism. In all four of the countries for which we have assembled data, Paganism is growing at a spectacular rate—far faster than any other religion. (Once again, keep in mind that Australian figures are for a five-year rather than for a ten-year period.) If this rate of expansion could be maintained, then Neo-Paganism—not Mormonism—would become the next "major world faith" to emerge before the end of the twenty-first century.

Rethinking the Religious Success Model

It is not my intention here to offer anything approaching a complete explanation of what went wrong with Stark's predictions, nor I am interested in thoroughly reformulating his theory of religious success. I would, however, still like to apply Stark's model to the Church of Scientology, so at least some sort of explanation is in order here.

Predicting the future on the basis of current trends is always a problematic enterprise, especially in complex modern societies like our own. Situations can change quickly, and in unpredictable ways. For example, who would have predicted that many lucrative, computer-related jobs would be exported to India? Based on the job market prior to the advent of overseas outsourcing, many Americans studied information technology in anticipation of obtaining great positions—only to be severely disappointed.

The situation with the Stark model is comparable, though there is probably no single factor like overseas outsourcing that can completely explain why groups like the Jehovah's Witnesses and the Latter-day Saints stopped expanding at rapid rates in Western industrialized nations. In terms of the economic analogy Stark often utilizes, perhaps certain religious groups simply reached a limit in their market penetration so that no amount of additional promotional activity enabled them to attract new customers. In the words of Roger Loomis, "Only a fraction of the population is interested in strict religions" and that "market is of limited size" (2002: 7). I also think that, at least in the United States, new forms of Protestantism have arisen (e.g., the "new paradigm churches" surveyed in Miller 1997 and the seeker churches analyzed by Sargeant 2000) that offer a more attractive and compelling alternative to comparatively straight-laced groups like the Witnesses and the LDS.[3]

The emergence of newer forms of religion that effectively compete with older religions can be explained within the horizon of Stark's theorizing, despite the fact that emergent movements like the new paradigm churches and the seeker-oriented churches tend to be less strict than their competitors (thus compromising Stark's ninth proposition). However, the expansion of a highly secularized church like the Unitarians is beyond the pale, and simply cannot be explained by the religious success model in its present form. Unitarians represent an entirely different kind of market for which the model breaks down completely. Though religions with "high costs" (Stark 2003 [1996]) may appeal to many religious consumers, they clearly do not appeal to everyone. Comparatively, most of us prefer to drive sedans on a day-to-day basis, but a minority prefer to ride motorcycles. So perhaps the Unitarian Universalist Church is a kind of religious motorcycle. Similarly, maybe Spiritualism and Neo-Paganism appeal to yet other niche markets.

Though my market analogy may not be compelling, the point should be clear enough. Namely, though Stark's theory of religious success may apply to many people—maybe even to most people—it seems there is a significant population of religious consumers for whom major components of his model simply break down. In its current form, Stark's approach is most illuminating when applied to Protestant sect movements and to the corresponding target audience culturally predisposed to become involved in such sects, but fails to pass muster as a truly comprehensive predictor of religious growth.

Despite these reservations, I nevertheless feel that applying Stark's model to the Church of Scientology could be an interesting and useful exercise. In the remaining sections of the present chapter, I will undertake this task.

Cultural Continuity

Continuity with the conventional faiths of a society is the initial proposition in Stark's original model and in his revised model. In the revised version, he discusses this point in terms of an economic metaphor, namely as the conservation of cultural capital: "For example, persons raised to be Christians have accumulated a substantial store of Christian culture—a store that can be conceived of as cultural capital." What Stark means by cultural capital is best clarified by the illustration he provides in his discussion:

> A young person from a Christian background and living in a Christian society is deciding whether to join the Mormons or the Hare Krishnas. By becoming a Mormon, this person retains his or her entire Christian culture and simply adds to it. The Mormon missionaries, noting that the person has copies of the Old Testament and the New Testament, suggest that an additional scripture, The Book of Mormon, is needed to complete the set. In contrast, the Hare Krishna missionaries note that the person has the wrong scriptures and must discard the Bible in exchange for the Bhagavad Gita. The principle of the conservation of cultural capital predicts (and explains) why the overwhelming majority of converts within a Christian context select the Mormon rather than the Hare Krishna option, with the reverse being the case in a Hindu context. (Stark 2003: 261 [1996])[4]

It seems to me, however, that Stark's emphasis on the West's Christian tradition misses the fact that there is a significant religious subculture in the West that is largely non-Christian, namely the spiritual strand that has been referred to variously as the "occult," "metaphysical," or "New Age" subculture (contemporary academic specialists tend to utilize "New Age" as the preferred etic term[5]). Stark and Bainbridge appear to reject the "occult milieu" (an alternate expression for the New Age) as a true subculture (1985: 322). (One issue for Stark may be that only an explicitly Christian movement is likely to ever truly *dominate* U.S. society.) But the New Age milieu appears to be cohesive and distinct enough to constitute a pool of potential recruits for certain types of non-Christian religions.

As reflected in the data from the NSRI-ARIS surveys and the Canadian, Australian, and New Zealand censuses, there exist a number of such religions and they are experiencing dynamic growth. We have already examined the relevant figures for Spiritualism and Neo-Paganism. Data from the NSRI-ARIS surveys also indicate that Eckankar—a religion owing little or nothing to Christianity—grew by 44 percent between 1990 and 2001 (from 18,000 to 26,000 members). Scientology, as noted earlier, grew by 22 percent during the same period (from 45,000 to 55,000).

In his initial article on the religious success model, Stark asks, "Is it impossible for a new religion to make its way if it lacks continuity with conventional religious culture? I am inclined to say yes" (1987: 15). Taken together, the data on Spiritualism, Paganism, Eckankar, and Scientology definitively refute Stark on this point. However, the cultural continuity proposition can be salvaged if we regard the New Age subculture as an alternate cultural tradition to Christianity—at least for the purpose of understanding a non-Christian religion's growth potential. Though one might not immediately think of the

Church of Scientology as a "New Age" religion (refer to Andreas Grünschloß's chapter [11] in the present collection), Scientology *does* share certain key beliefs with the New Age (e.g., beliefs in reincarnation and in the power of the mind to reshape "external" reality), and thus arguably has a degree of cultural continuity with this alternative spiritual milieu.

Another consideration is Scientology's appeal to the legitimating authority of science. As discussed in the introduction, people in contemporary industrialized societies tend to view science quasi-religiously, as the arbiter of "Truth." As a consequence, more than a few religions (e.g., Christian Science and Science of Mind) have clothed themselves in an aura of scientific authority. As Bainbridge argues in his contribution to the Bromley/Hammond volume mentioned earlier, "Scientology claims cultural continuity with science" (1987: 59):

> Scientology harmonizes with current developments in cosmology, and Hubbard's religion could gain strength by adding to the new scientific perspective on existence the hope and human meaning that only a transcendent creed can give. Both Scientology and the anthropic principle make Man, not God, the center of existence. In an age of religious transformation, we can predict that many people will join Scientology or other techno-scientific religions, seeking to be God rather than to find Him. (1987: 74)

Nonempirical Doctrines

The proposition that a group's doctrines should not be capable of being empirically disconfirmed was not part of the original model of religious success. This seems to be because this criterion is not an actual "trait" that a successful movement should have. Rather, it is a negative factor: A successful religion *lacks* such doctrines. As indicated by the subject heading in Stark's discussion of this point—"If Prophecy Fails"—he primarily has in mind concrete prophecies, such as setting specific dates for the end of the world. "Although prophesies may arouse a great deal of excitement and attract many new followers beforehand, the subsequent disappointment usually more than offsets these benefits" (Stark 2003: 262 [1996]). The Church of Scientology has never been involved in this kind of prophecy, or at least not in a major way.

Perhaps the most significant historical example of date setting was the Millerite movement. After an intensive study of the Bible, a Baptist layman, William Miller, became convinced he had deciphered the chronology pinpointing the end of his age. Miller dedicated ten years of his life to preaching and teaching his message of the imminent return of Jesus. His view was that 1843 was the year of the "cleansing of the sanctuary," which he derived from Daniel 8:14 and which he interpreted to mean the Second Coming (Miller 1842).

As the movement expanded, the Millerites became targets of ridicule. One of the more colorful bits of folklore about the Millerites was that they dressed themselves in white "ascension robes" (Ehrlich 1994 [1975]) in preparation for the Second Coming. The idea seems to have been that they would thus be wearing appropriately heavenly attire when they rose to meet Jesus in the air (I Thessalonians 4:17). It was even said that some Millerites sat on their rooftops on the appointed day to avoid bumping their heads against their ceilings as they floated upward during the rapture.

Miller gave himself a wide margin of error, predicting the end would come sometime between March 21, 1843, and March 21, 1844. When the Second Coming did not occur, adjustments were made so that October 22, 1844, became the revised return date. But once again nothing happened, and a "great disappointment" followed that left the Millerites in chaos. The great majority of participants defected from the movement. Miller came to regard himself as a failure, and soon retired. Some groups of followers decided to return to the original source of revelation and seek yet other dates for the end. Few of these groups lasted beyond their projected new dates.

One Millerite, Ellen G. White, developed the interpretation that Miller was not wrong about the *occurrence* of the eschatologically significant event, but that he was wrong about the *nature* of the event. Jesus did not return to earth in 1844, but he did begin the cleansing of the *heavenly* sanctuary (Hebrews 8:1–2). By 1863, White and others had brought together the network of remaining Adventists sufficiently to organize the Seventh-Day Adventist Church. Although the contemporary SDA Church eventually become a large, successful denomination, it never achieved the prominence the Millerite movement enjoyed in the 1840s.

Medium Tension

The theme of "strictness," embodied in propositions 3 and 9 of the success model, ultimately derives from H. Richard Niebuhr. For a variety of reasons, sectarian religious groups—groups that, at the time of their founding, tended to set themselves apart from the surrounding society—gradually accommodate themselves until they become mainstream denominations. Niebuhr examined this dynamic process in his classic work, *The Social Sources of Denominationalism* (1929). The primary way in which sects distance themselves from secular culture is by requiring their members to adhere to strict moral guidelines.

Stark asserts that strictness is an *attractive* trait that brings converts into a religion. At first glance, this proposition seems counterintuitive. Stark's argument here is—to oversimplify a bit—that the more participation in a religion "costs" members, the more they value their membership. Additionally, strictness tends to screen out "free riders"—individuals who want to enjoy the benefits of a collective enterprise without contributing to the group in any way. Once again, a concrete example is the best way to clarify this notion: "One need not look far to find examples of anemic congregations plagued by free-rider problems—a visit to the nearest liberal Protestant church will usually suffice to discover 'members' who draw upon the group for weddings, funerals, holiday celebrations, daycare and even counseling, but who provide little or nothing in return" (2003: 263 [1996]).

Finally it should be noted that strictness can be carried too far. It is not difficult to find churches that are too strict to grow in any significant way, which is why the ideal formula for growth is medium tension. The ninth proposition in the religious success model is that to maintain growth, a religion must maintain its strictness and resist the accommodation process analyzed by Niebuhr (i.e., a religion should resist the process of becoming a "liberal Protestant church").

Unlike other groups in the New Age milieu, the Church of Scientology puts forward strong, explicit ethical guidelines for its members (though this would be disputed by critics), as reflected in, for example, Hubbard's *Introduction to Scientology Ethics* (1968) and, more recently, the "Integrity and Honesty" chapter of the *Scientology Handbook* (Hubbard and the Church of Scientology, 1994). Every Scientology organization of any size has an "ethics officer" who is the first point of contact in a complex, internal justice system that takes actions again individuals whose actions are viewed as destructive. (Critics of the Church often portray this internal bureaucratic justice system as a form of social control.)

A second meaning of medium tension refers a movement's tension with its sociocultural environment. Though he focuses on the strictness aspect of tension in his article on the revised model of religious success, it is clear from examining his article on Christian Science that Stark has not abandoned sociocultural tension. There he notes that though "Christian Science was not especially strict, even concerning the resort to materialist medical treatments, it maintained a significant degree of tension with the surround culture on the basis of other aspects of its theology" (1998: 199).

To succeed and grow, an emergent religion should "not be viewed as so deviant that it wards off potential converts," yet it should be "unique and dissimilar enough from conventional religious bodies that it has saleability in the religious marketplace" (Lucas 1992: 40). High tension can be generated by excessive cultural discontinuity (e.g., the Hare Krishna example mentioned earlier) or by group actions that evoke the hostility of the surrounding society. I have already discussed the issue of cultural continuity.

With respect to social conflict, one might think that the Church of Scientology has provoked too much hostility to attract new members. However, as evidenced by the growth statistics cited earlier, this has not been the case. In fact, Scientologists I have spoken with tell me that *more*, rather than fewer, people have contacted and expressed interest in the Church of Scientology as a consequence of the free publicity generated by the relevant *South Park* episodes and by the high-profile remarks of Scientology celebrities like Tom Cruise.

Legitimate Authority

Unlike some of the other components of the religious success model, the need for the leadership to have authority that is recognized as legitimate by the membership is relatively straightforward. As Stark notes, "all successful social movements require effective leadership and this, in turn, requires that the authority of the leaders is seen as legitimate" (2003: 264 [1996]). Perhaps because this point appears obvious, Stark did not include it as one of the propositions in his original model.

The classic discussion of authority is Max Weber's tripartite schema of traditional, rational-legal, and charismatic legitimations of authority. He described charisma as follows:

> [A] certain quality of an individual personality by virtue of which he is set apart from ordinary men and treated as endowed with supernatural, superhuman, or at least specifically exceptional powers or qualities. These are such as are not accessible to the ordinary person, but are regarded as of divine origin or as exemplary, and on the basis of them the individual concerned is treated as a leader. . . . What is alone important is how the individual is actually regarded by those subject to charismatic authority, by his "followers" or "disciples." (1949: 329)

Hubbard never claimed superhuman status, though some have interpreted his "Hymn of Asia" as a claim to be Maitreya, the Buddha of the future.[6] Although not quite superhuman, the Church has portrayed Hubbard as an unparalleled genius whose therapeutic technology will solve all of humanity's psychological problems.

According to Weber, to avoid disintegrating in the wake of the death of a charismatic founder, a movement must routinize and institutionalize the leader's charisma until the organization comes to be viewed as embodying the founder's authority. To this end, the Church of Scientology has carefully cultivated Hubbard's "hagiography" (Christensen 2005), amplifying the already strong tendency within the organization to view him as the pinnacle of humankind. At the same time, in a variety of different ways the Church has emphasized its exclusive claim to the founder's legacy. To people within the organization, these complementary strategies effectively legitimate the authority of the Church of Scientology's leadership.

Religious Labor Force

The paradigms for Stark's religious labor force appear to be Mormon missionaries and Jehovah's Witnesses spreading their message door to door. He even goes so far as to assert, "Rapidly growing religious movements rely on their rank-and-file members to gather in the converts. If, during the next few years, you were to keep track of which religious groups have showed up at your door and how often, you would have a very accurate picture of who is growing and who is not" (2003: 265 [1996]).

In light of the data cited earlier, this observation is incorrect. I have never had Spiritualist, Pagan, or Unitarian Universalist missionaries show up at my doorstep. Yet, in the United States, all three of these movements are growing faster than either the LDS or the Jehovah's Witnesses (the Witnesses, as we saw, are actually declining). Even my own denomination, the Episcopal Church (a liberal Protestant church), is growing faster in the United States than either the Mormons or the Witnesses (by 13 percent between 1990 and 2001, according to the NRSI-ARIS surveys)—and I certainly have never been asked by my Church to go door to door preaching the Good Word.

As noted earlier, what appears to have happened is that groups like the LDS and the Jehovah's Witnesses have simply reached a saturation point in the United States and in certain other nations—a saturation point beyond which they are unlikely to grow. Additionally, as was also noted earlier, vigorous new Protestant bodies have emerged whose lively, contemporary styles are able to attract potential new congregants more effectively than door-to-door missionizing. Perhaps like door-to-door salesmen, door-to-door missionaries have been superseded by more effective merchandising practices.

Scientologists do not generally view themselves as missionaries, despite the fact that the smaller local branches of the Church are referred to as "missions." Instead, like many New Age groups, Scientology attracts potential participants via lectures, classes, and the infamous "free personality test" that critics dismiss as a deceptive recruitment tool (though only 18 percent of neophytes are recruited through this test, as noted in Rigal-Cellard's contribution to the present volume [chapter 16]). The goal is to *educate* people and to attract them into becoming clients for Scientology services rather than to *convert* them into card-carrying members of the Church.

This is not to say that Scientologists are not asked to disseminate Scientology. Over the course of my participant-observer research, I have regularly heard speakers encourage the audience to help with the task of healing the planet by bringing the "tech" to others. But this periodic prompting is quite different from a campaign requiring all active members to undertake door-to-door proselytizing every week.

The one aspect of Church teachings that purports to provide members with the tools to disseminate Scientology is the so-called "deadly quartet," which is taught as part of the London Congress on Dissemination and Help seminar (http://www.lrh-books.com/mailings/congress/lcdh.php). I attended this seminar when it was offered in Chicago in 2008. Simple in theory, the four steps of this process are actually quite awkward to apply in a coordinated fashion, and my impression is that the "quartet" was rarely utilized outside of the seminar room.

Other nontraditional religions such as Eckankar, the Ramtha School of Enlightenment, and so forth also seem to be growing quite well without missionaries. And though these organizations hold regular religious services, they tend, like Scientology, to attract new participants via lectures, workshops, and classes.

Despite these criticisms, this aspect of Stark's model can nevertheless be salvaged if we expand the meaning of "proselytize" to include the various activities that constitute these movements' educational outreach. In fact, Scientologists would probably agree to the relevance of this factor if it were changed to something like, "They can generate a highly motivated, volunteer, religious labor force, including many willing to engage in educational outreach activities," or, perhaps, "They can generate a highly motivated, volunteer, religious labor force, including many willing to share the teachings."

Growth Factors 6, 7, 9, and 10

There are a series of propositions in the religious success model that can be dealt with briefly. I have therefore brought together a consideration of four growth factors in this section, numbers 6, 7, 9, and 10 in Stark's revised model.

I was unable to obtain hard data on members' level of fertility (proposition number 6) or on their ability to sufficiently socialize their young (proposition 10). Unlike other religious groups I have researched, the Church of Scientology is burdened by a complex organizational hierarchy so that out-of-the-ordinary requests like permission to send out questionnaires to members—even to limited, local samples—must be approved by an officer at a national or even an international level. When the Chicago Scientology center passed along my request to conduct questionnaire research in 2006, the organization never responded. My guess is the request was so unusual that Church officials did not know how to respond, so they just tabled it and it got forgotten.

My informal observation is that Scientologists appear to have normal levels of fertility with respect to their demographic backgrounds. As for retaining offspring, I have interacted with a number of second-generation Scientologists in positions of authority, both in Los Angeles and Chicago. So my impression is that Church members do seem to succeed in adequately socializing their children.

One aspect of Scientology rarely noted by critics is that different levels of involvement are possible. Though core staff members are immersed in Scientology during most of their waking hours, the majority of Scientologists have regular jobs and participate in classes, events, and other services in a manner comparable to participants in mainstream religious organizations. In other words (and in short contrast to the "cult" stereotype), it is quite possible to be a casual member of the Church. This structure of variable involvement allows room for young people to experiment with other lifestyle options. They can even drop out of Scientology completely for a period of time and then return to the organization without suffering the kind of social ostracism they might experience from more traditional religious bodies. I would hypothesize that this fluid boundary is a big plus for retaining children.

With respect to Stark's ninth proposition, the Church of Scientology will almost certainly "continue to maintain sufficient tension with their environment—remain sufficiently strict" into the foreseeable future. As noted in the earlier discussion of the third growth factor, Scientology has an explicit system of ethics and a rather elaborate system for enforcing these ethics (or, more accurately, for dealing with the most egregious violations of ethical behavior). It also does not appear that the Church's tension with the larger society will diminish anytime in the near future.

The seventh condition in the religious success model is that rapid organizational growth is, in part, a function of competing "against weak, local conventional religious organizations within a relatively unregulated religious economy." By a *regulated* religious economy, Stark has in mind countries like China and certain Islamic nations in which new religions are actively repressed. These environments would obviously not favor the organizational growth of unconventional movements.

The related point about competing against weak, local conventional religions is reasonably straightforward. A new religion is likely to have more success expanding in, for example, a large city in California where local religious traditions tend to be relatively weak and fragmented (partly because of the many residents who have immigrated from other areas) than in the rural South where local churches are strong.

For the individuals Scientology is likely to attract, the Church has few rivals. Within the larger New Age subculture—the primary source of Scientology participants—there are relatively few organizations providing anything like the community and the "range of services" provided by a regular church. Many of the groups encountered in the New Age subculture are what Stark and Bainbridge would term "audience cults," meaning people who follow popular writer-lecturers like Deepak Chopra by reading their books, listening to their tapes, and attending their lectures. Other groups, such as therapy-oriented movements like EST, are what Stark and Bainbridge term "client cults." Client-oriented groups provide a limited range of services not typically available from an audience-oriented group, but for a fee. Neither of these kinds of groups are "cult movements," Stark and Bainbridge's term for religions in the full sense (Stark and Bainbridge 1979).

Few New Age groups are true religions in this sense. Buddhist and neo-Hindu groups draw many of their recruits from the New Age subculture, though both Buddhism and Hinduism still have the aura of being exotic transplants in the Western cultural environment (i.e., they lack cultural continuity). Nineteenth-century new religions like Theosophy, Spiritualism, and New Thought have also survived into the twenty-first century, largely by recruiting new members from the New Age subculture. Though organized Theosophy seems to have stagnated, both Spiritualism and New Thought are growing. These two latter movements and a few newer groups like Eckankar are the only organizations of significant size appealing to the same sorts of religious consumers as Scientology. So in terms of this growth factor, the Church is competing against relatively weak, local *un*conventional religious organizations—not the kind of stiff competition the Jehovah's Witnesses and the Mormons currently face from new paradigm and seeker churches.

Personal Networks

One of the most significant factors for understanding how people become involved in another religion is network ties. Community is such an important

aspect of a group's attraction that some analysts have downplayed all other factors; in Stark's words, "People do not join religious groups because they suddenly found the doctrines appealing. They convert when their ties to members
outweigh their ties to non-members—for most people, conversion consists of
aligning their religious behavior with that of their friends" (2003: 267 [1996]). In
addition to reinforcing one's commitment to the group and to the group's ideology, social relationships—the source of affection, respect, and companionship—
are some of the "tangible rewards of participating in a religious movement" (Stark
2003: 266 [1996]). Stark claims that weak internal networks have "doomed"
many religious movements. He further notes that this is one of the problems
with liberal Protestant denominations causing them to decline relative to Protestant sects: "Their congregations are more like theater audiences than groups,
for only small minorities of liberal Protestants report having close personal
friends among members of their local congregation. In contrast, large majorities
of members of Protestant sects report that most or all of their best friends are
members of their congregation" (Stark 2003: 267 [1996]). Though it is not the
precise focus of their analysis, the importance of community for Scientologists is
clearly implicit in Andersen and Wellendorf's discussion in the next chapter.

However, having a tight community can work *against* a movement's growth
if it becomes so all-consuming that forming relationships with people outside
the group becomes difficult. The first point of contact for many people who join
a religion is a friend, coworker, or family member who is already a participant.
A corollary of this observation is that a group that restricts its social relationships
to other members—a situation sometimes referred to as "social implosion"—
is unable to attract new members. Like the factor of medium tension, a religious movement thus needs to strike a balance between two extremes if it is to
grow effectively. A related consideration is that some movements attract "social
isolates"—meaning people with low social skills who tend to be loners—whose
relationships with outsiders are quite limited. A movement can grow up to a
certain point and then stop if it is mostly attracting this kind of individual.

Andersen and Wellendorf observe that Scientology has stopped growing in
Denmark. Though they do not use the term, their data would support the hypothesis that the Danish Church has "imploded." This does not, however, seem
to be the case in other parts of the world, where Scientology is experiencing a
healthy rate of growth. For example, in contrast to Andersen and Wellendorf,
I have never sensed the kind of "garrison mentality" in the American Church
they found among members of the Danish Church. So one cannot generalize
their findings to all Scientologists.

As discussed earlier, the majority of Church members (at least in the United
States) are not "full-time" Scientologists. This means the majority of Scientologists are plugged into other social networks through which it is possible
for non-Scientologists to become involved. It had been my impression that a
lower percentage of people became involved in Scientology through social networks than people who join other religious bodies. In contrast to the Jehovah's
Witnesses and the Latter-Day Saints, the average, nonstaff Scientologist is not
typically expected to bring new members into the fold (which is not to say that

they are never asked to promote Scientology services). As a result, it would be quite conceivable for one to work side by side with a Scientologist for years and never know she or he was a Church member. However, the Church's own statistics indicate that over half (52.6 percent) are recruited through friendship networks.[7]

Instead, as noted earlier, the high level of public controversy surrounding Scientology seems to be the key to the organization's steadily expanding membership. It appears that there are more than a few individuals who hear the Church being criticized in a variety of media, become curious, decide to look into Scientology for themselves, and then join. Thus, and not a little ironically, the people and agencies that attack the Church most vociferously end up being Scientology's best friends.

NOTES

1. If one performs the relevant calculations on the data in the *World Christian Encyclopedia*, Christianity holds a slight edge over Islam in terms of actual numbers of new converts. It appears, however, that the authors of the *World Christian Encyclopedia* have consciously or unconsciously overestimated the number of Christians and underestimated the number of Muslims (in this regard refer to Hsu et al. 2008).

2. Lucas (1992: 37–51) systematically applied Stark's early model to the Holy Order of MANS, and Palmer (2004: 77–79) utilized it in a summary fashion in her study of the Raelian movement. No one else other than Stark himself has applied the model in a detailed way (Stark 2006).

3. When I sent a preliminary version of my critical analysis of his model to Stark, he responded, "I am comfortable with the notion that evangelical Protestants are eating up the market" (Stark 2007).

4. I am certain the Hare Krishna movement would object to this characterization. Specifically, though some ISKCON devotees might indeed note that the Bhagavad Gita is a *higher* or more advanced scripture, they would never disparage the Bible as the *wrong* scriptures.

5. In this regard refer, for example, to Lewis 1992 and, more recently, to Chryssides 2007.

6. Refer to the first section of chapter 2 in this volume (William Bainbridge's contribution) where the relevant part of Hubbard's "Hymn of Asia" is discussed. "Hymn of Asia" is also quoted and discussed in Grünschloß's chapter 11.

7. Refer to the figures reported in Rigal-Cellard's contribution to the present volume (chapter 16).

REFERENCES

Bainbridge, William Sims. 1987. "Science and Religion: The Case of Scientology." In David G. Bromley and Phillip Hammond, eds., *The Future of New Religious Movements*, pp. 59–79. Macon, GA: Mercer University Press.

Bainbridge, William Sims, and Rodney Stark. 1980. "Sectarian Tension." *Review of Religious Research* 22: 105–124.

Barrett, David B., George Thomas Kurian, and Todd M. Johnson. 2001. *World Christian Encyclopedia: A Comparative Survey of Churches and Religions in the Modern World*. Oxford: Oxford University Press.

Bedell, Kenneth B., Alice M. Jones, and Jack Keller, eds. 1992. *Yearbook of American Churches, 1992.* Nashville, TN: Abingdon Press.

Bromley, David G., and Phillip E. Hammond, eds. 1987. *The Future of New Religious Movements.* Macon, GA: Mercer University Press.

Christensen, Dorthe Refslund. 2005. "Inventing L. Ron Hubbard: On the Construction and Maintenance of the Hagiographic Mythology of Scientology's Founder." In James R. Lewis and Jesper Aagaard Petersen, eds., *Controversial New Religions,* pp. 227–258. New York: Oxford University Press.

Chryssides, George. 2007. "Defining the New Age." In Daren Kemp and James R. Lewis, eds., *Handbook of New Age,* pp. 5–24. Leiden, Netherlands: Brill.

Ehrlich, James. 1994 [1975]. "Ascension Robes and Other Millerite Fables: The Millerites in American Literature," *Journal of Adventist Education* (October/November): 18–22. [This article originally appeared in *Adventist Heritage* (Summer).]

Finke, Roger, and Rodney Stark. 2005. *The Churching of American, 1776–2005: Winners and Losers in Our Religious Economy.* Piscataway, NJ: Rutgers University Press.

Hsu, Becky, Amy Reynolds, Conrad Hackett, and James Gibbon. 2008. "Estimating the Religious Composition of All Nations: An Empirical Assessment." *Journal for the Scientific Study of Religion.*

Hubbard, L. Ron. 1968. *Introduction to Scientology Ethics.* East Grinstead, U.K.: St. Hill Organization.

Hubbard, L. Ron, and the Church of Scientology. 1994. *The Scientology Handbook.* Los Angeles, CA: Bridge Publications.

Johnson, Benton. 1963. "On Church and Sect." *American Sociological Review* 28: 539–549.
———. 1987. "A Sociologist of Religion Looks at the Future of New Religious Movements." In David G. Bromley and Phillip E. Hammond, eds., *The Future of New Religious Movements,* pp. 251–260. Macon, GA: Mercer University Press.

Jung, Fritz. 2006. "Witches' Voice Monthly Summaries" (unpublished statistics). Personal communication with author, November 15, 2006.

Lewis, James R. 1992. "Approaches to the Study of the New Age Movement." In James R. Lewis and J. Gordon Melton, eds., *Perspectives on the New Age,* pp. 1–12. Albany: State University of New York Press.
———. 2002. "Numbering Neopagans." In Shelley Rabinovitch and James Lewis, *The Encyclopedia of Modern Witchcraft and Neo-Paganism.* New York: Citadel.
———. 2007. "The Pagan Explosion: An Overview of Select Census and Survey Data." In Hannah E. Sanders and Peg Aloi, eds., *New Generation Witches: Teenage Practitioners of 21st Century Witchcraft.* Hampshire, UK: Ashgate.

Loomis, Roger. 2002. "Mormon Church Growth." Presented at the Annual Meeting of the Association for the Sociology of Religion, August 15–17, 2002, Chicago, Illinois.

Lucas, Phillip. 1992. "Social Factors in the Failure of New Religious Movements: A Case Study Using Stark's Success Model." *Syzygy: Journal of Alternative Religion and Culture* 1(1): 37–51.

Miller, Donald E. 1997. *Reinventing American Protestantism: Christianity in the New Millennium.* Berkeley: University of California Press.

Miller, William. 1842. *Letter to Joshua V. Himes, On the Cleansing of the Sanctuary* [14-page pamphlet]. Boston: Joshua V. Himes.

Niebuhr, H. Richard. 1929. *The Social Sources of Denominationalism.* New York: H. Holt & Company.

Palmer, Susan J. 2004. *Aliens Adored: Rael's UFO Religion.* Piscataway, NJ: Rutgers University Press.

Sargeant, Kimon Howland. 2000. *Seeker Churches: Promoting Traditional Religion in a Nontraditional Way.* Piscataway, NJ: Rutgers University Press.

Singelenberg, Richard. 1999. "Comments on Rodney Stark's 'The Rise and Fall of Christian Science.'" *Journal of Contemporary Religion* 14(1): 127–132.

Stark, Rodney. 1984. "The Rise of a New World Faith." *Review of Religious Research* 26: 18–27.

———. 1987. "How New Religions Succeed: A Theoretical Model." In David G. Bromley and Phillip Hammond, eds., *The Future of New Religious Movements*, pp. 11–29. Macon, GA: Mercer University Press.

———. 1996. *The Rise of Christianity: How the Obscure, Marginal Jesus Movement Became the Dominant Religious Force in the Western World in a Few Centuries.* Princeton, NJ: Princeton University Press.

———. 1998. "The Rise and Fall of Christian Science." *Journal of Contemporary Religion* 13(2): 189–214.

———. 2003 [1996]. "Why Religious Movements Succeed or Fail: A Revised General Model." In Lorne L. Dawson, ed., *Cults and New Religious Movements: A Reader*, pp. 259–270. Malden, MA: Blackwell Publishing. [Originally published in *Journal of Contemporary Religion* 11: 133–146.]

———. 2005. *The Rise of Mormonism.* Edited by Reid L. Neilson. New York: Columbia University Press. [This is a collection of Stark's papers compiled and edited by Reid L. Neilson.]

———. 2006. Personal communication with author, January 23, 2006.

———. 2007. Personal communication with author, June 15, 2007.

Stark, Rodney, and William Sims Bainbridge. 1979. "Of Churches, Sects and Cults," *Journal for the Scientific Study of Religion* 18: 117–133.

———. 1985. *The Future of Religion: Secularization, Revival, and Cult Formation.* Berkeley: University of California Press.

Stark, Rodney, and Laurence R. Iannaccone. 1997. "Why the Jehovah's Witnesses Grow So Rapidly: A Theoretical Application." *Journal of Contemporary Religion* 12(2): 133–157.

Stark, Rodney, and Lynne Roberts. 1985 [1982]. "The Arithmetic of Social Movements: Theoretical Implications." In Stark and Bainbridge, *The Future of Religion*, pp. 346–365. [Originally published in *Sociological Analysis* 43: 53–68.]

Van Biema, David. August 4, 1997. "Kingdom Come: Salt Lake City was Just for Starters." *Time* magazine 150: 5.

Weber, Max. 1949. *Theory of Social and Economic Organization.* Edinburgh: Hodge.

———. 1968. *Economy and Society.* New York: Bedminster Press.

Wilson, Bryan R. 1987. "Factors in the Failure of the New Religious Movements." In David G. Bromley and Phillip E. Hammond, eds., *The Future of New Religious Movements*, pp. 30–45. Macon, GA: Mercer University Press.

PART III

Community and Practices

7

Community in Scientology and among Scientologists

Peter B. Andersen and Rie Wellendorf

The Church of Scientology has been seen as a privatized religion fitting into the present age with hardly any "communal expression or community activity"(Wilson 1990: 278, vide infra 146). Based on observations, interviews and a questionnaire handed out to about 500 core members of Scientology in Denmark between 1986 and 1999, the chapter argues that the teachings and organization of the Church of Scientology, gnostic and arcane though they may be, still allow for community in a religious sense of the word, but that it is established through other channels and therefore expresses itself in different ways than in, for example, a Catholic community in which all members have equal access to salvation through one initiation.

From the outside the Church of Scientology may be seen as an expression of an extreme individualism because its core service is auditing, which aims to help individuals progress along "The Bridge to Total Freedom." The ultimate goal—Scientology's equivalent of salvation—is to enable the individual's thetan, the equivalent to the soul in other religious systems, to move freely in time and space as it once did countless existences ago before it was bound to its current state of existence in the material universe. On the other hand, L. Ron Hubbard, who developed the therapy and philosophy behind the Church of Scientology, fitted it into a utilitarian framework that attacked the individualistic assumptions of Freudian psychology. At a later point in time, Hubbard's ideas also inspired the Church to undertake a number of charitable activities.

This chapter will analyze the social setting in and around the Church of Scientology insofar as it is relevant to identify a community within Scientology and among its members. The Church of Scientology and its related charities will then be investigated to determine whether they promote integration with the society at large or whether they should be viewed as an isolated island consisting of an alternative community. To this end, Putnam's conceptualization of social capital as either bridging or bonding will be utilized as an analytical frame. One reason for using Putnam's approach is that it keeps the analysis of social capital at a societal level. It also approaches different positions in terms of a continuum, rather than as absolute positions (as some sociology of religions classifications have tended to do). The history of the Church of Scientology occupies an important position in the development of approaches to religious growth at the end of the 1960s and during the 1970s, so we should fit the Church of Scientology into the analytical frame developed in a number of illuminating studies at that time.

Background and Sociological Approaches to the Church of Scientology

The Church of Scientology was founded in the United States in 1954 on the back of the Dianetics movement that L. Ron Hubbard initiated in the late 1940s and early 1950s. *Dianetics: The Modern Science of Mental Health,* Hubbard's first publication in this field, was written as a manual for do-it-yourself therapy. The Dianetics movement emerged soon after the publication of this book in 1950.[1] In the first phase of the movement, people audited each other and, drawing on their personal experiences, freely modifying and adding new elements to auditing therapy. Following an organizational and economic crisis, Hubbard founded a new organization that would enable him to guide the development of the movement. In contrast to the earlier do-it-yourself approach, auditors were accredited, and the development of auditing was kept under Hubbard's strict control. Sociologists (e.g., Wallis 1977), as well as official historians of the Church of Scientology,[2] note that some of the conflicts between the early backers of the Dianetics movement and Hubbard focused on his attempt to document exteriorization (out-of-body experience). The reason for the conflict was that a successful documentation of exteriorization would mean that man had a soul (the thetan) which was independent of his body. This represented a definite move from a formally secular therapy—the "science" of Dianetics—to a "religion," as Hubbard himself stressed in a lecture series in 1955 (Hubbard 2005 [1955]: 8).

Sociologist of religion Roy Wallis termed the change from the open-ended and uncontrolled Dianetics phase to the establishment of the Church of Scientology as a development from a "cult" phase to a "sect" phase. The cult phase was characterized by the attraction of open-minded seekers from the cultic milieu, an environment in which loosely organized cults pop up, only to disappear, though the milieu itself persists as people search for new experiences. The sect phase was characterized by the pressure to conform within Scientology, the notion that the sect possesses the only path to salvation, and fierce attacks on the foes of Scientology (Wallis 1977). This control was later amplified with the creation of the Sea Organization (Sea Org) in 1967 (e.g., Melton 2000).

In the sociology of religion, sects are generally seen as being in tension with the surrounding society—including, perhaps, tension with the dominant church—but there is a wide range of positions organizations can take with respect to their surroundings. Beckford partly explains the surrounding society's opposition to the Church of Scientology as due to the fact that the Church seriously tries to change the society. In Beckford's typology of new religious movements, which is based on the goods manufactured by the organization, this means that the Church of Scientology is a social revitalization movement in contrast to organizations that offer refuge from the society or release from the individual's present condition. Beckford is not, however, blind to the fact that Dianetic therapy offers release (Beckford 1985).

Generally, sociologists of religion expect that sectarian movements strongly opposed to society will be organized in a vertical authority structure under the leader or, perhaps at a later point in their history, horizontally as a network among members. Both scenarios create a hermetically sealed environment with a strong emphasis toward uniformity. So it is surprising that two of the early empirical studies of the Church of Scientology conducted by Wallis and Wilson have viewed Scientology as an instance of a religion with little or no community.

Wallis emphasized that the organization did not work to create any formalized community among the members during the development from Dianetics to Scientology. He observed,

> Scientology has more in common organizationally with mass political parties, institutions of mass education, or multinational corporations, than with traditional churches. Its followers are drawn into no collective communion but rather into an atomized mass, differentiated only by their level of attainment in the theory and practice of the gnosis. With few institutionalized links among the members, communication and authority flow downwards from the leaders to the members who face the authority-structure of the movement as an isolated individual. The only collective means of influencing the decision-making process is that in which the members 'vote with their feet' through defection or apathy. (Wallis 1977: 252–253)

Bryan Wilson takes the theme of the lack of community within the Church of Scientology even further in connection with the concept of privatization. Here privatization refers to a state in which laypeople compose their own beliefs and theology. This concept has been developed within the context of Thomas Luckmann's (1967) argument that urbanization has led to the dissolution of traditional religious communities that are typically structured in congregations in which educated theologians communicate the beliefs to the members in a systematized way. According to Wilson, it is exactly such a lack of community that allows the Church of Scientology to operate and expand in what he considers as a secularized age in which churches generally have lost contact with the population and congregations are dissolving, leaving individuals to compose their own religious picture of the world. He argues that the

Church of Scientology is a religious organization that offers the individuals this opportunity: They can compose their own religious view of the world and keep religious experience at a private level.[3] In his view,

> Scientology designates itself as a church, and that description embraces the entire organisation which, over all, bears little resemblance to a traditional church structure. The most explicitly church-like facets of the movement lies in its chapel service and, to some extent, in the activities of its chaplains, but these, it must be said, are not central to the movement's operation. The core activity is auditing. Sociation is generally loose, impersonal, and informal. Chapel congregations are not the salient pivot on which the organizational structure rests. Church services are only occasional, not particularly solemn, not well attended, and far from being the main nexus of attachment of individuals to the movement. Thus, scientology conforms to the concept of a privatized religion which relies hardly at all on communal expression of community activity. (Wilson 1990: 277–278)

If Wilson is right in this regard, his point is of great importance for understanding the organization of religious communities in a secular age. The problem is that Wilson's approach limits itself to one of many possible ways of indicating the existence of a community and it may be that there are other kinds of community present in the Church of Scientology if one searches. To do this, it is necessary to identify forms of community that are important in terms of the teachings of the Church of Scientology, to specify how they may be identified, and to propose some generalized conceptualization of community that will allow for comparisons between the Church of Scientology and other social institutions.

Utilitarianism and Social Responsibility at the Individual and Institutional Level in Scientology

Since the presentation of the Dianetics therapy in 1950, Hubbard stressed throughout his writings that "Various educational, sociological, political, military . . . studies" would be "enhanced by Dianetics" (Hubbard 1985 [1950]: 11). Dianetics asserts that man is regulated by four so-called dynamics, which cover the urge for the survival for the individual to the urge for the survival of mankind. The dynamics between the individual (first dynamic) and mankind (fourth dynamic) focus on the survival of the family (second dynamic, which includes sex and care of one's children) and man as a member of a group (third dynamic). "The reward of survival activity is *pleasure*" and "The ultimate penalty of destructive activity is death or complete nonsurvival, and is *pain*" (*italics* in original, Hubbard 1985 [1950]: 45) is classic utilitarianism (e.g., Mill 1972: 6). Hubbard admitted that there may be competition between the different levels of survival, but he assumed that the cleared mind would be able to handle these potential conflicts and bring about an optimal solution.[4] As he stated,

> Now, it happens that these four dynamics can be seen to compete, one with another, in their operation within an individual or a society. There is a rational reason for this. The phrase "social competition" is a compound of aberrated behavior and sentient difficulties.
>
>   Any man, group or race may be in contest with any race, group or man and even in contest with sex on an entirely rational level. (Hubbard 1985 [1950]: 40)

But then he lays out an equation for the solution of potential conflict,

> The equation of the optimum solution would be that *a problem has been well resolved which portends the maximum good for the maximum number of dynamics.* That is to say that any solution, modified by the time available to put the solution into effect, should be creative or constructive for the greatest possible number of dynamics. The optimum solution for any problem would be a solution which achieved the maximum benefit in all the dynamics. This means that a man, determining upon some project, would fare best if he benefited everything concerned in the four dynamics as his project touched them. He would then have to benefit himself as well for the solution to be optimum. In other words, the benefiting of the group and mankind dynamics but the blocking of the sex dynamic and the self dynamic would be much poorer than the best solution. The *survival conduct pattern* is built upon this equation of the optimum solution. It is the basic equation of all rational behavior and is the equation on which a *clear* functions. It is inherent in man. (*italics* in original, Hubbard 1985 [1950]: 40–41)

Even if it would be possible to formulate such an equation Hubbard did not do. But in a series of "Fundamental Axioms of Dianetics," which he published in 1950, he formulated equations at the level of each dynamic. He stated that a high potential value for survival for a cleared individual "by reversed vector, [would] result in a negative worth as in some severely aberrated persons." (Hubbard 1985 [1950]: 47–48).[5] Even if the discussion of how to balance the common good between the dynamics has not been a major issue since Hubbard extended the four dynamics of Dianetics to the eight dynamics of Scientology, his basic approach is the same. For the present discussion, it is not necessary to explore the ramifications of the four additional dynamics (fifth through the eighth dynamic) because the first four dynamics cover the social realm in which we are interested.

   The problem of the common good has been discussed in philosophy and the social sciences at least since the time of Jeremy Bentham and J. S. Mill. The problems of how to put it into a proper formula has never been solved (Sen and Williams 1999), and this chapter is not the place to address that issue. Here it will suffice to identify this philosophy's consequences for the community of Scientologists.

Approach and Source Materials

One of the problems in assessing the existence of a community within the Church of Scientology and the position of the Church in society is that the classification of the organization as a "sect" (Wallis 1977) should—according to the traditional sociological characterization of sects—usually indicate a very high degree of community and some kind of isolation from the rest of the society. Because Scientology does not fit neatly into the traditional sect category, we will, instead, refer to the classification of "integrating" or "disintegrating" organizations that have been described by Putnam (2000). In this terminology, an integrating organization is described as bridging (between different groups) and a disintegrating organization is referred to as bonding (of organizational members). Methodologically, he has offered a number of quantitative approaches for measuring civil participation in democratic societies at large. One set of measurements is built around individual participation in political organizations, campaign activities, and attendance in meetings. At a collective level, then, the number of clubs and organizations in civil society represents one measurement. As for churches, he considers the decrease of individual participation as a decrease in what he calls social capital. With respect to the privatization of beliefs, he does not count it as an indicator of social capital due to the fact that private beliefs are individual (Putnam 2000: 65–79). On the other hand, he considers the increase in the membership of national environmental organizations, the Moral Majority, and the National Abortion and Reproductive Rights Action League as indicators of growth in social capital. For the present discussion it is methodologically relevant that the increase of civil activities from opposing positions in the society is considered an indicator of increased social capital and an improvement in the general integration of the society. Putnam does not distinguish between religious and secularly motivated ideologies in his analysis, an approach that allows him to consider the growth of religious and secular bodies opposed each other as a general indicator of growth in social capital.

The following analysis will begin with a discussion of a questionnaire that was administered to about 500 core members of the Church of Scientology in Denmark. The surveys were conducted in 1986–1987, 1991–1992, and 1996, with an estimated percent of about 75 percent of the members among each of the surveys (DDA 13095). The 500 core members among the Danish Scientologists were selected on the basis of a list the Church of Scientology had established due to changes in the Danish law in 1986 ($N = 380$, DDA 01494), and on the basis of newly established lists of active Scientologists for the surveys in 1991 ($N = 450$, DDA 01605) and 1999 ($N = 526$, DDA 05680). In all years, however, there were an uncertain number of Scientologists outside this core group. In 1985 the Church of Scientology reported it had 10,000 members (Sundby

Sørensen in DDA 01494: 13), and in 2007 the bimonthly Danish journal *Frem-tid* was sent to about 23,000 postal addresses.[6] The explanation of this much larger group is that one may be considered a member of Scientology even if one has an extremely low degree of commitment. During certain periods, for instance, memberships have been offered for free with the purchase of books or course materials.[7] For this reason it is difficult to make a precise calculation of the number of people who identify themselves as Scientologists. We estimate between 2,000 and 4,000.[8] Due to the high degree of similarity among the three samples, analysis has been mostly descriptive within a single year. When possible, comparisons to the Danish population have been made by means of the Danish Value Surveys in 1990 ($N = 1030$) and 1999 ($N = 1023$) of about 1,000 people, both of which are based on cross-sectional samples of the Danish population drawn from civil registration numbers.

The presence of a community has been estimated through the answers to questions regarding feeling of community among the Scientologists, trust, and cohabitation habits. The figures will be considered as indicators of preference for community if the Scientologists' answers indicate they prefer each other over the rest of Danish society. Beliefs will be given special consideration as questions regarding beliefs offer a possibility of testing Wilson's privatization thesis. If Scientologists do not agree with each other on a consistent belief system, this will be seen as an indicator of privatization, and if they agree with each other, it will be seen as a weakening of the privatization thesis with regard to the Church of Scientology community.

In general there has been some confusion regarding the consequences of individualization and social attitudes in new religious movements. It has sometimes been suggested that new religious movements recruited their members from hippies who turned apolitical in the wake of the (American) counterculture (e.g., Robbins 1992 [1988]: 28–37). But the evidence for this has been scant and based mostly on isolated life stories, and there is no agreement on this point among the researchers (Robbins 1992 [1988]). This may be due to the fact that the political distribution of adherents and different subgroups within religious movements may vary even when there is agreement on some major issues. Such a situation has been documented by Bramwell (1989) in her historical study of the ecological movement and its many religious facets. In fact, Hubbard's critique of the classical psychiatrists such as Freud and Jung indicates that he took a different stance from other parts of the cultic milieu and the new religious movements that drew inspiration from them. So it is worth trying to determine how far Hubbard's utilitarian ideology has influenced Scientologists and what consequences they draw from it. The indicators on this point are questions regarding attitudes toward public social security as opposed to private charity, and the political affiliations of Scientologists. If they prefer private charity to public programs, it may be a reflection of the influence of Hubbard's utilitarian thought. A preference for right-wing parties will be taken as indication of the same general influence. If there are no significant patterns in the distribution of these attitudes, it may mean that Scientologists utilize the therapeutic parts of Dianetics therapy with little correlation between

Scientology and other spheres of their lives. That might be considered an indicator of privatization even if it is very different from the privatization of belief systems analyzed by Wilson.

The survey does not go beyond the core members of the Church of Scientology, but it would be interesting if some of the official, global statistics collected by the Church of Scientology could be utilized in a description of the form of community within the Church and analyzed to determine whether it has undergone any changes. There is always a risk that such figures may be inflated by the organization's interest in documenting expansion. For instance, different offices within the Church participate in a yearly competition in the so-called birthday game used to celebrate Hubbard's birthday—the office that documents the greatest expansion wins. On the other hand, the very same game likely prompts the Church to be wary of the reporting of inflated figures. It is thus difficult to test the quality of the organization's own figures. Another issue is that, when only global figures are presented, it obscures the differences among different countries.

The calculations compare the number of new people introduced to Scientology with the number of outlets (churches, missions, and organizations). If the proportion is constant, it could be considered an indicator of a continued expansion of the Church over the last fifty years. If there are fewer new people per outlet, it could be a consolidation of the Church, because it would mean the Church is changing its focus toward servicing those who are already members.

The Church of Scientology's attitude toward Hubbard's lectures and writings, which in some ways can be seen as evidence of an ongoing process of canon formation, raises some special problems for the sociological study of a living church. First of all, the Church formally insists that nothing has been changed since Hubbard's day, and that his writings are the Church's only source. From a historical point of view this may be investigated, and has already given rise to some conflicts between the Church and some former members (Rothstein 2008). From a sociological point of view, the problem is how to interpret the present discourse when most of the words came from a man who gradually withdrew from the public eye as early as the mid-1960s and died in 1986. One way of approaching this problem is to examine the current campaigns of the Church, the issues during Hubbard's lifetime that the Church has focused on in different periods, and the interpretations of his life presented in the *RON* series of publications that are released at major Church events. Regularly participating in a number of such events since 1997 and interviews (both informal and structured) have also been helpful for recognizing continuities and changes.

A Religious Community

Wilson concluded his presentation of the eight dynamics of Scientology by noting, "It has to be said that those who take up Scientology are not attracted specifically by this elaborate metaphysical system: the appeal is rather the promise of personal therapy" (1990: 272–273). Ninety-five percent of Scientologists did, however, report feeling fellowship with Scientologists in other parts of the world in response to a simple question regarding self-reported feeling of fellowship. Even after stressing to them that the item was about Scientologists they did not know, only some 4 percent changed their response (table 7.1). As a Scientologist explained in an interview, this feeling of fellowship is based on the fact that Scientologists have chosen to belong to the same religious universe. This Scientologist observed, "As a point of departure, we all agree upon many things I consider important—for instance, the notion that we are immortal beings. Scientologists all over the world learn expressions that are used only among ourselves. That is something a Chinese Scientologist and I have in common—that is, we use the same English terms. I would be able to communicate with a Chinese person via Scientology terms and expressions" (Anonymous interview November 1999).

A single Scientologist cannot, however, disprove Wilson's assumption of a high level of privatization of beliefs among the Scientologists. A theologically conscious person in any religion might well assume that the rest of the membership endorses the same theology as s/he does. Nevertheless, the Scientologist's assumption of agreement is reflected in the pattern of Scientologists' beliefs when compared with the Danish population at large (table 7.2).

The beliefs endorsed by the Scientologists are definitely in accordance with the system that can be found in the publicly accessible writings of Hubbard. Even if a belief in "life after death" holds a marginal place in the Scientology system, it is evidently in agreement with other important concepts. On the other hand, the negative attitudes toward beliefs relating to sin, punishment, and reward expressed in Christian terminology represent a specific rejection of the view of humanity upon which these notions are based. That belief in God scores so low is a consequence of Scientologists' belief in the eighth dynamic, which may be the God dynamic, but is, of course, a force, and not a God in the personal sense of the word (table 7.2).

Even if in-group indicators like "solidarity" and "confidence" are often highly related, it is relevant to give "confidence" special consideration. To deepen the understanding of the minority identity of Scientologists, they were asked about their degree of confidence in three different, not necessarily concentric, ingroups (table 7.3). In this regard, it is significant that the level of confidence in

TABLE 7.1 Communality between Scientologists

Questions Asked	% Answering "Yes" 1999	N
Do you feel fellowship with Scientologists in other parts of the world?	95	524
Is this true in spite of the fact that you do not know them personally?	91	522

TABLE 7.2   Religious Beliefs among Scientologists and Danes

Religious Beliefs	% Scientologists 1991	% Danish population 1990	P	% Scientologists 1999	% Danish population 1999	P	N Scientologists 1991	N Danish population 1990	N Scientologists 1999	N Danish population 1999
God	52	64	<0.001	45	69	<0.001	291	940	404	921
Life after death	98	34	<0.001	96	38	<0.001	405	891	509	857
Hell	4	8	<0.01	3	10	<0.001	365	970	487	939
Heaven	5	19	<0.001	5	18	<0.001	358	935	482	907
Sin	8	24	<0.001	7	21	<0.001	354	934	461	911
Resurrection	2	23	<0.001	2	—		362	911	476	—
The Soul	95	47	<0.001	88	—		394	901	498	—
The Devil	2	10	<0.001	2	—		360	975	481	—
Angels	—	—		13	—		—	—	428	—
Reincarnation	97	17	<0.001	96	17	<0.001	420	911	494	909
Past lives	—	—		98	—		—	—	515	—
The eighth dynamic[s]	—	—		95	—		—	—	483	—
Man is abberated	—	—		92	—		—	—	477	—
Karma	—	—		80	—		—	—	470	—

Note: P calculated according to two-tailed difference of proportion test.

Scientologists is at least as high as the level of confidence in their own family. Even if they know their family through lifelong contact, they do not have more confidence in them than in Scientologists in general, who constitute a global community at an abstract level. The great confidence in other Scientologists may originate from a realization of common aims, a common interpretation of the universe, and an experience of a common opposition against what is perceived as attacks from the outside. The reciprocal confidence can consequently be interpreted as an indicator of delimitation and a manifestation of the fact that all Scientologists are united by a communality of interests and that they have chosen to form a special group to fight for that.

The different attitudes indicate that there is a distinct feeling of solidarity, agreement, and reciprocal identification among Scientologists. This is reflected in their selection of partners and friends. Here it becomes evident that Scientologists in Denmark choose to segregate themselves socially in their choice of close personal relations. Between 87 and 93 percent of Scientologists have chosen a partner who is him- or herself a Scientologist. The pattern is slightly less clear in the choice of their best friends (table 7.4).

Individualization and Utilitarianism

Even if Scientologists' responsibility for their own salvation does not lead to a privatized religion in Wilson's sense, the stress on the individual's personal responsibility, as well as Hubbard's utilitarian emphasis on the common good, may have consequences for their social and political attitudes. However, in contrast to classical utilitarians as J. S. Mill, Hubbard was not optimistic in his evaluation of society's chances for positive development—a position he arrived at in response to the Church of Scientology's fight for existence in the United States during the late 1960s, and a position about which the current leadership of the Church reminded members in a number of selections from his writings at the end of the 1990s. In 1968 Hubbard wrote, "One of the reasons that this society is dying and so forth is that it's gone too far out-ethics. Reasonable conduct and optimum solutions have ceased to be used to such an extent that the society is on the way out." He defined the concept of "out-ethics" as, "By out-ethics we mean an action or situation in which an individual is involved, or something the individual does, which is contrary to the ideals, best interests and survival of his dynamics" (Hubbard 1998 [1968]: 15–16).

Hubbard saw contemporary society as dying due to the suppressive states and political systems covering the range of "-isms" from capitalism to communism via socialism. "Capitalism, communism, and socialism all wind up with man in the same situation—owned body and soul by the state" (Ron Hubbard 1997: 47). His response was: "There is an answer to all this. If these isms all tend to a total state, then the obvious rebuttal is a no-state. This alone would be an opposition to the total state" (Ron Hubbard 1997: 48).

TABLE 7.3 Trust in Three Different In-Groups Question: "How much do you trust in the following groups of people?"

Levels of Trust among the Scientologists	% Trusting Family 1991	% Trusting Family 1999	% Trusting Scientologists 1991	% Trusting Scientologists 1999	% Trusting Danes in General 1991	% Trusting Danes in General 1999
Trust them completely	70	74	75	76	14	14
Trust them a little	24	21	19	21	52	59
Neither trust nor distrust them	5	4	5	2	32	24
Do not trust them very much	1	1	1	1	3	2
Do not trust them at all	0	0	0	0	0	1
N =	440	518	441	521	437	518

Note: P calculated according to Mann-Whitney U, Family 1991 and 1999 $P = 0.140$; Scientologists 1991 and 1999 $P = 0.441$; Danes in general 1991 and 1999 $P = 0.035$.

TABLE 7.4 Spouse/Cohabitor and Best Friends Are Scientologists

Scientologist Relationship Statements	% Agree 1986	N	% Agree 1991	N	% Agree 1999	N
My spouse/cohabitor is a Scientologist.	93	230	88	279	87	302
My best friends are Scientologists.	83	326	77	388	78	457

Freedom of the Individual

In other words, the national system have become "out-ethics" due to the fact that it hampers the rational individual's freedom of action. If individuals were left alone without a suppressive state, rational individuals would organize society in an optimal way directed towards maximum survival on all dynamics.

The lack of confidence in the state's ability to create a just and ethical society and help people in need has prompted Scientologists all over the world to establish various institutions based on Hubbard's techniques to solve certain social problems. The emphasis on freedom from suppressive states does not mean the individual has no personal responsibility. Among these initiatives are Applied Scholastics, founded in 1972 with the aim of disseminating Hubbard's study techniques. According to Scientology, Applied Scholastics benefits about 30 million people on all educational levels all over the world. It was formally introduced in Denmark in 1974. Around 1985 the first two schools using its techniques were founded, and presently there are six combined elementary and junior high schools[9] (U.S. terminology; the schools cover grades 1 to 10), as well as one kindergarten and twenty-three active tutoring groups. The drug rehabilitation program Narconon began in 1966. In 2001, Scientology ran an advertising campaign in Denmark stating that it had saved 250,000 persons in the world from drug abuse. There is one Narconon center in Denmark. Criminon, which is a branch of Narconon, was started in New Zealand in 1970. According to some Scientologists, it is expected to be introduced in Denmark soon. The Way to Happiness foundation, established in 1980, has its background in Hubbard's booklet *The Way to Happiness*, published 1981 (2004), in which he argued for a general morality on the basis of natural law. Significantly, in this treatise it is clear that he has become more tolerant toward the state. It is, however, characteristic that all programs begin with empowering the individual by increasing the individual's rationality (just like the study programs in Applied Scholastics) or by ending drug abuse, thereby promoting rational thought. The programs never begin to improve the situation of individuals by changing ownership structures in a collective approach.

Before presenting the sociopolitical attitudes of the Danish Scientologists, a brief note on Danish politics is required.

Danish Politics

Political development in Denmark accelerated in the 1970s. Before that time only four parties dominated the parliament in Denmark—a fifth arrived in 1959. One could say that each party represented a particular section of the population and elections did not disturb the picture much. The parties remained at a certain size according to the number of voters in "their" section of the population.

The political picture changed in 1973. Recession and unemployment had spread all over the world. In Denmark, the oil crisis, for example, had a great impact on the economy. During the election of 1973, no less than five new parties entered the scene. One of them in particular received significant support from voters. Of a total of 179 mandates, this party got 28 mandates that year, based on an antistate ideology that suggested the elimination of all income taxes. Over the years, "Fremskridtspartiet" (the name of the party, which refers to progress) has toned down certain parts of its antistate ideology, and has instead moved toward an ideology hostile toward immigrants.

The development of the political scene in Denmark over the last thirty-five years has been due to the influence of recession and unemployment. Though the economy has been improving since the 1990s, issues like immigrants and the influx of refugees have had great impact on the last elections. In the mid-1980s, Denmark took in a reasonable number of refugees trying to escape the Iran-Iraqi war. In the late 1980s and early 1990s it was refugees from Somalia and the former Yugoslavia that dominated stories in the press. During 2007, there was some discussion about returning refugees to Iraq as well as the possibility of accepting some refugees when British and Danish troops left Iraq.

In the political game, these refugees and whatever immigrants Denmark already contains become important issues among the parties. The rhetorical war concerns the welfare state and the preservation of it, and immigrants and refugees often get caught in the crossfire when politicians refer to them as "problems" and talk about "the cost" and "the taxpayers' money." Presently, the burden of taxation is between 50 percent (according to the socialists) and roughly 60 (according to the liberal and conservative parties).

All parties address this set of issues as well as the question of the quality of public administration and services. Generally, the older parties have compromised by adopting a political middle position. Only a few parties on the outer left wing and issue-based parties on the right wing have refused to compromise their ideology. The balance in Danish politics, then, is centered around the middle in attempts to form coalitions. The government was led by the Social Democrats from 1992 to 2001, supported by various parties from the left and the middle, and since 2001 by the rightist party "Venstre, Denmark's Liberal Party" (the official translation).

For analytical reasons, the ten parties represented in the Danish parliament in 1999 have been divided in three groups consisting of socialist, middle, and liberal/conservative parties. The following diagram shows the Danish election of 1998. As explained above, Danish voters are balanced around the middle (figure 7.1).

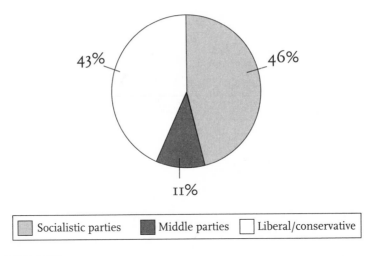

43%

46%

11%

Socialistic parties   Middle parties   Liberal/conservative

FIGURE 7.1

Sociopolitical Attitudes among Danish Scientologists

Core members of the Danish Church of Scientology display a somewhat different pattern of opinion when it comes to politics. The socialistic parties, for instance, would hardly be represented in the Danish parliament if the population adopted Scientologists' political values (figure 7.2).

Danish Scientologists do, indeed, seem to share a common value orientation when it comes to sociopolitical questions. Generally they follow Hubbard in his negative attitude toward socialism. After the fall of the Soviet bloc, the Church of Scientology reissued Hubbard's general statements against the state and national social welfare schemes in the publication *Ron The Humanitarian*, published 1997. That means that nearly all Scientologists vote for liberal/conservative parties on the right wing of Danish politics when they can easily find these attitudes expressed. In 1998 there were two antistate parties that were also very much against immigration and expressed a strong criticism of those international and European human rights conventions and agreements that the Danish government had ratified. Comparatively fewer Scientologists could be expected to vote for these parties, and it must be assumed that those who did vote for them identified with the antistate position rather than the anti-immigrant position, because Scientologists generally are pro-human rights and consequently do not criticize immigration.

It is, however, Scientology's conception of the human person that forms the core of the Church's sociopolitical attitudes. The freedom of the individual is the crucial point of departure, which is why a welfare ideology is incompatible with the ideology of a Scientologist. This is not to say that Scientological thought leaves the weak people in society behind. On the contrary, the point in Scientology is the universal human and spiritual potential that is ruined and paralyzed by the state and the regulations that hold the individual down.

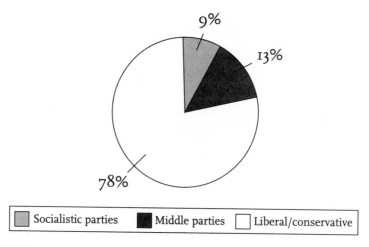

FIGURE 7.2

This conception of the modern state and the welfare system is clearly displayed in their reactions toward questions on social benefits and the expenses of public administration as well as in their preferences for private aid organizations for public benefits (tables 7.5 and 7.6).

The Anticollective Utilitarians and the Integration of Society

It is evident that the Scientologists prefer an individualistic utilitarian position for any collective position, and that the Scientologists insist that the utilitarian position is the one that demands they take upon themselves social responsibility for the common good. In this regard their stance reflects greater aversion to collective measures and a much higher confidence in the individual than has recently been common in Danish politics, even on the right wing. In this way, their opinions are coterminous reflections on individualism and utilitarianism, and one could see Hubbard and the Scientologists as representatives of a classical utilitarian position. The consistency of their opinions indicates the presence of a common Scientological value orientation. Because this value orientation springs from Hubbard's expressed ethical position, one can say that the ethical system is implemented by Scientologists in harmony with the religious system. As documented, Danish Scientologists also experience community with one another all over the world, and, on the local level, they have a higher confidence in each other than in the general population. The question is whether these findings have addressed the initial question regarding whether the Church of Scientology integrates or disintegrates the society.

In Danish society, as in the world in general, there are a number of critical voices who stress how the Church of Scientology isolates its members from the

TABLE 7.5 Sociopolitical Attitudes among Danish Scientologists 1999

Sociopolitical Statements	% Agree	% Disagree	N
We should spend more money on social security.	7	93	450
Private aid organizations usually get better results than the state.	94	6	378
Welfare payments pacify the receivers.	98	2	462

TABLE 7.6 Attitudes toward the Public Consumption among Danish Scientologists 1999

Expenditures	% Believing It's Too Much Money	% Believing It's Sufficient	% Believing It's Too Little Money	N
Unemployment benefit	63	36	1	478
Social security	68	30	2	464
Public administration	92	7	1	482

Technically the unemployment benefit is due to a policy taken out by a person in employment, but the benefit is heavily supported by the state, and the question, as well as the Scientologist's answers, reflects the discourse of public opinion in Denmark.

society at large. The overall picture the data present of Scientologists indicates the presence of a general mistrust and dissatisfaction with the state and the welfare system in Denmark. The numerous campaigns run by Scientologists against the official psychological and psychiatric therapeutic system, campaigns against the state's drug-rehabilitation programs, and attacks on foes of the Church have led many persons to hold a negative evaluation of Scientology. In sociological terms, the Church of Scientology is viewed as socially disintegrating.

Here Putnam's approach is useful because it considers organizations that are highly active in civil society as integrating in and of themselves, especially if other organizations in civil society address their activities in response. Because Scientology continuously manages to increase its global impact as measured by Internet activity (*What Is Scientology?* 1998: 558), newspaper coverage, and its members' involvement in community activities (*What Is Scientology?* 1998b: 583), the group definitely possesses a high level of social capital in Putnam's terms. The fact that in Denmark Scientologists are rightists, and globally they are middle class as indicated by their housing and education (*What Is Sociology?* 1998: 566–567), should not be counted against them when it comes to considering whether or not they are a positive factor in social integration.

Putnam has, however, another concern regarding the vitality of civil society, which is the increasing professionalization of nongovernmental organizations, churches as well as charities. As he says, "'Card-carrying' membership may not accurately reflect actual involvement in community activities. An individual who 'belongs to' half a dozen community groups may actually be active in none"

(Putnam 2000: 58). The expansion of the Church of Scientology, as well as its associated charities, may lead one to believe that Scientologists are more than "card-carrying" members, but when one calculates the figures, this impression may change. Regrettably, we do not have the figures for Denmark. But Scientology's international figures may indicate that the services of the Church to members are growing in comparison to the members' activities.

The primary evidence is that the number of people participating in Scientology for the first time per institutional outlet (churches, missions, and organizations) has been unsteadily decreasing from about 738 persons per institution in 1970 to about the half that at present (table 7.7). These figures are open to several interpretations. Scientologists have, for instance, stressed that they are building up for the next level of expansion; a new phase of "going public."[10] However this may be, the balance between new starters and institutional outlets in the Church of Scientology indicates that the membership pattern of Scientology has changed over the years. The change may not be from active to card-carrying members, but from active members in the process of building a new church to members who are serviced by the Church.

Integrating or Disintegrating?

At this juncture, we are in a position to consider our original question, namely, whether the Church of Scientology is integrating or disintegrating of society at large. Putnam's conceptualization of social capital as either bonding or bridging has made it possible to argue that in some ways the Church is integrating of the society at large, and in other ways has a less integrating effect. The major positive evidence for integration is that the Church is part of a general increase in debate in the public sphere, as the attempts of the Church to change the society have raised the general level of debate. At a more concrete level, the evidence for integration of the society is that Scientologists engage in a series of charitable activities. Both of these kinds of activities are what, in Putnam's terms, would be viewed as bridging between one part of society and another part of society. The evidence that points to a disintegrating effect is that the Scientologists join together in a closed community, which in a number of ways

TABLE 7.7 New Starters and Organizations in Scientology for Selected Years Globally

Institutions	1950	1960	1970	1980	1990	1997	2001	2001–2004
Groups/missions/churches	5	11	118	328	832	1,811	1,543	5,083
New starters			87,045	150,942	493,685	642.596		1,600,000
New starters by institution			738	460	593	355		315

Figures based on *What is Scientology* (1998) and calculations compiled by Ad Vulto, the Church of Scientology, received at a meeting with him and Anette Refstrup 2005.

isolates itself from the rest of the society. The main evidence here is that they do not trust people who do not belong to Scientology. As a consequence, they choose their friends and cohabitants within the Church.

One last consideration is that the professionalization of the Church may be evidence that it is no longer able to create the same level of activity around itself as it was able to generate in earlier times. The evidence for this professionalization is that the core group of Scientologists in Denmark seems to have been for the most part constant over the last twenty years, even if there are other indicators of "expansion." This was supported at the global level, where it was possible to create an index of the relation between the number of outlets compared to the number of new starters in the Church. In Putnam's opinion this kind of professionalization of an organization in the civic society indicates a decrease of social capital at large. In this regard, the Church of Scientology may be part of a trend in a number of the religious movements that began expanding in the middle of the twentieth century, and it may indicate that the values forwarded by the Church no longer address important areas of discussion in society at large. If this is the case, the process of canon formation around Hubbard's writings is not the way to expand the Church.

Acknowledgments

Major parts of this investigation are based on a survey of the core members of Scientology in Denmark. The survey was founded in 1985 by Associate Professor Merethe Sundby-Sørensen, who collected it in 1985 and in 1990. After her death in 1997 the Department of History of Religions trusted it to Peter B. Andersen to carry on the survey. In 1999 he collected it with the assistance of Rie Wellendorf using a grant from the Danish Research Council for the Social Sciences and from the research network RENNER founded by the Danish Research Council for the Humanities. The identification of community within Scientology was developed by Wellendorf, and some of the figures in this paper have earlier been published in Danish by Andersen and Wellendorf Riis (2002) and Andersen (2006). The Church of Scientology has generously provided us with addresses of core members for the surveys, and over the years we have been invited to participate in a number of Church events. A special thank you should be directed to the information officers, Karna Jensen and Anette Refslund, who have helped over the years, and Ad Vulto, who calculated the figures behind table 7.7 for this chapter. It should be stressed that responsibility for misinformation in this chapter rests solely with the Peter B. Andersen.

NOTES

1. The changes in the movement and organizational structure around various foundations are described by Wallis 1977: 77–100.

2. A video presentation from the official celebration of Hubbard's birthday as celebrated in 2007, which I later attended in Copenhagen, March 31, 2007.

3. Other approaches to secularization that might have involved rationalistic and scientistic claims as forwarded by Hubbard might well point to other conclusions (e.g., Willms 2005), but this is beyond the present argument, Wilson's as well as ours.

4. Melton (2000) has already stressed the utilitarian aspects of the Church of Scientology, and Heelas (1999) has pointed to a widespread kind of utilitarian thought in the New Age movement that the Church of Scientology in some ways can be considered as belonging to.

5. These axioms are different from the 194 Dianetic axioms put together during 1951 (Hubbard 1998b: 748–763) and presented as such in *What Is Scientology?*

6. Interview with Anette Refstrup July 1, 2007.

7. Sundby-Sørensen reported that an ad in the Danish daily *Det fri Aktuelt* March 1, 1985, offered a free membership for one year (DDA 01494: 13).

8. This figure does not consider the large number of Scientologists who pass through Copenhagen to take courses at the AOSH. But the estimate may be illustrated by the fact that information officer Anette Refslund from the Church of Scientology told us there were 1,200 persons who had registered for an event to celebrate L. Run Hubbard's birthday at a major hotel in Copenhagen March 31, 2007. This figure should leave space for a number of Scientologists who were not present, as the author also could see from personal experience.

9. Five of the schools receive support from the Danish state (interview with an anonymous scientologist at the Applied Scholastics office for Denmark September 5, 2007).

10. Interview with Anette Refstrup September 5, 2005 (Andersen 2006: 127).

REFERENCES

Data Materials Filed at the Dansk Data Arkiv

DDA 01494: Scientology som identitet og institution: kernemedlemmer, 1986–1987, primary investigator Merethe Sundby-Sørensen.

DDA 01605: Scientology som identitet og institution II: Opfølgning, 1991–1992, primary investigators Merethe Sundby-Sørensen and Jesper Demian Korsgaard.

DDA 05680: Scientology som identitet III, 1999, primary investigator Peter B. Andersen.

DDA 13095: Scientology som identitet I, II og III, 1986–1999.

DDA 01523: Den internationale værdiundersøgelse, 1990 (Denmark), primary investigators Peter Gundelach and Ole Riis.

DDA 15407: De europæiske værdiundersøgelser, 1999–2000, primary investigator Peter Gundelach.

Publications

Andersen, Peter B. 2006. "Scientology og 11. September 2001." *Chaos: Dansk-norsk Tidsskrift for Religionshistoriske Studier* [Thematic issue on "Religion og Krig" (Religion and War)] 45: 115–128.

Andersen, Peter B., and Rie Wellendorf Riis. 2002. "Kilder til et ikke eksisterende fællesskab." *Chaos: Dansk-norsk Ttidsskrift for Religionshistoriske Studier* 37: 9–20.

Beckford, James A. 1985. *Cult Controversies: The Societal Response to New Religious Movements.* London: Tavistock Publications.

Bramwell, Anna. 1989. *Ecology in the 20th Century: A History.* New Haven: Yale University Press.

Heelas, Paul. 1999. *The New Age Movement: The Celebration of the Self and the Sacralization of Modernity*. Oxford: Blackwell.

Hubbard, L. Ron. 1981 [2004]. *The Way to Happiness: A Common Sense Guide to Better Living*. Copenhagen: New Era Publications International.

Hubbard, L. Ron. 1985 [1950]. *Dianetics: The Modern Science of Mental Health, A Handbook of Dianetics Procedure*. Los Angeles: Bridge Publications.

Hubbard, L. Ron. 1997. *Ron The Humanitarian, Freedom Fighter: Articles and Essays*. Los Angeles: L. Ron Hubbard Library.

Hubbard, L. Ron. 1998a [1968]. *Introduction to Scientology Ethics*. Los Angeles: Bridge Publications.

Hubbard, L. Ron. 1998b. "The Dianetic Axioms," *What Is Scientology? Based on the Works of L. Ron Hubbard*. Los Angeles: Bridge Publication, 748–763.

Hubbard, L. Ron. 2005 [1955]. *Anatomy of the Spirit of Man Congress, Lectures 1–8*, Washington, DC, June 1955, Golden Era Productions.

Luckmann, Thomas. 1967. *The Invisible Religion: The Problem of Religion in Modern Society*. New York: Macmillan.

Melton, J. Gordon. 2000. *The Church of Scientology*. Studies in Contemporary Religions, series ed. Massimo Introvigne. Salt Lake City, UT: Signature Books.

Mill, John Stuart. 1972. *Utilitarianism: On Liberty and Considerations on Representative Government*, ed. H. B. Acton. London: J. M. Dent & Sons Ltd.

Putnam, Robert D. 2000. *Bowling Alone: The Collapse and Revival of American Community*. New York: Simon & Schuster.

Robbins, Thomas. 1992 [1988]. *Cults, Converts and Charisma: The Sociology of New Religious Movements*. London: Sage Publications.

Rothstein, Mikael. 2008. "Scientology, Scripture, and Sacred Tradition." In James Lewis and Olav Hammer (eds.), *The Invention of Sacred Tradition*. Cambridge: Cambridge University Press, 18–37.

Sen, Amartya, and Bernard Williams. 1999. "Introduction: Utilitarianism and Beyond." In Amartya Sen and Bernard Williams (eds.), *Utilitarianism and Beyond*. New Delhi: Cambridge University Press, [1982], 1–21.

Wallis, Roy. 1977. *The Road to Total Freedom: A Sociological Analysis*. London: Heinemann Educational Books Ltd.

What Is Scientology? Based on the Works of L. Ron Hubbard. 1998. Los Angeles: Bridge Publications.

Willms, Gerald. 2005. *Scientology. Kulturbeobachtungen jenseits der Devianz*. Bielefeld: Transcript Verlag.

Wilson, Bryan R. 1990. "Scientology: A Secularized Religion." In *The Social Dimensions of Sectarianism*, 267–288. Oxford: Oxford University Press.

8

How Should We Regard the Religious Ceremonies of the Church of Scientology?

Régis Dericquebourg

Foreword

It is difficult to write about Scientology because of the controversies that surround this movement. Those who view Scientology as a religion are labeled as apologists or crypto-Scientologists. For many people, the Church of Scientology is just a business with some religious varnish. For others, it is a dangerous religion or a wicked religion that does not deserve attention or interest. As for Scientology, it considers itself a religion and it is highly sensitive to anything written about it with a polemical mindset. If a sociologist focuses on the "false religion/true religion" issue, he/she becomes a party to the debate. Another solution consists in approaching the Church of Scientology with Weber's phrase in mind: "The question is about what exists, why something exists and not to express an opinion about what is desirable." This is our perspective. Scientology is a social movement that exists and that needs to be studied as any other "social actor." Otherwise, it retains its aura of mystery, which suits everybody except sociologists.

I have been studying the Church of Scientology since 1986 because this movement has some healing practices and I am interested in this topic. When I started studying healing churches, I met the spokesman for the Church in Paris and I submitted my proposed

---

This chapter is dedicated to Bryan Wilson, who read this article, gave some advice, and encouraged me to publish it.

project to him. Since then, I have been acting as a participant observer of the life of the Paris branch of the Church. I made a survey on the basis of a sample chosen at random from a list of its members with the aim of working out a sociological profile of French Scientologists. I submitted another sample of long-standing followers of the Church to the MMPI personality test. I have interviewed numerous Scientologists and, finally, I devoted a chapter to this church in my two books about healing religions (Dericquebourg, 1988, 2001). In doing so, I became a controversial researcher and I eventually gave up proposing two other articles to academic reviews, including this one about the ceremonies of the Church.

In his presentation at the CESNUR conference in Waco, Texas, Douglas E. Cowan (2004)[1] clearly says what I think, and I thank him for taking stock of this issue. Now I am more confident in my works about Scientology, and I am not afraid to publish this chapter. Religion or not, Scientology is a social phenomenon and must be studied as such without any prejudice. Reaching scientific truth about Scientology is not different from obtaining true data about any religion. Every church reconstructs its history and tries to build a good image of itself. Our work here consists in determining whether followers think they belong to a church or a business focusing on self-improvement, and only interviews with followers and surveys can inform us. Additionally, only a comparison with definitions of religion can inform us at to whether or not Scientology is a religion.

For sociologists, the questions are: How did Scientology appear in its cultural and historical context? Why do Scientologists act as they do? Has the Church of Scientology changed with time? Does affiliation with Scientology change the behaviors of its members in society? What are its links with the political and economic spheres? What is the origin of the controversial debates about this movement whose membership is very small? If it is a religion, what sort of religion is it? In this chapter, my question is, "What is the meaning of the ceremonies of the Church of Scientology?" There is nothing to make such a fuss about. The only relevant issue is "Does this research work meet scientific criteria?"

1. The Problem

The Church of Scientology is mainly known through Dianetics, a method of investigation into current and past traumatic incidents. These are said to be the cause of an individual's psychological and physical problems. By bringing back to consciousness past incidents and by reviving them mentally during an "oriented awake reverie," the person is said to release the traumatic charge associated to it and to achieve a better condition or healing (Dericquebourg, 1988). It is also known that Scientology proposes personal development sessions. What is less known is the exploration of past lives, which, according to Scientologists, leads to a high level of spirituality. Its religious ceremonies are almost totally ignored. In a sociological study on the Church of Scientology, Roy Wallis (1976) mentions them but considers them marginal practices. He does not analyze them. According to him, they would have simply been added to Dianetics when, it is alleged, L. Ron Hubbard decided to found a religion. Roland Chagnon (1979) grants them more importance but considers them as having a purely psychological aim. These explanations are not convincing because Scientology considers itself to be a form of wisdom, as a way of understanding and liberation based on personal experience. *A priori,* this type of Gnostic religion does not need any religious ceremonies (with collective practices or intercessions with an ethical and transcendent God). It does not need important moments in life sacralized in order to resemble a church. Even if they are not well attended and if they have been created to give the Scientology organization the appearance of a church, the ceremonies deserve a closer look because Ron Hubbard gave them a specific form and not another, a specific ritual and not another. Some specific words, which express a basic ideology, are used and not others. Whether they are artificial or not, the ceremonies of the Church of Scientology have a meaning and a function that the sociologist must decode. It is worth taking a closer look at them. Even if Hubbard invented ceremonies in order to give his organization the appearance of a church, these ceremonies do nevertheless have a form: They contain a particular ritual and specific words, expressing a basic ideology. The sense and the purpose of this can be easily explained.

There are two types of ceremony: the religious Sunday service and occasions of the passage of life (naming after birth, marriage, ministers' ordination, and funerals). An introduction of these almost unknown ceremonies is provided below and will be followed by an examination of their functions as compared to their theophilanthropic equivalent.

2. Description of the Ceremonies

The Sunday Service

In the Paris Scientology center, which was the first fieldwork site in my sociological study of Scientologists, the Sunday religious service takes place in a chapel inside the church alongside the administrative area, the auditing rooms, and the course room. The Paris Church of Scientology gave us a weekday religious service. A religious minister was kind enough to perform a celebration on its premises, with a few members present. Another time, we asked some veteran Scientologists to explain what importance these ceremonies held for them.

The chaplain gives a short welcome speech, then reads the principles of Scientology, which are summarized as follows: (1) The purpose of the Church founded by Ron Hubbard is to help man to understand that he is an immortal being, to help him find his place in relation to the physical universe by guiding him in his acknowledgment of the latter and in erasing his sins (called "aberrant acts"). This God is present in man, manifesting itself as an impulse for life. Its recognition leads to social tranquility and increases the potential for the survival of all mankind. (2) Man is soul. (3) He reincarnates. (4) Scientology is a road to freedom and wisdom by bringing about awareness of man's divinity. (5) One must love one's fellow man. (6) Scientology is a Gnostic faith. (7) Freedom is essential. It procures greater spiritual power. A prayer for total freedom is repeated. The chaplain then introduces a period of silent prayer by saying something like "rising to higher levels of survival is in itself a rising towards God." Afterward, the chaplain states the Church's creed (Church of Scientology, 1993a), reads a text by L. Ron Hubbard, and then gives a sermon that may also be a recording of one of Hubbard's lectures. At this time, members of the congregation are free to ask questions concerning what they have just heard. More prayers are then repeated: for justice, for an understanding of the Supreme Being, for greater understanding, for religious freedom, for spiritual advancement, and for religious enlightenment. Finally, the chaplain thanks the congregation for having participated in the service. He advises them to apply what they have just learned in their daily lives. He may also make announcements. A hymn or piece of music brings an end to the service. The prayer may be a short period of meditation, the assertion of a resolution, or an invocation similar to the following:

> May the author of the Universe enable all men to reach an understanding of their spiritual nature. May awareness and understanding of life expand so that all may come to know the author of the universe. And may others also reach this understanding which brings Total freedom. (Church of Scientology, n.d.)

At the Sunday service of the Los Angeles mission, the chaplain asked the assembly to do exercises that each Scientologist does during his/her individual training sessions. For example, the participants were asked "to look up at the ceiling, to look at the wall on the right, to look at the wall on the left, to look at the floor." This sequence, called group processing, is part of some training of a phenomenological nature that the Scientologist carries out to learn how to explore and occupy space. It is also meant to reconnect him/her to reality.

By recalling the principles and the values of Scientology and by reproducing the sequences of the individual training in a collective setting, the ceremonies also seem to be a digest of the training of the Scientologist (except the listening dimension, which can only be a strictly individual experience and therefore cannot be staged publicly).

Wedding Ceremony

The Scientology wedding ceremony is no different from a civil marriage ceremony. Each partner is requested to remain faithful to the other in happiness and misfortune alike and to help each other. When celebrated in the presence of Scientologists, the ritual is stated in Scientological language. For example, the partners are asked if they have "communicated" their love to each other and if they have both "acknowledged" such communication. The chaplain reminds the participants of the rings' symbolism for the Church of Scientology:

> The circle has been an emblem of permanency to man since time immemorial. In fact, it represents time and space—which are without ending. (Church of Scientology, n.d.)

The future spouses are asked to imagine an ARC (affinity-reality-communication) triangle inside the circles, this triangle being a symbol of successful communication. From a Scientological point of view, marriage is the mutual presentation of two thetans (primordial spirits that have incarnated as physical persons).

Funerals

The Scientological funeral rite is similar to that of the Antoinists (Dericquebourg, 1993). Having reminded the congregation of the mortal nature of the body and having affirmed that man progresses via successive reincarnations, the chaplain bids farewell to the deceased and invites him or her to take up another body: "Go now, dear (deceased) and live once more in happier time and place. Thank you (deceased)." In turn, the congregation says goodbye to the deceased. The chaplain then gives a speech of consolation: "Come friends, he/she is all right and he/she is gone. We have our work to do and he/she has his/hers. He/she will be welcome there. To man!" (Church of Scientology, n.d.).

The funeral service may be carried out in the church or in the deceased's home. In the first instance, a procession—pallbearers, minister, immediate family, other members of the family and friends—proceeds to the altar, in front of which stands a catafalque, to hear the religious service.

Naming Ceremony

This is a form of baptism. It based on the Scientology conception of reincarnation. Its main purpose is to help orientate the spirit (the thetan) who has recently taken over a new body. According to Ron Hubbard, the thetan is aware that the carnal envelope (body) is his own and that he is "operating" it.

> However, he has never been told the identity of is body. He knows there are quite a few adult bodies around, but he has not been told that there are specific ones who will care for his body until it has developed to where he can maneuver it thoroughly. (Ritual of the Church of Scientology, n.d.)

The chaplain introduces the incarnated spirit to his new body as well as those of his godparents. He reminds the parents—and, if need be, the godparents—of their duty in teaching and assisting the thetan. He reminds them that the child's education must be geared to his achieving freedom. He invites the members present to recognize the child as one of their group. This ceremony is not carried out for converted adults as they have already gained awareness of their incarnation in the course of their Scientology training. Furthermore, by becoming "Clear" (i.e., a person freed of all physical painful emotion from his/her life; the "Clear" is said to act totally rationally), an adult member has voluntary joined the group and this membership does not need to be made official by means of baptism. The idea is to welcome an incarnated thetan; an adult baptism would be meaningless.

Ministers' Ordination Ceremony

A Church of Scientology minister candidate is ordained upon an examination of his religious knowledge of the organization's codes and creed and his ability to give advice and celebrate the cult. The ordination consists of introducing the new minister to a congregation. The new minister reads the auditor's code (de-ontological rules for auditing) (Church of Scientology, 1993b) and the code of the Scientologist and promises to follow them. The officiant then announces, "On behalf of the Church's committee and before the witnesses present here before us, I hereby declare that this member (name) has proven his/her ability, competence and vocation in serving the Church of Scientology and is hereby recognized as a minister." An invocation is then said: "Through this invocation of the symbol of our Church, we hereby acknowledge X an ordained minister. He/she is hereafter a Church minister, entitled to all the rights and sacerdotal privileges to all the responsibilities which are expected of him/her as a minister." He/she is presented with the eight-pronged Church of Scientology cross on a chain:

> Before the witnesses here assembled, I hereby declare you responsi-
> ble for promoting the Church's spiritual work in every way, for hear-
> ing confessions, preaching, relieving the spiritual suffering of your
> fellow men and, in so doing, respecting total confidentiality. (Church
> of Scientology, n.d.)

The new minister's loyalty to the Church is evoked by the following:

> By accepting these titles, you are also agreeing to support at all times
> the religious and ethical doctrines, precepts and principles which are
> the cornerstone of our faith. (Church of Scientology, n.d.)

The ordination may be carried out during religious services. In this case, the postulants agree to respect the requirements of the position of minister. The congregation publicly accepts the candidate as a minister. The invocation is the same as for a pure ordination ceremony. Ordination is a simple enthrone-ment ceremony similar to the welcoming ceremonies of certain affinity groups like a brotherhood. It is not a sacrament designed to make the minister a sacred person. It is concerned only with the adherence to the norms and objectives of the organization. This is a consequence of the type of spirituality of the Church of Scientology. Spiritual work is undertaken with a minister, an ethics officer, and course supervisors. Spiritual perfecting does not necessitate the grace or powers of an ordained minister. The function of minister does not cover the other functions; it is a part of a whole. His role consists of celebrating rites of passage and leading prayers. He represents the principles and practices of the organization. He symbolizes the principles of immortality, the existence of a Supreme Being, and ethics.

3. Celebrations in Keeping with Reincarnationist Beliefs

The passages ceremonies practiced in Scientology (birth, marriage, and death) are strongly influenced by the doctrine of reincarnation. As we have already seen, they deal with helping an incarnated spirit (called a "thetan") to localize himself in a new body or to present him to another incarnated spirit with whom he has chosen to live. The funeral rite is similar to that of the Antoinist one in that its purpose is to help a spirit leave the body during the final farewell. Scientology revives the doctrine of primordial beings. Like the latter, thetans were around before the emergence of humanity, which itself came into being when the thetans took up human bodies in order to play the game of life on earth. They perpetuate this game by incarnating down through successive generations.

The other ceremonies are also similar in principle—even if they differ in form—to the initiation ceremonies of certain traditional societies in that they affirm man's sacred nature. They also contain reflections concerning communication and ethics. Reincarnation is just one element of Hubbard's teachings. He offers the individual the chance to develop and transform himself into a being freed of his carnal envelope and to regain his power as a thetan thanks to auditing, communication exercises, and the purification rundown. Man's regeneration by the adoption of Hubbard's "humanist" values is expected to bring about improved civilization and the survival of humanity. These values are affirmed over the course of Scientology religious ceremonies. For this reason, such ceremonies are closer to a ceremony in which morals for the benefit of mankind are recognized as a sacred man rather than a cult before a transcendental God or of the reincarnationist rite. For this reason, Scientology's religious services are more comparable to the theophilanthropic services.

4. Modern Theophilanthropy?

Theophilanthropy emerged during the French Revolution of 1789. It was put forward by certain revolutionaries in an attempt to replace Christianity and to make the republic a sacred entity. Mathiez (1903), who studied it at the beginning of the twentieth century, sees it as a kind of open freemasonry. It appears that the principles and rites of the Church of Scientology have much in common with theophilanthropy.

The Principles

The two principles upon which theophilanthropy is based give it a religious nature. These are the existence of God and immortality, "two essential truths necessary for preserving societies and guaranteeing happiness" (Mathiez, 1903).

This concept is present in Scientological vocabulary. As we have already seen, God is frequently evoked, as is the soul and immortality. The terms "Spirit," "soul," and "Spiritual nature" appear thirty-seven times in the ceremony text and twice in the church's creed. Immortality is mentioned eight times in the ceremony texts. A reference to immortality is made in the preamble of the Scientologists' religious service:

> Our aim in Scientology is simple and direct. It is to help the individual to become aware of himself as an immortal being and to help him achieve basic truths regarding his relationship with the supreme Being; Scientology has taught us that a man IS his own immortal soul. (Church of Scientology, n.d.)

In theophilanthropical funeral services, the words *"death is the beginning of immortality"* provided a reminder of man's spirituality. This is where the similarity ends, for although Scientology is reincarnationist, theophilanthropy was not. Theophilanthropy was a cult of the Supreme Being. In the Scientological ritual, the Supreme Being is God, "the supreme aim of all religious aspiration," "the initiator of the teachings and actions of the Buddhas and saints throughout time." The ceremonial text contains fifty-four expressions naming God in different ways as the Supreme Being. The creed contains two designations. Each man "inside himself" is an "intimate reality." This is the internal God, the God of all mankind cherished by the metaphysical groups. But he is more than just a spiritual principle—he is also "the maker of the universe" and the main player in the divinity of the great game of universal life. He reigns over spirits in human forms, and we address prayers to him. In him, all qualities come together. Through his role as the great organizer of the universe and cosmic keystone, he can be compared to the great architect of the universe in Anglo-Saxon freemasonry. However, unlike freemasonry, Scientology does not evoke him alone or purely formally urge its followers to glorify him. For them, he is also the divine principle, God of all religions, the divine part of man of the metaphysical groups. Besides the name, does the god of Scientology have any other analogies with the theophilanthropists' Supreme Being (also known as the author, the Eternal, the Father of the universe, the Highest intelligence, and the Creator)?

The Evocation of Wisdom

The theophilanthropical ritual contains the ethics of sages, in other words, "high truths present in religions, philosophers and poets." The Scientological rite proclaims "the freedom of the soul through wisdom" (mentioned five times in the ceremony text). As for Scientologists, their religion is the science "formed from ten thousand years of various philosophies. It considers itself as the result of research undertaken in Veda, Taoism, Buddhism and other religions." The search must lead to "infinite wisdom" driven by God. This result, considered to be illumination, which God is called upon to provide via "the prayer for religious illumination," is comprehension and knowledge of God and his ways. (Vocabulary connected with the understanding is very important in the Scientology ceremonies. *Comprehension, becoming aware, realizing,* and *understanding* appear thirty-three times. *Know, answer, question, not knowing,* and *discovering the truth* are mentioned thirty times in all.) Although the choice of references is more eclectic in the case of the theophilanthropist, both doctrines resort to a tradition of wisdom.

Assertion of the Same Values

The comparison can be taken further. Moral values—human rights, justice, freedom, and tolerance as proclaimed by the revolutionaries—are present in the Scientological service as the prayers for "total freedom" and human rights demonstrate. (*Freedom* is mentioned twenty-nine times, either with the reference to freedom or to the contrary: *trapped.* The word *freely* appears three times in the creed.) "At this time, we think of those whose liberty is threatened; of those who have suffered imprisonment for their beliefs; of those who are enslaved or martyred; and for all those who are brutalized, trapped or attacked. We pray that human rights will be preserved so that all people may believe and worship freely, so that freedom will once again be seen in our land." (The rights of men are mentioned three times in the creed). The prayer for justice and the prayer for religious freedom, which, even in the latter, went through a rough patch during the French Revolution, are in keeping with the spirit of the universal human rights declaration that underlies certain invocations. Justice is praised in terms like, "We pray that those whose task is to restore justice to mankind and to decide on the goodness or badness of human acts, may carry out their duty in full knowledge and awareness of the true nature of their task, which must be impartial and unprejudiced"; or otherwise, "And we the Church pray for the true justice, the beginning of a better understanding and greater freedom for all mankind" (Church of Scientology, n.d.).

The Concern of Survival of Mankind and Society

The highest appeal, in the revolutionary cult as in Scientology, is the "interest of the society." The Sunday service's preamble contains the following words:

> The Church of Scientology is made in such a way as to embrace
> the proofs of the Supreme Being and the spirit, which Man has the
> power to know. By using these proofs, the Church of Scientology
> intends a greater tranquility to the state, a public order and survival
> potential for Man on this planet. (Church of Scientology, n.d.)

The Sunday service's introduction evokes the dynamics that are man's impulse for survival. Among these dynamics are the groups and humanity, which "heroes and noble people" serve best when they are on the spiritual path. This will is asserted in the prayer for peace: "That all men may live in harmony and build a civilization without insanity, without criminals and without war, where man is free to rise to greater heights" (Church of Scientology, n.d.).

As in the revolutionary cult, this deals with putting morals to use for social well-being. The *Theophilanthropy Manual* affirmed that "goodness was all that contributes to saving and perfecting mankind." These notions of constructive goodness and destructive evil are present in Hubbard's works. They are translated into the Scientology ceremony by the will to preserve life and humanity's striving toward civilization. (Life-related words—*life/lives, survival,* and *living*—appear twenty-one times in the ceremony text and four times in the creed.)

Emergence from the Chaos Thanks to Reason and Awareness of God

In the Scientological ritual, the world that has no knowledge or understanding is in chaos, in ideological confusion, an unethical planet obsessed with materialism, given to hatred, slavery, and destruction. Man is lost in "ideological confusion." The following is an extract from the preamble of the cult's purpose:

> The first act carried out by a government wishing to deprave its
> people to such an extent where they accept the most treacherous and
> corruptive behavior is to abolish the concept of Divinity . . . Denial
> of the existence of a supreme Being as an intimate reality, has made
> prostitution the most ideal conduct for women, treachery and treason
> the highest level of ethics to which man can rise and total obliteration
> due to treachery, bombs and guns, the highest aim of a culture. As a
> result, no-one argues anymore about the reality of a Supreme Being.
> (Church of Scientology, n.d.)

The rationality of a godless world is as follows: The negation of God causes a disintegration of morals, which in turn pushes divinity into oblivion. The way to cure this is to recognize the creator, and to know and understand the divine plan. This is the result of reason: "Scientology is more an appeal to reason than the first science of understanding."

According to Mathiez (Mathiez, 1903), the theophilanthropist's prayer is "really intuition by awareness of this eternal and divine order," the judge of goodness and evil, who is the basis of morals, and "a large group of agnostic men who believe their crimes to be forever buried in their tombs would be a herd of ferocious beasts" (Mathiez, 1903, 93). The Supreme Being as the Scientological God enables ethics to be based on divine intuition. Hubbard asks men to have knowledge of the divine order before acting. Everything can be explained and understood. This is a rational system, which removes all mystery. Hubbard's appeal to reason in legitimizing religion is not so different from the approach of the philosophies of light.

Faith in Man and His Works

The text pronounced in Scientology's Sunday service expresses faith in man. The word *man* is spoken more often than *God*. (The words *men* and *man* appear in all fifty-seven times in the ceremony text and eleven times in the creed. In the former, individual appears nine times and person twice.) The creed of the Church of Scientology asserts that man is basically good, that he is seeking to survive, and that despite the fact that he loathes cruelty, he sometimes has to accept it but, by virtue of his "basic nature," he has the ability to reach "maximum survival." Our ancestors have proved this through their great works. Scientology's aim is to incite the regeneration of man with a view to building a harmonious world. There is no need to develop the fact that theophilanthropy was a human religion, a religion of beings who had been "renewed" by a revolution seeking to establish new sociability.

Formal Resemblances

Theophilanthropic baptism also involved naming. It also talked about the commitment of raising the child in keeping with natural religion, about the parent's roles as educators, and fosters and the roles of godmother and godfather, if the need were to arise. Marriage involved a presentation of rings and a reminder of the spouses' mutual duties.

The Scientology and theophilanthropical religious services (to which might be added the "religion of humanity" founded by Auguste Comte in 1851) are similar in form. They both share the invocation to God (Father of nature in theophilanthropy), the necessity of examining one's conscience, lectures, moral sermons, and hymns. They adopt the model of Christian religious services. Their ideologies have similarities. They share the purpose of focusing men on a common, spirituality legitimate, secular objective. For them, religion should be based on reason and therefore controlled by intelligence. Besides affirming God's existence and immortality, the contents of these religious services are civil. They express the desire to go beyond all existing religions and systems of thought by containing the best of all these in the form of wisdom. They place emphasis on man, on values of sociability, and on progress. Their values (freedom, human rights, survival of humanity, peace, and social harmony) are not those of a traditional religion. They are more akin to a declaration of human rights, to humanism as descended from the philosophy.

The similarities between theophilanthropy devised by freemasonry and Scientology are self-evident. Could this arise from the fact that Hubbard frequented a paramasonic lodge (Introvigne, 1993)?

5. The Functions of Scientology Ceremonies

Methodology

To understand the meaning of the religious ceremonies of the Church of Scientology as experienced by its faithful, we undertook nondirective interviews with a sample of fifteen Scientologists. We asked each of them the question, What do the ceremonies of the Church of Scientology mean to you? The interviews were recorded.

We chose members who had been in the organization for over five years because we assumed that they had had the opportunity to attend various ceremonies and maybe to have personally participated in some of them (marriage, baptism of a child, etc.). The technique of the nondirective interview does not involve a large number of interviews as sociologists and psychologists share the standpoint that in a sample, the number of opinions about a social phenomenon is limited and interviews quickly become repetitive. This was verified in our case. On reading the transcription of interviews, we noticed recurrent topics that could be classified into three categories: (1) those mentioning the community dimension, (2) those legitimizing the value and the project of Ron Hubbard, and (3) those asserting and transmitting the values of the Scientology belief system.

Due to the recurrence of these themes, we concluded that it was not necessary to conduct a quantitative analysis and so we limited ourselves to a qualitative analysis. This seemed sufficient to identify the functions.

We have isolated an extract of the interviews that illustrates each theme, and reproduced them as quotations below.

As has already been pointed out, the Church of Scientology does not need ministers and religious services, nor does it need to mark important moments of the existence in order to function as the spiritual path it prescribes via auditing and teaching by way of courses and manuals. As one Scientologist pointed out:

> Personally, I never or rarely attend the service held at the Church of Scientology. I am aware that some Scientologists go to a regular church service, but *that is not* what counts the most for me as far as Scientology religion is concerned. Put differently, that is not the main aspect of my commitment. The main thing for me is pastoral counseling, in other words the activities which revolve around processing and Scientology courses.

It does not call for the evocation of the commandments or the wishes of a personal and transcendental ethical God, and neither transmits a "grace" by way of sacraments, nor intercessions to such a God for receiving individual benefits on earth. L. Ron Hubbard used Asian religion as a model, not Christianity. He himself frequented an esoteric lodge, which perhaps inspired his choice of rituals. But when creating the ceremonies, Hubbard seems to have been inspired by Christian church (services with sermons and prayers and consecration of life passages). This is quite plausible. It is not, however, obvious why he should have combined a spiritual path based on personal psychological experience, which he assimilates to Buddhism, and faith, which he qualifies as Gnostic, with a religious service similar in form to a Christian one and with treatment of important life passages in a sacred way.

The Sunday service is similar to that of the Christian Science Church, in which extracts of *Science and Health* (Mary Baker Eddy, 1875) and the Bible are read in public. But their aims are different (Wallis, 1973). In the case of Christian Science, the texts allow for the Scriptures to be interpreted and therefore enable the followers to understand the curative nature of praying. Scientology ceremonies, however, neither explain nor legitimize auditing, which is the privileged tool used on Hubbard's spiritual path. It is also possible that the followers asked for celebrations during their biographical phases, in a quest for a religious life that was in keeping with other denominations. Such claims were made by Antoinists, and led the founder's successor to contrive short ceremonies aimed at separating existential transitions. However, Christian Science, for example, proves that it is possible to operate without these rites and to invite followers to seek them elsewhere. Because the Church of Scientology is not an exclusive group, the follower may participate in rites of passages and religious services with the aim of manifesting God in his church of origin or in another religious group of his choice. One Scientologist, for example, had the following to say:

> I have four children. All four of them got married in the Church of Scientology and three out of the four also had a marriage ceremony in a Catholic Church.

In this respect, Scientology resembles a number of metaphysical groups and cults. Moreover, if Hubbard was seeking to satisfy a demand for rites of passage, why did he also write a ritual for a religious Sunday service?

It would be possible to imagine the cult to consist of a simple teaching, as in the case of the Jehovah's Witnesses. However, learning in Scientology takes place in courses, for which the founder developed a very specific method, as detailed in conferences and books. Furthermore, this service does not appear to be regular. We took part in a Sunday service lecture in the course of our research on the Church of Scientology. This chaplain said it especially for us, on a weekday evening. According to followers I interviewed, the service is not given regularly. Some centers hold it more often than others, and, within any one center, there may be peak periods and slump periods as far as services are concerned. Having said that, we never stopped by during times at which the weekend religious services were scheduled to check whether or not they were actually held. At for the question of why Hubbard introduced these rites, several interpretations are possible. It is our opinion that the ceremonies serve social, legitimizing, and declarative purposes.

Awakening of the Community Dimension

One might think that a "client cult" such as Scientology would need to provide its members with a spirit of community by way of ceremonies. The Church of Scientology is organized bureaucratically. Followers are well aware of this as they study the organization chart and the way in which services operate. A Scientologist is confronted with the bureaucratic aspect of the organization and a personalization of one's spiritual life. The latter is a private and highly individual matter based on auditing and attendance at seminars. A follower can become more committed by "working for the org." This entails taking on a post in which he is asked to demonstrate his skills and contribute to his department's statistics. However, the Church cannot simply be an efficient organization in which each individual follows his own path, which simply crosses that of others. Such an approach would lead to social atomization.

When they do not ask for it themselves, the members must be reminded that the Church is a community. For example, one Sunday afternoon when I went to the Paris Church of Scientology to interview followers, most of them with whom I had appointments had left. A woman Scientologist had phoned to say that her baby had just died and that she wanted to be surrounded by co-followers. The services may fulfill this role by introducing a group dimension based on an emotion as expressed in these terms:

> The ceremonies are beautiful in the true sense of the word. They are simple unstaged affairs (the notion of stage being an innuendo). As a child, I was struck by the fact that in the main religion— Catholicism—funerals were conducted in a very dramatized way, to use a Scientological expression. One was expected to be downtrodden or sad. Naturally, it is sad to see someone go. It is a loss for everyone, even as a Scientologist, of course. But our ceremonies are simple and represent life.

And about the service itself:

> It is a short, good nature ceremony. I must say these (ceremonial) texts are very moving. They appeal to something very deep that, as spiritual beings, we all possess. (Interviewee is a Scientologist of thirteen years)

Assembling members at particular times helps create an "us." This notion is based on the results of our interviews; for example:

> Why did Ron Hubbard create services? I think Scientology is a way of advancing personally towards perfection, but one cannot survive alone. It the same reasons one does not go into politics without belonging to a Party—there is no point. It is as good a comparison as any other. In other words, one does not experience religion in isolation. Therefore, in Scientology, we have common tools for advancing. We also share tools for building Ethics between cohabiting Scientologists; I think the ceremonies are also manifestations of a shared spiritual religious existence. (Interviewee is a Scientologist of six years)

The "us" would help prevent the follower from feeling isolated. This translates as a psychological dimension of ceremonies that differs from that described by Chagnon (1979). The latter believes ceremonies encourage Scientologists to become more involved with the spiritual path offered by the Church. We, however, know that the Church of Scientology uses other means to keep members interested (conferences, advertising campaigns, reminders, etc.). We also know that, despite the fact that in their early stages the Dianetics "missions" needed to rally followers' interest in order to grow, they do not have a chapel or a chaplain.

The Legitimizing Role

By continuing the comparison with theophilanthropy, it is possible to identify a second role of religious services. The French revolutionists wanted to establish values, morals, and a new social order different from those of the old system, which were to be applied by new political practices and new social practices. Using Berger's and Luckmann's terms, we could say that the revolutionaries were proposing a symbolic universe "devised like a model of all the socially objectivized and subjectively real meaning in which historical society and the lives of individuals have their place."[2] The founders of the revolutionary cults and later figures, such as August Comte and his *religion of humanity*, which was an extension of such cults, sought to legitimize norms, reflecting values in people's conscience and making them sacred. In other words, they included them in the symbolic universe of which the Supreme Being was the keystone. It was also necessary to ensure that the new symbolic universe was passed on to future generations. Worship is certainly not the only method for achieving this aim, but it is inclined to create more of an impact with a view to embedding it in followers' memories. Scientology is also a symbolic universe integrating personal experience of spiritual regeneration, morals, and values that become instrumental—in other words, that must lead a mission of social transformation (Wilson, 1994). Ron Hubbard incites his disciples to "go up the bridge," which corresponds to building a fighting soul for oneself in order to regenerate civilization. Scientologists are always involved in a cause, based on their values, that is supposed to contribute to the advancement of civilization, and to fight against psychiatry, drugs, psychotropic medication, and Interpol. Their driving force is similar to that of a knighthood that strives to lead the world to greater spirituality and ethical heights (to use their own expression, "to clear the planet"). Roy Wallis (1976) attributes a legitimatization to these fights. From a Scientological point of view, this mission must be accomplished by beings who have recovered the power of original thetans via spiritual training. The first function of the Scientological service seems to be the legitimization of Hubbard's values and project. It puts this before incarnation, wherein the Supreme Being is surrounded by omnipotent and potent thetans that will establish him on earth. This is a characteristic of a retrogressive utopia.

The Assertive Function

The Scientology ceremonies also serve an assertive purpose. As has already been noted, the spiritual path is an individual one. The ceremonies provide a space and time for the social project and faith system—which make up the symbolic universe to be asserted in the group. Asserted as discoveries of what the "great men" of the past predicted, the ceremonies give meaning to the history of ideas and provide a common basis for reference for the projection of individual action into the future.[3] The Scientology ceremonies basically put forward a "permanent solution" to a "permanent" collective problem in such a way that "the potential players in institutional actions" are "systematically informed of this significance."[4] For this reason, it is not surprising that the services are often held when the Church is faced with difficulties. This is expressed as follows by a Scientologist:

> I remember for instance when the Church was faced with an enormous problem in 1985. I went to the United States, to Portland, to demonstrate with other Scientologists from all over the world. The Church had been ordered to pay five million dollars, which would have ruined it completely. There were collective prayers for total freedom and freedom of opinions, which had nothing to do with Catholic-type prayers. It was more a "postulate," which is a decision taken by the group that something will happen in a certain way. Such prayers are not a plea to a higher power such as God, but a way of being together and showing that we all made the decision to overcome the difficulties the group was going through. It was a more symbolic meaning. For me, it doesn't carry the same importance as in the Catholic Church. (Scientologist of thirteen years)

In the Church service ritual, Ron Hubbard describes Scientology as "a system of axioms and processes which solve life's problems," be they personal or social. The Scientology cult seems to be "social apparatus" designed to imprint the institutional significance of Scientology "in the individual's conscience in a powerful and lasting way."[5] From the reincarnationist perspective, which is Hubbard's, Scientology ceremonies affirm the true identities of the followers and of the spiritual being encased in their bodies. They also provide spiritual meaning in the biographical passages. Berger and Luckmann's formula states that the symbolic universe establishes a hierarchy of apprehensions the individual has in relation to his identity—from the "most real to the most fleeting."[6] In other words, "the individual can live in society knowing that he is really what he thinks he is when playing routine social roles, in the light of day and looked upon by others."[7] This notion applies to the Scientology ceremonies. In particular, in these ceremonies death is both located and legitimized. The assertion of values obviously plays a transmissive role. Auditing, now called "pastoral advice," does not transmit the values of Scientology or Hubbard's social project, nor do most of the personal development courses. The services may well be a vehicle for presenting Hubbard's social philosophy for the benefit of followers.

The services are poorly attended, probably because the followers feel they have understood most of what is to be learned after having attended a few of these events. Many Scientologists told us they had been to two or tree of the services or attended them whenever they could. However, the most committed members wish to and must become ministers in order to be competent in transmitting the organization's purposes.

Conclusion

Although the Scientology service addresses followers of a religious elite in a nonemotional way, and theophilanthropy was a mass religion aimed at winning people's consciences in a ceremonial and emotive manner, these two religions have definite similarities. To repeat Karel Dobbelaere (1993), we affirm that they are based on an expressive set of morals with an instrumental vocation aimed at allowing man to surpass himself by striving to improve civilization. Far from being an epiphenomenon, Scientology religious services may be a focal point of Hubbard's purposes, just as theophilanthropy was the center of the spirit of light for the revolutionaries. In both cases, what is asserted and legitimized is not revealed values of an otherworldly salvation but thinkers' morals aimed at providing greater sociability and a better civilization. We could consider them a result of an "inter-world" religiosity. Nevertheless, the lack of enthusiasm about these ceremonies manifested by certain Scientologist reveals tensions between the individual aspect of the spiritual path and the collective and organizational aspects of Scientology that the founder tried to impose in an effort to establish the Church.

NOTES

1. An expanded version of Cowan's paper is chapter 3 in the present collection.
2. Berger and Luckmann, *La construction sociale*, p. 133.
3. Ibid., p. 142.
4. Ibid., p. 99.
5. Ibid., p. 139.
6. Ibid., p. 141.
7. Ibid.

REFERENCES

Baker Eddy, Mary. (1875). *Science and Health with the Key to Scripture*. Boston, MA: The First Church of Christ Scientist.
Berger, Peter, and Thomas Luckmann. (1992). *La construction sociale de la réalité* [The Social Construction of Reality]. Paris: Meridiens.
Chagnon, Roland. (1979). *La Scientologie, une nouvelle religion de la puissance* [Scientology: A New Religion of Power]. LaSalle, Québec: Hurtubise HMH.
Church of Scientology. (n.d.). *Observance et doctrines de l'Eglise de Scientologie de France*, polytyped.
Church of Scientology. (1993a). "Le credo de l'Eglise de Scientologie" ["The Creed of the Church of Scientology"], in *Qu'est ce que la Scientologie?* Copenhagen: New Era, p. 579. The credo was written by Ron Hubbard on January 18, 1954.
Church of Scientology. (1993b). "Le code de l'auditeur" in *Qu'est ce la scientologie?*, Copenhagen: New Era, p. 580. The auditor's code was written by Ron Hubbard in 1947, first published in 1957. On June, 19, 1980, the Church of Scientology published the final text.
Cowan, E. D. (2004). "Researching Scientology: Academic Premises, Premises, Promises, and Problematics." Paper presented at the CESNUR 2004 International Conference, "Religious Movements, Conflict, and Democracy: International Perspectives," June 17–20, Baylor University, Waco, TX.
Dericquebourg, Régis. (1988). *Religions de guérison* [Healing Religions]. Paris: Cerf.
Dericquebourg, Régis. (1993). *Les Antoinistes*. Paris: Turnhout, Brepols.
Dericquebourg, Régis. (2001). *Croire et guérir: Quatre religions de guérison*. Paris: Dervy.

Dobbelaere, Karel. (1993). "Religion civile et differenciation fonctionnelle: étude critique." *Archives de Sciences Sociales des Religions*, 19, 509–534.

Hennis, William. (1996). La problématique de Max Weber. Paris: P.U.F., p. 80. Hennis quotes Max Weber, Colloquium of Frankfurt, 1910.

Introvigne, Massimo. (1993). *La magie, les nouveaux mouvements magiques* [Magic and the Magical New Movements]. Paris: Droguet et Ardant, pp. 232–233.

Mathiez, Albert. (1903). *La théophilanthropie et le culte décadaire* [Theophilanthropy and the Ten-Days' Cult]. Paris: Alcan

Mathiez, Albert. (n.d.). *Manuel de theophilanthropie* [A Guide to Philanthropy]. (n.p.), p. 94.

Wallis, Roy. (1973). "A Comparative Analysis of Problems and Processes of Change in Two Manipulationist Movements: Christian Science and Scientology." *Acts of the CISR: The Contemporary Metamorphosis of Religion*. Paris: CNRS.

Wallis, Roy. (1976). *The Road to Total Freedom*. London: Heinemann, p. 122.

Weber, Max. (1910). Colloquium of Frankfurt, 1910. Quoted in W. Hennis, *La problématique de Max Weber*. Paris: P.U.F., 1996, p. 80.

Wilson, Bryan. (1998). La Scientologie. In *Scientologie*. Copenhagen: New Era Publications, pp. 111–145.

9

The Development and Reality of Auditing

Gail M. Harley and John Kieffer

Introduction

The pioneering spirit of the United States was fertile ground for the development of new religious movements that promised health, healing and serene lifestyles, abundance, positive thought, and moments of bliss, as well as economic prosperity. Pluralism of religious thought became a keynote of American religious culture. Various forms of novel religions grew out of the American soil.[1] In the 1880s Christian Science developed with the passion of Mary Baker Eddy to pursue her religious viewpoints that wedded monism and healing to her carefully penned version of the Bible—*Science and Health with Key to the Scriptures*. One component of Christian Science is the healing aspect developed by Eddy, who asserted disease could be cured through spiritual and divine power without medical intervention, and in church doctrine medicines and doctors were seen as barriers to optimum health and spirituality; in fact, they represented an illusory dimension of ultimate reality.[2]

New Thought, organized in Chicago, under the tutelage and directorship of Emma Curtis Hopkins also during the 1880s, ushered in the advent of spiritual healing that she posited as the second coming of Christ (Hopkins 1923/1983). Humans, for Hopkins, were spiritual beings, in essence divine sparks of God who did not realize their own divinity. This lack of knowledge diminished the divine power of humans to know their spiritual inheritance, and subsequently erroneous thinking manifested as illness, poverty, and misery in the mundane world. She prescribed teaching that would transform the individual into a spiritual being with health, positive thoughts, and a serenity of countenance (Hopkins 1923/1983). The novel changes in theological thinking to a monistic philosophy had had a home in the transcendentalists movement in the 1840s when they imported Asian writing of a monistic nature to stimulate their world of experience beyond the normative New England provincial ideas. The appeal to the East was further stimulated by the World Parliament of Religions, held in Chicago in 1893 (Harley 2003: 26). The unorthodox theological precepts taught by Eddy, Hopkins, and other ambitious and eager minds set the theological stage for the emergence of a plethora of religions that placed responsibility for lifestyle choices on the individual, and saw the humans as divine beings who could take charge of their spiritual and daily life and deliver the methods needed for their own salvation.[3]

Industrial expansion, which was the hallmark of a growing technological America, took place around the same time as the expansion of religions that espoused an impersonal God as Divine Mind. Hopkins, who had been editor of the *Christian Science Journal* for Eddy, left that religion to teach her own understanding of what would soon become known as New Thought. As a trailblazer in religion in America, Hopkins, a mystic as well as a metaphysician, taught a theological oneness in which evil did not dwell. New Thought, unlike Christian Science, however, did not subscribe to the idea that medical treatment was harmful. Hopkins, a prolific teacher and writer, continued to teach her monistic ideas of the newer ways of thinking about health, healing, and spirituality until her death in 1925. *High Mysticism,* her magnum opus, is as avidly read today among religious seekers as Eddy's *Science and Health with Key to the Scriptures.*[4]

Concurrent with the midpoint of the new century (1950), what later became the Church of Scientology was introduced by founder L. Ron Hubbard (1911–1986). His seminal teachings would catapult this new religion into continual controversy, intriguing scholars and the lay public about their pacesetter position in the international arena of religious pluralism. Pluralism, a prominent feature of religion in America, had been established before the birth of Hubbard and underwrote the pioneering spirit of Hubbard to promote the religious precepts of Scientology by developing churches, centers, and organizations throughout the world. Today, there are Scientology organizations in more that seventy-four countries around the world. Hubbard's writings and church scripture have been translated into a number of languages.

Hubbard had an interesting childhood that provided the impetus to fuel his inquisitive mind. According to Gordon Melton, Hubbard, as a youth of six had been made a blood brother to the Blackfoot Indians near Helena, Montana. When Hubbard was twelve his father, a Navy officer, took the family east to Washington, DC, and there, in October 1923, young Hubbard met a student and disciple of Sigmund Freud, U.S. Navy Commander Joseph "Snake" Thompson. It was he who introduced Hubbard to the "inner workings of the mind being explored by depth psychology" (Melton 2000: 2). Depth psychology was a controversial new field of study then, and Hubbard, having acquired earth-centered spiritual experiences in an oral religious tradition with the Blackfoot Indians as a youth, was now introduced to a sophisticated psychology or form of mental healing based on talking out one's feelings, thoughts, traumas, and ideas, formulated by Freud, the father of psychiatry. He also found that Freud postulated that individuals had an unconscious mind replete with love, anguish, hate, lust, and violence.

In 1925, Hubbard returned to the family homestead in Montana having been suitably informed by the eclectic, military, international, and political milieu of Washington, D.C. He left home again in 1927 to set out on international journeys, which became the hallmark of his lifestyle and permitted him to associate with peoples of varied religions and exotic cultures. Encountering sages and teachers abroad during his journeys stimulated his curious quest to know different spiritual and theological phenomena. His philosophical thought, which diverged from mainline Christianity, placed him in a peculiar theological setting that allowed him to think outside of the traditional Judeo-Christian cultural milieu and provided impetus, as well as experiential fuel, for his theories about transformation that were later put into practice. Hubbard served in World War II and later supported himself as a screenwriter and pulp fiction author. During these years he worked on pulling together his theories and synthesizing his elementary philosophy.

Scientology had its preliminary origins in Hubbard's book *Dianetics: The Modern Science of Mental Health (DMSMH)*, developed in the 1940s and presented in book form in 1950. Because of the title of his book and its reference to mental health, Hubbard, a religious entrepreneur who considered himself a founder of a religion, was challenged.

Hubbard continued to work on theories and hypotheses until he felt that he could advance the precept that his work was of religious origin. His ideas transformed the individuals from suffering humans beneath the heaps of debris that cloaked them with mental uncertainty and emotional turmoil to someone with a recognition that they are divine, spiritual beings he called "thetans." Images of lifelong traumas he called "engrams" were contained in what he termed the "engram bank." This bank he called a called a "reactive mind," which operates on a "stimulus-response basis . . . [and is] . . . the single source of aberrations and psychosomatic ills" according to Hubbard (1981: 336). Hubbard in his reasoning had discovered a cure for these miseries caused by these engrams. This discovery was a method of transformation that he called auditing and could be administered in a number of ways to benefit human beings. In the 1950s, Hubbard's thinking about healing began to develop more along the lines of Eddy and her belief that medical treatment could be harmful. He began to advance his theories that good mental health was something that each human could acquire without the help of the psychiatric community and psychotropic medications.

Long after Hopkins and Eddy had developed their theologies of healing and religion, Hubbard developed his science of spirituality based on mental and physical health that, according to the teachings of William James in *The Varieties of Religious Experience*, written fifty years earlier, would place Hubbard's teachings in the arena of the mind cure movement or religion of healthy-mindedness (James 1902/2002: 75). Hubbard himself, apparently, did not see how his work dovetailed with the religions of healthy-mindedness. He assumed he was an original thinker or even avatar.

Hubbard hazards the question of his importance in his poem "The Hymn of Asia." The first three words are a query, "Am I Metteyya?"[5] Apparently, he beseeched others to validate him as a great world teacher, a pathfinder of the stature, or even the reincarnation, of Buddha who deserved reverence from his disciples and the world at large for his explorations into the inner dynamics of humanity and divinity and his thoughtful solutions to the painful predicaments of the human race that he thought were spiritual cures to age-old problems.

It was not until 1952 that Scientology became an officially designated title spoken first by Hubbard at Hubbard College in Wichita, Kansas, in early March 1952 (Christensen 1999: 2). The success of his book *Dianetics* and the evolution of his thinking about human spirituality had crossed the theological divide between mental health and a religious technology. His label for his religion reflected the paradigm shift that had occurred in the 1880s when founders of new made-in-America religions attempted to link science and technology with religion. Hubbard's interest in, and sponsored development of, a unique confessional device used in religious therapy, the E-Meter (which will be discussed later), took religious technology onward. Talking one-on-one about personal issues and challenges through auditing in a variety of ways was different from the silent mental treatments and autonomous affirmations of New Thought and Christian Science. Hubbard had created a link with technology that was not only a theory, but a creatively engineered engaged science.

In this way Hubbard sought to deliver humanity from a lifetime of suffering caused by the disastrous effects of the reactive mind. His goal was for students of Scientology to attain the state of "Clear," which is the result of many years of auditing involving the removal of engrams. This auditing process deals with the traumatic mental images stored over lifetimes that when restimulated caused misery, irrational behavior, even war. Hubbard's universal plan encompassed the welfare of the entire planet Earth. His detailed methods of salvation, such as the sacred practice of auditing, became the solution to restore ethics, sanity, and peace to the peoples of the planet. His all-encompassing vision was to "clear the planet."

Auditing Field Experience

This writer became interested in auditing, which is considered the most sacred process in Scientology. After extensive field visits to a number of Scientology centers, orgs, and FLAG bases, I enquired if I could be granted some auditing sessions. Throughout the past eight years, prior to and after September 11, 2001, I have conducted opportunistic surveys of people who were not Scientologists but who had unusual encounters with the auditing experience. Examples of anecdotal evidence came from several people, including a former university student of mine. A woman reported to me that as a young person she was on vacation in New York City and encountered a Dianetics center. Being curious, she went in and had a brief auditing session. She reported that a red blister appeared on her hand in the same place she had been burned in an accident as a child. As she worked the painful event through verbally, she reported that the red mark disappeared, that she subsequently no longer thought of it as a hurtful event, and that she simply went on with her life. She never returned to Scientology because, she stated, she was too busy searching and seeking out other spiritual practices. She still is! Another person, a retired professor, told me he had become involved with Scientology some years ago and had taken various courses. He had lost a dear friend in Vietnam and had never been able to deal with his grief over this loss. He said that during an auditing he was able to cry and mourn for the first time. His demeanor as he recounted this to me seemed to indicate he was at peace with his friend's death.

According to Roy Wallis in his *Road to Total Freedom* (1977: 113), there have been thousands of auditing techniques employed since the early work of Hubbard. Hubbard had worked with his Dianetic principles, refining and elaborating upon them prior to 1952. According to Christensen (1999: 2), Hubbard named the principles he developed "Scientology" after 1952, when Dianetics had already been established. New Dianetic ideas were established and developed from Hubbard's original auditing concepts, employed first as a self-help therapy and later as a sacred ritual. I have observed several types or methods of auditing during field observation in both Los Angeles and Clearwater, Florida, and asked officials at the Church if I could experience auditing. My preference was the auditing processes that used a device formally known as an "electropsychometer," or, simply, an "E-Meter."

I arranged for auditing in a mission facility in the Tampa Bay area. Though I realized that my request as a scholar was out of the ordinary, I was advised that I could receive auditing with experienced auditors using E-Meters. Due to my schedule, the only time that I had available was on Saturday after I had handled my responsibilities for that week. It was made clear when I spoke with the two auditors who were assigned to me that Scientology was offering me the auditing process not because I was a historian and scholar studying comparative religions but because I was a member of their version of the human family, a thetan. It is not the purpose of this chapter to discuss the controversies that abound regarding mental health, Scientology, and the viewpoints the Church holds about psychiatry. Nor will I draw parallels between auditing and psychotherapy. To be brief, Melton's (2000: 49) interpretation of Hubbard's thinking was that psychiatry was "built upon a false foundation" because it ignored the fact human beings were spiritual beings (thetan). I was not a Scientologist, but their view that I was a thetan included me in the company of Scientologists as a preclear. Noteworthy as well was that I was not excluded simply because I was a researcher. Ideally, a dedicated preclear attends sessions daily; however, my sessions were carried out intermittently from July to October 2001, due to my schedule and the 100-mile round-trip commute from the rural area where I lived. The first day that I arrived at the mission center I was cordially greeted, and chatted informally with Kathryn, the person chosen to be my auditor. We entered a modest office equipped with a heating blanket, a tiny fan, and a small desk with a dish of polished rocks to the side of the desk. These few tumbled rose quartz stones represented a "demo kit" and could have been any variety

of items. With some interest, Kathryn watched as I took a few out of the dish
and rolled them around in my hand, lined up several, and then carefully placed
them back. I advised her I was a rock collector of sorts and liked them there.
She beamed. I had just demonstrated one of Hubbard's premises that theory
must be combined with mass (Hubbard 1976e: 393). Adjustments were made
to the air-conditioning system so that I would feel comfortable: not too hot and
not too cold. Blankets were placed under my feet so there would be no drafts to
disrupt me. The blinds were drawn so the room had enough light for her to administer and chart the auditing process in a file folder. She chose several different can sizes for me to hold that were attached to the E-Meter. It was important
to find the correct fit for my hand size. After that I was given a hand cream to
use so that the silver metal cans made closer contact with my skin surface. The
process began. I was asked what I was thinking or seeing in my mind and, after
several minutes of this, Kathryn seemed have the E-Meter tailored for my specific electrical charge. By reading the needle on the meter, she could tell when
I was being affected emotionally. When I would reach an area that indicated
emotional charge, she would instruct me to elaborate more fully about it. As
I repeated the incident over and over, she responded with a corresponding series of positive, short acknowledgments, such as "good," "that's fine," or "got
it." When I became bored with the repetition and sighed, the auditing process
for that series of incidents had reached an end point as I had apparently released the emotional charge connected with it. In one instance, I had another
auditor, Shelly, who operated in much the same standard style that Kathryn did.
I got the impression that auditing is very precise, with oversight by case supervisors ensuring that each session follows a precise format and that variations
in standard protocol do not occur.

I no longer can recall the specifics of each and every session. Some were
determined by the auditor to be past life events held in my reactive mind
through what could have been a number of lifetimes. I do not know. Just as
a number of religions believe in rebirth or reincarnation, Scientology holds
this premise as well. Though I cannot validate that aspect of religious belief,
two sessions that took place on two different days several weeks apart could
possibly cause someone to rationalize it in that way. During these sessions
I became emotionally charged about scenes that I saw very clearly in my mind
at that time. These images were challenging and somewhat painful to talk
about; in fact, as I slowly related the incidents, a few tears streamed down my
cheeks. As in my previous auditing sessions, these incidents were run out to
an end point. To this day, I still recall those scenes as graphically as I did during
my auditing experience, except that there is no emotional response: They are
just pictures—intriguing pictures. I cannot explain the phenomena, at least not
in a scientific way. Perhaps they were vignettes from books I had read as a child
or clips from a movie that I had forgotten. Hubbard, of course, would posit that
these were past life recalls.

I do remember setting it up in my mind that I would use logical linear left-
brain functioning to keep track of what the reactive mind was doing and feeling. I found this experimental technique to be confusing and decided to go with

what was happening at the time—auditing—the release of the reactive mind to upsetting events and episodes. I would leave rational analysis for later.

On one Saturday I arrived at the mission tired and a bit achy. Kathryn tried to get a correct E-Meter reading on me to start the process of auditing for that day. She never did. Resourcefully, she changed gears and we set out on another path I had not explored before. We did what she called a "locational"— orienting the person to a specific area. We walked around the neighborhood as if we were taking a casual stroll, enjoying the weather. While pointing out various things—trees, buildings, plants, flowers, porches, shops and so forth—she would say, "Look at that" and name the item. I would reply, "I see," and she would acknowledge my response with the sort of short answers used in auditing. This procedure is designed to bring an individual into what is known as "present time and space."

On Monday, two days later, I was diagnosed with a minor eye infection. I cannot say if it was my immune system that was mobilizing to fight this infection that caused a somatic situation that dropped my energy level to the extent that I could not be audited. On another date in October, again Kathryn could not get me to register the appropriate energy on the E-Meter to be able to audit with it. Instead we walked again and she administered what is called a "touch assist." This is a gentle process in which the auditor systematically touches the person lightly on certain neutral areas of the body. Each touch was associated with a communication cycle that included the auditor's command "Feel my finger," a response from the individual such as "Yes," and the usual short acknowledgment by the auditor. This procedure is meant to bring the person back into communication or, more precisely, what is known as "ARC,"[6] with one's body.

Scientologists typically administer these locationals, assists, and other rudimentary processes following catastrophic events to help calm people who have become hysterical and disoriented. On Thursday, September 20, 2001 the New York Times published an article, "Changed Lives; Religious Leader Takes His Calling to Ground Zero," praising the efforts of volunteer ministers from Scientology for their response to the devastation of September 11, 2001. These locationals, similar to those applied to me, were given to the exhausted workers grappling with the devastating effects of human carnage after the attacks on the World Trade Center. Keeping the workers themselves grounded to the present, the outside world, instead of the horror within the rubble (Waldman, 2001). When other workers were sent home for the weekend, volunteer ministers of Scientology were asked to continue on along with other pivotal social and religious agencies such as the Salvation Army and Red Cross. Hubbard writes that in order for "a society to survive well, it will need at least as many Volunteer ministers as it has policemen" (Hubbard 199b: 870).

Training and Auditing through Primary Text Materials

"The only reason that [Scientology] orgs exist," according to an official policy letter written by Hubbard in 1983, "is to sell and deliver materials and service to the public and [to] get [into the] public to sell and deliver to" (Hubbard 1986: 66). Hubbard believed that it was through the delivery and application of his doctrine, or "Scientology tech," via a worldwide network of orgs functioning as frontline marketing, distribution, and service centers that the planet would have had any hope of being cleared. Thus, it is primarily through outreach programs managed at the org level that the human interface between Scientology and members of "the public" occurs. In these initial contacts, a member of "the public" is invited to visit an org, where she is guided by specially trained staff members to make an initial purchase of literature, audio recordings or, preferably, one of several introductory services.

Administered and supervised by trained staff at the org, the objective of the initial service is to create for the novice an acknowledged benefit or success, called a "win," which may spark interest in additional services. For the org, however, the service provides a valuable opportunity to establish a relationship with the individual to facilitate further involvement. These initial services include individual, self-paced courses and therapeutic one-on-one confessionals, or "auditing," such as the "Success through Communication Course" and "Introductory Dianetics (Book One) Auditing," respectively.

The full set of introductory services are listed and briefly described on a chart titled "The Bridge to Total Freedom: Scientology Classification Gradation and Awareness Chart of Levels and Certificates," otherwise known simply as "the Bridge." These and the many other services provided at the org—as well as those administered at advanced facilities—are organized on the chart in the following manner. The longitudinal axis on the left side of the chart identifies the numerical levels of auditor training classes and, on the right side, the auditing grades; the services listed are offered to qualified individuals who have successfully completed the prerequisite services listed below the level they wish to proceed to. Thus the introductory services are located at the base of the chart and the most advanced training and processes at the top; additional services of either type are listed on the sides of the chart and may be integrated within the progression of levels up the bridge through the recommendation by what are known as case supervisors. The training side of the Bridge proceeds through an initial five levels of training, identified as "Not Classed," from the "Method One Word Co-Audit Course" to the "Professional Metering Course." It then advances on to Class 0, I, II, III, IV, and so on to the highest shown, the Class XII Auditor. On the auditing side of the Bridge, processes begin with the "Purification Rundown," followed by the optional "TRs and Objectives" and "Drug Rundown"; next are "Happiness Rundown," "ARC Straightwire," and on to Grades 0, I, II, III, IV, "New Era Dianetics," "Expanded Dianetics," "Clear Certainty Rundown" and finally to "Clear." Beyond "Clear," several additional processes prepare the individual for the second major segment of auditing, the "OT" ("Operating Thetan") levels; these levels range from "OT I" through "OT XV." At the time of this publication, the Church of Scientology had released OT levels up through OT VIII. OT IX through XV will be released as Scientology achieves benchmarks in its goal to "clear the planet."

The rest of this chapter will engage the initial training phases that transform the newcomer to Scientology into an auditor and on the auditing side will discuss some forms of auditing that are administered both with and without the E-Meter.

Issues concerning the cost of these services have garnered some controversy throughout the course of Scientology's history. Hubbard's philosophy in this matter can be understood through his principles of ethics that posit, in part, that an exchange, defined as "something for something," must accompany any transaction. Moreover, to do otherwise, for instance to give or receive something for nothing, would in itself create a less-than-desirable condition that would be counterproductive to the physical, mental, and spiritual well-being of both parties to the transaction (Hubbard 1986: 394–397). Though the transaction is virtually always conducted through the exchange of money for services, there is the option that a motivated and qualified individual can be hired as a staff member in order to qualify for free services; however, except for training and student auditing, the full range of services offered at the org may not be available for free until she has attained a third level of staff ranking known as "Staff Status II" (Hubbard 1991a: 173, 191–192). Additionally, given that Scientology places greater importance on the individual who is trained to deliver auditing as a necessary asset to clear the planet over someone who has only been audited, a more economical (and usually encouraged) route is for the individual to purchase training and advance up the bridge by co-auditing the grades with fellow org students. This mode significantly reduces the individual's utilization of the org's staff auditors and, consequently, the monetary expense associated with processing through the various grade levels toward Clear.

The costs of the services, especially those that occur beyond the introductory phase, are private information and are provided at a time when the individual is qualified to advance to those services. Training is purchased as individual courses, in packages of several courses, or by placing money in an escrow account and drawing as necessary from it. Auditing is purchased in blocks called "intensives," which consist of at least twelve-and-one-half hours of auditing (Hubbard 1991a: 178). In a 1964 policy letter, Hubbard stated that the fee for a block of twenty-five hours of auditing was to be "computed as costing the same as three months' pay for the average middle class working individual" (Hubbard 1969: 95). John Kieffer, a former member of the International Association of Scientologists (IAS), reports that in the mid-1980s the cost of a twelve-and-a-half-hour intensive, including a 20 percent discount for IAS members, was $2,000 at the org in Tampa, Florida. In a phone call to that org in 2007, a staff member informed him that the fee for the twelve-and-one-half-hour block of auditing was currently $4,000, or $3,200 with IAS discount. To forecast the financial outlay of going up the Bridge for any given individual, however, is virtually impossible as each case represents a unique journey that can be made through many combinations of professional auditing and co-audited training. It is safe to say that for most it will necessitate numerous blocks of auditing and/or years of training.

All training courses are packaged as individual self-paced instructional programs that are worked on at the org during daily scheduled course room sessions administered by trained staff called course supervisors. These course packets contain a check sheet of requirements, pertinent policy letters, and lists of required Scientology texts, media, and other items necessary to complete the course. Some of these required items have to be purchased, whereas others are available for students' use while they are in the org's classroom. Students, whether staff or public, work on their courses only in the designated org course room and only during regularly scheduled course room hours. Students select and commit to course times and days on a schedule that fits within their schedule of work and personal obligations. This commitment requires students to be present for roll call in the course room at the time the session begins and engage in their course work throughout the three-hour class session with the exception of a ten-minute break period provided at the session midpoint. Those who are consistently late to class or have other challenges complying with the highly regimented protocols of the course room are counseled by the course supervisor or, if necessary, staff members at higher organizational posts in the org to correct the situation. Course packets remain in the classroom for the duration of the course and are turned back to the org through the course supervisor when all check sheet requirements have been completed.

Hubbard's name is kept in the forefront of activities and sacred processes. New students read Hubbard's premises as if he were still here and alive. For example, virtually every course pack begins with two of Hubbard's policy letters: the 3,400-word essay, "Keeping Scientology Working" and the roughly 600-word "Technical Degrades" (Hubbard 1991a: 7–13, 14–15). This format can be seen employed in the most current and publicly available, seven-volume *Organization Executive Course* that locates these directives on pages 7 and 14, respectively, in each volume. These documents are required to be read with the initial course and reread each and every time a subsequent course is taken; further, the student must be prepared to be spot-checked by the course supervisor concerning the definition of any word, abbreviation, or concept contained in the writing. If the spot check locates something that is unknown or misunderstood, a series of steps are required to fully understand the erred item and the spot check is resumed when the student feels she is sufficiently ready. Spot checks may occur for any of the several reading or audio assignments that comprise the training courses.

This ritual of verbal review is an example of Hubbard's principles of study, a key doctrine that is introduced early in the training of new auditors and staff members. Hubbard posits that there are three barriers preventing the successful comprehension and application of new material and, he asserts as well, that produce physical and emotional symptoms when these difficulties are encountered. The first factor, absence of mass, asserts that theoretical concepts must be engaged with counterpart physical components; to do otherwise makes the student feel "bent . . . bored, exasperated" (Hubbard 1976e: 393). Every table used for study in an org's course room is equipped with what are known as "demo kits," small containers filled with arbitrary and various small objects for students to demonstrate for themselves any text or concept that may be of such a complex nature that it eludes their immediate and full understanding. Additionally, a table with modeling clay is also available to demonstrate concepts in greater detail, either as required specifically by course check sheet instructions or by the case supervisor as she may deem necessary (Hubbard 1976c: 205). In cases in which the clay demo is a course requirement, these molded shapes must be able to easily relay to the course supervisor exactly what is being represented; it is only then that the student receives a pass for that particular check sheet item.

Ambitious students eager to advance faster than they can grasp the material will encounter a second barrier to study. Hubbard refers to this as "too steep a study gradient" (Hubbard 1976e: 393), and it occurs when students have not completely comprehended, or even skipped, prerequisite concepts. When this happens, the course supervisor will locate the last time the student was on target and require the student to proceed forward from that point.

The third barrier is the "misunderstood word" (Hubbard 1976e: 394). So vital is this factor to Hubbard that he asserts, "Stupidity *is* the effect of the misunderstood word" (Hubbard 1976e: 427). He further claims that the "manifestation of the blow [meaning a sudden and unexplained departure] from sessions, posts, jobs, locations and areas" (Hubbard 1981: 49) stems from this third aspect of study, which is the "misunderstood definition or the not comprehended definition, the undefined word" (Hubbard 1976e: 394). In other words, a reason that a student would suddenly quit a course of study, or for that matter leave any position in the org or even Scientology altogether, is that she had simply encountered an misunderstood word. Thus along with the demo kits, an adequate number of various types of dictionaries are required, by official policy, to be located in all Scientology course rooms.

All of these study concepts are encountered in the "Student Hat" course ("hat" means a job, duty, or position) by those individuals who have selected the training route up the Bridge. Upon its successful completion they are required to apply the principles of study tech throughout their future course work and, importantly, in their interactions with preclears as auditors.

Upon completion of the "Student Hat" course, the next step on the training side of the Bridge is the "New Hubbard Professional TR Course" (TR means training regimen) which will thoroughly reveal Hubbard's theories of communication. Fully understanding the concepts of communication is so critical to auditing that Hubbard asserts that "the magic of communication is about the only thing that makes auditing work" (Hubbard 1976e: 63). It is for this reason that each and every paragraph of a chapter on communication in Hubbard's book, *Dianetics 55!*, is demoed (demonstrated) in clay as one of the course requirements. The student must shape, organize, and label the clay in such a way that, as stated before, the course supervisor can easily spot the paragraph's premise in order to receive a pass and continue on to the next paragraph.

An excellent definition of communication can be found in the quote below. It will be presented exactly as Hubbard wrote it and then reworked in lay terms for easier understanding. As readers examine his definition, they may reflect back on the barriers to study just covered—abstraction requiring demo, too steep a gradient, and misunderstood words. Hubbard:

> Communication is the considerations and actions of impelling an impulse or particle from source-point across a distance to receipt-point with the intention of bringing into being at the receipt-point a duplication and understanding of that which emanated from the source-point. (Hubbard 1982: 32)

Substituting more tangible words, the definition may now read as follows: Communication is the intention and actions of sending a message or thing in some form from a sender across a distance to a receiver with the intention of having the receiver fully comprehend that which was sent by the sender.

Continuing further, if the receiver acknowledges the sender's communication, the event is known as a "communication cycle" (Hubbard 1981: 82). Auditing, at its most basic level, can be understood as a regimen of communication cycles between auditor and preclear.

Another fundamental concept of communication vital to the auditor concerns the structure of *understanding*. Hubbard asserts that understanding is "*knowingness* in action . . . a sort of solvent . . . that washes away everything" and is composed of "*affinity, reality* and *communication*" (Hubbard 1981: 454–455). According to Hubbard, affinity is "the feeling of love or liking for something or someone" (Hubbard 1981: 12); reality is "agreement as to what is" (Hubbard 1981: 82); and communication, defined earlier. These three components are abbreviated as *ARC*, an acronym that "has come to mean [to Scientologists] good feeling, love or friendliness" (Hubbard 1981: 20). *ARC* is usually depicted in Scientology texts as a triangle with one of each of the three letters in each corner. Doctrine posits these three components as interconnected and self-adjusting that convey a particular level of understanding. As one of the three components is expanded, for instance communication, the other two, affinity and reality, expand automatically and in equal proportion; consequently, understanding increases respectively. Conversely, as one of the components of ARC diminishes, so also do the other two and, with them, understanding.

As the student continues in her early training toward becoming an auditor, she must grasp the principles of the "Emotional Tone Scale," a linear chart of the range of emotional tones identified numerically and by description. This concept is important to the auditor for several reasons. First, it is used extensively as a tool in auditing in maintaining the "reality" component of ARC and thus maintaining communication with the preclear. The auditor achieves this by placing her own emotional level within proximity but slightly higher than that of the preclear.

Secondly, it is part of the methodology of how data about the preclear is inputted into the preclear's auditing worksheet to track the improvement or worsening of the preclear's case.

The range of emotional tones begins at the most desirable state for a thetan with a body, Tone 4.0 or *Enthusiasm*, and proceeds lower through diminishing tones of *Conservative, Boredom, Antagonism, Anger, Covert Hostility, Fear, Grief,* and *Apathy,* to Tone 0.0, *Being a Body (Death).* Emotional tones extend higher and lower than this range for the thetan scale: *Serenity of Beingness* is highest at Tone 40.0, and the lowest is Tone—40.0: *Total Failure.* These tone descriptions are an abbreviated representation of the complete fifty-nine emotional tones of the "Tone Scale in Full" (Hubbard, 1982: 108–110). Using partnered drills, the student demonstrates these tones with facial expressions as well as being able to quickly spot and identify variously produced emotional tones by her coach. In an auditing scenario, a preclear's yawn, for example, may indicate "Tone 2.5 Boredom" and, relative to a starting tone level, signal either an improvement or worsening of the preclear's case.

It is at this stage that a series of training drills, called "TRs," are introduced to all future auditors. These training actions proceed in a gradient of increasing difficulty and include the participation of another student, called a twin, that alternatively acts as either student or coach. Hubbard emphasizes the importance of these drills stating that "an auditor who can't do his TRs can't audit, period" (Hubbard 1976d: 253).

TRs prepare the student for her future role as auditor by training her to "confront," meaning "to be there comfortably and perceive" (Hubbard 1981: 88) another person without her own issues, or "case," becoming involved regardless of what that person may say or do. The drill "OT TR-0" requires the student and her assigned twin, acting as coach, to sit silently facing each other at about three feet from each other with eyes closed until such time that the student is able to do this effortlessly without any twitching, laughing, or other physical reactions (Hubbard 1976d: 348–349).

In "TR-0 Confronting," the difficulty level increases with the drill, as described previously, now conducted with each person looking directly at the other. The student must be able to do this with no outward emotional expressions or physical reactions. In most initial attempts, this exercise lasts for less than a minute or two before the coach declares a "flunk" for reactions such as watering eyes, excessive blinking, looking away, or laughing. With each endeavor, these reactions diminish until the student is able to confront the coach, eyeball to eyeball, for two uninterrupted hours in order to advance to the next level. This is a big win for the student.

Confident with her recent win, the student now tackles "TR-0 Bullbait." This exercise increases the gradient further with the coach taunting the student to locate her "buttons." A button triggers a response that creates discomfort, embarrassment, upset, or uncontrollable laughter. Hubbard specifies that buttons must be "tromp[ed] on hard" (Hubbard 1976d: 350). These activities invoke hysterical laughter from the student when her buttons are discovered. However, any emotional reaction would mandate the coach to "flunk" the student and restart the drill until the buttons are exorcized, or, in Scientology terminology, "flattened" (Hubbard 1976d: 350).

With additional wins, the student advances to the next set of exercises. In "TR-1" through "TR-3" students learn to deliver auditing commands and acknowledge responses. In "TR-1," the student arbitrarily selects quotations from the book *Alice in Wonderland* and delivers them to the coach as commands. In

"TR-2," the coach gives the commands from the book and the student acknowledges each in an appropriate manner. "TR-3" uses the commands "Do fish swim?" or "Do birds fly?" In this drill the student delivers either command to the coach and either acknowledges an appropriate response or repeats the command until a response relative to the question is rendered. Hubbard writes, "The student's job is to keep a session going in spite of anything, using only command, the repeat statement or the acknowledgement." If the coach, playing the part of the preclear, gets up and tries to leave, the student, enacting the role of the auditor, may, according to Hubbard's directive, "use his or her hands to prevent [the coach from leaving]" (Hubbard 1976d: 352).

It is important to reflect here on Hubbard's comments as they underscore the essence of his philosophy as seen in the training and auditing processes he formulated. In short, Scientology procedures are designed to confront the reactive bank. Below the level of Operating Thetan, Hubbard asserts that "the auditor plus the preclear is greater than the preclear's bank" (Hubbard 1976d: 352). The power of the dark side—the reactive bank—makes one incapable of confronting it alone. The auditor is there to get the preclear to confront her bank and annihilate its harmful force.

With the completion of this level of training, the individual will have been in Scientology long enough—anywhere from several months to years—to have experienced "case gain" and internalized the principles of the religion. The next step for this new Scientologist is to move to the auditor's side of the E-Meter with the "Hubbard Professional Metering Course."

Church literature uses the term E-Meter as a shortened form of "Hubbard Electrometer" or "electro-psychometer." It is an electronic device used for auditing that detects the stability or fluctuations in the electrical resistance of the preclear's body. An E-Meter handbook states that "technically it is known as a specially developed 'Wheatstone Bridge' . . . to measure the amount of resistance to a flow of electricity" (Hubbard 1975: 1). Several models of E-Meters are in use today, including the Mark V, VI, and VII;[7] for this research a Mark VI was evaluated.[8]

The system consists of electronic apparatus enclosed in a rounded, plastic housing measuring approximately 12" long × 8.5" high × 2.5" deep and weighing about three pounds. The most prominent feature is located on the right side of the E-Meter; it is an oval, glass-covered analog dial about 5.5" wide × 3" high enclosing a thin 2.5" pointer needle suspended over the dial face so as to allow it to sweep an arch across the dial's markings. The marked arch includes the following terms from left to right: "rise," "set," "fall," and "test." Situated around this window are two digital displays (a clock and tone arm counter). Moving from top left around to the bottom right are two rotating control arms on numbered scales, known as the tone arm (with numbers 1 through 6), and the sensitivity knob (with numbers 1, 2, 3, 4, 6, 8, 16, and 32); and three circular knobs, the sensitivity booster (three settings: 32, 64, and 128), mode (Off, On, and Test), and trim. The electrodes that connect the preclear with the E-Meter are composed of twin electrical cords that plug into the meter and extend seven feet to twin metal clips that attach to 5" long × 2.5" wide metal cans. The meter is powered by an enclosed rechargeable battery and can be used either with or without an external power source. Our Mark VI meter was tested to determine the electrical voltage that is delivered to the preclear through the electrodes. Depending on control knob settings, the voltage ranged from 1.0 volt to a maximum of 8.0 volts of DC current.

In an auditing session, the preclear completes the electrical circuit by holding each of the cans in her hands so that the electrical current flows through her. With the control knobs, the auditor can center the needle on a centrally located position of the dial labeled "set" and notice changes in position and motion that the needle registers to fluctuations in the electrical resistance of the preclear during an auditing session. Simply stated, the E-Meter measures the degree that the preclear's body either permits or impedes the electrical current flowing through her. Based on the movement of the needle, the auditor adjusts the voltage higher or lower with the control knobs to keep the needle within the parameters of the dial display.

There are ten main "needle actions" that an auditor is trained to spot, including a "fall," a smooth needle motion to the right; a "rise," a similar motion to the left; and a "free needle," or more commonly called a "floating needle," which is "a rhythmic sweep of the dial at a slow, even pace . . . back and forth." Other needle actions are identified as "stuck," "no reaction," "change of characteristic," "theta bop," "rock slam," "body reactions," and "stage four" (Hubbard 1982: 14–17). In E-Meter auditing these various needle actions, along with knob settings and digital tone arm counter information, are recorded throughout the auditing worksheet in relation to the preclear's responses to the auditing commands.

The student is trained to effectively use this device through a regimen of E-Meter drills that proceed from what would seem extraordinarily simple through an increasing gradient of difficulty. The student learns to set up the E-Meter, operate the control knobs, and recognize the various needle readings described earlier. Finally, the student auditor drills with another student to practice recognizing actual "reads" on the meter. In "Drill-21, E-Meter Steering" the student auditor, by observing only the needle's actions, learns to identify a specific thought that a student, acting as preclear, has at the moment she thinks it and to re-identify that exact thought when the student preclear rethinks it. This ability is crucial in E-Meter auditing.

Auditing

Auditing without the E-Meter

Some auditing techniques do not employ the E-Meter. "Book One Auditing," offered as an introductory service, is derived from Hubbard's early work laid out in "Book One" of *Dianetics: The Modern Science of Mental Health*. For a fee considerably less than charged for professional E-Metered auditing, an interested individual can choose to receive a series of sessions of this auditing from a trained staff auditor or she can attend a group seminar and learn how to do it.

In the latter method, the individual is twinned with another seminar attendee and the two practice this technique on each other.

"Book One" auditing is based on Hubbard's theories of the reactive mind.[9] The theory holds that this portion of the mind stores mental image pictures of times of physical pain and unconsciousness, called "engrams." Each of these engrams is associated with a "chain" of incidents that may include an assortment of other engrams, "secondaries,"[10] or "locks"[11] with similar content strung out over time. The technique is to start on a lock, identified as a recent upset, and work back along the time track[12] to earlier similar incidents on the chain until a secondary or engram is encountered. At each incident on the chain, the event is recounted several times; every time that it is described, fewer of the images and sensations, called "perceptics,"[13] remain until some single aspect of it will not erase.[14] The nonerasing perceptic associated with the incident is the connection to an earlier event on the chain. The objective of this sort of auditing session is to go through several incidents to "discover the basic[15] on that chain and reduce it" (Hubbard 1976a: 20).

In auditing Book One, the auditor sits at a table with pencil and paper facing the preclear, who is seated across from her; importantly, a box of tissues is required to be in reach of the preclear because most cases draw out tearful reactions. The auditor ensures that the preclear is comfortable, explains how the procedure works, and starts the session. The preclear is instructed to close her eyes,[16] which will remain closed until the end of the session, and is given the command to recall a "recent upset." When the preclear announces that she has located such an occurrence, the auditor gives her the command to go to the beginning of the incident and go through it. This is done as if the preclear were in the moment of the upset, as if experiencing it in present time, reporting what she sees, hears, and details of other perceptions as they unfold over the continuum of the event. The auditor writes brief notes about the incident, particularly the perceptics, apparent emotional tone levels, and any observed physical reactions. When the preclear seems to have reached the end of the event, the auditor queries if this is the end of the incident and, if so, acknowledges the preclear's reply. The auditor then gives the command to go back to the beginning of the incident and respond when she is there. When the preclear tells the auditor that she is at that point of the incident, the auditor again gives the command to go through it and report what she still perceives. The auditor enters additional data on her worksheet, noting particularly what perceptics continue to linger in the event. This is an important aspect of the process and one that the auditor must track to navigate the preclear toward the basic on the chain. As the incident is reexperienced in this state, the perceptics associated with the event will begin to fade and, after several more runs through the incident, all will erase except one that will not vanish. This is the link to an earlier similar event on the chain that may represent another lock, a secondary, or an engram.

At this point, the auditor gives the command to locate an earlier similar incident and to tell her when she has located it. When the event is located, the process is repeated as before. This procedure may run through several locks before a secondary or engram is encountered. When the preclear encounters such a secondary or engram the emotional tone of the preclear will reflect the perceived gravity of the event and may begin to weep, sometimes uncontrollably. Sometimes, within these highly significant life incidents, the preclear may enter the event so profoundly that she may stop reporting. In these cases, the auditor will nudge the session forward with, "What's happening?" or "Go on." Even though to the lay observer some of these events may not seem that serious, the auditor is trained to understand that any incident that has significance to the preclear must be acknowledged as such and audited to what is known as an "end phenomenon," or "E/P."[17]

As the auditor runs the event through the series of recalls she notes both the fading of precepts and subsequent elevation of emotional tone. In the first run-through, the preclear may have been at Tone .07 "Hopeless" or Tone .1 "Victim"; on subsequent runs, she may sequence through Tones .5 "Grief," 1.3 "Resentment," 1.5 "Anger," 2.5 "Boredom," and finally up to 2.6 "Disinterested," or 2.9 "Mild Interest." These last tones may be accompanied with the preclear smiling or chuckling, and some reflection about herself or the incident would be comprehended by the auditor as the E/P of the session.

Here the auditor will acknowledge the preclear's statements as she has done throughout the session, ask her to come to present time, and tell her to slowly open her eyes. Once the preclear has done this, a brief locational is usually administered to reintegrate her into present time and space. The auditor would note on the worksheet the final tone level and if the preclear was exhibiting very good indicators, annotated as "VGI." When this technique was created, the E-Meter had not yet been introduced. Today, however, at the end of such a session, a preclear may sometimes be evaluated by a case supervisor with an E-Meter to verify a good ending point, such as a floating needle. If so, she is informed, "Your needle is floating."

Another type of auditing achieved without an E-Meter is called the "Objective Processes." Categorized on the auditing side of the Bridge, Objective Processes fatigue the ego through mundane activities such as repeatedly observing and touching inconsequential objects in the auditing room designed to create an out-of-body experience. Hubbard uses the term "exteriorize" to describe the event of the thetan being out of the body (Hubbard 1976b: 395). The goal is to convince the preclear that she has a mind or consciousness that does not have to be connected to the human body. One of the Objective Processes, "Operating Procedure by Duplication," utilizes two dissimilar objects, such as a book and a bottle, located several feet apart in the auditing room, and employs a repetitive command-and-response cycle that can go on for hours. Once the auditor has started the session, the process flows in the following manner:

AUDITOR   "Go over to the book."
Preclear walks to within reach of the book.

AUDITOR   "Thank you, pick it up."
Preclear picks up the book.

AUDITOR   "Thank you, what is its color?"
Preclear answers the question.

AUDITOR   "Thank you, what is its temperature?"
Preclear answers the question.

AUDITOR   "Thank you, what is its weight?"
Preclear answers the question.

AUDITOR   "Thank you. Put it down in exactly the same place."
Preclear places the book back as it was.

AUDITOR   "Thank you. Go over to the bottle."
Preclear walks to within reach of the bottle.

AUDITOR   "Thank you, pick it up."
Preclear picks up the bottle.

AUDITOR   "Thank you, what is its color?"
Preclear answers the question.

AUDITOR   "Thank you, what is its temperature?"
Preclear answers the question.

AUDITOR   "Thank you, what is its weight?"
Preclear answers the question.

AUDITOR   "Thank you. Put it down in exactly the same place."
Preclear places the bottle back as it was.

AUDITOR   "Thank you. Go over to the book."

The process is repeated to an end phenomenon. During the procedure the pre-clear will eventually say or do something that breaks the regimen's standard flow of the procedure. This is known as an "origination," and the auditor must quickly determine whether it is a distraction or a "cognition": a major realiza-tion by the preclear about herself that would signal the end phenomenon of the session. If deemed a distraction, the auditor acknowledges the comment, repeats the command, and continues the process. If, however, it is a cognition, she will end the session and a case supervisor is called in to check the preclear for a floating needle on the E-Meter.

According to doctrine, the cognition is critically important in auditing. To understand this phenomenon two concepts need defining: "as is" and "aberra-tion." To "as-is" something means to see it exactly as it is without any distor-tions, at which moment it will vanish and cease to exist (Hubbard 1981: 24). "Aberration" is a departure from rational thought or behavior and false fixed ideas (Hubbard 1981: 24). They are the result of engrams in the reactive mind that prevent what would be a normal ability to think rationally. In other words, aberrations are persistent irrational views and behaviors brought about by en-grams that prohibit an individual's ability to as-is these distortions. Auditing eliminates engrams and permits the as-ising of the fallacious thinking associ-ated with them. Cognitions usually occur immediately after an erasure of an engram along with the chain connected to it (Hubbard 1976c: 373). Noteworthy is that the E-Meter's "floating needle" may confirm this end phenomenon (Hubbard 1982: 18).

Auditing with the E-Meter

As was discussed earlier, in E-Meter training the auditor has the ability to recognize a specific thought that occurs at the moment of a command. She can accurately locate items that may either exist below the level of the preclear's consciousness or unacknowledged items the preclear consciously does not wish to confront or admit. In these cases, the preclear is again given the same command. Every subsequent time that the command is given, the auditor looks again for that "read" and identifies it for the preclear with a "That's it" or "There it is."

In the first situation, in which the item is below a conscious level, the subsequent commands raise the item to the level of consciousness, which is then identified by the preclear in a response to the command. It is in these areas that past life events, known as "whole track," are sometimes reported. If the needle does not "float" with this reply, then the auditor queries deeper until the earliest incident is found on the track and "flattened." This means that there is no charge left in the incident and is producing a floating needle and possibly some type of cognition.

In the case in which the preclear consciously did not want to admit something, either she will eventually confess it, or, if she does not nor will not, the session moves on to additional levels of auditing queries to find its resolution. Sometimes the issue must be resolved as a nonauditing procedure handled by org staff members trained in the area of ethics before auditing can proceed. In this context, ethics are principles of right and wrong conduct. Such ethics challenges may deal with an array of illegal, immoral, and dishonest activities that the preclear does not want anyone, or at least the auditor, to find out.

One type of auditing that may induce the above scenarios is a preparatory auditing cycle known as "rudiments," which have to be administered to the preclear by her auditor at the beginning of the session before auditing can occur. Rudiment auditing includes what are known as "ARC breaks," "present time problems," "withholds," or other prepared lists (Hubbard 1976d: 46). These will be explained and shown how they are used in the following description of setting up a typical auditing cycle.

With the preclear sitting in front of the auditor, the auditor asks the preclear to pick up the E-Meter cans and starts by stating, "This is the session." The first command is, "Do you have an ARC break?" This condition is usually an emotional upset. If, upon the command, the meter "reads," the auditor informs the preclear of this fact and asks her about it. If the preclear cannot identify what could have caused the read, then a series of additional commands will locate the issue to obtain a floating needle. The next command is, "Do you have a present time problem?" If this reads, the issue is pursued in a similar manner to a floating needle. The last command in this rudiment cycle is, "Has a withhold been missed?" A "withhold" is an unspoken, unannounced transgression against a moral code. The question posed in the auditing command asks if someone, including the auditor, should have found out about (or almost found out about) a withhold that preclear was harboring. If it reads, the auditor indicates this to the preclear and is probed through a series of commands to a floating needle.

If a floating needle was not achieved in any of the three components of these rudiments, any auditing that the preclear was expecting to have done cannot proceed. In this case, the auditor would end the session and notify the case supervisor. The supervisor would review the auditing file, possibly speak with the preclear, and recommend a course of action for the preclear to rectify the situation so that she could get back on the Bridge.

Conclusion

The training and auditing described in this project is but the tip of the theological iceberg containing the doctrines, the teachings, and sacred rituals of Scientology. Hubbard, a pioneer in New Age technology, created a novel window of opportunity through his creative visions into the sacred ordering of the universe. Notable in his work is the notion of "clearing the planet" by training auditors throughout the world. Through the disciplined tenets of Scientology, humans in increasing numbers from every region of the globe can step into the stellar realms of awareness that Hubbard institutionalized through the auditing process. This is similar to the way adherents viewed and participated in the spiritual worlds created by religious entrepreneurs, reformers, and spiritual figureheads such as Buddha, Emma Curtis Hopkins, and Mary Baker Eddy who, in their time, structured their particular universe into novel paradigms of thinking.

Scientology's mystique is an enigma to the public, to scholars who study new religious movements, and to traditional religious groups, who feel threatened by the power and prestige presented through the sometimes eye-catching displays of architecture and media publications that earmark Scientology venues. The pluralism of religion in America nurtured its beginnings. Will the pluralism of America eventually spawn a rival religious movement that will encroach upon Scientology's power as a major player in the arena of new religious movements? Maybe. Maybe not. Auditing, its most sacred process, has yielded interesting results with a variety of people—rich, perhaps some poor, but mostly middle-class people—struggling to re-identify with their spiritual essence (called "thetan" in Scientology), within a world enchained in engrams resulting in a wasteland of chaos and debris.

For specific reasons detailed in this chapter, Scientologists find a unique salvation in the auditing process, a confessional of conscience, and pathway up the Bridge to enlightenment. Scientology has been zealous in defending its theological turf and has conspicuously grown from its theoretical beginnings with its founder L. Ron Hubbard (who grew up in a rural America) to have an uptown presence. Other made-in-America religions have similar histories. Old mainline Christian traditions are also caught in the crunch to keep membership high and attrition low. All religions face contemporary challenges, not only from a pluralistic cultural milieu, but from political, religious, and governmental hazards encountered with globalization, critical economic and environmental changes coupled with natural disasters. Scientologists have joined other religious organizations and groups upon the planet with a new theological method. As William James might have said, they are the new kids on the block of the mind cure movement. Their desire to become "Clear" through the auditing process and free of entanglements, not only for this lifetime but also in expectancy for others to come, is commendable in a world frequently cluttered with pain, sorrow, and poverty. The missionaries, ministers, and members of this religion are grappling with and against elemental and sophisticated forces of the human, natural, and spiritual universe to get to the ideal of "Clear" for the planet—meanwhile preparing themselves for lifetimes of dedicated service to the earth and its peoples.

NOTES

1. See Miller, *America's Alternative Religions.*

2. See Wessinger, *Women's Leadership.*

3. For further discussion see Neusner, *World Religions in America.* Articles by Dell deChant and Danny Jorgensen and other writers give excellent information about a number of made in America religions.

4. Eddy, *Science and Health.*

5. Metteyya is the Pali spelling for Maitreya (Buddhist 105).

6. ARC is an abbreviation for "affinity, reality and communication": the components of "understanding."

7. The Mark VII is essentially identical to the VI except for an additional digital display for the tone arm (TA) setting that is assessed on the VI as a position of the tone arm knob on a circular numerical scale.

8. Data plate on this Mark VI reads in part: "HUBBARD ELECTROMETER MANUFACTURING DIVISION," "SERIAL # 9355" and "DATE OKED TO AUDIT 7MAR90."

9. The *reactive mind, unconscious mind, reactive bank, engram bank,* and *bank* are synonyms for that portion of the mind that stores engrams (Hubbard 1981).

10. A "secondary," or secondary engram, is "a period of anguish brought about by a major loss or a threat of loss to the individual"; the secondary "depends for its strength and force upon physical pain engrams that underlie it" (Hubbard 1981: 377).

11. A "lock" is dependent on secondaries or engrams; it is a moment of severe restimulation of an engram; it is a "mental image picture of a non-painful but disturbing experience" (Hubbard 1981: 234–235).

12. The "time track" is "the consecutive record of mental image pictures which accumulates through the preclear's life or lives" (Hubbard 1981: 439).

13. Precepts are "specialized data from the standard memory or reactive banks which represent and reproduce the sense messages of a moment in the past" (Hubbard 1981: 296).

14. "Erase" means that "the engram has disappeared from the engram bank" (Hubbard 1981: 145).

15. The "basic" is "the first engram on any chain of similar engrams" (Hubbard 1985: 456); also "the first incident (engram, lock, overt act) on any chain" (Hubbard 1981: 38).

16. When the preclear closes her eyes she enters, according to Hubbard, an awakened form of consciousness called "reverie" (Hubbard 1985: 470).

17. An "end phenomenon," or "E/P," is defined as "those indicators on the preclear and E-meter which show that a chain or process is ended. It shows . . . that a basic on that chain . . . has been erased" (Hubbard 1981: 139).

REFERENCES

Christensen, Dorthe Refslund. "Rethinking Scientology: Cognition and Representation in Religion, Therapy and Soteriology." Ph.D. Diss. University of Aarhus, Denmark, 1999.
deChant, Dell and Danny Jorgensen. "The Church of Scientology: A Very New American Religion." In *World Religions in America*, 3rd ed., ed. Jacob Neusner. Louisville: Westminster John Knox Press, 2003.
Eddy, Mary Baker. *Science and Health with Key to the Scriptures*. Boston: Christian Science Publishing, 1935.
Harley, Gail M. *Emma Curtis Hopkins: Forgotten Founder of New Thought*. Syracuse: Syracuse University Press, 2002.
———. *Hindu and Sikh Faiths in America*. New York: Facts on File, 2003.
Hopkins, Emma Curtis. *High Mysticism*. Marina del Rey, CA: DeVorss, 1923/1983.
Hubbard, L. Ron. *The Book Introducing the E-meter*. Los Angeles: Bridge Publications, 1975.
———. *The Book of E-meter Drills*. Los Angeles: Bridge Publications, 1979.
———. *Dianetics: The Modern Science of Mental Health*. Los Angeles: Bridge Publications, 1950/1985.
———. *Dianetics and Scientology Technical Dictionary*. Los Angeles: Bridge Publications, 1981.
———. *E-meter Essentials 1961*. Los Angeles: Bridge Publications, 1982.
———. *Hymn of Asia: An Eastern Poem*. Los Angeles: Golden Era Productions, 2000.
———. *The Organization Executive Course: An Encyclopedia of Scientology Policy*, vol. 0, Basic Staff Volume. Los Angeles: Bridge Publications, 1986.
———. *The Organization Executive Course: An Encyclopedia of Scientology Policy*, vol. 3, Treasury Division. Los Angeles: Church of Scientology, 1969.
———. *The Organization Executive Course*, vol. 3, Treasury Division. Los Angeles: Bridge Publications, 1991a.
———. *The Organization Executive Course*, vol. 6, Treasury Division. Los Angeles: Bridge Publications, 1991b.
———. *Scientology 0–8: The Book of Basics*. Los Angeles: Bridge Publications, 1982.
———. *The Technical Bulletins of Dianetics and Scientology*, vol. I. Los Angeles: Church of Scientology, 1976a.
———. *The Technical Bulletins of Dianetics and Scientology*, vol. III. Los Angeles: Church of Scientology, 1976b.
———. *The Technical Bulletins of Dianetics and Scientology*, vol. VI. Los Angeles: Church of Scientology, 1976c.
———. *The Technical Bulletins of Dianetics and Scientology*, vol. VII. Los Angeles: Church of Scientology, 1976d.
———. *The Technical Bulletins of Dianetics and Scientology: Auditing Series*, vol. IX. Los Angeles: Church of Scientology, 1976e.

James, William. *The Varieties of Religious Experience: A Study in Human Nature.* London: Routledge, 1902/2002.

Melton, J. Gordon. *The Church of Scientology.* Salt Lake City: Signature Books, 2000.

Miller, Timothy, ed. *America's Alternative Religions.* New York: State University of New York Press, 1995.

Neusner, Jacob, ed. *World Religions in America,* 3rd ed. Louisville: Westminster John Knox Press, 2003.

Robinson, Richard H., and Willard L. Johnson. *The Buddhist Religion: A Historical Introduction,* 4th ed. Belmont: Wadsworth Publishing Company, 1997.

Waldman, Amy. "Changed Lives; Religious Leader Takes His Calling to Ground Zero." *New York Times,* Sept. 20, 2001.

Wallis, Roy. *The Road to Total Freedom: A Sociological Analysis of Scientology.* New York: Columbia University Press, 1977.

Wessinger, Catherine, ed. *Women's Leadership in Marginal Religions: Explorations Outside the Mainstream.* Urbana: University of Illinois Press, 1993.

PART IV

Sources and Comparative Approaches

IO

Scientology as Technological Buddhism

Frank K. Flinn

In several ways Scientology is the most interesting of the new religious movements. It describes itself as "an applied religious philosophy,"[1] but it does not fall easily under any exclusive label such as *religion, science, philosophy,* or *technique.* In a situation like this the chances are many for misclassification and misinterpretation. For the time being, some designation like "new religious movement" or "alternative religious movement" seems the most appropriate for describing these recently recognized religious phenomena.

Interpreting a New Religion

The traditional sociological classification derived from Ernst Troeltsch's *The Social Teaching of the Christian Churches* (church, denomination, sect, and cult) has encountered difficulties.[2] This is particularly true for the terms *sect* and *cult,* which have been most often applied to the newer religious groups. It is important to note that these are *relational* terms. Thus, the concept of sect takes on sharper definitional focus when related to organized churches that have become diffuse in doctrine and practice. Rodney Stark has captured this relational aspect well when he wrote that sects "reflect the efforts of the churched to remain churched."[3] The condition, then, for sect formation seems to be the presence of strongly organized churches. Conversely, the concept of cult takes on sharper definitional focus when related not to church, denomination, or sect, but to a prior condition of secularity. In Stark's words, the cult represents "efforts by the unchurched to become churched."

This definitional clarification, however, does not allow an unambiguous application of either cult or sect to Scientology. Sectarian movements are characterized by their "over-againstness" to organized religion, that is, they are separated from and contrasted to other religions. Yet, one characteristic peculiar to many of the new religions—including Scientology, Unificationists, and Charismatics—is the fact that they are *pluri-denominational,* or *trans-denominational* in the religious affiliation of their adherents. Scientologists can remain in good standing as Scientologists even if they continue to participate in their natal or previously acquired religion. This is a widespread phenomenon among many new religions and even among some traditional ones.

A year ago I attended a gathering of the Full Gospel Businessmen's Association in St. Louis. This Pentecostal movement was started in 1952 by Demos Shakarian.[4] At one point in the meeting the people in the audience were asked to identify their religious affiliation. About one-third identified themselves as belonging to some traditional Pentecostal group. The rest were fairly evenly distributed among Episcopalians, Lutherans, Roman Catholics, Reformed Church, and other mainline denominations. Conversations with these and other Pentecostals led me to think that they are not the churched striving to remain churched, but they are the churched trying to get a spiritual dimension into their lives.

Charismatic Catholics in particular react to the traditional "propositional" faith of the catechism. They want to "feel" or "experience" their faith. Hence, their emphasis is mainly on the energizing experience of "the gifts of the Holy Spirit." Yet these Charismatic Catholics still attend traditional religious services, often with renewed fervor. Scientologists have told me similar stories about returning to their natal religious group with a new understanding of what that traditional faith was all about. Instead of "over-againstness," there seems to be a "two-way traffic" between the traditional and the new in many of these movements. Postmodern faith seems to be getting poly*spheric* rather than simply "ecumenical" or, in sectarian terms, "exclusivistic." If this is sectarianism, then it is a new kind of sectarianism. Over time, the expectation is that Scientologists will center more and more on their own religious practices. And this seems, indeed, to be taking place.

The term *cult* presents its own problems. If understood as the effort of the unchurched to become churched, then it may be cautiously applied to Scientology. I have conducted numerous "spiritual autobiography" interviews with Scientologists and have been astounded by the number of different religious groups they have previously joined or associated with. Most members can be described as "seekers," but their search does not have a fixed pattern. Some tried various traditional religions, others tried born-again groups, and still others had been through more esoteric astrological and meditationist affiliations. Although Scientology may be just another stage in their search, most members, when asked what Scientology did for them that their prior groups did not do, replied with the words "the tech" (auditing technology). The "tech" is "standard," in other words, authoritatively set down by L. Ron Hubbard. As we shall see further, the development of a "standard" in the technology is functionally equivalent to "infallibility" in Roman Catholicism or to the "inerrancy" of Scripture in fundamentalist Protestantism. This characteristic does not correspond to "epistemological individualism," which is said to be the mark of a cult.[5] If one way of distinguishing a cult from a sect is to say that a cult is an aggregation of the "like-minded" whereas the sect is a congregation of the "like-committed," then Scientology falls in the camp of the sectarians.

Much of this depends upon where we are going to slice the pie. Although I do not want to say that the pie cannot or ought not to be sliced, the arbitrariness of the initial cut leaves me uneasy. I am uneasy, too, about what has happened to the word *cult* in the popular media. The popular image of a cult—a deranged, tyrannical leader; "brainwashing"; and bizarre beliefs and practices—may have rendered the word permanently damaged for analytic purposes. Furthermore, the word *cult* now impinges upon the legal interpretation and definition of what constitutes a religion. The U.S. Constitution uses only one word—*religion*—to designate the phenomenon we are talking about. Many anticultists believe that they have *ipso facto* established a religious group as a "pseudo-religion" if they have managed to get the group labeled as a "cult" in court proceedings. Elsewhere I have argued that, from a constitutional viewpoint, judiciary can determine only *that* a group is, or is not, a religion; it cannot describe *how* a group is a religion.[6] In other words, whether a group is a church, denomination, sect, or cult is constitutionally irrelevant. To make distinctions like these in court proceedings would be to establish certain religions (the traditional ones) over others (the innovative ones). If making such distinctions is not an actual establishment, it certainly is *respecting* an establishment.

The above reasons convince me that we need to temper sociological analyses with a more phenomenological and hermeneutical approach to the new religions. I take it as a primary hermeneutical principle that the interpreter must first interpret a text or tradition as it interprets itself. That is to say, I cannot presume that I understand the interpretant better than it understands itself.[7] For example, this principle states that I cannot read a religious text unless I let it in some way read me. For authentic interpretation to take place, there needs to be what Hans-Georg Gadamer calls a "merging of horizons," my own and the text's.[8] But this cannot take place unless I enter into the horizon of what the text intends and let its world of representation, categories, and figures of speech appear and speak to my own world of representation. This reciprocal principle of interpretation does not require that I believe *what* the believer believes but asks that I take a step in the direction of believing *as* the believer believes. In the attempt to understand Islam, for example, I do not become a Muslim. But I can approximate that which is "alien" to me in the Muslim's world of representation. W. Brede Kristensen writes, "By means of empathy (the historian or interpreter) tries to relive in his own experience that which 'alien,' and that, too, he can only approximate."[9]

The Ambiguity of Being "Clear"

Scientology bears many close resemblances to Buddhism. This affinity is part of Scientology's own self-understanding: "A Scientologist is a first cousin to the Buddhist."[10] The central Scientological term "Clear" is roughly equivalent to the Buddhist concept of *bodhi,* which describes "the one awake" or "enlightened one" who has gained releasement *(moksa)* from the entangling threads of existence and illusion.[11] By undergoing the auditing techniques, Scientologists hope to rid themselves of "engrams"—mental images or "facsimiles" of past pain, injury or harm that prevent the believer from being "at cause" over matter, energy, space, and time (MEST).[12] In interviews, Scientologists describe the state of being "Clear" as being active rather than passive over one's life situation. They also identify it with "freedom" and "awareness." Although Scientologists ascribe the discovery of the "auditing technology" to L. Ron Hubbard's independent "research," they nonetheless recognize the Buddhist tradition as part of the church's "antecedents and background." Indeed, the many levels and grades of the auditing process can be seen as a refinement and resignification of the Buddhist Eightfold Path in a space-age context.[13] In this respect, Scientology is Buddhism made applicable.

The term *Clear,* however, has another meaning in Scientology. It also refers to the button on the calculator that "clears" the machine of all previous entries and mistakes and allows for reprocessing of information. "Really, that is all a Clear is. Clears are beings who have been cleared of wrong answers or useless answers which keep them from living or thinking."[14] This technological image suggests that the "atomic elements" of Buddhism, obviously present in Scientology, have been transmuted into a new "molecular compound" that is characteristic of North American technologism. In *Scientology: A World Religion Emerges in the Space Age* the Buddhistic elements that coincide with Scientology are enumerated: (1) knowing for oneself, or personal experience, as the test of truth, (2) a scientific understanding of cause and effect in matters of the Spirit *(karma),* (3) Buddhism's "pragmatic" concern with human problem solving rather than metaphysics, (4) the Middle Path, which centers on Man and "the dynamics of Human development," (5) the democratic spirit in Buddhism, and (6) the emphasis on individual action.[15] Any one of these gems could have been taken directly from Bacon's *Novum Organon* or William James's *Pragmatism.* Notably absent from the list, as well as from technological pragmatism, is my emphasis on meditation and contemplation.

This analysis presents a special problem. How can the realm of "religion" include what we have come to know as "technology"? The popular mind places these two concepts miles apart, but their conjunction may be a characteristic peculiar to late modernity. By *technology* I mean the linguistic union of *techne* (craft, art, making) with *logos* (word, reason, rationale) so that "knowing" is copenetrated with "making" or "doing."[16] It is important to realize that, though the term *technology* is derived from Greek, the ancient Greek thinkers would have never joined these two words in this way. Knowing for the sake of knowing was an end in itself for the Greeks and could never be placed on the same level with "doing" or "action." *Technology* is a neologism that first came into use around 1615. Surprisingly, we discover that the Latin *technologia* made its first appearance in Puritan *theological* circles. The Puritan divine rejected the old-world *metaphysica,* by which the liberal arts were aimed in the direction of contemplation, prayer, and meditation, in favor of *technologia* or the rationale of the arts aimed in the direction of *eupraxia,* right use or employment. In the New England mind, Perry Miller wrote, "technologia and theology coincided."[17]

The New England primal opening to technologia paved the royal road for the reception of Francis Bacon's new "active science" by which nature was put "under constraint and vexed . . . when by art and the hand of man she is forced out of her natural state and squeezed and molded."[18] Technological Baconianism is much more than "applied science" or a methodology for making useful products. It is also a mode for apprehending the world that has imbued the fundamental thrust of all North American life, including its religion. What differentiates religious fundamentalism, for example, from theological liberalism in North America is not that the former rejects the findings of science and the latter accepts them, but that the fundamentalists accepted the Baconian wave of science whereas the liberals accepted both Baconian empiricism *and* Darwinian evolutionism.[19] Bacon interpreted the Book of Nature as an array of "instances" whereby mankind could wrest power from natural forces, whereas the fundamentalists scrutinized the Book of Scripture for "evidences" whereby one could find the right formula for the conduct of life. From this perspective, Scientology may be a variation of a hybrid seed planted long ago at Plymouth Rock.

Max Weber once contrasted Buddhism and Calvinism as "ideal types," respectively, of a "world-negating" and a "world-affirming" religion.[20] I think Weber's typology needs to be modified in light of a phenomenon like Scientology. Scientology has recast certain elements of Buddhism in a mold that nonetheless receives its shape from the egalitarian technologism pervasive in North American culture. Like pragmatism, the only indigenous philosophy to arise in North America, Scientology underlines the word *applied* in its self-definition as an "*applied* religious philosophy."

From Dianetics to Scientology

Before discussing the characteristics of Scientology as technological Buddhism, I need to say something about the transition from Dianetics to Scientology proper. In this regard, two of L. Ron Hubbard's writings are of paramount importance: *Dianetics: The Modern Science of Mental Health,* first published in 1950, and *Scientology: The Fundamentals of Thought,* first published in 1956. There were preliminary drafts of both works, as well as intermediate writings such as *Science of Survival* (1951), but the above two books clearly mark a watershed between the two phases of the movement.

Although Dianetics has many transempirical and religious overtones, it falls in the category of a "mind-cure" therapy. Many commentators claim that Scientology is mental therapy masquerading as a religion. The crux of the question, however, is whether one can separate "therapy" from "religion" or even from "philosophy" by a hard-and-fast rule. The word *therapeuo* (to heal, cure, restore) occurs frequently in the New Testament and refers to both spiritual and physical healings by Jesus of Nazareth.[21] Indeed, there seem to be many kinds of therapy, like the Platonic philosophical sequence: ignorance–conversion to dialectic–illumination, and the Christian religious sequence: sin–repentance through grace–salvation.[22] There are also many kinds of medical and psycho-analytic therapies, like the Freudian sequence: neurosis–analysis–normality; and the radical behaviorist therapy: nervous disorder–modification through psychotropic drugs/psychosurgery-altered behavior.

Dianetics, too, has its therapeutic sequence: aberration (reactive mind)–removal of engrams through auditing–"Clear" analytical mind. We shall dis-cuss later how this sequence was modified in the Scientology phase of the movement. In terms of the therapeutic models here exemplified, Dianetics stands closer to the philosophical and religious models than to the psycho-analytic and behaviorist models. The Scientology movement in both its phases has stressed that the term *psychiatry* literally means "healing the soul" and has always opposed physicalist solutions to what members consider mental and/or spiritual problems.[23]

Although Dianetics had religious and spiritual tendencies, it was not yet a religion in the full sense of the term. A number of factors can be pointed out here. First, Dianetics did not promise what may be called "transcendental" rewards as the outcome of its therapy. It did, however, promise "transnormal" rewards. In the book *Dianetics*, "Clears" are opposed to "preclears," neophytes striving to get clear, and "normals," the people on the street. Clears do not catch colds (p. 107), are unrepressed (p. 38), do paranormal mental computations and have "complete recall" (p. 179), have keener perceptions and improve their eye-sight (p. 32), and are entirely free of "all psychoses, compulsions and repressions (all aberrations) and . . . any autogenic (self-generated) diseases referred to as psycho-somatic ills" (p. 30). In sum, "the Dianetic Clear is to a current normal individual as the current normal person is to the severely insane" (p. 15). Second, in the Dianetics stage of the movement, engrams were traced back to the fetal stage at the earliest (pp. 265 ff.). Third, Dianetics had only four "dynamics" or "urges for survival"—self, sex, group, and mankind (p. 10). Fourth, the auditing techniques in the Dianetics phase were fairly developed, but the "E-Meter" (an electrogalvanometer commonly known as the "lie detector" and used to gauge electrical resistance on the skin), had not yetcome into use.

There has been much debate as to when Scientology began to be a reli-gion. One can point to the incorporation of the Hubbard Association of Sci-entologists in Phoenix, Arizona, in 1952, and then to the establishment of the Founding Church of Scientology in 1954. Legal incorporation, however, does not tell us when the specifically religious concepts took shape in the church's self-understanding. These debates, however, remind one of the nineteenth-century disputes on when Christianity began: during Jesus's lifetime? at Pente-cost? through the ministry of Paul and the Apostles? I think it is more helpful to see the transition from Dianetics to Scientology in terms of the four factors discussed above.

First, the transition between the two phases of the movement can be seen in the shift from the "transnormal" to the "transempirical" or "transcendental" in the understanding of "Clear." In the book Dianetics, a *Clear* is defined as "the optimum individual: no longer possessed of any engrams" (p. 426). In *Scientology: The Fundamentals of Thought* (1956) and thereafter, *Clear* was no longer defined simply as the optimization of mind and abilities but as "a thetan who can be at cause knowingly and at will over mental matter, energy, space, and time as regards the first dynamic (survival for self)."[24] The concept *thetan* no longer refers to a mental state but is analogous to the Christian concept of "spirit" or "soul" that is, it is immortal and is above both brain and mind. Secondly, the notion of *engram* chains was extended beyond the fetal state to include "past lives and past deaths." In *Science and Survival* (1951), Hubbard, voicing his wariness of "spiritualism," nonetheless cautioned auditors not to "invalidate" evidence for past lives and past deaths showing up in the auditing sessions. Thirdly, the four dynamics of the Dianetics phase were augmented to include "animal," "universe," "spirit" (thetan), and "Infinity" or "God."[25] Fourthly, there was the introduction of the "E-Meter" into the auditing session. Due to a court case, the church places a qualification on the use of the E-Meter: "The E-Meter is not intended or effective for diagnosis, treatment or prevention of disease."[26] From the perspective I am suggesting, however, the use of the E-Meter is better seen as a "technological sacrament." Just as Christians define a sacrament (e.g., baptism) as an "outward or visible sign of inward or invisible grace," so Scientologists see the E-Meter as an external or visible indicator of an internal or invisible state ("Clear").

The four factors that demarcate the transition from Dianetics to Scientology changed the fundamental character of the therapeutic sequence. No longer was the goal simply to get "Clear" but also to become an Operating Thetan (OT). Thus, the Gradation Chart was expanded to include levels both for pre-clear to Clear, and for post-Clear (Operating Thetan) and beyond. The introduction of the notions of past lives/deaths and "thetan" caused considerable dissension within the movement between those who wanted to retain the more empirical base of the earlier Dianetics and those who wanted to be more open to spiritual implications of the movement. The essential differences between Dianetics and Scientology can be summarized in the following diagram.

	Therapeutic Sequence		Dynamics	
Dianetics	pre-Clear fetal engrams	auditing verbal only	Clear	self sex group mankind
Scientology	pre-Clear past life/ death	auditing verbal+ E-Meter	clear+ Operating Thetan	four above animal universe spirit infinity/ God

After the development of the ideas specific to Scientology proper, the movement gradually assumed more characteristics of what is classically known as a "church." Most important was the centralization of authority in Hubbard and the Executive Council Worldwide and the development of an ecclesiastical policy. The relation between Hubbard and the Executive Council Worldwide looks remarkably like the relation between the Pope and the Roman Curia or between a bishop and his chancery. The policy statements, which are in a state of evolution, also remind one of Canon Law. Finally, there was also the formalization of a Creed, the introduction of religious ceremonials for "naming," marriage and burial, and the appointment of ministers.

The evolution of Dianetics into Scientology is both continuous and discontinuous. On one hand, in the church's current self-understanding, Dianetics remains a "substudy" of Scientology and is used for "Dianetic Pastoral Counseling."[27] Likewise, Hubbard introduced the notion of "theta" energy as a "postulate" to explain what he believed to be empirical and experimental evidence.[28] On the other hand, the notion of past lives/deaths and Operating Thetan, the use of the E-Meter, the addition of new "dynamics," and the centralization of authority are not continuous with what had gone on before. Whatever else may be said about the transition from Dianetics to Scientology, it is quite true that Dianetics promised "transnormal" rewards to its adherents, whereas Scientology is now promising "transcendental," "supranatural" rewards to its believers: total freedom, complete knowingness, the meaning of life and death, and the meaning of the universe.

Scientology's Self-Understanding: Seven Characteristics

In this section I discuss seven characteristics that are central to Scientology's self-understanding. These characteristics can be compared and contrasted to notions that inform the traditional religious consciousness of the West. The characteristics also tell us something about Scientology as a fusion of technology and Buddhism.

I. RESEARCH VERSUS REVELATION. Religions like Judaism and Christianity approach the dimension of the sacred "from the top down." The sacred is believed to come to humans in an external revelation (e.g., Moses and the burning bush), which is delivered from "above" and which is then codified into a sacred scripture. Other religious traditions, however, approach the dimension of the sacred "from the bottom up" or "from the inward to the outward." Instead of looking upward for a revelatory experience that is deemed beyond human capacity, this latter type of religion looks inward for the illumination of the sacred. Both Buddhism and Scientology fall into this second category. There have been examples of the second type within Christianity. Certain Christian groups like the Quakers, which have stressed the doctrine of Glorification/Sanctification (Holy Spirit) over the doctrines of Creation (Father) and Redemption (Son) have had a tendency to be illuminationist rather than revelationist. Scientology adds a "scientific" framework to its Buddhistic base. Scientologists universally express the belief that Hubbard's discoveries are founded on "research" even when this means examining religious teachings from other traditions. The research model has allowed the movement to be rather open-ended: This explains, for example, much about the transition from Dianetics to Scientology as well as the seemingly endless subdivision and expansion of the levels of auditing.[29] The research model also reinforces experimental and experiential knowing for oneself. The common expression is "If it is not true for you, it is not true." There are qualifications to this dictum.

2. STANDARDNESS VERSUS INFALLIBILITY/INERRANCY. Although Scientology places a high priority on knowing for oneself, there is one aspect of the religious system that functions as an absolute or near absolute. That is the "standardness" of "the tech." The standardness of the technology in Scientology can be compared to the doctrine of infallibility of the pope and magisterium in Roman Catholicism and the doctrine of the inerrancy in scripture in certain branches of Protestantism. Whereas infallibility and inerrancy guarantee the content of teaching ("the message"), the doctrine of standardness in technical application guarantees the form of the teaching in Scientology ("the medium").

The doctrine of standardness arose in response to splinter groups and competing "researchers" in the early phases of the movement.[30] In the crucial HCO Policy Letter, dated February 7, 1965, and entitled "Keeping Scientology Working," Hubbard arrogated to himself all the basic discoveries in the technology:

> In all the years I have been engaged in research I have kept my
> comm lines wide open for research data. I once had the idea that
> a group could evolve the truth. A third of a century has thoroughly
> disabused me of that idea. Willing as I was to accept suggestions and
> data, only a handful of suggestions (less than twenty) had long run
> value and none were major or basic; and when I did accept major or
> basic suggestions and used them, we went astray and I repented and
> eventually had to "eat crow."[31]

Today, when a question about the technology arises in auditing situations, individuals are discouraged from giving their own interpretation. Instead, members are required to check out in the technical manuals any subject that has come under question. Thus "standardness" is preserved. It may be assumed that after Hubbard's death "the tech" will assume canonical status. The control that Hubbard has exerted over the standardness of "the tech" can be compared with the efforts of sectarian leaders to maintain control over the printed word in order to hold in check the centrifugal forces that the spread of a movement sets into play.

3. KNOWINGNESS VERSUS FAITH/REASON. In the Western religious heritage there has always been a tension, and sometimes actual conflict, between faith and reason, or between the revealed will of God and what mankind can know

on its own. In particular, Christianity has stressed that salvation does not come through knowledge but through faith. In Scientology this tension or conflict does not form a part of the self-understanding of the adherents. Scientology defines itself as a "knowing how to know." "Knowingness," or "self-determined knowledge," is a comprehensive concept embracing what outsiders would distinguish as matters of faith and matters of knowledge.[32] Thus, Scientology includes within the notion of "knowingness" the knowledge of both spiritual and material things.

The self-understanding of Scientology as a *science* causes not a little confusion. In the culture at large, the term *science* is limited to knowledge that results from the observation of an experimentation with quantifiable material phenomena. However, we may note that the medieval theologians called theology the *scientia divina* or *scientia sacra* and even today the French refer to *les sciences religieuses*. Second, in North American religious circles, the self-interpretation of belief has had both an experiential and scientific coloring that dates from the Puritan conception of theology as *technologia*. Mary Baker Eddy, for example, called her principal theological treatise *The Science of Health: With a Key to the Scriptures*. Even the hermeneutics of the turn-of-the-century evangelical dispensationalists grounded itself on Scottish common sense philosophy and "a Baconian system, which first gathers the teachings of the word of God, and then seeks to deduce some general laws upon which the facts can be arranged."[33] Finally, Christians would tend to classify Scientology as a species of "gnosticism" or doctrine that "salvation comes through knowledge." Scientology, however, does not use the term *salvation* but *survival*.

4. ENGRAMS VERSUS SIN. Scientologists make a distinction between reactive mind and analytical mind. The reactive mind, roughly equivalent to the unconscious, records "engrams" or traces of pain, injury or impact.[34] *Engrams* are unconscious "mental image pictures" that result from traumas extending back to the fetal state and even to "past lives." Unless one is freed from these entangling engrams through the restimulation of the analytical mind (roughly, equivalent to consciousness), a person's survival ability, happiness, and intelligence are considered to be severely impaired. Engrams are discovered and eradicated through the techniques of the Dianetic auditing process. Someone freed from all engrams is called a "Clear." There are now levels of auditing for "post-Clears" or "Operating Thetans." The level "Clear" promises ability to be at cause over only the first dynamic (survival for self), but level OT VI and above, for example, promise "power on all 8 dynamics."[35]

The sequence engrams/Clear (and beyond) can be compared to the Christian sequence sin/justification or sin/forgiveness through grace. Consistent with its belief in an external revelation, Christianity maintains that the source of grace must come from outside. Consistent with its Buddhist-like notion of inner enlightenment, Scientology holds each member responsible for the eradication of engrams. Some have claimed that the addition of post-Clear levels of enlightenment amounts to a mystification of the notion of Clear. This kind of development, however, is not without precedent. St. Bonaventure's *Triplica Via* (threefold way divided into *purgatio, illuminatio,* and *perfectio*) was expanded into *sensatio, imaginatio, ratio, intellectus, intelligentia,* and *unio mystica* in his *Itinerarium Mentis in Deum.* All traditions of Zen Buddhism have multiple levels of meditation that developed over time.

5. ORGANIZATION VERSUS CHARISMA One of the unique features of Scientology has been the number of organizations that have been developed to apply the technology to areas like education, mental health reform, drug rehabilitation, prison reform.[36] One might even say that it is an organizational religion that meets the perceptions and needs of the organizational person of a mass society. Max Weber tended to see religious evolution as a transition from an original charismatic phase followed by a routinization of the charisma in rules, organizations, and specializations.[37] This model of interpretation needs to be modified to account for a phenomenon like Scientology. From one aspect, Hubbard functions as a "charismatic leader" and as the original "researcher." From another aspect, however, the "charismatic message" is the technology itself. It is as if technique and routinization were given charismatic legitimacy.

This aspect of Scientology invites us to rethink the definition of religion. *Webster's Dictionary* stresses only the system of beliefs, for example, a belief in the Supreme Being. Other definitions give equal weight to the cultus or rites. Few definitions, however, note the interplay between the belief system, the ritual practices and the organizational association, or congregation, which guarantees the maintenance of the beliefs and practices. The word *religion* is derived from *religare,* which means "to bind back together." This leads me to the broad definition of religion as a system of beliefs expressed in symbols that bind together the lives of individuals and/or groups, which issues in a set of religious practices (rituals), and which is sustained by an organized mode of life. The beliefs, practices, and mode of life bind together the lives of people so as to give their existence ultimate meaning. Although all religions have rudimentary elements of all three aspects, some, for example, stress the organizational system, or mode of life, over the belief system or the ritual practices. In Scientology we see an example of a group that began with religious practices (the auditing techniques), soon developed a strong ecclesiastical structure, and only then formalized its belief system into a creed. This does not mean that the belief system was not latent in the earlier phases of the church's evolution. It simply was not codified in a formal manner the way the organizational technology was from the start.

6. TECHNIQUE VERSUS CEREMONY. The ritual practice centers on the techniques of the auditing process. The church later instituted traditional ceremonies for initiation or christening, marriage, and funerals. This may simply be an accommodation to the standard image of religion in North America and the beginnings of an incipient denominalization. By their nature, ceremonies tend to be "world maintaining," confirmatory of the status quo, and dedicated

to preserving tradition. Ritual, on the other hand, is "person transforming," demarcative not of social states but of social transitions, and open to social innovation.[38] Scientology may be said to have "technological rituals."

In the narrow sense of the term, *technique* is the purposive-rational application of the empirico-analytic sciences for the sake of acquiring mastery over the external environment. Scientology inverts this understanding of technique and sees it as a symbolic-interpretative model for acquiring mastery over the internal environment of the psychic processes. This internalization of the model of technique seems common in technological civilization. Even "humanistic" management psychologists are now defining human beings as "information processing centers." This certainly illustrates Jacques Ellul's observation that "when technique enters into every area of life, including the human, it ceases to be external to man and becomes his very essence."[39] Many critics of technological consciousness, including Jacques Ellul, see in it the suppression of symbolic interaction in favor of purposive-rational work, the repression of the ethical, and the fettering of free and open communication in favor of technical problem solving. Scientology shares no such fears of technology. Rather, by internalizing and symbolizing the model of technological consciousness, Scientology expects to bring about total communication and total freedom. Whether the technological model ends up confirming or transforming the social status quo remains to be seen, but the aggressiveness and ingenuity with which the church has pursued the Freedom of Information Act, prison reform, drug rehabilitation and other social ends certainly speaks for the reformational and transformational role the church chooses for itself.

7. SURVIVAL VERSUS SALVATION. In the dominant religious tradition of the West the ultimate future is seen in categories like salvation/damnation or heaven/hell. By contrast, Scientology takes a Darwinian view of the ultimate future and speaks of survival/succumbing. The fundamental "dynamics" of all existence are seen in terms of survival.[40] The ultimate benefit of the Dianetic auditing process is to give the individual "the highest possible potential of survival." Survival is not limited to the biological survival of the fittest but also embraces survival as spirit ("thetan") and survival to infinity (the eighth dynamic). The emphasis on survival reflects Hubbard's view of the threat posed by World War II. Like many postwar revitalization movements, Scientology looks toward survival in "abundance." The belief in the ultimate survival of humanity rests on a belief in mankind's basic goodness. The Creed of the church states the following:

> *And we of the Church believe:*
>   That man is basically good.
>   That he is seeking to survive.
>   That his survival depends upon himself and upon his fellows,
> and his attainment of brotherhood with the universe.

The Creed also states that *"the laws of God forbid Man . . . to destroy or reduce the survival of one's companion or one's group."*

The notion of survival has been raised here to the status of a religious concept. This is no different from the Latin word *salvere*, "to preserve, keep whole," serving as a metaphor for *salvation* in traditional religious imagery. The elevation of the notion of survival also reflects a religious response to the global effect of World War II and the use of the ultimate weapon during that war.

Conclusion

In *The Genealogy of Morals* Nietzsche predicted the coming of a European form of Buddhism that would represent "the beginning of the end, stagnation, nostalgic fatigue, a will that had turned *against* life."[41] In one sense Nietzsche's prediction has been correct. The Western religious tradition has been subjected to the destructive onslaught of critical consciousness—the disenchantment of the world, the decoding of dreams, the demystification of economic forces, and the demythologization of the scriptures themselves. One of the consequences of critical consciousness, I think, has been the turning of the twentieth century Westerners to the East for the revitalization of religious consciousness. Scientology represents one aspect of this turning to the East. Where Nietzsche's analysis goes awry is his underestimation of the resourcefulness of symbols to give new life and meaning to existence. Scientology's employment of Buddhistic elements has not led to an enervation of the will in a technological civilization but to an investment of technology itself with symbolic power that gives meaning to the believer's existence. Some may think this is "illusion," and others may think that Scientology does not constitute a "new religious molecule" but an unstable "amalgam," yet Scientology stands out among the new religions as the indigenization of Buddhism within a society that has technology as its cultural base.

Hegel was the first to point out that modern religion (the Protestant principle of inwardness) terminated in the Christianizing of the saeculum, which led to the secularization of Christianity itself.[42] As an example of postmodern religion, Scientology represents the resacralization and remythologization of the saeculum. Some may have expected the revitalization of Christianity itself rather than a fusion of Buddhism and technology. Though there are many examples of Christian vitalizing movements, the turn to the East and the investment of egalitarian technologism with mythic meaning may be just an exemplification of H. Richard Niebuhr's acute observation: "In the course of succeeding generations the heritage of faith with which liberalism has started was used up. The liberal children of liberal fathers needed to operate with ever diminishing capital."[43]

NOTES

The following abbreviations for official Scientology publications will be used:

BCS: *The Background and Ceremonies of the Church of Scientology of California*, World Wide (1970).

DMS: Dianetics: The Modern Science of Mental Health, A Handbook of Dianetic Therapy. New York: Paperback Library, 1950.

FOT: Scientology: The Fundamentals of Thought (1956).

OEC: The Organization Executive Course: An Encyclopedia of Scientology Policy (1972 ff.) Volumes 0–6.

SOS: Science of Survival: Prediction of Human Behavior (1951).

SWR: Scientology: A World Religion Emerges in the Space Age (1974).

WIS: What Is Scientology? (1978).

1. *WIS*, p. 3.

2. For a creative reinterpretation of the taxonomy, see Roy Wallis, "Yesterday's Children," in Bryan Wilson, ed., *The Social Impact of New Religious Movements* (Barrytown, N.Y.: Unification Theological Seminary, distr. Rose of Sharon Press, 1981), pp. 117–121.

3. Rodney Stark, "Must All Religions Be Supernatural?," in Wilson, p. 168.

4. Demos Shakarian (as told to John and Elizabeth Sherrill), *The Happiest People on Earth* (Old Tappan, N.J.: Spire Books, 1975).

5. See Wallis, p. 119.

6. See my article, "Law, Language and Religion," *New ERA Newsletter*, 1, no. 2 (May–June 1981).

7. See Leo Strauss, *On Tyranny, Revised and Enlarged* (Ithaca: Cornell University Press, 1963), p. 24.

8. Hans-Georg Gadamer, *Truth and Method* (New York: Seabury Press, 1975), pp. 273–274.

9. W. Brede Kristensen, *The Meaning of Religion*, trans. John B. Carman (The Hague: Martinus Nijoff, 1960), p. 7.

10. *WIS*, p. 7.

11. See Heinrich Zimmer, *Philosophies of India*, ed. Joseph Campbell (Princeton: Princeton University Press, 1951), pp. 464–487.

12. *WIS*, p. 332, s.v. "Clear."

13. *BCS*, pp. 13–15.

14. *WIS*, p. 332, s.v. "Clear."

15. *SWR*, pp. 9–10.

16. See George Grant, "The computer does not impose on us the ways it should be used," in *Beyond Industrial Growth*, ed. Abraham Rotstein (Toronto: University of Toronto Press, 1976), pp. 117–131.

17. Perry Miller, *The New England Mind: The Seventeenth Century* (Cambridge, Mass.: Harvard University Press, 1967), p. 166.

18. Francis Bacon, *The New Organon and Related Writings*, ed. Fulton H. Anderson (Indianapolis: Library of Liberal Arts, 1960), p. 25.

19. See George M. Marsden, *Fundamentalism and American Culture* (New York: Oxford University Press, 1980), pp. 55–62.

20. Max Weber, *The Protestant Ethic and the Spirit of Capitalism*, trans. Talcott Parsons (New York: Scribner's, 1958), pp. 98–128.

21. There is renewed interest in healing even within mainline Christianity. See Morton T. Kelsey, *Healing and Christianity in Ancient Thought and Modern Times* (New York: Harper & Row, 1973).

22. See George Grant, "Conceptions of Health," in *Psychiatry and Responsibility*, ed. Helmut Schoeck and James W. Wiggins (Princeton: Van Nostrand, 1962),

pp. 117–134. Grant notes that modern therapies have a clear conception of disease but an unclear conception of health.

23. In particular, Scientologists are opposed to the stimulus-response conception of man proposed by Wilhelm Wundt. See *WIS*, pp. 97–98.

24. *WIS*, p. 332, s.v. "Clear."

25. Cf. *DMS*, p. 10, and *FOT*, pp. 36–39.

26. See *WIS*, publication page (v).

27. See "To the Reader," *DMS*, p. 2.

28. *SOS*, I: 3–5.

29. See *WIS*, pp. 56–65.

30. On the splinter groups, see J. Gordon Melton, *The Encyclopedia of American Religions* (Wilmington: McGrath, 1978), II: 223 ff.; Roy Wallis, *The Road to Total Freedom: A Sociological Analysis of Scientology* (New York: Columbia University Press, 1977), pp. 84 ff.

31. *OEC*, 5: 44.

32. *WIS*, p. 336, s.v. "Knowingness" and p. 339, s.v. "Scientology."

33. Arthur T. Pierson, *Addresses on the Second Coming of the Lord: Delivered at the Prophetic Conference, Allegheny, Pa., December 3–5, 1895* (Pittsburgh, 1895), p. 82, quoted in Marsden, p. 55.

34. *WIS*, p. 334, s.v. "Engram(s)."

35. *WIS*, p. 64.

36. See *WIS*, pp. 85–139, for a survey of the organizations initiated by Scientology.

37. Max Weber, *From Max Weber: Essays in Sociology*, trans. and ed. H. H. Gerth and C. Wright Mills (New York: Oxford University Press, 1946), pp. 267, 297.

38. On the distinction between *ceremony* versus *ritual*, see Victor Turner, *The Forest of Symbols: Aspects of Ndembu Ritual* (Ithaca: Cornell University Press, 1970), p. 95.

39. Jacques Ellul, *The Technological Society*, trans. John Wilkinson (New York: Vintage Books, 1964), p. 6.

40. *SOS*, I: x–xi.

41. Friedrich Nietzsche, *The Birth of Tragedy and the Genealogy of Morals*, trans. Francis Golffing (New York: Doubleday Anchor Books, 1956), p. 154.

42. G. W. F. Hegel, *The Philosophy of History*, trans. J. Sibree (New York: Dover, 1956), pp. 341–346.

43. H. Richard Niebuhr, *The Kingdom of God in America* (New York: Harper Torchbooks, 1959), p. 194.

II

Scientology, a "New Age" Religion?

Andreas Grünschloß

Introductory Remarks

In the German context, the term *New Age* has almost vanished completely from the discourses in society as well as in academics.[1] This is due to the fact that the New Age label has been replaced by a broader use of the term *esotericism* (*Esoterik*), and even in academia the term is used only in a narrow sense nowadays, with reference to the "historical" and formative phase of a movement or "discourse" in the 1970s and '80s.[2] Accordingly, and different from the usage of the term in Anglophone contexts, contemporary people with alternative or esoteric religious orientations would not refer to themselves as "New Agers" in Germany at all, as it would still be possible in, for example, Great Britain. Accordingly, the title of this essay refers to the wider and unspecific notion of "New Age" as it is still established in the Anglophone context. Scientology has often been questioned with regard to its "religious" nature, and several scholars in the new religious movements area have even refrained from a closer study of Scientology. If Scientology is viewed as a religion at all—an issue that is again and again debated both in academic religious studies as well as in the quarrels about the legal status of this organization in various countries—it is mainly perceived as a candidate that might fit into this "alternative" realm of modern religiosity denoted by such labels like *New Age* or *Esotericism*. Following its formal beginning in the 1950s, the "Church of Scientology" has gradually surfaced as the most hotly debated movement during the second half of the twentieth century, and it continued to stimulate ongoing discussions up to the present. For a differentiated and unbiased answer to the question concerning the religious "nature" or "function" of Scientology, it is therefore necessary to recapitulate the historical formation of Scientology, its basic anthropological, soteriological, and cosmological convictions, as well as its rituals and institutions, and to relate these findings to the wider realm of contemporary, or older, religious movements—a task that obviously exceeds the scope of this chapter. Certainly, several aspects of Scientology don't fit easily into "traditional" concepts of religion, whereas others appear definitely "religious" again. The question of this chapter therefore is whether Scientology could be perceived as a typical esoteric or "New Age" version of religion and "Weltanschauung" within the context of our postmodern industrial society.

Approaching the Subject Heuristically

As a researcher in religious studies, my analysis of Scientology tries to do justice to the self-perception as accessible through primary sources and informants, but nevertheless such an academic study will not always remain fully compatible with the self-understanding of people inside Scientology, because the comparative insights and systematic thoughts developed in such an analysis—starting with the points on which one is focusing to identify "religious elements" in Scientology!—tend to differ from *emic* constructions inside the movement.[3] Such an inevitable "tension with believers"[4] becomes even more apparent when "critical" issues are raised concerning certain practices or aspects of "ethics" in Scientology, but the hermeneutical principles of a religious studies approach are strongly rooted within the complementary enlightenment virtues of *tolerance, criticism* and *distance.*[5]

By raising the question of whether Scientology is a "New Age" movement, I have to clarify what I have in mind when using the term "New Age." Having become a catchphrase in the 1970s and '80s, it implies the expectation of an imminent global change, in which certain anthropological, soteriological, and cosmological hopes merge: evolutionary optimism; a monistic cosmology and anthropology; a holistic view of life (including a merging of "science" and "religion"); a striving for levels of higher consciousness with spiritual, paranormal, ecological and peaceful implications; a syncretistic openness to various traditional religious discourses and spiritual practices (from shamanism or Buddhist or Yogic meditation up to revitalizations and reinventions of "pagan" elements); incorporation of therapeutic endeavors and insights; reenchanted forms of an "alternative" technology and sometimes a strong emphasis on the higher, light, *spiritual reign* over against a lower, dark reign of *matter* (etc.). Transcending the closed systems of traditional Theosophy, "New Age" is nevertheless a successor to this older esoteric stream of spiritual knowledge, traceable back through the works of Alice Bailey and down to the grand "Madame" Helena Petrovna Blavatsky. So the question is, how does Scientology fit into this?

Scientology itself is also far from being an easy, handy topic. When we talk about Scientology, we are faced with a multifaceted international organization that cannot be labeled easily within established categories of academic research or public discourse. To mention just a few attempts to identify Scientology, is

it a profit-oriented "business" operating according to hard-sell market principles? Or a *bona fide* "religion" along traditional or modern esoteric lines? Is it
primarily a therapeutic practice and attempt to create mental health or efficient
attentiveness with only a little surplus of "Weltanschauung"? Or is it even a
dangerous, antidemocratic and subversive transnational aiming at total power
in the modern world?

Scientology has been credited with positive aspects here and there, but
more often it has been criticized and stigmatized. It certainly is the most hotly
debated new religion or *Weltanschauung* today—though the discussion takes
place in public media, Christian apologetics, hundreds of Internet sites, and
many court trials, rather than in the academic discourses of religious studies.
So we are faced with the *paradox* and *problem* that the most hotly debated movement of the last fifty years has provoked treatments here and there, but this has
not led to an encompassing, thorough, and solid religious studies book that
could be regarded as a valuable state-of-the-art and up-to-date reference work
covering all aspects of and approaches to the movement. We do not have this at
the moment, and that's actually a scandal.[6]

So I find myself in a twofold trouble: There is hardly a coherently established definition of what *New Age* is supposed to mean. Neither is there a final
solution to the question of whether Scientology can be regarded as "religion"
in the proper sense of the word.[7] Because many scholars have taken opposite
positions here, the whole issue is far from being settled, and many researchers
refrain from a closer study of Scientology for various reasons—be it the fear of
open hostility from the movement if they raise critical issues, or be it simply
that they do not consider it as a proper object for religious studies research.

For my purpose here, it may suffice to start with the heuristic principle that
Scientology becomes a legitimate subject of religious studies research if there
are elements in Scientology that show "family resemblances" to other—well-
established or "unquestioned"—*religious* traditions or elements thereof, or, in
the language of empirical multivariant statistical research, it is legitimate to
approach Scientology from the perspective of religious research if some of its
elements do obviously "load" on a religious "factor," so to say. I assume nobody
would object to this "soft" approach. Furthermore, Scientology seems to "function" in a "religious" manner for many of its adherents: They conceive of it as
their *community,* their place of help and guidance through life, and the writings of Hubbard are taken as a sort of sacred scriptures disclosing the one and
only relevant "religious technology" for them,[8] and so forth. This is also true in
the case of the "free Scientologists" who do not accept the leading role of the
Church of Scientology today, but who operate through the networks of their
independent "Free Zone."[9]

One problem with the application of the label "religion" to Scientology
seems to be the misunderstanding that once the label is granted to Scientology,
then somehow one has approved of its basic goodness.[10] Scientology's effort
to collect all kinds of positive statements by more or less established scholars
in favor of the religion issue is rooted in the idea that the bona fide status
of religion implies goodness and acceptability.[11] The religious studies view of

religion is of a different sort: As we know, religion is far from being "nice" all the time. It is, rather, a powerful force to create meaning in all dimensions, to motivate people, to safeguard them, to indoctrinate them, to liberate them, and to do harmful things to them and religious others. One does not need to turn to Mesoamerican ritual killings or to the events of September 11 to identify the dark side of religion: Religion is far from being simply pleasant or always "good," integrating or harmonizing social or personal life.

If researchers in religious studies come to the conclusion that Scientology could rightly be perceived as a religion of sorts, this does not imply that all practices of Scientology are automatically promoted as harmless, nice, good, and humane. The religion label is not an official license. It is in the hands of the authorities what to do with an alternative (religious) movement if it violates the law[12]—and in the eyes of many authorities Scientology has at least become very suspicious with its lengthy juridical record in many countries.[13]

From Dianetics to Scientology: The Formation of an Exclusivist Movement

I do not need to rehearse the details of Scientology's formative story, which Roy Wallis has already analyzed convincingly as a paradigmatic shift from an initial, informal, and popular phase of the movement to a closed and progressively more structured organization. After the unexpected success of his self-help bestseller *Dianetics: The Modern Science of Mental Heath*, initially published in 1950, L. Ron Hubbard tried to assert control over the various autonomous Dianetics groups spreading over the United States. He became involved in a series of organizations that followed each other rapidly in the early 1950s: Elisabeth Foundation, Wichita Foundation, Church of American Science, Church of Spiritual Engineering, and so forth. All of these organizations preceded—and some of them were directly connected with—the so-called Church of Scientology founded later in California in 1954 (some claim that this nomenclature was already used in New Jersey in 1953). In succession to the Dianetics book, which promised almost miraculous results in a person when successfully confronting and working through his or her traumatic memories ("engrams") on the memory track in the "reactive mind," the very topic "Scientology" took shape after Hubbard's move to Phoenix, Arizona, in 1952. Some of Hubbard's heaviest "mythological" writings and talks were delivered in the following years: "What to Audit" (1952; later titled: "Scientology: A History of Man"), the lectures on "The Time Track of Theta" (1952), the legendary "Phoenix Lectures" (1954), followed by "Have You Lived before This Life?" (1960), and several "Lectures on the Whole Track" (1959–1963), to name a few. They are all publicly available and are highly recommended reading—or listening, in the case of tape-recorded talks—for those who still ardently oppose any applicability of the religion label for Scientology.

Roy Wallis, well-known author of the first in-depth sociological study on Scientology, *The Road to Total Freedom* (1976/1977), has labeled this shift from an informal popular "cult phase" to the formation of an exclusivist alternative religion—in other words, a "sectarian" movement (in the sociological understanding of the terms *cult* and *sect*) propagating a message and practice that is said to be the definite and only workable solution to mankind's problems.[14] Scientology was gradually restructured into a hierarchical and centralized organization with a firm grip on all subgroups and local outposts—with Hubbard leading the movement from the top down in the manner of a naval officer. However, it is clear for Wallis that Scientology, "although it describes itself as a church, has only the most rudimentary of religious practices in any conventional sense."[15] How can this be related to the New Age issue?

"Scientology: The Philosophy of a New Age"?

The first and, on the surface, strongest hint that there might be something to this topic can be found in Hubbard's own writings. In a short text, published in late 1957 in Scientology's *Ability* magazine, Hubbard himself used the term *New Age* with reference to his brainchild Scientology.[16] This is quite early and still relatively close to Alice Bailey's first usage of the term in her book *Discipleship in the New Age* ([1]1950). Hubbard's work thus appears as one of the rare and early instances in which reference to "New Age" is used already in the original object language of an alternative spiritual movement or worldview—or, to borrow the language of ethnology, in the *emic* presentation of Scientology. Without doubt, Hubbard's usage also influenced the name of Scientology's main publishing company "New Era" ("Golden Era" for audiovisual media). The notion and idea of a new age or new era is far more than a mere metaphoric usage for Hubbard and Scientology. The publication of *Dianetics* in 1950 marks Scientology's new internal counting of eras, by which, for example, 1957 C.E. would be relabeled "AD7" (i.e., seven years "after Dianetics"). This fact is already clear in Hubbard's 1957 text "Scientology: The Philosophy of a New Age." A few excerpts might serve to illustrate Hubbard's perspective:

> We are the heralds of a New Age. Man, stuck for millennia in the rut of status quo can at first balk and even ridicule, but, Can He Survive?
> What will this world be? Atomic reactors giving unlimited power. Automatic machines providing for most of Man's animal wants. Space flight to the Solar System. New politics, new leisure, new hates, new loves. . . .
> Scientology for the individual is a passport to this new time. . . . Only a clear could think and act fast enough to live in a disaster and to make others live. Only a clear could survive in Space. Only a clear could enjoy the fast pace of the game to come. . . .
> Hence, Project Clear. That's our goal now. We can do it. We can teach you to get it done.
> It's taken seven years to iron out the kinks. Seven years isn't long against 73 trillion.

Today can be ours. Tomorrow can come. Let us be ready for it.

We are the prime movers in this, the new age. Forget the old. Face up to what will come. And let the dead yesterdays bury the philosophy of Authority and Capital Gains and Communist psychology cults. We're no longer tied to it.

The eons march on. Space Opera has again come to a planet on which we live. Always before it meant destruction.

Perhaps, this time, due to our efforts, a humanitarian world can exist. We, the Prophets of the Morrow, know the way.[17]

Hubbard declares Scientology as the "passport" into and "answer" to a dawning new age or era. "Survival," a basic category of Hubbard's philosophy, can be granted only through Scientology—as well as the project to "clear" humanity through Scientology processing ("Project Clear"). What are the signs of the new age? Technological advances like atomic power and space flights. But Hubbard also talks of some dangerous "space opera" reentering this planet and of seventy-three trillion years of human history. These are direct hints to the strong undercurrent linking Scientology with the formation of UFO-related movements within the same historical U.S. context of the 1950s. Having published mainly as a writer in pulp fiction and science fiction genres, Hubbard appears as an interesting person who himself oscillated between the production of fantasy tales and the successful formation of a socially organized *Weltanschauung* incorporating science fiction—or, as Hubbard likes to call it, "space opera"—tales as mythic core stories for its anthropology and cosmology.

"Space Opera" and "Whole Track" Memories

This appears already quite "New Agey," as we all know, because there have been many prophets of a dawning millennium during the last fifty years who claimed to bridge science and religion by a new revelation of space alien origin—or, at least, who posit themselves within a space-age scenario using many allusions to science fiction motifs. Hubbard's "space opera"[18] includes a huge intergalactic conspiracy, in which the evil agents of old, the "Marcabians" (or "Marcabian Confederacy"), try to enslave other beings. From within the perspective of Scientology it is ensured, however, that "space opera" is *indeed*

relating to time periods on the *whole track* millions of years ago which concerned activities in this and other galaxies. Space opera has space travel, spaceships, spacemen, intergalactic travel, wars, conflicts, other beings, civilizations and societies, and other planets and galaxies. *It is not fiction and concerns actual incidents and things that occurred on the track.*[19] (my italics)

Also, when Hubbard speaks of "73 trillion years" of history in his "New Age" text quoted above, it must be understood as a direct hint of the supposedly arcane mythic history related to the "whole track" memories hidden in a person's memory bank. The basic "historical" framework, which Hubbard formulated as his "discovery" as early as the 1950s, includes a nowadays famous—although arcane—story of an old incident by which earthly "thetans" (i.e., the "soul" unit of the person) have been brought into this sector of the universe by an evil galactic emperor. Thus, the memory banks of many people share certain elements of a "space opera" core story. These ideas have become less prominent in the public statements of the Church of Scientology today,[20] but they are still a major issue in the splinter groups of the "Free Zone," where it is maintained that the Church of Scientology has itself been taken over by these Marcabian forces of old, which are nowadays becoming active on earth (Hubbard's "New Age" text also alludes to such renewed space alien interventions).

However, L. Ron Hubbard never claimed any access to "revelation" or other numinous forms of privileged information of the "channeling" or "automatic writing" type.[21] He always reported his knowledge as the results of sober research and rational inquiry, almost scientifically proven, and allegedly well established by experiment and controlled analysis. The history of mankind, as it is displayed in one of Hubbard's most "mythological" writings publicly accessible—originally published under the title *What to Audit,* and later replaced by the title *Scientology: A History of Man*—is, according to Hubbard's own words, to be taken as "a cold-blooded and factual account of your last sixty trillion years."[22] Together with another highly mythological book, *Have You Lived before This Life?*,[23] the sketch of a far-reaching interplanetary scenario is already developed, locating earthly souls within a gigantic "space opera" mythology. Through Scientology auditing, it is claimed, memories of the "whole track" can be recollected—and these do contain memories from remote interstellar times and regions, as Hubbard insists.[24] Hubbard presents these alleged "recollections" as truths, established facts, not as "guided fantasies" as outside observers would be inclined to perceive them.

The spirit or soul unit, called the "thetan" according to Hubbard's terminology, can be compared to similar soul conceptions that became famous during the formation of esoteric movements: The Western strands of Theosophy and Esotericism had already introduced Indian style, "atman"-like concepts of the soul to Western spiritual seekers, and this concept of the soul was enlarged by UFO-related prophets and groups from the early 1950s onward in an interplanetary style—so-called "star seeds" or "walk-ins" from outer space. Earth is a garden, where these spiritual implants were supposed to grow, to mature, in order to be eligible for further evolution into higher realms. I cannot go into the fascinating details of UFOlogical anthropologies, but I simply want to draw attention to the fact that Hubbard's idea of the person and its role in interstellar history is very, very close to other UFOlogical spiritual movements in the 1950s and later.[25]

This UFOlogical connection is explicitly apparent in the foundation myth of Scientology's "Operating Thetan" (OT) anthropology. According to the secret doctrines of Scientology—which are nowadays far from arcane, as information about court trials and other disclosures by former members appear in hundreds of pages on the Internet—there once was a fierce intergalactic ruler named Xenu, who brought millions of thetans to this Earth (which back then carried the name "Teegeack"), and that is how their (i.e., our) life started in this region of the universe ("sector nine"). Amazingly, this story, which forms the central core myth in OT level III initiation teachings,[26] was rewritten by Hubbard as a mere science fiction novel in the late 1970s. As such, it carries the title *Revolt in the Stars,* and it has so far not been officially published. Copies of the manuscript circulate every now and then on the Internet. It is an amazing piece and trustworthy in terms of Hubbard's authorship—according to style, phrasing, and content.[27] This oscillation between the production of mythic core stories and mere fantasy tales is also a characteristic typical of modern esoteric traditions: Helena P. Blavatsky, for example, wrote fantasy tales beside her theosophical disclosures,[28] and Charles Hoy Fort's alternative, *anomalistic* science in his *Book of the Damned* (and the three follow-up volumes)[29] inspired fantasy authors like H. P. Lovecraft as well as esoteric seekers. Erich von Däniken, working along Charles Fort's lines, also oscillates between fantasy and fringe historiography/archaeology, and his "Ancient Astronaut" stories have often been often reabsorbed by esoteric and UFO-believing groups.[30] The framework story in Hubbard's *Revolt in the Stars* does, by the way, include the idea of a time capsule in the vein of the Ancient Astronauts' scheme.[31]

But Scientologists always feel uneasy when compared with or related to UFO-believing groups, especially because many critics dismiss Hubbard for his pulp fiction and science fiction involvements. Far more prestigious for Scientology is the reference to Buddhism mentioned in many publications by Hubbard, as well as in contemporary Scientology books.

The Alleged Buddhism Connection

I cannot go into the details here, but one thing is obvious to everybody familiar with at least a few basics of Buddhism: Hubbard had no sound knowledge about Buddhism when he wrote his early Scientology pieces—despite the hagiographic records in other Church of Scientology publications that claim that he had allegedly discoursed intensively with Tibetan Buddhist Lamas, among others.[32] Hubbard might have caught a few encyclopedia pieces about Buddhism here and there, and he had a very remote perception of the overall thesis in Blavatsky's *Secret Doctrine,* as becomes clear, for example, in the first few speeches of his *Phoenix Lectures,* in which he also alludes to the idea that some genuine ancient wisdom originated within the context of Indian Buddhism.[33] Hubbard does not come up with "ascended masters," to be sure, but he suggests that *dhyana* and *dharma* are nothing but ancient parallels to Scientology's term *knowingness.* Obviously, Hubbard has no idea at all what the Sanskrit words *dharma, dhyana*—or especially *bodhi* (enlightenment)[34]—denote.[35] Hubbard's reference to *dhyana* is a remote reverberation of Blavatsky's mysterious *Stanzas from the Book of Dzyan* (i.e., dhyana), which she identified as an (alleged) ancient source of wisdom in her *Secret Doctrine.*[36] Hubbard is also not aware of the fact—nor are still many contemporary Scientologists—that the "soul" concept of Scientology's "thetan" is directly opposed to what the Buddha taught about the person with his *anatta* ("no-self," Sanskrit *anatman*) doctrine. Buddhists have therefore convincingly argued that Scientology's claim to an analogy with Buddhism is entirely spurious.[37] But Hubbard went a step further and styled himself as the future Buddha *Maitreya* (Pali: *Metteya*). In his poetic booklet *Hymn of Asia,* recently set to music and republished together with an audio CD, he writes the following, among other things:

> Am I Metteyya? . . . I come to you in peace, I come to you as a
> teacher. . . . I come to bring you all that Lord Buddha would have you
> know of life, Earth and Man. I come to you with freedom, I come
> to you with science . . . to teach you. . . . Address me and you ad-
> dress Lord Buddha. . . . I am the beginning, I am the end. . . . In all
> these twenty-five centuries none came and spoke The Great Lessons
> again. . . . I am but a teacher, I bring you word of Lessons you have
> lost. . . . Study then, Be worked with then, Become Bodhi [sic].[38]

Hubbard then claims that the message of these "Great Lessons" is the herald of a dawning New Age: "We enter into a Golden age. We are Golden Men. We are the New Men, The spiritual Leaders of Earth." He further asserts that his mes-sage is presented in a "tongue of science" that was long ago "stolen from the East," and that Buddhist prophecies even predicted Hubbard's own revelatory appearance "in the Western World."

This poetic representation, however offensive it might appear to Bud-dhists, is in concordance with the opening chapters of *The Phoenix Lectures* and other descriptions by Hubbard or in Scientology publications. The reference to a "Western Buddha," for example, can also be found in the opening paragraphs of Scientology's *Volunteer Minister's Handbook.*[39] It might itself be traceable to Nicholas Roerich (Russian painter and Theosophist),[40] but it has no origin in the Buddhist (Pali) Scriptures, of course. Anyone familiar with H. P. Blavatsky will immediately realize her indirect influence in the idea that some occult or esoteric "science" originated in India, was kept hidden there, and is now dis-seminated again for the first time in renewed, perfected, and "scientific" fash-ion from a "New Western Buddha."

The only point at which Scientology could convincingly argue in favor of a plausible similarity to Buddhism is the issue of *reincarnation*—or "previous lives," as Hubbard/Scientology prefer to call it (because a transmigration to animals is denied). Hubbard not only styled himself in the manner of a Bud-dha, he also claimed to have gained certain paranormal insights into previous lives—a topic that constitutes a classic aspect of attaining full insight in the higher states of Buddhist perfection and meditation. In the so-called "Tathagata sermon," a formalized systematic account of the Buddhist path to enlighten-ment that can be found several times in the dialogues of the *Digha-Nikaya,*[41] the Buddhist attainment also implies access to the otherwise hidden memories of one's own previous lives—a realization that Siddhartha Gautama also achieved, according to canonical texts, during his final realization of Buddhahood under the legendary Bodhi tree. In an interesting little booklet displaying Hubbard's own "research" into his memories about previous lives along the shores of the Mediterranean Sea, called *Mission into Time*, Hubbard writes about his insights into these "whole track" memories:

> The idea of the whole track is very, very intriguing.—I am not in a position at the present moment to give you a complete history of it but I know quite a bit about it. I know with certainty where I was and who I was in the last 80 trillion years. The small details of it like what I ate for breakfast two trillion years ago are liable to go astray here and there, but otherwise it's no mystery to me.
>
> Whole track is the continuous record of time of the individual from the first moment he began to experience straight on through now, a 3D, 52-perception movie. It is not imaginary. The seconds go on, the minutes go on, and the days go on and all of it can be plotted out.[42]

The idea that a person can recollect all of his or her former lives—along Hubbard's idea of a tape-like record of memories—is also dominant in other esoteric strands of the 1950s. It is also prominent in the esoteric or theosophic versions of UFOlogy that surfaced during this time.[43] But there is another paranormal ability that can supposedly be acquired and trained during auditing: "exteriorization," the ability to leave the body at will and to move around freely. This rather important "faculty" can be well illustrated by the training process called "Grand Tour" guiding the person to extend his psychic center into the realm of "astral travel" or "projection": Here, the person (preclear) is instructed to "move" around in the stellar system ("Be near Earth," "Be near the Moon," "Be near the Earth," etc.), to find certain spots on these planets ("Now find a rock," "Be inside of it," "Be outside of it," "Inside," . . . "Be in the center of the Earth," "Be outside of Earth," . . . "Now move down slowly to the surface" . . . "Be near Mars," etc.) until he or she is "entirely used" to these planets and the solar system at large.[44] This playful routine works on the basis of Hubbard's central assumption that persons can indeed "exteriorize": Their "thetan" is supposedly able to leave the body at will. The quest for such paranormal faculties like *astral projection* is a common theme of esoteric movements and UFOlogical anthropologies alike, and one could easily document many instances in which Scientology commercials allude to the acquisition of such paranormal powers—powers which would have to be understood as fully "normal" powers of a liberated "Operating Thetan."[45]

All of the observations collected so far "load" on the "religious factor," as I have called it. In order to do justice to Scientology's self-reference, as well as to the perception of Scientology by the wider society, I would now have to open another, analogous box of examples that display the rather secular side of Scientology. In the early and formative book *Scientology: Fundamentals of Thought*, Hubbard already wrote the following:

> Probably the greatest discovery of Scientology and its most forceful contribution to mankind has been the isolation, description and *handling* of the human spirit, accomplished in July, 1951, in Phoenix,

Arizona. I established, *along scientific rather than religious or humani-tarian lines* that the thing which is the person, the personality, is sepa-rate from the body and the mind at will and without causing bodily death or derangement.[46] (my italics)

This reverence to scientific investigation and the notion of "technology" is typi-cal of Hubbard and Scientology: Hubbard's disclosures about Dianetics and Scientology are always referred to as "technological" disclosures. However, it is a quite "fantastic science"[47] or "technology" that is implied in allusions like this. The predominant emphasis on *inner-worldly* improvement (rather than "salvation"), a *commonsense* ethic, the absorption of "therapeutic man" (instead of *homo religiosus*), the absence of religious or spiritual-soteriological talk in the "success stories," the famous testing device of the so-called "Oxford Capac-ity Analysis" and the "E-Meter," as well as the dominant self-perception as an "applied philosophy," "technology," or "religious technology"—all that would point to the other side of the spectrum in which Scientology is locating its *Weltanschauung* and practice: within a commonly shared modern, secular, and rational worldview. Gerald Willms has devoted a book-length study to this sub-ject, to which I would simply like to refer here.[48] Therefore I will touch on this issue only a little bit, in a more thesis-like manner, in my final paragraph.

The Dialectics of Disenchantment and Reenchantment

Within the context of a fully secularized world, Max Weber identified the pre-requisite for an enduring power of religious worldviews in their creative, on-going capacity to provide a solid foundation for options in leading one's life. Scientology certainly operates within the framework of a fully disenchanted world; it even adopts the rules and market strategies of this immanent world, as well as the technological imagery of modern industrial societies—including such late modern psychological types like "therapeutic man," further aided by an electronic device, the "E-Meter." I have tried to illustrate aspects of Scien-tology's worldview in relation to the topic "New Age," putting those aspects in the center where recourse is taken to a reenchantment of the human condition: Man *is* "thetan," says Hubbard, a spiritual being who has to be aided "upon the Bridge" in order to gain a panorama of more or less paranormal abilities, "fullest" capacities "back." This is the "goal of Scientology"—"making the indi-vidual capable of leading a better life" and "the playing of a better game."[49]

But despite these scattered spiritual overtones, Scientology is not all that different from mainstream assumptions in the modern society—it even repro-duces them in concise form. Scientology offers guaranteed inner-worldly "suc-cess" (cf. the dominant success stories, the talk about "gains," and the up-going "statistics") and is far from preaching inner-worldly asceticism (maybe with the exception of the Sea Org staff personnel). With its quest for a "religious technology," Scientology presents itself as a modern way of being religious/spiritual,[50] technical, fully capable, and efficient at the same time.

Scientology is deviant from traditional religions in the form that its "religiousness" is portrayed as entirely producible, technologically makeable, and imposable by a sound system of "processes" and "technological" disclosures, which are, last but not least, all *registered trademarks!* Apart from the whole aura of profit-oriented dissemination and hard-sell strategies, it was mainly this *technical* and *instrumental* aspect that has led some German (Christian) critics to revive the term *magic* out of the religious studies' labels "wastebasket" in order to stigmatize Scientology with the (bad) label *magic* and the allusion of an "occult science" instead of attributing it with the (good) label religion.[51] Scientology declares with Hubbard that the former goals of religion/spirituality, including the old aspirations of the Buddha, as we have seen in *Hymn of Asia,* can now be "handled" with a sound technology: Scientology can therefore be displayed as a solidified and stable "fulfillment" of the Buddha's older (but back then futile) hopes and aspirations.

Is Scientology a New Age religion? It certainly is *the* technological *religion* of a fully disenchanted industrial world—or, to put it the other way round, a reenchanted therapeutic endeavor, a reenchanted secular technology. And that has also been an important hope for at least some New Age spiritual movements as well: to present applicable "tools" for spirituality. What exactly is "New-Agey" about Scientology? One needs only to visit an esoteric fair in order to find a huge array of booths presenting analogous (esoteric-religious) technologies: computerized I Ching analyses, aura photography, easy-to-handle crystal tools for every daily purpose, and much more. New religious movements of today—especially within the New Age realm—have grown out of the compartmentalized context of traditional Western "religion." They differ insofar as they not only have recourse to religious or spiritual issues on a global scale, but also absorb and amalgamate (aspects of) the *critique of religion,* a disenchanted worldview and the technological imagery of the modern context.

A Post-Religious Movement?

In absorbing the critique of religion, in explaining the supernatural in technological terms, *Scientology also posits itself as a modern and postreligious movement.* It does have religious facets, draws playfully on different sources (which alludes to the label *post*modernity rather than modernity), but it surely oscillates with regard to its religiousness because the "religious" facets are part of a playful side inventory of the system, and in many cases they appear hardly at the core center of the efficacy propagated by Scientology. As I said, religious themes are quite absent in the success stories, for example. Because the main focus is definitely on *inner-worldly success* and increased "abilities," the truly soteriological talk of a "liberation from matter" is simply an aside to the *primarily this-worldly focus.* If you visit a Church of Scientology, there is more affinity to the cool, efficient ambience of Western technological service, business perfection, and marketing ambience than to any (traditional) occult or esoteric spiritual practice.

But this is sometimes also true of other modern religious movements: Soka Gakkai chanting is said to evoke a flood of desired goods, be it a new car, a better TV, or simply money. One could also think of the crystal batteries in the Aetherius society, supposedly able to "store" prayer "energy" in order to "charge" certain Earthly spots with it later. Or take today's most disenchanted religion, the Raelian movement, in which the technique of cloning is propagated to finally achieve eternal life by technical means via such a "scientific reincarnation."

Now, is Scientology a New Age religion? . . . Sure, if you are inclined to use the New Age label at all. But Scientology is at the same time a postmodern and a postreligious movement—it is a "secularized religion," as Brian Wilson has put it,[52] and as such it is difficult to grasp. But so are many other movements that we do perceive as legitimate objects of religious studies: the Raelians, for example, based on their reductionist explanations à la Erich von Däniken and Robert Charroux, perceive themselves as an "atheistic" religion, enriched by stories about conversations with (alleged) space alien ancient astronauts. Here the supernatural is explained (away) in terms of the modern scientific worldview. And that is also a common feature of fantasy novels: They use religious imagery, but in the end it will be explained in terms of immanence. And in Scientology, we are confronted with the exciting case of a typical oscillation between fantasy genres (we've seen them reproduced in the "guided fantasies" during auditing) and a science fiction (or "space opera") mythology with anthropological, cosmological, and soteriological implications.

What do we make of this? In a postmodern world, Scientology can be perceived as one highly consolidated movement that is able to posit itself with totally different "faces" in differing contexts, able to adapt to differing challenges: The alleged analogy to Christianity—heavily displayed in the important current self-description, *What Is Scientology?*—is used within a Christian context, but within a wider (post-Christian) society the protagonists can switch to the exotic fascination with Buddhism dominant in the Western world, and in other contexts (former Eastern Block states) one can take recourse to the self-presentation as a fully secular science or technology, and in yet other situations one speaks of therapy and uses rather old-style Dianetics to get people attracted. Outsiders perceive that as oscillating, but from the point of system theory it is an evolutionary advance to incorporate different "faces" and to be able to adapt to different conceptual niches and discourses in the context—an extremely useful ability to sustain and procreate the system.

Scientology can best be viewed as a mixture of therapeutic, technological, and evolutionary fantasies, incorporating some neo-gnostic myths about world and man, and spreading, selling itself according to late-capitalistic marketing strategies. With older strands of theosophical and esoteric movements it shares certain anthropological elements, conspiracy theories, belief in reincarnation ("past lives"), and a special reverence to Buddhism (akin to Blavatsky's Secret Doctrine), as well as the hope for an approaching "New Age" with a new fantastic synthesis of science/technology and religion at hands to solve mankind's ultimate riddles. But the main accent, nevertheless, is on inner-worldly progress: to guarantee and secure success, profit, and improvement of faculties in life—with "certainty," as it is stressed. To be able to "handle" life easily ("playing a better game") is the promised goal—and the whole notion of "handling" is a very, very important and significant aspect in Scientology.[53] Despite the many critiques of the movement in political, legal, and public discourses, Scientology—with its massive slang of instrumental handling—has to be viewed as a very typical "product" of our late-modern Western industrial society, because it mirrors and reflects most of that society's basic economic convictions, instrumental fantasies of ongoing increasing success, as well as its tactics to maximize profit—and not all of them follow humane principles, either. With New Age movements it shares several aspects like reincarnation and the reverence toward Buddhism, the hope for paranormal faculties, and a dawning new age. But the spiritual elements are handled by a system of techniques and routines: Even the *spirit* can be "handled," as we have seen before.[54] Scientology, therefore, represents the *technological, strongly disenchanted side of the New Age movements*—and is closely linked to the UFOlogical ones. But the spiritual elements are caged in "technological," psychomanipulative tools.[55] Therefore I am probably ending with a paradox when I say that *Scientology can rightly be perceived not only as a postmodern, but also as a postreligious New Age religion.* And with all I have said so far, I hope that this makes sense and can shed light on our subject matter.

NOTES

1. This chapter is a revised version of my earlier contribution to the ASANAS-Conference, Milton Keynes, Great Britain, May 30–June 1, 2003. All Internet URLs referred to below were visited and checked for the last time July 25, 2007.

2. Cf. Christoph Bochinger's extensive study, *"New Age" und moderne Religion: Religionswissenschaftliche Analysen* (München: Kaiser, [2]1995); for an overview cf. the entry on "New Age" in the latest edition of the standard encyclopedia *Religion in Geschichte und Gegenwart,* Vol. 6 (Tübingen: Mohr, [4]2003), 265–268.

3. See, for example, the documentation of this problem in the preface (vi ff.) and appendix IV (265 ff.) to Roy Wallis, *The Road to Total Freedom: A Sociological Analysis of Scientology* (London: Heinemann, 1976; New York: Columbia Press, 1977).

4. Cf. M. Pye, "Methodological Integration in the Study of Religions," in T. Ahlbäck, *Approaching Religion, Part I* (Stockholm: Almqvist & Wiksell, 1999), 189–205; idem, "Participation, Observation and Reflection," in N. G. Holm et al. (eds.), *Ethnography Is a Heavy Rite: Studies of Comparative Religion in Honor of Julia Pentikäinen* (Åbo: Akademi University Press, 2000), 64–79.

5. Cf. Kurt Rudolph, "Die ideologiekritischen Traditionen in der Religionswissenschaft," in H. G. Kippenberg and B. Luchesi (eds.), *Religionswissenschaft und Kulturkritik* (Marburg: Diagonal, 1991), 149–156.

As a matter of fact, even my Scientology contacts have found such an approach helpful or at least acceptable—although I am addressing "critical" points in question every now and then. I definitely do *not* buy into the recent fad among some social and religious researchers who simply re-present the inner (emic) perception of a movement, arguing that only this would be "politically correct," and leave it at such a "theology from outside" (without academic discussion of any critical issues involved). Gordon Melton's little booklet *The Church of Scientology* (Salt Lake City: Signature, 2000) is an example for such a superficial and less helpful approach, leaving all "problematic" aspects of the movement completely out of the picture.

6. This is not to deny the existence of several helpful monographs from different perspectives, but one would expect that an up-to-date, encompassing reference work should be available.

7. In his essay "Scientology: Religion or Racket?" well-known religious studies researcher Benjamin Beit-Hallahmi develops twenty-six points of argument why Scientology cannot be regarded as a religious practice in the proper sense; cf. *Marburg Journal of Religion* 8 (2003); http://web.uni-marburg.de/religionswissenschaft/journal/mjr/beit.html.

8. L. Ron Hubbard's *A New Slant on Life* (Los Angeles: Bridge Publications, 1997; first edition East Grinstead/Sussex 1965), for example, is often used as a compact display of basic Scientological beliefs; cf. also Marco Frenschkowski, "L. Ron Hubbard and Scientology: An Annotated Bibliographical Survey of Primary and Selected Secondary Literature," in: *Marburg Journal of Religion* 4 (1999): 1; http://web.uni-marburg.de/religionswissenschaft/journal/mjr/frenschkowski.html.

9. Cf. Internet resources such as http://www.freezoneearth.org, http://www.ronsorg.com, http://www.fzaoint.net, http://www.freezone.de, and http://internationalfreezone.net.

10. A few years back, I had a fierce discussion with one state politician because she opposed the religion label for Scientology for such reasons; she even managed to have the exposition of Scientology items removed from the historical section of a museum in the city of Stuttgart, because Scientology would have been displayed "on the same eye height" with "established" religions like Christianity, Islam, and Judaism—which she perceived as "intolerable."

11. See, for example, Church of Scientology International (ed.), *Scientology, Lehre und Ausübung einer modernen Religion: Ein Überblick aus religionswissenschaftlicher Sicht* (Copenhagen: New Era Publications, 1998). There are many pages on the Internet (directly or indirectly related to Scientology) that also seek to display exclusively such *positive* evaluations of the religious nature of Scientology—pages that are then countered by a huge amount of analogous *anti*-Scientology arguments developed by critics.

12. For an overview concerning the legal problems and trials involving Scientology or Scientologists, cf. Werner Raik, *Scientology im Spiegel des Rechts: Strukturen einer Subkulturellen Ordnung zwischen Konformität und Konflikt mit den staatlichen Normen* (München: Wilhelm-Fink-Verlag, 2002); and Arnd Diringer, *Scientology—Verbotsmöglichkeit einer verfassungsfeindlichen Bekenntnisgemeinschaft* (Frankfurt: Peter Lang, 2000).

13. So far, Scientology is still a soft target of observation by intelligence services in Germany.

14. Roy Wallis, *The Road to Total Freedom: A Sociological Analysis of Scientology* (London: Heinemann, 1976; New York: Columbia Press, 1977).

15. Roy Wallis, *The Elementary Forms of New Religious Life* (London: Routledge & Kegan Paul, 1984), 28.

16. "Scientology: The Philosophy of a New Age," first published in *Ability—The Magazine of Dianetics and Scientology*, Washington, D.C., no. 60 (1957), reprinted in the collection of Hubbard Communications Office Policy Letters (Vol. 3, 153 f.). An online version can be found at the Toronto Canada Scientology News Blog, http://www.blogscientology.com/2007/03/philosophy-of-new-age.html, and a slightly abridged

version disseminated by "free Scientologist" Andreas Groß is available at http://freierscientologe.netfirms.com/newage.htm. Groß even takes this text as the "foundational text" (*Gründungsschrift*) of the whole New Age, and formulates the (historically incorrect) thesis that "the biggest part of the philosophical and practical repertoire of the New Age is based directly or indirectly upon Scientology and was originally developed and formulated by Hubbard" (my translation from http://www.freiescientologen.de/newageq.htm).

17. Cf. note 16.

18. The term appears in many writings and audiotapes by L. Ron Hubbard and relates especially to science fiction scenarios in human memories about previous lives. This has even led to an entry in Hubbard's formal *Technical Dictionary of Dianetics and Scientology* (Los Angeles: Bridge Publications, 1975), in which the term is defined with reference to Webster's dictionary as a piece of (science) fiction "featuring interplanetary travel," conflicts between space alien beings, and so forth.

19. Quoted from Scientology's Online Glossary of Scientology and Dianetics under the entry "space opera"; http://www.scientology.org/gloss.htm#SPACEOPERA.

20. As an impression from talks with my Scientology contacts, this might mainly be due to the fact that the science fiction tales and "space opera" issues are often taken up by critics to ridicule Scientology's belief system; furthermore, because the stories are to be kept arcane (because of their imminent danger for uninitiated people), Scientologists are anyway reluctant to talk with outsiders about these issues.

21. According to disclosures available on the Internet (one only has to search for "Christian Heaven," "Hubbard," and "1963"), Hubbard obviously related stories in a Hubbard Communications Office Bulletin dated May 11, 1963 ("A.D. 13") about his own "visit," on May 9, 1963, to the Christian heavens, which he allegedly found in a rotten state, badly maintained, and not all too enlightening.

22. L. Ron Hubbard, *Scientology—A History of Man* ['1952: *What to Audit*] (Los Angeles: New Era, 1988), 3.

23. L. Ron Hubbard, *Have You Lived Before This Life?* (Los Angeles: New Era, 1989 ['1960]).

24. Illustrative quotations from these alleged recollections in *Have You Lived before This Life?* can be found in my contribution to the *Oxford Handbook of New Religious Movements*, ed. James Lewis (Oxford: Oxford University Press, 2004), 419–444: "Waiting for the 'Big Beam': UFO Religions and 'Ufological' Themes in New Religious Movements." Compare also my entry on "Scientology" in James Lewis (ed.), *UFOs and Popular Culture: An Encyclopedia of Contemporary Myth* (Santa Barbara, CA: ABC Clio, 2000), 266–268.

25. For example, "Mrs. Keech" and "Mr. Armstrong" (pseudonyms), of the millennial UFO group in the famous sociopsychological study *When Prophecy Fails* (1956), had both been involved in Dianetics and Scientology prior to their commitment to this esoteric movement.

26. Robert Kaufman, *Inside Scientology* (London: Olympia Press, 1972) was among the first (if not *the* first) to publish a disclosure of this mythic story. Nowadays, even copies of Hubbard's handwritten sheets containing this story are circulating on the Internet.

27. It contains Hubbard's typical imagery of women, an evil psychiatrist, on the other hand "loyal officers," and the usual Star Wars scenario inside a "Galactic Confederation." Compared to other published fictional writings by Hubbard, it appears very genuine. (Probably due to legal reasons, no existing copy could be located via Web searches at the moment.) The story contains the struggle between the intergalactic

ruler Xenu and the "loyal officers" who, in the end, manage to overthrow his despotic rule after he murdered all disobedient subjects on the "extermination site" earth by bombing them on volcanoes (cf. esp. chapter 14).

28. Cf. Marco Frenschkowski, "Okkultismus und Phantastik: eine Studie zu ihrem verhältnis am Beispiel der Helena Petrovna Blavatsky," in: *Das Schwarze Geheimnis. Magazin für unheimliche Literatur* 4 (1999): 53–104. Or, take Heinlein's science fiction novel "Stranger in a Strange Land," which in turn inspired the formation of a neo-pagan movement calling itself actually "Church of all Worlds," like the neo-Martian religion in the novel. One could go on to the Star Trek culture, to Heaven's Gate, and the Raelians.

29. Charles Hoy Fort, *The Book of the Damned* (New York: Boni & Liveright, 1919); the books to follow were *New Lands* (1923), *Lo!* (1931), and *Wild Talents* (1932). There are several hypertext editions of the books available on the Internet: for example, see http://www.sacred-texts.com/fort (only books 1 and 2), or http://www.resologist. net/ (damnei.htm, landsei.htm, loei.htm and talentei.htm), prepared by a "Fortean" student.

30. Cf. my article " 'Ancient Astronaut' Narrations—A Popular Discourse on Our Religious Past," available online in *Marburg Journal of Religion* 11, 2006; http://web. uni-marburg.de/religionswissenschaft/journal/mjr/; for a slightly revised printed version see *Fabula* 48 (Berlin: W. de Gruyter, 2007), 205–228.

31. The framework story is located in our time: a strange object ("it might be something from outer space, it might be some archaeological wonder") is found on a U.S. beach, and after investigation it turns out to be a "time capsule" ("seventy-five million years old") containing an audiovisual record of the Xenu story. After listening to the record, the president of the United States denies its existence, pretending it was "just scrap metal."

32. Cf. on this issue already critically Stephen A. Kent, "Scientology's Relationship with Eastern Religious Traditions" in *Journal of Contemporary Religion* 11 (1996): 21–36.

33. Cf. especially the first three chapters of L. Ron Hubbard, *The Phoenix Lectures* [originally delivered in July 1954], in the first edition (Edinburgh: Publications Organization World Wide, 1968), 1–35. I have also used a separate version of these introductory chapters in a German translation, *Scientology—Ihr allgemeiner Hintergrund* [audio CDs and text] (Copenhagen: New Era, 2003).

34. Hubbard identifies *bodhi* mistakenly as "someone who is enlightened," as in "becoming a Bodhi" (*sic*) or "the individual who aspires to the attainment of perfect serenity"; Hubbard in fact *cannot* even distinguish at all between the attainment of "bodhi" and the person of an "awakened one" or "Buddha." He even writes, "We first find this Buddha called actually Bodhi, and a Bodhi [*sic*] is one who has attained intellectual and ethical perfection by human means," and "There were many Bodhis [*sic*], or Buddhas" (Hubbard, *Phoenix Lectures*, 1968, 18).

35. Hubbard takes *dharma* as the name for a "legendary Hindu sage" and goes on to say that "we have the word Dharma almost interchangeable with the word Dhyana" (*sic*); *Phoenix Lectures* (1968), 17.

36. Hubbard does not give direct quotations from or references to Blavatsky's text (it is very questionable that he did know it at all by firsthand reading), but the general setting of disclosing a new system of knowledge with mysteriously hidden roots in ancient Indian "dhyana/dzyan" is surely no coincidence.

37. See, for example, "Scientology: A Problem for Buddhists?," a short text by Goswin Baumhögger (staff member of the German Buddhist Union) in the journal *Lotosblätter*, no. 1 (1996): 59–61, which was written as a direct reaction to "Buddhist"

claims by Scientology, culminating in the statement that "the alleged connections between Scientology and Buddhism have to be interpreted as simply opportunistic and that the basic teachings of Buddhism are either not sought for at all or they are misunderstood" by Scientologists (my translation; an online version is currently still available athttp://www.religio.de/therapie/sc/hubbud.html).

38. L. Ron Hubbard, *Hymn of Asia: An Eastern Poem* (Copenhagen: New Era, 1965, 1972, 1974, 1984; recently published again together with audio CD in 2000).

39. I have used the German translation (*Das Handbuch für den Ehrenamtlichen Geistlichen*, Copenhagen: AOSH Publ., 1980); the U.S. original appeared first in 1959 with several editions to follow.

40. According to Marco Frenschkowski (by oral communication).

41. A good analysis of the Tathagata sermon, its history and function, can be found in Konrad Meisig, *Das Shramanyaphala-Sutra. Synoptische Übersetzung und Glossar der chinesischen Fassungen verglichen mit dem Sanskrit und Pali*, Freiburger Beiträge zur Indologie 19 (Wiesbaden: Harrassowitz, 1987), 39 ff.

42. L. Ron Hubbard, *Mission into Time* (Copenhagen: AOSH Publications Department, 1968; 1973), 69.

43. For example, Orfeo Angelucci reports in his *The Secret of the Saucers* (Amherst, WI: Amherst Press, 1955) about his "first contact" and space alien esoteric "initiation" that he suddenly gained access to all his former lives ("Every event of my life upon Earth was crystal clear to me—and then memory of all of my previous lives upon Earth returned"). I have used the German edition, Orfeo Angelucci, *Geheimnis der Untertassen* (Wiesbaden: Ventla Verlag, ²1983 ['1959]), cf. esp. page 60, and the online English version: http://www.galactic-server.net/rune/orfeo2.html.

44. L. Ron Hubbard, *The Creation of Human Ability* (Copenhagen, 1989; '1955), 65 f. In chapter 6 ("On a Clear Night You Can See Forever") of the famous Scientology story, *The Road to Xenu*, "Margery" Wakefield also reports about this "astral projection"-like training routine; http://www.cs.cmu.edu/˜dst/Library/Shelf/xenu/.

45. Cf. Andreas Grünschloß, "Die Konstruktion des 'para-normalen' Menschen—Übermenschliche Fähigkeiten als Bestandteil religiöser Anthropologien," in: Eilert Herms (ed.), *Menschenbild und Menschenwürde* (Gütersloh: Kaiser Vlg. & Gütersloher Verlagshaus, 2001), 497–528; for examples from Scientology publications, see esp. 516–524.

46. L. Ron Hubbard, *Scientology: The Fundamentals of Thought* (Copenhagen: New Era, 1986 ['1956]), 58.

47. This term was used both as an *emic* and *etic* description of the "Ancient Astronauts" discourse in the vein of Erich von Däniken; cf. Markus Pössel, *Phantastische Wissenschaft: Über Erich von Däniken und Johannes von Buttlar* (Reinbek: Rowohlt, 2000). The older Internet page of Erich von Däniken's giant "Mystery Park" in Interlaken (Switzerland) also carried the term as a catch phrase (the park was closed down in late 2006).

48. Gerald Willms (cf. his contribution to this volume, chapter 12) has published a detailed analysis of Scientology's self-understanding as being not "deviant," but primarily in full coherence with the optimistic, technicistic/technocratic, and rational worldview of modern industrial societies; *Scientology: Kulturbeobachtungen jenseits der Devianz* (Bielefeld: Transcript, 2005).

49. According to the mythic cosmology in Scientology, the thetans once "created" this universe (MEST = matter, energy, space, and time) in the style of a game convention, but then they got "trapped" in the game, and now they have to be led out of their own traps.

50. Hubbard referred to Scientology as a "religion of religions" in his well-known video interview in 1966, recently released again on DVD. I have used the edition with German subtitles, *An Introduction to Scientology* (*Eine Einführung in die Scientology*) (Los Angeles: Golden Era, 2006).

51. Cf. the extremely polemical work of Friedrich-Wilhelm Haack, *Scientology—Magie des 20. Jahrhunderts* (München: Claudius 1982, enlarged edition by Thomas Gandow, ³1995), and the later publication by Werner Thiede, *Scientology—Religion oder Geistesmagie?* (Neukirchen-Vluyn: Neukirchener Verlag, ²1995).

52. Brian Wilson, *The Social Dimensions of Sectarianism: Sects and New Religious Movements in Contemporary Society* (London: Clarendon Press, 1992), 267 ff.

53. Problems are "handled," and problematic cases and persons have to be "handled" (etc.).

54. Cf. the passage from *Scientology: Fundamentals of Thought* already quoted above (58): "Probably the greatest discovery of Scientology and its most forceful contribution to mankind has been the isolation, description and *handling* of the human spirit, accomplished in July, 1951, in Phoenix, Arizona" (my italics).

55. In 1998, the final report of the German government's Enquête Commission for alternative forms of spirituality could not come up with a final statement regarding the religious or *weltanschauliche* nature of Scientology; cf. Deutscher Bundestag (ed.), *Endbericht der Enquête Kommission "Sogenannte Sekten und Psycho-Gruppen"* (Bonn: Deutscher Bundestag, 13. Wahlperiode, Drucksache 13/10950, June 1998), http://www.bundestag.de/ftp/pdf_arch/13_10950.pdf and http://www.cesnur.org/testi/endber/ENDBER.HTM. In an additional statement ("Sondervotum," 158 f.) several specialists argued, however, that Scientology should be located within the realm of groups who are devoted mainly to a *behavioral modification* by some sort of *psycho-engineering*. This argumentation is to the point, because Hubbard presented Dianetics already in 1950 as an easy-to-handle "tool" in resemblance to engineer's (technological) knowledge: "Dianetics is an exact science and its application is on the order of, but simpler than, engineering" (ix); "In an engineering science like Dianetics, we can work on a push-button basis" (275); Dianetics "is entirely mechanistic and works with engineering precision" (525). The quotations are taken from the 1978 edition of L. Ron Hubbard, *Dianetics: The Modern Science of Mental Health* (Los Angeles: Scientology Publications Organization, 1978).

12

Scientology: "Modern Religion" or "Religion of Modernity"?

Gerald Willms

There are no tenets in Scientology which cannot be demonstrated with entirely scientific procedures.

—Hubbard, 1956a: 79

Introduction

Being a religion is one of the most important issues of Scientology's current self-representation. Although this claim seems to be supported by the majority of the (mainly Anglo-Saxon) scientific community, it is widely rejected in the public discourses throughout Europe, particularly in Germanophone countries, where the discourse is headed by a strong coalition of anti-Scientology activists, including church and state representatives, and backed by continuous hostile media coverage.

Apart from public opinions and court decisions, the mainstream of the scientific discourse is ruled by the *principle of charity* that rejects the questioning of the very substance of any religious self-portrayal. Hence, Scientology's claim of *being a religion* can hardly be denied from a scientific point of view, though Melton's emphasis, "in the fullest sense of this word," seems at best confusing because there is no scientific consensus on any "religion in the fullest sense" at all. If there were one, it would be on the common sense over the cited principle, which means in application: If Scientology claims to be a religion, we must first acknowledge this claim.

Yet we should be critically guided by a common but unexpressed scientific agreement on the "nature" of religions. The "enlightened" sociological point of view suggests that all religions contain an element of "irrationality" or, more neutrally, "nonrationality"; in other words, their members share a basic belief in some reality beyond reality as it can be discerned by the human senses—otherwise there is no reason to separate religions from secular ideologies. Hence, the primary essence of a "true" belief system is mostly represented through unquestionable, subjective, or nonrational assumptions and motives, incapable of empirical testing: the will of God(s), impersonal powers or transcendental forces, miracles, and so on. This means, in a more contemporary cultural perspective, assumptions and motives that are not backed by scientific/technical/functional knowledge and/or economic/individualistic rationality (see in detail Willms 2005: 131–151).

Although the nonrational, or religious, substance should not be questioned, and therefore should not be valued as more or less likely or appropriate, the analytical distinctions among religions are based on secondary aspects. Such characteristics emanate from or are at least legitimized by the primary religious context. Then, the primary aspects are likely to explain the more empirical or secondary aspects: the organization and the practice of the group, the individual or collective behavior, the rituals, the way of worshipping whatever, and so on. In a Weberian perspective the empirical or secondary aspects can therefore be interpreted as rational (actions) due to the primary nonrational (ideological) context.[1]

Religious Dimensions of Scientology

Prelude: Theta and Thetans

The *spiritual character of men* is definitely the most important issue of the Scientological construction of reality and the primary argument for considering Scientology a religion (Hubbard 1976: lxvii f).[2] Thus the thetan, the "immortal spiritual being," is interpreted as some sort of religious soul and therefore genuinely religious—even if it/he/she is nothing other than a synonym for the personal identity of the individual.[3] Though a human individual becoming aware of his/her own spiritual nature (= becoming aware of theta, or "life energy"), realizing his/her immaterial self as the cause of his/her own (and finally every) material reality—a reality caused by an act of volition to "play the game" of material life (Hubbard 1965: 28 ff., 95 ff.)—is seemingly a religious idea.

On closer scrutiny, however, we have to recognize that the metaphysical spiritual being is, generally speaking, irrelevant for Scientological reality. Either the spirit does not take part in life, in which case it is by definition nonexistent to any reality, or it plays the material game, in which case it/he/she has to accept the rules of the game: first and foremost, Hubbard's discovered universal qua natural laws of the life game—which are in fact a potpourri of philosophical buzzwords and everyday platitudes (from free market economics to popularized evolutionism), verbalized in the functional terminology of engineering.

Consequently, it does not make sense to become a "pure spirit," in other words, totally free, which means being an "unhappy nothing" (Hubbard 1965: 30), nor does it make any sense to be dead, in other words, "quitting the game."[4]

Thus to create a material reality (the world) to play the game (of life) is not a free decision of a free subject. *Playing the game* is the overall command that drives everything, including the immaterial spirit. Like this, there is a "spiritual command" that complements, not replaces, the former Dianetical and more biological command to survive. The one and only motive for any kind of human and social action follows from the "bio-spiritual" command to survive (Willms 2005: 165–168) and playing the "game of life"—in a demonstrative, successful way. Even if the latter is (nowadays) labeled a "spiritual" program, it can unequivocally be identified as a material (businesslike) enterprise in the here and now[5]—and, therefore, resembles more the religious-like business varieties of the *American Idea of Success* (Huber 1971).

It is typical modern misunderstanding (that may willingly be intensified by the Christian religion) to conceive of the spiritual being to stand in opposition to a rational secular being. In contrast, since Descartes and the days of Enlightenment, the "rational spirit" is, in fact, the sovereign of modern times (Rehfus 1990: 82). Hubbard's fundamental antagonism was designed between the spiritual (i.e., self-conscious, rational, and reasonable; see Hubbard 1951a: 40, 42, 130) and an animal-like material being. The latter was mostly, and, until the present, identified as the psychiatric idea of men. The way Hubbard describes the spiritual subject (the thetan) as a self-recognizing individual, analyzing reality (the material world) by spiritual means (rationality), acting consciously (meaning: in terms of economic-like competition), and in full control of his (functional) mind can be seen as an ideal type of a Cartesian subject—which has nothing in common with a sensitive religious soul.

At this point, I would suggest, there is no need to overinterpret the spirit or to go beyond the occidental philosophy, in other words, Durant's *Story of Philosophy* (see below). Hubbard's immortal spirit, which is due to Scientological processing some sort of "purified" or "cleared" thought, fits the immortality concepts of Aristotle's "pure thought" as well as Spinoza's "clear thought" (see Durant 1928: 84, 207).

The comprehensible version of the spirit or the spiritual self described above is connected to the overall modern image of Scientology. It is compatible to all self-help programs presented and advertised by Scientology, does not threaten the Scientological idea of offering a scientific technology, and fits the "Western" morals of individual freedom, economic competition, civilized behavior, or of "occidental rationality." Therefore, it is more or less unrelated to a genuine religious sphere of faith. As Hubbard said (still in 1959): "Scientology is not a heretic religion and demands no belief or faith and thus is not in conflict with faith."[6] But there exists a second, more religious context, explaining the Scientological idea of spiritual existence.

Religious "Subtext"

Aside from the above interpretation there are some other aspects of the Scientological construction of reality that are based on a more or less mythical subtext.[7] This subtext was already explicit in some early lectures given by

Hubbard, not to mention the significant role it plays in climbing the upper levels of Scientology's graduation chart. The mythical subtext is represented in the myth of *Xenu*, which, since the mid-1960s, has been an integral part of the more esoteric, so-called OT levels.[8] In short, the myth turns some ideas given early on by Hubbard in the *History of Man* into cosmic but also into "historical" facts (see Hubbard 1952b: 79 ff.; 1951b: 12 ff.). The myth of Xenu reveals the secrets of the terrestrial existence of the thetans (= human individuals) in form of an intergalactic adventure story. This mythical knowledge describes the extraterrestrial origin of the thetans, their unhappy doom under the rule of the evil leader Xenu, who deported them to earth ("Teegeeack") and wiped out their physical existence by atomic bombs in volcanoes. This story, which may otherwise be read as "bad science fiction" (Corydon 1992: 191), is in fact fundamentally different from common religious stories, not because it seems to be more or less plausible compared to the traditional or well-known religious stories of the origin of mankind or the universe, but because of its lack of transcendentalism. Of course, the incidents were said to have taken place in a different galaxy far away and some trillions of years ago, but they are presented as entirely material incidents, caused by flesh-and-blood persons, and related as historical facts.[9] Just because the thetans, in other words, their immortal spiritual selves, have personally witnessed these incidents on the "whole track" (see Hubbard 1973: 69 ff.) and recorded them as memorable material data, this reality can be experienced by each individual, measured by the Hubbard-E-Meter, and controlled by Scientological techniques.

Yet there is no "other" reality behind or beyond the material facts: neither a metaphysical Creator, nor ghosts or transcendental forces in any sense. The only metaphysical source remains the spiritual self that is "forced" to succeed in life and has to accept the universal laws and rules of the game (including all physical laws[10]). This is why Scientology's way of "freeing" the spiritual subject is so involved with teaching/learning/training and understanding/following laws and rules.

It is unquestionable that sociology and/or religious studies has to be willing to conceive of the myth of Xenu, in whatever shape, as a genuine religious theme. But (surprisingly?) neither Hubbard nor the Scientology organization has ever justified its religious legitimacy with the Xenu story (see LRH-L 1999: passim). In contrast, most Scientologists who explicitly refer to the more metaphysical and esoteric sphere of Scientology (like telepathy or the intergalactic adventures) are in conflict with the official Church—and, for that reason, we find those elements mostly in the context of the "Free Zone" and/or "Ron's Org," which are different splinter groups arguing that they are the true inheritors of Hubbard's "unaltered" doctrines.[11]

Nevertheless there are philosophical aspects in the Scientological idea that might be understood as more or less esoteric. The intrinsic connection between scientific and religious knowledge or the "spirit-mind-body" philosophy (Hubbard 1956a: 63 ff.) can be read in context of Blavatski's Theosophy—or more popularly as "satanism," as most critics call it.[12] But if we examine the mainstream of Hubbard's philosophical statements, we find *The Story of Phi-*

losophy (1928) by Will Durant (to whom Dianetics is dedicated). Apart from the outstanding importance of popularized psychological fragments, this *story* contains nearly everything that is basic to Hubbard's anthropological and, moreover, anthropocentric philosophy: the matter/mind problem as one of the most popular themes in the occidental philosophy (and also as basic problem of modern psychology, see Rohracher 1988: 12 ff.); the principle of pleasure and pain (i.e., Bentham's) as the one and universal motive of human action, the (pre-)utilitarian views on utility as virtue, and egoism as reason. The most impressive, sometimes literal source, however, is Durant's Spinoza, especially with regard to the view that the mechanical laws of nature have to be applied to the functions of mind. But also in the view that emotions are "motions" in a physical sense, on one hand, as well as individual "displays" of the conditions of existence, on the other hand: "He [man, G.W.] begins by making happiness the goal of conduct; and he defines happiness very simply as the presence of pleasure and the absence of pain"; "Pleasure is man's transition from lesser state of perfection . . . to a greater"; "Joy consists in this, that one's power is increased"; "Pain is man's transition from a greater state of perfection to lesser"; and "[A]ll emotions are motions, toward or from completeness and power."[13] All this can be found more or less literally in Hubbard's anthropocentric philosophy, so one can understand his *applied religious philosophy* as an attempt to realize Spinozism.[14]

In this philosophical rereading of basic Scientology assumptions, Hubbard's unwillingness to define or explicate the "eighth dynamic"—sometimes called "the Supreme Being"—seems to be less influenced by the Protestant *deus absconditus* than by the agnostic viewpoint of Herbert Spencer's "unknowable" (see Durant 1928: 395 ff.), even more if one recognizes how much Spencerism is included in the bio-spiritual evolutionism of Hubbard's Scientology.

In a more practical sense we may mention the "body thetans" (sometimes called "demons"), Hubbard's "proof" of rebirth,[15] or the different processes of auditing as a whole. But if we look at *Dianetics* we will recognize that nearly everything in this context is based on popularized psychological beliefs from the early twentieth century—often reinterpreted and renamed, or, as Hubbard would have said later on, "redefined." Everything in this context is of practical, more precisely therapeutic, use. We do not have to believe in the demons or in rebirth and we do not have to believe in Xenu or the whole bunch of incidents on the whole track or the *genetic entity*. All of this explains actual diseases of the individual which can be dis- and recovered by practicing Scientology. Understanding these as esoteric beliefs clearly means the goal of Scientology processing can be seen as a method to get rid of esoteric influences.

Religious "Meta-Text"

As a matter of fact it is redundant to scrutinize the details of this religious subtext because the Scientology organization and the scientific discourse are relating Scientology's religious character to the "big" traditional or universal religions. This is surprising because Hubbard's remarks on this topic are marginal and of a very general nature. The most concentrated discussion on traditional religions is about thirty-five pages in his *Phoenix Lectures* (1954), which can be seen as the intellectual basis for Hubbard's high-handed view that the Dao, Dharma, or Buddhism are all synonyms of spiritual knowledge (or knowledge of the spirit).[16] From this point of view that summarizes all Eastern philosophies as spiritual doctrines of knowledge (Hubbard 1954: 16 ff.), Hubbard describes Scientology as a successor of all Eastern religious philosophies[17] and in line with all spiritual (religious) leaders—a perspective that includes the Western spiritual leaders like Moses, Jesus, and Mohammed as well.[18]

Since the late 1970s, Buddhism has been most frequently cited as the tradition closest to Scientology. Hubbard mentioned Buddhism first in 1954 as a basic religious knowledge for Christianity (1954: 23 ff.)[19] but did not advance this theory until 1960. His poem *Hymn of Asia* (1974)—which bears a remarkably similarity between Hubbard himself and a returned new "occidental" Buddha—reflects a relationship between Scientology and Buddhism. However, Hubbard never gave reasonable arguments for his claim, nor can we find reasons for the additional claim of Hinduistic, Vedic, and Daoistic roots.[20]

Obviously, there are few deeper reflections on Scientological religious claims, but these are not made by Hubbard. A few of them are from broader Scientological contexts in the late 1960s until the mid 1970s (see Briggs et al. 1967; Thomas 1970; CS 1972; Oosthuizen 1975; SKD 1973, 1975), but most stem from scientific discourses (sociology of religion and religious studies). Several scholarly studies were published, predominantly in the 1990s, pointing to the alleged religious character of Scientology.[21] In 1998 they were summarized in a German Scientology anthology that clarifies the substantial affinities between Scientology and the overall scientific understanding of religion. In fact, this is one of the very rare Scientology documents widely compassing the "source," L. Ron Hubbard.

If Scientology, or at least some aspects of Scientological ideas or practices, are discussed in terms of their resemblances to Buddhism (Flinn 1983), Hinduism (Wallis 1976: 110 ff.; Wilson 1998: 139 ff.), Daoism (Wallis 1976: 110 ff.), Japanese Shinto religions (Sawada 1998: 232 ff.), or the universal religions of antiquity (Flinn 1998: 151) and, of course, Christianity (Wilson 1998: 130, 138), then the Scientological claim of being a "meta-religion" (or "religion of religions") seems to be correct (see CSI 1998a).[22] This reinforces the assumption of the existence of a Scientological religious doctrine or a systematic theology—which, as a matter of fact, is nonexistent (see Bednarowski 1989: 34, 63; Kent 1999a: 108 ff.).

To the contrary, the *Scientology Handbook* (CSI 1994), which grasps every essential issue[23] of Hubbard's construction of Scientological reality, contains four pages that may be seen as relevant to classical social scientific approaches to religion. Even before the introduction there is a short attempt to define religion according to common historical understanding—and without making any references to Scientology. The introduction then states that Scientology *is* a religious philosophy because it leads mankind to freedom and truth, followed by the doctrine of man as an immortal spiritual being. About 790 pages later, in the appendix, we can read the Scientological creed—that is more or less a reformulation of the 1948 UN Declaration of Human Rights, supplanted with the peculiar Scientological idea of "spiritual health" (CSI 1994: 795). In this way, the liberal or personal rights of the individual can be identified as the core of the Scientological creed—but these rights are the very essence of the modern culture, too. Without overseeing the religious (Christian) influence on the modern ideology, the liberal rights are actually reasoned in terms of natural philosophy and the philosophy of the Enlightenment (especially in continental Europe). This leads to the opinion that the Scientological creed is actually not based on faith but on rationality, and hence rationality is the genuine basis of the Scientological belief (Gollnick 1998: 137).

In fact Scientology's terminology has changed widely (since the beginning of 1960s) and in a very special way: The literal definitions (in the original texts) were not altered, but the subjects (the titles) were. So since the beginning of the 1960s, "philosophy" was often turned into "religion" or "religious philosophy," "knowledge" and "conditions" were transformed into "spiritual knowledge" and "spiritual conditions," "technologies" became (religious) "releases" (see Werner 2002: 102 ff., 310, and Dericquebourg 1998: 173), and so on. Maybe the best illustration for what is meant by changing-terms-not-content can be found in the *Volunteer Minister's Handbook* from the mid-1970s. The title (and the cover art) suggests a very traditional (Christian!) religious content, whereas the "normal" Scientologist is called a "minister" and his practice is turned into a religious practice. So the content emphasizes only the well-known duties and activities of a Scientologist described elsewhere: practicing Scientology "to make things better" (see Hubbard 1976: lxxii).

Also, the most recent "proof" given by the present Scientology organization in support of their claim to their religious identity (LRH-L 1999), a heavyweight, 1,000-page documentary, cannot conceal the religious deficiencies left by Hubbard. Aside from some general remarks on Hubbard's discoveries, the topic of religion, and the religious nature of Scientology, it contains a modernized version of *The Background and Ceremonies of the Church of California, World Wide* from 1959 (100 pages). Nearly 500 pages are filled with "group processing"—which is taken from Scientology beginner courses and should be given to an audience by a minister then "acting as an auditor" (LRH-L 1999: 512). And about 350 pages are dedicated to the so-called prayers of L. Ron Hubbard. These prayers, however, are just common texts from Hubbard's (mostly early) works, which are supposed to be utilized in the manner of prayers (see LRH-L 1999: 151–507).[24]

Institutional, Organizational, and Practical Aspects

We cannot deny that the present organization uses slogan-like, common religious terms like *church* or symbols like the (Scientology) cross (see CSI 1998a: 45–57; also earlier SKD 1973, 1974a, and 1974b). But if we look at Hubbard's books or the more internal writings, the organizational instructions, the training or education material, there is no equivalent to this symbolism (Werner 2002: 107). This gap is traceable to Hubbard himself because he—as the only source of Scientology's knowledge—never deepened the religious symbolism into an adequate practice. Only the Xenu story is transformed into practical therapeutic relevance—but this story is not, as has been said before, used for religious legitimacy.

Apart from Xenu, the rudimentary religious ideology vanishes entirely in the context of the Scientological product, although auditing and training are described as the "two central services of the Scientology religion."[25] In fact Scientological therapies (i.e., auditing and training) are commonly derived from the Dianetical background, which was always connected to (popularized) psychological or psychotherapeutic meaning systems without any religious intentions (Beit-Hallahmi 2003: 9)—though we shall notice that psychotherapy, too, has been located in the ambiguous Bermuda Triangle between philosophy, science, and religion ever since (Gross 1984: 69, 238 ff.). Moreover, the Dianetical therapeutic system was connected with Hubbard's scientism, in other words, the proto-positivistic ideology of measuring and engineering all individual and social conditions of existence. Although these conditions are now called "spiritual conditions," none of these conditions are related to transcendent or esoteric forms of conditions—they all can be measured in terms of (more or less) material gains.[26] Also, the Scientology graduation chart, the overview of the basic Scientology courses and the complete graduation system, displays no specific religious courses. This corresponds with the fact that we won't find traditional religious motives mentioned by customers (see Beit-Hallahmi 2003: 10, Thiede 2000a: 296 ff.; Dericquebourg 1998: 173). Finally, it is obvious that the other parts of the Scientological product, the management and/or administration technologies, are definitely not linked to metaphysical knowledge.[27]

Moreover, when we step into the churches,

> In the case of Scientology, where all major premises are kept in the same style, we find what most Europeans would identify as "American Style." Scientology celebrations all over the world are similarly carried out in a way quite unlike traditional European festivities, not to mention traditional Asian or African ways of celebrating important events. Scientology will stage a performance quite similar to the Oscar award show, and the religious content of such events will therefore be very different from traditional religious ways. (Rothstein 1996)

Thus, no fundamental changes have taken place since Wallis observed that "Scientology, although it describes itself as a church, has only the most rudimentary of religious practices in any conventional sense" (1984: 28).

Though it seems appropriate to discuss Scientology in line with traditional religions—for reasons stated elsewhere[28]—it is doubtful that we get at the heart of the matter when holding a religiously biased perspective.

Traditional Dimensions

Nevertheless, it would be wrong to interpret Scientology without traditional and therefore sometimes religious roots, which are intrinsically incorporated in modern culture. This means Christianity, or, more precisely: Protestantism, and, with respect to Scientology, mainly the American versions of Protestantism. The term *occidental,* or "Western civilization," is in fact often moralized and used by Christian apologetics to point out the intrinsic connection between Christianity and modernity. Especially in this context the tenuousness of Stephen Kent's insistence that no serious scientist would ever claim that Hubbard's thinking could be influenced by Christianity (Kent 1997a: 16) becomes apparent, even more so, because Kent demonstrates that Scientology has no arguable links to Eastern religious traditions (ibid: passim; see also Thiede 2000a: 297 ff.). So a possibly "modern" character of Scientology means—if there is a need to apply a classical religious approach—that a comparative perspective can be fruitful only when compared with "Western" religious traditions, in other words, Christianity. We can find support for this approach in Hubbard's statement that Scientology is "the first completely occidental endeavor to understand life" (Hubbard 1956b: 17) and moreover a specific "Anglo-Saxon" way.[29] It can indeed be shown that the announced Scientological value system is compatible with common Protestant, particularly "WASP," morals (see Hubbard 1981: passim).

Christian contexts may never be explicitly stated, but if we look, for example, at Scientology's church ceremonies, the recommended clothing, the forms of action, or the structure of the prayers (see, in general, LRH-L 1999), then it is evident that unquestioned Protestant traditions were dominating Hubbard's own religious mind (see Dericquebourg 1998: 174).

In a more explicit ideological sense we may examine the content and also the syntax of Scientology's "factors," which seem to be a "redefined" version of the biblical Genesis[30]—although the omnipotence of God is transformed into "life" and "consideration," and the "heaven-and-earth" terminology is replaced by a physically determined universe (see Hubbard 1953: 1 ff.).

Admittedly, there were a few disparaging remarks made by Hubbard about Christianity,[31] but we will find more (thought still very few) positive notes. *The Creation of Human Ability* (Hubbard 1955) opens with a motto from Luke, and Hubbard suggests a Scientological fulfillment of the promised goals of Christ: comfort, sanity, and immortality.[32] Jesus and Thomas Aquinas are adopted as ancestors of the Scientological idea.[33] Last but not least are the many thoughtless (or naïve?) mentions of "god," by which the Christian god is definitely meant, for example, in the last sentence of the Scientology creed: "[N]o agency less than god has the power to suspend these rights" (see CSI 1994: 795, my translation).[34]

Hubbard's alleged refusal of Christianity is part of a constant verbal rejection of any philosophy/ideology that is not "working" in a practical sense—and that refers (in his opinion) to any religious or secular social concept not grounded in individualism and (his) psycho-scientism: "Christianity and a million other-anities have struggled with this problem [of soul or spirit], and the result is a pot-pourri of answers, none of which can reconcile the problem."[35] Only Scientology has solved the key historical problem of the spirit or the soul (both interchangeable with the term *human mind*),[36] which causes the decline of all religions and civilizations.[37] And Scientology has reached all religious goals because the Scientological approach to the universal religious problem is not "subjective" but knowledge-based (read "scientific").[38]

Scientology as a Modern Religion?

"Dianetics is a science; as such, it has no opinion about religion, for sciences are based on natural laws, not on opinions."[39]—Hubbard never really abandoned this point of view (see also CSI 1993: 1). And he goes far beyond the subjectivism of psychotherapy when he claims that Dianetics is the "[f]irst fully validated psycho-therapy" (Hubbard 1955: 277). Thus he introduces Scientology as "a new word which names a new science."[40] And still in 1956, Hubbard emphasizes, "We're [in Scientology] studying hearable, measurable, weighable, meterable phenomena—right below the Static (...) And even the Static is experienceable."[41]

This is considered to be the most fundamental difference between Scientology and all other historical or contemporary philosophies/religions. It is a demarcation line between the claimed positive and functional knowledge of Scientology and all unproven forms of mere belief. Paying attention to this "line" is not only a primary legitimization of the basic Scientological idea, it is the justification for 100 percent functionality of all Scientological products, which never paid any credibility to metaphysical or transcendental uncertainties.

Hence, Scientology claims to be true not because it is a mere religion; Scientology claims to be true because of its provable workability: "The religion of Scientology provides a systematic path with exact procedures, which achieve standardized predictable results" (*Freiheit* 1997: 53, my translation).

The advertised 100 percent workability of all Scientological technology, of any therapeutic and/or administrative product, is guaranteed in that it is based not on subjectivism, transcendentalism, or just faith but on scientifically discovered knowledge and positive, universal, and functional laws. Scientology perceives itself as being functional in a proto-positivistic sense. Because the application of Scientology products makes men "free," "self-determined," "immortal," and "successful," Scientology claims to be a religion—not the other way round.

If we compare the outstanding relevance of "scientific" arguments—the "natural laws," the detailed description of universal "axioms," "logics," and the constantly advertised workability of all Scientology Tech(niques)—to the few (and superficially) existing religious arguments throughout the Scientological belief system, then it is obvious that a broader sociological approach should not be confined to the terminology and perspectives of a highly specialized *sociology of religion*.

Nevertheless, most scholars are actually interpreting Scientology as a very rationalized or secularized religion (see, for example, Wilson 1990: 267; Knoblauch 1997: 105)—nothing else is meant by categorizing Scientology as "world-affirming" (Wallis)—whereas, on the other hand, they concomitantly declare that Scientology is compatible or even in line with all traditional or universal religions. In the way, *occidental rationalism* could also be understood as a multireligious project, an argument that may be "politically correct" in some way but definitely wrong in any historical or sociological sense.

Again, there is a strong scientific consensus that Scientology has to be seen as some kind of scientism (Flinn 1983; Bainbridge 1987) and that Scientology is oriented to very individualistic (Bednarowski 1989) and (neo)liberal economic values and therefore displays "widely prevailing cultural themes" (Wallis 1987: 81). This means the main characteristics of Scientology are adjusted to the "normatively approved goals and values" of modern society (Wallis 1984: 4).

If we look at descriptions like "technological Buddhism" (Flinn 1983), "techno-scientific religion" (Bainbridge 1987: 74), or "modern gnosticism" (Bednarowski 1989: 34), it is obvious that sociological common sense can be found only in the first part of those terms. "Technological," "techno-scientific," or "modern" imply the same sociological context, whereas the latter words— not to mention the elsewhere-cited religious traditions like Hinduism, Daoism, Shintoism, Theosophy, UFOlogy, and so on[42]—are only weakly connected with the term *religion*. The expression "quasi-religion" (Bromley and Bracey 1998: 141) reflects this intellectual uncertainty in the case of Scientology.

The factual conformity of a religion to the broader cultural or social context defines (in modern societies) their grade of rationality or the "modernity" of a religious group or movement.

Without taking into account a specific religious background, we can see on closer scrutiny that Wallis's well-known analytical distinction between "world affirming/denying/accommodating" religions is guided by the idea of modern, cultural rationality: Some groups are apparently fitting into the rational conditions of a modern culture, and some groups are not. Translated in cultural terms, a world-denying group or movement stands in contrast to the standards of societal rationality—in a modern society that portrays its societal value system as rational in a very paradigmatic way.

In this sense, Scientology arguably is world-affirming, meaning that it is a very rationalized or modern religion, because of its assumed secondary aspects: the scientific "symbolism," technical "gestures," highly individualistic "appearance," and capitalistic "performance." Although in the case of Scientology these arguments could not be opposed, I suggest swapping the rank of the primary and secondary aspects to get a more adequate understanding of Scientology and to embrace a less "religious" and more sociological perspective.

Scientology as a Religion of Modernity?

As I have shown above, the assumed secondary, "rationalized," or "modern" aspects of Scientology can be seen as the primary aspects. Since *Dianetics*—the very fundamental ideology of Scientology's functional anthropology and the technical starting point for most Scientology processes and products until the present—every new doctrine has been introduced by Hubbard as purely "scientific" and based on "natural laws." Even the values of individualism and economic rationality, and also the more traditional Protestant morals, are exposed as scientifically demonstrated (natural) laws and/or evolutionary bio-spiritual necessity. There is no indication that Hubbard ever intended to reduce this very modern ideology as relative or secondary when he later claimed a religious character for his never-changed substantial doctrines. Moreover, the opinion that Scientology should be seen as the "religion of religions" is more likely to show resemblance to the cherished scientific hopes of the early Enlightenment, in other words, Auguste Comte's proposal of a future society that is ruled by positivistic means only—and in which sociology (not Scientology!) as the most complex meta-science will be established as the new societal religion.

If we take the whole bunch of modern values (scientism, technology, individualism, and capitalism)—and indeed rationality as a value of its own—as primary aspects and therefore as the incontestable substance of the Scientological belief system, we may also better understand the rationale of the more nonrational or religious aspects. Being a religion in Western societies means to have a privileged status. So it can be rational to claim some nonrational aspects to aspire to the economic and societal advantages given to religions—which then may enhance its own dynamic of rationalization (like prayers for mental health). The history of Scientology in fact displays this evolution, and Hubbard's internal remarks on this topic seem to confirm this perspective.[43] Beyond these sore points in the religious history of Scientology, there is evidence that allows a more adequate understanding of this reversed, and perhaps unintended, logic of rationalization. Following and generalizing Max Weber's theory of occidental rationalism, which reflects on the unintended consequences in the processes of occidental rationalization (summarized in the term *iron cage*), we may see these dynamics at work in the case of Scientology.

Being a "true," fully self-determined and free individual means, in consequence, being a godlike individual (a "super ego" in control of everything and therefore successful and not making any mistakes) and being free from social bounds or constraints. This primary ideological issue is reflected throughout all of Scientology's secondary aspects, and remains, above all, of paramount importance in all matters concerning (individual) "power" and "control," which are of elementary significance to all basic Scientological techniques and which are constitutive for interpersonal relations as well as for the external affairs of the organization (whose functionality is seen as identical to the functionality of an individual). Furthermore, the individualistic logic is displayed in a very sophisticated system of individual duties with its highly personalized structure of blaming and punishing individuals for any failure or malfunctioning of a group, as well as in "ethical" therapies suggesting abandoning social bounds to *suppressive persons*—a practice that was then criticized as the *disconnection order* by all public discourses, too. At last the all-embracing Scientological concept of universal individual rationality leads to the overall paradox of "total freedom": The more freedom the individual (or social group) acquires, the more rational and therefore predictable are his or her actions and the resulting consequences of acting. The highest level of individual freedom is being predictable ("rational") in every respect: Being totally free means, in fact, to be faced with Hobson's choice!

Applying the economic rationality of efficiency and the evolutionary imperative of steady growth to every aspect of individual and social life means to be necessarily successful in all things. And that means the evolution of a "super-sized" observer matrix, keeping everything under the surveillance of statistics, and valuing the whole social reality by measurable successes. This is the way the organization and its adherents have been described, measured, and advertised in a very economic language of growth, expansion, and success—and this fits the public perception of Scientology as a solely economic enterprise.

Finally, it is the outsized technoscientific belief system that is increased to a universal therapy for any problem of mankind and utilized as a religious-like concept. The "100 percent workability" of any *Scientology tech* is based on belief in the physical determination of the material world, the universal validity of the (mechanical) laws[44] of cause and effect, and Hubbard's axioms and logics[45]— given as scientifically proven laws. The doctrinal spin-offs from this positivistic belief then lead to "strange" secondary aspects like the sometimes merely understandable mumbo jumbo of technical terminology or seemingly useless abbreviations. The multiplicity of Scientological instruments charts and scales measuring (and ranking) all aspects of reality demonstrate the unlimited belief in positivistic scientism. Most notably the Hubbard E-Meter demonstrates this over-radicalized positivism as the ideological core of the Scientological belief system: not reclaiming limitations on the cognizance of natural sciences or their technical methods due to spiritual reservations, but to broaden the very material and positivistic worldview and techniques to the real paradox that the immaterial cause of life (the "spirit") now has to authenticate itself at the E-Meter. The Scientological belief in total knowledge of the overall conditions of existence and universal methods of handling any individual and social reality is intrinsically connected with this radical positivism—and it reveals its deformed consequences when unfoundedly applied to social reality.

This does not mean that Scientology cannot be taken seriously as a religion at all. Quite the opposite: If there is no scientific argument for questioning the nonrational substance of a belief system, then there is no argument for questioning the essential Scientological belief in Hubbard's scientism and his spiritual technology. There is no need to take up a competing scientific position, declaring that Scientology is not "true" science (which is obvious). This would be nothing other than the Counter Cult Movement's argument that Scientology is no "true" religion. Yet we need to change our perspective: The nonrational and therefore the so-called religious substance of Scientology is the unquestionable belief in the truth of Hubbard's scientism and the 100 percent workability of any Scientological technology, along with the ultimate truth of an ideal society ruled only by the "natural" laws of utilitarianism. To be sure, this has to be taken seriously only as a belief system—not more or less.

If we remember Durkheim's main thesis, that "the elementary forms of religious life" are a reflection of the most basic rules of human society, and hypothesize that modern society is "unique"[46] and represents a very distinct type of society—a real new society with fundamental (cultural) differences from any premodern society—then we have to ask what would be their elementary social forms and in which way would they be "symbolized" and "sanctified" in a corresponding religion. Perhaps Scientology gives one possible answer. In fact, Scientology has sanctified and ritualized science and technology as well as basic Western values like individualism and capitalism. The most constitutive ideological settings of modern culture are not reflected as ancillary societal conditions to Scientology but in contrast as universal truth, as universal, natural, or evolutionary laws, unchangeable by men, that have to be applied mandatory to anyone and anything. What would a specific belief in the very essence of the modern culture be called if not a "religion of modernity"?

Hence, why should we compare *standard tech* to the infallibility of the pope in the Roman Catholic tradition (Flinn 1983: 91)? Or interpret *auditing* in terms of traditional religious counseling, confessionals, or devotion (Flinn 1998: 161, Bryant 1998: 188 ff., Wilson 1998: 125)? These may all be well-reasoned approaches, but what does it take to interpret *standard tech* as a substantial reference to the proposed infallibility of modern technology? Or auditing as a substantial reference to the modern psychological understanding of the autonomous individual? Why not understand *Scientology ethics* as an unambiguous organizational briefing to improve the church's economic performance in the overall struggle for existence (see Willms 2005: 229)?

To compare Scientological doctrines and practices to traditional religious doctrines and practices, be they "Western" or "Eastern," seems a weak conclusion by analogy. Furthermore, this conclusion violates the substance of Scientological self-perception to be a practice based on natural sciences, which possesses a workable technology with the intended purpose of fabricating (better: rehabilitating) free and self-determined individuals as a precondition for personal and (mainly) material successes in the here and now. If the *principle of charity* suggests not questioning the self-perception of a religion, and rather following the subjective settings that are enrolled in the meanings of the basic idea, then it makes no sense to relate Scientology to patriarchal historic religions.

Conclusions

In sum, we can refer to Eileen Barker's proposal for "better understanding society" (1982) by analyzing a new religious movement. If a new religion reflects at least some main aspects of the host society from which its members are drawn, then it appears that Scientology reflects first and foremost the dynamics of "simple modernization" (Beck 1993: 180–187). Just as Scientology literally "preaches" (Hubbard's) technology and the "natural" laws of individualism and capitalism (assisted by a conservative framework derived from common WASP morals), the uncompromising way Scientology realizes their doctrines, primarily within their own structures, provides an idea of the turning points and the consequences of extensive and simplified rationalization. Expanding sciences, especially human (i.e., psychological) sciences to a religious-like enterprise of ultimate truth, abolishes any tolerance. Overestimating standardized technologies as universal problem solvers destroys the human capability to solve problems appropriately by using human intellect. Expanding the logic of economic rationality to every aspect of human life, in other words, reducing rationality to a mere instrumental meaning and therefore narrowing social reality to economic reality, eventually destroys humanity, which is primarily a social endeavor that can and should not be measured solely in terms of material successes. And "totally" freeing the human individual, developing the "super ego," means necessarily quitting any social reality.

NOTES

1. No primary religious context is, of course, ever labeled "irrational" (not by the religious themselves nor by religious scientists). Nevertheless, I would like to maintain this conceptual difference in accordance to a broader, at first not religiously biased, sociological perspective.

2. Some quotations by Hubbard/Scientology stem from German editions, which have been (re)translated into English for this article.

3. "One does not speak of MY thetan. . . . One would speak of ME" (Hubbard 1952a: 68).

4. There are no Scientology perspectives to any kingdom come.

5. Hubbard himself has well stated that otherwise, the individual endeavor to survive of a by definition immortal being is "based upon somewhat idiotic circumstances" (Hubbard 1975: 236).

6. HCO B, August 19, 1959, TB 1979, Vol. III: 514.

7. See, for example, Kin 1991: 29–44, 187 ff., Whitehead 1974, or C. Evans 1979: 49–54.

8. The most relevant part of the Xenu myth is revealed on "OT-III" (see http://www.xenu.net/archive/OTIII-scholar/, http://www.xenu.net/archive/OTIII-scholar/spaink-ot3.html, and http://www.xs4all.nl/~kspaink/fishman/ot3.html, all accessed April 7, 2004; see also Kin 1991: esp. 29–44, 60–63).

9. For a skeptical reading of "religious" science fiction see H. Evans 1998 and Grünschloß 2000.

10. See the Axioms of Dianetics and Scientology, esp. Dianetic Axiom no. 8. (A detailed interpretation can be found in Willms 2005: 184.)

11. See, for example, http://www.ronsorgusa.org/docs/excalhowto/excalchecksheet.shtml, http://www.fza.org/doc722.html#fz, http://www.freezone.de/german/cbr/d_teeg.htm, or the discussions about "ICAUSE" http://www.freezoneamerica.org/cgi-bin/discus/discus.cgi (all accessed July 7, 2003).

12. The public discourse refers to "satanist" aspects with respect to Aleister Crowley and the Ordo Templi Orientis (OTO), a gnostic group with which Hubbard seemed to have some connections during the 1940s (see, for example, Haack 1991: 34 ff.; Atack 1990: 89 ff.). Although the Scientology cross or the often-used triangles may be influenced by these symbols (or may not), there is no further evidence that "satanism" leaves any marks in Hubbard's doctrines. Those who suppose that the traces of satanism are displayed in the ideology of the autonomous individual (like theologian Haack 1991: 35 ff.) have a poor understanding of the political anthropology of modern societies at all.

13. Spinoza cited from Durant 1928: 197 ff.; compare Hubbard 1950a: 34–56 and CSC-WW 1973: 18.

14. See in detail Willms 2005: 54–58.

15. In *Mission into Time* Hubbard claimed to have self-tested his theories of the "whole track" and "past lives" by predicting special archaeological locations that were unknown before, which he found because he allegedly knew them from past lives (see Hubbard 1973: 31 ff.).

16. In his article "Why Doctor of Divinity" Hubbard denies that the idea of Scientology can be classified in traditional religious terms at all. Moreover, he states that the reason for describing Scientology as religion is of practical nature and can be seen only in the societal legitimization of religion (see *PAB* 1954, No. 32, 7.8.1954 in *TB* 1979, Vol. II: 72 ff). See in general Hubbard's article on religion in CS 1973 (24 ff.) and the collection of religious citations made by Hubbard in SKD 1975 (esp. 55 ff.).

17. Hubbard, *Ability*, Minor 5, 1955, *TB* 1979, Vol. II: S. 214 ff.

18. Hubbard 1954: 23 ff.; Hubbard, *Ability*, Minor 5, 1955, *TB* 1979, Vol. II: 210 ff.

19. See CSC 1978: 7; *HCO B*, 18, April 1967, *TB* 1979, Vol. VI: 195 (first: *HCO B* 21.6.1960).

20. Hubbard 1954: 13 ff.; Hubbard, *Ability*, Minor 5, 1955, *TB* 1979, Vol. II: 210. See also CSC-WW 1973: 10–19.

21. See http://www.humanrights-germany.org/experts/index.htm, accessed March 24, 2007.

22. See CSI 1993 (544). It was probably simply overlooked that Scientology could be seen as a forerunner of *New Age*, too. See Hubbard's article "The Philosophy of a New Age," *Ability*, Issue 60, 1957, *TB* 1979, Vol. III: 153. See also Andreas Grünschloß: "Scientology: A 'New Age' Religion?" (chapter 11 in this edition).

23. The original edition of the authoritative Scientology work is introduced by Scientology spokeswoman Lisa Goodman: "The definitive reference work on Scientology is *What Is Scientology?*, an 833-page work that describes the philosophy and beliefs, catechism, creeds and codes, services and scriptures of the Scientology religion." Cited in http://www.theta.com/goodman/wis.htm, accessed June 16, 2003.

24. This sheds light on the increasing tendency in organizations of worshipping Hubbard not only as "founder" or "source" of Scientology but as a real "saint" who was not lecturing but "preaching" his technologies, and whose "holy" scriptures are designed to be engraved on stainless steel tablets, encased into titanium capsules, and enshrined deep in mountain vaults protecting them from disasters of all kinds, including a nuclear blast.

25. See http://www.whatisscientology.org/, accessed August 23, 2006.

26. See, for example, CSI 2000, in which "spiritual" betterment is always "proven" by more or less material gains/successes.

27. Hall 1998 (conclusions).

28. Theologian Frenschkowski states that solely the concept of religion possesses the analytical requirements for a definition of Scientology (2000: 266). For direct objection see Thiede (2000a).

29. To differentiate from the Latin *medicin*, from German *psychologie* (Wundt), from Austrian *psychoanalysis* (Freud), and from Russian *psychatrie* (Pavlov), Hubbard defined the science of Scientology more precisely as "THE ONLY ANGLO-SAXON developed science of mind and spirit"; see. "Selling," *PAB*, No. 61, 16.9.1955 in *TB* 1979, Vol. II: 265.

30. Factor 1: "Before the beginning there was a cause"; Factor 8: "And thus there is light"; Factor 10: "And thus there is life," and so forth.

31. See, for example, *PAB* 1954, No. 31, July 31, cited in Kent (1997a: 16); see also Kent 1999a: 105 ff., 108.

32. *Ability*, Major 1, 1955, *TB* 1979, Vol. II: 152.

33. "To a Roman Catholic," *HCO B* v. 19. August 1959 in *TB* 1979, Vol. III: 514.

34. See also Hubbard's opinion of the undisputable reality of a Supreme Being (1951a: 97), which is not compatible with Buddhism at all. Further, see Briggs et al. 1967 and Oosthuizen 1976.

35. "The Limitations of Homo Novis" [*sic!*], *JoS*, Issue 17-G (June 1953) in *TB* 1979, Vol. I: 404.

36. Logic 24 states: "The resolution of the philosophical, scientific and human studies (such as economics, politics, sociology, medicine, criminology, etc.) depends primarily upon the resolution of the problems of the human mind" (see CSI 1993: 594).

37. *Ability*, Minor 5, 1955, *TB* 1979, Vol. II: 212 ff. For failure of Buddhism, see CSI 1993: 17; for Daoism, see ibid. 26. And the failure of practical understanding is also the reason for the decline of the Egyptian, Greek, and Roman civilizations (see ibid. 14, 33, 41, and Dericquebourg 1998: 173).

38. *Ability*, Major 1, 1955, *TB* 1979, Vol. II: 152. Finally, it is the E-Meter, whose functions are based on physical laws—and therefore raised above objection—that indicates the "reality," in other words, the positive and measurable quality of the spirit (see Hubbard 1961: 8, 30).

39. Hubbard, *DAB* 1(4), October 1950; *TB* 1979, Vol. I: 38.

40. *JoS*, Issue 1-G (August 1952) in *TB* 1979, Vol. I: 268; see also *JoS*, Issue 16-G (June 1953) in *TB* 1979, Vol. I: 376 ff.

41. "Randomity and Automaticity," *Ability*, Issue 36, October 1956 in *TB* 1979, Vol. II: 535. See also Haack 1991: 262 ff.

42. A German apostate also noticed religious borrowings from the Hawaiian kahunas (Jacobi 1999: 12). In sum, it seems to be more likely that Hubbard was inspired by popular themes of "New Thought," which was very popular at that time. Especially the syncretism of "plundered" Eastern religion, Christianity, and scientific fragments drawn from "physics, chemistry, psychology, and the applied science of industrialism" (Huber 1971: 167) bears a remarkable resemblance to Hubbard's writings at all.

43. See note 16. In 1962, Hubbard internally clarifies that every part of Scientology has to be seen as of a religious nature. He also points out in which ways the E-Meter from then on should not longer be defined as a scientific but a religious tool (see "Religion," *HCO PL* 29.10.1962 in *OEC-V*: 282).

44. "[E]ven the laws of Newton can be found operative in thought" (Hubbard 1952a: 17).

45. "The Logics" of Scientology given by Hubbard, which can be read as some kind of prolegomena to a mathematical-based positivism, are described as "basic common denominators of all education" that "form a gradient scale of association of facts necessary to understand and resolve any problem" (see CSI 1993: 594).

46. For the principal differentiation between "one" modern and the "many" premodern culture(s), see Latour 1995: 130 ff. and Beck 1993: 75.

REFERENCES

The bibliographical items from "Hubbard 1950a" to "Hubbard 1981" are referenced with the year of the (assumed) first publication. The year of the edition cited is noted at the end of each item.

Abbreviations

DAB = *Dianetic Auditor's Bulletin*
HCO B = *Hubbard Communication Office—Bulletin*
HCO PL = *Hubbard Communication Office—Policy Letters*
JoS = *Journal of Scientology*
PAB = *Professional Auditor's Bulletin*

Atack, J. 1990. *A Piece of Blue Sky: Scientology, Dianetics and Hubbard Exposed.*
New York.

Bainbridge, W. S. 1987. "Science and Religion: The Case of Scientology." In *The Future of New Religious Movements*, ed. D. G. Bromley and P. E. Hammond, 59–79.
Macon, Ga.

Barker, E. (ed.). 1982. *New Religious Movements: A Perspective for Understanding Society.*
New York.

Beck, U. 1993. *Die Erfindung des Politischen*. Frankfurt.

Bednarowski, M. F. 1989. *New Religions and the Theological Imagination in America.*
Bloomington, Ind.

Beit-Hallahmi, B. 2003. "Scientology. Religion or Racket." *Marburg Journal of Religion*,
8(1). http://www.uni-marburg.de/religionswissenschaft/journal/mjr.

Briggs, C., et al. 1967. *A Manifest Paralleling the Discoveries of L. Ron Hubbard with the Holy Scriptures.* East Grinstead.

Bromley, D. G., and M. L. Bracey Jr. 1998. "The Church of Scientology: A Quasi-Religion." In *Sects, Cults, and Spiritual Communities: A Sociological Analysis*, ed. W. W. Zellner and M. Petrowski, 140–156. Westport, Conn.

Bryant, D. 1998. "Scientology. Analyse und Prüfung einer neuen Religion." In CSI
1998a, 177–191.

Corydon, B., 1992. *L. Ron Hubbard: Messiah or Madmen?*, Revised, updated and expanded ed. Fort Lee/N.J.

CS [Church of Scientology, ed.]. 1972. "Scientology: The Other Case." N.p.

———. 1973. *Whatever Happened to Adelaide?: A Report on the Select Committee on the Scientology (Prohibition) Act to the Government and People of South Australia.* N.p.

CSC [Church of Scientology of California, ed.], 1978. *What Is Scientology? Based on the Works of L. Ron Hubbard, Founder of Dianetics and Scientology.*
Los Angeles, Calif.

CSC–WW [Church of Scientology of California–World Wide, ed.]. 1973. *Der Hintergrund und die Zeremonien der Scientology Kirche.* Feldafing.

CSI [Church of Scientology International, ed.]. 1993. *Was ist Scientology?* [What Is Scientology?]. Copenhagen.

———. 1994. *Das Scientology Handbuch* [The Scientology Handbook]. Copenhagen.

———. 1998a. *Lehre und Ausübung einer modernen Religion. Scientology. Ein Überblick aus religionswissenschaftlicher Sicht.* Copenhagen.

———. 1998b. *Vom Rechtsstaat zur Inquisition. Hinter den Kulissen der Bonner Enquete-Kommission "Sogenannte Sekten und Psychogruppen,"* 2nd ed. Los Angeles, Calif.

———. 2000. *Was Scientologen über Scientology sagen.* Los Angeles, Calif.

Dericquebourg, R. 1998. "Scientology. Kosmologie, Anthropologie, Ethik und Methodologie." In CSI 1998a, 163–175.

Durant, W. J. 1928. *The Story of Philosophy: The Lives and Opinions of the Greater Philosophers.* London.

Evans, C. 1979. *Kulte des Irrationalen. Sekten, Schwindler, Seelenfänger.* [Cults of Unreason: Sects, Deceivers, and Soul-Catchers]. Reinbeck/Hamburg.

Evans, H. 1998. *From Other Worlds. Alien, Abductions and UFOs.* London.

Flinn, F. K. 1983. "Scientology as Technological Buddhism." In *Alternatives to American Mainline Churches*, ed. J. Fichter, 89–110. New York.

———. 1998. "Scientology." In CSI 1998a, 147–161.

Freiheit. 1997. [Irregularly published German Scientology magazine].

Frenschkowski, M. 2000. "Den Religionsbegriff rein halten? Thesen und Beobachtungen zur Debatte um Scientology und anderer Neuer Religiöser Bewegungen." *Evangelische Theologie,* 60: 257–269.

Gollnick, R. 1998. *Studien zur Ethik und Pädagogik der Scientology.* Sankt Augustin.

Gross, M. L. 1984. *Die psychologische Gesellschaft. Kritische Analyse der Psychiatrie, Psychotherapie, Psychoanalyse und der psychologischen Revolution.* Frankfurt.

Grünschloß, A. 2000. *Wenn die Götter landen . . . Religiöse Dimensionen des UFO-Glaubens.* EZW-Texte 153. Berlin.

Haack, F.-W. 1991. *Scientology—Magie des 20. Jahrhunderts,* 2nd ed. Munich.

Hall, D. 1998. "Managing to Recruit: Religious Conversion in the Work Place." *Sociology of Religion,* 54(4): 393–410. http://www.innernet.net/joecisar/sosh.htm accessed on 02/21/2003.

Hubbard, L. R. 1950a. *Dianetik. Der Leitfaden für den menschlichen Verstand.* [Dianetics: The Modern Science of Mental Health]. Dreieich (1990).

———. 1950b. *Dianetik: Die Entwicklung einer Wissenschaft.* [Dianetics: The Evolution of a Science]. Copenhagen (2002).

———. 1951a. *Science of Survival. Prediction of Human Behaviour. Part One: The Dynamics of Behaviour.* Leicester (1968).

———. 1951b. *Advanced Procedure and Axioms.* Los Angeles (1974).

———. 1952a. *Scientology 8–80. The Discovery and Increase of Life Energy in the Genus Homo Sapiens.* Copenhagen (1979).

———. 1952b. *A History of Man. A List and Description of the Principal Incidents to Be Found in a Human Being.* Copenhagen (1988).

———. 1953. *Scientology 8–8008.* Los Angeles (1974).

———. 1954. *The Phoenix Lectures.* The Celebrated Lecture Series Given by L. Ron Hubbard to the Professional Course, Phoenix Arizona, July 1954, Compiled into Book Form by the Editorial Staff of Publications Organizations World Wide. Letchworth, Hertfordshire (1968).

———. 1955. *The Creation of Human Ability: A Handbook for Scientologists.* Letchworth, Hertfordshire (1968).

———. 1956a. *The Fundamentals of Thought.* Los Angeles, Calif. (1988).

———. 1956b. *Die Probleme der Arbeit. Scientology angewandt auf den Bereich des Alltags* [The Problems of Work: Scientology Applied to the Workaday World], 2nd ed., Copenhagen (1974).

———. 1960. *Haben Sie vor diesem Leben gelebt? Eine wissenschaftliche Untersuchung. Eine Studie über den Tod und den Nachweis früherer Leben* [Have You Lived before This Life? A Scientific Survey]. Copenhagen (1979).

———. 1961. *Wesentliches über das E-Meter* [E-Meter Essentials]. Copenhagen (1982).

———. 1965. *Scientology. Eine neue Sicht des Lebens.* [Scientology: A New Slant of Life]. Copenhagen (1979).

———. 1968. *Einführung in die Ethik der Scientology.* [Introduction to Scientology Ethics] Copenhagen (1980).

———. 1973. *Mission into Time.* Copenhagen (1973).

———. 1974. *Hymn of Asia.* Los Angeles, Calif. (1974).

———. 1975. *Dianetics and Scientology: Technical Dictionary.* Los Angeles (1975).

————. 1976. *Das Handbuch für den ehrenamtlichen Geistlichen* [The Volunteer Minister's Handbook]. Copenhagen (1980).

————. 1981. *Der Weg zum Glücklichsein* [The Way to Happiness]. Hollywood (1988).

Huber, R. M. 1971. *The American Idea of Success*. New York.

Jacobi, J. 1999. *Scientology. Ein Blick hinter die Kulissen*. Kevelaer.

Kent, S. A. 1997a. "Scientology und östliche religiöse Tradition." *Berliner Dialog*, 3(1): 16–21.

————. 1999a. "The Creation of 'Religious' Scientology." *Religious Studies and Theology*, 18: 97–126.

————. 1999b: Scientology—Is This a Religion? *Marburg Journal of Religion*, 4(1). http://www.uni-marburg.de/religionswissenschaft/journal/mjr.

Kin, L. 1991. *Scientology. Mehr als ein Modetrend? Die Entwicklung zur monetären Heilslehre. Die Philosophie im Klartext*, Vol. 1. Wiesbaden.

Knoblauch, H. 1997. "Scientology aus der Sicht der Gesellschaftswissenschaften." In *Referate zum Symposium: "Scientology: Kirche, Konzern? Totalitäre Bewegung?"* [Schriftenreihe der Hochschule der Polizei 1997, No. 13], ed. W. Müller-Franke, 97–111.

Latour, B. 1995. *Wir sind nie modern gewesen. Versuch einer symmetrischen Anthropologie*. Berlin.

LRH-L [L. Ron Hubbard Library (ed.)]. 1999. *Ursprung, Geistliches Amt, Zeremonien und Predigten der Scientology-Religion*. Copenhagen.

Malko, G. 1970. *Scientology: The Now Religion*. New York.

Melton, G. J. 1981. "A Short Study of the Scientology Religion." http://www.neuereligion.de/ENG/melton/page01.htm, accessed February 7, 2007.

Moreau, P. F. 1994. *Spinoza. Versuch über die Anstößigkeit seines Denkens*. Frankfurt.

OEC [Church of Scientology of California (ed.)]. 1976. *The Organization Executive Course: An Encyclopedia of Scientology Policy*. 8 vols. Los Angeles, Calif.

————. *OEC-0*. "Basic Staff" (Volume 0).

————. *OEC-I*. "HCO Division" (Volume I).

————. *OEC-II*. "HCO Dissemination Division" (Volume II).

————. *OEC-III*. "Treasury Division" (Volume III).

————. *OEC-IV*. "Technical Division" (Volume IV).

————. *OEC-V*. "Qualifications Division" (Volume V).

————. *OEC-VI*. "Distribution Division" (Volume VI).

————. *OEC-VII*. "Executive Division" (Volume VII).

Oosthuizen, G.C. 1975. *The Church of Scientology: Religious Philosophy, Religion and Church*. N.p.

Rehfus, W. D. 1990. *Die Vernunft frisst ihre Kinder. Zeitgeist und Zerfall des modernen Weltbildes*. Hamburg.

Rohracher, H. 1988. *Einführung in die Psychologie*, 13th ed. Munich.

Rothstein, M. 1996. "Patterns of Diffusion and Religious Globalization. An Empirical Survey of New Religious Movements." *Temenos* 32: 195–220. http://www.abo.fi/comprel/temenos/temeno32/rothsten.htm, accessed May 5, 2003.

Sawada, F. 1998. "Scientology im Verhältnis zu anderen Religionen." In CSI 1998a, 226–233.

SKD [Scientology Kirche Deutschland (ed.)]. 1973. *Glaube und religiöses Brauchtum der Scientology-Kirche*. Munich.

————. 1974a. *Der Klerus der Scientology-Kirche*. Munich.

————. 1974b. *Kultus und Dogmatik der Scientology Kirche in Deutschland*. Munich.

————. 1975. *Scientology. . . . . . eine Religion. Ausführungen über den Hintergrund und die Lehren sowie ihre Anerkennung als religiöse Gemeinschaft*. Munich.

TB [Church of Scientology of California (ed.)]. 1979. *The Technical Bulletins of Dianetics and Scientology by L. Ron Hubbard, Founder of Dianetics and Scientology.* Volumes I–XII, 1950–1979. Los Angeles, Calif.

Thiede, W. 2000a. "Scientology—eine Religion. Reflexionen zu einem unabgeschlossenen Thema." In *Dialog und Unterscheidung. Religionen und neue religiöse Bewegungen im Gespräch,* ed. R. Hempelmann and U. Dehn. Stuttgart.

———. 2000b. "Den Religionsbegriff differenziert anwenden. Warum die Einschätzung von Scientology als Religion problematisch bleibt." *Evangelische Theologie,* 60: 270–278.

Thomas, R. H. 1970. *Scientology and Dianetics.* N.p.

Wallis, R. 1976. *The Road to Total Freedom: A Sociological Analysis of Scientology.* London.

———. 1984. *The Elementary Forms of the New Religious Life.* London.

———. 1987. "Hostages of Fortune: Thoughts on the Future of Scientology and the Children of God." In *The Future of New Religious Movements,* ed. D. G. Bromley and P. E. Hammond, 80–90. Macon, Ga.

Werner, R. 2002. *Scientology im Spiegel des Rechts. Strukturen einer subkulturellen Ordnung zwischen Konformität und Konflikt mit den staatlichen Normen.* Munich.

Whitehead, H. 1974. "Reasonably Fantastic: Some Perspectives on Scientology, Science Fiction, and Occultism." In *Religious Movements in Contemporary America,* ed. I. I. Zaretsky, and M. P. Leone. Princeton, N.J.

———. 1975. *What Does Scientology Auditing Do?.* Ph.D. diss., University of Chicago.

Willms, G. 2005. *Scientology. Kulturbeobachtungen jenseits der Devianz.* Bielefeld.

Wilson, B. R. 1990. *The Social Dimensions of Sectarianism: Sect and New Religious Movements in Contemporary Society.* Oxford.

———. 1998. "Scientology. Vergleichende Analyse ihrer religiösen Lehren und Doktrin." In CSI 1998a, 111–145.

PART V

Controversy

13

The Nature of the New Religious Movements–Anticult "Culture War" in Microcosm: The Church of Scientology versus the Cult Awareness Network

Anson Shupe

During the 1980s and 1990s evangelical Christians wrote books, articles and editorial columns in such magazines as *Christianity Today* proclaiming their conservative theologies, lifestyles, and values under attack by a hostile alliance of liberal Christians, agnostics, atheists, hedonists, radical feminists, pro-abortionists, and others. They referred to the presumed struggle between themselves ("the forces of godliness") and the proponents of a secular America (presumably "the forces of darkness") as a "culture war."

Meanwhile, however, there was a parallel "culture war" that had started earlier during the mid-1960s. Its protagonists were unconventional new religious movements (hereafter NRMs): some Christian-based (such as the Unification Church and the Children of God, now The Family); some of foreign origin (such as the International Society for Krishna consciousness, or Hare Krishnas, and the Divine Light Mission); and some more like New Age psycho-technologies (such as est). In particular was one that has endured longer and larger than most: the Church of Scientology International.

The antagonists in this other culture war were family-based, grassroots groups with emotive names such as Love Our Children, Inc., Citizens Engaged in Freeing Minds, the American Family Foundation, and the Citizens Freedom Foundation. They were all dedicated to (1) rallying official and popular support for repressing NRMs they referred to as "destructive cults" and (2) seeking extraction of their loved ones (some minors, some legal adults) from NRMs, sometimes forcibly (employing a controversial abduction "shock" tactic they termed *deprogramming*). Together these two groups constituted what has been termed the anticult movement (hereafter the ACM). One long-lasting group in the ACM, ultimately the largest and most influential on both national (U.S.) and international levels, was the Cult Awareness Network (hereafter CAN) headquartered in Chicago, Illinois.

Scientology and CAN were the organizational personifications of NRM and ACM forces in this older culture war. This chapter reports on their respective public strategies, tactics, and entanglements over roughly a ten-year period until CAN, buried under a barrage of resource-consuming lawsuits (many, but not all, instigated by individual Scientologists), succumbed to bankruptcy. Scientology can indirectly take some credit for NRMs' "defeat" of CAN (though CAN's own *sub rosa* activities played a major role as well), but unlike wars between nations, it was social science observers, not the victors, who wrote the account of CAN's demise.

A Word on Sources

There are two general categories of materials upon which assertions in this chapter rely. One is the author's over-thirty-five years' collecting and reviewing ACM records and published literature along with interviews and correspondence with select ACM activists/leaders. Included also would be approximately 400 boxes of CAN files assigned as assets to a Chicago, Illinois, bankruptcy court trustee (including court transcripts, correspondence, and so forth concerning more than fifty lawsuits against CAN and thirty-two boxes just on receipts, audits, and other materials concerning CAN's finances). These were eventually auctioned off by the trustee, and the purchaser graciously permitted repeated access to them for scholarly purposes (for further details see Shupe and Darnell, 2006). In addition, this author served as a consultant/expert witness in several of the above-mentioned lawsuits for an attorney prosecuting clients' claims against CAN, including the seminal JASON SCOTT, PLAINTIFF V. RICK ROSS, A/K/A RICKEY ALLEN ROSS, MARK WORKMAN, CHARLES SIMPSON, CULT AWARENESS NETWORK, A CALIFORNIA NONPROFIT CORPORATION AND JOHN DOE 1–JOHN DOE 20, DEFENDANTS, Case No. C94–00796, November 29, 1995, which spelled the economic and functional Waterloo for CAN.

The second category of materials is a cumulative published literature on the modern ACM (plus linkages to past countermovements in U.S. history) and international parallel groups, much of it authored by Anson Shupe and David G. Bromley (see particularly Shupe and Bromley, 1979, 1980, 1982, 1985, 1986, 1993, 1994, 1995; Shupe, Bromley, and Oliver, 1984; Shupe, Hardin, and Bromley, 1984; Shupe, Spielmann, and Stigall, 1977; Bromley and Shupe, 1979, 1982a, 1982b, 1987). There have been relatively few other assessments of the ACM (e.g., Garay, 1999; Beckford, 1985), some bibliographic (Saliba, 1990), others merely derivative (Shinn, 1987), or some even misleading to sympathetic of side-issue considerations (Zablocki and Robbins, 2001). Almost all points of interest and the capstone of the Shupe-Bromley corpus of work is subsumed by Shupe and Darnell (2006), from which legal information in the second half of this chapter is almost exclusively derived.

Social Movement Environment for the NRM/ACM Culture War

NRMs, as a large number of scholars in history, religious studies, and sociology have witnessed, have been ubiquitous in North American history. I leave it for others to discuss why the ebb and flow of popular sociopolitical movements provide at times opportunities for religious movements to seize hold of at least a critical mass of supporters at least for a time. (See, for two brief attempts, Shupe and Darnell, 2006: 3–7; Bromley and Shupe, 1979: 87–96.) In the current culture war a perceived onslaught of NRMs emerged starting in the late 1960s and blossomed into something resembling a minor national scare from the late 1970s to the mid-1990s. This was a scare aided by such highly publicized, if anomalous, self-destructive groups as the Peoples Temple, the Branch Davidians, the Order of the Solar Temple, and the Heaven's Gate UFO cult.

To concerned (often middle- and upper-class) citizens, many of whom were directly touched by the phenomenon as their family members became involved in an array of NRMs, these groups seemed to emerge with dramatic speed through aggressive recruitment strategies. Some seemed to amass enormous followings and financial resources from or gathered by members. Many aggrieved families, initially considering their crises as personal tragedies and unaccountable disappointments, gradually discovered one another and coalesced to frame a common interpretation of their problems. Attempts to work through existing social control agencies, such as law enforcement agencies and political representatives at every level, to remedy their situations by finding assistance to remove their (frequently) adult family members from NRMs often proved futile. Thus the ACM was established in grassroots fashion as a third-party social control institution. When families tried to remove by force loved ones from these controversial groups they resembled the vigilante committees of America's frontier past.

ACM spokespersons quickly were able to draw selectively on post–Korean War POW psychological literature and in doing so generated a self-justifying ideology maintaining that NRMs employed socially subversive, individually harmful, encapsulating brainwashing/mind control techniques. CAN in particular (emerging out of its earlier California incarnation, the Citizens Freedom Foundation) claimed that this mental enslavement could be countered by experts who understood these esoteric practices and who could, on dramatic occasions, implement the specialized intervention antidote of deprogramming. (Deprogramming consisted of holding the NRM member against his/her will for a time and browbeating the latter with negative information on the NRM in question and on all NRMs as a threatening genus). CAN served as a clearinghouse to provide aggrieved families both negative information on any group it chose to label a "cult" (and the long list found in CAN files was impressively indiscriminate) as well as referrals to deprogrammers. Indeed, CAN maintained a select list of these ersatz mental health "experts" and derived about a third of its overall annual income from kickback fees paid by contacted deprogrammers (Shupe and Darnell, 2006).

Alternately, the Church of Scientology was founded by Lafayette Ron Hubbard, unquestionably an indefatigable adventurer and explorer, entrepreneur, and writer. His ideas for a new psycho-technology, which he came to call Dianetics, came together during the late 1940s and then were officially promulgated in 1951 with publication of his book *Dianetics*.

Eventually, after much conflict with the U.S. Food and Drug Administration, as well as increasing visibility, Hubbard incorporated his growing movement as the Church of Scientology and international branches were cultivated (Bainbridge and Stark, 1980; Wallis, 1977; 21–76). By the mid-1980s Scientology had replaced the maturing, less millennial, and controversial Unification Church of South Korean Industrialist the Rev. Sun Myung Moon as the ACM's *bête noire* and became CAN's personal archnemesis.

Here I present only Scientology's fortunes in the North American culture war with CAN. For its harsher European experiences, alongside which its hostile American encounters easily pale, see Shupe and Darnell (2006: 125–238), Davis (2000). Shupe and Bromley (1994), Beckford (1985), and Shupe, Hardin, and Bromley (1984). On both continents, however, the issue for Scientologists was the same: freedom of unrestricted religious (and related business) practice, especially from government interference and scrutiny.

Social Movement Strategies

Both sides in this culture war accused the other of more than being simply misguided. Each threw out charges of deliberate duplicity, heavy-handedness, even illegalities. They each sought litigation (criminal and civil), spread propaganda about the other and tried to sway popular opinion against the other, and accused the other of hate mongering. For example, when an ex-Scientologist in an Internet message threatened to bomb Scientology church facilities, CAN supporters publicly dismissed it as a joke (Shupe and Darnell, 2006: 17). When Scientologists pointed to CAN's rather poorly disguised referral system for families seeking coercive deprogrammings, CAN spokespersons piously denied they ever advocated anything illegal and encouraged only benign "exit counseling" (which was really a euphemism for deprogramming). When Scientologists accused CAN (and other ACM groups) of disseminating only negatively slanted, alarmist information on NRMs, CAN claimed it was only trying to provide an alternative voice to sometimes "slick" NRM influence in the media and, among other audiences, academics.

At some level these counterinterpretations—misunderstandings, self-serving embellishments, even crafted lies—are to be expected in any culture war. However, there was much more involved. It has now been shown that although the Church of Scientology was often accused of using "dirty tricks" to embarrass and harass CAN, CAN for its part acted out not just as a rallying point for anticult sentiment and a disseminator of anti-NRM materials but, more important, served as a referral agency to connect desperate families with vigilante deprogrammers. According to CAN's own salvaged archives, these deprogrammers, paid upward of $25,000 per intervention (plus miscellaneous costs such as travel, lodging, and bodyguards) by the families, then kicked back percentages of their fees to CAN, which laundered the monies as operating funds and "donations." The deprogrammers' kickbacks were in exchange for being kept on a select list in order to obtain future referrals. (These are serious matters of illegality for any group, much less an ostensible nonprofit, and readers are referred to Shupe and Darnell, 2006: 73–122, 163–194 for corroborating details, including those of an investigation into CAN by the Federal Bureau of Investigation.)

However, the above facts were virtually unknown except by rumor to many CAN supporters and certainly during the 1970s and 1990s to Anson Shupe, David G. Bromley, and other academic researchers (so far as I know) until the aftermath of CAN's demise in the mid-1990s. Therefore, here I discuss only the publicly recognized profiles and strategies of CAN and Scientology. The two primary combatants in the culture throughout the 1980s and 1990s seemed forced by necessity to adopt distinctly different methods of attacking their opponents and defending themselves. I say "by necessity" because of their respective differing resources and abilities to identify with (i.e., gain sympathy from) mainstream American culture.

The Public Relations Strategy of CAN

CAN's primary strategy was to cultivate its image of possessing NRM expertise in the forum of public opinion and to press the advantage of mass media receptiveness to its alarmist message of "cult dangers," which increasingly concerned the Church of Scientology by the early 1990s. Although there is insufficient space here to describe CAN's East Coast counterpart, the American Family Foundation (AFF), it is fair to say that AFF, compared to CAN in terms of leadership and activities, seemed to be composed of more degreed professionals and acted more as a "think tank" examining the "cult problem" with white paper reports, a professional journal, and academic conferences. CAN, for its part, aggressively handled more of the media/public relations opportunities, particularly on television. It was CAN that was more likely to respond to anguished families seeking interim actions of intervention rather than intellectual understanding of NRM dynamics. Compared to groups such as Scientology, with its lawyers and official spokespersons who often appeared formal and on the defensive when journalists allowed it equal time responses to prior CAN assertions, CAN held the cultural majoritarian advantage. This was true in five intertwined respects.

First, CAN claimed the moral high ground as representative for ordinary grassroots American families whose loved ones had become involved in poorly understood NRMs, some so obscure they could offer no spokespersons to respond to CAN allegations against them or some as large as multidimensional Scientology and therefore suspect as actually slick business enterprises in spiritual disguise. CAN could resonate empathically and sympathetically with noninvolved families who shared similar concerns for the lifestyles, career trajectories, and religious beliefs/practices of their own offspring. CAN spokespersons, such as its executive director, Cynthia Kisser, presented an earnest, serious, straightforward demeanor along with promoting the appearance of a no-nonsense, firm nonprofit group specializing in exposing "cult" realities.

Second, it helped CAN immensely to deal with a largely naive mass media that in entrepreneurial fashion fed on the drama of distraught families, torn parent-child relations, heroic rescuers, and the stereotypes of mysterious, possibly nefarious, "cults" that might be pseudo-religions up to no eventual good. Observed Bromley and Shupe (1987: 227):

> The media disseminated in uncritical fashion ACM claims and apostate accounts to create widespread public acceptance of the "mind-control" and "cult" stereotypes. Although toward the end of the ACM's first decade of operation, there could be seen a gradual trend toward "balanced coverage" (as anticultism alone ceased to be newsworthy), the mass media were still dominated by negative images of many religious groups.

CAN delivered up "good copy" for journalists by way of catchy sound bites and oversimplifications that most NRMs had difficulty immediately countering. It is no wonder that when a *Night Line, 60 Minutes,* ABC's *Prime Time,* or other television news magazine was faced with a fast-breaking sensational story on a Branch Davidian or Heaven's Gate–type group, CAN spokespersons like Cynthia Kisser, "exit counselors"/deprogrammers like Rick Ross and Steven Hassan, or CAN sympathizers like Drs. Margaret Singer and Louis "Jolly" West were more likely to be found in news producers' Rolodex files to be tapped for commentary rather than the virtual legion of mainstream social scientists and religion specialists who actually researched such groups and their issues.

Third, CAN could without much effort produce the "apostates," or angry ex-NRM members who often became outspoken "whistle-blowers" on their groups after coaching by deprogrammers and coaxing by CAN and journalists. To be sure, there were the NRM victims of failed deprogrammings, but as Shupe and Darnell (2006) found out in their research, one usually had to find the right lawyers who had the affidavits and notarized testimonies buried in their files.

Fourth, CAN was adept at "pushing the buttons" of ethnocentrism, xenophobia, and racism concerning the average American's unfamiliarity with many foreign-born NRMs. This is a pattern little discussed in the academic literature on the conflict. (See Shupe and Darnell, 2006, footnote 1 of chapter 2, for a brief exploration of this phenomenon.) Perhaps CAN's adeptness was not unrelated to the fact that CAN's executive director had a background in cultural anthropology and therefore had to have been well aware of how fanning certain flames of fear could work to CAN's advantage (as it did in constructing a working list of over 1,500 "dangerous and questionable" groups in American society, from the Roman Catholic Church to the Unification Church, to the National Democratic Party, to Mary Kay Cosmetics—see Shupe and Darnell, 2006: 39).

Fifth, CAN, like many ACM predecessors, readily made common cause with traditional faith communities (Protestant/Catholic/Jewish) that regarded NRMs as natural (but excessively aggressive) competitors and even poachers in the "gentlemen's club" of coexisting pluralistic mainline American faiths. Churches and denominations were also natural allies for such "child-saving" (hence family-protecting) crusades (Shupe and Darnell, 2006: 30–32; Shupe and Bromley, 1980: 47–56, 63–76). Thus, in the NRM/ACM struggle, even before the formal existence of CAN, Shupe and Bromley (1980: 241) could argue: "The balance of power was weighted heavily in favor of the familial [ACM groups] . . . because of their much greater capacity to form alliances with other institutions possessing symbolic and behavioral sanctioning capacity."

The Legal Strategy of Scientology

The Church of Scientology came to realize that, given CAN's image as a family protector that lent it an affinity for journalists sympathetic with that theme (and themselves generally inexperienced in covering minority religions), it was difficult if not frustratingly ineffectual to try to refute CAN's press releases and spokespersons. The Scientology equivalents of names like Cynthia Kisser and Rick Ross were not on the ready call lists of most journalists and editors. Accordingly, Scientology chose to fight CAN with litigation through attorneys, sometimes in the process enlisting a more dedicated, disciplined corps of adherents than CAN possessed. To anticipate the overall thrust of select brief examples presented below, it appears that a consequence of Scientology's litigious strategy was to erode CAN's resources with recurrent lawsuits even if this procedure was often not able to mute that ACM group's uncompromisingly anti-Scientology rhetoric and ideology.

During the late 1980s and early 1990s CAN was repeatedly declared to be "a going concern" in its annual audits by respected accounting firm KPMG Peat Marwick. CAN took in sufficient revenues from book and literature sales, newsletter subscriptions and membership dues, and deprogrammer kickback fees to cover office expenses and staff salaries, provide funds to manage costs of overseas travel for several spokespersons like executive director Cynthia Kisser to attend international ACM meetings, and collect monies to stage its own annual conventions. In addition, CAN could use the revenues to pay lawyers' fees during the early 1990s when Cynthia Kisser filed lawsuits against two local Illinois Scientology congregations and their leaders, alleging libel. (CAN lost both suits.) Within a few years, however, CAN's financial (and other) fortunes had turned.

One major reversal was due to the disastrous deprogramming attempts conducted by some "big name" deprogrammers whose names, home addresses and telephone numbers, and NRM "specialty targets" were staples in CAN files. A sampler:

> One fiasco was led by the venerable father of deprogramming, Ted Patrick, who in 1990 conducted a failed deprogramming of an Old Order Amish woman in rural LaGrange County, Indiana. Her husband, concerned that his beloved wife was "straying" from the strict faith, paid Patrick somewhere near $20,000 to abduct her and deprogram her "back" into the fold. She escaped her abductors, reconciled with her husband, Patrick fled back to his home in San Diego, California, and Indiana news services gave it much coverage.
>
> Another disaster was the dramatic abduction of Boise, Idaho's LaVerne Collins-Macchio, a thirty-nine-year-old member of the Montana-based New Age group the Church Universal and Triumphant (CUT), in front of her four young children. Despite days of constant shuffling among locations, twenty-four-hour-a-day confinement, harangues against CUT, and forcing her to watch videos of the Roman Catholic Church, the Church of Jesus Christ of Latter-day Saints, the Unification Church, and the Hare Krishnas (all of which, she was told, used similar mind-control techniques), the deprogrammers—led by CAN veteran Joe Szimhart—eventually gave up. They let her go, and Collins-Macchio went to the police. Szimhart fled Idaho for Santa Fe, New Mexico, and was eventually returned to Idaho by police detectives who tracked him south with an arrest warrant. Other deprogrammer colleagues had fled to New Jersey but were similarly apprehended and returned to Idaho. The "Idaho Seven" all initially pleaded innocent to kidnapping or aiding/abetting kidnapping; several won acquittal in a lower court; then after the Idaho Supreme Court rejected their "necessity" defense, four of the team agreed to plead guilty to felony charges of second-degree kidnapping.
>
> As just one more deprogramming bungle: former private detective-turned-high-profile-coercive deprogrammer Galen Kelly, who once contracted to provide security at CAN annual conferences, famously botched a 1992 deprogramming by the kidnapping of Debra Dobkowski, mistaking her for the intended deprogrammee roommate Beth Brukert.

Another factor in CAN's reversal of fortunes was an internal scandal that Scientology, through its *Freedom Magazine* and other publications, heartily publicized. During the early 1990s a most spectacular form of embarrassment occurred: The Reverend Michael G. Rokos, an Episcopalian minister, chaplain in the Maryland State Police, and CAN president from late 1989 to fall 1990, was discovered to have been arrested in 1982 for public lewdness and soliciting sex from an undercover police officer passing as a male prostitute. Rokos was eventually drummed out of the Maryland State Police and even considered *persona non grata* by CAN officials (Shupe and Darnell, 2006: 174).

Scientology, at least indirectly, also took the initiative in fomenting opportunities for litigation directed at CAN. During the 1980s and 1990s more than twenty-five lawsuits were filed against CAN by Scientology members (not by the Church itself on their behalf) who had attempted to register at CAN's annual conferences and/or join the not-for-profit group. CAN saw them as infiltrators (or at least troublemakers) and tried denying them conference admission (or if detecting them, ejected them) as well as membership. The individuals then claimed that tax-exempt CAN was discriminating, hence acting illegally as a not-for-profit. In its final years (mid-1990s), after undoubtedly feeling itself being "nibbled to death by ducks" in court, CAN finally conceded those Scientologists membership rights, as testified to by the number of relevant cancelled checks in CAN's archives (Shupe and Darnell, 2006: 18). This type of problem was not nearly as serious as the economic cataclysm of the Jason Scott deprogramming lawsuit (below), but these punitive legal actions and others by Scientology-related groups such as Sterling Management Systems (which sued CAN for libel) began to take their toll. Altogether at its height, CAN had more than fifty lawsuits against it pending. CAN's once comfortable cash flow, impaired by not just the tightening noose around the once-thriving deprogramming practice but also by the expense of constantly mounting attorneys' fees, began to pose a serious financial drain. By the mid-1990s letters to CAN from attorneys and auditors, found in the CAN archives, demonstrate clear fiscal stress. KPMG Peat Marwick continually throughout the 1990s expressed concerns. Indeed, one cause for concern was the costs of the lawsuits. CAN had made no "rainy day" fund allotments for such crises. In its audit of 1993–1994, Peat Marwick expressed its overall concern for CAN's continued solvency:

> The Organization [CAN] had not obtained new insurance coverage
> for legal costs and these is no assurance such insurance coverage can
> be obtained. Additionally, the organization had a deficit fund balance
> at December 31, 1994 of $121, 161. If the costs of [legal] defense, cou-
> pled with the organization's other expenses exceed the organization's
> ability to generate support and revenue, the organization would be
> unable to continue as a going concern. (For further details, see Shupe
> and Darnell, 2006: 174–180.)

That warning proved prophetic, coming at a time when CAN increasingly found itself defaulting on bills as mundane as for its telephones and continually in arrears to its lawyers for their legal costs.

Here, in brief, is how Scientology used the legal strategy (ironically in the end with CAN's own assistance) to triumph in the culture war.

CAN versus Scientology: The Jason Scott Deprogramming Case

The attempted but failed deprogramming of eighteen-year-old Jason Scott constitutes the precipitating event in setting up CAN's demise. A Church of

Scientology member and private attorney, Kendrick Moxon, had been a thorn in CAN's side for years through numerous lawsuits lodged against it by Scientologists, and there is little doubt that he saw the Scott case as offering a superb opportunity to use the legal process of "discovery" to implicate CAN officials and operative in deprogramming referrals. The following brief narrative is based on testimonies, CAN records, and assorted materials related to the case Scott v. Ross/CAN, November 29, 1995, as well as the author's firsthand experience as a consultant to Moxon and sole expert witness in the case (called on behalf of Jason Scott).

In essence, Jason Scott was one of three brothers (the others sixteen and thirteen years of age, respectively) whose mother, Kathy Tonkin, belonged to the Life Tabernacle Church, a Seattle, Washington, branch of the United Pentecostal Church International. Over several related issues involving another congregational member and the pastor, Tonkin abruptly quit the church and encouraged her sons to do the same. They would not. She subsequently ejected her two youngest sons from her home. (One went to live with grandparents, another with a church family.) Meanwhile, Jason continued to live with his mother and seek reconciliation.

Through Shirley Landa, a local CAN contact person (and cofounder of CAN) Tonkin was placed through to Arizona deprogrammer Rick Ross, self-styled "Bible-based exit counselor" (and a convicted jewel thief with a prison record). Tonkin retained Ross to deprogram her two younger sons; Ross came to Seattle with assistants and successfully abducted the two teenagers and convinced them to leave the church, and then added "for muscle" to his "security team" a karate black belt for Jason's deprogramming. Also, besides being physically large and athletic, Jason was a legal adult, so Ross upped his deprogramming fee to Tonkin. When Scott visited his grandmother's house one evening to see his brother, the deprogrammers surprised him, wrestled him to the ground after a violent scuffle, and dragged him to a waiting van, the windows of which were covered by towels taped over to mask the inside. While one man held Scott's torso, another sat on his legs, and a third pinned his head and shoulders to the floor of the van. They handcuffed his wrists, tied his ankles with tape, and gagged him from ear to ear with duct tape. Finally, during the trip to a remote oceanside cottage, Jason was kept on his stomach, his hands beneath him, while one of the deprogrammers (weighing 300 pounds) sat on his back.

After this dramatic kidnapping Ross et al. confined Jason Scott for five days, at times in a bathroom shower stall, on a nylon leash, but always in the cottage complete with motion sensors and thick nylon straps riveted in a mesh-like pattern over all the windows. When Jason finally faked his "awakening" out of mind control by renouncing the Life Tabernacle Church, the deprogrammers took him to a restaurant to celebrate, foolishly allowing him to go to the men's lavatory alone. Jason immediately ducked out a back door and called the police from a telephone across the street. The deprogrammers were immediately taken into police custody.

The deprogrammers were prosecuted on criminal charges, but the trial ended in a hung jury. In late 1995 Jason Scott sought damages in a civil trial (represented by attorney Moxon). A nine-member jury unanimously agreed that the defendants were negligent and that their actions were both physically and psychologically injurious to Jason, that the defendants had deprived him of his civil liberties, and that they had "intentionally or recklessly acted in a way so outrageous in character and so extreme in degree so as to go beyond all possible bounds of decency and to be regarded as atrocious and utterly intolerable in a civilized community." Compensatory and punitive damages totaling almost $5 million were awarded to Jason Scott. (One million dollars was levied against CAN itself.)

CAN for its part received an insurance settlement to absorb the cost of its fine, but it used the money instead to pursue stubbornly an unsuccessful appeal in Jason Scott, Plaintiff Appellee v. Rick Ross, aka Rickey Allen Ross; Mark Workman; Charles Simpson, Defendants and Cult Awareness Network, a California Non-profit Corp, Defendant-Appellant, United States Court of Appeal for the North Circuit Before Mary M. Schroeder and Robert B. Beezer, Circuit Judges, and William W. Schwarzer, Senior District Judge, Case No. 96–35050, Seattle, WA, September 11, 1997.

Insurance claim money spent on that unsuccessful appeal, plus the burden of numerous unpaid legal bills from previous lawsuits, led in a major way to a bankrupted CAN. On October 23, 1996, CAN entered a Chapter 11 bankruptcy, hoping but failing ultimately to develop a reorganization plan. Scott's attorney, Kendrick Moxon, vigorously opposed such a plan, and it was not approved by the United States Bankruptcy Court for the Northern District of Illinois. Scott began collection proceedings as CAN filed for the Chapter 7 bankruptcy in June 1996. There was a period of frantic ACM efforts to obtain CAN's files and logo, and there was even a brief attempt by scrambling ACM activists to resurrect the group, but CAN was irreparably broken. Eventually a new CAN *did* emerge, but it was headed and staffed at its Los Angeles office largely by Scientologists and sympathizers of that church (Shupe and Darnell, 2006: 184–191).

The Cultural War Dissolved by Default

With CAN gone, neither the American Family Foundation nor any of the sporadic contenders to duplicate CAN could replace its vital ACM role as both a disseminator of alarmist anti-NRM propaganda to the media and a clearinghouse for coercive deprogramming referrals. No other ACM group could or did step up to assume CAN's mantle as primary ACM spokesgroup.

Indeed, by the dawn of the twenty-first century both AFF and the entire NRM/ACM culture war, or "cult scare," were moribund. Groups like the Unification Church, the Family, or the Hare Krishnas had weathered their own internal issues, their members had aged (many were now grandparents), and their organizations had matured in sociologically predictable ways. Most important, NRMs had lost or outgrown the cultural "rough edges" that had earned them so much acrimony and public distrust. Many had simply faded from public controversy.

The irony is that overall CAN, with its public relations and successes and easy access to media outlets that enabled it to shape much of the public debate about "cults" and that won it so many television news magazine victories over groups like Scientology, ultimately still lost the culture war. These ACM media and other cultural successes were foreseen a quarter of a century earlier when Shupe and Bromley (1980: 245) noted (even before CAN had been formed out of CFF):

> While the ACM was unable to move the new religions or their members into a position where legitimated management or outright coercive repression was possible, they were nevertheless highly successful at achieving symbolic degradation of these movements. Affixing the label "cults" to the new religions (however imprecise from sociological and even theological viewpoints), along with all the stereotypical attributes we have described . . . was both more easily accomplished and also extremely effective in locating these movements beyond the pale of public morality.

However, at the time when Shupe and Bromley wrote that analysis, as relevant as it seemingly was for much of CFF's and CAN's existence, CAN's role in cultivating a criminal corporate climate by sponsoring and facilitating as accessory after the fact illegal deprogrammings was largely unknown except to ACM insiders and activists. CAN's financial undoing was the result partly of Scientology's litigious harassment but also importantly from the legal costs incurred by CAN's own numerous illegalities. Again, not knowing the full extent of these activities even a decade earlier, the prescient sociologists David G. Bromley and Anson Shupe nevertheless anticipated such a possible demise for ACM groups like CAN. These authors' assessment below refers mainly to the ACM's cavalier, indiscriminate labeling of so many diverse groups as questionably "cults." But it also serves as a fitting obituary for CAN, which could not wean itself from the financial rewards of criminal abductions: "The most likely outcome is decline into relative obscurity and impotence, for the kinds of changes needed to ensure future successes involve disavowal of practices upon which past successes have been built (Bromley and Shupe, 1987: 233)." There was no official armistice signed for the NRM/ACM culture war, but for all practical purposes—for now—it is over by default.

REFERENCES

Bainbridge, William Sims, and Rodney Stark. 1980. "Scientology: To Be Perfectly Clear." *Sociological Analysis* 4 (2): 128–136.

Beckford, James A. 1985. *Cult Controversies: The Societal Response to the New Religious Movements*. New York: Tavistock.

Bromley, David G., and Anson D. Shupe, Jr. 1979. *"Moonies" in America: Cult, Church, and Crusade*. Beverly Hills, CA: Sage.

———. 1982a. *Strange Gods: The Great American Cult Scare*. Boston: Beacon Press.

———. 1982b. "Repression and the Decline of Social Movements: The Case of the New Religions." Pp. 325–347 in Jo Freeman (ed.), *Social Movements of the 1960s and 1970s*. San Francisco: Longman Publishers.

———. 1987. "The Future of the Anticult Movement." Pp. 221–234 in David G. Bromley and Phillip E. Hammond (eds.), *The Future of New Religious Movements.* Macon, GA: Mercer University Press.

Davis, Derek H. 2000. "Religious Persecution in Today's Germany: Old Habits Renewed." Pp. 107–124 in Derek H. Davis (ed.), *Religious Liberty in Northern Europe in the Twenty-First Century.* Waco, TX: J. M. Dawson Institute of Church State Studies, Baylor University.

Garay, Alain. 1999. *L'activisme anti-sectes de l'assistance a l'amalgame.* Lewiston, NY: The Edwin Mellen Press.

Saliba, John A. 1990. *Social Science and the Cults: An Annotated Bibliography.* New York: Garland Publishers: 618–652.

Shinn, Larry D. 1987. *The Dark Lord: Cult Images and the Hare Krishnas in America.* Philadelphia: Westminster Press.

Shupe, Anson, and David G. Bromley. 1979. "*The Moonies and the Anti-Cultists: Movement and Countermovement in Conflict.*" *Sociological Analysis* 40 (Winter): 325–356.

———. 1980. *The New Vigilantes: Deprogrammers, Anticultists, and the New Religions.* Beverly Hills, CA: Sage.

———. 1982. "Shaping the Public Response to Jonestown: The Peoples Temple and the Anti-Cult Movement." Pp. 105–32 in Kenneth Levi (ed.), *Violence and Religious Commitment.* College Park, PA: Penn State University Press.

———. 1985. "Social Responses to Cults." Pp. 58–72 in Phillip E. Hammond (ed.), *The Sacred in a Secular Age.* Berkeley, CA: University of California Press.

———. 1986. *A Documentary History of the Anti-Cult Movement.* Arlington, TX: Center for Social Research Press.

———. 1993. "Organized Opposition to New Religious Movements." Pp. 177–98 in Jeffrey K. Hadden and David G. Bromley (eds.), *Religion and the Social Order: The Handbook on Cults and Sects in America.* Greenwich, CT: JAI Press.

———. 1994. *AntiCult Movements in Cross-Cultural Perspective.* New York: Garland Publishers.

———. 1995. "The Evolution of Modern American Anticult Ideology: A Case Study in Frame Extension." Pp. 411–116 in Timothy Miller (ed.), *America's Alternative Religions.* Albany, NY: State University of New York Press.

Shupe, Anson, David G. Bromley, and Donna L. Oliver. 1984. *The Anti-Cult Movement in America: A Bibliography and Historical Survey.* New York: Garland Publishers.

Shupe, Anson D., Jr., David G. Bromley, and Joseph E. Ventimiglia. 1979. "Atrocity Tales, the Unification Church, and the Social Construction of Evil." *Journal of Communication* 29 (Summer): 42–53.

Shupe, Anson, and Susan E. Darnell. 2006. *Agents of Discord: Deprogramming, Pseudo-Science, and the American Anticult Movement.* New Brunswick, NJ: Transaction Publishers.

Shupe, Anson D., Bert Hardin, and David G. Bromley, 1984. "A Comparison of Anti-Cult Movements in the United States and West Germany." Pp. 177–192 in Eileen Barker (ed.), *Of Gods and Men: New Religious Movements in the West.* Macon, GA: Mercer University Press.

Shupe, Anson, Roger Spielmann, and Sam Stigall. 1977. "Deprogramming: the New Exorcism." *American Behavioral Scientist* 20 (July/August): 941–956.

Wallis, Roy. 1977. *The Road to Total Freedom: A Sociological Analysis of Scientology.* New York: Columbia University Press.

Zablocki, Benjamin, and Thomas Robbins (eds.). 2001. *Misunderstanding Cults: Searching for Objectivity in a Controversial Field.* Toronto: University of Toronto Press.

14

Scientology in Court: A Look at Some Major Cases from Various Nations

James T. Richardson

Introduction

Scientology, which claims to have churches in 150 countries with
ten million members in all (Church of Scientology, 2007), has been
perhaps the most litigious religious group in modern history. Since
its inception in 1954 it has filed innumerable lawsuits against governments, individuals, and organizations in a long-running effort to establish itself legally as a religion, and to defend itself from allegations
made by outsiders, former members, and government officials. Indeed, it has been said that Scientology uses legal action as a weapon
against those with whom it has disagreements. Whether this is the
case or not, it has been noted that large numbers of lawsuits have
been filed by Scientology organizations in many different countries.
For instance, when the Internal Revenue Service in the United States
finally decided to grant tax-exempt status to the Church of Scientology, as a part of this controversial settlement, the *New York Times* reported that Scientology agreed to withdraw dozens of lawsuits against
the IRS (Frantz, 1997).[1]

Scientology has also been forced to defend itself from civil suits
and even criminal charges, as well, with former members claiming
that they were tricked into participating in Scientology and paying
significant sums for the auditing courses offered by the organization.[2] One such civil case was that brought by former member Larry
Wollersheim in 1988 in California. He was initially awarded a total of
$30 million by a civil jury (including $25 million in punitive damages) that accepted his claims even though they were based in part
on unscientific evidence concerning "brainwashing."[3] Similar cases
were brought against Scientology over several decades in America,

with some significant judgments being rendered against the organization. Most awards were, however, overturned on appeal, as Scientology legal teams moved the cases from trial courts to appeal courts where judges were perhaps more objective than American juries in their decision-making process and more informed of the applicable law.[4]

In both these situations involving Scientology as either a plaintiff or a defendant, the organization has entered the legal arena vigorously, using its considerable legal prowess to its advantage.[5] Obviously this use of the legal system will be more effective in certain contexts, but Scientology has managed to act effectively in many different societies to defend its interest in court.[6] It is the prototype of what sociologists of law refer to as a "repeat player" within the legal arena. Its attorneys generally know the law relevant to its issues of concern as well as the way a given legal system operates. Consequently it generally has been effective when engaged in litigation. Those with whom it deals within this arena are often at some disadvantage in that they may well be less experienced than the representatives of Scientology who are adversaries in a given case. This can be the case even in situations in which Scientology is suing a governmental agency. The vigor and deliberateness with which Scientology makes use of the legal system is impressive, and it has probably caused some who would criticize or even research the organization to reconsider before doing so.[7] It may be fitting to call Scientology's approach to litigation a form of "disciplined or vigilante litigation," terms developed by Cote and Richardson (2001) to describe the very focused and deliberate use of the legal system by the Jehovah's Witnesses in recent decades, not only in the United States but elsewhere, such as in the European Court of Human Rights (Richardson and Garay, 2004).

The analysis of the experience of Scientology in court will be organized around two issues. One will be cases in which Scientology has attempted to define and defend itself as a genuine religion. This has often been within the context of seeking tax-exempt status within a nation. Another type of case concerns registration in societies that demand registration of religious groups before they can achieve tax-exempt status and other privileges. These types of cases, and others where relevant, will be discussed by country, with certain countries being selected that are particularly telling in terms of legal precedents and the impact of the decisions.

Before beginning this examination of selected countries' experience with Scientology legal cases it will be useful to summarize the global situation as reported by Scientology itself. In a recent publication (Church of Scientology, 2007) the organization claimed that it was properly registered as a religion in the following European countries that require some sort of registration of religious groups: Sweden, Portugal, Hungary, Slovenia, Croatia, and Albania. Other European countries that do not require registration have also recognized Scientology through various bureaucratic or judicial processes. These include, according to Scientology, Italy, Denmark, Austria, Germany, the United Kingdom, and Norway. Noticeably absent from either list is France, which has been a major battleground over recognition of Scientology. France will not be examined herein, however, given that Susan Palmer's chapter in this same collection recounts that busy history of conflict well (see chapter 15 in this volume).[8]

The same document that recounts the European countries that have recognized in one form or another also lists a number of other countries that have recognized Scientology, according to its claims. These include the United States, Australia, New Zealand, Canada, South Africa, Nepal, Tanzania, Kenya, Zimbabwe, Taiwan, Kazakhstan, Kyrgyzstan, Venezuela, Ecuador, Costa Rica, Brazil, India, Philippines, and Sri Lanka.[9] It would be impossible given space demands to discuss each of these countries in terms of how Scientology gained recognition as a religion. Therefore, several will be selected to demonstrate the various ways this has occurred. It will be noted that recognition usually involved litigation of one form or another. The nations selected for examination herein include Australia, Germany, Italy, the United States, the United Kingdom, and Russia.

Australia

Australia will be included although another chapter herein will discuss the boarder context concerning Scientology in that country, as well as report some revealing research on media coverage of the organization (Possamai and Possamai-Inesedy, chapter 18 in this volume). The inclusion is based on the significance of a case involving Scientology for Australia, but also because the opinion itself is quite thorough and impressive, and is cited in case law of other countries.

The case that will be discussed was decided in 1983 in Australia, and involved an effort to gain tax-exempt status in the State of Victoria. The Church had been granted that status in some other Australian states, but there had been a long history of efforts to exert control over Scientology in various Australian states. "Various state psychological practice acts had banned Scientologists from registering, advertising, teaching, or receiving payments for services, while granting exemptions to ministers of other faiths who practice counseling" (Richardson, 1995, 2005). Also, the Australian Companies Code had at one point listed the terms Scientology and Dianetics in its Prohibited Names Directive. .

When the State of Victoria sought to collect payroll taxes on salaries paid by Scientology to its member workers, the Church appealed and eventually sued to overturn that administrative decision, because the law clearly stated that such taxes were not to be charged against religious and benevolent organizations. The case was dismissed at the trial court level in Victoria, and an appeal was dismissed by the Supreme Court of Victoria. Scientology then appealed to the High Court of Australia, eventually winning a quite significant victory in that Court. The lengthy and erudite judgment carefully defined attributes of a religion, using a quite sophisticated analysis. The opinion cites such scholarly figures as Clifford Geertz, Max Weber, Emile Durkheim, James Frazer, Bryan Wilson, along with many others, in an effort to determine useful criteria that might be used to establish whether an organization was a religion. The opinion also discussed major cases from other countries on the issue, especially United

States case law, and laments the fact that no Australian case has dealt in depth with the issue prior to the present case before the Court.[10] After doing a thorough analysis the Court stated unequivocally that Scientology met the criteria establishing itself as a religion, and therefore should be granted exempt status for tax purposes. The Court went on to state that a religion did not have to be theistic, and that a religion involved both belief and behavior, thus avoiding the crude dichotomy promulgated by the famous polygamy case in America in 1897. This case is still the leading case in Australia defining religion, and is cited in other courts and countries as well.

It is worth noting, however, as did Gaze and Jones (1990), that in the same year, 1983, Scientology lost a significant High Court case in which they were seeking redress from surveillance by the Australian Security Intelligence Organization (ASIO), which had been involved in monitoring the activities of Scientologists in Australia for some time. ASIO was identifying Scientologists and reporting the association of individuals with Scientology when they applied for a government post. So, although it may seem odd, in the same year Scientology was affirmed strongly as a real religion, the government also upheld surveillance of Scientology members for the purpose of keeping them from obtaining government jobs.

Russia and the European Court of Human Rights

Perhaps the most important registration case involving Scientology developed in the context of contemporary Russia, a former communist country, attempting to regulate religious groups within its borders (Richardson, Krylova, and Shterin, 2004). Scientology had registered as a religion under the quite liberal laws approved in 1990 in Russia, achieving registration in January 1994. Indeed, it achieved some apparent degree of acceptance in a number of areas of Russia, and managed to place collections of Ron Hubbard's books and other publications about Scientology in many libraries throughout Russia, and to have contact with some high-level Russian officials. But the situation changed rapidly for Scientology and other minority faiths, as a resurgent Russian Orthodox Church (ROC), working hand in hand with conservative politicians (many former communist officials), made efforts to subvert and change the law (Shterin and Richardson, 1998, 2000). Eventually a new law was passed in Russia in 1997 requiring, among other things, that all religious groups reregister, and stating that no religious group could register unless it could demonstrate that it had legally operated in Russia for at least fifteen years. This law was designed to weed out the certain groups that had registered during the halcyon days after the fall of communism—groups such as Scientology.

Scientology officials in Moscow attempted to reregister a total of ten times after the new law came into effect. However, the convoluted trail of applications, court cases, and appeals followed by Scientology resulted in its being thwarted at every turn for reasons that were disingenuous and involved obvious subterfuge. Apparently a decision had been made on high that the organization was not going to be reregistered no matter what it did. The tortured history of these efforts by Scientology even involved some lower court rulings in their favor, but decisions made clearly demonstrated the lack of autonomy and authority of the judicial system in Russia, and initial rulings were ignored by the Moscow Justice Department, or overturned on review by judicial authorities.

Scientology filed another reregistration case from a different region (Izhevsk) with the Russian Constitutional Court, claiming that the 1997 law was unconstitutional in that it violated provisions of the Russian Constitution that guaranteed religious freedom and the ability of religious groups to function. Although similar suits were won before the Constitutional Court by the Salvation Army, Jehovah's Witnesses, a Protestant group, and the Society of Jesus, Scientology's suit was dismissed on a technical ground that seemed again like a subterfuge (Richardson et al., 2004).

After being rebuffed within the legal system of Russia for years, Scientology carried the Moscow case to the European Court of Human Rights (ECHR) in Strasbourg, France. This was possible because Russia had joined the Council of Europe, along with a number of other former communist countries, and had thereby agreed to subject itself to the jurisdiction of the ECHR. The Scientology case was admitted by the Court, and in April of 2007, the ECHR ruled in favor of Scientology, and ordered the Russian government to register them. Modest money damages were awarded as well. The opinion recounts the convoluted history of the ten attempts to reregister, the many court cases and other machinations engaged in by the government entities involved, and in very strong language castigates the Russian government for its refusal to intervene and effect a reregistration. The opinion also makes it clear that the series of events involved with this effort were violative of the international agreements to which Russia was a signatory, including especially the European Convention on Human Rights, the governing document for the ECHR.

Russia filed a notice of appeal on the case seeking a hearing before the full Court (the decision was made by a subset of five justices). However, the initial decision, which was quite critical of the Russian government, and stating unequivocally that Scientology should have been allowed to reregister, was not overturned.

This decision is a major victory, as the ECHR has jurisdiction over forty-seven countries with over 900 million citizens in them. The decision should serve as a precedent in other countries in the Council of Europe concerning the status of Scientology as a religion. Indeed, given the reputation and influence of the ECHR around the world, this could well be the most important legal victory ever for Scientology, rivaling even the major decision of the IRS in the United States to grant tax-exempt status to Scientology.

The United States

The United States does not register religious groups officially, and does not have any official hierarchy of religious groups, as do many other nations around the world. This is a result of historical interpretations of the free exercise and anti-establishment clauses of the U.S. Constitution. However, the governmental bureaucracy, particularly when dealing with taxes, has to have some way of deciding whether a group claiming to be religious is genuine for purposes of granting tax-exempt status. Thus, perhaps the most important decision made on this question in America is that of the tax authorities, both federal and local (see Davis, 2004, for a careful analysis of the criteria used by the IRS). Scientology had been fighting for years for federal tax-exempt status, making many requests and filing a large number of lawsuits against the federal IRS. They were rebuffed in these efforts, even when such cases were heard by the U.S. Supreme Court. This occurred in spite of the fact that for a few years in the 1950s the Church of Scientology had been granted tax-exempt status, a position that was reversed and defended for years by the IRS on the ground that Scientology was mainly a commercial activity (Davis, 2004).

However, in a dramatic reversal of policy, in 1993 the IRS agreed in a settlement to recognize Scientology as a religious group warranting tax-exempt status. A part of this settlement required Scientology to seek dismissal of all its pending suits against the IRS. This unexpected turn of events was major news in the United States, and there was much discussion in the media concerning reasons for the decision. Frantz (1997) wrote in the *New York Times* that the decision was suspicious, and may have involved undue pressures brought by Scientology against IRS officials, which Frantz said had been under surveillance by Scientology investigators. Both the IRS and Scientology denied any wrongdoing or undue pressure, and claimed that the decision was based on the merits of the case.[11] According to Frantz (1997), the IRS claimed that Scientology had demonstrated is worthiness for tax-exempt status for three reasons. Those involved in earlier illegal activities against the IRS had been purged (see below), no one was getting rich off Scientology since the death of Ron Hubbard a few years before, and the funds raised by Scientology were being used for exempt purposes.

It should be noted that Scientology had been involved in a number of other legal matters in the United State prior to this major victory with the IRS. This background contributed to the level of surprise by legal scholars, journalists, and others about the unexpected IRS decision in 1993. For instance, in the early 1980s eleven Scientologists, including Hubbard's wife, were convicted in criminal court of trying to plant spies in federal agencies, breaking into government offices and taking files, and bugging at least one IRS meeting. Much controversy had also surrounded Scientology's decision to establish its headquarters in Clearwater, Florida, and accusations were made that it was attempting to completely take over the local government of that city. There had also been a number of lawsuits brought in civil court by former members of Scientology, such as the Wollersheim case mentioned above. There was, as well, a long-running battle with the federal Food and Drug Administration in the 1950s and '60s over whether the "E-Meter," a device used in Scientology "auditing" rituals, was being falsely advertised as effective in healing various maladies.

Scientology eventually won the battle with the FDA, but these various legal battles, coupled with the proclivity for Scientology to file suit against critics, has made Scientology a well-known group, and one with a generally negative connotation when referred to in the media and in public discussion.

The IRS decision was, of course, immediately broadcast worldwide, and used in efforts to attain registration or tax-exempt status in other countries. It also contributed to the U.S. State Department criticizing Germany in reports issued in 1995 and 1996 about the status of religious freedom around the world. Those criticisms of Germany caused a diplomatic flap that was well publicized on both sides of the Atlantic.

Germany

The situation concerning Scientology in Germany has been especially controversial. This may be partially explicable given Germany's past, and its concern about organizations that are perceived by some as seeking power if not dominance in society. The level of animus between the German federal government and Scientology has been high. And some German Lands (states) have been particularly rigorous in efforts to exert control over Scientology, with surveillance and policies against hiring Scientologists for government jobs in at least one German state, Bavaria. Noted entertainers and movie stars associated with Scientology have been discouraged in various ways from performing in Germany, a policy that has provoked considerable controversy in America, from whence these well-known figures have come. As indicated, some of these actions have resulted in official criticisms by the U.S. State Department of Germany for violations of religious freedom of Scientologists. Also, an immigration court in Florida ruled a few years back in favor of a Scientologist who was seeking asylum in the United States on the ground that she would be persecuted and unable to find a job if she returned to Germany.

As might be expected, Scientology has fought against the policies of the Germany government and its Lands. Many court cases have been filed, most around the issue of tax-exempt status for the organization, which was refused for many years in a series of decisions rendered by various courts in Germany. However, in more recent times court decisions have favored Scientology, and it now claims to have achieved tax-exempt status in at least some locales in Germany (Church of Scientology, 2007; Davis, 2004). These more recent decisions seems to indicate that compared with some other nations (such as Russia), the German judicial system operates with some degree of autonomy (a very important variable; see Richardson, 2007) and is shielded somewhat from pressures of a very negative attitude toward Scientology (and some other minority faiths) that exists among the general public and some political groups in Germany.

In an important related development, the Germany *Bundestag* (parliament) established an Enquete Commission to study sects and other similar groups in Germany. This commission, established in large part because of concerns about Scientology, worked for several years before producing a voluminous report (discussed by Seiwert, 2004, who was a member of the commission). Unlike such governmental bodies established to study sects in some other European countries (Richardson and Introvigne, 2001), the Enquete Commission actually funded considerable research on such groups, and some of its members also visited the United States to learn more about how the American government was dealing with minority religious and psychological groups (Seiwert, 2004). The final report was internally self-contradictory, in that none of the research done by the commission revealed any serious problems caused by the groups studied. However, the commission did recommend some forms of action that were motivated by desires to control such groups. Included was a recommendation that Scientology remain under surveillance. Notably, there was a strong dissenting opinion filed by a minority of the commission members, who pointed out that the research done did not justify the recommendations made by the majority report of the commission.

United Kingdom

Scientology has fought fierce legal battles with the government of the United Kingdom, where is has a major headquarters that serves the European region. For many years Scientologists were denied entry into the United Kingdom if their affiliation with Scientology was known. This posture was officially revoked in the late 1980s, however, as being ineffectual and without adequate basis in law.

One famous legal case coming out of the U.K. context involved a female citizen of the Netherlands named Yvonne van Duyn, who brought an action before the European Court of Justice in 1974 as a result of being refused entry into the United Kingdom because she was a Scientologist moving there to work at the Scientology headquarters in East Grinstead (Richardson, 1995). The European Union had clear official rules allowing citizens of any member nation to travel to other member nations for the purposes of employment. Van Duyn, however, lost her legal action, as the Court, while affirming the right of European Union citizens to travel freely for purposes of employment, nonetheless ruled that the United Kingdom had the prerogative to deny her entry if it was deemed in the national interest to do so. This strange logic puzzled some observers, but it clearly demonstrated the animus toward Scientology that existed not only in the United Kingdom but elsewhere in Europe at the time.

Scientology claims that it has achieved some modicum of official recognition in the United Kingdom (Church of Scientology, 2007; also see Davis, 2004), and lists several developments to support this claim, including rulings by HM Customs and Excise officials, Inland Revenue, the Ministry of Defense, and the Department of Trade and Industry, that Scientology is due treatment as a genuine religion or charity. It also cites decisions to allow it to advertise as a religion in mass media in the United Kingdom. However, the national Charity Commission has consistently ruled against Scientology, claiming that it does not meet the criteria for an officially recognized charity within U.K. charity law. A 1999 decision faults Scientology for not engaging in what is normally thought of as public worship and also cites the considerable negative attention paid to Scientology in the United Kingdom and elsewhere.

Because the United Kingdom is a member of the Council of Europe, it will be of interest to note whether the recent ECHR decision concerning Scientology in Russia will have any impact on the posture of the U.K. government toward the organization.

Italy

Scientology's religious nature has been judicially recognized in Italy.[12] But this victory was not without a long legal battle with many skirmishes. Some courts in Italy had not recognized Scientology as a bona fide religion, despite repeated directions for the Supreme Court (Corte Suprema di Cassazione) to do so. The line of cases that led to recognition involved criminal charges against a number of Scientologists for aggressive recruiting tactics that allegedly took advantage of weak individuals. The case brought by the public prosecutor of Milan claimed that the entire organization was criminal, but the case was initially dismissed at the trial court level, and then reinstated on appeal at the Criminal Court of Appeal of Milan in 1993. On appeal, a new trial was ordered by the Supreme Court in 1995, but this, too, resulted in another decision against Scientology by the Court of Appeal in Milan in 1996. Again the decision was overturned by the Supreme Court of Italy, and a third new trial ordered in 1997, with strong direction given to recognize the religious nature of Scientology and to reject the application of Christian-based definitions of religion that would exclude Taoism, Buddhism, and many other polytheistic, shamanistic, or animistic religions. Also, the decision ordered the Appeal Court not to assume that the acts of a few members and leaders could be used to condemn the entire organization. The issue was finally resolved on October 5, 2000, with an Appeal Court opinion that followed the directions given by the Supreme Court.

In another case, concerning the tax-exempt status of Scientology's Narconon drug rehabilitation program, which was decided March 1, 2000, the Italian Supreme Court restated its opinion that Scientology is a religion and criticized the lower courts for not considering international precedents for so designating Scientology. However, the decision, which was made by a "section" of the Supreme Court that usually hears tax cases only, did require Scientology to pay taxes on some of its Narconon-related activities that were viewed as commercial in nature.

Conclusions

Scientology has grown at a phenomenal rate since 1954, when groups that had organized around the famous *Dianetics* volume written by L. Ron Hubbard coalesced and defined themselves as a religion. Its claims concerning number of members (ten million members in 150 countries as of 2007) may be inflated and count everyone who has every taken a beginning auditing course. But even discounting that figure leaves one with the impression of a group that has gained considerable momentum in recent decades, and it has done so in spite of quite significant opposition in many areas around the world. Scientology is disliked by political and religious officials, treated negatively by the media, and viewed with suspicion by many in the general public. But in spite of that animus, Scientology has attracted many participants and grown and spread around the globe (Melton, 2000).

That growth has been contested, but Scientology leadership has been more than willing to assert itself and deal with whatever opposition it has encountered in quite sophisticated ways, even if some critics define its methods as heavy-handed and overly aggressive. The description of how Scientology dealt with the IRS in America (Frantz, 1997), even if only partially accurate, demonstrates this mode of operation well. The Scientology organization will use many tactics to accomplish it ends, with one of the preferred ones clearly being use of the legal system when this is possible. In some parts of the world, access to a judicial system that operates with a semblance of following the rule of law is rare, if not impossible (Richardson, 2007). But in most modern Western-oriented nations, Scientology and other minority faiths can access courts that have some degree of autonomy, and they can expect to have a reasonable chance of success in such an arena.

Thus Scientology has defended itself and succeeded in being defined as a genuine religion in many nations. As it has done so, it has also paved the way for other minority religious groups to enjoy more access to the legal system and have more success within that arena. Indeed, as Susan Palmer reports in her chapter herein on France, and as this writer has noted in other contexts, Scientology has sometimes become a major organizer of coalitions to defend minority faiths and fight groups that would attack them. Thus, like the Jehovah's Witnesses in the 1950s in nations such as America and Canada, and within the last two decades in the European arena with the European Court of Human Rights, Scientology, even if sometimes acting too aggressively for some, has worked diligently to spread its message and also has assisted in making it easier for other minority faiths to practice their own religion.

NOTES

1. Davis (2004) says that thousands of lawsuits were filed against the IRS by individual Scientologists to supplement those filed by Scientology organizations.

2. This discussion will not include coverage of criminal matters involving Scientology, such as the major controversy over the death in 1995 of Lisa McPherson at Scientology facilities in Clearwater, Florida.

3. The award was reduced to $2.5 million on appeal, but Scientology refused to pay for years. Over twenty years later Wollersheim was paid $8.7 million by Scientology to settle the case, the majority of which went to pay his legal fees (Wollersheim, 2007).

4. There is a very long history of "cult brainwashing" cases in America and else-where. See Anthony (1990), Richardson (1991, 1993, 1996) for an overview of this area of jurisprudence, and DeWitt, Richardson, and Warner (1996) and Pfeifer (1999) for experimental evidence of the impact of such claims on potential juries.

5. For an analysis of Scientology and other controversial new religions in both situations see Richardson (1998).

6. Conditions allowing successful use of a legal system in defense of religious freedom vary greatly, as discussed in Richardson (2007).

7. See Douglas Cowan (2004) for a thoughtful discussion of the problematic affects of this perception of litigiousness on academic researchers who might be inter-ested in studying Scientology.

8. Note that Derek Davis (2004) does report that France has granted official recognition to Scientology as a religion as early as 1980.

9. Davis (2004), citing Scientology sources, also includes Japan, Switzerland, Taiwan, and Mexico as countries recognizing Scientology as a religion. Why the dis-crepancy exists between the two listings is not known.

10. It is worth noting that a few years later Chief Justice Mason, who was the lead author of the main opinion in the 1983 Scientology case, in another context offered the opinion that American Supreme Court case law in the area of religion is a "bewilder-ing array of confusing decisions" (Mason, 1989).

11. McDonald (1997) says that Scientology paid $12.5 million to settle all claims and obtain an agreement that no Scientology operation would be audited for any pre-1993 activities.

12. My thanks to Massimo Introvigne for reading a draft of this section and clarify-ing the complicated legal situation concerning Scientology in Italy.

REFERENCES

Anthony, Dick (1990). Religious movements and brainwashing litigation: Evaluating key testimony. In T. Robbins and D. Anthony (eds.), *In Gods We Trust* (pp. 295–344). New Brunswick, NJ: Transaction Books.

Church of Scientology (2007). Scientology: Religious recognition in Europe and around the world. Obtained from Scientology.

Cote, Pauline, and James T. Richardson (2001). Disciplined litigation, vigilante litiga-tion, and deformation: Dramatic organizational change in the Jehovah's Wit-nesses. *Journal for the Scientific Study of Religion* 40: 11–26.

Cowan, Douglas (2004). Researching Scientology: Academic premises, promises, and problematics. Presented at CESNUR conference, Baylor University. Available at http://www.cesnur.org.

Davis, Derek (2004). The Church of Scientology: In Pursuit of Legal Recognition. Presented at CESNUR conference, Baylor, University. Available at http://www.cesnur.org.

DeWitt, John, James T. Richardson, and Lyle Warner (1996). Novel scientific evidence in controversial cases: A social psychological analysis. *Law and Psychology Review* 21: 1–26.

Frantz, Douglas (1997). The shadowy story behind Scientology's tax-exempt status. *New York Times*, March 9.

Gaze, Beth, and M. Jones (1990). *Law, Liberty, and Australian Democracy.* Sydney: The Law Book Company.

Mason, Anthony (1989). A Bill of Rights for Australia. *Australian Bar Review* 5: 79–84.

McDonald, Elizabeth (1997). Scientologists and the IRS settle for $12.5 million. *The Wall Street Journal*, Dec. 30.

Melton, Gordon (2000). *The Church of Scientology*. Salt Lake City: Signature Books.

Pfeifer, Jeffrey (1999). Perceptual biases and mock jury decision making: Minority religions in court. *Social Justice Research* 12: 409–420.

Richardson, James T. (1991). Cult/brainwashing cases and freedom of religion. *Journal of Church and State* 33: 55–74.

Richardson, James T. (1996). "Brainwashing" claims and minority religions outside the United States: Cultural diffusion of a questionable concept in the legal arena. *Brigham Young University Law Review* 1996: 873–904.

Richardson, James T. (1998). Law and minority religions: "Positive" and "negative" uses of the legal system. *Nova Religio* 2: 93–107.

Richardson, James T. (2007). The sociology of religious freedom: A structural and socio-legal analysis. *Sociology of Religion* 67: 271–294.

Richardson, James T., and Alain Garay (2004). The European Court of Human Rights and former communist countries. In D. Jerolimoc, S. Ziniscak, and I. Borowik, *Religion and Patterns of Social Transformation* (pp. 223–234). Zagreb: Institute for Social Research.

Richardson, James T., and Massimo Introvigne (2001). "Brainwashing" theories in European parliamentary and administrative reports on "cults and sects." *Journal for the Scientific Study of Religion* 40: 143–168.

Richardson, James T., Krylova, Galina, and Marta Shterin (2004). Legal regulation in Russia: New developments. In J. T. Richardson (ed.), *Regulating Religion: Case Studies from around the Globe* (pp. 247–258). New York: Kluwer.

Seiwert, Hubert (2004). The German Enquete Commission on Sects: Political conflicts and compromises. In J. T. Richardson (ed.), *Regulating Religion* (pp. 85–101). New York: Kluwer.

Shterin, Marat, and J. T. Richardson (1998). Local laws restricting religion in Russia: Precursors of Russia's new national law." *Journal of Church and State* 40: 319–342.

Shterin, Marat, and J. T. Richardson (2000). Effects of the Western anti-cult movement in development of laws concerning religion in post-communist Russia. *Journal of Church and State* 42: 247–271.

Wollersheim, Lawrence (2007). In *Wikipedia: The Free Encyclopedia*. http://en.wikipedia.org/wiki/Lawrence_Wollersheim

15

The Church of Scientology in France: Legal and Activist Counterattacks in the "War on *Sectes*"

Susan J. Palmer

Michel Raoust is a Parisian Scientologist whose wedding day was spoiled by anticult propaganda. He joined the Church in 1975, when he was a university student. Over the years, he has taken Scientology courses in Paris and in East Grinstead, and steadily climbed "up the grades" to become an Operating Thetan 5 and a Class 5 Auditor. Through the Church he met A—and asked her to marry him. On December 3, 1994, their wedding day, they arrived at a friend's garden where the ceremony was to be held to find that over half of the wedding guests were missing.

I interviewed Michel Raoust at the Church of Scientology in Paris, 7 rue Jules Cesar, on the evening of October 9, 2007. As I stood waiting in the hall I reflected on the controversial status of Scientology in France, when I noticed the doors to L. Ron Hubbard's study were open—the small shrine room that is a standard feature of every CoS in the world: his desk, a fifties typewriter, a fountain pen and inkwell, and an early wooden cased model of the E-Meter. Hubbard visited France briefly in the 1950s. In 1978 he was tried and convicted in France for fraud *in absentia* and never bothered to appeal. Michel Raoust is another controversial figure, and has been described as a "spy" and a "very dangerous Scientologist" in the French media, but when he came down the hall and introduced himself, I saw only a thin, shy, balding man in his mid-fifties. I asked him to tell me about his wedding.

"My beau frère (brother-in-law) had gone to ADFI and they had given him articles that were critical of Scientology and some about me," he replied. "These articles were linked to a discrimination case involving my company."

He explained that in 1991 his computer company had a contract with the Ministry of the Interior, but when the media announced in news reports that he was a Scientologist, the Ministry cancelled the contract. A few articles then came out in the press that defamed him:

They said that I was spying for Scientology, that I was a very danger-ous person. There was an article about me in *Libération* that was complete bullshit! I pursued *Libération* for defamation, and I won. They did not appeal, the journalists just admitted to the judge they had made a mistake, that they had lied, and they apologized—it was very strange, I have never seen anything like it.

Altogether, I have won four major lawsuits against the media. When my beau frère went to ADFI, however, they gave him only the *lying* articles accusing me, and nothing that mentioned my successful lawsuits that exonerated me. They were very selective, as always. My beau frère copied the *Libération* article and sent it out to all the wed-ding guests with a letter denouncing me as a very dangerous person, a spy, who was high up in a dangerous *secte*. The result was, half of the guests decided not to come. We had invited around 150 guests to our wedding, and only 70 showed up. My wife was very upset. There had been no problems with her parents—it was only the brother. Of course he did not show up either.

After the wedding, my wife wrote to the guests and explained the situation (you would think they would know that the media sometimes lie) but we have had no further communication with her brother. Years later, I attended a conference where ADFI was present, and I stood up and told my story, right in front of Janine Tavernier, who was the president at the time—and she said absolutely nothing!

Mr. Raoust's "dangerousness" appears to reside not from a position of lead-ership, but rather from his activism in fighting the anticult movement. In 1985 he created the *Comité français des Scientologues contre la discrimination*. I asked him why.

Because of the *McCarthyisme* I saw happening in France. I have been the president of the Comité for most of the years. We help scientolo-gists who face discrimination at work or in their private life and alert the media about the persecution of philosophical minorities in France. I have written articles for *Ethique et Liberté*.[1]

Years later, in 2005, Raoust was part of a class action suit against ADFI, the French anticult organization (see below). But since 2003 he has become one of the heroes in the Sect Wars because he is the very first member of a new religious movement to gain access to his RG (Renseignements Generaux) file. Because hundreds of people had been turned down, I asked him why he decided to apply for it.

"Because transparency is one of my subjects of interest," he said. "I don't like a police that spies on people's philosophy or religious beliefs and keeps secret reports on them."

Michel Raoust's story is a miniature version of the "French cult wars." He is one of the many members of NRMs whose professional and family life has been adversely affected by the French "war on sects"—in this sense a "victim"—but he is one of the few who decided to fight, and the trajectory of his battle, between the 1980s to the present, reflects the gradual "lightening up" of the fierce opposition to unconventional religions in France.

"NRMs ordinarily face formidable opposition and challenges to their legitimacy," Stuart Wright (2007) notes. But over time, he argues, the very elite groups and institutions that oppose NRMs are often subject to cultural and social structural changes. Social movement theorists have observed that these kinds of changes "precipitate shifts in the power alignments that may provide expanded political opportunities that enable movements to overcome obstacles to collective action and sustain a challenge to institutional opponents" (Wright, 2007: 190). The history of the Church of Scientology in France, in its struggle for social legitimacy within the context of the "cult wars"—from 1978 to the present—provides an excellent example of this pattern.

The story of Scientology in France is the story of a ferocious battle. On one side of the field, we find a new religion surrounded by a militantly secular society, struggling to survive, and appealing to foreign troops and standards to support their demands for religious recognition and freedom. On other side, we have France's cult-watching, secte-fighting movement—which since 1996 has gained status as a government body. The action (aside from a few bombs tossed into Scientology centers) is nonviolent and quite legal. It takes place in the administrative and criminal courts, in the appeals court, and in the Supreme Court. But this bureaucratic war is nevertheless fraught with passion and invective. It is a "war of words," of name-calling, deviance-labeling, and defamation suits.

Unlike most NRMs in France, Scientology is a wealthy and international organization and receives strong support from its "Mother Church." Dianetics was first "implanted" in France in 1959. According to my source,[2] "Hubbard asked a concert pianist named Mario Feninger to bring Dianetics to France. Feninger came to Paris and gave recitals in friends' houses to raise interest for the first Dianetics center on rue de Londres.[3] It later moved to the Quartier Latin, where Hubbard's book on Dianetics was translated into French. Today, in 2008, Scientology boasts five churches in France and ten missions (small churches and institutes that provide services for new members). Its two main churches, declared in 1995 as associations, according to the 1901 law, are ASESIF (Association Spirituelle de l'Eglise de Scientologie d'Ile de France) and ASES-CC (Association Spirituelle de l'Eglise de Scientologie—Celebrity Center). There is also a commercial enterprise for the sale of L. Ron Hubbard's books, called Scientologie Espace Librairie (SEL). Parallel to each of the five churches there are five associations registered per the law of 1905, in other words, as worship associations (associations culturelles), for example, the "Eglise de Scientologie Spirituelle d'Ile de France." Scientology produces a newsletter that focuses on religious freedom issues in France (Éthique et Liberté). Scientology claims a membership list of around 45,000 associate members and 4,500 active members in France.[4]

The Church of Scientology has an important role in the French Sect Wars for two reasons. Other NRMs, notably Aumisme and the Témoins de Jéhovah, have defended their associations from discrimination in the courts with remarkable tenacity and some success. But the CoS has reacted not merely defensively, but offensively. The CoS has posed a dramatic head-on challenge to its enemies—both to organizations and individuals. It has demanded the dissolution of anticult organizations such as UNADFI. It has called into question the professional qualifications of officials involved in the "war on sects"—judges, a court-appointed psychiatrist, UNADFI officials, and even politicians in the government cult-fighting ministries MILS and MIVILUDES—and requested they be retired from their posts. Thus, the CoS stands out in France's Sect Wars for the sheer aggressiveness of its counterattacks against groups and individuals belonging to the anticult movement.

Second, CoS is the only NRM that has reached out to other religious and philosophical minority groups in order to build solidarity and launch a resistance movement among the 172 groups named as "sectes" on the Guyard list.

Considering that France is a highly developed, sophisticated culture with freedom of conscience enshrined in its constitution, it is oddly hostile to foreign and nontraditional religions. This paradox has been brilliantly explained within discussions of the concept of the laïcité by French sociologists (Baubérot, Déricquebourg, Hervieu-Lèger, and others), and so it will not be dealt with here. This chapter focuses more narrowly on Scientology's battle in France—a battle that reflects larger trends in its host society and shows us how unconventional religions are "managed" in the République. By studying Scientology's battles against the forces of antisectisme, we can observe the contours of the French Sect Wars. The case of Scientology provides a tool to measure the limits of religious freedom in France, and its legal battles are experiments that test the possible avenues for extending those freedoms.

Before we can make sense of this battle, however, it is necessary to examine the terrain on which it was fought and the arsenal of weapons employed. To this end I will give a brief description of France's anticult movement.

The Rise of France's State-Sponsored Antisecte Movement

The French law of 1905 established the principle of secularism as a rational means to separate church and state. But this principle has since developed into a militant and highly politicized form of secularism. The principle of la laïcité tolerates the Catholic Church but distrusts philosophical "obscurantisme," exotic imported spirituality, and foreign expressions of overtly mystical or enthusiastic religiosity. Thus, the principle of freedom of religion became a cry for freedom from religion. In the 1970s, the first cult-watching/fighting organizations sprang up. By the mid-1990s these private groups were supported and subsidized by the French government, so that they gained recognition as public service organizations.

France's closest equivalent to the old Cult Awareness Network in the United States is UNADFI (*Union Nationale des Associations de Défense des Familles et de l'Individu*), a grassroots organization that developed in the early 1980s with help from Catholic countercult groups. In 1996 UNADFI was recognized as a public service organization and became eligible for large subsidies from the government. Many NRMs in France trace the origins of their conflicts with society to their local ADFI, whose officials contact the media and the local mayor with discrediting information about *sectes* in their area. Another anticult movement was founded by Roger Ikor, called *Centre de documentation, d'education et d'action contre les manipulations mentales* (CCMM). A law passed in June 2000 (section 105) entitles anticult groups like UNADFI to initiate criminal proceedings against *sectes* and *secte* members on behalf of the victim, even without the latter's consent or knowledge.

In 1995 the OTS (*l'Ordre du Temple Solaire*) staged a third "transit," or mass suicide/homicide, this time in France. As Jonestown was to the American ACM, this tragic event proved to be a catalyst for the French *antisecte* movement, which gathered momentum and government support. That same year, the *Renseignement Généraux* compiled information in a list of 172 groups that was adopted by the first Parliamentary Board of Inquiry into the *secte* phenomenon, headed by Jacques Guyard and Jean-Pierre Brard. In December 1995, this Guyard Commission submitted a report to the National Assembly, and the controversial list of 172 *sectes* became official. Academics who specialized in the study of esoteric movements complained of not being consulted during this process,[5] and the groups could not challenge their inclusion on the stigmatizing list.

In May 1996 an *Observatoire Interministériel sur les sectes* was created by Prime Minister Alain Juppé. It was replaced in 1998 by MILS (*Mission Interministérielle de Lutte contre les Sectes*), whose director was Alain Vivien. Alain Vivien had written a report for the Prime Minister Pierre Mauroy (*Les sectes en France*, 1983), which was the first major anticult book. In 1999 a second parliamentary board of inquiry was set up to investigate the (presumed shady) financial dealing of *sects*, and the results were published in the 1999 report *Sectes et Argent*.

On November 28, 2002, MILS was replaced by MIVILUDES (*Mission Interministérielle de vigilance et de lutte contre les dérives sectaires*). As its title demonstrates, this new interministerial mission gave up trying to fight *sectes* directly, and focused instead of the *derives* (derailments or harm) issuing from the *sectes*. A new law designed to target cult leaders who cause harm to their followers—the About-Picard law—was passed in June 2001. This law incorporated a diluted notion of brainwashing theory into France's Common Law, by making "*abus de faiblesse*" (abuse of weakness) a misdemeanor (see Dericquebourg 2003; Palmer 2006).

All of these different government-sponsored bodies identified new, problematic issues having to do with *sectes*. By launching investigations that relied on auditions with anticult officials, hostile ex-members, and RG files (secret police records whose contents could not be divulged), and by studiously ignoring academic input and producing a reports based on these findings, these government officials were able to instigated new social control strategies intended to eradicate sectarian movements from French soil. These actions included tax audits, seizure of documents and computers from NRM centers, arresting and holding citizens for questioning, prosecutions for the illegal practice of medicine and nonassistance to a person in danger, and new laws to discourage or closely monitor homeschooling.

Scientologists complained that "the obstruction of NRMs at the echelon of the national, regional and local government and civil service was decided at the most senior level . . . The MILS and then the MIVILUDES have been created under the direct authority of the Prime Minister" (*Ethique & Liberté* 2004: 8).

Thus, what with the government funding and recognition of private, grassroots anticult groups, and the creation of a series of parliamentary commissions by the National Assembly specifically designed to fight the *sectes*, by the mid-1990s France was well equipped to eradicate cults from its social landscape. But unlike other countries (e.g., China), France promises religious liberty, nondiscrimination, and freedom of expression, as in its Constitution of 1958 (Article 2), which states, "France . . . ensures the equality of all citizens before the law . . . It respects all beliefs." Moreover, the European Convention for the Protection of Human Rights and Fundamental Freedoms of 1950, Articles 9, 10, and 14 guarantee freedom of thought, conscience, and religion, and freedom of expression (as in religious proselytism). This has created an interesting situation and has given the CoS fuel for its legal battles.

The Early Conflict: 1970–1994

The first major challenge to the CoS was in 1970 when a criminal investigation for fraud was opened regarding the Dianetics center in Paris. After eight years, three successive presidents were tried, along with L. Ron Hubbard (*in absentia,* since he never lived in France and was never notified in person of the trial). On February 14, 1978, L. Ron Hubbard was condemned to four years in prison in a judgment rendered by the Tribunal de Grande Instance (TGI) in Paris.[6] The three presidents were subsequently fully acquitted in the appeal. As for Mr. Hubbard, Georges Levasseur, emeritus professor of the University of Law, Economy and Social Sciences, notes that "There are strong indications that it would have been likewise for Mr. Ron Hubbard had he too been given the possibility of a retrial."

In 1983 *le parquet de Paris* [public prosecutor] opened another investigation into fraud (*escroquerie*). Many Scientologists were arrested and held for questioning in 1985, and again in 1989.

On July 4, 1990, two Scientology centers in Paris were raided by the police and documents seized. Twenty Scientologists were then arrested and held in *garde à vue* (police custody) for police interrogations. A Scientologist who was there described her experience:

> The President of the Celebrity Center in Paris, the President of
> the Church, and I and most of the staff in Lyons were arrested—
> eighteen people were put in prison in Lyon for a month. Then, we

were put in vans, held in a little cell, and put on the train to Paris. There we were held in a Paris jail for two days.

The CoS magazine *Ethique et Liberté* featured an article in which the president of the International Church of Scientology, Heber Jentzsch, declared that this was a "conspiracy of the French Intelligence Service."

The investigation that had been opened in 1983 dragged on for sixteen years. When the Scientologists who had been charged demanded at the end of 1998 that their case be resolved, as a statute of limitations had meanwhile passed due to three years of court inactivity, the judge of instruction announced that one and a half volumes of the case had disappeared in an internal transfer between courts. A rumor was then circulated in the press that it was the Scientologists who had stolen the file. On September 8, 1999, a news report in *Libération* announced, "Scientology files destroyed. Three tons of documents disappeared from the Court of Marseilles." The very next day, *Libération* wrote, "The destruction of documents placed under seal in the Marseilles court raises the question of infiltration by the cult." The MP and president of MILS, Alain Vivien, was quoted saying, "Any organization that attempts to lay its hands on the civil service should be dissolved." The minister of justice, Elizabeth Guigou, announced, "We need to consider banning the Church of Scientology."

That same week, however, the public prosecutor of Marseilles issued an official statement: "As a result of an error that occurred in the management of the documents under seal, a certain number of documents seized in the case . . . were prematurely destroyed at the same time as a batch of material that is assembled every year and earmarked for destruction. As it happens, this operation concerned 1,788 other case files amounting to more than three tons of material."

At that point, the sixteen Scientologists under investigation demanded that the case be resolved because they were suffering from a *prejudice moral*. In the judgment, the Scientologists obtained a condemnation of the French state for *faute lourd* (grave error). Nevertheless, the rumor of a Scientology theft of court documents continued to flourish in the media. Mme Tavernier told journalists that the disappearance of the 1983 dossier concerning the Church of Scientology at the Palais de Justice in Paris "could have been accomplished by the Scientologists themselves."

The eleven Scientologists in the case responded by suing her for defamation, but she won the case in 2001 at the seventeenth chamber of tribunal correctional, which rejected the defamation action. But the judge in the case did admit that "the disappearance of the dossier and the non-reconstruction are facts indicating a dysfunctioning of the public service of justice, constitutive of a *faute lourde*" (*La Croix*, Paris, October 5, 2005, Agence France-Presse).

The Treatment of Religious Minorities after the Guyard Report

The CoS experienced minor conflicts with the state during the 1980s, but it was after the Guyard Report in 1996 that the anticult movement gathered force.

Many of the groups on the list of 172 claimed they were being persecuted and that their members were experiencing discrimination in the workplace. In an earlier paper (Palmer 2002) I identified six strategies of social control exerted against 14 groups on the 1996 Guyard list of 172 during the period of 1996–2001. These were deviance labeling in the media, financial pressure (fiscal control), public humiliation of leaders, ostracism from public space, prosecutions for the illegal practice of medicine, and exposure of professionals in the workplace.[7] Examples of all these social control methods can be found in the history of Scientology, particularly after 1995.

The Church of Scientology responded to the new wave of discrimination in various ways and, whenever possible, by a legal challenge. One case was filed before the Conseil d'Etat in September 2003 contesting the validity of two ministerial circulars regarding sects, one of which had a list of *sectes* (drawn up by the parliament and having no normative value) attached to it. Although the Church of Scientology did not win the case canceling the circular letters, the Conseil d'Etat admitted that the contested circular letters about how the state prosecutors should treat *sectes* did "not contain any disposition of a legislative or statutory nature" and the fact that the list of *sectes* was attached was declared "of an informal nature." The Conseil d'Etat did not and could not ratify the use of a list of *sectes* by the state in any official capacity. Moreover, possibly due to this case, shortly afterward Prime Minister Raffarin decreed on May 27, 2005, that all ministerial directives issued by his predecessors should be brought up to date based on the guidelines set out in this circular—an indirect victory for the Scientologists who had contested these circular letters.

Bombs and Demonstrations

There was an outbreak of bomb attacks on the headquarters of various NRMs after their names appeared on the Guyard list. A bomb exploded in front of the Unification Church, which subsequently closed down. On March 15, 1996, a paint bomb was thrown into the Church of Scientology in Lyons, and later that year on December 5, a bomb threat was received by the "Scientology school" Ecole de l'Éveil. Again, on March 7, 1997, a bomb was placed in the CoS in Angers, and on November 7, 2002, the ASESIF (CoS in Paris) received a bomb threat. The worst incident, however, occurred when a bomb exploded in front of the Paris Celebrity Center, injuring a member who became handicapped for life on November 7, 2002.

Several public demonstrations were organized by Scientologists to protest their treatment by the state. Scientologists demonstrated outside the UNADFI office and ADFI in Lille and Lyon respectively and also in front of the home of the vice president of UNADFI (BULLES de 3ère trimester 1992).

In October 2005, Anne Hidalgo, *premiere adjoint socialiste au maire de Paris* and president of the Committee of Vigilance against Sects, organized a demonstration outside the CoS headquarters in Paris. She told a journalist from the Catholic newsletter *La Vie*, "Paris is a veritable hunting ground for large sectarian movements like Scientology or New Acropolis. One knows that Scientology has infiltrated the seats of power. For example, Tom Cruise was received by Nicolas Sarkozy and by the Mayor of Marseilles and made an honorary citizen of the city."

The Investigation of the Suicide of Patric Vic, 1988–1996

The next confrontation between the CoS and the state occurred after a member committed suicide, and this raised the specter of brainwashing and the issue of "abuse of weakness" that later provided a rationale for the creation of France's controversial About-Picard law in 2001.

In March 1988, Patric Vic, thirty years old, who had joined the Church in Lyon for two months and was about to sign up for the purification process, committed suicide by "defenestration." According to newspaper reports,[8] the president of a Scientology mission in Lyon, Jean-Jacques Mazier, had tried to convince Vic to take out a loan of 35,000 FF for a purification cure. A police investigation was carried out on request of the prosecutor, who shelved it on March 31, 1988 concluding that the suicide was due to "the depressive state of the deceased." Vic's wife filed a second complaint, and a criminal investigation was launched that lasted for eight years. The prosecutor shelved the case a second time, concluding that Vic's death could not be attributed to any third party. During this period there were many stigmatizing reports on Scientology in the mass media.

Before the case went to court, the investigating judge, George Fenech, appeared on television programs that dramatized the danger of cults. According to CoS executives, Fenech discussed the Lyon case and publicly disclosed information from his case file.[9]

The CoS retaliated by requesting before the court that Judge Fenech be dismissed for unprofessional behavior, but it was rejected by the *Cour de Cassation* in December 1991.[10]

When the widely publicized Lyon trial finally took place, in September 1996, twenty-three Scientologists were tried for attempted and accomplished fraud, for complicity to commit fraud, and for breach of trust. After Vic's wife had filed the initial charges, thirty-eight more individuals filed charges, but only seven of the plaintiffs lasted until the trial. The CoS claims these plaintiffs were sought out by UNADFI and the police to reinforce the prosecution's case.

Dr. Jean-Marie Abgrall, a psychoanalyst and leading figure in France's anti-secte movement, testified on the fourth day of trial. He claimed to have perused over a hundred files retrieved from the Church in Lyon and argued that CoS used marketing techniques to impose guilt on their clients, to harass and blackmail. He offered a postmortem psychoanalysis of Patric Vic (whom he had never met), arguing that he had been faced with an "impossible choice" between his family and Scientology, and thereforehis suicide was ineluctable. Abgrall also claimed that the megavitamin doses used in the purification process causes problems in the kidney, hepatitis, and brain: "The disciple poisons himself with his own waste products, his liver and kidney stop working." He claimed that "the adherent sees himself . . . in the form of a snail. He talks to plants. He is told that he should go back in time . . . he finds himself as an Egyptian mummy or as a sage in Tibet" (*Libération*, October 4, 1996). Another witness, financial expert Etienne Mozul, said that Scientology's financial records were "fluffy," and that their earnings were sent straight out of France into U.S. coffers.[11]

A leading anticultist, Yvette Genosy, testified that CoS was neither a psychotherapy nor a religion. A journalist, Serge Faubert, author of the anti-Scientology book, *Une Secte au coeur de la République* (Editions Calmann-Levy, 1993), asserted that Scientology was controlled from the United States by the OSA (Office of Special Affairs) and that the French branch of Scientology was just "window dressing."

Jean-Jacques Mazier was given eighteen months in prison convicted of fraud and involuntary homicide, and fined 500,000 FF. On July 28, 1997, the Court of Appeals of Lyon upheld the conviction, but acquitted several Scientologists and converted Jean-Jacques Mazier's prison sentence to a conditional one. Twelve other Scientologists were given suspended sentences for theft, complicity, or abuse trust. The charges against ten others were dropped.[12] Spokespersons from the international Church called the ruling a "heresy trial" that was "politically motivated."

It is interesting to note that the lawyers Jouglas and Pesenti, who worked for UNADFI, were present. They would later be involved in another "cult suicide" trial featuring the first application of "abus de faiblesse."[13] Pesenti told the journalists that Scientology was a "war machine." Jouglas summed up the Lyon trial years later: "This trial was emblematic. It helped to understand the psychological influence that Scientology can have on individuals. It also helped to realize that the laws were inadequate to fight efficiently cult abuses. This allowed the development of a law to prevent psychological subjection."

In its ruling, on July 28, 1997, the Court of Appeals of Lyon upheld the conviction, but CoS won an unexpected victory. Duvert (2004: 45) writes, "Charges of fraud were not upheld against most of the Scientologists on trial, for the court decided they were sincere believers and [despite its controversial status] Scientology could be considered *a bona fide* religion." The court announced that it was in no position to judge whether or not Scientology was a religion: "Scientology is entitles to call itself and religion and to freely develop within the framework of existing laws, its activities" (Court of Appeals decision, July 28, 1997). This ruling was sharply criticized by Lionel Jospin, the prime minister, who declared he felt "concerned" about its implications.[14] According to Duvert (2004: 45) this is just one indication of how the anticult movement has gained influence in the highest levels of government of France.

Scientology: Religion or Commercial Enterprise?

Between 1991 and 1996 a legal battle was waged over the payment of taxes to l'Administration fiscale ("le fisc") and to URSSAF (*Union de Recouvrement des*

Cotisations de Sécurité Sociale et d'Allocations Familiales [social security admin-istration]). The *Tribunal administratif* claimed that Scientology was a business pretending to be a religion, whereas Scientologists insisted they were indeed a religion. As a Scientologist at the Paris center explained,

> Between 1985 and 95 we fought with the tax office. We took the U.S. view that as a religion we should have to pay no tax on income from auditing and courses, and also that our books were tools for religious practice. We went to court many times, but we lost, lost, lost year after year—until 1995. Then we were under threat of bankruptcy because we lost the appeal. We were asked to pay $48 million francs, which included tax plus interest and penalties for 15 years.

In April 1995 the Mother Church proposed to help the French church by paying the taxes, but the transfer of the money was refused on the pretext that it was from a foreign bank and the sources of the funds were unknown. Conse-quently, on November 30, 1995, the Tribunal of Commerce of Paris declared the CoS bankrupt for nonpayment of taxes. A document obtained under the U.S. FOIA (Freedom of Information Act) revealed later that the French refused the transfer only because they wanted to stop CoS activities in France.

An official from the American Embassy in Paris noted, on December 18, 1997, that after contacting the Department of Investments in the French Min-istry of Finance, he was informed that by refusing to authorize investments in France by the Church of Scientology International "the Economy Minister's goal was to put an end to the activities of the Church of Scientology (Paris)," and that the minister of finance had deliberately refused to authorize "a trans-fer . . . because this could regularize the Church of Scientology's (Paris) finan-cial status, i.e., bring it out of bankruptcy and allow normal operation."

Scientology lawyers challenged the refusal of the transfer before the Ad-ministrative Court of Paris and won, so that the decision of the French State was cancelled. This judgment was confirmed by the Administrative Court of Appeals on December 16, 2004.

At that time the Church of Scientology moved to its new premises at 7 rue Jules Cesar and set up three different structures:

1. An association, according to the 1901 law (l'Association Spirituelle de l'Eglise de Scientologie d'Ile-de-France), declared in December 1995.
2. A worship (*culte*) (Eglise de Scientologie d'Ile de France) association ac-cording to the 1905 law.
3. SARL, a commercial enterprise dedicated to sales of the works of L. Ron Hubbard (Scientologie Espace Librairie).

Enter the Brainwashing Expert, Dr. Jean-Marie Abgrall

Dr. Abgrall testified as an expert witness in three of the major Scientology trials (described above). These involved members of the Churches in Nice,

Marseilles, and Paris who were primarily charged with fraud. The prosecution's case in each trial relied heavily on what Anthony refers to as "Abgrall's appropriation of CIA brainwashing theory."[15] His argument was that the defendants had managed (or tried to) convince prospective members of the truth of Scientology doctrines through applying techniques of cultic brainwashing, thereby committing fraud (Anthony 2004: 128). Influenced by a report submitted by the American psychologist Dr. Dick Anthony on behalf of the defense, in which he attacked the scientific credibility of the brainwashing theory, the three courts decided that the Scientologists on trial did not brainwash.

Dr. Abgrall also testified in the Bader case, which put Scientologists in the Paris Church on trial for the CNIL violation of continuing to send mail to several old members who had requested their name be removed from the Church's list. The prosecution argued that the defendants committed false advertising and fraud by mailing out brochures announcing upcoming courses and events of the Church, which the recipients did not attend. Dr. Abgrall argued this was an attempt to "brainwash." The stakes were very high, because the About-Picard ("brainwashing") law had just been voted in, which mandated the dissolution of an organization for two or more criminal convictions of the organization itself or of two of its leaders. Fraud and deceptive advertising qualified as crimes under the new redefinition of "abus de faiblesse."

The fact that the court found the Scientologists innocent of the charges in the Bader case is significant. Anthony (2004: 144) notes that "the French court system may serve as a barrier to the legislative and legal use of the cultic brainwashing ideology as a social weapon for eliminating . . . minority religions."

The Birth of a Resistance Movement: CAP

The Church of Scientology joined forces with two activists who opposed the "thought police." One of these was Joel Labruyère, a journalist and artist who founded the human rights newsletter *Omnium des Libertés*. The other was Thierry Bécourt, founder of Psychoanimie, a therapeutic group based on the teachings of Alice Bailey. They worked together to drum up solidarity among the 172 groups on the Guyard list in order to form a resistance movement. First, they contacted the Friends of United Nations, an American NGO dedicated to promoting the Universal Declaration of Human Rights. A public hearing was set up by its president, Irving Sarnoff, to hear the testimonies of NRM members who spoke before a panel of experts on religious freedom issues from Belgium, the United Kingdom, and the United States.

This took place on March 3, 2000, at the Forum de Grenelle in Paris. Out of this meeting a new coalition was formed. It was called CAP (*Coordination des Associations et Particuliers pour la Liberté de Conscience*). A Scientologist explained how it began:

> Between 1995 to 2000 there was a *chasse des sorcières* (big witch hunt).
> If a person burned incense or practised yoga, he or she could be

denounced by a neighbour as a member of a *secte*. It was crazy! So, several members of minority religions got together and decided to fight against the report as a coalition. So, we made a big call to all the people who had suffered discrimination because their association was on the *liste*. They were invited to testify in front of a panel of experts. Members from 40 different groups were there. CAP was born that day!

I first heard about CAP when I interviewed a Scientologist in Paris in July 2001. He explained,

> In the 1990s the fight was all about *associations*. We realized it was more useful, it had more impact, to emphasize the fact that the *individual's* rights and civil liberties were being violated by the repercussions of the Guyard list. If we cried out, "the different groups—*les sectes*—are threatened with extinction!" of course no one would care—in fact they would be happy. But if we de-emphasise the *group* that people belong to—these associations—and if we highlight the fact that these are all *French citizens* who are suffering—then we get a response![16]

CAP held its first public meeting in the Forum Grenelle on March 3, 2000. Several *communiqué de presses* were sent out to announce that Friends of the United Nations was holding public hearings in front of a panel of international experts. They would be studying MILS's violations of the French Constitution and the European Convention of the Rights of Man.

The meeting was set up as a trial. Three empty chairs sat on the stage, labeled with the names of the "accused": Alain Vivien (president of MILS), the mayor of Paris, Jean Tiberi (founder of a watchdog group to counter *sectes*), and senator Nicholas About (coauthor of the projected antibrainwashing law). Behind a red-carpeted table sat the "judges," ten religion experts: Joel Labruyère; Irving Smarnoff of Friends of United Nations; Reverend N. J. L'Heureux, Methodist minister and director of the Federation of Churches in Queens, New York; and others.

The "plaintiffs" were 50-odd members from the 172 groups on the Guyard list. They were invited to come up on stage and share the assaults on their civil liberties suffered in their professional and personal lives. Members from the Raëlian Movement, Soka Gakkai, the Family, Raja Yoga, Mandarom, Horus, and more obscure, local groups took the stand and told their testimonies of discrimination and antireligious prejudice. Their anecdotes featured examples of refusal of French citizenship, ostracism in the workplace, the arbitrary closing down of bank accounts, administrative harassment, and damages. They described themselves as living in targeted ghettos as "subcitizens." Many blamed their local ADFI chapter and the infamous list of 172. Alain Vivien was accused of using his official function to create "laws of exception" that made members "subcitizens" of France, and of reinterpreting the Constitution . . . in order to exclude . . . religious minorities."[17] The audience clapped in support of their fellows, and many were wearing the yellow star (evocative of Jews under the Nazi regime) glued to their arms. After the "hearing" the participants were invited to sign a petition, to commit themselves to establishing a new coordination against the new inquisition, and to meet every three months. The media were invited to be present and to interview adepts. The highly theatrical aspect of this meeting was noted by the journalists.[18] One marveled that "never before have we seen assembled in such a large number, members of religious minorities confirmed in their participation."[19]

The "judges" then deemed that Vivien had abused his official function, and demanded he respond to this convocation concerned with MILS's violations of the French Constitution and the European Convention of the Droits de l'Homme.

CAP is still very active today. Under the direction of Thierry Bécourt, CAP distributes a newsletter and stages protests. As a member noted, "A recent study found that we have 2500 visitors per month on our Web site." Although I have heard CAP dismissed as Scientology-driven activist organization, Scientologists assure me that CAP is in fact composed of many different interest groups and individuals, most of them involved with alternative medicine. A group of lawyers interested in human rights and religious freedom are available for legal council through CAP.

The Condemnation of the Church of Scientology as a *"Personne Morale"*

In 2000 there was an attempt to dissolve *l'Association Spirituelle de l'Eglise de Scientologie d'Ile de France* (ASESIF) on the grounds of a new law whereby a corporation could be dissolved if the legal entity had been created for the specific purpose of defrauding people or committing other crimes. In France (as in Belgium and other countries) there is a law whereby a criminal organization is defined as group of three or more persons, existing over period of time, whose aim is the "concerted commission of criminal offenses to obtain . . . material advantages, by using intimidation, threats, violence, fraud or corruption . . . to hide or facilitate the commission of such offenses."

The conflict began when an ex-member complained of receiving unwelcome mail from ASESIF after she had requested that her name be removed from the mailing list. The ex-member complained *to La Commission nationale de l'informatique et des libertés* (CNIL) an association that protects confidential information of citizens. ASESIF and its president were charged with noncompliance with the data protection law and fraud and were indicted by the investigating judge for the criminal court of Paris. (As one of my informants explained, "We have over 40,000 names on our mailing list—we sometimes make mistakes. . . . CNIL had received over 100 complaints the same week but they chose to pursue only one—the one involving Scientology.")

This case had wider repercussions. The judge of instruction, when sending this case to trial, noted in his order of March 28, 2001, that there were "aggravating circumstances, in that the legal entity had been created for the purpose of committing such offense." This statement provided the rationale for threatening a penal dissolution of the Church of Scientology in Paris (ASESIF) as a legal entity, under a French law that defines an organization or corporation as a "moral person" that can be punished. The notion that "La Scientology was threatened with *dissolution*" was broadcast in the newspapers. *Le Parisien*[20] noted, "For the first time . . . *a tribunal correctionel* condemned the Church of Scientology as a "moral person."[21]

The judge of the first instance trial, however, dismissed all the charges except the charged based on the erroneous mailing in 2002. And upon appeal in 2003, ASESIF and its president received only a conditional fine of 5,000 euros each. Far from the announced condemnation as a moral person, the appeal court estimated that ASESIF had violated only the law *Informatique et Libertés* toward one person. Additionally the court rejected UNADFI as a civil party from the procedure. In October 2003, the *Cour de Cassation* (Supreme Court) confirmed the judgment.

This trial occurred at a time when the National Assembly was about to vote on the About-Picard law, which gives the justice the right to order the dissolution of an organization whose aim is "exploitation and physical or psychological subjection of persons" if the association in question has been condemned at least two times.

Libération (May 16, 2002) announced, "*Le tribunal correctional de Paris*, 13th chamber held an audience to render a judgment on Scientology as a 'moral person.'" Scientology was accused of attempted fraud (*escroquerie*), public misrepresentation, and assault on the rights of persons via computer files (*fichage informatique*).The deputy prosecutor (*substitut du procureur*) recommended the dissolution of the group that presents itself as a religion, "although the National Assembly considers them a *secte* and a racketeering enterprise."

Although this threat was never realized, it carried a symbolic weight and paved the way to giving the state the power to dissolve NRMs in the future. As a lawyer for ADFI (and one of the civil parties in the process), Olivier Morice, told the press, "The dissolution . . . can be pronounced as soon as two condemnations are acquired. *Unadfi* will give a *rendez-vous* to Scientology in other tribunals . . . you must not underestimate the *portée symbolique* of this decision! It is the first time that that this association is condemned as a moral person. That opens the way for other trials later on. We will encounter Scientology again in Justice."

Scientology spokespersons were quoted in the news commenting on the situation: Daniele Gounord noted that "the banal concern over a mere filing error shows they are lacking more serious matters, and this clearly illustrates the political hysteria surrounding this affair." Anne Lelièvre complained that Scientology was perceived as "violation of the Laïcité," and that there was a tendency in France to sanction those who "think differently!"[22]

The Closing of the "Scientology" School

Although the state did not succeed in dissolving the Church of Scientology itself, other institutions associated with it were closed down. In 1996 there were a series of complaints concerning *l'École de l'Eveil* in Paris, a private school that had incorporated some of the methods of L. Ron Hubbard into its pedagogy. Many of the parents and some of the teachers were Scientologists. The school closed its doors in 1997 due to what Scientologists described as "continuous harassment by officials on building codes." The school principal was fined 30,000 FF for circulating misleading publicity about the school.[23]

Scientology's Challenge to the ACM

The CoS has responded to France's social control efforts in a manner that is quite unique among NRMs. It has systematically questioned, opposed, and even attempted to destroy virtually all of the anticult organizations in France: MILS, MIVILUDES, UNADFI and its local ADFI chapters.

In 1987 the CoS successfully contested the agreement UNADFI had made with the Ministry of Youth and Sports to extract extra subsidies for anticult activities. In 1992 Scientology's lawyers demanded an annulment of the subsidy given by the minister of social affairs to an anticult observatory, *Centre de documentation, d'education et d' action contre les manipulations mentales* (CCMM), which amounted to 100,000 FF. The administrative court rejected the Scientologists' demand.

Between 2001 and 2005, the CoS assisted the European Law Center based in Sofia, Bulgaria, with circulating a petition against FECRIS, which was gaining consultative status at the Council of Europe. FECRIS (*Fedération Européenne des Centres Recherche et d'Information sur le Sectarisme*) is a coalition of small, local grassroots *antisecte* groups in Europe. The petition was unsuccessful. It was, however, recently revealed through the public documents access law CAP that FECRIS had been financed all the way exclusively by the French government (and no other European government), receiving between 40,000 to 50,000 euros per year.

In January 1992, the Church of Scientology's lawyers went before the *tribunal de grande instance* in Paris to demand that UNADFI and ADFI (recognized as pubic service organizations since 1996) be dissolved as an association. They did not win.

In 2005 a similar demand made by a group of lawyers on behalf of ten plaintiffs (one of them was Scientologist Michel Raoust, described above) who complained of serious damage or harm in their professional and personal lives as the result of UNADFI and ADFI's interference and dissemination of stigmatizing misinformation concerning their "*secte*" involvements. These lawyers were affiliated with CAP, and they demanded that UNADFI be dissolved as an organization on the grounds that its fundamental aims violated the laws of the Republic, particularly those governing religious freedom. The plaintiffs described UNADFI as "the thought police" and argued it had engaged in illicit activities and published highly stigmatizing portraits of sectarian movements. They also complained about UNADFI's role in forging the About-Picard law of June 2001. (Catherine Picard, the coauthor of the law, after working to have it passed in the National Assembly, then became the president of UNADFI.)

The case was dismissed in December 2005 by the TGI of Paris, and the judgment stated that "it could not seriously be held that the aims of UNADFI were contrary to the Republic, and that the law of 2001 had been set in place to reinforce that prevention and the repression of sectarian movement that attacked the rights of man and fundamental liberties." The tribunal also deemed CAP guilty of "bad faith" in leveling accusations that were "completely unfounded," condemned the plaintiffs to pay a fine of 10,000 euros in damages plus interest,[24] and ordered them to publish the judgment in eight journals of their choice.[25]

In March 2007 the appeals court of Paris examined the demand for the dissolution of UNADFI and its branch, Nord/Pas de Calais. In 2007 the plaintiffs appeared in the court of appeals, where their lawyer, Jean-Marc Florand, presented his clients as "people crushed by the judicial system due to a simple denunciation by UNADFI." He called UNADFI "a threat to the laws of the *Republique,* to freedom of conscience, of religion and of thought"[26]

The judge said the proof against UNADFI was insufficient. In the first court, the plaintiffs were condemned to publish the judgment in eight *journaux*— amounting to 40,000 euros. In the appeals aourt, however, the judge annulled that condemnation. She (the judge) also waived the plaintiffs' obligation: the payment of the fees of the lawyers of UNADFI. A Scientologist noted, "99% cases do this, in application of the article 700 of the new civil code, fees amounting to 10,000 euros. It is very unusual for a judge to do this. It seems she realized something was wrong."

The Panda Software Scandal

The Panda Software scandal tells us much about how Scientology is perceived in France. Scientology is considered to be a quintessentially *American* phenomenon. The fear is often expressed in media reports that via Scientology, U.S. corporations (and possibly even the CIA) can infiltrate government ministries, conduct espionage, copy secret files, and funnel money out of the *Republique* into the United States. It appears the publicizer of this conspiracy theory was the journalist Bruno Fouchereau, whose article appeared in 2001 in *Le Monde Diplomatique,* titled, "Sectes: Trojan horse of the United States in Europe." Fouchereau argues that the imperialistic policies of the U.S. government and the influence of American corporations are infiltrating France *via* the sects. Quebecois scholar Benjamin-Hugo LeBlanc comments on the "Trojan horse" theory of sects, pointing to France's "longstanding anti-American sentiment [that] led some French media to identify *sectes* with the United States" and its "ultraliberal" policies. He also describes an investigative documentary (*Sects and Big-Time Espionage*) that promoted an anti-American rumor that some "cults" could actually be used as front groups for international espionage.[27]

A Spanish Scientologist had developed a new antiviral protection system during the 1990s, and founded the company Panda, which specialized in protecting information. Panda was soon established in thirty-five countries and became one of the most popular antivirus protection systems in the world.

In April 2001 a series of media reports came out warning the public about Panda's connection to Scientology. *Le Parisien* (April 12, 2001) issued a warning of "*Infiltration and espionage Americain*":

> Since several weeks, one has seen that at least 12% of computer software of the Ministry of the Interior of France is provided by Scientologists, just as is the Ministry of Education. The American magistrates know of the infiltration of Scientology through the wheels of French and American administration. One was quoted, as follows: "When I say to the French, if you don't pay attention to Scientology, it will happen what happened in Clearwater (FL). They reply, "Not in France. It is impossible." But I say, watch out!

The article concludes, "Everyone is talking about it. *L'emotion est grande.*" Next, fifteen articles came out in other newspapers suggesting that Panda was a covert U.S. espionage operation funneled through Scientology. *L'Express* and *Libération* (April 12, 2001) suggested that the money generated by Panda went straight into the coffers of WISE, the World Institute of Scientology Enterprises in the United States. They noted the company's founder had given a donation of 40,000 FF to WISE in 1996. All the articles suggested that Panda was designed not just to *shield* confidential information, but also to actually *penetrate* into the bases of ultraconfidential information of the minister of the interior. A member of the cabinet was interviewed who "swore to the press that Panda Software . . . could not penetrate into the bases of the confidential information of the *ministere*" (*L'Express,* April 12, 2001).

Several broadcasts then explored the theme of Panda-like infiltration of *les sectes* into business enterprises. As the result of all this bad publicity, Panda lost half its clientele within a few days.

In 2007 the Panda scandal was resurrected. *Libération* and *Parisien* both mentioned that Panda software was used by *L'Association E-Enfance* in their campaign to protect children by blocking pornography on the net (Jean-Marc Ducos, April 27, 2007). This article cites the 2006 MIVILUDES report that claimed that the U.S. president and the international president of Panda were members of WISE.

Two years earlier, in 1999, the second parliamentary commission created to investigate the problem of cults had claimed to discover several cases of "infiltration" of *sectes* into the business world. The commission's report claimed that *sectes* offered courses in sales motivation and training. The example given was that Transcendental Meditation had acquired SAPITEX (a clothing manufacturing firm) and was imposing daily meditation séances on its employees.[28] The commission expressed a concern about "gourous [gurus] in white ties" who "dissimulate" by pretending to be respectable personnel management experts, in order to "infiltrate" the business networks by offering training programs and workshops.[29] It appears likely that the Panda scandal was influenced by this report.

Attacks on Individuals and Defamation

The history of Scientology in France is riddled with defamation suits. These have been launched from both sides, but although Scientology's name-calling is no worse than, and almost identical to, that of its enemies, Scientology nearly always loses in court. This appears to be a clear indication of France's deeply entrenched distrust of religious minorities.

Between 1996 and 1998, UNADFI successfully sued the Scientology newsletter *Ethique et Liberté* for calling UNADFI "irresponsible" and "manipulative," and claiming it had participated in "criminal actions."

In 2002, the court of appeal condemned *Éthique et Liberté* and its president for defamation against Janine Tavernier and Olivier Morice of UNADFI, for comparing UNADFI's activities to "the Gestapo in the Third Reich" in a 2000 publication (ADFI BULLES 75 (3): 2002).

In September 1991 Tribunal correctional of Paris rejected Scientology's lawsuit directed against Dr. Jean-Marie Abgrall. Dr. Abgrall in turn sued Scientologists for stealing his "snail mail," making threatening phone calls, damage to his car, and generally putting pressure on him to make him *"craquer."*[30] He filed charges against a Scientologist who was the head of the *Comité des Citoyens pour les Droits de 1'Homme,* an association that researches and denounces psychiatric abuses in France. She was accused of inciting two young students to steal letters out of Dr. Abgrall's mailbox in Toulons. Although she admitted instructing them to investigate his professional activities, she denied ordering them to commit postal theft. The students admitted to stealing the letters spontaneously, explaining they were "caught up in the amusing game of being a detective." She was exonerated, but one of the students was convicted of the serious crime of mail theft.

In October 1993 a Scientologist, well-known actor Xavier Deluc, lost his suit against Janine Tavernier, the president of ADFI who distributed anticult literature in order to discredit his antidrug association.[31]

On the May 18, 1992, the Court of Appeals of Douai condemned the Centre Hubbard de Diantetique de Lille to pay 9,000 FF in damages and interest to ADFI of Lille for defamation.[32]

The Exposé of Alain Vivien and MILS

After years of experiencing stigmatizing media reports on their church and losing their defamation suits against UNADFI officials, Scientology finally launched a successful attack on the reputation of MILS and its president. On July 23, 2002, a press conference was held in Paris, where Danièle Gounord, Scientology's *porte parole* [spokesperson] unveiled an embarrassing finding concerning the spending habits of MILS officials. Alain Vivien had just retired as MILS was withdrawn in favor of the new cult-fighting, government-sponsored interministerial mission, MIVILUDES. Through the *Commission d'Acces aux Documents Administratifs* (CADA), Scientology had obtained information on the spending habits of MILS. They discovered that within a three-year period, members of MILS made eighty-eight voyages in forty-three countries "costing taxpayers dearly."

Several articles on the theme of "MILS in the Tropics" were published in Scientology newsletters. *Ethique et Liberté* notes that for the year 2001, 35 percent of MILS's budget was spent on foreign travel, amounting to around one million euros. Similarly, the budget for 2000 was 1,083,824 euros, and almost all of it was spent on travel. The article suggests that Vivien may have retired after receiving pressure from CADA to control public expenses and obliging MILS to communicate their accounts.[33]

Also mentioned was the fact that Vivien and his wife attended an anticult conference in Beijing in November 2001. At that time, the Falun Gong were claiming that the Chinese government had tortured and killed over 100 Falun Gong practitioners. China's anticult officials invited MILS to share its cult-fighting techniques, hoping to create a law in China modeled on the About-Picard law. Scientology deplores the fact that "these globe trotters and zealots, waging a holy war, are given the right to represent the name of France in the international community of the rights of man."

Ironically, Vivien received the Prix de Leipzig human rights award in 2002 from the "The European-American Citizens Committee for Human Rights and Religious Freedom in the USA," who praised him for opposing "new totalitarian organizations." The Prix de Leipzig has been awarded exclusively to critics of Scientology during its three-year existence, between 2000 and 2003. The committee congratulated Vivien on his "aim to protect society" and individuals menaced by the "totalitarian" Scientology, and commended his "demonstration of public courage" despite "pressure from a new form of totalitarianism exercised by Scientology."[34]

The Ostracism of Scientologists from Public Space

There are many incidents in which Scientologists have been ostracized in France by being refused jobs or promotions on the basis of their religious affiliation. Teachers have been fired, and singers, actors, and concert pianists have found their performances cancelled at the last minute. Public officials who consort with Scientologists find themselves the object of criticism. On June 27, 2006, a deputy of Loire-Atlantique, Michel Hunault, who was also member of the *commission parlementaire sur les sectes*, accepted an invitation from Scientology to attend a conference called La Commission des Citoyens pour les Droits de l'Homme (CCDH), which is tied to Scientology. Cameras caught him talking to Michel Grossman, president of CCDH. The parliamentary *commission d'enquête sur les mineurs* warned Hunault against associating with Scientologists. Hunault claimed his presence was "purely fortuitous" and should not undermine his legitimacy or work in the region (Claude Askolovitch, "La faute du depute Hunault," October 23, 2006, *Nouvel Observateur*).

This "scandal" indicates the strong taboo against officials having contact with sects, even if it is actually their job to investigate them. This brings to mind the remarkable statement of the former president of UNADFI, Janine Tavernier, in a talk show: "We make it a point of never having anything to do with the groups we are fighting against."

The Roots of Anti-Scientology Sentiments

It is very clear that Scientology features prominently in French conspiracy theories of "infiltration" that circulate through the mass media and in anticult literature. This fear of infiltration is conveyed by the title of Serge Faubert's book alone: *Une secte au Coeur de la République: les reseaux français de l'Eglise de Scientologie*. Thus the most common allegation most frequently leveled against Scientology is that it is a "Trojan horse" for American imperialism, a multinational corporation constructed on American business and cultural principles that "funnels" money straight to the United States, and sends its spies out to "penetrate" the institutions of France: public schools, business corporations, the Justice Department, the government, and even the Ministry of the Interior(!). Scientology is accused of trying to impose its peculiarly American brand of utopianism on Europe. But, unlike the Unification Church, Scientology is less interested in saving the world than in "clearing the planet." That is to say, the utopianism that one finds in many "totalistic" NRMs (notably the Unification Church) that strives to unite all nations into one theocracy (ruled by Reverend Moon, Lord of the Second Advent) has been downplayed in Scientology. Scientologists today pursue a capitalist ideology that promotes individualistic values oriented toward success in the world (Luca 2004; Wallis 1984). The Church of Scientology is imbued with American cultural values that encourage its adepts to purchase symbolic products that promise to enhance their success in their individual private and professional lives. These cultural values are, of course, no longer distinctly American, although they may have originated there before the Industrial Revolution transformed Europe. Nevertheless, according to French anthropologist Nathalie Luca, "Scientology is regarded in Europe as an extension of the American culture of consumerism" (Luca 2004: 59). Scientology evokes fears of the hegemony of American culture that is threatening to take over Europe. Catherine Picard warns the French public that one of the dangers of cults is "American imperialism . . . the advanced liberalism symbolized by the commercialization of education, belief."[35] Indeed, there is a rumor circulating in France that the U.S. government is a puppet of Scientology. Philippe Vuilque, a *depute* in the National Assembly, declared that "the High American Administration has the Scientology pox."[36] Jean-Pierre Brard, another *depute* renowned for his anticult activism, even suggested that President George Bush belonged to the

Church of Scientology![37] Cyrille Duvert (2004: 46) a French lawyer, comments on this trend, noting that France's "nervous parliamentarians" account for the U.S. State Department's critiques of France's treatment of religious minorities by alleging that the highest levels of the American administration have been infiltrated by cults, and "especially by Scientologists."

Scientology's declared goals are often misquoted (or mistranslated) in government reports and on *antisecte* Web sites in order to support this paranoid view. An amusing example appears in MILS Report (2001: 58–59), which claims that Scientology's aim is to "clean" the planet. The Scientology motto is "Clear the Planet!" meaning everyone should be audited and erase their engrams so that humanity can become "Clear" (the Scientology version of enlightenment). But MILS officials have evidently not studied Dianetics, so they imagine a sort of fascistic ethnic cleansing to "purify the planet from crime, war and insanity." This mission implies the "elimination of all parasites all antisocial people who hinder the world from progressing," MILS claims, disapprovingly.

It is useful to study the theories developed by French sociologists who analyze the Sect Wars within the context of the development of *laïcité* and the decline of the Catholic Church's power in society after the French Revolution. Their arguments shed light on the three main criticisms leveled against Scientology: its commercial enterprise, its "American" character, and its uncanny mastery and ruthless application of brainwashing techniques.

An epithet applied frequently to Scientology is *"escroc"* (fraud): the notion that is not a religion, but a business pretending to be a religion so as to bilk its gullible "congregation." But, as Nathalie Luca points out, the French are quite unfamiliar with the concept of a religion that charges money, as Scientology does for its auditing services. The French Revolution saw the overthrow of the one religion that dominated France for many centuries, the Catholic Church, the religion that enjoyed ultimate economic *"puissance."* Part of the reform of the Catholic Church after the French Revolution, Luca notes, has been to allow the congregation free access to symbolic products and to sacraments. The post-Revolution cost-fee availability of Catholic religious services is considered normal, is taken for granted. Thus, it is difficult for the French to accept the "extension of the reign of merchandise into the sphere of production and of consumption of religious symbolic products . . . the idea that money could be associated with religion is today, in the French context, something that scandalizes people" (Hervieu-Léger 2001: 119). Considering the historical context, it is possible to understand the outrage expressed in the 1999 government report *Sectes et Argent* (Guyard and Brard 1999: 10), as well as the media's constant harping on the private wealth of *gourous* and their fraudulent exploitation of their members' pocketbooks. New reports on the business innovations and economic success of groups like Scientology, the Unification Church, and Soka Gakkai are guaranteed to shock and amaze the French people. It is assured that because Scientology is a successful business enterprise it cannot also be an authentic religion.

The third aspect of Scientology that is feared by the French is their putative mastery of the techniques of *manipulation mentale*. French sociologist Jean

Baubérot argues that the France's "Sect Wars" is really a struggle to protect "freedom of thought."

He distinguishes between the notion of "freedom of conscience" and "freedom of thought," and he argues that *laïcité* is located at the intersection of the two ideal types (Luca 2004: 68). The first guarantees religious liberty and freedom of belief, but the second emphasizes a peculiarly French concept of "freedom of thought" that is opposed to "the promulgation of beliefs that prevent a person from being critical of them" (Luca 2004: 68).

The struggle against *sectes* obviously contravenes "freedom of conscience," but it is considered justified, Baubérot notes, because *sectes* could destroy their members' capacity for critical thinking by using bad, if not stupid, spiritual merchandise to make them change their minds (Baubérot 1999: 326).

Thus, to combat Scientology is to struggle against its uncanny, totalitarian control over the mind. Catherine Picard (2002) argues that we cannot favor freedom of conscience when freedom of thought is at stake, so she creates a hierarchy, placing "thought" above "conscience."

Because Scientology, as all religions do, offends reason by espousing spiritual, nonempirical realities (such as recapturing the powers of the thetan), and its rituals are based on myth (reincarnation and Prince Xenu), it must be uprooted in France.

Luca writes that "it is one of the duties of the State to provide education for its citizens that promotes critical thinking." Thus, it is the duty of the state to "denounce all things that seem dangerous for good development of Reason" (Luca 2004: 69).

The Future of Scientology in France: Implications for Change?

As the events described above demonstrate, the anticult movement in France is so powerful and pervasive, its stereotypical, value-laden perspectives on unconventional religion extending into the government ministries and the National Assembly, that it appears virtually impossible for any NRM, once it is labeled a *secte*, to receive recognition as a minority religion—or even respect as an alternative philosophical system. Given its many defeats and the impossible odds it faces, it seems remarkable that the Church of Scientology has persisted in fighting this battle in France.

But Scientology is inclined to wage this battle for several reasons. First, Scientologists are motivated by L. Ron Hubbard's ideas on human rights and religious freedoms. Second, the CoS is mature and quite secularized, thus better able to grasp and cope with legal and political realities than some of the newer, smaller, sectarian groups in France. Third, l'Église de Scientologie has imbibed American standards of religious freedom and human rights—as well as an American litigious approach to achieving its goals. These influences have mingled with the ideals of *liberté, egalité,* and the notions of freedom of conscience enshrined in the Declaration of the Rights of Man. Fourth, l'Église de Scientologie has received support, both legal and financial, from its headquarters in the United States. Thus, the CoS in France is but one phalanx of a vast army belonging to a fifty-seven-year-old religion that is currently waging an international battle for recognition as a religion.

Recent developments and rulings in France and other countries may have an impact on the status of Scientology in France. The Church of Scientology in Moscow gained a legal victory in April 2007 when the state's refusal to reregister Scientology as a religion was overturned by European Court of Human Rights ("Scientologists 1, Russia 0," *Independent Online,* South Africa, April 5, 2007). This applies to case law and jurisprudence in all the states of the European Council, to which France belongs.

In December 2004 the mayor of Angers tried to ban Scientologie Espace Librairie from selling the books of L. Ron Hubbard in the outdoor market on the grounds that "the litigious books come from a sectarian group and could endanger a young or psychologically weak public." The administrative court in Nantes, however, cancelled the mayor's order and noted, "Neither the contents of a book for sale, nor the personality of its author can by itself trouble public peace." The mayor was condemned to pay 1,200 euros to SEL.[38]

In Belgium a Brazilian evangelical congregation, the Universal Church of God's Kingdom, complained of being referred to as a "criminal organization" and described as extorting money from their members, in the 1997 parliamentary report (similar to the Guyard Report of the previous year). They sued the Belgian Parliament with acting in an irresponsible fashion and won their case in the appeals court on June 28, 2005. The Parliament is now taking the case to the Supreme Court. Three other groups on the parliamentary list are following this obscure Brazilian church's lead.

Over the years Scientology has suffered many defeats in the French court system. "*Les demêlés judiciaire de la Scientologie*" are displayed, gloatingly, on the Web site (http://www.antisecte.net) of Roger Gonnet, who is Scientology's French "arch apostate."[39] And yet, Scientology has also won some of its cases.

In July 2003 a Scientologist won his case against the *Renseignement generaux* (France's equivalent to the American CIA). In 1992 Michel Raoust had requested permission to see his RG file (traditionally top-secret material) after many Scientologists in the past had made the same request and been refused. The RG had argued that the Church of Scientology was a sectarian movement that posed a threat to public security and that the Minister of the Interior kept the file in the Renseignement generaux because the file could not be communicated without violating public safety or the security of the state" (Case 242812).

Michel Raoust explained how he persisted:

> I took it before the Tribunal Administratif, it was refused again. Then I took it before the Cour administratif d'appel, and they upheld the decision. Finally, I took it to the highest level, the Conseil d'Etat, and in 2003 I obtained a positive decision—they gave me the right to see my file. This has created a jurisprudence so other Scientologists, and people from other groups, have access to their files.

When I asked him what he found in his file, he replied, "Not much!":

I think they took away all the papers that could create difficulties. It said I was born in Argentina (I already knew that), that I was a scientologist, that I was president of the Comité, that I had marched in demonstrations . . . I saw nothing embarrassing.

This was a significant breakthrough, because the Guyard Commission had been able to create a "blacklist" of sects based on *secret* information obtained from the RG—information that no one could double-check or challenge. Even if the Guyard Commission had been unable to find negative reports on a specific group, they could pretend the RG had and dub the group as potentially "dangerous." This cycle of misinformation has been broken.

Social movement theorists (Wright 2007: 190) have observed that groups and institutions that oppose NRMs are themselves subject to cultural and social structural changes that may open up new opportunities for NRMs to overcome obstacles in their struggle to attain religious recognition and social legitimacy. There are several indications that this could occur in France.

Michel Raoust expressed his hopes in this respect:

The fact that France has close links to the U.S. and other European countries that value and protect religious freedom—this will put pressure on France. I think MIVILUDES will reform and UNADFI will become more and more isolated. I am very optimistic for the future. The OSCE are amazed that this occurs in a democratic country. As long as we shed light on what they do we are on our way to becoming a more tolerant society.

It appears likely that under Nicolas Sarkozy's leadership France may develop provide a more favorable ecology for NRMs. Sarkosy is known for his conservative stance on law and order, but he is of mixed parentage and his grandparents suffered anti-Semitic persecution under the Nazis. In his book *La Republique, les religions, l'ésperance,* Sarkozy reveals a deep respect for religiosity. In his speeches,[40] Sarkozy expresses his hopes for a society based on a *laïcité ouverte* and *positive*—where religious beliefs and diversity are respected.[41] His new minister of the interior, Michèle Alliot-Marie, has proclaimed that it is the role of the *pouvoirs publics* to protect freedom of belief and respect for "*toutes les spiritualités.*" She has made it clear that the new policy of law enforcement will not be based on a "*vision arbitraire, stigmatisant a priori.*"[42]

Predictably, the leading officials with UNADFI and MIVILUDES have protested, saying they support religious freedom, of course, but that *sectes* do not qualify as religions.[43] They question Sarkozy's objectivity—for after all, he did shake hands with Tom Cruise!

Acknowledgments

My understanding of the important role played by the CoS in what Stuart Wright calls the "French CAPS sect wars" is based on interviews with members of other NRMs who cooperated (or refused to cooperate) with Scientology in its attempts to build a resistance movement to combat the anticult movement. My data collection method involved the examination of news reports, Scientology texts, and anticult literature, and conducting interviews with Scientologists in Paris and Brussels in June 2001, February 2001, and June 2007. An earlier version of this chapter was presented as a paper at the ISSR meeting in Leipzig, Germany, July 22–27, 2007.

NOTES

1. This is a Scientology magazine in France, similar to the CoS's *Freedom* magazine in the United States.

2. Interview with Jean-Louis Gagnot, Paris, 2006.

3. Mario Feninger recently performed a concert December 17, 2005, at the Salle Gaveau in Paris.

4. This data was given to me in March 2006 by Daniele Gounord and Jean-Louis Gagnot, who are *responsables* at the Church of Scientology in Paris.

5. See my interview with a professor at the Sorbonne, Antoine Faivre, who was actually arrested and held for questioning because he had the temerity to ask why no academics were consulted by the Guyard Commission (Palmer Nova Religio, Field Notes, February, 2008).

6. "Les démêlés judiciaires de Scientologie en France." http://prevensectes.com/france.htm.

7. Palmer, Susan, "Field Notes: France's Anti-Sect Wars," *Nova Religio: The Journal of Alternative and Emergent Religions* 6, no. 1 (October 2002): 174–182.

8. Bernard Fromentien, "Choisir entre sa famille et la scientology" *Libération* 4 (November 1996); Jean Perilhon, "Jail for Scientology Official," Associated Press, November 22, 1996 (http://www.whyaretheydead.net/Patrice_Vic_31/ap96n22.txt).

9. "Religious Intolerance in France; the Emblematic Case of Scientology, "*Ethique et Liberté* (September 2004): 28.

10. *Bulletin de liaison du CCMM,* May 1991.

11. The Church's lawyers, however, demonstrated that the accusations on the amount of money transfers were false, and Dr. Abgrall had some embarrassing moments when his expert claim that Vic's misfortunes were caused by the purification rundown was discredited when records showed Vic never went through this particular church service.

12. *Associated Press,* November 22, 1996, by Jean Perilhon.

13. Mr. Pesenti later became the prosecuting lawyer in the 2002 trial of Arnaud Mossy of Néo-Phare, which would become another celebrated "cult suicide" case (see Palmer 2006).

14. "L'arrêt sur la scientologie préoccupé Lionel Jospin," *Le Monde,* August 1, 1997.

15. "Rapport sur l'Eglise de Scientologie, Les techniques de Scientologie, La Doctrine Dianetique, Leurs Consequences Medico-Legales" (1990) par Dr. Jean-Marie Abgrall.

16. Interview with Martin Weightman, July 2001, in Paris.

17. "Communiqué de Press: Alain Vivien, Nicolas About, et Jean Tiberi convoqués devant un panel d'experts internationaux" (http://prevensectes.com/desinfo02.htm).

18. Xavier Ternisien, "A Commission Organized by Scientology Denounces the 'New Inquisition,'" *Le Monde,* March 7, 2000.

19. See http://www.lemonde.fr/article/0,2320,45320,00.html.

20. May 18 by Nelly Terrier.

21. "La Scientologie condamnée comme personne morale," Agence France-Presse, May, 18, 2002.

22. Agence France-Presse, May, 15, 2003, by Francois Ausseil.

23. *Libération,* December 3, 1997.

24. "Le TGI refuse de dissoudre l'UNADFI," *Nouvel Observateur,* December 14, 2005.

25. *Nouvel Observateur,* December 14, 2005. "Tribunal de grande instance (TGI) in Paris deboute un group of avocats tied to CAP who demanded the dissolution of UNADFI."

26. Agence France-Presse, March 27, 2007.

27. *Religion in the News* 3, no. 4 (fall 2001).

28. Stephane Haik, "Sectes et Entreprises—Ressources humaines et gourous," March 11, 2005 (http://www.anti-scientologie.ch/formation-entreprises.htm).

29. It is interesting to note that the unworldly *sectes* (i.e., the communal and or millenarian groups like Néo-Phare and Tabitha's Place) who refuse to participate in society's business and political realms are accused of cutting themselves and their children off from "reality" and the advantages of a pluralistic, democratic education and lifestyle full of choice. On the other hand, when *les sectes* prove they can be very effective in participating in the everyday realms of business and education, then they are accused of "infiltration."

30. UNADFI Bulles, third trimester 1992.

31. "Blaming the Secret Police," November 1991, "Les démelés judiciaries de la Scientologie en France" (http://www.preventsectes.com/france.htm).

32. BULLES, first trimester 1993.

33. See http://www.freedommag.org/french/E134/page02.htm.

34. "Prix de Leipzig" (http://www.leipzig-award.org/franzoesisch/begruend ung_2002.htm). This humanitarian exultation of Alain Vivien stands in sharp contrast to the official declarations the newly elected French government did in 2002 faced with increasing criticism for its antisect fight. In its official declaration before the OSCE (Organization for Security and Co-operation in Europe) the French representative, talking about the MILS, stated, "We are aware that this mission has generated incomprehension and has conveyed an image which does not correspond with the French reality. The government has started a deep reflection on the objectives, the role and the structure of the inter-ministerial mission, the President of which has not been replaced since June."

35. Quoted in Xavier Ternisien's article, "Le Senat adopte la proposition de loi anti-sectes" (*Le Monde,* May, 5, 2001).

36. *Journal Officiel Assemblie National* (JOAN) May 30, 2001, p. 3685.

37. JOAN, June 22, 2001, p. 5728.

38. *Le Courrier de l'Ouest,* May 10, 2007.

39. Interview with Roger Gonnet at the ICSA meeting in Brussels (June 30, 2007). I noticed him because of his T-shirts that featured anti-Scientology slogans and advertised his own and other anticult Web sites (http://www.preventsectes.com; http://www.antisectes.net; http://www.prevensectes.com; http://www.antiscientologie.ch).

40. These speeches were delivered at Saint-Jean de Latran, December 20, 2007, and at Riyad, January 14, 2008.

41. See http://www.lemonde.fr/societe/article/2008/02/05/face-aux-sectes-le-ministere-de-1-interieur-adopte-une-politique-liberale-mais-ferme_1007600_3224.html#ens_id = 1007694.

42. *Le Monde*, February 5, 2008.
43. See http://www.cicns-news.net/soutien_reforme_lutte_anti_sectes.htm.

REFERENCES

Anthony, Dick, and Thomas Robbins. 2004. "Pseudoscience versus Minority Reports: An Evaluation of the Brainwashing Theories of Jean-Marie Abgrall." In *Regulating Religions*, ed. James T. Richardson, 127–150. New York: Kluwer Academic/Plenum Publishers.

Baubérot, Jean. 2001. "Mutations la laïcité française face au pluralisme et à ses mutations." In *Chercheurs de Dieux dans l'espace public* [Frontier Religions in Public Space], ed. Pauline Coté. Ottawa: University of Ottawa Press.

Dericquebourg, Régis. 2003. "From the MILS to the MIVILUDES: France's 'Sect' Policy since the Fall of the Socialist Government." Paper presented at the CESNUR 2003 Conference, Vilnius, Lithuania, April 9–12, 2003. http://www.cesnur.org/2003/vii2003_dericquebourg.htm.

Duvert, Cyrille. 2004. "Anti-Cultism in the French Parliament." *Regulating Religions*, ed. James T. Richardson, 41–52. New York: Kluwer Academic/Plenum Publishers.

Gest, Alain (Président), and M. Jacques Guyard (Rapporteur), Députés. 1996. "Rapport fait au nom de la commission d'enquête sur le sects," no. 2468. Paris: Assemblée Nationale. http://www.assemblee-nationale.fr/11/rap-enq/r2468.asp.

Guyard, Jacques, and Jean-Pierre Brard. 1999. "Les sected et l'argent," no. 1687. "Rapport fait au nom de la commission d'enquête sur le sects sur la situation financiere, patrimoniale et fiscale des sectes, ainsi que sur leurs activites economiques et leurs relations avec les milieux economiques et financiers." Paris: Assemblée Nationale.

Hervieu-Léger, Danièle. 2004. "France's Obsession with the 'Sectarian Threat.'" In *New Religious Movements in the 21st Century: Legal, Political and Social Challenges in Global Perspective*, ed. Phillip Charles Lucas and Thomas Robbins, 57. New York: Routledge.

Introvigne, Massimo, and J. Gordon Melton, eds. 1996. *Pour en finir avec les sectes* [To Put an End to Sects]. Turin, Italy: CESNUR-Di Giovanni.

Luca, Nathalie. 2004. "Is There a Unique French Policy of Cults? A European Perspective." *Regulating Religions*, ed. James T. Richardson, 53–72. New York: Kluwer Academic/Plenum Publishers.

Palmer, Susan. 2002. "Field Notes: France's Anti-Sect Wars." *Nova Religio: The Journal of Alternative and Emergent Religions* 6, no. 1 (October), 174–182.

Palmer, Susan. 2006. "The About-Picard Law and Néo-Phare: The First Application of *Abus de faiblesse*." Presented at the July 2006 CESNUR conference in San Diego, California. http://www.cesnur.org/2006/sd_palmer.htm.

Picard, Catherine, and Anne Fournier. 2002. *Sectes, démocratie et mondialization*. Paris: Presses Universitaires de France.

Wright, Stuart. 2007. "The Dynamics of Movement Membership: Joining and Leaving New Religious Movements." In *Teaching New Religious Movements*, ed. David G. Bromley. New York: Oxford University Press.

PART VI

International Missions

16

Scientology Missions International (SMI): An Immutable Model of Technological Missionary Activity

Bernadette Rigal-Cellard

The following study looks at the way religions undergo transformations when they migrate from the country in which they were born to other cultures. With all the problems it has engendered in Europe in particular, where it is mostly held as the Trojan horse of American imperialism, the Church of Scientology offers a perfect case study. How do its missionaries, called *mission holders,* react to their new environment: Do they try to adapt to it, or, on the contrary, do they seek to adapt it to their own vision of the world? I will present here only the foundation of SMI, its European missions, its franchise system, and the duty of the mission holders.

The Foundation of Scientology Missions International (SMI)

Strangely enough, SMI, that is the mission system, properly speaking, was set up only in 1981 once the Church had already expanded worldwide. Before this date the term used, instead of mission, was "franchise." The authorities have explained that the foundation of a specific branch devoted to missions corresponded to a new era, "a new dawn within the Church" (*Qu'est* 1998, 483), when several administrative changes were operated to put an end to the activities of the Guardian Office (GO), which had been created in 1966 to counterattack the criticisms leveled against the Church, but which was now found to have grown into an isolated and autonomous branch that did not abide by Hubbard's rules (see Melton 2002: 27). It was also at that time that Hubbard retreated somehow from the direction of the Church to dedicate himself to his writing.

His successors created the Church of Scientology International (CSI), to coordinate all the branches of the Church worldwide (these remain administratively independent) and SMI, called the superior ecclesiastical body that supervises all the missions (*Qu'est* 1998, 483). SMI manages the whole infrastructure and the training of the mission holders, with the guidance of the International Hubbard Ecclesiastical League of Pastors (IHELP).

European Missions

The number has been increasing tremendously in the last twenty-five years due to the intensification of the crusade launched by David Muscavige. Europe ranks second after the United States for the number of missions: In 1983, there were 40 missions, which had grown to 197 as of 2002. Missions can be found in most countries, and as of 2006 or 2007, there were 2 in Austria, 2 in Belorussia, 1 in Croatia, 6 in the Czech Republic, 3 in Denmark, 2 in Finland, 10 in Germany, 1 in Georgia, 23 in Hungary (33 as of 2002), 2 in Ireland, 51 in Italy (33 as of 2002), 1 in Latvia, 1 in Lithuania, 2 in Macedonia, 1 in Romania, 44 in Russia in 2007 (80 in 2002), 1 in Slovenia, 14 in Slovakia, 5 in Spain (4 in 2002), 6 in Switzerland, 17 in Ukraine and on the fringe of Europe, and 9 in Kazakhstan (10 in 2002).

Internationally, the latest figures available (on the Web site) give 3,200 missions, churches, and groups; there were 2,600 in 1998. The French edition *of What Is Scientology?* reported 1,811, in 133 countries as of 1997 (*Qu'est* 1998, 451). In 2008 the Web site says 129 countries. In France, 7 missions were operative as of 2006 (5 in 2002); Avignon, Bordeaux, Toulouse, Marseille, Montpellier, Nice, Vannes, and others were ready to open. (All figures for 2002 given in personal correspondence with an SMI officer for the EU, January 25, 2002; for 2006–2007 found on http://www.smi.org/address/index.htm and http://www.scientology.org/en_US/news-media/stats/pg006.html, consulted January 17, 2008.)

Figures vary greatly according to sources: In 1999, the Associated Press reported 30,000 Church members in Germany (Associated Press, December 1), whereas the official Web site of the German embassy in Washington, DC, estimated their number at between 5,000 and 6,000 in 2008 (http://www.germany.info/relaunch/info/archives/background/scientology.htm; August 19, 2008); in France, the Church says 40,000, whereas observers give much lower estimates: 2000 and 4000.[1] The European center of SMI is in Copenhagen and is managed by Sea Org members. Great Britain (6 missions as of 2007) is not included in the European mission zone, but is in itself an autonomous zone, with its headquarters in Sussex. South Africa is itself attached to Australia. What matters most for our purpose here is that whatever the region, missions always operate in the same way.

Administrative Functioning of SMI

The missionizing will be spiritual, technical, and as always cultural, even if the mission holders do not realize it.[2] Though it can be called a mission with only three members, it is mostly once the mission holder has converted about twenty people that his mission is formally established. It may then either grow into a church or remain a mission. The largest in the world is the one in St. Petersburg that, even though it has a staff of over 150, remains "a mission" (SMI Officer European Union, January 25, 2002; it was still such a mission in 2007).

Missions function as franchises, even though the term stopped being used in 1981, whose official program was set up in 1959. They operate as commercial companies, of the associative type, and have their own local administration board that is responsible for the overall financial management of the mission. Minute accounting is extremely important for the Church of Scientology. Traditional Christian missionaries had to report on the progress they made to their authorities and also to their bankers but never with the same accuracy. In a society obsessed with figures, digits, feasibility, projects, results, and with the instantaneous transmission of orders from the hierarchy and from its accountants, the Scientologist mission holder cannot improvise nor remain vague on his or her daily activities. Goals are set and constantly repeated to keep up the stamina of the missionary. It is this intense financial management that has led critics to see in Scientology a major transnational firm, more interested in its bank accounts than in true spiritual teachings, unlike the major traditional evangelizing Churches. Typically, in his 1999 study, "The Globalization of Scientology: Influence, Control and Opposition in Transnational Markets," Stephen A. Kent explained how Ron Hubbard fought against the American government and wooed international elites in order to establish the respectability of the group. He also described the publicity campaigns on the path to happiness organized in foreign countries. However, if Scientology missionaries are great PR managers, they operate like most missionaries throughout the world and throughout the ages with the latest communication tools at hand.

What differentiates SMI missionaries is their constant recourse to acronyms, to an infinite variety of numbers to represent the various initiation stages and also to evoke the planets where mankind is supposed to have lived before. Hubbard's texts do not bear regular titles but numbers and acronyms that function like a code understood by members only, but which is translated in the books on the Church for anyone to read. These figures and letters are meant to guarantee scientific efficiency and are used by most companies and administrations in our own societies as well with the same intended purpose.

What is original is that mission holders embark on this enterprise without any financial or material aid from SMI, like Latter-day Saints who must somehow finance all their expenses. Yet Latter-day Saints do not choose the location of their mission: They gravitate around fixed LDS centers or explore new territories under the guidance of the authorities, whereas Scientologists are left completely free to pick up their territory. They can start a mission at home, or nearby, or much farther. They can go alone or in a group. Before departing they undergo specific training in an *Org* or in an existing mission and they need to run the gamut of all the activities. Once they have successfully completed all the levels on the list, they are declared operational. Afterward they are left to fend for themselves. If they do not gain any converts, all of their investments will be lost. At the same time, if they gain many converts and need money to expand, they cannot borrow any funds from the Church. They have to provide everything for themselves and the mission from their own personal networks.

SMI has prepared a shortlist of requisites to open a mission. Franchised mission holders are considered pioneers who must display the greatest perfection (*SMI Newsletter* 1, no. 13: 2). The term "pioneer" recurs very often in the literature: "Pioneer New Worlds" is the title of their application file. The missionaries undergo their training in an Org or in a mission, and they work in all of its departments in order to be prepared to hold any kind of function. Once they have gone through all the levels of the mission they are considered fully trained and ready to open their own mission center.

Again, unlike most traditional missionaries who may have only a few books and aids to work with, Scientologists have to take along masses of cases containing books and aids, the practice of Scientology requiring an exact knowledge of all the writings of Ron Hubbard. They must also carry the *tech* (the technology used in the spiritual work of the Church). None of these books or machines are rented or lent by the Church; mission holders must buy them with their own money, and it must be said that they cost quite a lot. The basic *Mission Starter Package* costs $35,000, the *Scientology Handbook,* $80, and the *Volunteer Minister Course Pack,* $15 (2001 prices).[3] The *Package* contains a full bookshop, a video set, *Public Film System,* films, dissemination brochures, prepared courses, and an *E-Meter* for auditing. The first *Package* in a foreign language appeared in German in 1981 (*SMI Newsletter* 1, no. 4: 2). The *Ultimate Collection,* containing eighteen hardback books and a thirty-four lecture series (six DVDs), cost U.S. $7,850 in 2008 (http://bpi.goldenageofknowledge.net/), with package prices ranging from $5,000 to $5,500.

Though they are fully autonomous in the management of their mission, the pioneers must remain in constant contact with the Church. They are given advice, in particular in the form of personal testimonies coming from other missionaries: tips on how to succeed or things to avoid; again, recipes for success that will be passed on within all missionary enterprises the world over. They must take part in various operations, such as Franchise Promotion Musts. If they are good they can become Field Staff Members (FSM), that is to say, members officially recognized and rewarded for their dissemination activities.

In 1969, Hubbard spelled out in great detail what they had to do monthly, for example, they must explain FSM projects to people during meetings, give paper and envelopes to them so that they can write directly to the nearest Scientology Orgs for advice, or, better still, the staff can even mail the letters directly. "AT THIS MEETING, EXPLAIN TO THEM THAT THEY MAY SELECT EVERY PERSON THEY BRING INTO SCIENTOLOGY, and that if they have not done so in 2 weeks, the Mission will select them. This chance for them to make some money creates a terrific body and money flow for the Mission" (LRH PL 11 Nov. 69 III; extract from "Franchise

Promotion Musts" printed under the title "Successful Actions," *SMI Newsletter* 1, no. 13: 2). Pioneers must also take part in a game, which used to be called the "LRH Birthday Game for Missions." It is meant to stimulate competition between missions. They each receive grades according to their statistics.

> EVERY MISSION WHICH SCORES 1500 POINTS BY THE END OF THE BIRTHDAY
> GAME WILL BE AWARDED A VERY SPECIAL GOLD CERTIFICATE IN RECOGNITION OF
> THEIR CONTRIBUTION TOWARD RON'S BIRTHDAY PRESENT!! (LRH, "Playing the
> Game," *SMI Newsletter* 1, no. 13: 3)

I was told the birthday present that Hubbard demanded was simply a good rating for proselytism activities.

Hubbard defined the Musts in 14 points for the opening of SMI, such as to keep doing what has been successful so far and that can always help the mission to expand and prosper, and to promote Scientology through advertisement in order to present all the services available to the community. Number 4 advised: "Start a campaign to get EVERY Scientologist in your area to select and bring in at *least* one new person per month into the Mission and then make sure that the person is well handled by Div 6 or Div 4 so that he continues up the Bridge." The basic material, *Dianetics* and *Scientology* books, have to be displayed in all bookshops and all possible outlets. Fellow Scientologists have to be constantly contacted, "revitalized, enthused and excited and made active." People have to be helped up the Bridge by being moved to higher orgs. Rallies and training sessions must be organized. Number 10 reads:

> DELIVER; DELIVER; DELIVER 100% STANDARD TECH to FULL EP on every public
> person so that they rave about the standardness of the results and
> continue on up *BOTH* sides of the Bridge.

The clear motto is to expand constantly so that floods of new members can reach the mission and require further help, notably training courses. LRH ends his injunction with number 14:

> Remember that the keynote to handling any antagonistic element is
> to FLOURISH and PROSPER. Realize that there is no more deadly way to
> get even with a suppressive or antagonistic person or a downgrading
> society than by FLOURISHING and PROSPERING . . .
>   Love
>   Ron
>
> (LRH ED 326–1R INT 1981–1982, "Playing the Game," *SMI News-
> letter* 1, no. 13: 3)

Proselytism

The mission holder must recruit people whom he will help through the early stages of their teaching and will later send to more established centers to follow higher classes in order to climb on the Bridge that will take the person onto the path of inner discovery. If the mission holder is himself allowed to audit new members he can start the auditing process. The missions are thus seen as the gates to the Bridge. The mission holders explain to the non-Scientologists what the activities of the Church are, what it can achieve for them. Hubbard defined all the steps missionaries must follow in order to "open the door of expansion" for neophytes. Theses steps could be found in any missionary manual in a chapter on how to entice strangers to listen to you. LRH advised people to choose a set, yet unique, approach and react according to the specific situation. First, personal contact must be achieved, the person must be "handled" if she or he is not so open to the contact as one would expect, the negative conditions of that person must be uncovered and accepted as unwanted in order to "salvage" the individual, and finally *"Bring to understanding:* Once the person is aware of the ruin, you bring an understanding that Scientology can handle the condition found in 3 . . . It is the right moment on this step that one hands the person a selection slip, or one's professional card . . ." (LRH HCO PL 23 Oct. 65 "Dissemination Drill," quoted in "Open the Door to Expansion," *SMI Newsletter* 1, no. 15: 2).

The mission holder will be able to disseminate successfully once his or her goal is made apparent to the potential trainee. LRH advises, "Show him that something about himself and the battle is pretty much won. We try too often for a total effect on people and try to tell them everything there is in a single moment. The motto here is: don't try to overwhelm, just penetrate" (LRH HCO B15 Sept 59, "Dissemination Tips," reprinted in "Successful Actions," *SMI Newsletter* 1, no. 15: 2).

According to Church stats, in 52.6 percent cases, it is through friends that the newcomers will be recruited. Publicity (4.8 percent) and lectures (3.1 percent) are less efficient. Scientology's famous personality test, *Test Oxford Capacity Analysis,* is said to be in fact not very useful, and only 18 percent of neophytes are recruited in this way (http://www.scientology.org/en_US/news-media/stats/pg001.h; January 17, 2008). This personality test is the trademark of the Church, like the door-to-door evangelization campaigns of the Jehovah's Witnesses, the pairs of Mormon missionaries, or the Christmas carols of the Salvation Army. The test contains 200 questions meant to understand the personality of the respondent and his or her shortcomings. It is filled out on the spot, or on the Internet, or mailed. The answers are thoroughly analyzed and the results explained to the respondents with the solutions offered by the Church. Scientologists estimate only about 10 percent of the respondents will actually go beyond the lower stages of initiation and embark on the auditing process.

The Immutability of Scientology

Here we have the major characteristic of SMI missions: Absolutely no adaptation, whether cultural or doctrinal, is to be authorized. Unlike most religions, which feel the necessity to adapt and accept to mutate either over time in the same location or when they export themselves to another culture, Scientology imposes itself as an unadulterable compound. Hubbard conceived it as a universal model that would function exactly the same way everywhere in the world. To observers, though, it may not be so much a universal system as the global imposition of a marked Western model, or, better still, an American model.

For example, when one looks at the 200 questions of the personality test, one can see that it is typically the product of Western society. The questions bear on social relations, on the ways of expressing one's feelings, on one's emotions. Asian cultures, for example, do not behave socially as we do in the West; in many of their societies people are not meant to show their feelings. Even in Europe, there are great varieties from one country to another in terms of the expression of emotions. Yet when people take the test, whatever their cultural origins, they have to answer the same questions Americans are given. To counter this criticism, Scientologists explain that cultures do not modify the mental process of each human brain at all: Hubbard and his successors have always rejected the assumption that a given culture impacts an individual's symbolic imagination. For Hubbard, all human beings share the same mental makeup, whatever their social milieu, their education, or their genetic heritage. Scientologists state that this refusal to adapt to foreign cultures is not the mark of a colonizing spirit but that it simply derives from the conviction that the findings of Hubbard were precise, exact, perfect, and universally efficient. Were they even slightly altered, the whole system would collapse. This is why the *tech* must either be accepted in its most minute details and as a whole, or rejected altogether.

The keeper of this perfect transmission, the Religious Technology Center (RTC), was founded in 1982. All the clergy and all the mission holders depend on it for their teaching and their own progression. RTC guarantees the purity of the doctrine and the correct standard and immutable use of technology. The recourse to the *tech* is of course another difference between SMI and other missionary religions, but I do not need to speak about this here. Each local church and each mission sign a formal agreement with the Church of Scientology that gives them the right to use its trademark. The idea is that when a symbol associated with the Church is used in a particular mission, the participants can rest assured everything is performed according to the general prescriptions of Hubbard and of his successors. Scientologists thus guarantee equal access to spiritual freedom to all potential recruits the world over, whatever regional or ethnic culture and emotional training they have experienced until then.

Conclusion

SMI is a fabulous tool that strangely serves two diverging purposes: On the one hand it trains mission holders to develop survival skills in any conditions without relying on the material support of the hierarchy or of the group (that will, however, morally support its missionaries). It encourages competition in a business-like environment and thus prepares its members to succeed within the society at large, which corresponds to the belief of the Church that one should not depend on social aid but triumph through one's hard labor.

On the other hand, through the interdiction against modifying, however slightly, the doctrine and the *tech,* SMI imposes a strict discipline all over its international centers that must remain perfectly obedient to RTC and SMI authorities. The center, that is Hubbard's word and the presidency, firmly holds together the pioneers who are otherwise sent into the wild world to play the game of the survival of the fittest. In the case of SMI, missions do not adapt to their foreign milieu; they force their neophytes to conform to what the pioneers teach. Their current success may be due partly to their riding the wave of globalization that engenders the standardization of behavior on the Western model. We know that throughout history, missionaries have always benefited from the power of seduction their country of origin exerted on the evangelized population, either in a strictly colonial setting or in more general cultural imperialist mode. Once Europe receded as a world model, the United States became the leading evangelist power, and the success of so many American-born religions in the world cannot be interpreted without an understanding of the desire of potential converts to benefit from the riches of the United States. Reversely, in some areas, notably in Western Europe, in France and Germany in particular, the fact that a religious group has American roots is definitely not a plus but a handicap so that Mormon or Scientologist missionaries often have a hard time trying to minimize their "Americanness." Neither group will modify its core doctrine, yet Mormons will develop various adaptive strategies to make up for the bad reputation of their home county, whereas Scientologists will hold firm. They will explain that their view of the brain and the *tech* are not American per se but truly universal, and their only adaptation will be to the market economy of their mission surroundings.

SMI offers thus a rare case, for even though it refuses to evolve, which has been found to be one of the major conditions for missionary success, Scientology is still progressing. The near future will tell us whether such unconditional obedience to the founder's words, such refusal of any possible interpretation or commentary, will remain a viable model of international missionary activity.

Acknowledgments

I wish to thank here especially Danièle Gounord, the spokesperson for the Church of Scientology in France, for her kindness and her help, as well as Scientology President Heber Jentzsch, who gave me a lot of his time at the headquarters in Hollywood, and Leisa Goodman for her kindness there as well. And as usual, Massimo Introvigne and Gordon Melton, whose names and friendship are a wonderful sesame to open all doors.

NOTES

1. Figures given by Jean-Louis Gagnot, Paris, December 2001. In the issue "L'offensive des religions: Manière de Voir," *Le Monde Diplomatique,* November–December 1999, one finds 4,000 in the article written by F. Beaucé (p. 76), and 2,000 in the article by F. Lenoir (p. 80).

2. See the advice George J. Jennings gives to missionaries so that they will be conscious of their own inculturation before trying to adapt to their new milieu: "American Missionary Candidates—Out of These Worlds." *Missiology* 21, no. 2 (April 1993): 207–222.

3. Prices given in SMI magazine, now called *Centre,* no. 75 (2001). All the issues of *SMI Newsletter* can now be found in the *American Religions Collection,* UCSB.

REFERENCES

Church of Scientology Publications Consulted

Description d'une Religion: la Scientologie. D'après le Manuel de Scientologie. Copenhagen: New Era Publications, 1994.

Hubbard, L. Ron. *Dianetics: The Modern Science of Mental Health.* New York: Hermitage Press, 1950.

———. *Éthique, justice et civilisation.* Los Angeles. L. Ron Hubbard Library, 1995.

Guide *Au service de la communauté et de ses besoins.* Église de Scientologie Internationale, 1998.

Qu'est-ce que la Scientologie. D'après les travaux de L. Ron Hubbard. Copenhagen: New Era Publications, 1992, 1993, 1998.

Scientology: Theology and Practice of a Contemporary Religion. Los Angeles: Bridge Publications, 1998. French edition: Copenhagen: New Era Publications, 1998. Includes an article by Bryan Wilson.

Sivertsev, Michael A. *La Scientologie: une voie pour se trouver.* Los Angeles: Freedom Publishing, 1995.

SMI Newsletter 1, no. 4 (Howard D. Becker, editor).

SMI Newsletter 1, no. 13 (Howard D. Becker, editor).

SMI Newsletter 1, no. 15 (Howard D. Becker, editor).

What Scientologists Say About Scientology. International Association of Scientologists. USA, 2000.

Independent Studies Consulted

Aries, Paul. "La Scientologie contre la République" in "L'offensive des religions: Manière de Voir," *Le Monde Diplomatique* (November–December 1999): 86–87.

———. *La Scientologie, laboratoire du futur: Les secrets d'une machine infernale.* Lyon: Golias, 1999.

Associated Press. "Switzerland: Scientology Spying by a German Official Spurs Jail Term." December 1, 1999.

Bainbridge, William Sims, and Rodney Stark. "To Be Perfectly Clear." *Sociological Analysis* 41, no. 2 (1980): 128–136.

Beauge, Florence. "Vers une religiosité sans Dieu" in "L'offensive des religions: Manière de Voir," *Le Monde Diplomatique* (November–December 1999): 74–78.

Bromley, David, and Mitchell L. Bracey, Jr. "The Church of Scientology: A Quasi-Religion." In William W. Zellner and Marc Petrowsky, eds., *Sects, Cults and Spiritual Communities.* Westport, Conn.: Praeger Press, 1998, 141–155.

Delattre, Lucas. "L'Église de Scientologie suscite des tensions transatlantiques." *Le Monde* 30 (January 1997): 3.

Dericquebourg, Régis. *Croire et guérir: quatre religions de guérison.* Paris: Dervy, 2001. (Nouvelle édition augmentée de *Religions de guérison.* Paris: Éditions du Cerf/ Fides, 1988)

German Embassy. "Scientology and Germany: Scientology Organization." Background Papers. German Embassy, Washington, DC. Available at http://www.germany. info/relaunch/info/archives/background/scientology.html. Accessed August 19, 2008.

Flinn, Frank K. "Scientology as Technological Buddhism." In J. Fichter, *Alternatives to American Mainline Churches.* Barrytown, N.Y.: Union Theological Seminary, 1983.

Fouchereau, Bruno. "Les sectes, cheval de Troie des États-Unis en Europe." *Le Monde diplomatique* (May 2001): 26–27.

Introvigne, Massimo, and Gordon Melton, eds. *Pour en finir avec les sectes: le débat sur le rapport de la commission parlementaire.* Paris: Éditions Dervy, 1996.

Lenoir, Frédéric. "Controverse à propos des sectes," in "L'offensive des religions: Manière de Voir," *Le Monde Diplomatique* (November–December 1999): 79–81.

Kent, Stephen. "Scientology's Relationship with Eastern Religious Traditions." *Journal of Contemporary Religion* 11 (1996): 21–36.

———. "The Globalization of Scientology: Influences, Control and Opposition in Transnational markets." *Religion* 29 (1999): 147–169.

Mayer, Jean-François. *La Scientologie en Suisse. Rapport préparé à l'intention de la Commission consultative en matière de protection de l'État.* Publié par le Département fédéral de justice et police (CH), July 1998.

———. "Les activités missionnaires transatlantiques des mouvements religieux contemporains." In C. Lerat and B. Rigal-Cellard, eds., *Les mutations transatlantiques des religions.* Pessac: PUB, 2000, 265–278.

Melton, J. Gordon. *L'Église de Scientologie.* Turin: Editrice Elledici, 2002.

Rigal-Cellard, Bernadette. "Introduction: échanges transatlantiques." In Christian Lerat and Bernadette Rigal-Cellard, eds., *Les mutations transatlantiques des religions.* Pessac: PUB, 2000, 11–21.

Internet Sources

http://www.cesnur.org
http://www.cesnur.org/testi/se_scientology.htm
http://www.scientology.org
http://www.whatisscientology.org
http://www.dianetics.org
http://www.theology.scientology.org

17

The Church of Scientology in Sweden

Henrik Bogdan

New Religious Movements in Sweden

In September 1998 the Swedish Ministry of Health and Social Affairs published a report on new religious movements (NRMs) in Sweden, titled *I God Tro—Samhället och nyandligheten* (In Good Faith—Society and the New Spirituality).[1] The report was 378 pages long, and its primary object was to ascertain the extent to which former members of NRMs needed help from the government when leaving their groups. Although the premises for the report were implicitly negative regarding the effects of membership in NRMs, the authors showed an awareness that general information about NRMs in Sweden was polarized between criticism from the anticult movement and an apologetic approach from the members themselves. It was furthermore stated that research into NRMs in Sweden was largely nonexistent, and that the few scholars dealing with NRMs agreed that more research needed to be done in this particular field. One of the main conclusions of the report was the suggestion that a governmentally funded association for information about and research into NRMs should be created, the so-called Kunskapscentrum för Livsåskådnings-och Trosfrågor (KULT). Although this laudable enterprise never materialized, the report itself was nevertheless an important step forward for official recognition that NRMs are an established and integrated part of the Swedish religious landscape—a landscape that has changed drastically over the past decades with new actors competing against traditional institutions such as the Swedish State Church (on January 1, 2000, the Church of Sweden was separated from the state). One of the more well known new actors is the Church of Scientology, which has been active in Sweden since 1968.

Until the 1960s Sweden was—in comparison with most other European countries—a comparatively homogenous country, both from an ethnic and a religious perspective. The official evangelical-Lutheran religion as formulated and propagated by the Swedish State Church was characterized by nationalism, unity, and homogeneity, whereas other forms of religion were often met with hostility and suspicion. In effect, being Swedish actually meant being a member of the State Church, and the only other practiced forms of religion from the Reformation to the nineteenth century were those of immigrant Jews and Catholics. It was not until 1860 that Swedish citizens were allowed to leave the State Church, but only on the condition that they became members of congregations approved by the state, which in practice meant the Catholic Church and the Methodists. (Andersson and Sander 2005). From the mid-nineteenth century various new Christian denominations were established throughout Sweden, such as the Church of Jesus Christ of Latter-day Saints (1850), the Plymouth Brethren movement (1876), Seventh-day Adventists (1880), Jehovah's Witnesses (1899), and Christian Science (1905), along with a number of alternative forms of religion including various spiritualist organizations and esoteric movements such as the Theosophical Society (1888), the Martinist Order (1890s), and the Hermetic Brotherhood of Luxor (1890s). However, these new organizations posed no real threat to the hegemony of the State Church, and membership in the new organizations was very limited compared to that of the State Church.

It was not until 1951 that freedom of religion was formally established in Sweden through the passing of the law of religious freedom that granted Swedish citizens the right to leave the State Church and to choose their own religious beliefs and practices. From the 1960s on the religious landscape in Sweden changed dramatically both with regard to the number of new Christian denominations and churches and the increased presence of non-Christian religious institutions. The primary reason for the changes was the increase of immigrants into Sweden who brought with them new forms of religion. The increased presence of new denominations and non-Christian religious traditions occurred while the whole of Swedish society was undergoing profound changes due to the impact of secularization, globalization, and processes of modernity/late modernity. The notion that the established religious institutions were the only legitimate and accepted forms of religion was questioned, and religious seekers began to look for alternative answers and solutions—as people were already doing in other parts of Europe and in the United States.

The 1960s and 1970s saw the establishment in Sweden of a number of international NRMs that reflected the broader trends of contemporary religious changes in the United States and Western Europe. The first Transcendental Meditation group in Sweden was established as early as 1961, only fours years after Maharishi Mahesh Yogi founded the Spiritual Regeneration Movement in Madras. The formation of the Transcendental Meditation group was probably prompted by the fact that Maharishi had visited Sweden in 1960 on his travels around the world. The Unification Church was established in 1969—that is to say, around the same time as the Church of Scientology—and two years later the Family/Children of God appeared in Sweden. Other international NRMs that established themselves in Sweden at this time included the International Society of Krishna Consciousness (ISKCON) in 1973, with Bhaktivedanta Swami Prabhupada visiting Sweden the same year, and the Osho movement in 1978 (Frisk 1998; Ståhl and Persson 1971).

The Church of Scientology in Sweden

When the Church of Scientology came to Sweden in 1968 it was during a period of social and political turmoil characterized on the one hand by university students protesting against the Vietnam War and agitating for socialist and communist changes (often in the form of revolution), and on the other hand by an increased interest in alternative forms of religion among members of the counterculture movement in Sweden. The commotion was particularly intense at the universities, and many students joined or formed radical political groups, whereas others turned their attention to alternative forms of religion, joining existing NRMs or coming into contact with religious groups in other countries. It is thus not surprising that the first forms of Scientology activity were organized by a small group of students in the university town of Lund (Ståhl and Persson 1971: 104). In Stockholm the first Scientology group met at the home of a young art student, Tomas Tillberg, who had visited the Church of Scientology headquarters at Saint Hill in East Grinstead, Sussex, during the spring of 1968. After another visit to Saint Hill a few months later, during which he completed a course in communication, Tillberg set up a Scientology group at his home on Birkagatan 33, in the Vasastan area of Stockholm. In April 1969 the group was elevated to the status of a formal church by the headquarters at Saint Hill. In Göteborg the Church of Scientology established itself in a similar manner with people interested in Scientology traveling to Saint Hill in 1967, and then setting up a group in May 1968. As was the case with the Stockholm group, the group in Göteborg initially had the authority only to teach the course in communication.

The Church of Scientology spread quickly across Sweden with a number of centers established in various cities such as Eskilstuna and Örebro, but it was in the three largest cities, Stockholm, Göteborg, and Malmö, that the Church of Scientology would be most successful. The Church of Scientology apparently attracted a large number of members during the first couple of years, and according to one source the number of sympathizers had reached around seven thousand in 1970 (Ståhl and Persson 1971: 104), although it must be stated that this figure appears to be unduly high. The organizational structure of the Church of Scientology in Sweden followed the same pattern as the Church of Scientology in other countries, and when the Citizens Commission on Human Rights was established in 1969, with the aim of fighting against "human rights crimes" performed by mental health professionals, it took only a year before a Swedish branch, Kommittén för Mänskliga Rättigheter, was set up. Nineteen-seventy also saw the start of the publication of *Freedom* in Sweden, this being the official newsletter of the Church of Scientology. Other organizations linked to Scientology in Sweden include Criminon, dedicated to the rehabilitation of criminals, and Applied Scholastics Sweden, which promulgates study techniques based on the teachings of L. Ron Hubbard. However, it is Narconon—its drug rehabilitation program established in Sweden in 1972—that is the perhaps the best-known Scientology organization in Sweden.

From 1970 onward the Church has been very active in translating and publishing books by L. Ron Hubbard, including *Dianetics: utvecklandet av en vetenskap* [Dianetics: The Evolution of a Science] (1970); *När du tvivlar, kommunicera* [When in Doubt, Communicate: Quotations from L. Ron Hubbard] (1971); *Scientologi: tankens grunder* [Scientology: The Fundamentals of Thought] (1972); *Dianetik: den moderna vetenskapen om mental hälsa* [Dianetics: The Modern Science of Mental Health] (1973); and *Scientology: tjugonde århundradets religion* [Scientology: Twentieth-Century Religion] (1974).

It would take thirty years for the Church of Scientology in Sweden to be legally recognized as a so-called voluntary organization with a religious purpose, and on November 23, 1999, the tax authorities decided to grant the Church of Scientology tax exemption. The following year, on March 13, 2000, the Church of Scientology was registered as a religious community by the National Judicial Board for Public Lands and Funds following a new law, titled the Act on Religious Communities (Swedish Code of Statutes 1988: 1593), which took on effect on January 1, 2000, with the separation of the Church of Sweden from the state. On June 10, 2000, the first legal Scientology wedding in Europe was celebrated in Stockholm.

In 2008 the Church of Scientology has churches in Stockholm, Göteborg, and Malmö, and Narconon has two centers in Huddinge and Eslöv, and, according to their Web site, the number of active Scientology members in Sweden is around 3,500.[2] In addition, there is an independent school, Studemaskolan, in Bandhagen, Stockholm, that uses the study techniques of Applied Scholastics. The school was founded in 1991 and is open from first to ninth grade and has about 100 students. Ever since its start the Church of Scientology has maintained an active profile in Swedish society with activities ranging from demonstrations against the National Board of Health and Welfare and—in the past few years—the erection of large yellow tents in central locations in major cities where volunteer ministers offer help (Åkerbäck 2008: 329). In comparison with other NRMs active in Sweden, the Church of Scientology maintains an open attitude toward academics and students, and interest among students is illustrated by the fact that on their Web site the Church of Scientology offers information to students at compulsory high-school and university levels.

Scientology in the Swedish Media

Its active role in society has made the Church of Scientology one of the most well known NRMs in Sweden, but it has also attracted a lot of negative attention. Many of the misconceptions and prejudices found among the public often stem from the yellow press, which has accused the Church of Scientology of being manipulative and dishonest. Chief among the allegations is the notion that the Church of Scientology practices brainwashing and that members are being forced to spend huge amounts of money on the courses offered by the Church. The latest trend in the gossip press is to focus on celebrities such as Tom Cruise and to emphasize what is often seen as "weird" or "strange" in the Church of Scientology. There are, however, two particular events that stand out in the history of Swedish Scientology and that have attracted a lot of attention even from the more respectable media: namely, the "E-Meter case" in the 1970s and the controversy over the "Bible of Scientology" during the late 1990s.

The "E-Meter case" was brought about by criticism leveled against the content of a number of advertisements placed in the Swedish Scientology magazine *Start* in 1973. According to the advertisements, the E-Meter could measure the mental state of human beings, a position that attracted the opposition of psychiatrists and certain members of the heath department. The advertisements were reported to the Consumer Ombudsman, and in 1976 the Swedish Market Court banned the Church of Scientology from formulating their advertisements in such a manner. The decision was appealed by the Church of Scientology on the grounds of religious freedom. The case eventually reached both the Supreme Court and the European Commission of Human Rights, however, without any results. The case received widespread media attention, and it became clear that Scientology and Dianetics stood in sharp contrast with the more traditional forms of psychiatric health care. Criticism from psychiatrists was fierce, and it was argued that information provided by the Church of Scientology was misleading and false. The criticism was reflected in the rhetoric of the Church of Scientology, which argued not only that traditional forms of psychiatry violated human rights, but also that psychiatry's use of diagnoses is not based on scientific or medical premises and that the treatments used by psychiatry (particularly the use of drugs) has a negative effect on patients. The debate was thus highly polarized, and the general public, through the media, tended to side with the psychiatrists and representatives of health-care institutions and viewed the use of the E-Meter as something suspect or fraudulent. But as Swedish sociologist of religion Jonas Alwall (2000) has argued, the critics did not take into account the fact that the use of the E-Meter is an integrated part of the religious belief system of Scientology, and that the claims of effectiveness of the E-Meter should be placed in the wider religious discourse of Scientology. The controversy surrounding the use of the E-Meter was not, however, something new in the history of Scientology. In fact, as early as the 1950s the U.S. Food and Drug Administration had investigated whether unwarranted medical claims were being attached to the E-Meter by the Church of Scientology. The investigation led to a raid on January 4, 1963, at the Founding Church of Scientology in Washington, D.C., and all the E-Meters present in the building were confiscated, only to be returned eight years later after the issue had been resolved in court. The E-Meter was declared to be a legitimate religious artifact (Melton 2000: 13, 14).

Alwall argues that a similar lack of contextualization of Scientology within the broader context of religious discourse underlies some of the criticism leveled against Scientology in connection with the much-publicized "Bible of Scientology" case of the late 1990s. On June 1, 1996, Swedish citizen Zenon Panoussis posted a number of secret—and copyrighted—OT-level documents on the Internet, which the media erroneously labeled the Bible of Scientology. However, the posting of the material on the Internet was not something new in itself, but reflected what had been going on for a while in other countries as well (Melton 2000: 36–38). According to the Church of Scientology in Sweden, the material that Panoussis posted was not only in violation of copyright law, it was furthermore claimed that the material had been stolen from the Church. The Web site was closed down following a court decision, but this did not deter Panoussis from trying to spread Scientology materials. Through an appeal to the Swedish constitution and the principles of public domain, Panoussis deposited copies of the documents in question at public institutions such as the Ministry of Justice, the Chancellor of Justice, and the Riksdag (the Swedish parliament), thereby making them accessible to the public. This stratagem worked for a while, but in October 1997 the government decided to place the documents under secrecy, thereby restricting them from the public. The official reason for this decision was that the documents were protected by foreign secrecy, "i.e., the rule that states that information pertaining to citizens or legal persons in another country shall be protected by secrecy if its publication threatens to interfere with Swedish foreign relations" (Alwall 2000: 112). It became known that the Swedish government had come under pressure from the United States in this particular case, a fact that prompted critics of Scientology to also criticize the Swedish government. The case of the "Bible of Scientology" did not, however, end here but sometime later the decision of the government was overruled by the Supreme Administrative Court, only to be challenged by the proposition of a new law by the government. The legal implications notwithstanding, it was the content of the OT-level documents that received the most attention from the public. The documents were often described as "bad" science fiction and it was questioned on what grounds normal persons could believe in the truth of the documents. As in other countries, Scientologists were often ridiculed for believing in the religious worldview formulated by Hubbard, but as with the "E-Meter case," the critics tended to overlook the fact that the documents should be interpreted in the light of religious discourse. Religious texts are more often than not interpreted in symbolic and allegorical ways, and they are often characterized by self-contradiction and nonempirical arguments.

The practice of regarding the Church of Scientology as not falling into the domain of religious discourse has a number of reasons, one of which is to be found in the language of Scientology itself and the way the Church presents itself to the public, which is often interpreted as a form of pseudo-science falling in a liminal position somewhere between science and religion. This state of liminality is illustrated by the fact that Scientology in Sweden is often perceived as not being a true or proper form of religion, and at the same time failing to meet the standards of scientific criteria. However, it is not only in the public mind that Scientology is often separated from religious discourse. This can also be seen as central to the criticisms leveled against Scientology by the Swedish anticult movement. The anticult group FRI, arguably the fiercest opponent of the Church of Scientology in Sweden, has as its motto on its Web site, "It is not about religion but about manipulation," while stating at the same time that groups such as the Church of Scientology do indeed have religion as a basis for their activities.

Scientology and the Swedish Anticult Movement

Criticism against the Church of Scientology has been expressed in the Swedish media right from the very outset in the late 1960s, but it is the anticult movement and individuals connected to it that have been the strongest opponents. The leading anticult group in Sweden, Föreningen Rädda Individen (FRI; the Save the Individual Association), was founded in 1984 by a group of friends and relatives of members of various "destructive sects" (in Sweden the term *sect* has negative connotations similar to the term *cult* in the United States). Since 2002, FRI has had a suborganization called SESAM that consists of former members of "destructive" and "totalitarian" groups. Since April 2001, FRI has been a member of the Fédération Européenne des Centres de Recherche et d'Information sur le Sectarisme (FECRIS, or the European Federation of Centers of Research and Information on Sectarianism). According to Liselotte Frisk (1998: 216), the primary arguments expressed by FRI against movements such as the Church of Scientology are that they exploit the insecurity and idealism of youths, they are dishonest about their real objectives, they systematically break down their members through techniques that aim to change the behavior of the members, the movements confiscate the assets of their members, religion is often used as a cover for receiving tax-exempt status, their true goals are power and money, they use psychological and sometimes physical violence against their members, they represent a fascist ideology and ethics, they have authoritarian leaders, and they practice mind control or brainwashing.

According to their website FRI has been in contact with over 500 defectors, out of whom about 200 have been subjected to deprogramming, and according to Frisk FRI claimed that between 20 and 30 of these deprogrammed individuals had belonged to the Church of Scientology. In discussing the Church of Scientology on their Web site, FRI enumerates four aspects that Scientology allegedly shares with other "totalitarian" groups. First, they manipulate their members by withholding important information and by using suggestion during the auditing process and in their courses. Second, they control their members through confessions and surveillance and by encouraging members to inform on one another. Third, they restrain members through the notion that the words of L. Ron Hubbard are a law that is forbidden to change or discuss. Fourth, Scientology offends its members through bullying if one does not make any progress, and by questioning the judgment of members if they do anything wrong. FRI is frequently used by the Swedish media as an expert body when the subject of NRMs is being discussed.

Another example of an anticult spokesperson is the priest Karl-Erik Ny-lund, who frequently appears in the press as an "expert on sects." Nylund is the author of a well-known book titled *Att leka med elden: sekternas värld* [To Play with Fire: The World of Sects] (2004), in which he identifies the Church of Scientology as the most dangerous sect in the world. According to Nylund the five most dangerous sects in the world are (1) the Church of Scientology, (2) the Raëlian movement, (3) the Unification Church, (4) the Family/Children of God, and (5) ISKCON. In Sweden the top five dangerous sects are a bit different, but it is still the Church of Scientology that is identified as number 1. The other groups in the top five include (2) the Raelian movement, (3) the Unification Church, (4) Kristi Församling, and (5) Linbufonden (Nylund 2004: 301). According to Nylund manipulative sects are characterized by four criteria, namely (1) *aggression* toward members who think differently, (2) *aversion* toward outsiders, (3) *alienation* from society, and (4) claims to *absolute truth* (Nylund 2004: 58–60). In discussing the Church of Scientology, Nylund addresses in particular the ways whereby the Church tries to silence its critics, and he states quite bluntly that Scientology—which he identifies as a "psychotherapy characterised by occult science-fiction"—is about money. In common with other critics, he dismisses the religious dimension of Scientology, stating that after reading some of the OT-level documents he came to the conclusion that it was nothing but rubbish (Nylund 2004: 218).

What is significant about the criticism directed against the Church of Scientology by FRI and authors like Nylund is that they are not criticizing the religious beliefs and practices as such, but rather the claims of what Dianetics can accomplish, the cost of the courses and auditing sessions, and what they see as deceptive behavior. This type of criticism is part of an international anticult movement that is secular in character, as opposed to religious countercult groups that largely base their criticism on theological grounds. FRI shares many similarities with other anticult groups in Europe, such as British organization FAIR (Family, Information and Resource), and it is perhaps not surprising that both organizations belong to FECRIS (Arweck 2006: 111–201).

Concluding Remarks

Although Christianity is still the dominant religion in Sweden—about 75 percent of the Swedish population are members of the Swedish Church—the religious landscape has changed dramatically since the 1960s with a wide range of new religious traditions on the scene. The Church of Scientology and other international NRMs established themselves in Sweden at a time when the whole of Swedish society was undergoing profound changes and when Swedes were increasingly looking for alternative religious answers. Although most of the NRMs active in Sweden have a comparatively small number of members, they have nevertheless received a lot of attention from the public through the media and from the academic world, as well as from the anticult movement. Government recognition of the importance of NRMs in Swedish society was made evident by the report commissioned by the Swedish Ministry of Health and Social Affairs in 1998. As one of the largest and most active NRMs in Sweden, the Church of Scientology stands out as perhaps the best-known NRM but also as one of the most controversial groups in Sweden. As discussed above, the controversy surrounding the Church of Scientology stems to a large extent from the "E-Meter case" in the 1970s and the controversy over the "Bible of Scientology" during the late 1990s. These two events were not only hotly debated and received wide attention from the media, but they are also illustrative of the conflict and tension that can arise when secular and religious worldviews meet. The E-Meter was questioned on scientific grounds, and the controversy over the OT-level documents posted on the Internet and later deposited in public institutions focused on questions of copyright and freedom of speech. But from the perspective of the Church of Scientology, both controversies were ultimately seen as an infringement on the freedom of religion, or the right to exercise and to protect religious beliefs and practices.

Moreover, the criticism from the anticult movement has added to the controversy that sometimes surrounds the Church of Scientology in that spokespersons from the anticult movement are frequently used as "experts" by the media. When comparing the development of the Church of Scientology in Sweden with that of its development in other countries, one is immediately struck by the apparent lack of idiosyncratic tendencies and, for that matter, controversies. The establishment and later development of the Church in Sweden parallels that in many other countries, and the organizational structure is identical for the Church of Scientology in all countries. Both the "E-Meter case" and the posting of OT-level documents is something that echoes conflicts that the Church of Scientology has experienced in other countries, as is the tendency to answer criticism from outsiders in an often polemical fashion and to use the legal system to protect the Church. The criticism from the anticult movement, but also the anticult movement as such, resembles what we see in many other countries.

NOTES

1. Statens offentliga utredningar (SOU), *I God Tro—Samhället och nyandligheten* (Socialdepartementet, Betänkande av Krisstödsutredningen, no. 113, September 1998).

2. According to the report published by the Swedish Ministry of Health and Social Affairs, in 1998 the Church of Scientology was estimated to have about 1,000 active members and about 10,000 passive members. This can be compared with other NRMs such as Summit Lighthouse with about 200 members, ISKCON with about 150–180 "full-time" members and 1,000–2,000 affiliated members, and the Raëlian movement, which has only about 10 members.. According to Swedish scholar Peter Åkerbäck (2008: 328), the estimated number of active members is about 500.

REFERENCES

Åkerbäck, Peter (2008). "Scientologikyrkan." In Ingvar Svanberg and David Westerlund (eds.), *Religion i Sverige*. Stockholm: Dialogos Förlag.

Alwall, Jonas (2000). "Scientologerna och samhället: Dialog eller konflikt?" In Carl-Gustav Carlsson and Liselotte Frisk (eds.), *Gudars och gudinnors återkomst: studier i nyreligiositet*. Umeå: Institutionen för religionsvetenskap, Umeå Universitet.

Andersson, Daniel, and Åke Sander (eds.) (2005). *Det mångreligiösa Sverige—ett landskap i förändring*. Lund: Studentlitteratur.

Arweck, Elisabeth (2006). *Researching New Religious Movements: Responses and Redefinitions*. London: Routledge.

Frisk, Liselotte (1998). *Nyreligiositet i Sverige: Ett religionsvetenskapligt perspektiv*. Nora: Nya Doxa.

Statens offentliga utredningar (SOU). (September 1998). *I God Tro—Samhället och nyandligheten*. Socialdepartementet, Betänkande av Krisstödsutredningen, no. 113

Melton, J. Gordon (2000). *The Church of Scientology*. N.p.: Signature Books.

Nylund, Karl-Erik (2004). *Att leka med elden: Sekternas värld*. 2nd ed. Stockholm: Sellin & Partner Bok och Idé AB.

Ståhl, Bo R., and Bertil Persson (1971). *Kulter, Sekter, Samfund: en studie av religiösa minoriteter i Sverige*. 2nd ed. Stockholm: Proprius Förlag.

Internet Sources

"Scientologikyrkan firar trettio-års jubileum," at http://www.freedommag.org/swedish/A06/page03.htm (accessed September 1, 2007).

"Scientologi-kyrkan i Sverige," at http://www.scientologikyrkanisverige.info/ (accessed August 5, 2008).

"Föreningen Rädda Individen," at http://www.fri-sverige.se/ (accessed August 5, 2008).

18

Scientology Down Under

Adam Possamai and
Alphia Possamai-Inesedy

Introduction

Australia is a country that has seen its religious groups being diversified over the years; as part of this growing diversity, many new religious movements (NRMs) have found a niche (e.g., Bouma, 1998; Hume, 2000; Ireland et al., 2000; Possamai, 2003; Possamai and Lee, 2004). However, several legal battles have surrounded the case of, for example, the Church of Scientology (Kohn, 1996), the Children of God, or the Family (Kohn, 1996; Sheen, 1996), and Ananda Marga (Richardson, 1996). Some "cults" have also been mistreated and/or misrepresented in the media. Richardson (1996) examined Australian media and new religions and concluded that Australian media relates to NRMs the way American journalists did a decade or so ago. In 1996, Australian journalists appeared to know little objective information about NRMs and as a consequence represented them negatively.[1] These negative sentiments, needless to say, create a sense of fear toward new forms of religion.[2]

Although the believers of these groups are legally protected, their protection in Australia is not of the same high level as the American model (Richardson, 2004). The Australian Constitution includes Clause 116, which protects religion: "The Commonwealth shall not make any law for establishing any religion, or for imposing any religious observance, or for prohibiting the free exercise of any religion, and no religious test shall be required as a qualification for any office or public trust under the Commonwealth." Unfortunately, Clause 116 does not apply to the Australian states; nevertheless, it does prevent federal laws that violate religious freedom. Of the six Australian states, Tasmania is the only one with a guarantee of religious freedom in its state constitution. Victoria and Queensland have statutes that afford some protection for minority faiths, but New South Wales has explicitly rejected adding religious freedom to its antidiscrimination statutes (Richardson 2004: 205).

At the governmental level, two recent reports have dealt with the freedom of religious beliefs. These are the *Commonwealth of Australia, Human Rights and Equal Opportunity Commission Article 18: Freedom of Religion and Belief*, July 1998 (CA98), and the *Commonwealth of Australia, Joint Standing Committee on Foreign Affairs, Defence and Trade, Conviction with Compassion: A Report into Freedom of Religion and Belief*, November 2000 (CA00).

Reflecting on these two reports and the way they portray "cults," Hill (2001: 120) claims that they lapse into popular stereotypes. "The problem with these reports is that they failed to recognise the appropriate expertise on which reliable conclusions might be based and sound policies developed; they lent themselves to the agendas of interest groups. One has to conclude that in their attempts to investigate the nature of NRMs the reports are expensive but largely futile exercises." Richardson (1999: 263) believes that the *Article 18* report suggests that more animosity exists toward new religions "than one might expect, given the long history of relative openness toward new religious groups" in Australia.

Although the Australian case is far from being close to the French and Belgian ones (Possamai and Lee, 2004), the Australian "fair go" attitude (see, for example, Possamai, 2008) does not seem to apply to all religious groups with the same intensity. This chapter thus explores the Church of Scientology as a case study to map out this possible level of animosity toward NRMs. This group arrived in Australia in 1957 and is well situated in Australia as Sydney is the regional headquarter of the Asian/Pacific region. There are six churches in Australia and four missions (these are smaller churches delivering introductory services).[3]

This chapter first analyzes census data to situate the group in Australia, then explores court cases and governmental reports involving the Church, and finishes with an updated analysis of the media and its representation of Scientology. It is the argument of this chapter that the tensions toward the Church have decreased over the years, but that the Church is still stereotyped.

The Church in Australia According to the Census

Between 1996 and 2001, the Church experienced a growth rate of 36.6 percent, which is an increase from 1,488 self-reported members to 2,032. Nine hundred and seventy-nine members (48.2 percent) of them live in New South Wales and more particularly Sydney. Other states have a much lower number, with Victoria being the next most represented (18.5 percent). Taking into account the level of hostility that the Church has experienced over the years in Australia (see below), we might expect a certain number of Scientologists who are not willing to reveal their religion for a governmental census.

Other NRMs that have grown in Australia between these two censuses are, for example, Baha'i (23.3 percent), Spiritualism (14 percent), Theosophy (14.3 percent), and Wicca/Witchcraft (373.5 percent). There are, of course, less successful stories among NRMs such as Caodaism (–15 percent), Satanism (–14 percent), Eckankar (–9.9 percent), and Swedenborgian (–15.3 percent).

The data in table 18.1 for the Church also include statistics from the Baha'i faith and Caodaism. The data from these three groups were purchased from the Australian Bureau of Statistics at the same time, and the choice of these groups was partly for the purpose of another research project (Possamai and Possamai-Inesedy, 2007). The reason why the Church is statistically compared and contrasted with these two groups, even if they do not have the same belief system and religious practices, is that they are all recently imported groups to Australia. The 2001 census reports 11,036 members from the Baha'i faith in Australia, with half reported to be Iranians, and 824 Caodaist members in Australia, which is a decline of 140 since the previous census (Possamai and Possamai-Inesedy, 2007).

Table 18.1 lists the birthplace of Scientologists, and shows that a large majority of Scientology Church members (67 percent) were born in Australia; this is in line with the country's average (72.6 percent). In contrast to the Iranian Baha'i faith (33.5 percent) and Vietnamese Caodaism (18 percent), which are new migrant religions also trying to attract Westerners (Possamai and Possamai-Inesedy, 2007), Scientology, even if it is a transnational movement, is well established among the Australian population. Even though this

TABLE 18.1 Birthplace of Scientologists, Bahaists, Caodaists, and the General Population

Birthplace by Percentage	Scientologists (%)	Bahaists (%)	Caodaists (%)	Australians in General (%)
Australia	67	33.5	18	72.6
Vietnam	0	0.1	73	0.8
New Zealand	7	2	0.5	1.9
United Kingdom	6	4	0	4.5
Iran	0	45	0	0.1
Italy	1	0.1	0	1
Japan	1	0.1	0	0.1
Taiwan	3	0.05	0	0.1
United States	1	1	0	0.3
South Africa	2	0.2	0	0.4
Other	11	8.5	6.5	14.71
Not stated	2	6	2	5.4

Source: From Australian Bureau of Statistics 2001 census.

religion is an American import, it is far from being a religion for American migrants.

In table 18.2, we discover that there is a much higher proportion of members who are between the ages of 25 and 54 (58 percent), which is where baby boomers and the Generation Xers are situated. On the other hand, children (16 percent) are underrepresented compared with the national average (20.8 percent) and the two other groups (22 percent and 20 percent). This high proportion in the 25–54 group, which is the most active in terms of recognized work, might be the reason for the higher income found among members of the Church (see below).

In terms of income, table 18.3 is quite revealing. In regard to people earning more than $1,000 a week, we find 10 percent of Scientologists, which is higher than the overall population of 8 percent. However, we have a slightly higher number of Scientologists earning less than $300 a week (36 percent) than the average population (31 percent), but there is a much higher level among the two new migrant religious groups (40 percent and 47 percent). Although it can be claimed that there is more wealth among Scientologists than the average population, one should be aware that there is a proportion of low-income earners. On the other hand, if we add the low-income earners with the persons under 15 (52 percent), we can discover an almost identical level with the Australian average (53 percent), and a much lower one than with the two other groups (62 percent and 67 percent).

The reasons for these higher wages is found in table 18.4, where we can discover that a higher percentage (7 percent) of Scientologists (in comparison with the whole of Australia, 4 percent, and other groups, 3 percent and 2.5 percent) are managers, professionals, and associate professionals. Further, only a small percentage of Scientologists are not employed (36 percent) compared with the Australian average (56.5 percent). Although data are not available, it is fair to expect Scientologists to be more educated than the average population. This finding from the Australian case offers a continuation with that of Wallis (1976) in his early work on the Church claiming that many Dianeticians were

TABLE 18.2 Age Group Cohorts for Scientologists, Bahaists, Caodaists, and the General Population

Age by Percentage	Scientologists (%)	Bahaists (%)	Caodaists (%)	Australians in General (%)
Birth–14	16	22	20	20.8
15–24	15	16	15	13.7
25–54	58	46	50	43.5
55–64	5	8.5	7	9.4
65+	6	7.5	8	12.6

Source: From Australian Bureau of Statistics 2001 census.

TABLE 18.3 Individual Weekly Income for Scientologists, Bahaists, Caodaists, and General Population

Weekly Income by Percentage	Scientologists (%)	Bahaists (%)	Caodaists (%)	Australians in General (%)
Less than $300	36	40	47	31
$300–$499	14	11	13	13
$500–$999	22	15	13	20
$1000+	10	7	3	8
Not stated	2	5	4	6
Not applicable (persons under 15)	16	22	20	22

Source: From Australian Bureau of Statistics 2001.

TABLE 18.4 Occupations of Scientologists, Bahaists, Caodaists, and the General Population

Occupation	Scientologists (%)	Bahaists (%)	Caodaists (%)	Australians in General (%)
Occupation managers and administrators	7	3	2.5	4
Professionals	14	11.5	3.5	8
Associate professionals	7	4	2.5	5
Tradespersons and related workers	6	4	5.5	5.5
Advanced clerical and service workers	2	1	0.5	1.5
Intermediate clerical, sales, and service workers	12	5	2	7
Intermediate production and transport workers	4	2.5	7	3.5
Elementary clerical, sales, and service workers	5	3.5	1.5	4
Laborers and related workers	5	2	5.5	4
Inadequately described	2	0.5	0.5	0.5
Not stated	. . .	0.5	1	0.5
Not applicable (those not in employment)	36	62.5	68	56.5

Source: From Australian Bureau of Statistics 2001 census.

relatively highly educated with regard to academic, scientific, and professional background (cited in Locke, 2004: 123).

In conclusion from the analysis of the census data, Scientologists in Australia tend to be baby boomers and Generation Xers with high-income jobs. They represent a much higher percentage than average in active employment, and although Scientology is a NRM imported from the United States, it is nevertheless attractive to those born within Australia.

The Church in Australian Courts and in Government Reports

Following complaints from health professionals, government health authorities, and the public, Scientology became in 1963 the subject of an inquiry by Kevin Anderson, QC. In 1965, a Victorian Board of Inquiry reported in the first paragraph of its prefatory note that "Scientology is evil; its techniques evil; its practices a serious threat to the community, medically, morally and socially; and its adherents sadly deluded and often mentally ill" and that Scientology is not a religion. The inquiry board sat to receive evidence and to hear submissions and addresses for 160 days. It listened to oral evidence on oath from 151 witnesses covering 8,920 pages of transcript.

Reading through this report, one can easily discover that the board viewed the Church as a (pseudo)-science affecting the mental health of its members. In chapter 27 of the report titled "Scientology and Religion," the board interpreted that when the Church claimed to be a religion, it was for improving their defense tactics by pretending to be persecuted because of their religious beliefs. Further, the board did not seem to accept that a religious group could have a non-Christian perspective:

> Scientology is opposed to religion as such, irrespective of kind of denomination. The essence of Hubbard's axioms of scientology is that the universe was created not by God, but by a conglomeration of thetans who postulated the universe. Sometimes God is referred to as the Big Thetan. Many of the theories he propounds are almost the negation of Christian thought and morality. (Chapter 7)

It is clear from this statement (and a few others in the same chapter) that the legal system of that time did not reflect the type of autonomous judiciary system (in this case, independent from a Christian perspective) required for religious freedom for minority groups as described by Richardson (2007). This lack of independence from external systems, be it religious or secularist, is demonstrated quite strongly in the conclusions of the report when describing Scientologists' accounts: "These ardent devotees, though quite rational and intelligent on other subjects, are possessed of an invincible impediment to reason where scientology is concerned." A further conclusion is also worth quoting: "Though the practice of scientology has many undesirable features, such is the novelty of many of its activities that it is difficult to classify them precisely as being in breach of existing laws. That scientology practices and activities are improper and are harmful and prejudicial to mental health is evident." In its recommendations, the board admits that invoking the criminal law in respect to past conduct of the group will be of little significance, "like prosecuting a bank robber for driving his get-away car against the traffic lights."

The board then decided that "in order to control Scientology, it is necessary to strike at the heart of the problem":

> Hubbard claims that scientology is a form of psychology and the evidence shows it to be psychology practises in a perverted and dangerous way by persons who are not only lacking in any qualifications which would fit them to practise psychology but who have been indoctrinated and trained in beliefs and practices which equip them to do more than apply dangerous techniques harmfully and indiscriminately.

The board envisaged a system of registration of psychologists that would prohibit the advertising and practicing of psychology for fee or reward unless registered. It was the board's opinion that Scientology qualifications should not entitle a person to register as a psychologist. It admitted that to limit the practice of Scientology, it would involve the surveillance of practices and conduct by persons other than Scientologists. This report led to the Psychological Practices Act 1965 (Vict.), which made the teaching of Scientology an offense. However, this Act did not apply to "anything done by any person who is a priest or minister of a recognised religion in accordance with the usual practice of that religion." These provisions were repealed in 1982 (Psychological Practices [Scientology] Act 1982 [Vict.]). It is also worth noting that the Australian *Companies Code* used to include the terms *Scientology* and *Dianetics* as part of its Prohibited Names Directive.

The Church became recognized as a religious denomination under s.26 of the *Marriage Act 1961* in 1973, and was then exempted as a religious institution from payroll tax in South Australia, Western Australia, New South Wales, and the Australian Capital Territory.

However, in Victoria, in 1983, the Church faced a legal battle on the issue of being defined as a religion for tax purposes in the *Church of the New Faith v. Commissioner for Payroll Tax* (*Vic.*). The court was asked to decide if the Church was a religious institution for the purpose of tax exemption. The Church was first listed as a foreign company, as the Church of the New Faith Incorporated, in 1969 in Victoria. When the Church of the New Faith was asked to pay taxes from 1975 to 1977, it objected on the basis that it was a religion, and thus claiming its wages were not liable to payroll tax. After many rejections to this objection, the "corporation"/Church applied for an appeal at the High Court of Australia. The court investigated whether this "corporation" was, during the relevant period, a religious institution. Instead of focusing on the writings of Hubbard, as previously done (see above), the court focused instead on whether "the beliefs, practices and observances which were established by the affidavits and oral evidence as the set of beliefs, practices and observances accepted by Scientologists are properly to be described as a religion." Taking into account that religion had received little judicial exegesis in Australia since 1943 (*Company of Jehovah's Witnesses Inc. v. The Commonwealth*), that religions in Australia were no longer exclusively Christian and theistic because it recognized itself as a multicultural country since the early 1970s, and that protection is required for the adherents of religions rather than for the religions themselves, the court held that beliefs, practices, and observances of this church did constitute a religion in the state of Victoria. Through this case, the legal definition of religion in Australia was redefined by Acting Chief Justice Mason and Justice Brennan to include as its two elements:

- belief in a supernatural Being, Thing, or Principle
- the acceptance of canons of conduct to give effect to that belief (though canons of conduct that offend against the ordinary laws are outside the area of any immunity, privilege, or right conferred on the ground of religion)

Justices Wilson and Deane, instead of a single definition of religion, referred to some guiding principles:

- a particular collection of ideas and/or practices involving belief in the supernatural
- ideas that relate to the nature and place of humanity in the universe and the relation of humanity to things supernatural
- ideas accepted by adherents requiring or encouraging the observation of particular standards or codes of conduct or participation in specific practices having supernatural significance
- adherents constituting an identifiable group or identifiable groups, regardless of how loosely knit and varying in beliefs and practices these adherents may be
- adherents themselves seeing the collection of ideas and/or practices as constituting a religion

However, in the same year, Gaze and Jones (1990: 222, 282–284) report that the High Court offered little help when Scientologists complained about the Australian Security Intelligence Organisation (ASIO) (*Church of Scientology v. Woodward* [1983] 154 C.L.R. 25 [High Ct.]). The Australian intelligence services were claimed to keep them under surveillance and were reporting members' church affiliation to Commonwealth agencies when applying for jobs. The matter was heard and ASIO's activities were regarded as not being subject to judicial review. Using this case as an example of ASIO's lack of accountability in the light of the new antiterror laws, Head (2004) underlines how the agency was shielded from legal scrutiny.

In New South Wales, the New South Wales Anti-Discrimination Board (1984) published an extensive report on discrimination and religious conviction in New South Wales and Australia. It reports, in an unprejudiced way, and among many other things, the Church of Scientology as a case study of Australian intolerance and prejudice toward minority religions. According to the board, the reason for this attitude is that the public is inadequately informed about religion in general, and minority groups in particular (section 5.5). It underlines that pressure on federal and NSW governments to make extensive inquiries into the "cults" in general has been resisted by both federal and the state attorneys-general. Such inquiries, the board argues, would infringe religious freedom, and specific breaches of the law can be dealt adequately under existing legislation. It follows the view that "controversial activities of unpopular minority religious groups belong rather in the province of public discussion than in that of governmental regulation by legislation or other action" (section 5.183). It recommends (section 5.241) to educate people working in governmental agencies (e.g., police, local governments, health, and education) more on issues of religious prejudice.

In 1998, the Australian Human Rights and Equal Opportunity Commission investigated freedom of religion and belief in Australia and discovered, for example, that some Scientologists would not disclose their affiliation when applying for accommodation, fearing that this would affect their chances (1998: 77). This report uses the case of the Church as part of its subsection 5.2 on experiences of vilification and incitement to hatred for nonmainstream religions and other beliefs (90–93). This subsection explores the large group of submissions received from members of the Church who complained of vilification and harassment on the basis of their membership. For example, a member made reference to the Church being publicly vilified in a state parliament by derogatory claims about the Church targeting the recruitment of children through its schools in Australia (e.g., the Athena school). The report also quotes a former member of the Church who surveyed sixty Scientologists and who claimed that despite the gradual recognition and tolerance of the group in Australia over the last thirty years, many still experience intolerance and discrimination.

Australia offers limited protection against religious vilification and when antidiscrimination at the federal and state levels makes incitement to religious hatred unlawful in some form, it covers mainly ethnically based religions. This led a former Scientologist to state, in this Article 18 report, that "Scientologists come from all racial and cultural backgrounds. This . . . means that they are not protected by any discrimination legislation in Australia" (96).

In 2000, an inquiry into freedom of religion and belief was investigated by the Joint Standing Committee on Foreign Affairs, Defence and Trade (2000). One chapter is devoted to "cults" and falls into using stereotypes (Hill, 2001). It includes the Church of Scientology (10.12) as a "cult" but does not address the group much more. This chapter acknowledges that this "cult" issue raises a number of complex issues that remain outside government or other controls and recommends the same recommendation as in Article 18 above—that is, that the "Commonwealth Attorney-General give consideration to the convening of an inter-faith dialogue to formulate a set of minimum standards for the practice of cults" (10.47).

More recently, in 2002, a case in the Australian Capital Territory involved the government's attempt to define Scientology's "Purification Rundown" as a "health practice" and thus subject to regulation.[4] The Supreme Court of the Australian Capital Territory ruled that the "Purification Rundown" is a religious practice because it is "essentially provided for religious purposes and not for the benefit of the health of participants" (28), and thus public officials are not allowed "to intrude into areas which predominantly concern matters of religious belief and practice" (24).

Although this last case illustrates that there is still tension between the authorities and the Church of Scientology, we are nevertheless a long way from the 1965 Anderson report.

The Church in Australian Media

"The mass media are one of the major forces that mold and shape social movements, which challenge the established order and prescribe different paths along which change should take place" (van Driel and Richardson, 1988: 37). Media analyses of various societal issues have dominated social science research for the last several decades. However, regardless of the consensus that has arisen among social science scholars that the media does not represent a balanced, neutral view but rather is an active participant in the construction of information and accordingly individual opinion, there is little analysis of the representation of new religious movements within Australian society.

Four relevant studies can be mentioned as the exception; Deborah Selway's (1989) analysis (as cited by Richardson, 1996) of the representation of NRMs within the *Sydney Morning Herald* over a decade demonstrates a negative representation of these movements. Selway's research was most likely fueled by the NSW Anti-Discrimination Board's 1984 publication (see above), where the following was argued: "Many feature articles about minority religious groups re-interpret new information to conform with old material held on file, whose tone is usually pejorative. Negative stereotypes are perpetuated, the more so as what is already in print tends to be believed. The same material is also repeated and distorted" (1984: 195). Again, negative representations were further analyzed in Selway's (1992) study of print religion journalists in Australia. Her study demonstrated that the journalist respondents not only lacked experience in the field, but also held various suspicions of the marginal religious groups. The journalists admitted that their reporting was far from comprehensive in covering all sides of the issues revolving around the groups, and was often limited and uniformed. Interestingly, most of the journalists did not "hold any concerns about reporting the minority religions" (Selway, 1992: 21).

Selway's work was followed by Richardson's (1996) examination of journalistic bias toward NRMs within Australia. Richardson demonstrates that despite the media being subject to ethical standards such as the Australian Press Council's Statement of Principles and findings such as the NSW's Anti-Discrimination Board's (1984: 275) argument that "irresponsible sensationalism should not be able to hide under the shield of 'public interest,'" the media appear to function as "moral entrepreneurs" on many occasions (Richardson, 1996: 290).

The extensive study conducted by NSW's Anti-Discrimination Board can be seen as an unsuccessful attempt to get religion included in the NSW anti-discrimination law. Nevertheless, it provides valuable data that present clear evidence of media bias against NRMs within Australia during a particular time period.

Although an up-to-date analysis of media representation of NRMs is sorely needed within Australia, for the purposes of this chapter the following section provides an analysis of the representation of Scientology only. Central to this analysis, as discussed in the introduction, is the "lag theory" argument purported by Richardson (1996), in which Australian media's objectivities to NRMs demonstrates tendencies that are behind the American media by a decade. His 1996 analysis concluded by presenting Australian journalists as quite negative toward NRMs, and confirming Selway's findings that many journalists seemed to know little objective information about them and that there appeared to be an alliance between various journalists and anticult organizations.

Although this section does not deal with journalistic attitudes, it explores Scientology's more recent representation within two print media outlets, the *Australian* and the *Sydney Morning Herald* (*SMH*).

The *SMH* is Australia's oldest newspaper. It has been continuously published since 1831[5] and is often seen as the paper of the white-collar middle class. Although its circulation is smaller than its competitor the *Daily Telegraph*,[6] its inclusion within this study relates to its readership. As van Driel and Richardson (1988) argue, "[t]he conflict between the new religions and their critics is basically an upper-middle-class phenomenon" (39). Further justification for the inclusion of this particular media outlet is the fact, as noted above, that Sydney is Scientology's regional headquarters of the Asia Pacific region.

The *Australian* has a much weaker circulation than the *SMH* or the *Daily Telegraph*, with a reported weekday circulation of approximately 130,000 to the *SMH*'s 211,700 copies per weekday.[7] However, it is the only national daily newspaper of Australia. Similar to the *SMH*, its readership stems from the "white-collar middle class, yet they are also identified as the political elite and the business class."[8] Individuals from this particular stratum of society, it can be argued, are also responsible for the social reality of NRMs.

The data from these two newspapers were collected over a six-year period—January 1, 2000, until December 31, 2006. A thematic analysis was undertaken, and following van Driel and Richardson's (1988) approach in their longitudinal study of NRMs within the print media of the United States, themes were evaluated for their positivity or negativity by ranking them along a Likert scale with five values: extremely positive, somewhat positive, neutral, somewhat negative, and extremely negative. As defined by van Driel and Richardson, the "extremely positive" category encompasses any report that defends or supports, in this case, Scientology, and/or rejects allegations of opponents to the group. This value also highlights that there should be no sign of suspicion or rejection of the movement within the report. "Somewhat positive" involves a report that has a favorable approach to Scientology and/or an unfavorable approach to any of its opponents. This value, unlike the first, denotes that the report implicitly or explicitly communicates reservations and/or suspicions of the Church. The third, "neutral," value indicates that the report avoids taking a position on issues raised: There is no support voiced for Scientology or any of its opponents. Moving along the Likert scale we find the "somewhat negative" value. Reports that can be categorized into this section of the scale portray Scientology with ridicule, suspicion, and/or doubts. Importantly, this value denotes that the group is not being severely criticized; however, it also indicates that there is no unambiguous support for the Church. The final value on the scale, "extremely negative," indicates that Scientology is attacked or outright rejected, and/or any opponents of the Church are given sympathy and support (van Driel and Richardson, 1988: 48–49).

As stated above, Richardson (1996) argued for a lag theory in relation to Australian print media and its approach to NRMs. Although there is no current American media analysis of its treatment of NRMs, Richardson and van Driel (1997) do provide a follow-up study of their 1988 longitudinal content analysis of print media coverage of NRMs. The authors report on research carried out in the United States on misinformation and possible bias among American journalists toward new religions. Their sample of individual religious news writers revealed a slight increase in the amount of distrust for new religions among the journalists surveyed. This is in opposition to their earlier findings in which a more neutral approach characterized the U.S. 1980s media representation of these groups. They conclude by stating that "the U.S. media coverage of NRMs will continue to be problematic when compared to standards of objectivity and fairness" (1997: 128). This proclamation might be a replicate of the 1996 conclusion of Australian journalists and their approach to these groups. Accordingly, when taking into consideration Richardson's lag theory, one would assume that current media representations of new religions, for the present study, Scientology, within Australia will be quite negative, with an apparent incorporation of material from anticult organizations (Richardson, 1996: 296).

Keywords such as "Scientology," "Hubbard," and "Dianetics" were used to find newspaper articles for this chapter. Out of 161 articles from the Australian and 119 from the Sydney Morning Herald, 47 and 39, respectively, were not considered applicable to the study. These articles were just making a reference to any of these three terms without discussing the group's activities and/or beliefs.

The high number of articles found for this analysis tends to reflect the celebrity culture we currently live in. Not only are there numerous celebrity members of Scientology, but there is also a gossip-magazine style of reporting that has unfortunately infiltrated "serious" newspapers. Indeed, much of the current analysis could have easily been seen as an analysis of present-day celebrities within the media. A large percentage of this form of reporting was dedicated to the actor Tom Cruise. Initial accounts of the actor and his links with Scientology were portrayed in a favorable or at least neutral light. Interestingly, this quickly changed to a more negative approach after Cruise became more public about his religious beliefs to the point where he was being accused of proselytizing, which will be discussed below.

As detailed in tables 18.5 and 18.6, there are very few articles that present Scientology in an "extremely positive" or "somewhat positive" manner. In fact, out of the 194 newspaper articles examined across both of the described papers, only 5.5 percent are situated within the first two values. The six articles represented within the first value were found exclusively within the *Australian*. Of these six, two were actual letters provided by the vice president of the Church of Scientology. The other four, interestingly, reported on the Citizens Committee on Human Rights (CCHR) and their approach to ADHD and the commonly used drug for its treatment, Ritalin. These particular stories portrayed the group that was founded by Scientology as a "community advocate." All four of these articles made a clear link between CCHR and Scientology. Of the five articles that were found to be "somewhat positive" in their approach to Scientology, four were based on reports revolving around public personas, and half of these were dedicated to Tom Cruise before his downfall, as discussed above. These articles describe actors such as Cruise and singers such as the Australian Kate Cebrano as benefiting from the "tools" that Scientology had provided them that have contributed to their extremely successful lives. The fifth article represented a journalist's experience with the Church and its personality test. Rather than present the information in a satirical fashion, as most of the reports did (see below), the reporter described her interaction with the Church and concluded that she was impressed by the courteous and nonpressured exchange.

The neutral value of the scale was found to hold the second largest amount of reports on the group, with a 40 percent allocation. As discussed above, it is widely publicized that numerous Hollywood actors are actively involved in the

TABLE 18.5 The Church of Scientology in the *Australian* (2000–2006; 114 articles)

1 Extremely Positive	2 Somewhat Positive	3 Neutral	4 Somewhat Negative	5 Extremely Negative
6 (5%)	3 (3%)	44 (38%)	51 (45%)	10 (9%)

TABLE 18.6 The Church of Scientology in *The Sydney Morning Herald* (2000–2006; 80 articles)

1 Extremely Positive	2 Somewhat Positive	3 Neutral	4 Somewhat Negative	5 Extremely Negative
0	2 (3%)	33 (41%)	45 (56%)	0

movement. The neutral quality of these reports is usually based on a star sighting at the Sydney Scientology headquarters or the simple linking of the stars' names and their current projects to the fact that they are Scientologists. This includes the Australian media tycoon heir James Packer and his dalliance with Scientology. The many articles that are devoted to the representation of Scientology as part of this celebrity culture is contraindicative, for this current case of Scientology in Australia, of Beckford's claim that "the most elementary observation about print and broadcast media's portrayal of NRMs is that the movement's activities are newsworthy only when conflicts are involved" (1994: 20).

The majority of the reports were classified within the "somewhat negative" value. As outlined above, any media stories categorized into this section portray Scientology with ridicule, suspicion, and/or doubts. Importantly, the Church is not being severely criticized in these reports, yet they are also not receiving support. Across both papers there were ninety-six articles that were classified as such. Although there were quite a few reports that approached the Church with suspicion and unambiguous doubt, much of the tone was more satirical than overtly critical or foreboding. Again, many of these reports were linked to celebrity stories, with the majority of these linked to the actor Tom Cruise. Cruise's proselytizing behavior was closely scrutinized and reported but was often delivered in a comical fashion. It became apparent that at least half of the reports that could be categorized into this value were strongly related to the actor and his supposed downfall from public favor. Behaviors such as setting up a Scientology tent on the *War of the Worlds* set, bringing potential costars and reporters on tours of Scientology centers, and of course the public endorsement of some of the central tenets of the religion during interviews were all met with suspicion, yet reported in a mocking style. In this case Scientology is indeed being portrayed in a negative manner; however, its satirical presentation negates the group's ability to be the type of public menace that the earlier court reports alluded to (see section above).

Finally, the last value of "extremely negative" contained only ten articles. An outright attack on the group or overt support for its opponents was rare. However, in instances in which the group was attacking central tenets of Western society such as free speech, journalists were quick to respond. Examples that can be included here are the closure of Internet sites such as the anti-Scientology site http://www.zenu.net, as well as the censoring of a free speech forum because it published a quotation of a copyrighted text by Scientology. Furthermore, the retraction from circulation of the infamous Scientology *South Park* episode was handled in the same critical manner. It can be argued that in the case of Scientology it is only when it threatens conventional society and its central principles that it will be presented in the extremely negative manner.

It appears from this analysis that Scientology is no longer portrayed as a societal danger by the Australian press. Indeed, there were no reports on the Church within the chosen media outlets, or indeed any other mainstream Australian newspapers or magazines, that analyzed the group to the extent of the American *Time* publication "The Thriving Cult of Greed and Power" (Behar,

1991), or *Rolling Stone*'s recent critical report "Inside Scientology" (Reitman, 2006).

At face value the results of this research align with the "lag theory" proposed by Richardson (1996), in which the majority of the media reports are classified within the "somewhat negative" and "extremely negative" value. However, rather than an increase or even unvarying presence of anticult network (such as the Cult Awareness Network, CAN) information, it seems there is no presence or very little presence. Indeed, of the 194 articles examined, there was only one that involved an anticult network. This story involved the reporting of a suit brought by the National Union of Associations for the Defence of Families and the Individual against Scientology in France. Furthermore, as argued above, the "somewhat negative" reports do not represent the Church in a controversial or dangerous manner, but rather in a satirical fashion. This style of reporting and its impact on its readership should nevertheless not be devalued, as there is a clear bias represented. Although the media is not informing its readers to fear Scientology, it is stigmatizing the group into a "joke" and presenting its central doctrine as a "comic story."

Conclusion

This chapter has demonstrated that Scientology has come a long way in its migration process from the United States to Australia. More people are claiming to be Scientologists in official censuses, the media is less hostile to the group, and although the group has had dealings with the law, this has become low key since the 1990s.

This demonstrates that minority religions in Australia have a much better "lifestyle" than in France (see Possamai and Lee, 2004), but their protection is not fully settled. Indeed, "Freedom of religion in Australia depends on the goodwill of those in power at any given time, a majoritarian approach that may offer little solace to members of the growing minority faiths which are trying to practise their faith within Australia" (Richardson 1995b, 1999).

As illustrated by the 2002 case against the "Purification Rundown" practice in the Australian Capital Territory, the discourses of "fear" (Possamai and Lee, 2004) and demonization of the Church of Scientology lay dormant in Australia. Such fear has reared its head briefly on other occasions, as was highlighted above, without ever becoming all-pervasive. Further, these fears have lost their intensity in the media, which appears to have moved toward a more satirical approach to the group rather than an openly hostile one.

NOTES

1. The most infamous examples of this in Australia are the vilification of the Ananda Marga sect following the Sydney Hilton bombing and similarly the persecution of Lindy Chamberlain, a Seventh-day Adventist, following the death of her daughter Azaria, who was killed by a dingo at Ayers Rock.

2. Richardson (1995a) details the role of the media in the Waco tragedy involving David Koresh and the Branch Davidians and explores how the media, through its involvement with the government, prepared the general public to accept as justified the violence against a group labeled as deviant.

3. Data obtained from the Australian Church of Scientology's Web site at http://www.scientology.org.au, November 1, 2007.

4. *Vicki Marie Hanna and Church of Scientology Inc. v. The Commissioner Community and Health Services Complaints Australian Capital Territory [2002] ACTS 111* (November 6, 2002).

5. See http://www.smh.com.au/aboutsmh, accessed December 1, 2007.

6. See http://www.fxj.com.au/readershipcirc.htm, accessed December 1, 2007.

7. See http://www.fxj.com.au/readershipcirc.htm, accessed December 1, 2007.

8. Ibid.

REFERENCES

Australian Human Rights and Equal Opportunity Commission (1998). *Article 18—Freedom of Religion and Belief.* Canberra, Commonwealth of Australia.

Beckford, J. A. (1994). "The Mass Media and New Religious Movements." *ISKCON Communication Journal* 4: 17–24.

Behar, R. (1991). "The Thriving Cult of Greed and Power." *Time,* May 6, 1991.

Bouma, G. (1998). "New Religions in Australia: Cultural Diffusion in Action." In M. Cousineau (ed.), *Religion in a Changing World: Comparative Studies in Sociology.* Westport, Conn.: Praeger, 203–212.

Gaze, B., and M. Jones (1990). *Law, Liberty, and Australian Democracy.* Sydney: The Law Book Co.

Head, M. (2004). "ASIO, Secrecy and Lack of Accountability." *Murdoch University Electronic Journal of Law* 11(4). http://search.astlii.edu.au/au/journals/muruejl/2004/31,html, accessed December 1, 2007.

Hill, M. (2001). "Cult-Busters in Canberra? Reflections on Two Recent Government Reports." *Australian Religious Studies Review* 14(1): 113–121.

Hume, Lynne (2000). "New Religious Movements: Current Research in Australia." *Australian Religion Studies Review* 13(1).

Ireland, R. (1999). "Religious Diversity in the New Australian Democracy." *Australian Religious Studies Review* 12: 94–110.

Ireland, R, P. Hughes, A. Possamai et al. (2000). "Other Religions." In P. Hughes (ed.), *Australia's Religious Communities: A Multimedia Exploration. CD-Rom Professional Edition.* Melbourne: Christian Research Association.

Joint Standing Committee on Foreign Affairs, Defence and Trade (2000). *Conviction with Compassion: A Report on Freedom of Religion and Belief.* Canberra, Commonwealth of Australia.

Kohn, R. (1996). "Cults and the New Age in Australia." In G. Bouma (ed.), *Many Religions, All Australians: Religious Settlement, Identity and Cultural Diversity.* Melbourne: Christian Research Association, 149–162.

Locke, S. (2004). "Charisma and the Iron Cage: Rationalization, Science and Scientology." *Social Compass* 51(1): 111–131.

New South Wales Anti-Discrimination Board (1984). *Discrimination and Religious Conviction.* Sydney: New South Wales Anti-Discrimination Board.

Possamai, A. (2003). "Alternative Spiritualities, New Religious Movements and Jediism in Australia." *Australian Religion Studies Review* 16(2): 69–86.

Possamai, A. (2008). "Australia's 'Shy' De-secularisation Process." In A. Imtoual
and B. Spaler (eds.), *Religion, Spirituality, and Social Science*. Bristol: Polity
Press, 23–35.

Possamai, A., and M. Lee (2004). "New Religious Movements and the Fear of Crime."
The Journal of Contemporary Religion 19(3): 337–352.

Possamai, A., and A. Possamai-Inesedy (2007). "The Baha'i Faith and Caodaism:
Migration, Change and De-secularisation(s) in Australia." *Journal of Sociology* 43
(3): 301–317.

Reitman, J. (2006). "Inside Scientology." *Rolling Stone* 995: 55–66.

Richardson, J. T. (1995a). "Manufacturing Consent and Koresh: The Role of the Media
in the Waco Tragedy." In S. Wright (ed.), *Armageddon in Waco: Critical Perspectives
on the Branch Davidian Conflict*. Chicago: University of Chicago Press, 153–176.

Richardson, J. T. (1995b). "Minority Religions ('Cults') and the Law: Comparisons of
the United States, Europe and Australia." *University of Queensland Law Review* 18:
183–207.

Richardson, J. T. (1996). "Journalistic Bias toward New Religious Movements in Australia." *Journal of Contemporary Religion* 11(3): 289–302.

Richardson, J. T. (1999). "New Religions in Australia: Public Menace or Societal Salvation?" *Nova Religio: The Journal of Alternative and Emergent Religions* 4(2): 258–265.

Richardson, J. T. (2004). "New Religions in Australia: Public Menace or Societal Salva-
tion?" In P. Lucas and T. Robbins (eds.), *New Religious Movements in the Twenty-
First Century: Legal, Political, and Social Challenges in Global Perspective*. New York:
Routledge, 203–210.

Richardson, J. T. (2007). "The Sociology of Religious Freedom: A Structural and Socio-
Legal Analysis." *Sociology of Religion* 67(3): 271–294.

Richardson, J. T., and B. van Driel (1997). "Journalists Attitudes toward New Religious
Movements." *Review of Religious Research* 39(2): 116–136.

Selway, D. (1989). *Religion in the Print Media: A Study of the Portrayal of Religion in
the Sydney Morning Herald 1978–1988*. Unpublished honors thesis, University of
Queensland.

Selway, D. (1992). "Religion in the Mainstream Press: The Challenge of the Future."
Australian Religion Studies Review 5(2): 18–24.

Sheen, J. (1996). "Living within the Tensions of Plurality: Religious Discrimination
and Human Rights Law and Policy." In G. Bouma (ed.), *Many Religions, All Australians: Religious Settlement, Identity and Cultural Diversity*. Melbourne: Christian
Research Association, 163–180.

Van Driel, B., and J. T. Richardson (1988). "Print Media Coverage of New Religious
Movements: A Longitudinal Study." *Journal of Communication* 38(3): 37–61.

Wallis, R. (1976). *The Road to Total Freedom: A Sociological Analysis on Scientology*. London: Heinemann.

PART VII

Dimensions
of Scientology

19

"His name was Xenu. He used renegades . . .": Aspects of Scientology's Founding Myth

Mikael Rothstein

Introduction

The study of new religious movements has, since the inception of NRM studies in the late 1960s, primarily been sociological in its orientation. The many groups that emerged in the wake of the counter-cultural revolution in Europe and the United States have, in most cases, been identified as societal responses to changing cultural conditions. The application of sociological analysis has therefore been the obvious choice. At the same time, however, the groups in question are all *religions* with all the features and qualities that go with the category (however defined). Consequently, they also lend themselves to other kinds of academic analysis. The sociological perspective should never be avoided, but in many cases historical studies, hermeneutic analysis, performance and ritual theory, cognitive studies, art history, and phenomenology, just to mention a number of academic approaches rarely found in NRM-studies, are just as relevant. In the case of Scientology a number of studies have been completed by scholars from the perspective of comparative religion (or history of religions), but they are few in number compared to the numerous sociologically inclined studies.[1]

In this chapter I shall contribute along the same lines and offer an analysis of one of Scientology's more important religious narratives, the text that apparently constitutes the basic (sometimes implicit) mythology of the movement, the *Xenu myth,* which is basically a story of the origin of man on Earth and the human condition. In doing so I take the study of a postmodern religion back to the fabric of traditional *Religionswissenschaft*, the philologically based study of religious ideas and notions as they come to life in religious texts. This is not to highlight this approach as more relevant than others, but to provide a more thorough understanding of a religious narrative otherwise only mentioned in the passing in academic studies of Scientology.[2]

In the public and legal sphere Scientology rightfully demands to be treated as any other religion, and in this chapter (in the academic context) I intend to do just that (as in previous works).[3] The critical, scientific investigation into Scientology's religious narratives, however, does not support the proclaimed self-perception of the organization. What I have to say will generally contradict or question official Scientology claims. This independent scholarly interpretation should therefore not be confused with Scientology's theological teachings.

I shall gradually approach the text itself. First, however, it is necessary to discuss the conditions under which the Xenu myth originated and thrives.

Text, Initiation, and Control

Scientology is primarily a religion of action. Even if the religious goals are ultimately defined according to a Gnostic formula, the religious lives of Scientologists center on an ongoing line of ritualized practices, "courses," that gradually, from an emic point of view, pave the way toward religious enlightenment. In this perspective Scientology has taken speculative or intellectualistic religion into a new realm, leaving the disregard for rituals and initiations in Gnostic traditions behind. Through the application of various therapeutic techniques, so it is believed, the individual is gradually transformed from a state of deluded consciousness to that of "Clear," and from that point on to ultimate enlightenment, and eventually "freedom." This ritual process, and the theoretical elaborations behind it, was developed and designed by Scientology's founder, L. Ron Hubbard (1911–1986). In an impressive number of so-called *Technical Bulletins* he laid the foundation for how the procedures should be carried out and how they should work, and it is the unconditional obligation on the part of the therapist, the "auditor," to follow Hubbard's instructions in minute detail. In the everyday lives of most Scientologists these kinds of (technical) guiding texts remain the most important. They are frequently used, and considered the concrete tools in the quest for religious fulfillment.

In this chapter, however, I shall explore another kind of religious text with a more indirect impact on the religious lives of Hubbard's devotees: the narrative that ultimately, but not necessarily openly, provides the mythological framework for Hubbard's Gnostic soteriology, and thus the machinery of the (often quite expensive) courses that take the patient devotee step by step over the "Bridge to Total Freedom," Scientology's metaphor for the path of salvation.

To most attendees and practitioners of Hubbard's religious techniques, this mythological level will be (and, as people drop out, in most cases remain) virtually unknown. Scientology is an esoteric religion, and it is necessary to progress on the Bridge to the advanced stages before the participant is exposed to the myth about Xenu, which, in the shape of a science fiction–inspired anthropogony, *explains* the basic Scientological claims about the human condition.[4]

The cosmology and anthropology that permeate the entire soteriological system in Scientology, also the initial levels the neophyte encounters, are presented without this reference but explained in other ways until the neophyte reaches the esoteric level known as OT-III, an initiatory level in which the "inner spiritual being" (believed to be present in every human) called the "thetan," reaches fulfillment and becomes an "Operating Thetan" (OT) on the third level. However, in order to understand even the more *exoteric* formulations properly, it is necessary to dive into the parts of Hubbard's religious imagination that are kept as esoteric secrets.

But this is no simple venture: Scientology will always deny the uninitiated access to esoteric documents, and it is well known that the organization will take legal measures to secure its sacred teachings from any unauthorized or religiously inappropriate scrutiny. At the same time, however, a number of former Scientologists have (sometimes illegally; these matters are often quite blurred) put the esoteric material at the public's disposal. For many years copies of various texts have circulated among anticultists, and critical reporters have, on many occasions, been able to obtain the texts. Scholars have had the same possibilities, but for ethical reasons there has been some reluctance to publish texts from organizations that consider them secret and sacred. Furthermore, scholars and others have had unsettling experiences with relation to such materials: In 1997, following an incident from the year before, in which a private person, wishing to counteract Scientology, had deposited a number of esoteric Scientology texts (the so-called OT-II and -III files to which I shall return) in the Swedish Parliament in Stockholm in order to make them publicly available (according to Swedish law all documents in the governments position are, in principle, accessible), I received a copy of the texts from a Danish reporter (I have no knowledge of his contacts).[5] He wanted my comment, and I said that the texts would mean nothing to the uninitiated, myself included. At that point I was unable to make any concrete use of the documents, and the political climate did not encourage anything of the kind. I browsed through the papers, felt reassured that this could mean something only to devoted Scientologists and the very patient scholar, and placed the material in a drawer at my university office. When I, at a later point in time, wanted to work a bit on them, they were gone. I have been through all of my shelves, drawers, and boxes but to no avail. The texts are not in my possession any longer. I have no clue as to where they are, but neither a specific indication of either intrusion or theft. My case is not unique. My colleague Dorthe Refslund Christensen, at that time with the Department of the Study of Religion, University of Aarhus, had a similar experience, and, in order to keep possession of the texts, a Christian anticult organization in Denmark, the Dialog Centre, kept its Scientology documents in a safe. This in itself, the ongoing conflicts, and the sense of uncertainty that seems to adhere to the texts, explain why many scholars over the years have been rather reluctant to take on the challenge of interpreting Scientology's esoteric myths.

Scientology officials at the organization's European headquarters in Copenhagen, Denmark, have told me that they find it offensive whenever esoteric texts are published, and that they expect the scholarly community to abide by certain standards.[6] In general they have been content with the scholarly community's reluctance to expose Hubbard's esoteric writings to the public. Scientology, in this respect, argues along the same lines as, for instance, Aboriginal Australians who have claimed the right not to have their sacred, esoteric songs or iconographic *churingas* published or otherwise shown to the public by anthropologists, reporters, and others. They are the intellectual heritage of their people, they maintain, and therefore not available to just anyone.

The question, however, is not so simple, no matter how susceptible Scientology (or the Australians, for that matter) may be, and at this point, in my judgment, the professional obligation on the part of the scholar pulls in another direction. Not because the moral codes that formerly protected religious groups is irrelevant, but because conditions regarding the availability of the texts have changed fundamentally.

With the breakthrough of the Internet an entirely new situation has been created. The texts are now, to a large extent, made available on many different home pages, and the ethical considerations on the part of scholars should change accordingly. Pretending that the texts are *not* there is ridiculous, and acting as if anyone with potential interest in the subject is unaware of this material equally meaningless. The texts are there, almost waiting for scholarly inspection and analysis.

It should be recognized, of course, that the texts that can be found on the Internet might vary from what is, in fact, used during Scientology's religious procedures, for two reasons: First, it is possible that renegades and people who work to destroy Scientology have chosen to misrepresent the organization by leaving out material or changing things. Second, it is certainly possible that the organization, in order to maintain its esoteric intention, has changed the substance of the texts used during high-level initiations. We have no definite way of knowing whether such changes have taken place, but it is wise to assume some kind of uncertainty in the material. I shall return to this problem later.

Double-Level Mythology

Scientology officials I have spoken with recognize that the texts (in one version or another) are available to anyone who might be interested, and even if it disturbs them on the level of principle, they know that little can be done about it. The solution to the problem, they maintain, is that the texts become religiously meaningful only in the ritualized context of the courses (grades of initiation) to which they belong, an argument previously used by Freemasons in a similar situation when a book was published with minute descriptions of rituals and ritual texts (Mogstad 1994).

Being unable to prevent outsiders from reading the texts, Scientology has taken measures to protect unprepared Scientologists from doing so. The idea is that although the texts are incomprehensible and irrelevant to the curious outsider, they will certainly corrupt the progression on the Bridge for those who have embarked on the esoteric Scientology voyage. Scientology has, in my judgment, done the only viable thing by acting inward and trying to prevent members from exposure to esoteric materials designed for people on higher initiatory levels. The argument is religious and resembles what many other esoteric movements have said again and again: The texts may be harmful, if not straightforwardly dangerous, if you are unprepared and uneducated. Rumor has it that the uneducated will die from pneumonia if he or she should read the text, a notion derived from the text itself, as we shall see.

As always a promoting or qualifying narrative, in effect a myth in its own right, surrounds the myth. This mythological wrapping is quite similar to what we find in most religions. The Qur'an, for instance, is enveloped in the *hadith* of how Muhammad received it through channeling mediated by the angel Jibril, and the Book of Mormon is legitimized through the myth that recalls how the young Joseph Smith, through divine intervention, was instructed to dig out the golden tablets with the original text on them. Sacred texts (not least founding myths) are themselves very often carried by a myth. In the case of Scientology "the myth about the myth" maintains that it is dangerous to approach the text without the proper initiation.[7] This double-level mythological structure is quite important as the myth about the myth effectively creates an atmosphere of authority around the mythological narrative, an atmosphere that remains a precondition to the *functioning* of the myth. Myths are not only myths because of their remarkable content. They are myths because a second-level narrative promotes them as authoritative and divine, and in one way or another supports them.

In ironic commentary on the Xenu myth (to which I shall return shortly), former Scientologist and decades-long zealous campaigner against Scientology, Jon Atack, makes use of this second-level narrative: "To save the brain strain of reading this purportedly lethal material in the original Ronspeak, and to save any danger of litigation for violation of copyright, this version is humbly tendered as a gift to mankind."[8] This should, in principle, allow Scientologist to read along, as Atack's text is not the *real* version. However, the question of what the reader learns or does not learn may not be the key issue. It remains an internal, theological problem. It may be more important to note that Scientology's officious attempt to keep "undergraduates" in the initiatory system away from the texts also has to do with rather non-esoteric aspects of the religion such as power and money. Courses are expensive, and the logic that underlies the entire system is that no step along The Bridge can be surpassed. A similar structure is found in Scientology's didactical principles pertaining to reading and education in general. Most official Scientology publications carry a statement that warns the reader not to proceed from one word to another until the word is properly understood (large Scientology dictionaries are available). Should the reader fail to comply, he or she will understand nothing, it is claimed. Hierarchy, social and intellectual, is a strong pillar in Scientology. It would therefore be quite disastrous for Scientology's educational (religious as well as secular) programs and business strategy (which are synonymous with the religious aspirations of the organization) if knowledge of what lies ahead became known to the average attendee.

And perhaps Scientology *has* something to worry about. Not because people die or get pneumonia from encounters with the esoteric texts, but because it makes them abandon Scientology. It is well documented that potential high-level initiates have left the organization once they learned (through unofficial information) what waited at the more advanced stages. A woman had, for instance, read about the Xenu material in a newspaper (following the Stockholm incident mentioned above) and subsequently decided to discontinue her engagement with Scientology. Her explanation: "It was simply too silly, too stupid. Who would take such a story seriously? Certainly not me!"[9] In this particular case the impact of Scientology's religious education had been too weak to keep the potential high-level initiate on the track: She obtained the newspaper even though Scientology discouraged members from doing so. Had she been more advanced along the Bridge she might have refrained from reading the article, or perhaps the outcome of reading it could have been different. I have also encountered active Scientologists that were reluctant to accept the existence of stories such as the Xenu narrative. They found Scientology to be a workable, scientific method and did not identify with stories of that kind.

This mechanism should not be seen as something special to Scientology. It is, for instance, perfectly normal for members of Europe's and the United States' majority religion to reject *some* mythological elements in their own religion while accepting others: They will most probably believe in a creator god, but not necessarily accept the notion of bodily resurrection—even if both ideas are constructed and entertained in the same mythological corpus, in this case, the Bible. In the case of Scientology, of course, the phenomenon of esotericism adds another dimension, but the basic idea is the same. Certain things from the bulk of religious possibilities are embraced; other things are rejected.

Apparently some mythological statements or religious claims are more believable than others, and a mixture of cognitive and sociological conditions will determine which succeeds and which fails. In Scientology people learn to accept religious notions through carefully designed educational procedures and general social interaction with co-believers. One of the things they learn is, as mentioned, to keep away from texts that belong to higher initiatory levels. Abiding by such requirements is to recognize the authority of the organization. Questioning the regulations or the very existence of the material is an expression of a looser commitment.

On the other hand, it seems unrealistic to suppose that no dedicated Scientologist would peek into what is available on the Internet, no matter what warning they are given by Scientology and disregarding their general recognition of Scientology's authority. Some will, of course, abide by the organization's rules and accept the second-level narrative as true. Others most certainly will not. Anticult movements have claimed that in 1998, when the Internet was still new and not as diffused and uncontrollable as it has become, Scientology began issuing a CD containing the browser Netscape Navigator to its members. This CD, it was said, would secretly install a "censorware program" that would make it impossible to access Web sites with critical information regarding the movement, including sites that carried the esoteric texts.[10] I have been unable to confirm this information from Scientology sources, but the very rumor indicates how the emergence of the Internet has pushed the conflict over the texts into new realms.

First and foremost, however, the CD rumor shows how anticult propaganda constructed what we may term a third-level narrative about the secret texts: The esoteric texts themselves represent one level, Scientology's emic-style narratives about the texts another, and anticult propaganda, which seeks to demolish the texts, a third. In all instances the texts are perceived as the core of the Scientology religion, which makes the discussion about Scientology's esoteric writings a case of *scripturalism,* the misperceived notion that sacred texts, so to speak, contain the entire religion. They do not, but obviously the texts provide a point of mythological departure as well as a permanent point of reference once they have been brought into the social reality of (in this case) Scientologists.

The Xenu Myth: Presenting the Text

To my knowledge no real analysis of Scientology's Xenu myth has appeared in scholarly publications. The most sober and enlightening text about the Xenu myth is probably the anonymous article on Wikipedia (English version) and, even if brief, Andreas Grünschloss's piece on Scientology in Lewis (2000: 266–268).[11] Scientology's opponents have, as we have seen, offered discussions of the text. Predictably, anticultists and ex-Scientologists want to expose the absurdities of the narrative and its irrational nature. The implicit argument is that the true status of Scientology as fraudulent and ridiculous is revealed once the core teachings of Hubbard become known.

This rationalistic approach, which is in itself quite humorous and enlightening, has little to do with scholarship in terms of understanding a religious myth. Needless to say, no religious myth will escape the rationalistic verdict should it be put on such a trial. Nevertheless, the scholarly analysis may benefit from attempts made by anticultists and others. The nonprofessional discussions of the Xenu myth, for instance, include, as far as I can judge, all the available material and a number of facts are often available regarding time of writing, distribution, usage, and so on. The best example is probably Peter Forde's "scientific scrutiny" of the OT-III material originally produced in 1996.[12] This analysis builds on prominent anti-Scientology activists such as Jon Atack, but primarily on a semiautobiographical text, *The Road to Xenu,* by Margery Wakefield. Apparently "Margery is a fictionalized character whose story combines Wakefield's own experiences with those of other Scientologists."[13] In the partly fictitious story told in *The Road to Xenu,* Margery's first encounter with the OT-III material is dramatized. In her real autobiography the context is different and less elaborate. The mythological text referred to, however, is more or less the same.[14] I first quote from the briefer version in which the author has joined the OT-III program:

I was given the secret materials in a brown folder and let into the locked room where OT3 was taught. I opened the folder and began to read:

"The head of the Galactic Confederation (76 planets around larger stars visible from here, founded 95,000,000 years ago, very space opera) solved overpopulation (250 billion or so per planet—178 billion on average) by mass implanting. He caused people to be brought to Teegeeack (Earth) and put an H-bomb on the principal volcanoes (incident 2) and then the Pacific ones were taken in boxes to Hawaii and the Atlantic ones to Las Palmas and there "packaged." His name was Xenu. He used renegades. Various misleading data by means of circuits, etc., was placed in the implants. When through with his crime, Loyal Officers (to the people) captured him after six years of battle and put him in an electronic mountain trap where he still is. "They" are gone. The place (Confederacy) has since been a desert.

The length and brutality of it all was such that this Confederation never recovered. The implant is calculated to kill (by pneumonia, etc.) anyone who attempts to solve it. This liability has been dispensed with by my tech development.

In December '67 I knew somebody had to take the plunge. I did and emerged very knocked out but alive. Probably the only one ever to do so in 75,000,000 years. I have all the data but only that given here is needful. Good luck."

At this point the author takes over:

In the subsequent OT3 bulletins, Hubbard explains further. It was very hard reading. Other students in the classroom were watching me as I read to see my reaction, to see if I "got it."

According to Hubbard, millions of years ago, an evil dictator named Xenu decided to solve the overpopulation problem in his galaxy by rounding up people, freezing them, and shipping them to earth on space ships.

They were deposited on two volcanoes, one at Las Palmas and one in Hawaii. Then nuclear explosions were set off, blowing these frozen souls into the stratosphere where they were collected by "electronic ribbons" (force fields) and brought back to earth where they were packaged into clusters.

After packaging, they were subjected to implants in which they were shown many different scenes on huge screens. Then they were released.

And so, according to Hubbard, the great secret of this sector of the universe is that each person on earth is not just a single person, but a collection ("cluster") of hundreds of different entities.

What I was going to learn on OT3, was how to telepathically locate these other entities of mine and audit them through the nuclear explosion and implanting that occurred 75,000,000 years ago. Then these entities would be freed, and able to fly off and find a body of their own.

The closest we get to a transcript of Hubbard's handwritten account, and thus the original version, is what Margery Wakefield provides in her more elaborate version (81–82):

> The head of the Galactic Federation (76 planets around larger stars visible from here) (founded 95,000,000 years ago, very space opera) solved overpopulation (250 billion or so per planet, 178 billion on average) by mass implanting. He caused people to be brought to Teegeeack (Earth) and put an H-bomb on the principal volcanoes (Incident II) and then the Pacific area ones were taken in boxes to Hawaii and the Atlantic ones to Las Palmas and there "packaged." His name was Xenu. He used renegades. Various misleading data by means of circuits etc. was placed in the implants.
>   When through with his crime loyal officers (to the people) captured him after six years of battle and put him in an electronic mountain trap where he still is. "They" are gone. The place (Confederation) has since been a desert. The length and brutality of it all was such that this Confederation never recovered.
>   The implant is calculated to kill (by pneumonia etc.) anyone who attempts to solve it. This liability has been dispensed with by my tech development. One can freewheel through the implant and die unless it is approached as precisely outlined. The "freewheel" (auto-running on and on) lasts too long, denies sleep etc. and one dies. So be careful to do only Incidents I and II as given and not plow around and fail to complete one thetan at a time.
>   In December 1967 I knew someone had to take the plunge. I did and emerged very knocked out, but alive. Probably the only one ever to do so in 75,000,000 years. I have all the data now, but only that given here is needful. One's body is a mass of individual thetans stuck to oneself or to the body. One has to clean them off by running Incident II and Incident I. It is a long job, requiring care, patience and good auditing. You are running beings. They respond like any preclear. Some large, some small. Thetans believed they were one. This is the primary error. Good luck.[15]

Hubbard's text has been rendered into more coherent prose on many occasions, most reliably by the anonymous author of the Xenu entry on Wikipedia, which includes a number of details not mentioned in the text referred to above. Some of Hubbard's subsequent explanations and additions taken from other sources have been added (notes and references removed):

> In Scientology doctrine, Xenu (also Xemu), pronounced [ˈzi.nuː], was the dictator of the "Galactic Confederacy" who, 75 million years

ago, brought billions of his people to Earth in DC-8-like spacecraft, stacked them around volcanoes and killed them using hydrogen bombs. Scientology holds that their essences remained, and that they form around people in modern times, causing them spiritual harm. The existence of Xenu as part of Scientology is vehemently denied by Scientologists. These events are known to Scientologists as "Incident II," and the traumatic memories associated with them as The Wall of Fire or the R6 implant.[16]

A more detailed study of Hubbard's text requires a good knowledge of Hubbard's writings in general. To my awareness the discussion on Wikipedia is the only example in which such an analysis is attempted. In principle, this kind of knowledge could be established from a position outside of Scientology after a long time and hard work. It is, however, possible (perhaps even likely) that the anonymous Wikipedia contributor has knowledge from within the organization. Had the author been a scholar, his or her analysis would have reached the academic community more directly, but it has not. In the following I shall build on the Wikipedia material (bearing in mind that these particular sources are outside traditional academic control) but primarily try to say something different from what eloquently has been presented there. The reader, however, is directed to Wikipedia, in which many important details, not least historical and theological data that I will ignore, are available.

A Discussion of Hubbard's Text

Myths are literary products, sometimes in the shape of oral traditions, sometimes as texts. They do not rise from the collective deep of a culture, nor do they emerge miraculously. In this case, the myth was produced at Hubbard's desk along with many other stories. Hubbard was a rather industrious and prolific science fiction author, and it is quite clear that his contributions in that field overlap his religious work, and perhaps no division between such categories should be made. It appears Hubbard considered the genre of science fiction to reveal some kind of collective recollection of what had happened to humankind (the thetans, rather) a very long time ago in other parts of the universe.[17]

Hubbard's science fiction novels and short stories are to a certain extend preoccupied with UFOlogical scenarios, just as most other science fiction during the 1950s and 1960s. He started out as a writer of popular novels, and then transformed his fascination with science fiction into a therapeutic practice (Dianetics), which was subsequently developed into a religious philosophy (Scientology).[18] The notion of UFOs, space beings, remote universes, and so on remained part and parcel of his work. Therefore it is the *use* or the *emphasis* laid upon such stories, not the stories themselves, that are significant if we are to understand Hubbard's mythological creativity in the context of the Scientology religion.

In this connection it would be wrong not to pay attention to the wave of religious interest in UFOs and extraterrestrial visitation that swept over the

United States at exactly the time of Hubbard's writings. Hubbard's notion that human souls—thetans—are spiritual implants that originate in another world is, for instance, quite parallel to religious assumptions expressed by UFO religions such as Ashtar Command and other propagators of the "walk-in" or "Star Seed" hypothesis that claims humans to be incarnated extraterrestrials presently bound to earth. Hubbard's teachings explain how the single thetan carries a unconscious "track" of memory that stretches all the way back to its origin. After Xenu's sinister deeds ("Incidents I and II" in the myth) the thetans were trapped in the material universe known as MEST (as it is constituted by Matter, Energy, Space, and Time) and declined into physically constrained beings. The intention, by means of Scientological wisdom, is to free the thetans from their prison-like state by awakening them and giving them full self-awareness and the ability to transgress the limits of the three-dimensional universe.

The demonology in Hubbard's story is not typical of mid-twentieth-century religious UFOlogy, but the rest is by no means special. The Theosophical trends in religious UFOlogy of those days as expounded by contactee movements (Rothstein 2003c) or actual UFO religions such as the Aetherius Society (Rothstein 2003b, Smith 2003) or the Unarius Foundation (Tumminia 2003), are very much concerned with the mind-body complex and the impact of extraterrestrials. Hubbard was not original in that respect. In fact, Hubbard echoes the early contactees in many ways, for instance, when he describes the fashion and style of Xenu's times. Apparently people would dress very much like people in Hubbard's day. The same was the case when the first famous UFO contactee, George Adamski, told how people men on Venus looked a few years before Hubbard revealed his knowledge.[19] Furthermore, Hubbard's science fiction is highly appreciated by Scientologists as entertaining literature. They consider Hubbard a leading author, and Scientology promotes his productions with fervor and energy.[20] The link between their literary interest and their religious aspirations may be much stronger than they are aware of.

Already in his book *Scientology—A History of Man* (originally published as *What to Audit,* 1952) UFOlogical themes are dealt with and all the substantial claims from the Xenu story are detectable. Today the book, which—to say the least—escapes all kinds of rationality, is no longer a precondition to the auditing ritual, but it is required material at the more advanced esoteric levels.[21] According to Hubbard, he "plunged" into the depth of human history in December 1967 to be the first in innumerable years to realize the deepest causes of the human condition. "Plunging," in this case, means going back along the "time track" by means of the religious technology he had developed. From a historical point of view, what he did was in fact to transform the basic outline in *Scientology—A History of Man* into a genuine religious myth that would enhance Scientology's ambition of developing a soteriological strategy.

It appears the myth of Xenu entails more than simple explanation. It also offers a ritual procedure and implies a structure of power and authority. Having read about Xenu's brutality and the fate of the thetans, the reader (who is supposed to be attending the OT-III program) is warned that "the implant is calculated to kill anyone who attempts to solve it." However, thanks to Hubbard's "tech development," this liability is no longer a threat, providing his instructions are followed. There is only one way of doing that: subject oneself to the procedures in the advanced courses on the Bridge, most profoundly, the OT-III program. Recognizing the myth of Xenu as true therefore implies recognizing Hubbard as the only authority, and as his charisma is routinized in his writings and in the soteriological rituals of Scientology, compliance with the course program is the only way. The myth is an account of primordial events, but indirectly it also promotes Hubbard as the savior of humankind and Scientology (being the guardian of the soteriological rituals) as his tool. Furthermore, developing the ability to perform the feats promised in the OT program, the devotee is positioned on the same path as Hubbard himself. The Xenu text explains how the religious genius paved the way back in time and achieved all necessary knowledge needed to move forward. Now helping others to go back on the time track (by means of the "tech") Scientology, realizing Hubbard's legacy, is creating a reborn super race of thetans, free from bodily constraints, beings that will resume "the full cause" over the physical universe (MEST) and act independently of time and space mastering time travel, bilocation, telepathy, levitation, and so on.

The ritual time travel back along the "track" is probably one of the more important preconditions to the success of the myth. I have made no systematic examination of the problem, but I suspect that people partly rely on Hubbard's recollection of what transpired when he made his "plunge," because they are able to get similar experiences themselves during auditing, as we shall see further below. Auditing files are personal and not public, but Scientology has published a sample of accounts in which people (anonymously) tell all sorts of stories about previous lives encountered during auditing therapy. The material was gathered in 1958 when Hubbard was a science fiction writer as much as the head of a new religion. The book *Have You Lived before This Life?* (originally published in 1960) is intended to prove what happens during the process, but it is certainly also possible that it serves as a matrix for what people claim to have experienced during their trip back through earlier incarnations in all sorts of universes. The UFOlogical elements are abundantly clear, and it is likely that this particular book (which is still promoted with no hesitation) was an important precondition to Hubbard's subsequent launch of the Xenu story. In subsequent books more is added, and when the Xenu text was issued for internal use around 1967, numerous UFOlogically inclined texts and oral presentations (on tape) by Hubbard were at hand.[22] In order to get an impression of the standardized narratives of "lives before this life," refer to the Wikipedia article's examples from *Have You Lived before This Life?*[23]

The following statement was collected from a Danish Scientologist in 2005.[24] The man recalls what he has experienced during auditing therapy and makes a point that these events are very important elements in his self-perception. His story clearly reflects Hubbard's institutionalized narratives, but where Hubbard's stories serve as collective myths, this story—and those mentioned above—could be described as examples of individual or highly personalized mythologies that work in conjunction with Hubbard's basic stories. The official standard mythology and the individuals' personal creativity go hand in hand:

> It was just an ordinary life. My father was a powerful and influential man on the planet where I, as a young man, joined the Space Academy. This was what all boys wanted, to join the Space Academy, but in order to be accepted you had to be quite good at maths, but I was, so I was accepted. At the Space Academy we were assigned different jobs—to patrol various places in the galaxy, for instance, and other planets. I was appointed Head of the Security Organisation which is supposed to control the "outer security" and check for invading forces, those that come from other planets and other solar systems.
>
> I remember [from the auditing session] what my office looked like when I had that position. I was a big office where the ceiling was a dome, and when you pushed a button the dome became totally transparent and you could see the stars above, and when you pushed the button again, the dome protected against the sun—so there I was, able to watch all the solar systems and galaxies.
>
> I lived with my family on a small castle. It was fabulous. It was situated on a mountain slope by a great lake. The atmosphere was ordinary, just like on Earth, but there were no roads extending from our castle. You would reach the place with a small UFO that you would fly. Next to our house there was a big water fall that you would always hear, and we had a bathing jetty down by the lake. You could fish and everything—it was exactly like on Earth. Whenever you should do some shopping or go to the office you would take your UFO, just like in Starwars. That place, that lifetime, is very important to me. This is from where I come. That is my point of departure.

The Xenu story, in that context, is a culmination, not an innovation. The text itself reveals that Hubbard, with the Xenu story, has taken his science fiction fantasies into a new epistemological realm. It is no longer fictitious; it is supposed to reveal reality: "very space opera," Hubbard writes, referring to the 95,000,000,000-year-old Galactic Federation of seventy-six planets. In Scientology's comprehensive dictionaries the entry *space opera* is explained as follows:

> of or relating to time periods on the whole track millions of years ago which concerned activities in this and other galaxies. Space opera has space travel, spaceships, spacemen, intergalactic travel, wars, conflicts, other beings, civilizations and societies, and other planets and galaxies. It is not fiction and concerns actual incidents and things that occurred on the track.[25]

"Space opera," then, denotes a certain historiography, Hubbard's introduction of a new reality, a new foundation for everything, indeed a new anthropogony that is already detectable in the auditing narratives that predate his writing of the Xenu myth. With the Xenu narrative, however, we now know for sure where the thetans come from, what their precise problems are, and how these problems can be solved. Until the text was formulated and deployed in advanced courses in the latter half of the 1960s, only fragments of that knowledge existed. Scientologists were taught about the thetans and the relation between thetans and the physical body, but not with the kind of etiological insight provided by the Xenu story. On the OT-III level they finally get to know exactly why the human composition is the way it is—what really constitutes a human being.

The esoteric nature of the Scientology religion, however, does not allow this information to spread uncontrolled. It is restricted to people who are advanced on the Bridge. What separates those of high initiatory standing from those on lower levels, then, is, among other things, access to privileged knowledge of humanity's history. Everybody in Scientology is, in principle, following the same path toward salvation, but only the more advanced have knowledge of what lies behind it all.

According to Scientology dogmatic, Hubbard single-handedly solved the riddle of human existence. Nothing was revealed to him. He discovered truth in the same way any scientist uncovers hitherto unknown facts about nature (Refslund Christensen 2005). To devoted Scientologists this makes the narrative about Xenu a scientifically proven *fact* rather than a religious *belief,* as the "tech" provided by Hubbard is understood to be a reliable tool that leads to objective insights. By means of the same techniques as those applied in Scientology's therapeutic rituals, Hubbard was able to attain absolute knowledge of things otherwise out of reach of ordinary humans, and parts of what he learned he shared with his disciples—for instance, what transpired when Xenu was in power. Accepting the religious techniques as authoritative and workable (partly because the disciple him- or herself will experience something structurally similar during audition therapy) (1), and adoring Hubbard as the most sublime human being that has ever lived (2), a third dogma follows logically: What the man experienced by means of his marvelous techniques is by definition true (3). The very existence of the myth, consequently, in the *emic* perspective, points to the unprecedented and unparalleled genius and importance of Hubbard.

In Scientology everything written by Hubbard is "scripture," and everything pertaining to the Scientology religion has to be "on source," in other words, based and argued with direct and specific reference to Hubbard who *is* "source" (Rothstein 2007). The Xenu narrative is definitely "source," which means that even if the peculiarity of this particular text may tempt some Scientologists to focus their religious interest on something else, it is impossible to bypass. The cult of the religious leader forces devotees to accept the Xenu story as highly important. The intellectual weaknesses of the text, and the absurd claim that it should be scientific, is overpowered by the urge to honor Hubbard as the greatest individual that has ever lived. In effect the myth adds to the hagiographic construction and maintenance of Hubbard as savior (Refslund Christensen 2005, Rothstein 2001: 184–217).[26] After all, present-day Scientologists, who have never met Hubbard, are able to hear him talk of Xenu in his own voice, and samples of his explanations are even available on the Internet.[27]

The independent analyst should be cautious not to follow Scientology dogmatics too closely. There are good reasons to consider the cult of Hubbard the real issue and the soteriological aspirations in the text as means to that end.

A Closer Look at the Text

A simple analysis of Hubbard's story about Xenu leads to a number of interesting interpretations that allow us to see how it relates to or grows from the social reality and general cultural context of Hubbard and his organization.

On a more general level, the myth deals with the same problems as any religious narrative about "the human condition": It explains what human beings are, and where they came from. We hear of no creator god, but the composition of the human entity, and the existential problems it faces are made clear. In the tradition of Gnostic dualism the forces of good and evil are very important. Xenu, of course, represents evil, and good by the (eventually) successful soldiers who managed to trap him in his (very) long-lasting prison. The real hero, though, is Hubbard himself. He has no part in the actual narrative, but through his "plunge" he transcends time and space, learns what is necessary to escape Xenu's transformations of the thetans, and provides the tools for human salvation. The scene is set in a distant past, but the problem has been with humanity until recently, when Hubbard finally solved it. As in so many other myths, the world that existed prior to the events that lead to present conditions is now gone. The Confederation, which constituted a first-level world, was dissolved, and its "place" transformed into a desert. Humans, for a very long time, lived in a second-phase world, where the thetans still were trapped, but now, thanks to Hubbard, a third phase has emerged in which the thetans can be freed again.

The notion of a "Galactic Federation" is not unique to Hubbard. George King, for instance, the founder of the Aetherius Society and one of the most successful innovators in the tradition of UFO religions, claimed to have been appointed "Terrestrial Mental Channel" by representatives of an "Interplanetary Parliament" in 1954. Other so-called contactees of the 1950s held similar views. Though Hubbard, faithful to his traditional style, operates with time spans and numbers that transgress what anyone else has come up with, the structure is the same: Man on earth is inferior to space beings elsewhere in the universe. The notion is still entertained in science fiction and popular fantasy literature (the political structure of the universe is, for instance, a central theme in the *Star Wars* series), which may further its presence in Scientology's religious apparatus.

Similarly the idea of overpopulation was a popular theme in 1950–1960 science fiction nourished by the actual growth in postwar Western society. Most authors envisioned a future with crowded megacities, and foresaw explorations into deep space as a way of finding new places for people to live.[28] Hubbard, being a professional science fiction writer, followed the same trend, but placed his demographic drama in the remote past. Also, in this case, the problem has stayed with us: Overpopulation remains one of the more demanding challenges in today's world, a fact that makes Hubbard's religious narrative pertinent even today.

Additionally, the H-bomb mentioned in Hubbard's text is typical to writings of the time. The H-bomb was tested by the United States for the first time in 1952 on the Marshall Islands of the Pacific, and the following year the Soviet Union joined in. The H-bomb (or atom bombs at large) was the symbol of the gradually developing Cold War. As religious imaginations always draw upon the prevailing resources (people are usually unable to escape the social and cognitive reality to which they belong), it is no coincidence that Xenu in the myth uses the same weapons as humans in the early 1950s. The major advantage, of course, is that the participant in OT-III courses will think of the primordial event as something real and intelligible. Furthermore, it has been shown on many occasions that the driving force in the creation of the UFO or flying saucer myth that swept through the United States during the 1950s (and into which Hubbard inscribes his work) was based on Cold War fears, especially people's concern about atomic bombs and cynical politicians (Rothstein 2003c). Hubbard was in alignment with the minds of his contemporaries when he formulated the myth.

During the early 1950s UFOlogy was dominated by the so-called nuts-and-bolts theory. What people saw in the skies was interpreted as real, physical machines piloted by intelligent beings from another world. It was, however, impossible to explain precisely how the propulsion systems worked and how the pilots performed their miraculous maneuvers. Pseudoscientific explanations were abundant, and all sorts of illogical and technically impossible phenomena were mentioned. Hubbard's notions of "electrical circuits," "electronic mountain traps," and "implants," not to mention the remodeled DC-8 airplanes, are expressions of the same reasoning. Hubbard is balancing between things familiar to a 1950–1960 audience and the extraordinary world that belongs to his mythological imagination, thus—unknowingly—achieving the right balance of believable (intuitive) and challenging (counterintuitive) components in his belief system.[29] We could, of course, add the mention of pneumonia here, an illness that throughout Hubbard's lifetime had been known as a severe disease, and thus the best candidate for something that everybody would fear at his time of writing.

As any other myth, the Xenu narrative builds on human standards. A political villain is at center of things, but it is implied that the tyrant actually violates the political intentions of the Galactic Federation. Hence he is defeated by a group of opposition officers serving the people. He is taken to prison and pacified. Apparently the political lust for power, the legal system, and the public morality sometime between 95,000,000 and 75,000,000 years ago are very similar to what we know today. The "space opera" setting is a mythological realm in its own right, but the usual anthropomorphism of almost any myth is also quite apparent here.

On a more general level the Xenu myth shares features with, in principle, any myth. It is set in primordial times before the beginning of the present era, it involves superhuman beings with obvious anthropomorphic features, and it tells of extraordinary events that transcend the laws of nature. Hubbard claimed his findings to be scientifically valid, but everything in his story is contradicted by science. Trivial geological facts (just to mention an example) contradict Hubbard's vision. Mauna Loa, one of the volcanoes on Hawaii's Big Island (the one called Hawaii) is at the most 1,000,000 years old, possibly as young as 600,000 years old. Hubbard talks as if it were ninety-five times older. However, myths should not be tested against facts, and Hubbard's scientific claims should count as a religious discourse strategy.[30] This became evident when I encountered two Scientologists on a private pilgrimage to Hawaii's National Volcano Park. Preparing a study of the goddess Pele, who is mythologically linked with the Kilauea volcano, I spent some time on the slopes of Mauna Loa and happened to meet these people (winter 2006). They were amazed to learn that I had some understanding for their project, but they were not prepared to accept the information about the volcanoes that is made available at the park's visitor center. They found it convincing, and not at all strange, that Xenu had captured the thetans in ice cubes that were later dissolved in the volcano.[31]

In many cases religious myths are reenacted or "made alive" in rituals—so-called ritual dramas. At first glance the Xenu myth does not seem to have a corresponding ritual, but this is not entirely true. The myth explains how the thetans were captured, and Hubbard lays out the basic directions for solving the problems. In order to do that, it is necessary for the active Scientologist to perform the prescribed rituals and go back in time, encounter the traumatic events describes in the text, and thereby free the thetans step by step. In principle, the serious Scientologist will enliven the events described by Hubbard again and again. The myth, in this way, makes it way into the world of present-day humanity.

Hubbard talked about Xenu and the "Incidents" on several occasions. He even took the story into a screenplay. These sources (see note) add a few details to the story:

> With the assistance of "renegades," he defeated the populace and
> the "Loyal Officers," a force for good that was opposed to Xenu.
> Then, with the assistance of psychiatrists, he summoned billions of
> his citizens together to paralyze them with injections of alcohol and
> glycol, under the pretense that they were being called for "income tax
> inspections."[32]

It is no coincidence that psychiatrists are joining forces with the evil character. Scientology has been engaged in a lengthy conflict with psychiatrists, who remain the organization's favorite hate objects. Elsewhere I have tried to explain the deeper structures of this conflict (Rothstein 2003d). Here it suffices to note that Hubbard's disgust for psychiatrists predates the Xenu story, and that he obviously wanted to provide a mythological explanation for the fight with the psychiatric community by making them Xenu's allies. Fighting psychiatrists today, an obligation on the part of any serious Scientologist, has its roots in the dawn of time and is an integrated dimension of the fight against cosmic evil. In this way, the myth provides an important basis for the organization's persistent and intense operations against psychiatry, and thus its insertion into modern society.

One thing more seems to be mythologically rooted in the Xenu story, the elite group within Scientology, the *Sea Org*. According to the anonymous writer on Wikipedia, the Sea Org members, who have dedicated millions of future lives to Scientology, are supposed to mirror the team of "loyal officers" that helped overthrow Xenu. In Scientology they are supposed to be loyal to Hubbard and his organization. The article continues as follows:

> Its logo, a wreath with 26 leaves, represents the 26 stars of Xenu's Galactic Confederacy. According to the Dianetics and Scientology Technical Dictionary, "the Sea Org symbol, adopted and used as the symbol of a Galactic Confederacy far back in the history of this sector, derives much of its power and authority from that association." In the Advanced Orgs in Edinburgh and Los Angeles, Scientology staff were at one time ordered to wear all-white uniforms with silver boots, to mimic Xenu's Galactic Patrol.[33]

Xenu may be much more alive in the imaginations of Scientologists than first thought. The typical explanation for the dress code of the inner movement is, by the way, very different. For decades I have been told that Sea Org members dress in maritime clothing because Hubbard's soteriological project, in the early days of his organization, was closely connected with water (advanced auditing took place on a boat), and that "Ron loved the sea."

Finally, of course, the Xenu myth is basically a story about the fight between good and evil. Xenu is evil, the officers who captured him are fairly good, but the real hero in the story is, of course, Hubbard himself. He made the plunge, went through "the Wall of Fire," and only now, due to his feat, humans can be saved. In that way, he inscribes himself in the narrative of otherwise primordial events. He "emerged very knocked out, but alive," but thanks to this fight everybody else can access the past and clear up all their problems.[34]

The constructive use of the myth in order to create and maintain the culture of Scientology is its most significant function but not the only one. There is a significant parallel that works the other way around: The Xenu story is also used as a strong weapon against Scientology.

The Xenu Myth as Anticult Target

Operation Clambake is one of the more prominent among several anti-Scientology projects especially dedicated to "fight Scientology on the net."[35] On the project's Web page a folder presenting the background for and intentions of Operation Clambake can be downloaded.[36] The accusations against

Scientology are harsh and unconditional, but the main way of exposing Scientology as a sinister and fraudulent organization (Scientology is generally not recognized as a religion by its opponents) is to recapitulate the central religious narrative. It is taken for granted that Scientology's religious notions are so strange, so absurd, and so unsubstantiated that exposing them will in itself harm Scientology. Under the heading "Who is Xenu?" the folder reads, "Would you like to hear a wild story? Are you sitting comfortably? Right, let's begin." The reader proceeds to a brief text about the space ruler Xenu and his evil deeds, and then the question is raised, "Well what did you think of *that* story? What? You thought it was *ridiculous*? Sort of like Battlefield Earth?" (see note 21).

Operation Clambake clearly believe Scientology's myth about Xenu to be so utterly stupid that it unwillingly provides the best argument why people should denounce L. Ron Hubbard's teachings and altogether avoid the organization he founded. Granted, to the nonbeliever, and even to many Scientologists with no esoteric education pertaining to the myth, and thus the necessary socialization, the story *is* silly. But *this* is not a unique situation reserved for Scientology's myths. It is a common feature in Europe's religious traditions that the stories of "the others" are absurd or untrustworthy, whereas one's own are meaningful and true. It is interesting to observe, for instance, that many of Scientology's critics who would deem the Xenu myth absurd and irrational believe that (as already mentioned above) the world was created in six days by the god God, and that the man-god Jesus came back to life after his execution. The power of Western society allows the myths of Christianity to flourish as respectable or even true narratives, whereas Scientology's myths have no such status. It is not about the narratives themselves; it is about the *status* they are able to achieve. Under the present social conditions it *is* very easy to ridicule the Xenu myth, especially because it is written in Hubbard's very personal and untraditional style, "Ronspeak" among the critics, and because Hubbard appears less than persuasive to non-Scientologists when he talks about Xenu.

John Atack claims that Hubbard was abusing alcohol and so forth while composing the myth.[37] This, however, would not—whether it is true or not—make Hubbard's text less religious or less relevant. Religious specialists have always used toxicants of all sorts, and there is absolutely no reason why a modern mythologist should abstain from various kinds of consciousness-changing substances. Clarity in language and content is not necessarily a religious virtue, and drugs and alcohol may help construct the kind of counterintuitive components that characterize religious narratives. As pointed out by Pascal Boyer, "most religious traditions routinely flout the requirement of consistency." In fact, he maintains, some religious claims are precisely designed to violate it. Religious systems are unable to produce clarity, and when they try yet a new level of inconsistency emerges (Boyer 2001: 300). Explaining this phenomenon is almost explaining the phenomenon of religion. Indeed, it is much more difficult to make a new myth catch on than it is to carry on with myths that are thousands of years old, well institutionalized, and already subjected to long-standing interpretations. In the case of Hubbard's mythological creativity, the important thing is that Scientologists will confer *meaning* to the Xenu narrative, even if it is literarily poor, incomplete, and confusing. They are doing so in order to engage themselves in their own soteriological process, in order to uphold the dogmatics they have been taught, and in order to revere the saint that made this insight possible. As time goes on, the myth about Xenu and the thetans may become as respectable and uncontroversial as so many other fantastic accounts in the history of the world's religions.

NOTES

Most references in this chapter are URL addresses on the Internet. All of them were accessed successfully on July 6, 2007.

1. Most notably Refslund Christensen 1999a, 1999b, 2005. The present discussion is, by the way, linked with what I have already presented in another article, "Scientology, Scripture, and Sacred Tradition," in James Lewis and Olav Hammer (eds.), *The Invention of Sacred Tradition*, Cambridge University Press, forthcoming.

2. For a discussion on how the study of myth more generally is relevant with relation to new religions, see Tumminia and Kirkpatrick 2004.

3. See references.

4. I have discussed Scientology's esoteric nature at some length in Rothstein 2001: 138–160.

5. The incident is described by yet another campaigner against Scientology at http://xenu.xtdnet.nl/court/1.html.

6. Conversation at Scientology's Copenhagen premises, June 2007.

7. This is certainly a rather common feature in esoteric religions. Members of Kabbalistic movements have, for instance, claimed that anyone reading the *Zohar* without the proper training would risk insanity, and members of Eckankar have warned against something similar (author's personal experiences during interviews over the years).

8. See Jon Atack, "OT III: Scientology's 'Secret' Course Written for Beginners," http://www.spaink.net/cos/essays/atack_ot3.html. Accessed September 3, 2008.

9. I have talked to the woman on several occasions. Apparently she had a number of reasons to leave Scientology, and the Xenu affair was the trigger. In that, her reversed conversion carrier is quite typical.

10. See "Church of Scientology Censors Net Access for Members," http://www.xenu.net/archive/events/censorship/. Accessed September 3, 2008.

11. It is well known that this open source facility may contain fraudulent and erroneous material. However, what I have been able to check seems to be valid and well researched. This is not surprising as this particular entry is a "WikiProject" and as such it is more thoroughly watched than other entries. Furthermore, the Xenu part is termed a "featured" article, which testifies to its credibility. See http://en.wikipedia.org/wiki/Wikipedia:WikiProject_Scientology. At the time of writing this (June 2007) the Xenu entry was disabled and locked for further editing until July 7. No reason was given. However, as far as I have been able to check, the information given is trustworthy and well documented. See http://en.wikipedia.org/wiki/Xenu.

12. See Peter Forde (June 1996), "A Scientific Scrutiny of OT III," http://www.spaink.net/cos/essays/forde_volcanos.html#1.1. Accessed September 3, 2008.

13. The text, including this note, is found at http://www.cs.cmu.edu/~dst/Fishman/Xenu/xenu.html.

14. See Margery Wakefield, *Testimony*, http://www.cs.cmu.edu/afs/cs/Web/People/dst/Library/Shelf/wakefield/testimony-get.html. Accessed September 3, 2008.

15. "The Road to Xenu: A Narrative Account of Life in Scientology" by Margery Wakefield. See http://www.cs.cmu.edu/~dst/Library/Shelf/xenu/xenu.html. Hubbard's handwritten text can be found on several Internet sites, for example, see http://www.bringyou.to/apologetics/xenu.htm.

16. See "Xenu," http://en.wikipedia.org/wiki/Xenu. Accessed September 3, 2008.

17. See "Galactic Confederacy," http://en.wikipedia.org/wiki/Galactic_Confederacy. Accessed September 3, 2008.

18. This process is discussed in detail in Refslund Christensen 1997.

19. See "Space Opera in Scientology Scripture," http://en.wikipedia.org/wiki/Space_opera_in_Scientology_scripture. Accessed September 3, 2008.

20. See, for instance, the promotion home page for Hubbard's novel *Battlefield Earth,* including the site for the screen version, which is loved by Scientologists and denounced as extremely poor by film critics: http://www.battlefieldearth.com/index.htm and http://battlefieldearth.warnerbros.com/. See also Rothstein forthcoming.

21. See "Scientology: A History of Man," http://en.wikipedia.org/wiki/Scientology:_A_History_of_Man. Accessed September 3, 2008.

22. Not least the tape-recorded lectures known as *Time Track of Theta* (apparently also used during the more advanced OT-VIII course: http://www.cs.cmu.edu/~dst/NOTs/OT8summary.html) and the popular book *Have You Lived before This Life?* (1960).

23. See "Scientology: A History of Man," http://en.wikipedia.org/wiki/Scientology:_A_History_of_Man. Accessed September 3, 2008.

24. This is a sample from an interview conducted by Lisbeth Rubin during preparations for her M.A. degree at the University of Copenhagen.

25. This entry is taken from an abridged version available on the Internet: http://www.scientology.org/p_jpg/gloss.htm#SPACEOPERA.

26. For a parallel analysis, see Rothstein 2003.

27. The site http://www.bringyou.to/apologetics/xenu.htm has several audio clips and links to even more material.

28. See "Overpopulation," http://en.wikipedia.org/wiki/Overpopulation. Accessed September 3, 2008.

29. I hereby refer to Pascal Boyer's (1994) cognitive theory, which claims that religious notions need to stay within certain boundaries in order to be believed.

30. The relation between science and religion in the new religions is a rather complicated matter that I have pursued elsewhere; see Rothstein 2004.

31. The persons I encountered understood my position and acknowledged that I knew what I knew from the leaks on the Internet. Our communication, however, did not go beyond what they would consider common knowledge to anyone peeking into the sites hostile to Scientology I have, apart from that, no knowledge of pilgrimage to Hawaii as a common thing among Scientologists.

32. See "Xenu," http://en.wikipedia.org/wiki/Xenu. Accessed September 3, 2008.

33. Ibid.

34. There are claims that Hubbard's "plunge" had a physical character, and that he was actually injured during his time travel. Ordinary Scientologists do not suffer physically during the auditing ritual.

35. To learn more about Operation Clambake (including its name), see "Operation Clambake," http://en.wikipedia.org/wiki/Operation_Clambake. Accessed September 3, 2008.

36. See "Who is Zenu?" http://xenu.net/archive/leaflet/Xenu-A4.pdf. Accessed September 3, 2008.

37. See Jon Atack, "OT III: Scientology's 'Secret' Course Rewritten for Beginners," http://www.spaink.net/cos/essays/atack_ot3.html. This claim is strongly supported by sources referred to on http://en.wikipedia.org/wiki/Xenu.

REFERENCES

Boyer, Pascal 1994, *The Naturalness of Religious Ideas*, University of California Press, Berkeley.

Boyer, Pascal 2001, *Religion Explained: The Evolutionary Origins of Religious Thought*, Basic Books, New York.

Lewis, James (ed.) 2000, *UFOs and Popular Culture. An Encyclopedia of Contemporary Myth*, ABC-Clio, Santa Barbara.

Mogstad, Sverre Dag 1994, *Frimureri. Mysterier, Fellesskap, Personlighetsdannelse*, Universitetsforlaget, Oslo, Norway.

Refslund Christensen, Dorthe 1997. *Scientology: Fra Terapi til religion* [Scientology: From Therapy to Religion], Gyldendal, Copenhagen.

Refslund Christensen, Dorthe 1999a, *Rethinking Scientology. Cognition and Representation in Religion, Therapy, and Soteriology*, Unpublished Ph.D. dissertation.

Refslund Christensen, Dorthe 1999b, *Scientology. Fra terapi til religion*, Gyldendal, København.

Refslund Christensen, Dorthe 2005, "Inventing L. Ron Hubbard: On the Construction and Maintenance of the Hagiographic Mythology of Scientology's Founder," in James R. Lewis and Jesper Aagaard Petersen (eds.), *Controversial New Religions*, Oxford University Press, New York, pp. 227–258.

Rothstein, Mikael 2001, *Gud er (stadig) blå*, Aschehoug, København.

Rothstein, Mikael 2003a, "Hagiography and Text in the Aetherius Society: Aspects of the Social Construction of a Religious Leader," in Mikael Rothstein and Reender Kranenborg (eds.), *New Religions in a Post-modern World*, Aarhus University Press, Aarhus, pp. 165–193. Reprinted in Diana Tumminia (ed.) 2007, *Alien Worlds: Social and Religious Dimensions of Extraterrestrial Contact*, Syracuse University Press, New York, pp. 3–24.

Rothstein, Mikael 2003b, "The Idea of the Past, the Reality of the Present, and the Construction of the Future: A Case Study of the Aetherius Society," in James Lewis (ed.), *Encyclopedic Handbook of UFO Religions*, Prometheus Books, New York, pp. 143–156.

Rothstein, Mikael 2003c, "The Rise and Decline of the First Generation UFO Contactees: A Cognitive Approach," in James Lewis (ed.), *Encyclopedic Handbook of UFO Religions*, Prometheus Books, New York, pp. 63–76.

Rothstein, Mikael 2003d, "Sociale oppositioner og religiøs kreativitet. Magtudøvelse og modstand som paradigme for religiøs innovation," *CHAOS* 40: 103–114.

Rothstein, Mikael 2004, "Science and Religion in the New Religions," in James Lewis (ed.), *The Oxford Handbook of New Religious Movements*, Oxford University Press, Oxford, pp. 99–118.

Rothstein, Mikael 2007. "Scientology, Scripture, and Sacred Tradition," in James Lewis and Olav Hammer (eds.), *The Invention of Sacred Tradition*, Cambridge University Press, Cambridge.

Smith, Simon G. 2003, "Opening a Channel to the Stars: The Origins and Development of the Aetherius Society," in Christopher Partridge (ed.), *UFO Religions*, Routledge, London, pp. 84–102.

Tumminia, Diana 2003, "How Prophecy Never Fails: Interpretive Reason in a Flying Saucer Group," in James R. Lewis (ed.), *Encyclopedic Sourcebook of UFO Religions*, Prometheus Books, New York, pp. 173–190.

Tumminia, Diana G., and R. George Kirkpatrick 2004, "The Mythic Dimensions of New Religious Movements: Function, Reality Construction, and Process," in James Lewis (ed.), *The Oxford Handbook of New Religious Movements*, Oxford University Press, Oxford, pp. 359–377.

20

Celebrity, the Popular Media, and Scientology: Making Familiar the Unfamiliar

Carole M. Cusack

The Church of Scientology, a new religion founded by L. Ron Hubbard in 1954, is strange and unfamiliar to the majority of Western people. This is for several reasons: New religions are generally misunderstood and little known; Scientology is numerically small and has a strong emphasis on secrecy concerning its teachings; and, in company with other new religions, Scientology has received negative publicity which impacts upon community perceptions. However, there is an important dynamic in modern Western culture that contributes powerfully to rendering Scientology "familiar" and "mainstream." This is the all-pervasive culture of celebrity, which involves all forms of media (film, television, radio, and print journalism) in the nonstop coverage of the lives of the rich and famous, for enthusiastic consumption by the general public.

Celebrities function in Western consumer society as icons to be worshipped, role models to be emulated, and, most important, as exemplars of the perfected life (through their wealth, beauty, larger-than-life profile, and the fact that their existence is conducted entirely in the spotlight). Scientology is a religion with high-profile celebrity members (the American actors John Travolta and his wife Kelly Preston, Tom Cruise and his wife Katie Holmes, Kirstie Alley and actor-turned-musician Juliette Lewis, and in Australia millionaire James Packer and his wife model-turned-singer Erica Baxter, and pop singer Kate Ceberano, to name but a few). Through constant media coverage Scientology is rendered familiar, and even (despite some bad press) potentially desirable to many, in that it forms a core element of the lives of these celebrities. Further, insofar as they are admired and emulated by the public, the celebrity conscious may develop an interest in Scientology simply because it is a religion professed by Hollywood stars, rock musicians, millionaires, and other famous people.

The Role of Celebrity in Contemporary Western Society

Although there have always been famous individuals (royalty, saints, and heroes spring to mind), it can be argued that the celebrity is a peculiarly modern phenomenon. The *Concise Oxford English Dictionary* defines the noun *celebrity* as "a well-known person" and "*fame*," noting its derivation from the Latin *celeber-bris,* as "frequented, honoured" (Thomson, 1995: 210). The construction of fame in contemporary Western society is largely dependent on the mass media. Newspapers, audio recordings, photography, radio, and motion pictures were either developed or attained increased prominence in the nineteenth century, and television and the Internet appeared in the twentieth century. Thus, as Daniel Boorstin observes, "especially since 1900, we seem to have discovered the processes by which fame is manufactured" (2006: 73). The media, traditionally associated with the dissemination of information and political critique, has in the late twentieth and early twenty-first centuries become increasingly dominated by entertainment and diversion (Turner et al., 2000: 1), which reflects the increased importance of celebrities (including actors, rock musicians, models, and reality television "stars") for media consumers.

One important strand of the argument of this chapter is that celebrities have taken on certain functions and significances that traditionally belong to religious figures. It is therefore important to sketch some of the changes that have affected religion and the role of religious institutions in the West since the late nineteenth century. Secularization, which Peter Berger defined as "the process whereby sectors of society and culture are removed from the dominance of religious institutions and symbols" (1967: 107), has resulted in the retreat of institutional Christianity in Western cultures, but the demise of religion predicted by Marx, Freud, Frazer, and others at the beginning of the twentieth century has not eventuated. Rather, religion in the West has been transformed by the introduction of religions from other cultures (for example, Hinduism, Buddhism, and Islam) and the emergence of a myriad new religions (for example, Wicca, Scientology, the Raelians, the Family of Love, and the Unification Church). When revisiting the secularization paradigm, recent scholarly treatments note the effect of a diminished public role for the Christian churches, which is linked to the emergence of the individual self as the locus of identity and personal choice as the main medium of identity construction. These shifts reinforce the prevalence of consumer capitalism (Bruce, 2002: 10–26) and have resulted in the separation of the "sacred" from traditional religion and its manifestation in many areas of life previously regarded as "profane" (Demerath, 2000: 4).

Rock music, environmentalism, sport, both physical and mental personal cultivation, and certain consumer products and brands have all been identified as sources of the sacred and transcendent experiences for eclectic spiritual seekers (Chidester, 1994). The main concern of spiritual seekers (Campbell, 1972) is self-transformation, reflecting the increasingly psychological orientation of the West and affirming Jung's assertion that "individuation" constituted the primary religious process for modern individuals (Tacey, 2001: 20, 39). There are many who are reluctant to accord truly religious status to this *mélange* of concepts and practices, but within studies in religion the important subdiscipline of "implicit religion" (Bailey, 1998) or "quasi-religion" (Greil and Robbins, 1994) has become established, significantly broadening the understanding of religion and deepening the knowledge of the ways in which contemporary Westerners construct the self with reference to the sacred (Lyon, 2002 [2000]: 72–96).

This has special relevance as the Enlightenment project had as one of its aims the disenchantment of nature and the privileging of rational and scientific discourse (Cashmore, 2006: 251). However, recent decades have seen a reenchantment emerge, with, as Campbell observes, "significant sections of the educated middle-class . . . turn[ing] to magic, mystery and exotic religion, manifesting a marked alienation from the culture of rationality and a determined anti-puritanism" (2005 [1987]: 3). Campbell argues that this re-enchantment springs from the all-pervasive legacy of Romanticism, which can be seen in contemporary Western culture, particularly in its patterns of consumption. Philosophical Romanticism, the emergence of the romantic novel and marriage for love, and the modern consumer revolution are all traceable to the eighteenth century, the era of the Enlightenment. However, they represent the affective and imaginative "other" to the rationality espoused by the Enlightenment thinkers. Campbell concludes that daydreaming and fantasy are crucial in the creation of modern consumerism, in that they facilitate "imaginative speculation about the gratification novel products might bring" and encourage desires that know no limits (2005 [1987]: 95).

It is in this context that the religious dimensions of celebrity are best investigated. Within traditional Christianity the role models offered by the Church to the believing populace were the saints. These exceptional Christians had throughout history achieved heroic levels of holiness, piety, self-denial, and other virtues (Brown, 1981). This made them worthy of emulation, and exemplars of the closest that human beings might hope to come to perfection. Within Roman Catholic and Orthodox Christianity they acquired the function of intermediaries between God and the faithful: They were human, but their holiness participated in the perfection of God (bringing them closer to Jesus Christ, the incarnate god-man whose death and resurrection made salvation possible). The doctrine of the "treasury of merit" meant that sinful humans could receive spiritual benefits through praying to the saints and thus advance toward salvation by having their sins forgiven (www.concise.britannica.com). Fascinatingly, a majority of medieval Christian saints were aristocratic, which may have intensified both the perception of their piety and their potential to be emulated (Stark, 2003: 5–19). Christians sought to emulate the saints and because the values espoused by Christianity included poverty, asceticism, chastity, and unwavering devotion to God, these were the qualities that were esteemed as worthy and desirable. This remained the case after the Protestant Reformation in the sixteenth century, when the Puritan ethic "one of the most powerful anti-hedonistic forces which the world has known" (Campbell, 2005 [1987]: 101) encouraged the suppression of desires and heroic self-denial.

Even those academic commentators who disapprove of the contemporary culture of celebrity frequently acknowledge that its roots lie in Christianity, and that celebrities function as contemporary saints, idols, and/or demigods of the post-Christian world. For example, Boorstin caustically observes that in the past "when a great man appeared, people looked for God's purpose in him; today we look for his press agent" (2006: 72), and Chris Rojek more neutrally notes that the relation of fans to celebrities "has inescapable parallels to religious worship . . . reinforced by the attribution by fans of magical or extraordinary powers to the celebrity. Celebrities are thought to possess God-like qualities . . . others—experiencing the power of the celebrity to arouse deep emotions—recognize the spirit of the shaman" (2007: 390). Ellis Cashmore perceptively analyzes the phenomenon of fandom and the para-social relationships fans have with celebrities they have never met (Cashmore, 2006: 80), though he fails to note the similarity that such a devotional orientation has to that of believers with their gods, between whom exist classic para-social relationships (the worshipper never actually meets the god(s) and interacts at the level of icons or aniconic representations and via symbolically charged objects).

Further, the contribution of celebrity to the construction of identity in the contemporary West has been extensively commented upon. This is one important issue that well illustrates the shift away from traditional understandings to eclectic self-constructions. Prior to the twentieth century, identity was largely a matter of family, religion, and local and national community, resulting in an individual who was understood interdependently. Each level of society placed obligations upon the individual, and inherited tradition (familial, religious, social—in terms of class—and political) was a dominant factor (LeGoff, 1980: 53–57). Consequently, identity was a relatively stable concept. Contemporary society is radically detraditionalized, and the sources upon which significantly isolated individuals draw upon to construct their identity are secular, consumerist, and media-driven, and result in fluctuating and shifting identities (Bauman, 1995). The ubiquity of consumerism diverts attention from character to personality (Boorstin, 2006: 83), from inner virtues to external image. The sources for constructing identity are drawn from the media, in addition to the influence of friends and family, and Graeme Turner notes that in relation to celebrities, individuals have "a multiplicity of choices available—identities through which they might construct their own" (2006: 494).

Lawrence Grossberg insists on the active and ongoing nature of this process of identity construction (2006: 583), and Cashmore argues that "fans" potentially will develop three types of relationships with celebrities that are self-defining and that often result in personal and social transformation: an extraordinary psychological relationship; regarding the celebrity as a role model; and, most powerfully, the adoption of the perceived attributes of the celebrity (both their values and behavior) (2006: 83). So who are today's celebrities, and what version of the perfected life do they offer the public for emulation? Celebrities garnering significant print and visual media attention range from actors, musicians, and models (for example, Tom Cruise, Brad Pitt, Angelina Jolie, Bono, Pete Doherty, Kate Moss, Madonna, and Claudia Schiffer); television hosts, popular authors, and the children of famous people (for example, Oprah Winfrey, Jeffrey Archer, and Nicole Richie); and royalty, sports stars, and the extremely wealthy (the late Princess Diana, David Beckham, and Paris Hilton). These people are all deemed worthy of admiration and emulation, chiefly because they are perceived to "have it all." From this perspective, it is not their talents or achievements that make them worthy of attention, but their ability to conspicuously consume material goods, to command the spotlight, and to constantly reinvent themselves for an eager public. It has been objected that "the celebrity is nothing greater than a more publicized version of us" (Boorstin, 2006: 89), but this is rational within a self-oriented society. Further, it is evidence of the profound shift from a God-centered to a human-centered universe. Also, as Campbell notes, the multitude of possibilities is what makes the consumerist life-world so powerful (2005 [1987]: 77–95). That the self-realization takes place largely through the imagination removes the risk of attempting to do so in reality.

One final question that must be noted is that academic commentators are divided as to whether the contemporary West's focus on the acquisition of wealth and consumer gratification, and identification with or emulation of celebrity, should be interpreted in broadly positive or negative terms. Boorstin believes the celebrity "is morally neutral" (2006: 79), but Christopher Lasch claims that, "the media give substance to and thus intensify narcissistic dreams of fame and glory, encourage the common man to identify himself with the stars and to hate the "herd" and make it more difficult for him to accept the banality of everyday existence" (1980: 21). In contrast to Lasch's negative assessment, many media writers argue trenchantly that celebrity neither trivializes the media nor dupes the public. Rather, it is asserted that major political issues are no longer being determined by elites but are democratically constructed through popular media, including the Internet and talk shows (Shattuc, 1997). Fans are also more discriminating than is usually recognized (Grossberg, 2006: 582). Further, identification with a particular celebrity's life experiences may be empowering; for example, Jane Caputi argues that the late Princess Diana's "mass mediated narrative," which involved "an unhappy childhood, a loveless marriage, an eating disorder, loneliness [and] insecurity" functioned as an archetypal female journey, and as she "faced and healed these wounds" she offered to her female audience a path to independence and achieving selfhood (1999: 117–118). This issue generally carries moral overtones; those, like Lasch and Boorstin, who assess celebrity negatively disapprove of certain aspects of contemporary culture (materialism, individualism, narcissism, preoccupation with image, fantasy, constant change, and the collapse of high and low cultures into an undifferentiated whole), whereas those who assess celebrity positively embrace precisely these aspects of contemporary culture.

Scientology's Relation to Contemporary Culture

The *Concise Oxford English Dictionary* defines *Scientology* as "a religious system based on self-improvement and promotion through grades of esp. self-knowledge," noting its derivation from the Latin *scientia*, "knowledge" (Thompson, 1995: 1236). The Church of Scientology was founded by science fiction author L. Ron Hubbard (1912–1986) in 1954 after the success of the Dianetics movement, which he launched in 1950 with the publication of *Dianetics: The Modern Science of Mental Health*. Dianetics (a neologism derived from the Greek *dia*, "through," and *nous*, "mind") was a blend of scientific, psychological, and religious concepts that Hubbard characterized as a "science of the mind" (1986 [1950]: 7) The postwar public enthusiastically took up Hubbard's book, which explained how the human mind was comprised of two parts, the analytical mind, which is "accurate, rational, and logical," and the reactive mind, which "is the repository of a variety of memory traces, or what Hubbard calls engrams" (Urban, 2006: 365). Through the process of auditing, in which the auditor regresses the patient (who is termed the "preclear") to the original painful event, these engrams can be erased. Hubbard claimed that achieving the state of Clear was accompanied by "a variety of intellectual and physical benefits" enabling the Clear to experience "the world in a radically new way" (Urban, 2006: 365).

It is interesting to attempt to locate Hubbard's "science of the mind" and the Church of Scientology that built on its insights in the context of cultural and religious shifts that were occurring in the mid-twentieth century. Hugh Urban (2006) has observed that the Church of Scientology's concern with secrecy arises from Cold War America's concern with enemies and spies, and is thus explicable in terms of Hubbard's life experiences (he was in the navy during World War II). Richard Fenn has noted that bureaucracy is on powerful source of the "quasi-sacred" (1994: 266), and Scientology is organized hierarchically, like the military or a corporation. One early critic, psychologist Erich Fromm, concluded in a review of *Dianetics* that the audience of the book were "readers who look for prefabricated happiness and miracle cures" (1950: 7). Fromm also comments on Hubbard's concern with contemporary trends; the biological orientation of the survival instinct he posits; and the psychological, interiorizing orientation that characterizes the modern and contemporary West. Urban has linked the positive message of Dianetics, that all illnesses and problems can be cured through auditing, with the postwar need for hope in the face of a possible nuclear holocaust: "Dianetics offers new hope amidst a society struggling in the aftermath of World War II and its devastation, a hope that human beings could turn their powers to self-betterment rather than self-annihilation" (2006: 367).

Dianetics was very successful, and Hubbard acquired celebrity followers early on, including actress Gloria Swanson and jazz musician Dave Brubeck

(Martin, 1989: 205). Moreover, although the 1960s is the decade most often associated with the formation of new religions and the breakdown of traditional Christian authority in Western countries, it is possible to argue that the 1950s functioned as an important incubator of these trends. Several new religions were founded in the 1950s, including Scientology in 1954, Wicca (heralded by the publication of Gerald Gardner's *Witchcraft Today* in 1954), George King's Aetherius Society in 1955, Mark L. Prophet's Summit Lighthouse (later the Church Universal and Triumphant) in 1958, and Discordianism (founded by Malaclypse the Younger and Omar Khayyam Ravenhurst in 1959). Intellectuals and bohemians also experimented with Buddhism and Hinduism (Kripal, 2007).

The Church of Scientology was a more formal context through which Hubbard's message, the central aim of which is "a civilization without insanity, without criminals and without war, where the able can prosper and honest beings have rights, and where man is free to rise to greater heights" (Hubbard, 1956: 112), could be promoted. The auditing process was extended to involve both past lives and existences on planets other than earth. Human destiny was characterized in terms of the eight dynamics, here summarized by Stoddard Martin:

> (1) survival via self-preservation, (2) survival via procreation and sexual relations, (3) survival via family or race, (4) survival via identity with all mankind, (5) survival as a life organism, (6) survival as part of the physical universe of Matter, Energy, Space and Time (MEST), (7) survival as a *thetan* (variously defined as "thought, life-force, *élan vital*, spirit or soul"), and (8) survival as part of the Supreme Being. (1989: 210)

From its inception the Church of Scientology attracted negative publicity, chiefly because more conservative elements were unwilling to accord it the status of a "real religion" and also because Hubbard's teachings were regarded as outlandish and the practice of charging for religious services earned widespread disapproval. However, these issues can all be viewed as "cultural boundary conflicts" (Bednarowski, 1995: 385) that reflect the changing nature of modern religion. Christianity is normative in the West, and religions that are not Christian have struggled for recognition, and "new" religions are subjected to particular scrutiny. Moreover, even academic treatments of the founders of new religious movements often characterize them in entirely negative terms. Stark and Bainbridge's model of "cult formation" suggests that new religions emerge due to the founder's psychopathology, entrepreneurialism, or through subcultural evolution (1979: 283–295).

Moreover, religions have always been concerned with money, and Nikos Passas has argued that Scientology is not distinguished from "real religions" by its financial practices. His argument is part of a larger thesis that new religions are disadvantaged *vis à vis* established religions, and often engage in money-making activities to make good that disadvantage (1994: 217–240). This results in established religions and conservative social forces using these money-making activities as the justification for "withholding from these groups the right to claim the religious label" (Greil and Robbins, 1994: 15). In the late twentieth and early twenty-first centuries even traditional religions have become less inhibited about accruing and displaying conspicuous wealth. Christian churches employ the techniques of popular culture (Internet sites, rock concert dynamics, product placement, and reliance on celebrity members) to win converts and preach a gospel of success and prosperity (Connell, 2005). In doing this, they abandon the traditional Christian position of critiquing society, exemplified by the New Testament's urging that Christians be "strangers in the world" (John 17:15 in Jones, 1970: 136) and reflect the dominance of late capitalist consumerism. Therefore, both new and traditional religions have adapted to the secularized, materialistic society in which they function.

Hubbard elaborated his theology over the years, promulgating a creed and developing the "Bridge to Total Freedom," a complex and hierarchical system of enlightenment. This includes the controversial Operating Thetan levels, which were originally believed to be only eight in number but now appear to extend to fifteen (Urban, 2006: 370). Each of these levels incorporates training and study and unveils a particular revelation. Because the Church of Scientology is secretive about the content of these revelations, what is known has usually been released onto the Internet by disgruntled former Scientologists or has been tabled as evidence during legal proceedings against the Church (Bracchi, 2007: 54–55). Although respecting a religion's right to keep its doctrines esoteric, it is significant in the light of the argument I have been pursuing that Scientology is a recognizable product of its historical and social milieu, that the secret teachings often refer to extraterrestrials (for example, the seventy-six-planet Galactic Federation headed by Xenu) and other themes that are found in science fiction, of which genre Hubbard was a successful author. Science fiction films were also very popular in the 1950s, and the theme of the "alien messiah" can be traced to *The Day The Earth Stood Still* (1951), in which the alien Klaatu, analogously to Jesus Christ, came to Earth to bring a message of salvation, was killed by ungrateful and ignorant humanity, rose from the dead, and returned to outer space (Etherden, 2005).

L. Ron Hubbard was fascinated by Hollywood, and actively pursued "stars" by promoting the Church of Scientology among the rich and famous. That celebrities joined the Church became a powerful draw card for Scientology, in that it rendered membership desirable. Robert Frank has drawn attention to reference group theory, which suggests that personal reference groups tend to be disproportionately drawn from "others who are similar in terms of . . . education, and various other background variables" (1985: 111). When this is coupled with the literature on identity formation, which suggests that emulation of desired characteristics forms a significant part of an individual's identity, in that what Manuel Castells call "project identity" (that which the individual desires to be and is moving toward) is as important as their current state (Lyon, 2002 [2000]: 90), the significance of celebrity Scientologists is immediately apparent. Sundry new religious movements apart from Scientology have also sought celebrity members; these include Anton La Vey's Church of Satan (Jayne Mansfield, Sammy Davis Jr., and, of late, Goth rocker Marilyn Manson), Transcendental Meditation (the Beatles, radio shock jock Howard Stern, and film director David Lynch), the International Society for Krishna Consciousness (George Harrison, Boy George, and English rock musician Crispian Mills of Kula Shaker) and more recently, the Kabbalah Centers (Shakespeare, 2006: 12–19). Scientology has established a network of celebrity centers, including those in Los Angeles and Bayswater. Hubbard had stated that "[a] culture is only as great as its dreams and its dreams are dreamed by artists" (http://www.scientologytoday.org/Common/question/pg38.htm). At Celebrity Center Churches it is argued that the famous may work on their spiritual development in peace, without being pursued by the press or pressured by fans (http://www.scientologytoday.org).

Gradually, hostility to Scientology has diminished and the Church has won legal status as a religion in many countries, including the United States and Australia. This positive step has been resisted in Britain, where Scientology was denied charitable status in 1999 (Gledhill, 1999: 6) and is still regarded with suspicion, despite the 2007 European Court of Human Rights affirming "freedom of thought, conscience and religion was a cornerstone of a "democratic society" as guaranteed by the Human Rights Convention" (Anonymous, 2007a: 17). To reinforce this legally granted status as a legitimate religion, Scientology has encouraged scholars of studies in religion to investigate its doctrines and practices to determine whether they constitute a "religion" as traditionally understood (Flinn, 1998). A collection of these papers was published by the Church as *Scientology: Theology and Practice of a Contemporary Religion* (1998). Interestingly, and perhaps importantly, Scientology has not insisted that becoming a Scientologist invalidates other religious allegiances. Rather, the Church of Scientology "insists that membership in Scientology is not incompatible with being a Catholic, Protestant, or Jew and goes so far as to encourage dual membership" (Bednarowski, 1995: 389).

The Church of Scientology now has a complex hierarchical structure, with the Church of Scientology International (CSI) and the Religious Technology Center (RTC) at the top. Other branches include Scientology Missions International (SMI), Celebrity Center Churches, and the Sea Organization (which is a uniformed branch of especially committed Scientologists that has been likened to the Jesuit Order within Roman Catholicism), from which many Scientology leaders are drawn (Flinn, 1998). Rather surprisingly, the Church also runs the most recent incarnation of the Cult Awareness Network, rebranded as "New CAN" (Urban, 2006: 380). Scientology has more than six thousand churches, missions, and groups, with approximately ten million members, in more than one hundred and fifty countries (Saleh, 2006: 84). Moreover, important "secular" outreaches of Scientology include corporate motivational programs (Hall, 1998: 393–410), educational initiatives such as Applied Scholastics (Lussier, 2007: 1; Botting, 2006: 8–9), and welfare initiatives, including disaster relief after both September 11, 2001, and Hurricane Katrina (Digance and Cusack, 2003: 153–171; Hanrahan, 2006).

Scientology Celebrities: Scandals, Weddings,
and the Effect of Constant Coverage

Much of the media coverage of Scientology celebrities takes the form of brief items in newspapers and illustrated "spreads" in magazines. This chapter will consider the profile of actor John Travolta and his wife, actress Kelly Preston; actor Tom Cruise and his wife, actress Katie Holmes; actress-turned-singer Juliette Lewis; Australian millionaire James Packer and his wife, model-turned-singer Erica Baxter; and singer Kate Ceberano in determining how celebrity coverage aids in normalizing Scientology. John Travolta (born 1954) has led the way as a Hollywood celebrity committed to Scientology. He achieved early success in the 1970s television series *Welcome Back, Kotter* (in which he played rebel student Vinnie Barbarino), and his film career was boosted by appearances in *Carrie* (directed by Brian de Palma, 1976) and the cult classic *Saturday Night Fever* (directed by John Badham, 1977) (Schneider, 2003: 631). His film career has swung wildly between critical successes (*Pulp Fiction*, directed by Quentin Tarantino in 1994; *Primary Colors*, directed by Mike Nichols in 1998) and flops (*Staying Alive*, directed by Sylvester Stallone in 1983; *Two of a Kind*, directed by John Herzfeld in 1983; and, most notoriously, *Battlefield Earth*, directed by Roger Christian in 2000, from the novel of the same name by L. Ron Hubbard).

Travolta converted to Scientology in 1975, and wife Kelly Preston is also a Scientologist. Travolta has been a constant advocate of Scientology. His official Web site promotes Scientological enterprises such as Youth for Human Rights International and the Way to Happiness Foundation (http://www.travolta.com/news.htm). He is outspoken in asserting the centrality of Scientology to his personal life and career success:

> In January of 1975 I was working on my first film in Durango, Mexico. There I met an actress who gave me the book *Dianetics* . . . That was when I became involved in Dianetics—because it worked. When I returned to the United States I began Scientology training and auditing. My career immediately took off and I landed a lead role on the TV show *Welcome Back, Kotter* and had a string of successful films. I have been a successful actor for 17 years and Scientology has played a major role in that success. I have a wonderful child and a great marriage because I apply L. Ron Hubbard's technology to this area of my life. As a Scientologist I have the technology to handle life's problems and I have used this to help others in life as well. I would say that Scientology put me into the big time. (http://www.whatisscientology.org)

Travolta's involvement in Scientology has attracted a variety of negative comments, including accusations of homosexuality and news articles alleging that his elder child, son Jett, has autism and that Travolta and Preston have concealed this because of Scientology's teaching that auditing cures all aberrant conditions, both physical and mental (Anonymous, 2007b: 43).

However, the actor's popularity is undeniable, and his fans remain loyal and passionate. Fan sites are almost always aware of Travolta's membership of the Church of Scientology, and they are not disapproving. For example, on one site amid interesting facts, such as Travolta's favorite band being the Beatles and favorite underwear white Calvin Klein briefs, is mention of Travolta and Preston having had two marriage ceremonies, as "the first wedding on the 5th [September 1991] was considered illegal as a Scientologist minister did it" (http://www. geocities.com/Hollywood/Picture/2773/jtfacts.html). Rumors about Travolta's sexuality have recently been revisited, as the gay community was outraged over his reprisal of the role of Edna Turnblad (created by Divine) in a remake of John Waters' camp classic *Hairspray*, which was released in July 2007. Travolta himself has never condemned or criticized homosexuality, but gay activists have asserted that Scientology takes a hard line on sexual preference. Kevin Naff, managing editor of the gay-oriented *Washington Blade*, noted that "Travolta, a prominent Scientologist, has no business reprising an iconic gay role, given his [religion's] stance on gay issues. It's well-known that Scientology rejects gays and lesbians as members" (http://www.huffingtonposst.com/rumor-control/gossip-column-deja-vu_b_52247.html). Fan sites, unsurprisingly, are uninterested in the sexual politics and reflect uncomplicated delight in Travolta's performance. Examples include "John Travolta is so cute as Edna Turnblad," "I can't wait for this movie . . . I just wish there was more John Travolta in the trailer!" and, with reference to the dolls of each character, "I want the John Travolta one so badly!" (http://www.seriouslyomg.com/?cat=38).

In recent years Travolta's advocacy of Scientology has intensified, and he is now very nearly as vocal in its defense as fellow actor Tom Cruise. On May 8, 2007, BBC journalist John Sweeney's documentary "Scientology and Me" was screened. During filming, Sweeney lost his temper at Scientologists, and the program presented the religion entirely negatively. It also discussed links between the Church of Scientology and the City of London Police (Murray, 2007: 14–15; Laville, 2006: 3). At Starpulse, a celebrity blog, fans dissected Travolta's angry reaction to the documentary, which aired early in 2007. Overwhelmingly they asserted the primacy of freedom of religion, with one fan noting that "Travolta has a right to his own religion. I really think this journalist went too far with his personal beliefs on religion. I think Travolta was right to address this matter. I would be angry also if I had some journalist yelling at me, that I was the head of a cult" (http://www.starpulse.com/sp_comments/viewcomments.php?object_id=42345). It is easy to conclude that fans do perceive their idol as tarnished through his membership of a new religion, and the intimacy they feel for John Travolta is unaffected by negative journalism (Cashmore, 2006: 12–13). As Barry Divola remarks, "blind devotion, sense of ownership and need to defend the honour of your beloved are what being a fan is all about" (Divola, 2006: 57).

American actor Tom Cruise is the most prominent Scientology celebrity of the early twenty-first century. Thomas Cruise Mapother IV was born in 1962 and entered the film industry with a supporting role in Franco Zeffirelli's (1981) *Endless Love* (Karney, 1993: 102). He has had a long and distinguished film career, moving seamlessly between serious acting roles with action blockbust-ers. In 2006 he married his third wife, actress Katie Holmes (mother of his only biological child, Suri), in a lavish ceremony in Bracciano, a small town north of Rome (Hooper and McMahon, 2006: 29). His first wife, Mimi Rog-ers, was a devout Scientologist and introduced Cruise to Scientology during their three-year marriage. His second wife, Australian actress Nicole Kidman (a Roman Catholic), undertook basic instruction but never formally joined the Church of Scientology. Cruise and Kidman divorced in 2001 after ten years of marriage and two adopted children, Isabella and Connor (Ehrenstein, 1998: 327). Cruise has also received negative publicity, partly due to his involvement with Scientology, partly due to persistent rumors about his sexuality, and partly due to his determined efforts to control his public image (Lawson, 2006: 34).

As this chapter is concerned with the power of celebrity journalism to nor-malize otherwise unusual or fringe phenomena, such as membership of the Church of Scientology, attention will be paid to Cruise and Holmes's courtship and marriage. These subjects are the staple fodder of women's magazines and represent the apogee of achievement for many women (Turner, Bonner, and Marshall, 2000: 119). After his separation from Kidman, Cruise was involved with his *Vanilla Sky* (2001, directed by Cameron Crowe) costar, Spanish actress Penelope Cruz (Hattenstone, 2006: 18–20). This relationship lasted two-and-a-half years and Cruz has remained friendly with Tom Cruise. She has publicly defended his involvement with Scientology (Anonymous, 2006a), and sent 100 white roses as a wedding gift to Cruise and Holmes (Watson, 2006: 3). Cruise and *Dawson's Creek* star Holmes (born 1979) had a very public courtship, with Holmes admitting that she had fantasized as a young girl about marrying Tom Cruise (Shevlin, 2007: 8). The couple's daughter Suri was born in April 2006, and plans for the wedding dominated the press from that date on.

Weddings are exemplary occasions for the amassing of public sentiment, and the Cruise-Holmes nuptials provided opportunities for the Church of Sci-entology to showcase its beliefs and its marriage ceremony, just as Suri's birth had enabled Cruise to explain the concept of the "silent birth," advocated by L. Ron Hubbard as a method of preventing damaging engrams taking root in the reactive mind of infants being born (Anonymous, 2006b: D3). Through the TomKat (as the couple is popularly known) wedding, the reading public learned that Scientology weddings

> have much in common with those of mainstream Western denomi-
> nations, right down to guests tossing rice . . . The minister typically
> wears a clerical collar and displays the church's "eight-pointed cross,"
> representing the eight "dynamics" of existence . . . Some couples
> choose to fashion rings with the church's ARC triangle, referring to
> affinity, reality and communication. Bride and groom choose from
> among five versions of the wedding ceremony, ranging from the
> Traditional to the Double Ring. (Anonymous, 2006c)

Discussion of the vows, which involve the groom promising to provide his spouse with "a pan, a comb, perhaps a cat" (Brozan, 2006: 18) enabled the

Church to explain that these lines were part of a 200-line poem authored by L. Ron Hubbard (Saleh, 2006: 84), and the posited compatibility between Scientology and other religions was underlined by reporters who claimed that some Catholic elements would be present in the wedding service, as Holmes's parents are devout Roman Catholics (Brozan, 2006: 18).

The celebrity factor reinforced the intrinsic appeal of the marriage of two of Hollywood's stars. The ceremony took place in the impressive castle, the "property of the Odescalchi family," (Hooper, 2006: 27), and the guest list included star footballer David Beckham and his wife Victoria, the former Posh Spice; director Steven Spielberg; and actor Will Smith, among approximately 300 guests (Popham, 2006: 21). Despite some negative publicity (chiefly insinuations that the couple are not happy together) since the wedding, fan sites are enthusiastic about Tom and Katie and their daughter Suri. One fan, commenting on photographs of the Cruise family visiting the Riviera to attend James Packer's wedding, rhapsodized, [1]"Tom is reportedly officiating! I really cannot get over how sophisticated and mature Katie looks! She has always been a beautiful girl however she dressed, but looks almost overly elegant for her age. In some of the pics she looks so Jacki [sic] O!" (http://babyrazzi.com/baby/cat egory/Katie-holmes-tom-cruise/). A final issue that deserves comment is the recent announcement by the Church of Scientology that Tom Cruise has been designated a Christ figure for his religion. It is claimed that Cruise has reached the level of Operating Thetan VII, and the Church's head, David Miscavige, has revealed to Cruise his role as a "messiah" figure. When in 1966 John Lennon proclaimed that the Beatles were "more popular than Jesus" (Cleave, 1966) there was a huge uproar. Forty years later, secularization has progressed so far that the attribution of Christ-like qualities to Tom Cruise has attracted only mild comment. Australian academic Vincent O'Donnell wittily notes that "[i]n a world which is increasingly barren of religious affiliation, humankind's desire to find guidance and spiritual direction has been replaced by stars. They've become role models . . . though I thought he'd be a bit short for Christ" (Gilchrist, 2007: 5).

Rather different from Travolta and Cruise is Juliette Lewis, the precocious Hollywood actress who now fronts a rock band, Juliette and the Licks. Whereas Travolta and Cruise are interested in presenting a "squeaky-clean" image to the press, and advocate "family values," Lewis (born 1973) is frank and passionate about her faith in Scientology while admitting to a wild lifestyle. She became famous as a teenager and in her early twenties underwent drug rehabilitation through the Church of Scientology (Iley, 2006). L. Ron Hubbard established Narconon, a program that has considerable success in curing addiction. Lewis also appears likeable and independent, feisty and self-critical, in magazine and newspaper interviews. With regard to her faith, she states, "I'm a very questioning person and what's so great about it is that it follows my defiant nature . . . It's thought-provoking. I find it stimulating and intelligent . . . Technically it's a religion, but it's more broad-based than that. It brings in a lot of eastern-style philosophies and gives you life tools. Simple stuff that deals with communication" (Iley, 2006: 16). Journalists interviewing Lewis appear genuinely to like her. The *Guardian's* Chrissie Iley concludes her lengthy interview with Lewis by saying, "It's a rare thing when someone talks therapy-speak to you yet still manages to make you warm to them. Juliette Lewis believes in herself at least, so she makes you feel the same" (2006: 17).

With her drug use now in the past, Lewis still cultivates a bohemian image and is far from conventional. She is attractive, but does not fit the Hollywood stereotype. Although she was romantically involved with actor Brad Pitt from 1989 to 1993, she is not a mainstream actress like Pitt's other famous partners, Gwyneth Paltrow, Jennifer Aniston, and Angelina Jolie. Her roles are often edgy, and include parts in two serial killer films, as Adele in *Kalifornia* (1993, directed by Dominic Sena), Mallory in *Natural Born Killers* (1994, directed by Oliver Stone), and ex-prostitute Faith in the violent dystopian thriller *Strange Days* (1995, directed by Kathryn Bigelow) (Schneider, 2003: 842, 853). Her personal assessment of stardom is "Stardom is about being desirable to men in suits but I laugh too loud; I talk with my mouth full" (Harris, 2007). Music critic Bernard Zuel's assessment of Lewis is that her music is not particularly good but Lewis herself is definitely cool (2007: 4).

Scientology has always been part of Lewis's life, as her father, actor Geoffrey Lewis, was one of L. Ron Hubbard's earliest Hollywood converts (Meyer, 2000). Internet fan sites testify to Lewis's attractiveness and emulatability. Fan sites rarely mention Scientology, but make frequent reference to her individuality, her opinions, and her unconventionality.

Lewis is an empowering role model for girls because of her refusal to conform. A young female fan comments that she likes Lewis because, "she is pretty and she has a cool voice . . . And I like her character, from what I know she seems pretty cool. She has an interesting life, and I love to read about her. When I see her I feel like this power, I can't stop smiling, she makes me happy" (http://members.tripod.com/~menni/index-3.html). Another young fan, noting the sources of Lewis's fame and appeal, does link her belief in Scientology to her success and appeal, "Juliette Lewis has been a long time Scientologist . . . Her band Juliette and the Licks is totally rock-and-roll . . . Juliette is quite a character . . . She can be wild and have fun at the same time" (http://spiritualbeing.wordpress.com/2007/05/23/juliette-lewis-success-with-scientology). Other fan sites provide evidence that Lewis is up-front about her beliefs in her dealings with her fans. One German fan posts that Lewis sent her a German version of L. Ron Hubbard's *The Way to Happiness* pamphlet (http://my-autographs.de/lewis.htm), and another fan responded to a complaint about Lewis's membership of the Church of Scientology with "I've been around Juliette . . . and other Hollywood Scientologists and no one has EVER spoken about it or tried to get me to join" (http://www.dlisted.com/mode/10952).

Two Australian examples of the magnetic power of celebrity Scientologists will conclude this section of the chapter: Hawaiian born singer Kate Ceberano, and millionaire James Packer and his new wife, model Erica Baxter. Kate Ceberano (born 1966) is a third-generation Scientologist who had a pioneering role in familiarizing Australian music fans with the doctrines of the Church. In the 1980s she sang with the sophisticated soul-funk band I'm Talking and has had a successful career, most recently with an album of 1980s songs she loved as a teenager. She married filmmaker Lee Rogers in 1996, and they have one daughter, Gypsy (http://www.answers.com/topics/KateCeberano?cat =entertainment). Ceberano, a down-to-earth figure, credits her happy life to the tenets of Scientology. When she was singing as a teenager in Melbourne music venues, "[s]he was never corrupted. She never took drugs . . . She simply watched . . . She watched them snort cocaine. She watched them drink" (Dalton, 2007). Ceberano's commitment to her religion led her to reject international success. She sacked her manager, preferring to be managed by her mother, Cherie. Kate Ceberano has been an actress, has recently appeared in the hit television show *Dancing with the Stars,* and retains an attractive girl-next-door reputation, even as she distributes copies of L. Ron Hubbard's *The Way to Happiness* to journalists who interview her (Dalton, 2007).

James Packer (born 1967) is a media mogul and Australia's richest businessman. His grandfather Frank created a media empire in 1960, which was substantially expanded by his father Kerry, who died in 2005. James Packer has recently shifted his business interests from the media to gaming (Dennehy and McMahon, 2007: 7). Erica Baxter (born 1977) became involved with Packer after the failure of his first marriage, to model and fashion designer Jodhi Meares. After a four-year romance, Packer and Baxter were married on June 27 with a civil ceremony at the Antibes Hotel de Ville in the morning and a Scientology ceremony in the presence of over 100 guests at the Hotel du Cap Eden Roc (Lang, 2007: 4–7). Premier celebrity Scientologists Tom Cruise and Katie Holmes were guests at the wedding, which was conducted from the Church of Scientology's mission in Nice (Hudson, 2007: 13). Cruise is believed to have been instrumental in effecting Packer's 2002 conversion, as he and wife Katie may prove to be in the case of David and Victoria Beckham, who have recently moved to the United States, where Beckham will see out his career playing for the Los Angeles Galaxy (Nichols, 2007: 3). Packer says of Scientology, "I think it has been very good for me . . . It has been helpful. I have some friends in Scientology that have been very supportive. But I think it's just helped me have a better outlook on life" (McMahon, 2007: 32). Packer's great wealth makes him worthy of emulation by many seeking riches and power. His identification of the positive effect of Scientology in his life would therefore be an incentive for those seeking to emulate him.

Erica Baxter is more glamorous than Kate Ceberano, but in many ways has the same sort of girl-next-door appeal. Born in the remote country town of Gunnedah, Baxter's modeling career began when she was a schoolgirl at Abbotsleigh, an Anglican private school in Sydney. Beautiful and successful, Baxter fits the description of the modern "goddess":

> an easy label for a beautiful or adored woman . . . Western secular
> society is inundated with role models. Scarlett Johansson, Princess
> Diana, Madonna and Angelina Jolie are regularly labelled modern
> goddesses, admired and emulated by millions of women . . . These
> modern "deities," who appear as visions on films, magazines, books,

television, and red carpets, have global powers. Our appetite for them is clearly huge. (Low, 2006: 8)

Baxter's romance with James Packer has catapulted her into the star-studded world of the rich and famous. Before their wedding she and Packer held a "private beach party" for their guests aboard nine cruisers moored off the Hotel du Cap Eden Roc (Dale and Iaccarino, 2007: 22). The growing friendship between Baxter and Packer and Tom Cruise and Katie Holmes has attracted media attention (Anonymous, 2007c: 8–10) and Australian women's magazines consistently present Baxter's rise to fame and success as desirable and positive. Details of her $100,000 "couture gown by Christian Dior designer John Galliono" (Lang, 2007: 5) and multiple photographs of the wedding have been posted on the fan site http://www.tomcruisefan.com.

Conclusion

The all-pervasive nature of the culture of celebrity in the contemporary West is readily apparent. The functions performed by celebrities have been analyzed here as primarily contributing to the construction of individual identity in a radically detraditionalized social context. Contributing substantially to the phenomenon of celebrity are the lack of alternative, persuasive role models for Western people, and a significant shift in taste that devalued "high" culture and created "an openness to appreciating everything" (Peterson and Kern, 1996: 904). Coupled with a Romantically charged participation in consumer capitalism (Campbell, 2005 [1987]), the contemporary self individuates through a process of acquiring and discarding possessions and through the emulation of those in society who are deemed to "have it all," celebrities.

The list of Scientology celebrities is extensive; it is vastly more than the small number of figures discussed in this chapter. Soul musician Isaac Hayes, famous as the voice of Chef in *South Park* (Carlson, 2006); Nancy Cartwright, the voice of Bart Simpson (Anonymous, 2006d); and music stars Beck Hansen, Chaka Khan, Doug E. Fresh, Courtney Love, and Van Morrison are all either members of the Church of Scientology or have professed to have been inspired by L. Ron Hubbard's teachings (Leggett, 2006: 4). It has been shown that fans feel intimately connected to the celebrities they admire (Grossberg, 2006: 587), and journalists present the celebrities in attractive and seductive ways to their audiences (Marshall, 2006b: 316–317). Academic and popular critics alike assert that audiences take notice of the doings of celebrities (McInnes, 2007: 27), and Cathleen Falsani has noted the willingness of celebrities to discuss their religious beliefs and the power to persuade of such celebrity religious utterances:

> Public conversation has become more receptive to people incorporating their spiritual life into their everyday life. Celebrities, in the sense of being those most talked about, trade in the sphere of public conversation, "their currency is their status, and in some cases

they're spending it in the way of faith . . . it's a very natural thing to evangelize—to share what we feel is most transformative." (Orme, 2006: D7)

It is very difficult to determine how many fans might be influenced to experiment with Scientology due to the saturated media coverage received by major celebrities like John Travolta, Tom Cruise, Juliette Lewis, and James Packer. However, given the power of the media in offering contemporary Western people a vast array of potential images on which to model their self-concept or identity, coupled with the fact that the future of religion and spirituality appears to lie in variety, eclecticism, and invention (Rowbotham, 2006: 17), and the inevitability of the permeation of celebrity into the lives of the media's audiences, it seems that the profession of faith in Scientology by celebrities must have a normalizing and familiarizing effect, rendering the Church of Scientology mainstream rather than fringe, attractive rather than unattractive, associated with wealth and success, and thus desirable rather than otherwise.

Acknowledgments

During the writing of this paper my research assistant, Alex Norman, did considerable work, for which I am grateful. My thanks are also due to Don Barrett for his sympathetic interest in my researches and his patience in discussing issues and assisting me to clarify my ideas prior to, and during, the writing process.

REFERENCES

Anonymous. (2006a) "Cruz Praises Scientology for Anti-Drugs Work," *World Entertainment News*, August 7.
———. (2006b) "Cruise Explains a Scientology Birth," *The Boston Globe*, April 14, D3.
———. (2006c) "Tying the Knot, Scientology Style," *The Toronto Star*, November 19.
———. (2006d) "The Parlance of Our Times," *National Post*, May 17, AL1.
———. (2007a) "Scientologists Win Landmark Ruling," *Aberdeen Press and Journal*, April 6, 17.
———. (2007b) "Travolta's Son 'Autistic,'" *Sunday Telegraph*, June 3, 43.
———. (2007c) "James and Erica's Beach Party: Suri Is the Star Guest as She Makes Her Big Splash," *Woman's Day*, July 2, 8–10.
Bailey, E. (1998) *Implicit Religion*. London: Middlesex University Press.
Bauman, Z. (1995) *Life in Fragments*. Oxford: Blackwell.
Bednarowski, M. F. (1995) "The Church of Scientology: Lightning Rod for Cultural Boundary Conflicts," in Timothy Miller (ed.), *America's Alternative Religions*. Albany: State University of New York Press, 385–392.
Berger, P. (1967) *The Social Reality of Religion*. London: Faber and Faber.
Boorstin, D. (2006) "From Hero to Celebrity: The Human Pseudo-Event," in P. David Marshall (ed.), *The Celebrity Culture Reader*. New York: Routledge, 73–90.
Botting, C. (2006) "Attention Welcome for Scientologists," *Inner Western Courier*, May 30, 8–9.

Bracchi, P. (2007) "Church of Hate Tried to Destroy Me," *Daily Mail*, May 19, 54–55.

Brown, P. (1981) *The Cult of the Saints: Its Rise and Function in Latin Christianity.* Chicago: University of Chicago Press.

Brozan, N. (2006) "For Mrs. Cruise, Perhaps a Cat," *New York Times*, November 12, 18.

Bruce, S. (2002) *God Is Dead: Secularization in the West.* Oxford: Blackwell.

Campbell, C. (1972) "The Cult, the Cultic Milieu and Secularization," *A Sociological Yearbook of Religion in Britain*, 5: 119–136.

Campbell, C. (2005 [1987]) *The Romantic Ethic and the Spirit of Modern Consumerism.* York: Alcuin Academics.

Caputi, J. (1999) "The Second Coming of Diana," *National Women's Studies Association Journal*, 11:2, 103–123.

Carlson, E. (2006) "'South Park'—Scientology battle rages," *Associated Press*, March 18.

Cashmore, E. (2006) *Celebrity/Culture.* Abingdon: Routledge.

Chidester, D. (1994) "The Church of Baseball, the Fetish of Coca-Cola, and the Potlatch of Rock'n'Roll," *Journal of the American Academy of Religion*, 64(4): 743–766.

Cleave, M. (1966) "How Does a Beatle Live? John Lennon Lives Like This," *London Evening Standard*, March 4, http://www.geocities.com/nastymcquickly/articles/standard.html.

Connell, J. (2005) "Hillsong: A Megachurch in the Sydney Suburbs," *Australian Geographer*, 36(3): 315–332.

CSI International. (1998) *Scientology: Theology and Practice of a Contemporary Religion.* Los Angeles: Bridge Publications.

Dale, D., and Iaccarino, C. (2007) "Cruisers Galore but Tom's below the Horizon," *Sydney Morning Herald*, June 20, 22.

Dalton, T. (2007) "Song Bird," *Herald Sun*, June 2.

Demerath, N. J. III (2000) "The Varieties of Sacred Experience: Finding the Sacred in a Secular Grove," *Journal for the Scientific Study of Religion*, 39(1): 1–11.

Dennehy, L., and McMahon, S. (2007) "Secrets, Celebs and Mega-million Deals: Wedding of the Year," *Herald Sun*, June 2, 7.

Digance, J., and Cusack, C. (2003) "Religious, Spiritual Secular: Some American Responses to September 11," *Australian Religion Studies Review*, 16(2): 153–171.

Divola, B. (2006) "Fan Tales: Shrines, Stage Doors and Sex. Meet the True Obsessives," *Madison*, July, 56–60.

Ehrenstein, D. (1998) *Open Secret: Gay Hollywood 1928–1998.* New York: William Morrow and Company, Inc,

Etherden, M. (2005) "*The Day the Earth Stood Still:* 1950s Sci-Fi, Religion and the Alien," *Journal of Religion and Film*, 9(2): at http://www.unomaha.edu/jrf/previous.htm#vo19–2.

Fenn, R. (1994) "The Quasi-Sacred: A Theoretical Introduction," *Religion and the Social Order*, 4: 253–271.

Flinn, F. K. (1998) "Scientology: The Marks of a Religion," in CSI International (ed.), *Scientology: Theology and Practice of a Contemporary Religion.* Los Angeles: Bridge Publications, 147–161.

Frank, R. H. (1985) "The Demand for Unobservable and Other Nonpositional Goods," *The American Economic Review*, 75(1): 101–116.

Fromm, E. (1950) "Dianetics—For Seekers of Prefabricated Happiness," *New York Herald Tribune Book Review*, September 3, 7.

Gilchrist, I. (2007) "Christ, Tom Stars New Gods in Cult of Celebrity," *MX*, January 25, 5.

Gledhill, R. (1999) "Church 'Fails Test' for Charity Status," *The Times*, December 10, 6.

Greil, A. L., and Robbins, T. (1994) "Exploring the Boundaries of the Sacred," *Religion and the Social Order,* 4: 1–23.

Grossberg, L. (2006) "Is There a Fan in the House? The Affective Sensibility of Fandom," in P. David Marshall (ed.), *The Celebrity Culture Reader.* New York: Routledge, 581–590.

Hanrahan, K. (2006) "Scientology Missions Spring Up in Hurricane-Damaged Areas," *Associated Press,* May 15, at http://www.factiva.com.

Hall, D. (1998) "Managing to Recruit: Religious Conversion in the Workplace," *Sociology of Religion,* 59(4): 393–410.

Harris, S. (2007) "Juliette Lewis: The Actress and Singer on Love, Drugs and Scientology," *Independent on Sunday,* June 3, at http://news.independent.co.uk/people/profiles/article2602597.ece.

Hattenstone, S. (2006) "Homecoming Queen," *The Guardian Weekend,* August 5, 16–20.

Hooper, J. (2006) "Mission Impossible: Find the Cruise Wedding Site," *The Guardian,* November 11, 27.

Hooper, J., and McMahon, B. (2006) "Poor town's fairytale come true," *The Guardian,* November 18, 29.

Hubbard, L. R. (1986 [1950]) *Dianetics: The Modern Science of Mental Health.* Los Angeles: Bridge Publications.

Hubbard, L. Ron (1956) *The Fundamentals of Scientology.* Los Angeles: Church of Scientology of California.

Hudson, F. (2007) "Religious Chief Hints at Packer Wedding," *Daily Telegraph,* June 5, 13.

Iley, C. (2006) "Rock On," *The Guardian,* September 25, 14–17.

Jones, A. (ed.) (1970) *The New English Bible.* Cambridge and Oxford: Cambridge University Press and Oxford University Press.

Karney, R. (1993) *Who's Who in Hollywood.* London: Bloomsbury Publishing Limited.

Kripal, J. (2007) *Esalen: America and the Religion of No Religion.* Chicago: University of Chicago Press.

Lang, J. (2007) "James and Erica's Lavish Wedding," *Woman's Day,* July 2, 4–7.

Lasch, C. (1980) *The Culture of Narcissism.* London: Abacus.

Laville, S. (2006) "Gala dinners, Jive Bands and Tom Cruise: How the Scientologists Woo City Police," *The Guardian,* November 22, 3.

Lawson, M. (2006) "Too Batty for the Box Office," *The Guardian,* August 25, 34.

Leggett, J. (2006) "Keeping the Faith," *The Guardian,* March 25, 4.

Le Goff, J. (1980) "A Note on Tripartite Society, Monarchical Ideology, and Economic Renewal in Ninth- to Twelfth-Century Christendom," in J. LeGoff, *Time, Work and Culture in the Middle Ages,* trans. Arthur Goldhammer. Chicago: University of Chicago Press.

Low, L. A. (2006) "The Goddess Next Door," *Sydney Morning Herald,* October 7–8, 8–9.

Lussier, C. (2007) "Class, Scientology Linked—Educators Say School Benefiting," *The Baton Rouge Advocate,* May 29, 1.

Lyon, D. (2002 [2000]) *Jesus in Disneyland: Religion in Postmodern Times.* Cambridge: Polity.

Marshall, P. D. (ed.). (2006a) *The Celebrity Culture Reader.* New York: Routledge.

Marshall, P. D. (2006b) "Intimately Intertwined in the Most Public Way: Celebrity and Journalism," in P. David Marshall (ed.), *The Celebrity Culture Reader.* New York: Routledge, 315–323.

Martin, S. (1989) *Orthodox Heresy: The Rise of "Magic" as Religion and Its Relation to Literature.* New York: St. Martin's Press.

McInnes, W. (2007) "Twinkle, Twinkle, Earnest Star, Celebrity Alone Won't Get You Far," *Sydney Morning Herald,* January 13–14, 27.

McMahon, N. (2007) "Meet Mrs. Packer," *The Sydney Magazine, Sydney Morning Herald,* May 30, 32.

Meyer, C. (2000) "Juliette Lewis Is All Grown Up: Actress Moves Beyond Her Intense, Troubled Image," *San Francisco Chronicle,* September 3, at http://sfgate.com/cgi-bin/article.cgi?file=/chronicle/archive/2000/09/03/PK78825.DTL.

Murray, J. (2007) "MPs Call for Tax Probe into Cult Shamed on TV," *The Sunday Express,* May 20, 14–15.

Nichols, A. (2007) "Score for Scientology? Cruise May Have Lured Becks," *New York Daily News,* January 13, 3.

Orme, B. (2006) "Book Looks at Why Celebrities Highlight Religion: In the God Factor Cathleen Falsani Examines the Faith of Public Figures," *Dayton Daily News,* July 22, D7.

Passas, N. (1994) "The Market for Gods and Services: Religion, Commerce, and Deviance," *Religion and the Social Order,* 4: 217–240.

Peterson, R. A., and Kern, R. M. (1996) "Changing Highbrow Taste: From Snob to Omnivore," *American Sociological Review,* 61(5): 900–907.

Popham, P. (2006) "Hollywood Invades Lake Town for Scientology's Big Event," *The Independent,* November 17, 21.

Rojek, C (2006) "Celebrity and Religion," in P. David Marshall (ed.), *The Celebrity Culture Reader.* New York: Routledge, 389–417.

Rowbotham, J. (2006) "Holy Marketeers Want Your Soul," *The Weekend Australian,* December 23–24, 17.

Saleh, L. (2006) "Is It Science or Fiction?" *The Daily Telegraph,* December 2, 84.

Schneider, S. J. (gen. ed.) (2003) *1001 Movies You Must See before You Die.* London: Quintet Publishing Limited.

Sethi, A. (2006) "Where Is Tom Cruise's Baby?" *The Guardian,* July 28, 3.

Shakespeare, J. (2006) "Hollywood and Divine," *The Observer Magazine,* August 27, 12–19.

Shattuc, J. (1997) *The Talking Cure: TV Talk Shows and Women.* London: Routledge.

Shevlin, I. (2007) "Behind Closed Doors," *Sunday Tribune,* May 27, 8.

Stark, R. (2003) "Upper Class Asceticism: Social Origins of Ascetic Movements and Medieval Saints," *Review of Religious Research,* 45(1): 5–19.

Stark, R., and Bainbridge, W. S. (1979) "Cult Formation: Three Compatible Models," *Sociological Analysis,* 40(4): 283–295.

Tacey, D. (2001) *Jung and the New Age.* Hove: Brunner-Routledge.

Thompson, Della (ed.). (1995) *The Concise Oxford Dictionary of Current English,* 9th ed. Oxford: Clarendon Press.

Turner, G. (2006) "Celebrity, the Tabloid, and the Democratic Public Sphere," in P. David Marshall (ed.), *The Celebrity Culture Reader.* New York: Routledge, 487–500.

Turner, G., Bonner, F., and Marshall, P. D. (2000) *Fame Games: The Production of Celebrity in Australia.* Cambridge: Cambridge University Press.

Urban, H. B. (2006) "Fair Game: Secrecy, Security, and the Church of Scientology in Cold War America," *Journal of the American Academy of Religion,* 74(2): 356–389.

Watson, J. (2006) "Tom's 2.5m Happy Ending," *Scotland on Sunday,* November 19, 3.

Zuel, B. (2007) "Rocks in Their Heads," *Sydney Morning Herald: Metro,* February 16, 4.

Web References

http://babyrazzi.com/baby/category/Katie-holmes-tom-cruise/
http://members.tripod.com/~menni/index-3.html

http://my-autographs.de/lewis.htm

http://news.independent.co.uk/people/profiles/article2602597.ece

http://sfgate.com/cgi-bin/article.cgi?file=/chronicle/archive/2000/09/03/PK78825.
DTL

http://spiritualbeing.wordpress.com/2007/05/23/juliette-lewis-success-with-scientology

http://www.answers.com/topics/Kate-Ceberano?cat=entertainment).

http://www.concise.britannica.com

http://www.dlisted.com/mode/10952

http://www.factiva.com

http://www.geocities.com/Hollywood/Picture/2773/jtfacts.html

http://www.huffingtonposst.com/rumor-control/gossip-column-deja-vu_b_52247.html

http://www.scientologytoday.org

http://www.seriouslyomg.com/?cat=38

http://www.starpulse.com/sp_comments/viewcomments.php?object_id=42345

http://www.tomcruisefan.com

21

Sources for the Study of Scientology: Presentations and Reflections

Dorthe Refslund Christensen

Introduction to the Source Material and Its Usage

The amount of material on Dianetics and Scientology is extensive, to say the least. This material is composed of books by L. Ron Hubbard (including basic books on Dianetics and Scientology philosophy and technology, technical bulletins, a technical dictionary, and bulletins on Hubbard's management technology); compilations of his works; taped lectures; auditor training materials (books, tapes, films, and portfolios); course packages; booklets; a large number of magazines and annuals; and video recordings of the major annual events such as the L. Ron Hubbard Birthday Celebration Event and the May 9th Event (anniversary of the publication of *Dianetics: The Modern Science of Mental Health,* [*DMSMH*]). In this chapter, I will provide an introduction to two different types of Scientology material. I have prioritized books by their importance and provide thorough presentations of the *Technical Bulletins of Dianetics and Scientology,* the basic books of Dianetics (eleven) and Scientology (fifteen), and a few additional books (seven). I shall furthermore present an overview analysis of the video recordings of two major annual events from 1986 and forward. Finally, I will briefly cover Scientology periodicals, magazines, booklets, and pamphlets.

This prioritization means I am leaving out taped lectures by Hubbard (there is another world out there!) and course packages used in the auditor training including the training films. In future research, this material will have to be included in order for the ritual practice of Scientology to be satisfyingly analyzed. I am also leaving out all periodicals, magazines, booklets, pamphlets, films, flyers, and so forth published by the Church. This kind of material typically addresses very specific subjects such as a single kind of training material, a particular event, certain localities such as the *Freewinds* ship,[1] certain projects such as drug rehabilitations in certain areas, and the like.[2]

For each type of material, I will argue, work by work, how it can be used in analyses of therapeutic and religious activities in Scientology. It is my intention to make it possible for readers to get oriented within the labyrinthine world of Scientological material without having to spend the same inordinate amount of time working their way into it that I did when I started out as a young student.

On Representativity and Theology

It is impossible to single out any part of the Scientological material and claim it to be representative of Scientologists in general. This is not merely, as one might expect, due to the fact that the Scientological soteriology is hierarchical and that individual Scientologists study different materials at different points of the *Bridge*, the soteriological system. For this reason, one would expect the material to be representative of Scientologists at any part of the Bridge, and for these particular Scientologists alone. Accordingly, one could claim that a gradual accumulative process takes place in relation to accessed material from the bottom of the Bridge to a given level, which represents the Scientologists who had actually reached these soteriological steps.[3] However, recent cognitive research indicates that the acquisition and entertainment of religious ideas by individual subjects involves very dynamic interactions of cognitive and conceptual processes. The process of acquisition is underdetermined by formal tuition (Boyer 1994a: 26f; 1994b: 396f). Furthermore, the relations between a religious system and individual subjects engaged in this religion are not characterized by deduction but by *abduction* (see, e.g., Boyer 1994a: 146 ff.). This means that there is no automatic, mechanical process for acquiring information about the way things relate, in terms of a representation stated by a religious authority being automatically utilized by actual subjects.

Scientology is not a heavily theological or dogmatic religion in the sense that Scientology—like many other religions—is not a religion of belief, but a religion of practice. Scientologists are not supposed to study the Hubbard material and apply each and every principle to their own lives. They are supposed to study the principles to grasp an understanding of why the technology that they encounter in the ritual practice *auditing* works, and to obtain a deeper understanding of Hubbard's achievements in the religious and therapeutic fields dealt with in the material.

Even though Scientology is nontheological and nondogmatic, and despite the fact that, cognitively speaking, the material is not normative in the sense that any certainty can be claimed in the way individual subjects actually entertain the material (or parts of it), the Hubbard material still plays the role of a theology in a loose sense of the word. In Scientology this material is considered to constitute the religious philosophy "these particular teachings as opposed to others that are not part of Hubbard's ideas." Even though each idea is represented a number of times in highly different ways, there are of course limitations in terms of what a concept can mean. Each concept has several meanings when accounted for by Hubbard (and even more in the minds of individuals) depending on the actual situation in which the representation was made. Having said this, it should be stressed that a concept cannot mean just anything; it is not without content.[4] The term *theology* then, can be construed as meaning the total of singular expressions made by Hubbard, making up the set of concepts entertained in some way within the *cultural repertoire* that makes up Scientology—subdivided in two actual repertoires, that of religion and that of therapy.

The Legacy of L. Ron Hubbard

Having described the material in this fashion, I must immediately make certain reservations. The first of these has to do with the origin of the material. What does it mean that the material is Hubbard's?

Practically speaking, it means that, for example, the writings, such as the technical bulletins and the books issued and published in his name, are claimed to be his. This is not unproblematic, however, because his name in its different forms (Ron, LRH, Hubbard, the LRH seal symbol and the Ron signature [e.g., CSI 1993b: 83]) are all registered trademarks and service marks owned and licensed by the Religious Technology Center (RTC).[5] There are two aspects to this. First, the writings and material issued during Hubbard's lifetime, such as the *HCO Bulletins*,[6] are always concluded with "L. Ron Hubbard. Founder." However, it was the practice since the beginning of Dianetics and Scientology history that others wrote the bulletins and signed Hubbard's name. Although Hubbard always referred to himself as "I" and always implicated a first-person perspective in his writings, in single particular cases a bulletin reveals itself to have been produced by somebody else. One example is a staff member who, sharing some experiences of the establishment of Saint Hill,[7] refers to "Ron" (TB, vol. V: 209 f.). Hubbard made a general announcement in 1977 stating, "It is now forbidden to write an HCOB or a HCO PL and sign my name to it" (TB, vol. XI: 14). This case suggests that tasks were divided within the HCO and that Hubbard did not, in fact, write all the bulletins himself, but might have dictated the contents to staff members who did the actual writing.

A second aspect of this problem became relevant after Hubbard's death on January 24, 1982.[8] RTC was formed in 1982 by Hubbard and a small number of devoted Scientologists.[9] The aim was to form a unit within the Church structure that could take over the trademarks, service marks, and all other aspects that entail the management of what is considered "Ron's legacy." Already in February 1965 an initiative had been taken to establish the *Keeping Scientology Working* series, the aim of which was, and still is, to keep the organization "clean" of those who violate church policy and to correctly apply the technology.[10] This initiative was carried out within the framework of RTC. Today RTC is in absolute control of the L. Ron Hubbard brand because this unit owns the trademarks and service marks, thus controlling for what, and by whom, they can be used.

On a more profound level, the material is considered to be Hubbard's, in the sense that Hubbard is perceived as the *source,* as the ultimate discoverer and conveyer of wisdom. According to this understanding, nothing can be added to his discoveries, nor can they be altered in any sense, because this would make them "off source."[11] The material consists of a large number of singular expressions on different subjects such as prenatal traumas, radiation, marital problems, the existence of an immortal life force, studying, and so forth. There exists no concordant comment on, nor interpretation of, the writings of Hubbard because this is not necessary (according to the idea of Hubbard as ultimate source), and, ultimately, profoundly unacceptable, because one cannot alter what is already perfect.

This does not mean, however, that the writings of Hubbard are left untouched by the Church. They are not. Studying the basic books of Dianetics and Scientology clearly shows that an editorial process has been going on since very early in the history of Scientology. I shall deal briefly with the contexts of these editorial initiatives. First, as mentioned above, Scientology is a religion of practice. The technology developed by Hubbard is considered the most valuable and workable tool in the universe today for handling mental and spiritual human problems and suffering. However, like in many other religions, the ritual tools are not considered workable if they are applied with even just a tiny deviance from the standards, hence the idea of *Standard Technology.* Scientologists are not supposed to study the material in a random fashion but, instead, at a stepwise process along the Bridge, "getting reality on" why the tools are workable. They do not study the books and other material out of random interest, but because they want to apply them. This means that the data given in the material must be absolutely accurate and *on source,*[12] especially when dealing with the technology. In this context, the editorial process can be seen as one part of the keeping scientology working agenda. Because more or less all of the material contains ritual tools that are supposed to work only if correctly applied, it has been natural to see to that the data contained in the written material were gradually edited according to Hubbard's new findings and ideas. One example of this editorial context concerns the technology called New Era Dianetics (NED). This was developed by Hubbard and released in 1978. However, earlier bulletins were revised according to these new findings because NED actually replaced older auditing techniques.[13]

Second, during the early years of Scientology, Hubbard developed new concepts such as *thetan, whole track,* and *MEST.*[14] Already during the summer of 1950, shortly after the release of *DMSMH* (May 9), Hubbard moved on to new discoveries, publishing these in bulletins and sharing them at lectures. During this process some minor alterations of terms from the early writings were made as he gradually developed and partly integrated the old concepts into the new context. At some point, however, this seems to have stopped. This occurred when he realized that there were going to be two systems, Dianetics and Scientology, and not simply a new and reformulated Dianetics. An early example is the book *The Dynamics of Life* (1951a; originally titled *Dianetics: The Original Thesis*). In the 1970 edition the "Editor 1951" states that the manuscript reflects "the original Dianetics" (Hubbard 1970: 10). One minor example that indicates that this is not the case can be seen in the fact that the chapter on the *dynamics*[15] lists eight dynamics. Eight dynamics is a Scientological idea, whereas originally in Dianetics Hubbard operated with only four dynamics.

The third context in which to comprehend the editorial initiatives taken by the Church has to do with the construction and maintenance of Hubbard as source and ultimate legitimizing resource of Scientology. This kind of editing, which originated in Hubbard's lifetime, is preoccupied with "writing back history" to make the implicit or explicit claim that Hubbard knew all along where he was headed and how to get there.[16] This is done by referring to a former edition of some kind of material in order to claim that this was written early on and published later.[17] An early example of this is found in the presentation of the book *Scientology: A New Science*.[18] According to this presentation

> the basic science was named "Scientology" in 1938. In 1947 L. Ron Hubbard[19] changed its name to "Dianetics" in order to make a social test of publication and popularity. That test completed, in 1952 he changed the science back to its original name, SCIENTOLOGY. This was done to inhibit its being monopolized for private purposes. This work in its first manuscript form was called *Scientology: A New Science*. This was changed soon by L. Ron Hubbard to *Abnormal Dianetics* for offerance to the medical profession. (TB, vol. 2: 331)

This quote reflects both the "writing back" of history and the instrumental attitude in publishing and editorial matters.

The fourth context in which the editorial initiatives can be comprehended is solely practical. It reflects developments within publishing and trends in layouts and indexing. All of the latest editions of books are supplied with footnotes and indexes, in addition to those elements present in older editions such as advertisements for other Hubbard books, glossaries, and biographical notes on Hubbard.

Eventually I would like to mention a revision that has only to do with *Dianetics: The Modern Science of Mental Health* (Hubbard 1950a). In the 1950 and 1951 editions of this book there is a foreword written by medical doctor Joseph A. Winther. Doctor Winther, according to sociologist Roy Wallis, helped Hubbard during the early stages of developing Dianetics, but the two came to an impasse in relation to the development of ideas on past lives and therefore ceased working together (Wallis 1976: 21 ff.). There is only one mention of Dr. Winther in Scientology (TB, vol. 1: 186), and his possible influence is not mentioned in today's Scientology.[20] Furthermore, the 1950 edition of *DMSMH* has four appendixes, three of which were written, respectively, by Will Durant,[21] John W. Campbell, Jr., and D. H. Rogers, whom Hubbard collaborated with at the time. The first two appendixes were already removed in the 1951 edition. It has not been possible to find out when the foreword by Winther and the last appendix were removed. Apart from the hostility that seems to have arisen between the various men, one might of course argue that a forty-year-old foreword by an unknown medical doctor is not relevant anymore, though it was a highly legitimizing factor at the time.

Despite the critical comments made above, my pragmatic approach used in the following presentation has been to consider the written material as L. Ron Hubbard's because in Scientology and to Scientologists this material is Hubbard's. An analysis that wishes to reflect how this material is used in a religious system and by individual subjects must therefore take the approach that Hubbard was the originator—supplemented, of course, by critical analyses of how the Church and RTC are administering Hubbard's legacy.

A similar pragmatism has guided the priority of using the latest editions of books in my quotes. There is all the reason in this world—from a source-critical point of view—to be critical of the latest editions of manuscripts, but the Church will always recommend and display the latest editions of material. Thus any approach that tries to correlate with the Church's self-identity must accordingly utilize the material that is in use within the religion studied.[22]

The Technical Bulletins of Dianetics and Scientology

The technical bulletins (in short TB, also called the *technical volumes* or the *red volumes*) include thirteen chronological volumes (TB), four subject volumes (TB, Source Volume) and one index volume, comprising, all in all around 12,000 pages. The thirteen chronological bulletins are a collection of all of L. Ron Hubbard's technical issues and articles, journals, and HCOTBs[23] published from 1950 to 1991[24] ("I wrote and documented as I went" [CSI 1993b: 44]) as well as a collection of handwritten manuscripts and lists of lectures given by Hubbard throughout the years. The four subject volumes are a collection of specific auditing techniques on different subjects. For each year, there is a brief description of Hubbard's activities, among these: travel, dissemination in new countries, main book releases, and new technical breakthroughs. The text in the red volumes is printed in four different colors according to the Scientological printing system (*flash colors*): "Red on white," that is, red text on white paper, shows that the issues dealt with regard technical training. This means that the recipients of the text are auditors and auditor trainees.[25] "Black on white" shows that the issues dealt with are of a more general character. The recipients here are everybody, including the public. "Green on white" means that the text is a policy letter and concerns directions for Church policy. "Blue on white" are LRH executive directives (EDs), that is, immediate directions on, for instance, certain initiatives. The validity of these EDs ends automatically when the particular initiative is completed.

As with most other Dianetics and Scientology material, the technical bulletins are not studied "at random" by Scientologists or whenever they feel like it.[26] Included in the *Classification, Gradation and Awareness Chart of Levels and Certificates,* colloquially *The Bridge to Total Freedom* or just *the Bridge,* the full record of all salvational steps of the ritual hierarchy in Scientology, is a plan on which material (written or taped lectures) the preclear[27] is supposed to study at the different steps. The technical bulletins are not studied by Scientologists until the OT preparation step, the levels preparing the preclear (pc) for solo auditing and the OT steps that comprise the esoteric part of the soteriological hierarchy. Hubbard wrote in 1973, "A chronological study of materials is necessary for the complete training of a truly top-grade expert in these lines. He can see how the subject progressed and so is able to see which are the highest levels of development" (CSI 1993b: 44 f.).

The technical bulletins were originally released in August 1976 in ten volumes. They were the first attempt by the Church to release all of Hubbard's technical issues known at the time into one collection. In 1991 a new set of volumes were released containing the technical issues up to 1991 and presenting to Scientologists a lot of, until then, unknown materials including notes by Hubbard, data sheets, process sheets, and a number of magazine articles by Hubbard not publicly known or published. According to Scientology, this material had been found due to the work of Sea Org members[28] (CSI 1993a: 44).

The technical volumes are highly valuable sources because they comprise almost four decades of Hubbard's representational redescriptions in the development of Dianetics and Scientology. They can provide the reader with valuable data on Hubbard's different activities as well as organizational development and Hubbard's rhetoric and style. However, to the new student in the field this is not the place to start because they are very technical and demand some knowledge of the system, including language competences.

Books on Dianetics and Scientology

There are eleven basic books on Dianetics and fifteen on Scientology. Below I give a brief introduction to each basic book and seven additional books to provide an overview of the contents and history of each book as well as point out where on the Bridge it is studied. I hope this section proves to be a fruitful and time-saving tool when working oneself into the material and, at the same time, I want to demonstrate how the gradual development of Dianetics and Scientology came about.

Dianetics: The Modern Science of Mental Health (*DMSMH;* Hubbard 1950/1989), colloquially known as *Book One*, contains all basic principles on Dianetics in its original form.[29] Hubbard introduces the three different minds and their functions and interactions, and argues that these functions are the source of irrationality, mental aberration, and psychosomatic illness. He introduces the idea of the time track[30] and Dianetics therapeutic technology, auditing, and explains how a person can be relieved of his or her mental and psychosomatic pain by applying this technology. Although Dianetics has been transformed and integrated into Scientological soteriology, this book remains the book most often referred to, and it is an important promotional and dissemination tool. The book can be studied by Scientologists at any level of the Bridge.

Dianetics: The Evolution of a Science (Hubbard 1955a/1989) was first published as a book-length article in May 1950 in the then esteemed science fiction magazine *Astounding Science Fiction* (pp. 43–87) to which Hubbard contributed regularly.[31] The book covers the development of Dianetics theory and practice in its different phases and aspects, for instance, an account of why it was so important for Hubbard to develop his own distinct terminology and language to denote his findings. The book can be studied at any level of the Bridge and is recommended to newcomers as a way of getting to know Dianetic ideas on how the mind works and can hold one back if not dealt with.

The Dynamics of Life (Hubbard 1951a/1989), according to Scientology, was originally written by Hubbard in 1947 under the title *Scientology: A New Science*.[32] After retitling it *Abnormal Dianetics*, Hubbard offered it to the medical and psychiatric professions. However, these professions turned him down and, instead, according to the Church, thousands of copies were circulated all over the world and Hubbard wrote *Dianetics: The Modern Science of Mental Health* and *Dianetics* to meet the public demand on the new subject. The first hardcover edition was published in December 1951 entitled *Dianetics: The Original Thesis*. In 1983 the book was retitled once again as *The Dynamics of Life*. That book, according to Scientology, covers the earliest formulations of the Dianetics principles on how the mind works, including three early case stories. The book can be studied at any level of the Bridge.

Self Analysis (1951c/1989) is a "do-it-yourself" book on how to apply the then newest auditing technique, *straightwire*, developed by Hubbard during the summer 1951. The fundamental principle in auditing up until that time had been *engram running* and *engram running by chains*. In engram running the auditor helps the preclear to go back on the time track and *relive* painful incidents. When performing engram running by chains one relives chains of incidents on the time track, incidents that are connected in different ways. The aim is to find the basic engram (*basic basic*) and to erase its influence. Straightwire as a technique denotes the performance of a straight memory line from cause to effect aiming to understand the cause and limit its harmful effects on life at present. *Self Analysis* contains the Hubbard Chart of Human Evaluation[33] for a person to perform his or her own measuring of his or her own levels of awareness and possibilities of improvement. Straightwire, as introduced in *Self Analysis*, was also new in another sense: The preclear could perform all this by him- or herself without any auditor.[34] *Self Analysis* is now studied by Scientologists at the level *ARC Straightwire Expanded*.

The Basic Dianetics Picture Book (1971a/1991) was first published in 1971 to form an aid for the auditor to tell newcomers in text and pictures about what Dianetics is and how to apply its principles. It contains all of the basic Dianetics principles (compare to *DMSMH*), and it is considered part of the basic material. It can be studied at any step of the Bridge.

Science of Survival: Prediction of Human Behavior (originally subtitled *Simplified, Faster Dianetics Techniques* 1951b/1989) was written during the spring of 1951 and presented in limited form at the First Annual Conference of Hubbard Dianetics Auditors in Wichita, Kansas, June 25–28, 1951. It was published in

August 1951. *Science of Survival* contains the most detailed accounts of each level of the *Tone Scale* (Hubbard Chart of Human Evaluation) and a practical introduction to the auditing techniques developed at that time. However, the most important aspect of this book, in relation to the present context, is that the *theta-MEST theory* appears for the first time. The theta-MEST theory introduces the idea that all life is constituted by a battle between MEST (matter, energy, space, and time), that is, the physical universe, and theta (taken from the Greek letter), the invisible, immortal, and eternal life force.[35] The book is studied by Scientologists at *Grade 0* on the Bridge.

Dianetics 55! A Guide to Effective Communication (1955b/1989) was distributed to the Unification Congress in December 1954 and published in April 1955. *Dianetics 55!* is often referred to as *Book Two*. It is the most extended book on the subject of communication in Scientology. Communication is considered vital to the workability of Dianetics and Scientology because the barriers in communication will be barriers in, for example an auditing session if the auditor or the preclear can not communicate productively. Because communication can be influenced by the reactive mind or by the analytic mind, the result of the communication implementing one of those minds will be very different. *Dianetics 55!* is studied by Scientologists at *Grade 0 Communications Release*.

Advanced Procedures and Axioms (1951d/1989) was published in November 1951 in Wichita, Kansas. It provides data on *Effort Processing*, processing that focuses on the efforts and counterefforts of the individual and against the individual that make him or her realize that his or her own self-determinism is crucial for happiness and well-being. Secondly, it introduces *Postulate Processing*, processing that focus on the individual's ability to make postulates and change them. The book is studied at *Grade 1 Problems Release*.

Handbook for Preclears (1951e/1989) was released in December 1951, at the Second Annual Conference of Hubbard Dianetics Auditors, as a companion textbook to *Advanced Procedures and Axioms*. The book addresses the auditor or the individual preclear and provides him with tools, including a new Hubbard Chart of Attitudes to complement the Hubbard Chart of Human Evaluation for the preclear to estimate his stage of awareness and make him move up the *Tone Scale*. The book is studied at *Grade 1 Problems Release*.

Child Dianetics (1951f/1989) is a compilation of Hubbard materials dealing with children's mental well-being, intelligence, self-respect, and sane development and how to establish a good relationship with children. On a practical level, it teaches parents how to apply Dianetics to children. The book can be studied at any level of the Bridge.

Notes on the Lectures (1955d/1989) was based on a series of lectures given by Hubbard in Los Angeles in November 1950 and the notes and chalkboard diagrams from these lectures made by Hubbard Dianetics Research Foundation staff members. It was published under its present title and in its present form in 1955. It is considered the most comprehensive text on *ARC, affinity-reality-communication*, which combined denotes understanding in Dianetics and Scientology. Furthermore, the book contains several different scales complementing the Tone Scale in determining the individual's level regarding emotion, reality, and ability to communicate, as well as an extended description of the *dynamics,* the different spheres of life.[36] The book is used on the level *ARC Straightwire.*

Scientology: The Fundamentals of Thought (1956a/1989) were originally written by Hubbard as a résumé of Scientology for use in translations, and it is an early summation of the basic principles of Scientology. It gives an important explanation of the two different *cycles of action,*[37] the *apparent* and the *actual;* and of the conditions of existence, *be, do,* and *have;* the parts of man and how the individual's attitude toward his existence and these cycles will have very different outcomes in that the person's attitude will determine whether the person is *cause* (active subject) or *effect* (passive object) in his or her life. The book is considered fundamental and can be studied at any level of the Bridge as an introduction to Scientology.

A New Slant on Life (1965a/1989) is a compilation of thirty[38] philosophical essays by Hubbard on very different aspects of life. It is considered in Scientology to be an interesting introductory book to Hubbard's thought and rhetoric, and it is studied for inspiration by Scientologists.

The Problems at Work (1956b/1989) is a self-help book, written by Hubbard on board the ocean liner *Queen Elisabeth* as he was on his way to England for the London Congress in October 1956. At that time Hubbard had realized that practical problems prevented many auditors from having success, and so he wrote this book as a practical tool providing Scientology principles on handling such issues as efficiency, communication, exhaustion, injury at work, and how to get a job and keep it. The book is considered a basic book and can be studied at any level of the Bridge.

Scientology 0–8: The Book of Basics (1970/1989) is a compilation of technical data first printed in 1970 and extended in 1976 and 1988. It includes all scales, codes, axioms, and basic principles such as the original axioms of Dianetics, the newer axioms of Dianetics, the axioms of Scientology, and the *Factors.*[39] The number 0 refers to a preclear's present state and the number 8 to the eighth dynamic, infinity; 0–8 refers to how the techniques will increase the awareness of the individual from zero to infinity. It is studied at *Grade III Freedom Release.*

The Basic Scientology Picture Book (1971b/1997) is based on the works of Hubbard and comprises, in text and pictures, the basic principles of Scientology such as the cycle of action, the conditions of existence (be, do, and have), the eight dynamics, ARC triangle, and the principles of auditing. It is used as an introductory book for newcomers and is, as such, part of the basic material.

Clear Body, Clear Mind: The Effective Purification Program (1990) is a compilation of material that Hubbard wrote on the effects of drugs and chemicals from the 1960s. The Purification Program was released in 1979 under the name the Sweat Program, and in Scientology it is considered the only effective tool in recovering from drug abuse or other kinds of pollutants that, according to Hubbard, reside in the fatty tissue in the body and cause long-term physical, mental, and spiritual effects. The book also contains the different practical steps out of these barriers. The book is studied as part of the Purification Rundown, the first step on the Bridge.

Purification: An Illustrated Answer to Drugs (1984) demonstrates in text and pictures how drugs and chemicals affect the body, mind, and spirit of the individual, and illustrates how these problems, including long-term effects, can be dealt with. The book is a part of the Purification Rundown.

All About Radiation (1957/1989) was published in May 1957 and, according to Scientology, written by Hubbard in cooperation with a medical doctor.[40] It was Hubbard's response to the increasing fear of an atomic blast and nuclear radiation that existed in the 1950s. According to this book, most of the effects can be handled through participation in the Purification Rundown (and the book is used at this level of the Bridge) and through the correct doses of niacin.[41]

Scientology 8–8008[42] (1952a/1989) was published in December 1952 and presented as a textbook at the opening of the Philadelphia Doctorate Course. From April 1953 to 1956 Hubbard added five chapters as he developed his ideas on *theta*, the life force. The book contains an extensive explanation of Hubbard's ideas on how the individual, as a spiritual being, can restore his or her capacities to be *at cause* in this universe. It extends the explanation of the *theta-MEST theory*, first introduced in *Science of Survival* in 1951 and connects this theory to his ideas on ARC, the cycles of action, and the different universes and the individual's relations to these fields. Hubbard goes on to explain *Postulate Processing*,[43] *Creative Processing*,[44] the *Six Levels of Processing*,[45] and *Games Processing*.[46] The book is studied as part of the level *Clear*, the first major salvational step on the Bridge.

Scientology 8–80[47] (1952c/1989) was based on an earlier manuscript, *Scientology 88*, and complements *Scientology: A History of Man* (see below) on a very technical level. According to Hubbard's ideas, the human spirit, the thetan, uses simple flows, explosions, implosions, and retractor waves when he[48] deals with the physical universe, but these phenomena can also affect him harmfully. In this book Hubbard presents what is considered to be a very complete description of what a thetan is and how he can be rehabilitated. The book is a part of the level Clear and is considered vital for everybody who wants to proceed to the OT levels.

Scientology: A History of Man (1952b/1989) was a result of Hubbard's idea of the *whole track* developed in late 1951. Whole track is an extension of the time track, introduced in early Dianetics. It originally referred to the recordings of mental and physical traumas in a person's life from conception to death. Whole track is two time tracks combined. The first is the physical memory line (the *genetic entity*, or *GE*), and the second is all the mental and spiritual memory parts of the thetan, the individual spirit, including all of the incarnations he has been through during the last sixty trillion years. All of these memory parts and all of the physical pain throughout evolutionary history are aberrative to the individual[49] and must be audited. In the book Hubbard unfolds the most mythological narrative broadly available in Scientology on the trappings of the thetans, the principal aberrative incidents in evolutionary history, and the relationship between a thetan and his body.[50] The mythological narratives were fundamental in the development of the OT levels. The book is studied at the level Clear.

The Creation of Human Ability (1955c/1989) was first published in its present form in April 1955 after some additions to the first limited edition, titled *Scientology Auditor's Handbook,* presented by Hubbard at the closure of the 7th American ACC in Phoenix, Arizona. The subject of the book is how the individual is enslaved by the physical universe and how this same individual can regain his natural abilities through different auditing techniques. Technically speaking, the book contains several specific techniques such as *SOP 8-D* and *Short 8.*[51] The book is applied at the level *Grade IV Ability Release.*

In *How to Live though an Executive* (1953/1989) Hubbard presented the first book on business management, later developed into a full management technology[52] in accordance with which Scientology is organized and on the basis of which courses are offered to business organizations. The book contains the organization's communication system and can be studied at any level of the Bridge.

Introduction to Scientology Ethics (1968/1989) was first published at Saint Hill and later, in 1988, released with Hubbard's additions on the ethics technology. The book contains all principles of ethics and justice that are to be applied by the individual in everyday life and within Scientology. If not applied, the individual will achieve no wins in his or her life and if not applied in the organization, Scientology and Dianetics will not succeed. The book contains an overview presentation of the Scientology Organizing Board and is studied at the level *Grade II Relief Release.* It is also one of the fundamentals of all Scientology organizing.

Have You Lived before This Life? (1960/1989) was first published in 1960 and it is made up of forty-one case histories of preclears audited on a new engram-running technique at the Fifth London Advanced Clinical Course in October and November 1958. The expanded 1977 version contained additional articles by Hubbard, for example, on the subject of death. The book is considered a documentation of what happens after death and on the effects of past lives on the present existence. It is studied at the level *New Era Dianetics (NED),* which is one of two present routes to the state Clear.

In addition to these basic books, I want to present seven other books because they can throw light on Scientological theory and practice and Scientological self-understanding and representations.

The Scientology Handbook (CSI 1994) is based on the works of L. Ron Hubbard and includes an introduction to different subjects related to the practice of Scientology and the organization, such as *assists,* different actions of healing and comforting injured or hurting persons, and on the ethics and organizational affairs in the organization and so forth. *The Scientology Handbook* can be studied at any level of the Bridge, but it is not considered a part of the soteriological system.

The same can be said about *What Is Scientology?* (*WIS* 1992). This book, too, is a compilation based on the works of L. Ron Hubbard. It was written to introduce the religious philosophy and practice and to present different kinds of material and activities conducted by the Church and to L. Ron Hubbard. When first published, it was distributed by the Church to libraries, educational institutions, politicians, and so forth in order to present Dianetics and Scientology to a broader audience.

E-Meter Essentials (1961/1988) was written and published by Hubbard in 1961 and contains all of the basic principles and skills of operating an E-Meter.[53] The book explains, on a very fundamental level, how the mind works when preclear is asked to think of something and how this is registered by the meter. It also covers a technical introduction to the meter and to the sixteen main needle reactions.[54] The book is studied at the level of Clear.

The Book of E-Meter Drills (1965b/1997) is a compilation of Hubbard's writings. It was revised in 1988 after the appearance of the new Hubbard Professional Mark Super VII E-Meter.[55] It provides standard drills for the auditor to get well trained in the operation of the meter in any situation, from basic metering to track dating. The book is used at the level Clear.

Introducing the E-Meter (1966/1988) was compiled under the direction of Hubbard in 1966 and revised in 1988. The book provides technical skills in setting up the meter before a session, how to check the meter's efficiency, how to operate the tone arm, and read the needle. The book is used at the level Clear.

Understanding the E-Meter (1982/1989) was compiled and published in 1982 to provide the auditor with a more detailed understanding of the interrelations between the thetan and the body, the thetan and electrical charge, and how to understand the E-Meter in relation to these factors. The book is used at the level *Grade 0 Communications Release*.

The books by L. Ron Hubbard, as presented above, all deal with one or several aspects of the philosophy and practice of Scientology. As such, they are, of course, a main source of information for research purposes. Each aspect is dealt with in a rather detailed fashion and provides an insight in a single class of representations made at a certain point in the developmental history of the system. However, their detail is not solely advantageous because it is easy to get wrapped up in all the detail, losing an overview and broader perspective.

Video Recordings of the Major Annual Events

The video recordings of the two major annual events in Scientology, that is, "The L. Ron Hubbard Birthday Celebration Event" (in short, the Birthday Event) held on March 13, and "The May 9th Event" (the anniversary of the first publishing of *DMSMH*) from 1986 and forward, are excellent source material if one wants to keep updated on the redescriptions of practices, Church structuring and restructuring, Church rhetoric, new campaigns, key figures, changing key issues, and so forth.

Both events are celebrated by Scientologists all over the world; however, on the actual dates the events have been celebrated most years at Flag Landbase, Scientology's headquarters in Clearwater, Florida. The central celebration at Flag is videotaped and then distributed to every single Scientology organizational unit in the world, and the following weekend the video provides the core of the celebration at individual Scientology organizations worldwide. Besides celebrating L. Ron Hubbard and his works, both events are a celebration of Scientology and Scientologists and, ultimately, of individual and group efforts and expansion.

Both events display a similar dramaturgy in composition. A typical event will have the following structure: (1) welcome address by RTC chairman of the board, David Miscavige, including a presentation of, and a special welcome to, new countries and new organizations in the Church hierarchy; (2) expansion news presented by a highly positioned Scientologist, including the worldwide dissemination of Dianetics and Scientology (new initiatives, etc.) and some statistics on individual expansion on the Bridge; (3) a special presentation, usually bringing focus and attention to a single or a few aspects of what are considered Hubbard's contributions to the world and often presenting material not released beforehand; (4) the Birthday Game, presented by executive director of CSI, Guillaume Lesèvre, including the announcement of the winners in each category;[56] and (5) special release presented by David Miscavige, which might be a new translation initiative taken by RTC,[57] new materials released on the Internet, new technical training issues, and so forth. After the formal program there will be a buffet and jazz music in the garden of Ford Harrison.[58]

The following weekend, after the tape has been played for Scientology organizations in the rest of the world, there will usually be spectacular birthday cakes and informal conversation. Besides the formal program, the events play a social role, because many Scientologists do not see each other that often because they come to their organization for training and auditing at different times. The social aspect therefore has the character of old friends meeting and "hanging out."

NOTES

1. *Freewinds* is the ship where the highest levels of training and auditing are obtained.

2. The Ron Mags are a special kind of magazine introducing all aspects of the claimed skills of the founder. I have analyzed these magazines in context in Christensen 2005.

3. In fact, this is the actual claim of anthropologist and psychologist Harriet Whitehead (1987), whose theory on the acquisition of religious competence in Scientology, according to the Piagetian ideas of cognitive development, focuses on how Scientologists acquire increased competence in correlation to each step on the Bridge. See Refslund Christensen, in press, for a brief discussion of this hypothesis.

4. Boyer discusses the idea of *empty notions* in Boyer 1990.

5. According to Carl Helt from the juridical department of Church of Scientology International, this registration was effectuated in 1982. I give a presentation of RTC and its role in Scientology in Christensen 1999.

6. HCO stands for Hubbard Communication Office.

7. In 1959 Hubbard purchased Saint Hill Manor in East Grinstead, Sussex, England, and moved Hubbard Communications Office Worldwide and himself to this manor. Saint Hill was Hubbard's home and Scientology's center for a number of years and is still in the Church's possession.

8. I analyze this aspect at length, including the role of RTC, the application of *standard technology,* and keeping Scientology working, in Christensen 1999 and 2005.

9. Among these, Mr. Lymon Spurlock, RTC, who has shared valuable aspects of his experiences and reflections with me.

10. For a full understanding of the *Keeping Scientology Working* series, see TB, Subject Volume 2: 3–90, in which *KSW* series 1–33 are described.

11. I have analyzed this construction of Hubbard as related to the hagiographic material and the idea of *standard technology* with a focus on the legitimating potential in Christensen 1999 and 2005.

12. One explanation of this is found in TB, Subject Volume 2: 15 f.

13. The development of New Era Dianetics in 1978 led to revisions of earlier technical materials on Dianetics from 1969; see Technical Bulletins from 1969.

14. *Theta* denotes the immortal life force; *whole track* denotes a person's whole existence in the universe throughout all incarnations the person has been through; *thetan* denotes the individual as an immortal spiritual being (and is always referred to as *he*); *MEST* stands for *m*atter, *e*nergy, *s*pace, and *t*ime and denotes the physical universe as well as the material substance.

15. The term *dynamics* denotes the subdivisions of the primary survival dynamic.

16. A tendency very conspicuous in the hagiographic production. For an analysis of this aspect, see Christensen 1999 and 2005.

17. This can also be said of the rhetorics used in regard to the esoteric OT materials that make up the upper part of the Bridge. According to the Church, eight of these have been released, whereas the levels 9–15 are said to have been produced by Hubbard but they cannot be released until a certain numbers of Scientologists are ready for them and a certain number of organizations reach the size of Saint Hill. According to one of my informants, as many as thirty-four OT levels have been prepared by Hubbard. This esoteric factor related to RTC's control of trademarks and service marks again stresses the actual power of RTC.

18. The book is found in the references under the title *Dianetics: The Evolution of a Science,* 1955a.

19. Please note that this presentation is written in third person but ended by "L. Ron Hubbard. Founder."

20. See Wallis 1976: 21 ff. for an analysis of Hubbard's collaborations with Dr. Winther. See also Winther 1951.

21. Will Durant, the originator of *general semantics,* a philosophical idea about how meaning and form are related in words, was mentioned in an "Associate Newsletter," May 1953, as one of the writers worth studying as a supplement to the Hubbard materials (TB, vol. 2: 71).

22. This is not done blindly. I attempted in my thesis to make a historic-critical construction of the early formative years (Christensen 1994). My text studies, and the fieldwork I have carried out in the Church on and off since 1991, have convinced me that a historic-critical approach is not the right path to choose in that the historical correctness is of no importance to the Church or its individuals. For a full analysis of the Church's representations of its theological development, see Christensen 1999.

23. HCOTBs are Hubbard Communications Office Technical Bulletins.

24. Hubbard died in 1986, but his articles continued to be published for some years hereafter; see TB, vol. 13.

25. In Scientology there is a distinction made between *auditors,* individuals that are being trained to perform the ritual practice *auditing,* and *publics,* people who receive auditing but have not chosen to get trained to perform it themselves. Within the

Scientological hierarchy, auditors are superior because they are considered more active in achieving the goals of Scientology, *Clearing the Planet*.

26. According to the Church, some books may be studied at various points (CSI 1993b: colophon). See also the presentations of each Hubbard book below.

27. A *preclear*, or just *pc*, originally denoted a person who was not Clear. In Scientology today the term is also used for any person receiving Dianetics or Scientology auditing.

28. The Sea Organization (in short, *Sea Org*) was formed by Hubbard in 1967 and is the elite group of highly dedicated Scientologists. For a full presentation, see, for example, *Management Dictionary*: 464.

29. The term *original form* refers to Dianetics theory and practice *before* it was integrated in the Scientological soteriology. I do *not* refer to the book being published today in its original form.

30. At this time, the time track is the engrams (mental traumas) of this lifetime as recorded in the *memory banks*.

31. Chief editor John W. Campbell got interested in Hubbard's ideas on the mind in the late 1940s and played a part in the development of Dianetics. As the editor of one of the most esteemed science fiction magazines at that time, he was part of an influential network of publishing, and his introduction of Hubbard's ideas in the May 1950 volume might have played an important legitimizing role. Second, it was he who introduced Hubbard to Dr. Joseph A. Winther, who seems to have assisted Hubbard in the development and promotion of the first publications on Dianetics. For analyses on the cooperation of Hubbard, Winther, and Campbell, see Wallis 1976: 22 ff.; Whitehead 1974: 572 f.; and Whitehead 1987: 55 ff. For an account of Hubbard's science fiction and fantasy production, see Day 1979. See also Winther 1951.

32. It has not been possible to confirm this early usage of the term *scientology* outside the Church. According to Scientology, it was retitled *Abnormal Dianetics* when it was offered to the medical and psychiatric professions in early 1948.

33. Later known as the *Tone Scale*.

34. Today, auditing over the level of *Auditor Course, Part I*, is solo auditing, in which the person involved is both object and performer on the E-Meter at the same time. The Church promotes the idea of self-auditing in *Self Analysis* in this way: "This is not 'self-auditing.' Anyone who gets this book and follows the procedure, is in fact being processed by Ron himself" (CSI 1993b: 12). In Christensen 1999, I demonstrate that Hubbard is always present in an auditing session and, in fact, that it might be asked whether or not he is always the performer of the practice by means of representations made during session.

35. I have argued that this theory marks the beginning of the religious era in Hubbard's ideas, and that it is the foundation of the religious ideas of Scientology (Christensen 1994: 68 ff.), and that the theory is the first religious idea to intensify Dianetics (Christensen 1999).

36. At that time, there were seven dynamics: (1) self, (2) sex/family, (3) group, (4) mankind, (5) animal, (6) universe, and (7) spiritual dynamic. Eventually an eighth was added: (8) infinity or the highest being.

37. For an analysis, see Christensen 1994: 78 f.

38. The number thirty refers to the update version from 1989.

39. The Factors comprise a narrative on how the conditions of man as a spiritual being came into being and how things went wrong (see, e.g., Hubbard 1970/1989: 99 f.). For an analysis, see Christensen 1997a: 100 ff.; Christensen 1999.

40. The name of the doctor remains unknown in the written material.

41. Niacin was recommended repetitively by Hubbard for its positive influence on processing; see, for instance, TB, vol. VII: 740; IX: 595.

42. The numbers in this title refer to raising the individual to infinity (the eighth dynamic) by reducing the influence from the physical universe from infinity (eight) to zero and building the individual's universe from zero to infinity (eight) (TD: 371).

43. A type of processing that increases the individual's awareness of his ability to make postulates and change these as he wishes.

44. A type of processing that helps the preclear drill his ability to *mock up* the physical universe and things in it. A *mock-up* is a thing, created by the thetan, as he postulates that it is there.

45. A type of processing in six levels, each dealing with a certain aspect of the individual's relation to the physical universe and the mock-ups of it.

46. A type of processing that helps the preclear to deal with life as a game, including the communication with others.

47. The numbers in this title were explained by Hubbard as follows: "The '8–8' stands for 'infinity-infinity' upright, the '0' represents the static, theta" (CIS 1993b: 32).

48. The *thetan* is always referred to as *he*.

49. I have analyzed this extension of the time track into whole track in Refslund Christensen 1994: 84 f. and developed my arguments and extend the analysis in Christensen 1999.

50. I have argued that with *Scientology: A History of Man*, Hubbard transcended the goals of Dianetics and presented the new soteriology, Christensen, 1999.

51. SOP 8-D is elaborated on in TB, vol. 2: 329 ff., whereas information on Short 8 is found in TB, vol. 2: 73 ff.

52. I have not dealt with Hubbard's management technology in any of my work. It could be interesting, however, to make parallel analyses of Dianetics and Scientology theory and practice and the application of these fields to the Hubbard management technology.

53. The E-Meter was introduced by Hubbard in June 1952 as a technical device utilized in auditing for measuring different kinds of emotions and thoughts. The E-Meter is used today in all auditing. I have argued that the E-Meter is a substitute for Hubbard in auditing sessions; see Christensen 1999 and.

54. The movements of the meter are what is read by the auditor, and the sixteen different needle movements all indicate different things about the case.

55. The E-Meter type used today is the Mark VII Super Quantum. For a brief history of the meters, see *May 9th Event* 1996 (video recording).

56. The Birthday Game is a game in honor of Hubbard, the aim of which is that each organizational unit in the world produces as much expansion as possible. Rules of the Birthday Game can be found in CSI 1998b. Please note that point 4 is only relevant in the Birthday Event. Points 2–4 can be switched in regard to sequence of the single elements.

57. It is an ultimate goal of the Church to be able to provide all materials in all languages.

58. Ford Harrison is the 1920s hotel where Flag Landbase, Clearwater, is situated.

BIBLIOGRAPHY

The books are sequenced according to the year of the first copy printed. The year placed after each publication is the year I have used in my analysis.

Books by L. Ron Hubbard

Hubbard, L. Ron. 1950. *Dianetics. The Modern Science of Mental Health*. New Era Publications International, Aps., Copenhagen, 1989.

———. 1951a. *The Dynamics of Life*. New Era Publications International, Aps., Copenhagen, 1989.

———. 1951b. *Science of Survival: Prediction of Human Behavior*. New Era Publications International, Aps., Copenhagen, 1989.

———. 1951c. *Self Analysis*. New Era Publications International, Aps., Copenhagen, 1989.

———. 1951d. *Advanced Procedures and Axioms*. New Era Publications International, Aps., Copenhagen, 1989.

———. 1951e. *Handbook for Preclears*. New Era Publications International, Aps., Copenhagen, 1989.

———. 1951f. *Child Dianetics*. New Era Publications International, Aps., Copenhagen, 1989. (Compilation based on Hubbard's writing on the issue).

———. 1952a. *Scientology 8–8008*. New Era Publications International, Aps., Copenhagen, 1989.

———. 1952b. *Scientology: A History of Man*. New Era Publications International, Aps., Copenhagen, 1989.

———. 1952c. *Scientology 8–80: The Discovery and Increase of Life Energy in the Genus Homo Sapiens*. Scientology Publications Organization, Copenhagen, 1979.

———. 1953. *How to Live though an Executive*. New Era Publications International, Aps., Copenhagen, 1989.

———. 1955a. *Dianetics: The Evolution of a Science*. New Era Publications International, Aps., Copenhagen, 1989.

———. 1955b. *Dianetics 55! A Guide to Effective Communication*. New Era Publications International, Aps., Copenhagen, 1989.

———. 1955c. *The Creation of Human Ability*. New Era Publications International, Aps., Copenhagen, 1989.

———. 1955d. *Notes on the Lectures*. New Era Publications International, Aps., Copenhagen, 1989.

———. 1956a. *Scientology: The Fundamentals of Thought*. New Era Publications International, Aps., Copenhagen, 1989.

———. 1956b. *The Problems at Work*. New Era Publications International, Aps., Copenhagen, 1989.

———. 1957. *All about Radiation*. New Era Publications International, Aps., Copenhagen, 1989.

———. 1960. *Have You Lived before This Life?* New Era Publications International, Aps., Copenhagen, 1989.

———. 1961. *E-Meter Essentials*. New Era Publications International, Aps., Copenhagen, 1988.

———. 1965a. *A New Slant on Life*. New Era Publications International, Aps., Copenhagen, 1989.

———. 1965b. *The Book of E-Meter Drills*. New Era Publications International, Aps., Copenhagen, 1997. (Compilation based on Hubbard's writings on the issue.)

———. 1966. *Introducing the E-Meter*. New Era Publications International, Aps., Copenhagen, 1988. (Compilation based on Hubbard's writing on the issue.)

———. 1968a. *Introduction to Scientology Ethics*. New Era Publications International, Aps., Copenhagen, 1989.

———. 1968b. *The Phoenix Lectures*. The Publications Organization Worldwide, Los Angeles.

————. 1970a. *Scientology 0–8: The Book of Basics*. New Era Publications International, Aps., Copenhagen, 1989.

————. 1970b. *The Background and Ceremonies of the Church of Scientology Worldwide*. Church of Scientology Worldwide, Los Angeles.

————. 1971a. *The Basic Dianetics Picture Book*. New Era Publications International, Aps., Copenhagen, 1991.

————. 1971b. *The Basic Scientology Picture Book*. New Era Publications International, Aps., Copenhagen, 1997.

————. 1982. *Understanding the E-Meter*. New Era Publications International, Aps., Copenhagen, 1988. (Compilation based on Hubbard's writings on the issue.)

————. 1984. *Purification: An Illustrated Answer to Drugs*. New Era Publications International, Aps., Copenhagen.

————. 1990. *Clear Body, Clear Mind: The Effective Purification Program*. New Era Publications International, Aps., Copenhagen. (Compilation based on Hubbard's writings on the issue.)

The Technical Bulletins of Dianetics and Scientology (TB). AOSH DK Publications Department A/S, Copenhagen, 1976. Volumes 1–12. (Old edition of the Technical Bulletins.)

The Technical Bulletins of Dianetics and Scientology (TB). New Era Publications International, Copenhagen, 1991. (New edition of the Technical Bulletins.)

Dianetics and Scientology Technical Dictionary (TD). New Era Publications International, Copenhagen, 1983.

Knowingness: Quotations from the Works of L. Ron Hubbard, Vol. I. Bridge Publications Inc., Los Angeles, 1991.

Knowingness: The Universal Solvent, Quotations from the Works of L. Ron Hubbard, Vol. I. Bridge Publications Inc., Los Angeles, 1991.

Modern Management Technology Defined: Hubbard Dictionary of Administration and Management. New Era Publications International, Copenhagen, 1991.

Other Materials

Books

What Is Scientology? (WiS 1992). New Era Publications International, Copenhagen, 1992. (Compiled by LRH Book Compilations staff of the Church of Scientology International.)

The Scientology Handbook (CSI 1994). New Era Publications International, Copenhagen, 1994. (Compiled by LRH Book Compilations staff of the Church of Scientology International.)

Images of a Lifetime: A Photographic Biography. New Era Publications International, Copenhagen, 1996.

The Ron Series

L. Ron Hubbard: A Profile. L. Ron Hubbard Library, Los Angeles, 1995.

Ron. Letters and Journals: Early Years of Adventure. L. Ron Hubbard Library, Los Angeles, 1997.

Ron. Letters and Journals: Literary Correspondence, L. Ron Hubbard Library, Los Angeles, 1997.

Ron. Letters and Journals: The Dianetic Letters. L. Ron Hubbard Library, Los Angeles, 1997.

Ron. The Adventurer/Explorer: Daring Deeds and Unknown Realms. L. Ron Hubbard Library, Los Angeles, 1996.

Ron. The Artist: Art & Philosophy. L. Ron Hubbard Library, Los Angeles, 1998.

Ron. The Auditor: From Research to Application. L. Ron Hubbard Library, Los Angeles, 1991.

Ron. The Humanitarian: Rehabilitation of a Drugged Society. L. Ron Hubbard Library, Los Angeles, 1996.

Ron. The Humanitarian: The Educator. L. Ron Hubbard Library, Los Angeles, 1996.

Ron. The Humanitarian: Freedom Fighter, Articles and Essays. L. Ron Hubbard Library, Los Angeles, 1997.

Ron. The Humanitarian: The Road to Self-Respect. L. Ron Hubbard Library, Los Angeles, 1995.

Ron. The Master Mariner, Issue I: Sea Captain. L. Ron Hubbard Library, Los Angeles, 1991.

Ron. The Master Mariner, Issue II: Yachtsman. L. Ron Hubbard Library, Los Angeles, 1994.

Ron. The Music Maker. L. Ron Hubbard Library, Los Angeles, 1995.

Ron. The Philosopher: Rediscovery of the Human Soul. L. Ron Hubbard Library, Los Angeles, 1996.

Ron. The Philosopher, Issue I: The Quest for Truth. L. Ron Hubbard Library, Los Angeles, 1991.

Ron. The Philosopher, Issue II: The Spirit of Man. L. Ron Hubbard Library, Los Angeles, 1991.

Ron. The Poet/Lyricist. L. Ron Hubbard Library, Los Angeles, 1996.

Ron. The Writer: The Shaping of Popular Fiction. L. Ron Hubbard Library, Los Angeles, 1997.

Ron. The Writer: Issue I, The Legend Begins. L. Ron Hubbard Library, Los Angeles, 1989.

Ron. The Writer: Issue II, Changing a Genre. L. Ron Hubbard Library, Los Angeles, 1992.

Videos

L. Ron Hubbard Birthday Event. 1986–forward. Golden Era Productions, Los Angeles.

May 9th Event. 1986–forward. Golden Era Productions, Los Angeles.

The Classification, Gradation and Awareness Chart of Levels and Certificates. Lecture by L. Ron Hubbard, Sept. 9, 1965, at Saint Hill Special Briefing Course (CSI 1965).

Additional Materials

L. Ron Hubbard: A Chronicle of Research. New Era Publications International, Los Angeles, 1993 (CSI 1993a).

The Bridge of Knowledge: Books Containing Ron's Legacy of the Tech. New Era Publications International, Los Angeles, 1993 (CSI 1993b).

Religious Technology Center. New Era Publications International, Los Angeles, 1993 (RTC 1993).

Ron: Portraits of His Life. New Era Publications International, Los Angeles, 1998 (CSI 1998a).

LRH Birthday Game 1998/99: Rules and Tips. Bridge Publications International, Los Angeles, 1998 (CSI 1998b).

Scientology News Magazine, Issue 2. Bridge Publications, Los Angeles, 1996.

Research Literature

Boyer, Pascal. 1990. *Tradition as Truth and Communication: A Cognitive Description of Traditional Discourse.* Cambridge University Press, Cambridge.

———. 1994a. *The Naturalness of Religious Ideas: A Cognitive Theory of Religion*. University of California Press, Berkeley.

———. 1994b. "Cognitive Constraints on Cultural Representations: Natural Ontologies and Religious Ideas" in Hirschfeld, Lawrence A. and Susan A. Gelman (eds.), *Mapping the Mind: Domain Specificity in Cognition and Culture*. Cambridge University Press, New York.

Christensen, Dorthe Refslund. 1994. *Fra Terapi til Religion. En religionshistorisk analyse af centrale begreber i henholdsvis Dianetics og Scientology med særligt henblik på forskellene i diskurs og mål*. Department for the Study of Religion, Aarhus University.

———. 1997a. *Scientology. Fra Terapi til Religion*. Gyldendal, Copenhagen.

———. 1997b. *Scientology. En ny religion*. Forlaget Munksgaard, Copenhagen.

———. 1997c. "Legenden om L. Ron Hubbard—et eksempel på en moderne hagiografi. Om konstruktionen af et mytologisk livsforløb og brugen af det i Scientology" i *CHAOS, dansk-norsk tidsskrift for religionshistorie*, nr. 28.

———. 1999. *Rethinking Scientology. Cognition and Representation in Religion, Therapy, and Soteriology*. [PUBLISHING CO., CITY].

———. 2002. "Church of Scientology," in Melton, J. Gordon & Martin Baumann (eds.), *Religions of the World. A Comprehensive Encyclopedia of Beliefs and Practices*. ABC Clio, Santa Barbara, Calif., pp. 331–332.

———. 2005. "Inventing L. Ron Hubbard: On the Construction and Maintenance of the hagiographic Mythology on Scientology's Founder," in Lewis, Jim, and Jesper Aagaard Pedersen (eds.), *Controversial New Religions*. Oxford University Press, Oxford, pp. 227–259.

Day, Donald B. (ed.). 1979. *Index to the Science Fiction Magazines 1926–1950*. Revised edition. G. K. Hall & Co, Boston.

Wallis, Roy. 1976. *The Road to Total Freedom: A Sociological Analysis*. Heinemann Educational Books Ltd., London.

———. 1986. "The Social Construction of Charisma" in Wallis, Roy, and Steve Bruce, *Sociological Theory, Religion and Collective Action*. Queens University, Belfast: 129–154.

Whitehead, Harriet. 1974. "Reasonably Fantastic: Some Perspectives on Scientology, Science Fiction and Occultism" in Zaretsky, Irving I., and Mark P. Leone (eds.), *Religious Movements in Contemporary America*. Princeton University Press, Princeton, N.J., pp. 547–587.

———. 1987. *Renunciation and Reformulation: A Study of Conversion in an American Sect*. Cornell University Press, Ithaca, N.Y.

Winther, Joseph A. 1951. *A Doctor's Report on Dianetics: Theory and Therapy*. Julian Press, New York.

PART VIII

Appendix

22

Pastoral Care and September 11: Scientology's Nontraditional Religious Contribution

Carole M. Cusack and Justine Digance

Maintaining a presence at Ground Zero was a complex process, in that no religious group could set up there to provide pastoral care unless recognized by the authorities, city, state, and federal. These groups were overwhelmingly Christian churches, Catholic and Protestant. The one exception was the Church of Scientology, which is perhaps the quintessentially modern American religion, founded by L. Ron Hubbard (Bednarowski, 1995). Scientology shares certain features with New Age religions, such as the desire to interpret September 11 as an event that should result in peace, not war, and a hierarchical organizational structure resembling initiatory groups within the Western esoteric trajectory (Martin, 1989). However, in many ways it is quite different from New Age religion, having an institutional structure and a definite, articulated belief system.

   Scientology was the only nontraditional religion to provide pastoral care at Ground Zero. This unique status could be explained by the extensive network of powerful members the Church of Scientology possesses (show business celebrities and politicians being the most visible). It could also be explained by the fact that the Church

As noted in the acknowledgments, this appendix was originally a section in Carole M. Cusack and Justine Digance's article, "Religious, Spiritual, Secular: Some American Responses to September 11," which was published in the *Australian Religious Studies Review* 16:2 (Spring 2003). The editor of the current volume has slightly altered the original version of this section by dropping or rewording references to other sections, and by converting the spelling and punctuation into the conventions of American English.

   The authors would like to thank members of the Church of Scientology for providing some of the material that is used in this chapter.

of Scientology, despite a controversial history, has become powerfully involved in corporate motivational and charitable activities in America, often providing these secularized services to government agencies (Martin, 1989; Bednarowski, 1995).[1]

Scientology has developed a Volunteer Minister Program, first envisaged by Hubbard in 1973 and fleshed out in 1976. This program is unique in that it is open to anyone. That is, it is an example of the more secularized services that Scientology provides generally to the community rather than only to its members, recalling the continuum of contributions referred to above. Although not precisely trained counselors, Volunteer Ministers provide help in times of need, which may include counseling-type duties. They are also trained in performing a specifically Scientological therapy: Assists (for example, a Contact Assist or a Touch Assist). These are actions "undertaken to help a person confront physical difficulties" (CSI, 1994: 3). Assists may be administered to aid people in "periods of intense emotional shock" (CSI, 1994: 7). They thus resemble the traditional Christian practice of "laying on hands."

Scientology Volunteer Ministers arrived at Ground Zero within hours of the Twin Towers' collapse. Like Christian pastors, the Ministers' role was to counsel and support the workers who were engaged first in rescuing survivors, then in clearing away rubble and bodies over a period of months. Gail Armstrong, editor of Scientology's *Freedom* magazine, condemned the attackers: "[It is the] continuing tragedy of our times that fellow human beings can be twisted into killers who believe their acts of hatred, revenge, and cowardly acts of murder and suicide are justified" but quickly shifted focus to the courage and determination showed by the relief workers, which caused "the one result that the authors of destruction did not want; a stronger and united force for good, bound by that courage and determination to defend what is honorable and decent, a people joined and committed to the preservation of freedom for all" (http://www.freedommag.org/english/press/page03.htm).

Scientology is a minority religion that has created, and sought strenuously to maintain, strong ties with other minority religions, which demonstrates its deep understanding of the changed Western religious situation: secularization resulting in a varied religious climate, in which the traditional religion of the West, Christianity, retains its position while gradually losing authority (Wilson, 1995). Armstrong praises the efforts of the Red Cross and the Salvation Army, and extracts a theme of unity from what could have been a shattering experience (Armstrong, 2002). One unique feature of Scientology that remains to be noted is that it is the only nonconventional religion in the United States that was in a position to take a leading role alongside mainstream religions and secular charitable rescue workers.

In practical terms, the Volunteer Ministers, clad in distinctive and instantly identifiable yellow shirts, set up places where they could minister to rescue personnel who were stressed, drew up organizing charts, and undertook to provide food and water. All of these efforts might be classified as "secular," but what qualifies Scientology's contribution as nonconventionally religious is the practice of "assists." A Church of Scientology publication proudly asserts that the Volunteer Ministers provided something far more valuable, Scientology technology. Time after time, a fireman who'd lost a fellow firefighter in the tragedy would receive a special technique, called an "assist," to help him deal with his loss. Even though workers crawled over mountains of twisted steel, on no sleep, injuries were almost non-existent; and firefighters attributed it to assists received from the Volunteer Ministers. (CSI, 2001:8)

This is, of course, a biased source. However, it is interesting in that it demonstrates the Church's own self-understanding of its role at Ground Zero. Finally, Scientology shares with the New Age a belief in the perfectibility of humanity, but its approach is more rational and pragmatic. Thus, welfare work, rather than rituals, was performed on site.

NOTE

1. It has not been possible to discover precisely the way in which Scientology's Volunteer Minister Program was granted permission to undertake such a high-profile role in the response to September 11. There is, at present, no academic literature on the subject, and CSI publications tend not to supply details, but concentrate on the aspects of the successful outreach by the Church of Scientology and the garnering of positive publicity (e.g., CIS publications reproduce letters of thanks from the mayoral office, the emergency services, and so on).

REFERENCES

Armstrong, G. M. 2002. "A Message from the Editor." *Freedom* (July 2). CSI (Church of Scientology International).
Bednarowski, M. F. 1995. "The Church of Scientology: Lightning Rod for Cultural Boundary Conflicts." In *America's Alternative Religions*, ed. Timothy Miller, 385–392. Albany: State University of New York Press.
CSI (Church of Scientology International). 1994. *Assists for Illness and Injuries*. CSI.
CSI (Church of Scientology International). 2001. *The Volunteer minister Program*. CSI.
Martin, S. 1989. *Orthodox Heresy*. New York: St. Martin's Press.
Wilson, B. 1995. *Religious Toleration and Religious Diversity*. Santa Barbara: Institute for the Study of American Religion.

Index

Aberration, 21, 185, 200, 214, 417
Abgrall, Jean-Marie, 303, 305, 313
About, Nicholas, 307
Aetherius Society, 395
Alley, Kirstie, 389
Alliot-Marie, Michèle, 319
Alwall, Jonas, 339
American Family Foundation, 269
American Medical Association
    (AMA), 23
Amway, 97
Ananda Marga, 345
Anderson, Kevin, 349
Aniston, Jennifer, 402
Anti-Cult Movement (ACM). *See* also
    Cult Awareness Network (CAN)
    effect of the Guyard Report on, 301
    formation of, 270
    media coverage of, 274
    use of POW psychological
        literature, 271
Antisecte Movement, 298–300
Applied Scholastics Program
    barriers to learning, 98, 192–193,
        338, 397
    described, 397
    in Denmark, 155
ARC (Affinity, Reality,
    Communication)

breaks, 201
description, 95, 194
Archer, Ann, 9
Archer, Jeffrey, 393
Assists. *See* auditing
Atack, Jon, 369–371, 383,
Auditing
    "beingness," capacity for
        restoring, 42
    book one, 198
    changes in process of, 144, 215–216
    cost of, 191
    description of, 5, 425n25
    first published account of, 21
    first training materials for, 22
    levels of, 94, 191–192
    process of, 94, 95, 198–199, 412
    results of, 187
    techniques, specific, 187–189,
        198–199, 201–202
    training of, 5
    use of E-meter (*see* E-meter)
Australian Human Rights and Equal
    Opportunity Commission, 353
Australian Security Intelligence
    Organisation, 352

Baha'i, 347
Bainbridge, Sims, 56, 60–63, 68

Barrett, Justine, 109
Bauman, Zygmut, 104
Baxter, Erica, 389, 398, 402
Beckham, David, 393, 401
Beckham, Victoria, 401
Beliefs, common to all members, 111–112
Bellah, Robert, 83
"Bible of Scientology," 340
Blavatsky, Helena, 232–233
Bono, 393
Boy George, 397
Boyer, Pascal, 103, 109, 383, 385n29
Brard, Jean-Pierre, 315
Branch Davidians, 271, 274, 360n2
Brainwashing
    accusation of, 271
    civil suits against Scientology, 283
    criticisms of Scientology, 316, 339, 341
    cult description, 211
    dismissal of term, 113
    Picard Law of, 299
    Scientology proven innocent, 306
Bridge
    as precursor to paranormal abilities,
        235
    description of, 92, 107, 190, 396,
        412, 417
    international mission, 329–330
    relationship to world view, 108
Bridge to Total Freedom. See bridge
Bromley, David G., 270
Brubeck, Dave, 394
Brukert, Beth, 276
Buddhism
    Hubbard's knowledge of, 232–233
    Scientology's relationship to, 37,
        212, 233
Bush, George W., 315

Campbell, John W., 426n31
Caodaism, 347
Cartwright, Nancy, 404
Cebrano, Kate, 357, 389, 398, 402
Celebrity, 389–390
    and Christianity, 391
    and consumerism, 389–390
    construction of identity, 392
    followers of Hubbard, 394–395
    importance of in Scientology, 396
Celebrity Center Churches, 397

Centre de documentation, d'education
    et d'action contre les manipulations
    mentales (CCMM), 299
Ceremony
    functions of, 175–181
    funeral, 169
    ministers' ordination, 170
    naming, 169–170
    overview and importance of, 166–167
    Sunday Service, 168
    wedding, 168–169, 400
Children of God, 345
Christian conservative response to ACM,
    269
Christianity. See also Protestant
    Reformation
    as advantaged over NRMs, 395
    changes in original form, 74n4
    CoS in contrast to, 151, 218
    CoS mythology in relationship to, 92
    in contrast to CoS, 93
    saints as celebrities, 391
    therapy and, 213
    values worthy of honor, 391
Christian Science 123–127, 130–132,
    176–177, 183, 186, 336
Church of Jesus Christ of Latter-day
    Saints, 117–120, 122–129, 327, 332
Church of Satan, 397
Church Universal and Triumphant, 395
Citizens Commission on Human
    Rights, 337
Citizens Committee on Human Rights,
    357
Citizens Engaged in Freeing Minds, 269
Citizens Freedom Foundation, 269, 271
Clear
    changes in Scientology's
        understanding of, 214–215
    as parallel to Buddhist bodhi state, 212
    description, 5
    progression to state of, 92, 186, 218,
        366, 394
    status, evaluation of, 43
Closed source religious tradition, 61–62
Collins-Macchio, LaVerne, 276
Commission des Citoyens pour les Droits
    de l'Homme (CCDH), 314
Commission nationale de l'informatique
    et des libertés (CNIL), 308

Community of COS
  ceremony to support, 175
  growth of (*see* growth rates)
  in Denmark, 151–160
  individualist community, 143
  lack of, 145
Contractualism
  as atypical structure for religion, 86
  COS as a prophetic contractual
    organization, 84
  defined, 85
  in relationship to COS
    mythology, 93
  other religious groups using, 97
  types of relationships formed by, 86
Controversy
  Australia's response to, 24–25
  Britain's response to, 24–25
  court cases (*see* names of court cases)
  FDA raid, 6 24
  guardian's office, 7, 25
  IRS involvement with, 7, 24, 66–67
  summary of, 6–7
Cooper, Paulette, 25
Coordination des Associations et
    Particuliers pour la Liberté de
    Conscience (CAP), 306
Covenantalism, 84–86
Criminon, 97–98, 155, 338
Cruise, Suri, 400
Cruise, Tom, 3, 70, 132, 303, 319, 339,
    356–358, 389, 393, 398, 399, 400,
    401, 403, 404, 405
Cult Awareness Network (CAN)
  fiscal problems of, 276–279
  Jason Scott legal action against, 270
  relationship with media, 274, 359
  Scientology legal action against 6,
    270–272
  Scientology takeover of, 279, 397
Culture War, 269–272
Cyber-culture
  cyber-religion as form of, 45
  defined, 44
  versus traditional religion, 45

Davis, Sammy Jr., 397
Deprogramming
  defined, 270–271
  CAN as referral agent for, 278

ethical issues, 279–280
  failed effort at, 276–277
Deprogrammers
  CAN's referral to, 275–276
  failures of, 276
Dianetics
  as a foundational practice of CoS, 166
  as compared to classic utilitarianism,
    146–147
  as compared to psychoanalysis, 43
  as considered a science, 254
  differences in application of, 94
  in France, 297
  founding of, 5
  rationale for, 44
  transition to Scientology, 144, 213–215
*Dianetics: The Modern Science of Natural
    Health*
  anniversary of, 411
  as a "science of the mind," 394, 417
  popularity of, 87
  public reaction to, 21
  revisions, 415
Discordianism, 395
Dissemination Drill, 330
Divine Light Mission, 269
Dobkowski, Dbra, 276
Doherty, Pete, 393
Durkiem, Emile, 56–57, 65, 77–78, 257,
    285
Dynamics of Scientology, Eight, 395, 415,
    426n36

"E-Meter Case," 339, 423, 426n53
Eckankar, 347
Eddy, Mary Baker, 176, 183–185, 202, 218
Electropsychometer (E-meter)
  as new religious technology, 186
  description of physical features, 196
  description of use, 22, 94, 96, 196,
    201–202
Ellul, Jacques, 220
Emotion Tone, 194–195, 199
Engram
  bank, 185, 196
  basic, 418
  definition of, 5, 218
  description of, 90
  removal of, 394
  running, 418

Erhard, Werner, 36
Esotericism
   and New Age, 226, 435
   astral projection and Scientology, 234
   construction of myth and, 232
Exteriorizing, 234

The Family. *See* Children of God
Family of Love, 390
Fédération Européenne des Centres de
      Recherche et d'Information sur le
      Sectarisme (FECRIS), 341
Field Staff (FSM), 328
Franchise Promotion Musts, 328–329
Fouchereau, Bruno, 311
Föreningen Rädda Individen (FRI), 341
French, George, 303
Fresh, Doug E., 404
Frisk, Liselotte, 341

Galactic Federation, 396
Gardner, Gerald, 395
Garrison, Omar, 23
Giddens, Anthony, 104
Gnosticism, 218, 237, 255, 366
Golden Dawn, 43
Government interaction with CoS
   in foreign countries, 285–291, 351
   IRS, 24, 66–67, 287–289, 283, 292,
      294
Growth rates
   major world religions, 118
   of Scientology, 120, 149–150, 346
Guardians Office
   action in Clearwater, FL, 27
   controversy about, 7, 27
   disbanding of, 28
   establishment of, 25
   infiltration of government offices, 27
Guyard, Jacques, 299
Guyard report/list, 301–302, 307

Hagiologizing, 63
Hansen, Beck, 404
Hare Krishnas, 269, 397
Harrison, George, 397
Hassan, Steven, 274
Hayes, Isaac, 7, 9, 404
Heaven's Gate UFO cult, 271
Heelas, Paul, 104

Hegel, 221
Hein, Anton, 57
Hermetic Brotherhood of Luxor, 336
Hilton, Paris, 393
Hinduism, 395
Holmes, Katie, 389, 398
Hopkins, Emma Curtis, 183, 202
Hubbard, L. Ron
   as omnipresent in auditing, 426n34
   biographical information, 87, 184–185
   collaboration with Joseph A. Winther,
      415
   criminal investigation of, 300
   Crowley, connection to, 21, 31n10
   death of, 29
   goals for society, 395
   as Maitreya, 233
   published works (*see under* published
      works by L. Ron Hubbard)
   resignation of administrative duties,
      25, 87
   retreat from public life, 325–326
   soteriological system in the writing of,
      106
   Stephen Kent on, 327
Heaven's Gate, 271, 274
Hunter, James, 83
Hymn of Asia
   aspirations of the Buddha, 236
   Hubbard claims to be Maitreya, 134,
      233, 250

International Society for Krishna
      Consciousness. *See* Hare Krishnas

James, William, 185, 203, 213
Jentzsch, Heber, 22, 66, 77, 301
Jehovah's Witnesses, 123–127, 336, 352
Johansson, Scarlett, 403
Jolie, Angelina, 393, 402–403
Jospin, Lionel, 304
Jung, Carl, 391

Kabbalah Centers, 397
Kaufmann, Robert, 16, 25,
Kent, Stephen A., 57–59, 72–75, 241,
      253, 327
Kelly, Galen, 276
Khan, Chaka, 404
Kidman, Nicole, 400

King, George, 395
Kisser, Cynthia, 274–275
Koresh, David, 360n2
KPMG Peat Marwick, 275
Kula Shaker, 397

Landa, Shirley, 278
La Vey, Anton, 397
LeBlanc, Benjamin-Hugo, 311
Lennon, John, 401
Lewis, Geoffrey, 402
Lewis, Juliette, 389, 398, 401
Love, Courtney, 404
Love Our Children, Inc., 269
Lynch, David, 397

Madonna, 393, 403
Maharishi Mahesh Yogi, 336
Malaclypse the Younger, 395
Mannheim, Karl, 65, 68
Mansfield, Jayne, 397
Manson, Marilyn, 397
Marriage. *See* ceremony
Martinist Order, p.336
Mary Kay Cosmetics, 275
Masons, 43, 368
Mazier, Jean-Jacques, 303
McPherson, Lisa, 70
Membership in CoS, 54–56
MEST (matter, energy, space and time)
    creation of, 212, 414
    defined, 18, 91
    Hubbard's legacy to undo, 376
    levels of freedom from, 92, 395, 419
    relationship to engrams, 212
Miller, William, 130–131
Mills, Crispian, 397
Miscavige, David, 29, 55, 88, 326, 401,
    402, 424
Mission Interministérielle de vigilance
    et de lute contre les dérives sectaires
    (MIVILUDES), 299
Mission Interministérielle de vigilance et
    de lute contre les sects (MILS), 299,
    307
Moon, Rev. Sun Myung, 272, 315
Mormons. *See* Church of Jesus Christ of
    Latter Day Saints
Morice, Olivier, 309
Morrison, Van, 404

Moss, Kate, 393
Moxon, Kendrick, 278
Mozul, Etienne, 304
Muscavige, David, 326, 401

Narconon
    as addiction cure, 401
    in Denmark, 155
    in Sweden, 338
    international services, 97
    taxation for services of, 291
National Democratic Party, 275
New Acropolis, 303
New Era Dianetics (NED), 414
New Thought, 183–186, 261
Nietzsche, 221
Nixon, Richard, 66–67
Nylund, Karl-Erik, 342

Open Source religious traditions, 61
Operating Thetan (OT)
    functioning of, 92–93, 234
    levels of, 94, 218, 396
    mythology regarding, 91, 231–232
    nature of, 32n30, 91, 185
Operation Clambake, 382–383
Order of the Solar Temple, 271
Ordination. *See* ceremony
Ordo Tempi: Orientis (OTO), 20, 59, 259
Ordre du Temple Solaire (OTS), 299
Organization structure. *See also* Sea Org
    corporate structure, 98
    changes in, 144
    description, 97, 394
    financial structure, 99
Oxford Capacity Analysis, 330–331

Packer, James, 389, 398, 402–403
Paganism, 117, 124–127
Paltrow, Gwyneth, 402
Panoussis, Zenon, 340
Patrick, Ted, 276
Peoples Temple, 271
Picard, Catherine, 310, 315, 317
Pitt, Brad, 393, 402
Plymouth Brethren Movement, 336
Pre-clear. *See* clear
Present Time Problems, 95, 201
Preston, Kelly, 389, 398
Principles of Scientology, 167–168

Prix de Leipzig, 314
Prophet, Mark L., 395
Prophetic
  CoS as prophetic religion, 84
  leadership and contractually oriented
    group, 87
  persona for leader, 84
  versus priestly method of
    authority, 85
Protestant Reformation, 392
Psychiatry, 98, 187, 381
Psychology
  APA's response to Scientology, 23
  claims of harm done by CoS, 349–351
  combination of therapy and religion in
    CoS, 99
  Hubbard's training in, 18
Published works by L. Ron Hubbard
  Abnormal Dianetics, 418
  Advanced Procedures and Axioms, 419
  All About Radiation, 421
  The Basic Dianetics Picture Book, 418
  The Bridge to Total Freedom (The
    Bridge), 416
  Basic Scientology Picture Book, 420
  The Book of E-Meter Drills, 423
  Child Dianetics, 419
  Clear Body, Clear Mind: The Effective
    Purification Program, 420
  The Creation of Human Ability, 422
  Dianetics 55! A Guide to Effective
    Communication, 419
  Dianetics: The Evolution of a Science,
    418, 425n8
  Dianetics: The Modern Science of Mental
    Health (DMSMH), 21, 87, 394, 411,
    415, 418
  Dianetics: The Original Thesis, 418
  The Dynamics of Life, 415, 418
  E-Meter Essentials, 423
  Have You Lived before This Life?, 422
  Handbook for Preclears, 419
  How to Live though an Executive, 422
  Introducing the E-Meter, 423
  Introduction to Scientology Ethics, 422
  A New Slant on Life, 420
  Notes on the Lectures, 419
  The Problems at Work, 420
  Purification: An Illustrated Answer to
    Drugs, 421
  Science of Survival: Prediction of Human
    Behavior, 418, 419
  Scientology 0–8: The Book of Basics, 420
  Scientology 8–80, 421
  Scientology 8–8008, 421
  Scientology: A History of Man, 421,
    426n50
  Scientology: A New Science, 415, 418
  Scientology Handbook, The, 422
  Scientology: The Fundamentals of
    Thought, 420
  Self Analysis, 418
  technical bulletins (TB), 416
  Tone Scale, 419
  Understanding the E-Meter, 423
  What Is Scientology?, 422
Purification Program (a.k.a. Sweat
  Program), 420

Raelians, 390
Raoust, Michel, 295
Ravenhurst, Omar Khayyam, 395
Reincarnation
  addition of to the CoS mythology, 90
  Buddhism and, 233
  controversy within board of directors
    about, 22
  doctrine of, 5, 414
  funeral ceremony, 169
  healing of the human experience, 90
  importance in ritual, 171
  space opera myth in, 230–231
Religious technologies
  description of, 8–9, 212–213
  psycho-technologies, 269
  uses of, 10
Religious Technology Center (RTC),
  28–29, 62, 64, 68, 74, 88, 331–332,
  397, 413, 416, 424–425
Richie, Nicole, 393
Rituals. See ceremony
Robbins, 83
Rogers, Lee, 403
Rokos, Rev. Michael G., 276
Roman Catholic Church, 275
Rosicrucian, 43
Ross, Rick, 270, 274

Sarkozy, Nicolas, 303, 319
Satanism, 347

Schiffer, Claudia, 393
Scott, Jason, 270, 277–279
Science Fiction, 35–51
Scientology Missions International
    (SMI),
    administrative function, 326–330, 397
    financial responsibilities, 327–328
    foundation of, 325
    locations in Europe, 326
Sea Organization (Sea Org)
    controversy about, 26–27
    current membership of, 27
    establishment of, 87
    function of, 26–27
    as high investment members, 58, 60
    introduction to, 5
    members as ascetics, 235
    role in larger CoS structure, 97, 99,
        133, 397
Seventh Day Adventists, 336
Simpson, Charles, 270, 279
Singer, Margaret, 274
Smarnoff, Irving, 307
Smith, Will, 401
Social outreach, 9–10. See also
        Narconon; Criminon;
        Applied Scolastics
Soteriological System, 105–113, 236
        366–367, 379, 412, 417
Spielberg, Steven, 401
Spiritualism, 347
Standard Technology (Standard Tech)
    as compared to Christian dogma, 36,
        217
    defined, 90, 329
    as infallible, 217
    rationale for, 414
    Soteriological System using, 108
Stark, Rodney, 16, 60, 117–138
Stern, Howard, 397
Storey, John, 103, 104
Summit Lighthouse. See Church
        Universal and Triumphant
Suppressive Person, 9–10
Swanson, Gloria, 394
Swedenborgian, 347
Szimhart, Joe, 276

Témoins de Jéhovah 298
Theophilanthropy, 171–176

Theosophical Society, 336
Theosophy, 347
Thetan; See also Operating Thetan
    Body Thetans, 92
    description of, 43
    introduction of concept of, 22, 414
    in relationship to social contract of
        CoS, 93
    theological meaning of, 22
Thomson, Joseph "Snake", 18, 39–41
Tiberi, Jean, 307
Tillberg, Tomas, 337
Time magazine, 358
Time track, 417
Tipton, Robert, 83
Tonkin, Kathy, 278
Training, 5–6, 192–194
Training Routines (TR), 94, 195–196
Transcendental Meditation (TM), 97, 336,
        397
Travolta, John, 389, 398, 405
Tribunal de Grande Instance (TGI), 300
Troeltsch, Ernst, 209

UFOlogy, 225, 230–231, 375–379, 397,
Unification Church, 97, 275, 315, 390
Union de Recourrement des
        Cotisations de Sécurite
        Sociale et d'Allocations
        Familiales (URSSAF), 304–305
Union Nationale des Associations de
        Défense des Familles et de l'Indindu
        (UNADFI/ADFI), 295–296,
        298–299, 302
Unitarian Universalist Church, 128
Utilitarianism, 146–147

Vic, Patric, 303
Vivien, Alain, 307
Vuilque, Philippe, 315
Volunteer Minister program, 436

Wakefield, Margery, 371
Wallis, Roy, 56, 84
Way to Happiness Foundation, 398
Weber, Max, 213
White, Ellen G., 131
Whitehead, Harriet, 56, 108
Whole Track. See reincarnation
Wicca, 347, 390, 395

Willms, Gerald, 235
Winfrey, Oprah, 393
Winther, Joseph A., 415
Withholds, 95, 201. *See also*
    auditing
Wollersheim, Larry, 283

Xenu Myth
    and the book of Mormon, 369
    description of, 91, 231–232, 317

implant, 375
and the Qur'an, 369
as religious narrative, 365–366
as space opera, 377
UFOlogy themes in, 375–376

Youth for Human Rights International,
    398

Zuel, Bernard, 402